Progressive Concepts for Semantic Web Evolution:
Applications and Developments

Miltiadis Lytras
University of Patras, Greece

Amit Sheth
Wright State University, USA

INFORMATION SCIENCE REFERENCE

Hershey · New York

Director of Editorial Content:	Kristin Klinger
Director of Book Publications:	Julia Mosemann
Development Editor:	Julia Mosemann
Publishing Assistant:	Deanna Zombro
Typesetter:	Michael Brehm
Quality Control:	Jamie Snavely
Cover Design:	Lisa Tosheff
Printed at:	Yurchak Printing Inc.

Published in the United States of America by
Information Science Reference (an imprint of IGI Global)
701 E. Chocolate Avenue
Hershey PA 17033
Tel: 717-533-8845
Fax: 717-533-8661
E-mail: cust@igi-global.com
Web site: http://www.igi-global.com/reference

Copyright © 2010 by IGI Global. All rights reserved. No part of this publication may be reproduced, stored or distributed in any form or by any means, electronic or mechanical, including photocopying, without written permission from the publisher.

Product or company names used in this set are for identification purposes only. Inclusion of the names of the products or companies does not indicate a claim of ownership by IGI Global of the trademark or registered trademark.

Library of Congress Cataloging-in-Publication Data

Progressive concepts for Semantic Web evolution : applications and developments / Miltiadis Lytras and Amit Sheth, editors.
    p. cm.
  Includes bibliographical references and index.
  Summary: "This book unites research on essential theories, models, and applications of Semantic Web research, focusing on mobile ontologies and agents, fuzzy databases, and new approaches to retrieval and evaluation in the Semantic Web"--Provided by publisher.
  ISBN 978-1-60566-992-2 (hardcover) -- ISBN 978-1-60566-993-9 (ebook) 1. Semantic Web. 2. Ontologies (Information retrieval) 3. Mobile agents (Computer software) I. Lytras, Miltiadis D., 1973- II. Sheth, A. (Amit), 1959-
  TK5105.88815.P76 2010
  025.042'7--dc22

British Cataloguing in Publication Data
A Cataloguing in Publication record for this book is available from the British Library.

All work contributed to this book is new, previously-unpublished material. The views expressed in this book are those of the authors, but not necessarily of the publisher.

Advances in Semantic Web & Information Systems Series (ASWIS)

ISBN: 1935-3626

Editor-in-Chief: Miltiadis Lytras, Athens University, Greece

SOCIAL WEB EVOLUTION
Integrating Semantic Applications and Web 2.0 Technologies

Miltiadis D. Lytras & Patricia Ordóñez de Pablos

Semantic Web-Based Information Systems: State-of-the-Art Applications
CyberTech Publishing • copyright 2007 • 317 pp • H/Cover (ISBN: 1-59904-426-9)

As a new generation of technologies, frameworks, concepts and practices for information systems emerge, practitioners, academicians, and researchers are in need of a source where they can go to educate themselves on the latest innovations in this area. Semantic Web Information Systems: State-of-the-Art Applications establishes value-added knowledge transfer and personal development channels in three distinctive areas: academia, industry, and government. Semantic Web Information Systems: State-of-the-Art Applications covers new semantic Web-enabled tools for the citizen, learner, organization, and business. Real-world applications toward the development of the knowledge society and semantic Web issues, challenges and implications in each of the IS research streams are included as viable sources for this challenging subject.

Semantic Web-Based Information Systems
State-of-the-Art Applications

Amit Sheth and Miltiadis Lytras

Social Web Evolution: Integrating Semantic Applications and Web 2.0 Technologies
Information Science Reference • copyright 2009 • H/C (ISBN: 978-1-60566-272-5)

As semantic technologies prove their value with targeted applications, there are increasing opportunities to consider their usefulness in social contexts for knowledge, learning, and human development. Social Web Evolution: Integrating Semantic Applications and Web 2.0 Technologies explores the potential of Web 2.0 and its synergies with the Semantic Web and provides state-of-the-art theoretical foundations and technological applications. A reference edition for academicians, practitioners, policy makers, and government officers eager for knowledge on Web 2.0 and social Web, this book emphasizes practical aspects of the integration of semantic applications into social Web technologies.

IGI GLOBAL
DISSEMINATOR OF KNOWLEDGE

Hershey • New York

Order online at www.igi-global.com or call 717-533-8845 x10 –
Mon-Fri 8:30 am - 5:00 pm (est) or fax 24 hours a day 717-533-8661

Editorial Advisory Board

Gottfried Vossen, *University of Muenster, Germany*
Martin Hepp, *University of the German Federal Armed Forces, Germany*
Karl Aberer, *Institute for Core Computing Science, Switzerland*
Richard Benjamins, *Universiteit van Amsterdam, The Netherlands*
Abraham Bernstein, *University of Zurich, Switzerland*
Chris Bizer, *University of Berlin, Germany*
Paolo Bouquet, *University of Trento, Italy*
Francois Bry, *University of Munich, Germany*
Christoph Bussler, *Merced Systems, USA*
Jorge Cardoso, *SAP Research, Germany*
Vassilis Christophides, *ICS-Forth, Greece*
Oscar Corcho, *Intelligent Software Components, Spain*
John Davies, *British Telecom, UK*
Dieter Fensel, *University of Innsbruck, Austria*
Farshad Fotouhi, *Wayne State University, USA*
Asuncion Gomez-Perez, *Polytechnic University of Madrid, Spain*
William I. Grosky, *University of Michigan, USA*
Nicola Guarino, *STC-CNR - National Research Council, Italy*
Manfred Hauswirth, *DERI Galway, Ireland*
James Hendler, *Rensselaer Polytechnic Institute, USA*
Vasant Honavar, *Iowa State University, USA*
Lakshmi S. Iyer, *University of North Carolina, USA*
Ramesh Jain, *University of California - Irvine, USA*
Anupam Joshi, *University of Maryland - Baltimore County, USA*
Vipul Kashyap, *Partners Healthcare, USA*
Henry M. Kim, *York University, Canada*
Ralf Klischewski, *University of Hamburg, Germany*
Matthias Klusch, *German Research Center for Artificial Intelligence, Germany*
Shiyong Lu, *Wayne State University, USA*
Miltiadis D. Lytras, *Athens University of Economics and Business, Greece*
Michael Maximilien, *IBM Research, USA*
Mark Musen, *Stanford University, USA*

Ambjorn Naeve, *Royal Institute of Technology, Sweden*
Jeff Z. Pan, *University of Aberdeen, Scotland*
Demetrios Sampson, *University of Piraeus, Greece*
Miguel-Angel Sicilia, *University of Alcal, Spain*
Rahul Singh, *University of North Carolina, USA*
Susie Stephens, *Eli Lilly and Company, USA*
York Sure, *GESIS and University of Koblenz-Landau, Germany*
Bhavani Thuraisingham, *University of Texas at Dallas, USA*
Ubbo Visser, *University of Bremen, Germany*
Gerd Wagner, *Brandenburg University of Technology at Cottbus, Germany*
Yong Yu, *Shanghai Jiao Tong University, China*
Lina Zhou, *University of Maryland - Baltimore County, USA*

Table of Contents

Detailed Table of Contents

Chapter 1
Ulrich Küster, Institute of Computer Science, Germany
Birgitta König-Ries, Institute of Computer Science, Germany
Matthias Klusch, German Research Centre for Artificial Intelligence, Germany

In recent years, a huge amount of research effort and funding has been devoted to the area of semantic Web services (SWS). This has resulted in the proposal of numerous competing approaches to facilitate the automation of discovery, composition and mediation for Web services using semantic annotations. However, despite of a wealth of theoretical work, too little effort has been spent towards the comparative experimental evaluation of the competing approaches so far. Progress in scientific development and industrial adoption is thereby hindered. An established evaluation methodology and standard benchmarks that allow the comparative evaluation of different frameworks are thus needed for the further advancement of the field. To this end, a criteria model for SWS evaluation is presented and the existing approaches towards SWS evaluation are comprehensively analyzed. Their shortcomings are discussed in order to identify the fundamental issues of SWS evaluation. Based on this discussion, a research agenda towards agreed upon evaluation methodologies is proposed.

Chapter 2
Vasileios Baousis, University of Athens, Greece
*Vassilis Spiliopoulos, University of the Aegean and National Centre of Scientific Research
    "Demokritos", Greece*
*Elias Zavitsanos, University of the Aegean and National Centre of Scientific Research
    "Demokritos", Greece*
Stathes Hadjiefthymiades, University of Athens, Greece
Lazaros Merakos, University of Athens, Greece

The requirement for ubiquitous service access in wireless environments presents a great challenge in light of well-known problems like high error rate and frequent disconnections. In order to satisfy this requirement, this chapter proposes the integration of two modern service technologies: Web Services and mobile agents. This integration allows wireless users to access and invoke semantically enriched Web Services without the need for simultaneous, online presence of the service requestor. Moreover, in order to improve the capabilities of Service registries, the authors exploit the advantages offered by the Semantic Web framework. Specifically, they use enhanced registries enriched with semantic information that provide semantic matching to service queries and published service descriptions. Finally, they discuss the implementation of the proposed framework and present their performance assessment findings.

Chapter 3

Jari Veijalainen, University of Jyvaskyla, Finland

The number of mobile subscribers in the world will soon reach the three billion mark. Ontologies are an important ingredient towards more complicated mobile services and wider usage of mobile terminals. This chapter first discusses ontology and epistemology concepts in general. After that, the author reviews ontologies in the computer science field and introduces mobile ontologies as a special category. It seems reasonable to distinguish between two orthogonal categories, mobile domain ontologies and flowing ontologies. The domain of the former one is in some sense related with mobility, whereas the latter ones are able to flow from computer to computer in the network. This chapter then discusses the creation issues, business aspects, and intellectual property rights (IPR), including patentability of mobile ontologies. The chapter also discusses some basic requirements for computer systems architectures that would be needed to support the usage of mobile ontologies.

Chapter 4

Massimo Paolucci, DoCoMo Communications Laboratories Europe GmbH, Germany
Gregor Broll, Medieninformatik, Ludwig-Maximilians-Universität, Germany
John Hamard, DoCoMo Communications Laboratories Europe GmbH, Germany
Enrico Rukzio, Lancaster University, UK
Matthias Wagner, DoCoMo Communications Laboratories Europe GmbH, Germany
Albrecht Schmidt, University of Bonn, Germany

The last few years have seen two parallel trends emerge. The first of such trends is set by technologies such as Near Field Communication, 2D Bar codes, RFID and others that support the association of digital information with virtually every object. Using these technologies ordinary objects such as coffee mugs or advertisement posters can provide information that is easily processed. The second trend is set by (semantic) Web services that provide a way to automatically invoke functionalities across the Internet lowering interoperability barriers. The PERCI system, discussed in the chapter, provides a way to bridge between these two technologies allowing the invocation of Web services using the information gathered from the tags effectively transforming every object in a service proxy.

Tommaso Di Noia, Politecnico di Bari, Italy
Eugenio Di Sciascio, Politecnico di Bari, Italy
Francesco Maria Donini, Università della Tuscia, Italy
Michele Ruta, Politecnico di Bari, Italy
Floriano Scioscia, Politecnico di Bari, Italy
Eufemia Tinelli, Politecnico di Bari and Università degli Studi di Bari, Italy

This chapter proposes a novel object discovery framework integrating the application layer of Bluetooth and RFID standards. The approach is motivated and illustrated in an innovative u-commerce setting. Given a request, it allows an advanced discovery process, exploiting semantically annotated descriptions of goods available in the u-marketplace. The RFID data exchange protocol and the Bluetooth Service Discovery Protocol have been modified and enhanced to enable support for such semantic annotation of products. Modifications to the standards have been conceived to be backward compatible, thus allowing the smooth coexistence of the legacy discovery and/or identification features. Also noteworthy is the introduction of a dedicated compression tool to reduce storage/transmission problems due to the verbosity of XML-based semantic languages.

Patrick J. Hayes, Institute for Human and Machine Cognition, USA
Harry Halpin, University of Edinburgh, UK

URIs, a universal identification scheme, are different from human names insofar as they can provide the ability to reliably access the thing identified. URIs also can function to reference a non-accessible thing in a similar manner to how names function in natural language. There are two distinctly different relationships between names and things: access and reference. To confuse the two relations leads to underlying problems with Web architecture. Reference is by nature ambiguous in any language. So any attempts by Web architecture to make reference completely unambiguous will fail on the Web. Despite popular belief otherwise, making further ontological distinctions often leads to more ambiguity, not less. Contrary to appeals to Kripke for some sort of eternal and unique identification, reference on the Web uses descriptions and therefore there is no unambiguous resolution of reference. On the Web, what is needed is not just a simple redirection, but a uniform and logically consistent manner of associating descriptions with URIs that can be done in a number of practical ways that should be made consistent.

Valentina Presutti, ISTC National Research Council (CNR), Italy
Aldo Gangemi, ISTC National Research Council (CNR), Italy

One of the main strengths of the Web is that it allows any party of its global community to share information with any other party. This goal has been achieved by making use of a unique and uniform mechanism of identification, the URI (uniform resource identifiers). Although URIs succeed when used for retrieving resources on the Web, their suitability for identifying any kind of thing, for example, resources that are not on the Web, is not guaranteed. This chapter investigates the meaning of the identity of a Web resource, and how the current situation, as well as existing and possible future improvements, can be modeled and implemented on the Web. In particular, the authors propose an ontology, IRE, that provides a formal way to model both the problem and the solution spaces. IRE describes the concept of resource from the viewpoint of the Web, by reusing an ontology of Information Objects, built on top of DOLCE+ and its extensions. In particular, the authors formalize the concept of Web resource, as distinguished from the concept of a generic entity, and how those and other concepts are related, for example, by different proxy for relations. Based on the analysis formalized in IRE, the authors propose a formal pattern for modeling and comparing different solutions to the problems of the identity of resources.

Chapter 8

The expected utility of the Semantic Web (SW) hinges upon the idea that machines, just like humans, can make and interpret statements about "real world" objects, properties, and relations. A cornerstone of this idea is the notion that Uniform Resource Identifiers (URIs) can be used to refer to entities existing independently of the Web and to convey meanings. In this chapter, when a URI is used in this manner we will say that it is used declaratively, or that it is an R-URI. The key question is this: when an R-URI is used declaratively on the SW how is an agent, especially a non-human one, supposed to "understand" or "know" what it is intended to refer to or mean?

Chapter 9

This chapter offers an approach that combines a hierarchy of concepts and ontology for the task of identifying Web documents in the environment of the Semantic Web. A user provides a simple query in the form a hierarchy that only partially "describes" documents (s)he wants to retrieve from the Web. The hierarchy is treated as a "seed" representing user's initial knowledge about concepts covered by required documents. Ontologies are treated as supplementary knowledge bases. They are used to instantiate the hierarchy with concrete information, as well as to enhance it with new concepts initially unknown to the user. The proposed approach is used to design a prototype system for document identification in the Web environment. The description of the system and the results of preliminary experiments are presented.

Chapter 10

Ontology is an important part of the W3C standards for the Semantic Web used to specify standard conceptual vocabularies to exchange data among systems, provide reusable knowledge bases, and facilitate interoperability across multiple heterogeneous systems and databases. However, current ontology is not sufficient for handling vague information that is commonly found in many application domains. A feasible solution is to import the fuzzy ability to extend the classical ontology. This chapter proposes a fuzzy ontology generation framework from the fuzzy relational databases, in which the fuzzy ontology consists of fuzzy ontology structure and instances. The authors simultaneously consider the schema and instances of the fuzzy relational databases, and respectively transform them to fuzzy ontology structure and fuzzy RDF data model. This can ensure the integrality of the original structure as well as the completeness and consistency of the original instances in the fuzzy relational databases. The fuzzy RDF data model is used to represent the fuzzy ontology instance.

This chapter presents a novel approach to fuzzy description logic programs (or simply fuzzy dl-programs) under the answer set semantics, which is a tight integration of fuzzy disjunctive logic programs under the answer set semantics with fuzzy description logics. From a different perspective, it is a generalization of tightly coupled disjunctive dl-programs by fuzzy vagueness in both the description logic and the logic program component. The authors show that the new formalism faithfully extends both fuzzy disjunctive logic programs and fuzzy description logics, and that under suitable assumptions, reasoning in the new formalism is decidable. The authors present a polynomial reduction of certain fuzzy dl-programs to tightly coupled disjunctive dl-programs, and analyze the complexity of consistency checking and query processing for certain fuzzy dl-programs. Furthermore, the authors provide a special case of fuzzy dl-programs for which deciding consistency and query processing can both be done in polynomial time in the data complexity.

Chapter 12

This chapter presents a method based on clustering techniques to detect possible/probable novel concepts or concept drift in a knowledge base expressed in Description Logics. The method exploits an effective and language-independent semi-distance measure defined for the space of individuals, that is based on a finite number of dimensions corresponding to a committee of discriminating features (represented by concept descriptions). A maximally discriminating group of features can be obtained with the randomized optimization methods described in the chapter. In the algorithm, the possible clusterings are represented as strings of central elements (medoids, w.r.t. the given metric) of variable length. Hence, the number of clusters is not required as a parameter since the method is able to find an optimal choice by means of the evolutionary operators and of a proper fitness function. An experimentation with a number of ontologies proves the feasibility of this method and its effectiveness in terms of clustering validity indices. Then, with a supervised learning phase, each cluster can be assigned with a refined or newly constructed intensional definition expressed in the adopted language.

Chapter 13

Artem Chebotko, University of Texas - Pan American, USA
Shiyong Lu, Wayne State University, USA

Relational technology has shown to be very useful for scalable Semantic Web data management. Numerous researchers have proposed to use RDBMSs to store and query voluminous RDF data using SQL and RDF query languages. This chapter studies how RDF queries with the so called well-designed graph patterns and nested optional patterns can be efficiently evaluated in an RDBMS. The authors propose to extend relational algebra with a novel relational operator, nested optional join (NOJ), that is more efficient than left outer join in processing nested optional patterns of well-designed graph patterns. They design three efficient algorithms to implement the new operator in relational databases: (1) nested-loops NOJ algorithm, NL-NOJ, (2) sort-merge NOJ algorithm, SM-NOJ, and (3) simple hash NOJ algorithm, SH-NOJ. Using a real life RDF dataset, the authors demonstrate the efficiency of their algorithms by comparing them with the corresponding left outer join implementations and explore the effect of join selectivity on the performance of these algorithms.

Chapter 14

Peter Scheir, Styria Media Group AG, Austria
Peter Prettenhofer, Bauhaus University Weimar, Germany
Stefanie N. Lindstaedt, Know-Center Graz & Graz University of Technology, Austria
Chiara Ghidini, Fondazione Bruno Kessler, Italy

While it is agreed that semantic enrichment of resources would lead to better search results, at present the low coverage of resources on the Web with semantic information presents a major hurdle in realizing the vision of search on the Semantic Web. To address this problem, this chapter investigates how to improve retrieval performance in settings where resources are sparsely annotated with semantic information. Techniques from soft computing are employed to find relevant material that was not originally annotated with the concepts used in a query. The authors present an associative retrieval model for the Semantic Web and evaluate if and to which extent the use of associative retrieval techniques increases retrieval performance. In addition, the authors present recent work on adapting the network structure based on relevance feedback by the user to further improve retrieval effectiveness. The evaluation of new retrieval paradigms - such as retrieval based on technology for the Semantic Web - presents an additional challenge since no off-the-shelf test corpora exist. Hence, this chapter gives a detailed description of the approach taken to evaluate the information retrieval service the authors have built.

Preface

Semantic Web technologies and applications have become increasingly important as new methods for understanding and expressing information are discovered. This work, titled Progressive Concepts for Semantic Web Evolution: Applications and Developments, unites research on essential theories, models, and applications of Semantic Web research. Contributions focus on mobile ontologies and agents, fuzzy databases, and new approaches to retrieval and evaluation in the Semantic Web, among other topics.

Chapter 1, "*Evaluating Semantic Web Service Technologies: Criteria, Approaches and Challenges,*" by Ulrich Küster, Birgitta König-Ries, and Matthias Klusch presents a criteria model for SWS evaluation and comprehensively analyzes existing approaches towards SWS evaluation. The authors discuss shortcomings in order to identify the fundamental issues of SWS evaluation. Based on this discussion, a research agenda towards agreed upon evaluation methodologies is proposed.

Chapter 2, "*Semantic Web Services and Mobile Agents Integration for Efficient Mobile Services,*" by Vasileios Baousis, Vassilis Spiliopoulos, Elias Zavitsanos, Stathes Hadjiefthymiades, and Lazaros Merakos proposes the integration of two modern service technologies: Web Services and mobile agents. This integration allows wireless users to access and invoke semantically enriched Web Services without the need for simultaneous, online presence of the service requestor. Moreover, in order to improve the capabilities of Service registries, the authors exploit the advantages offered by the Semantic Web framework. Specifically, they use enhanced registries enriched with semantic information that provide semantic matching to service queries and published service descriptions.

Chapter 3, "*Mobile Ontologies: Concept, Development, Usage, and Business Potential,*" by Jari Veijalainen discusses ontology and epistemology concepts in general. After that, the author reviews ontologies in the computer science field and introduces mobile ontologies as a special category. It seems reasonable to distinguish between two orthogonal categories, mobile domain ontologies and flowing ontologies. The domain of the former one is in some sense related with mobility, whereas the latter ones are able to flow from computer to computer in the network. This chapter then discusses the creation issues, business aspects, and intellectual property rights (IPR), including patentability of mobile ontologies.

Chapter 4, "*Service Provisioning through Real World Objects,*" by Massimo Paolucci, Gregor Broll, John Hamard, and Enrico Rukzio discusses the PERCI system, which provides a way to bridge technologies that support the association of digital information with Semantic Web services. This allows the invocation of Web services using the information gathered from the tags, effectively transforming every object in a service proxy.

Chapter 5, "*Semantic-Based Bluetooth-RFID Interaction for Advanced Resource Discovery in Pervasive Contexts,*" by Tommaso Di Noia, Eugenio Di Sciascio, Francesco Maria Donini, Michele Ruta, Floriano Scioscia, and Eufemia Tinelli proposes a novel object discovery framework integrating the application layer of Bluetooth and RFID standards. The approach is motivated and illustrated in an innovative u-commerce setting. Given a request, it allows an advanced discovery process, exploiting semantically annotated descriptions of goods available in the u-marketplace. The RFID data exchange protocol and the Bluetooth Service Discovery Protocol have been modified and enhanced to enable support for such semantic annotation of products. Modifications to the standards have been conceived to be backward compatible, thus allowing the smooth coexistence of the legacy discovery and/or identification features.

Chapter 6, *"In Defense of Ambiguity Redux,"* by Patrick J. Hayes and Harry Halpin contends that reference is by nature ambiguous in any language. So any attempts by Web architecture to make reference completely unambiguous will fail on the Web. Despite popular belief otherwise, making further ontological distinctions often leads to more ambiguity, not less. Contrary to appeals to Kripke for some sort of eternal and unique identification, reference on the Web uses descriptions and therefore there is no unambiguous resolution of reference. On the Web, what is needed is not just a simple redirection, but a uniform and logically consistent manner of associating descriptions with URIs that can be done in a number of practical ways that should be made consistent.

Chapter 7, *"Identity of Resources and Entities on the Web,"* by Valentina Presutti and Aldo Gangemi chapter investigates the meaning of the identity of a Web resource, and how the current situation, as well as existing and possible future improvements, can be modeled and implemented on the Web. In particular, the authors propose an ontology, IRE, that provides a formal way to model both the problem and the solution spaces.

Chapter 8, *"Ontological Indeterminacy and the Semantic Web,"* by Allen Ginsberg argues that the expected utility of the Semantic Web (SW) hinges upon the idea that machines, just like humans, can make and interpret statements about "real world" objects, properties, and relations. A cornerstone of this idea is the notion that Uniform Resource Identifiers (URIs) can be used to refer to entities existing independently of the Web and to convey meanings. This chapter contends that when a URI is used in this manner, it is used declaratively, or that it is an R-URI. The key question is this: when an R-URI is used declaratively on the SW how is an agent, especially a non-human one, supposed to "understand" or "know" what it is intended to refer to or mean?

Chapter 9, *"Ontology Driven Document Identification in Semantic Web,"* Marek Reformat, Ronald R. Yager, and Zhan Li offers an approach that combines a hierarchy of concepts and ontology for the task of identifying Web documents in the environment of the Semantic Web. A user provides a simple query in the form a hierarchy that only partially "describes" documents (s)he wants to retrieve from the Web. The hierarchy is treated as a "seed" representing user's initial knowledge about concepts covered by required documents. Ontologies are treated as supplementary knowledge bases. They are used to instantiate the hierarchy with concrete information, as well as to enhance it with new concepts initially unknown to the user. The proposed approach is used to design a prototype system for document identification in the Web environment.

Chapter 10, *"A Fuzzy Ontology Generation Framework from Fuzzy Relational Databases,"* by Z.M. Ma, Yanhui Lv, and Li Yan proposes a fuzzy ontology generation framework from the fuzzy relational databases, in which the fuzzy ontology consists of fuzzy ontology structure and instances. The authors simultaneously consider the schema and instances of the fuzzy relational databases, and respectively transform them to fuzzy ontology structure and fuzzy RDF data model. This can ensure the integrality of the original structure as well as the completeness and consistency of the original instances in the fuzzy relational databases. The fuzzy RDF data model is used to represent the fuzzy ontology instance.

Chapter 11, *"Tightly Coupled Fuzzy Description Logic Programs under the Answer Set Semantics for the Semantic Web,"* by Thomas Lukasiewicz and Umberto Straccia presents a novel approach to fuzzy description logic programs (or simply fuzzy dl-programs) under the answer set semantics, which is a tight integration of fuzzy disjunctive logic programs under the answer set semantics with fuzzy description logics. From a different perspective, it is a generalization of tightly coupled disjunctive dl-programs by fuzzy vagueness in both the description logic and the logic program component. The authors show that the new formalism faithfully extends both fuzzy disjunctive logic programs and fuzzy description logics, and that under suitable assumptions, reasoning in the new formalism is decidable. The authors present a polynomial reduction of certain fuzzy dl-programs to tightly coupled disjunctive dl-programs, and analyze the complexity of consistency checking and query processing for certain fuzzy dl-programs.

Chapter 12, "*Evolutionary Conceptual Clustering Based on Induced Pseudo-Metrics,*" by Nicola Fanizzi, Claudia d'Amato, and Floriana Esposito presents a method based on clustering techniques to detect possible/probable novel concepts or concept drift in a knowledge base expressed in Description Logics. The method exploits an effective and language-independent semi-distance measure defined for the space of individuals, that is based on a finite number of dimensions corresponding to a committee of discriminating features (represented by concept descriptions). A maximally discriminating group of features can be obtained with the randomized optimization methods described in the chapter. In the algorithm, the possible clusterings are represented as strings of central elements (medoids, w.r.t. the given metric) of variable length. Hence, the number of clusters is not required as a parameter since the method is able to find an optimal choice by means of the evolutionary operators and of a proper fitness function. An experimentation with a number of ontologies proves the feasibility of this method and its effectiveness in terms of clustering validity indices.

Chapter 13, "*Nested Optional Join for Efficient Evaluation of SPARQL Nested Optional Graph Patterns,*" by Artem Chebotko and Shiyong Lu studies how RDF queries with the so called well-designed graph patterns and nested optional patterns can be efficiently evaluated in an RDBMS. The authors propose to extend relational algebra with a novel relational operator, nested optional join (NOJ), that is more efficient than left outer join in processing nested optional patterns of well-designed graph patterns. They design three efficient algorithms to implement the new operator in relational databases: (1) nested-loops NOJ algorithm, NL-NOJ, (2) sort-merge NOJ algorithm, SM-NOJ, and (3) simple hash NOJ algorithm, SH-NOJ. Using a real life RDF dataset, the authors demonstrate the efficiency of their algorithms by comparing them with the corresponding left outer join implementations and explore the effect of join selectivity on the performance of these algorithms.

Chapter 14, "*An Associative and Adaptive Network Model for Information Retrieval in the Semantic Web,*" by Peter Scheir, Peter Prettenhofer, Stefanie N. Lindstaedt, and Chiara Ghidini investigates how to improve retrieval performance in settings where resources are sparsely annotated with semantic information. Techniques from soft computing are employed to find relevant material that was not originally annotated with the concepts used in a query. The authors present an associative retrieval model for the Semantic Web and evaluate if and to which extent the use of associative retrieval techniques increases retrieval performance.

Progressive Concepts for Semantic Web Evolution: Applications and Developments provides focused coverage on research and applications in the Semantic Web discipline, investigating key considerations, frameworks, models, and methodologies that continue to inform and redefine information retrieval, services, and technologies in the Semantic Web.

Chapter 1
Evaluating Semantic Web Service Technologies:
Criteria, Approaches and Challenges

Ulrich Küster
Institute of Computer Science, Germany

Birgitta König-Ries
Institute of Computer Science, Germany

Matthias Klusch
German Research Centre for Artificial Intelligence, Germany

ABSTRACT

In recent years, a huge amount of research effort and funding has been devoted to the area of semantic web services (SWS). This has resulted in the proposal of numerous competing approaches to facilitate the automation of discovery, composition and mediation for web services using semantic annotations. However, despite of a wealth of theoretical work, too little effort has been spent towards the comparative experimental evaluation of the competing approaches so far. Progress in scientific development and industrial adoption is thereby hindered. An established evaluation methodology and standard benchmarks that allow the comparative evaluation of different frameworks are thus needed for the further advancement of the field. To this end, a criteria model for SWS evaluation is presented and the existing approaches towards SWS evaluation are comprehensively analyzed. Their shortcomings are discussed in order to identify the fundamental issues of SWS evaluation. Based on this discussion, a research agenda towards agreed upon evaluation methodologies is proposed.

INTRODUCTION

To foster reuse, state of the art software engineering has been driven over decades by the trend towards more and more component based software development. In recent years another trend towards more and more distributed and more loosely coupled systems could be observed. Service oriented architectures (*SOAs*) are the latest product of this long-reaching development. Web services in particular have become increasingly popular and are currently the most prominent implementation of a SOA. The grand vision of the web service paradigm is to have

DOI: 10.4018/978-1-60566-992-2.ch001

Copyright © 2010, IGI Global. Copying or distributing in print or electronic forms without written permission of IGI Global is prohibited.

a rich library of ten thousands web services available online that provide access to information, functionality or resources of any kind and that can be easily integrated into existing applications or composed in a workflow-like fashion to form new applications.

Even though this promising technology has already proven to be an effective way of creating widely distributed and loosely coupled systems, the integration of the services is still labor intensive and thus expensive work. Thus – following the vision of the semantic web (Berners-Lee et al., 2001) – the idea of semantic web services (*SWS* in the following) was introduced (McIlraith et al., 2001), applying the principles of the semantic web to the web service paradigm.

SWS related research has attracted a huge amount of effort and funding recently. Within the sixth EU framework program[1] alone, for instance, at least 20 projects with a combined funding of more than 70 million Euros dealt directly with semantic services. This gives a good impression of the importance being put on this field of research. The huge amount of effort (and money) spent into SWS research has resulted in numerous proposals of ontology based semantic descriptions for component services (Klusch, 2008b). Based on such descriptions, a plethora of increasingly sophisticated techniques and algorithms for the automated or semi-automated dynamic discovery, composition, binding, and invocation of services have been proposed (Klusch, 2008a).

However, despite of this wealth of theoretical work, recent surveys have shown that surprisingly little effort has been spent towards the comparative evaluation of the competing approaches (Küster et al., 2007b, Klusch and Zhing, 2008). Until recently there were no comparative evaluations and it was impossible to find two systems which had been evaluated on the same use cases. Evaluations were mostly concentrated either on artificially synthesized datasets under questionable assumptions or based on one or two use cases for which it was not clear, whether they were reverse engineered

from the solution. In other words: "There are many claims for such technologies in academic workshops and conferences. However, there is no scientific method of comparing the actual functionalities claimed. [...] Progress in scientific development and in industrial adoption is thereby hindered" (Lausen et al., 2007).

There are striking parallels to this situation in the history of related areas:

"[in the experiments] ...there have been two missing elements. First [...] there has been no concerted effort by groups to work with the same data, use the same evaluation techniques, and generally compare results across systems. The importance of this is not to show any system to be superior, but to allow comparison across a very wide variety of techniques, much wider than only one research group would tackle. [...] The second missing element, which has become critical [...] is the lack of a realistically-sized test collection. Evaluation using the small collections currently available may not reflect performance of systems in large [...] and certainly does not demonstrate any proven abilities of these systems to operate in real-world [...] environments. This is a major barrier to the transfer of these laboratory systems into the commercial world."

This quote by Donna Harman (Harman, 1992) addressed the situation in text retrieval research prior to the establishment of the series of TREC conferences[2] in 1992 but seems to perfectly describe the current situation in SWS research. Harman continued:

"The overall goal of the Text REtrieval Conference (TREC) was to address these two missing elements. It is hoped that by providing a very large test collection and encouraging interaction with other groups in a friendly evaluation forum, a new thrust in information retrieval will occur."

From the perspective of today, it is clear that her hope regarding the positive influence of the availability of mature evaluation methods to the progress of information retrieval research was well justified. This corresponds to a finding of Sim and colleagues who have developed a general theory of benchmarking (Sim et al., 2003). They observe that the creation and widespread use of a benchmark within a research area is frequently accompanied by rapid technical progress and community building:

"Creating a benchmark requires a community to examine their understanding of the field, come to an agreement on what are the key problems, and encapsulate this knowledge in an evaluation. Using the benchmark results in a more rigorous examination of research contributions, and an overall improvement in the tools and techniques being developed. Throughout the benchmarking process, there is greater communication and collaboration among different researchers leading to a stronger consensus on the community's research goals." (Sim et al., 2003)

We follow these lines and argue that today in the area of SWS related research an established evaluation methodology and standard benchmarks that allow the comparative evaluation of different frameworks are needed for the advancement of the field.

The development of such benchmarks requires answers to the fundamental research questions related to the evaluation of SWS technology: What are the appropriate criteria for evaluation? How can various fundamentally different SWS approaches be compared effectively? How can such comparison be guaranteed to be unbiased and balanced? Generally, how can the relative advantage of some SWS technology over another one, and ultimately over existing conventional programming techniques be reproducibly proven or disproven?

Without the ability to perform verifiable comparisons among different SWS technologies and of SWS technology with other software engineering techniques, SWS will remain an art, but not become a science. However, only if we succeed in transforming SWS research from art to science, industrial adoption and widespread recognition of research results will become reality. The development of commonly agreed upon evaluation methodologies and standard benchmark suites is thus absolutely indispensable.

The authors of this article have worked on establishing successful international SWS evaluation campaigns for about three years now. In the course of these activities we have learned that today, there is neither a consensus on what to evaluate nor on how to evaluate. Furthermore, the development of objective and reliable evaluation methodologies is generally far more complex than anticipated.

This article attempts to step back and discuss the general issues related to evaluating SWS technology. The approach is to learn from the existing efforts. Their current shortcomings and pitfalls are analyzed in order to develop an understanding for the general scientific problems related to SWS evaluation. Based on this analysis, a proposal of a further research agenda for SWS evaluation is laid out.

The rest of the paper is organized as follows. In the following section, an answer to the question of *what* to evaluate is presented. A comprehensive, general model of the suitable criteria for evaluation is derived from a requirement analysis for SWS. The remainder of the paper is devoted to the question of *how* to evaluate. First, the existing efforts in the area of SWS evaluation will be introduced and related to each other according to the presented criteria model. This will be followed by an in-depth analysis of the metrics and measures used to evaluate SWS. Current shortcomings are examined to identify and discuss the underlying research problems that need to be solved. Finally, the paper concludes by proposing a research agenda towards the development of standard evaluation methodologies in SWS research.

SWS EVALUATION CRITERIA

The first important question related to any evaluation endeavour regards the criteria according to which the object of interest should be evaluated, i.e. *what* to evaluate. As will be shown in the following Section, different SWS evaluation initiatives have so far focused on very different criteria and there has not been a discussion on why those criteria have been chosen or how they relate to each other. To establish a comprehensive, general model of the suitable criteria for evaluation, we follow the well established Goal-Question-Metric (GQM) approach to software evaluation. The GQM paradigm is a mechanism for defining and evaluating a set of operational goals, using measurement. It has been developed in 1984 at NASA, been used in various software engineering projects worldwide and is a recommended gold practice of the US Department of Defense Information Analysis Center[3] (Basili, 1992).

GQM is based on the assumption that the evaluation of any system should be an evaluation of fitness for purpose. Thus, any evaluation activity should be preceded by the identification of the engineering goals behind the system or technology to be evaluated. The goals are defined in an operational, tractable way by refining them into a set of quantifiable questions. These questions, in turn, are then used to define a specific set of metrics and identify the necessary data to measure according to those metrics (Basili, 1992).

The obvious overall goal of SWS is to support or (partially) automate the process of consuming functionality offered as a service. However, the precise use case motivating particular approaches to SWS is often not clearly identified. To identify the main objectives motivating SWS, we performed a review of published work with detailed and specific descriptions of envisioned

use-cases(Sîrbu et al., 2006, Cobo et al., 2004, Preist et al., 2005, Friesen and Namiri, 2006, Preist, 2007, Küster et al., 2007a, Preist, 2004, Stollberg, 2004, Küster and König-Ries, 2007, Li and Horrocks, 2003, Ragone et al., 2007, Colucci et al., 2005, Balzer et al., 2004, Friesen and Grimm, 2005, Gugliotta et al., 2006, Klein et al., 2005). While this review is clearly not exhaustive, we believe that it is representative for the majority of SWS projects. We found that the published use cases can be roughly divided in two types of application domains.

The first type envisions to enable late dynamic service discovery, selection and binding at runtime. In mobile environments, the non-availability of stable services forces to discover and bind services dynamically, e.g. booking local attractions via mobile devices while travelling (Sîrbu et al., 2006, Klein et al., 2005). In B2B scenarios, the dynamic and autonomous reaction to changes in the service landscape allows taking advantage of the appearance of better or less expensive services or recovering from failures by automatically replacing faulted or offline services (Cobo et al., 2004). Many scenarios involve the dynamic selection of service instances based on similar re-appearing goal instances in B2B relationships: the location of suitable carriers to provide transportation services (Preist et al., 2005, Friesen and Namiri, 2006, Küster et al., 2007a), an intelligent procurement management for non-critical supplies (Preist, 2007, Küster et al., 2007a) or the location of the most appropriate notification service to contact a customer (Cobo et al., 2004). In B2C scenarios, SWS are often motivated by the desire to delegate a search for the best among many options to autonomous agents. In these scenarios, many providers offer similar services and the best provider depends on the concrete goal or varies over time. Typical scenarios of this type involve the discovery of the best deal to purchase a set of items, e.g. books (Preist, 2004), furniture (Stollberg, 2004), computers (Küster and König-Ries, 2007, Li and Horrocks, 2003), or used cars

(Ragone et al., 2007), to find the best matching offer in an apartment rental scenario (Colucci et al., 2005), or to make travel arrangements and flight or hotel bookings (Balzer et al., 2004).

The focus in all of the above mentioned contexts is on discovery, matchmaking and precise filtering or ranking of many possible options. Usually a high degree of automation is sought, in some scenarios complete automation is required.

The second type of application scenarios deals with supporting developers in establishing or maintaining rather stable B2B or B2C relationships and setting up distributed applications. Such scenarios root in application domains like Business Process Management (BPM) and Enterprise Application Integration (EAI). In these fields, SWS are motivated by the desire to decrease the programming time and cost by semi-automating very time consuming tasks like the establishment of data and process mediation procedures. Scenarios in this category include the provision of value added services by bundling or mediating external contractors (Friesen and Grimm, 2005), the semi-automated design of processes to manage virtual ISP problems (Preist, 2004), or the development of an emergency management system in the e-government domain (Gugliotta et al., 2006).

The main focus in these scenarios is on mediation and composition rather than discovery. The goal of employing SWS in such settings is to ease the process of integrating remote systems, master the encountered heterogeneity, and decrease the level of coupling between the components. Full automation is usually not required.

In this work, we focus on the first class of application scenarios, leaving the other class to be dealt with in future work. We traced back the use cases of that first class of application scenarios to three main high-level goals of SWS. Following the GQM approach these are defined in a tractable way by refining them into a set of quantifiable questions. The goals and the defining questions

are described in the following, referenced with the use cases from which they have been derived.

Goal 1 *Allow the dynamic and transparent usage of functionality in mobile or P2P environments where the availability and reliability of that desired functionality is not under local control (Sirbu et al., 2006, Klein et al., 2005).*

1. Does the framework allow use of external functionality as if it were locally available? Is the framework able to hide the fact that the functionality is dynamically discovered and bound and supports full automation?
2. Does the framework guarantee correctness to allow for full automation?
3. If required, does the framework work under the requirements of P2P environments or the limited resources of mobile devices?

Goal 2 *Minimize the cost or optimize the quality of a consumed functionality by dynamically reacting to changes in the service landscape (Cobo et al., 2004, Preist et al., 2005, Friesen and Namiri, 2006, Preist, 2007, Küster et al., 2007a, Preist, 2004, Stollberg, 2004, Küster and König-Ries, 2007, Li and Horrocks, 2003, Ragone et al., 2007, Colucci et al., 2005, Balzer et al., 2004, Friesen and Grimm, 2005, Klein et al., 2005).*

4. Does the usage of the framework decrease the time necessary to find a good enough or the optimal option? To what extent?
5. Does the usage of the framework increase the quality of the option discovered? To what extent?

Goal 3 *Reduce failures or down-time by automatically replacing faulted or unavailable service components in a distributed application (Cobo et al., 2004, Preist et al., 2005, Preist, 2007, Küster et al., 2007a, Preist, 2004, Friesen and Grimm, 2005, Gugliotta et al., 2006).*

Figure 1. A model of the dimensions of evaluation in the field of automating service consumption using SWS frameworks

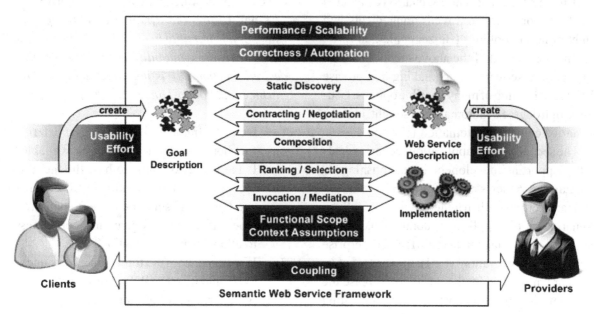

6. Does the framework support to react autonomously to detected failures?

7. If a human still needs to be in the loop, to what extent does the framework support that human and reduces the time necessary to recover from failures?

Furthermore, there are a number of questions related to all three goals:

8. How tightly coupled are service providers and consumers in the framework?

9. How much effort is it to use the framework, e.g. to publish service offers or formalize goals with the framework?

10. How much effort is it to set up and maintain the framework as such (e.g. agree on common ontologies if that is necessary)?

11. How good is the framework in locating and using externally available functionality? Does it act like the user it acts on behalf of? How often does it fail to find a solution even though one exists? How often does it find the optimal solution? How short of optimal

is the solution chosen by the framework if it is not the optimal one?

12. How well does the framework scale?

Finally, it is essential to keep in mind that the performance of any framework will depend on the specific context parameters at hand and must not be easily generalized:

13. For which types of applications, services or use cases are the answers to the previous questions valid? How do the answers change in a changing context?

According to the GQM methodology, the questions defining the software engineering goals motivating SWS are used to define the set of criteria that should be employed to evaluate SWS with respect to the goals. An analysis of the correlations among the questions was performed to derive the conceptual criteria model for the evaluation of SWS frameworks displayed in Figure 1. This model comprises the following five dimensions of evaluation.

Performance / Scalability

Regards the runtime performance and scalability characteristics of a framework. It is typically measured by the computing resources required (e.g. processor time or memory). Questions 3 and 12 are related to this dimension.

Usability / Effort

Regards the usability of the framework in terms of how much effort is required to set it up, maintain it, and use it. This dimension is influenced for instance by the complexity of the framework and the available tool support. Questions 4, 5, 7, 9, and 10 are related to this dimension.

Correctness

Regards the quality of the support offered by the framework, i.e. to which degree a framework acts precisely like the user it acts on behalf of. This dimension is closely related to the often used notion of *expressivity*, that captures how precisely and comprehensively a service's capabilities and a user's needs can be formalized in a framework. Questions 1, 2, 4 – 7, and 11 are related to this dimension.

Coupling

Regards how tightly coupled the providers and the consumers of services are in this framework, e.g. whether they have to agree on common ontologies or not. Questions 8 and 10 are related to this dimension.

Supported Scope and Automation

Define the context for the other dimensions, since assessments made with respect to these will always depend on assumptions regarding the scenarios at hand. The notions of the scope of a framework and the supported degree of automation are closely related. The former defines the phases during service consumption covered by a framework (see Figure 1) while the latter defines the degree of automation that the framework provides for these phases. Questions 1, 2, 6 and 13 are related to this dimension.

Three remarks about this model need to be made. First, it is quite obvious, that some of the criteria dimensions are correlated negatively. A framework supporting full automation even for complex use cases requires a highly expressive language. On the other hand, less expressive languages will likely be easier to use and yield better runtime performance. Therefore, SWS frameworks need to aspire a balance between competing requirements. It is thus important to evaluate the dimensions identified above conjointly to make the corresponding tradeoffs explicit.

Second, this model has been primarily designed with the use cases of the first application type in mind. These involve the automation of tasks that previously, i.e. using established technologies, always involved a human in the loop. Therefore, such tasks do not always allow a direct comparison of SWS-based approaches with conventional software engineering approaches. Nevertheless it is important to keep in mind that SWS approaches do not only need to be comparable to each other, but that it is additionally necessary to show their relative advantage over traditional software engineering approaches. This regards primarily the *effort* dimension.

Third, designing a criteria model like the one proposed above involves some degree of freedom how to design it. We have followed the GQM methodology because this methodology directly links engineering goals to evaluation criteria through the questions that are first used to define the goals and then to derive the criteria. Thus, if properly implemented, this methodology ensures that the evaluation model is complete with respect to the identified engineering goals.

Table 1. Overview of dimensions of evaluation covered by existing initiatives

	S3 Contest	SWS Challenge	WS Challenge	DIANE Benchmark
Performance & Scalability	Query response time for static discovery	n.a.	Runtime for WS composition algorithms	n.a. (not generalizable to other approaches)
Usability & Effort	n.a.	Evaluates effort to react to changes in problem scenarios	n.a.	Preliminarily accessed via questionnaire
Correctness	Matchmaking recall and precision for given test collections in specific formalisms	n.a. (solutions are only submitted if they solve a scenario correctly)	Tests for validity of solutions, extra credit for minimal composition length	Evaluates correct formalization of given sample service requests
Coupling	Decoupled setting, descriptions provided by organizers	n.a. (offers and goals formalized by the same developers)	Decoupled setting, data provided by organizers	Tests correctness of results in an explicitly decoupled setting
Scope & Automation	So far limited to static discovery only	Differentiates functional coverage via hierarchy of problem scenarios	Limited to static composition only	Assumes full automation of discovery, selection and invocation

CURRENT EVALUATION INITIATIVES

The criteria model presented above allows examining the existing approaches to SWS evaluation in a systematic manner. In this section, we lay the basis for such analysis by introducing to the state of the art in SWS evaluation. An overview of the different approaches is shown in Table 1.

S3 Contest on Semantic Service Selection

The S3 Contest on Semantic Service Selection[4] is an annual international contest for the comparative performance evaluation of implemented SWS matchmakers. Its first two editions were held in 2007 and 2008 in conjunction with the 6th and 7th International Semantic Web Conferences, a third edition will be held in conjunction with the 8th International Semantic Web Conference in Washington D.C., USA (October 2009). Depending on the availability of service retrieval test collections, the 2007 edition focused on OWL-S service matchmaking, while the 2008 edition broadened its scope to also cover SAWSDL matchmakers. Basic task of semantic service selection is to return a ranked set of service offer descriptions that are semantically relevant to given service request descriptions. The retrieval performance of matchmaker implementations is evaluated by measuring the classical retrieval performance in terms of recall/precision and F1-values (*correctness* and completeness of semantic service matching and ranking), as well as the *runtime performance* in terms of the average query response time and the aggregated runtime to match the complete test collection selected.

For comparative performance evaluation, the S3 contest readily provides the first publicly available semantic service matchmaker evaluation environment SME2[5] together with test collections OWLS-TC3 and SAWSDL-TC2 for OWL-S, respectively, SAWSDL services. As of today, both collections are widely used in practice with a reasonably high number of downloads for each. For example, OWLS-TC with around 10.000 downloads is comprised of 1.007 OWL-S services from 7 domains, 29 queries with respective binary and gradual relevance sets (in its current version OWLS-TC3). This collection has been jointly created by more than 30 users from different institutions based on the semantic annotation of public WSDL services and the inclusion of readily available OWL-S services as well. Regarding the definition of query relevance sets, binary and gradual relevance judgements of services followed the standard NIST-TREC with union average pooling.

At the 2008 edition, three OWL-S and two SAWSDL matchmaker implementations participated in the contest6. For the upcoming 2009 edition, six OWL-S matchmakers and four SAWSDL matchmakers are planned to be comparatively evaluated and discussed.

Semantic Web Services Challenge

The SWS Challenge Initiative[7] (Petrie et al., 2008b) was launched in March 2006 and has organized seven workshops and events since then. The challenge's main purpose is to provide a certification of SWS frameworks. The W3C SWS Testbed Incubator Group[8] aims to develop a standard evaluation methodology based on experiences gathered within the SWS-Challenge (Petrie et al., 2008a).

The approach of the SWS-Challenge is to define a set of detailed and realistic scenarios, each organized in different problem levels. Participants of the challenge try to solve these scenarios with their SWS technology. So far, two mediation scenarios involve building mediators to integrate systems in a purchase order and payment management scenario. Three more discovery scenarios target the automated discovery and invocation of suitable service providers for given specific service needs.

Until 2008, nine teams have participated in the challenge and were evaluated with respect to two aspects. Based on the set of increasingly complex problem levels in the Challenge's problem scenarios, the *functional coverage* of different SWS approaches is evaluated by assessing the extent to which approaches actually solved particular problem levels. This way a certification of the capabilities of particular technologies is provided. Additionally, but so far only for the mediation scenarios, the challenge tries to evaluate and

compare the level of *effort* involved in adapting solutions to changes in the underlying problem scenario. By doing so the challenge tries to investigate the fundamental assumption of SWS that an increased usage of formal, declarative semantics will make solutions more flexible and easier to adapt to change.

WS Challenge

The IEEE Web Service Challenge (Bleul et al., 2009)[9], hosted annually at the IEEE Conferences on E-Commerce Technology (CEC) and Enterprise Computing, E-Commerce and E-Services (EEE), focuses on evaluating the correctness and runtime performance of web service discovery and composition algorithms. It was started in 2005 with the evaluation of syntactic service matchmaking and composition based on the string equivalence of WSDL part names. In 2006, this was complemented by a track on semantic matchmaking and composition based on the compatibility of XML schema types (Blake et al., 2006). In 2007 and 2008, the syntactic and matchmaking tracks have been discontinued to solely focus on semantic composition (Blake et al., 2007, Bansal et al., 2008). However, the semantics used by the challenge are much less expressive than usually employed in SWS frameworks. Semantic descriptions do not include service categories, pre- or postconditions, but are restricted to input and output parameters. These parameters are defined with respect to an XML-Schema type hierarchy that, from 2007 on, is represented in a simplified OWL version. So far, no semantics beyond inheritance relationships are used in the challenge.

The challenge provides a test environment and a test data generator. It evaluates the runtime of the composition algorithms and the correctness and quality (completeness, composition length, exploitation of parallel invocations in the compositions) of the discovered compositions. In 2009 the quality of compositions will be evaluated using their response time and throughput which must be computed from the provided response time and throughput of the component services. Additionally, there is an award for the best solution architecture (Bleul et al., 2009).

DIANE Benchmark

Within the DIANE project[10], a service description language (called DSD) and an accompanying middleware supporting service discovery, composition, and invocation have been developed. DIANE is one of the projects taking part in the SWS Challenge. In addition to the evaluation provided by the challenge, considerable effort has been put into devising a benchmark suite for semantic service description frameworks[11]. This benchmark has then been applied to DSD/DIANE (Fischer, 2005).

The DIANE Benchmark focuses on three aspects. The *effort* required to use the framework is assessed by measuring the initial effort to model the necessary ontologies as well as the continuous effort to maintain and update ontologies and service descriptions with the framework. The *correctness* of the framework is evaluated by assessing how well the semantics of given services can be captured by descriptions based on the employed formalism. Finally, the level of *coupling* is evaluated by determining to which degree the framework still yields correct results, if services and goals are formalized by different people in a completely decoupled way. The Benchmark also deals with the runtime performance and the correctness of the framework's implementation. However, since the corresponding parts cannot be easily generalized from DSD to other languages, they are not relevant for this article.

Other Approaches

Toma et al. (Toma et al., 2007) presented a framework for the evaluation of semantic matchmaking frameworks by identifying different aspects of such frameworks that should be evaluated: query and advertising language, scalability, reasoning support, matchmaking versus brokering, and mediation support. They evaluate a number of frameworks with regard to these criteria. The focus of the work is rather on the survey than on the comparison framework itself. While the framework does provide guidance for a structured comparison, it does not offer concrete test suites, measures, benchmarks or procedures for an objective comparative evaluation.

Moreover we have looked into the evaluation results of various SWS research projects (see for instance (Sîrbu et al., 2006, Sîrbu, 2006, Unspecified, 2006)). Most have spent a surprisingly small share of resources on evaluation or not published details about any evaluation performed. For example RW[2], an Austrian funded research project[12], has implemented different discovery engines for request and service description in different logical languages, respectively different granularity. However, as evaluation only a relatively small set of a couple of dozen handcrafted services exist. The EU projects DIP and ASG, for instance, have also developed similar discovery engines. With respect to evaluation they quote industrial case studies which, in essence, are also just a small set of service descriptions. Moreover, due to intellectual property rights restrictions the situation is even slightly worse, since not all descriptions are publicly available and a comparative evaluation is thus impossible.

Just recently, the EU funded SEALS project (Semantic Evaluation At Large Scale) has started in June 2009[13]. The goal of SEALS is to provide a reference infrastructure for automated benchmarking in the areas of ontology engineering tools, storage and reasoning systems, matching tools, semantic search tools and semantic web service tools. Furthermore, it will organize two international benchmarking campaigns for these research areas in 2010 and 2011. The formation and funding of this project is an important step towards better and more standardized evaluations, but since the project has just started, no results are available yet.

ANALYSIS OF EVALUATION METRICS AND MEASURES

This section presents an in-depth critical analysis of the measures that the four main approaches introduced above use for evaluations along the criteria dimensions of the evaluation model introduced above. An understanding for the fundamental research problems involved in SWS evaluation is developed by identifying current shortcomings and discussing possible improvements. This allows proposing a research agenda towards standard evaluation methodologies and benchmarks in the conclusions.

Performance / Scalability

Status

A comparative evaluation of the runtime performance of different matchmaking algorithms is primarily provided by the S3 Contest. The experimental task to perform is to compare a given set of OWL-S (or SAWSDL) based request descriptions with a given set of OWL-S (or SAWSDL) based offer descriptions and identify the set of relevant offers for each request. This task is executed by the participating matchmaker implementations multiple times and the average query response time for single queries as well as the average total time to match all requests are measured. In 2007, the results for two matchmakers were roughly similar (11 respectively 9 minutes) whereas a third matchmaker required more than 20 hours to perform the task on a significantly downsized version of the test collection. Unfortunately, a detailed interpretation of the results is not available so far. An analysis of the causes for the poor performance of the third matchmaker would be important to investigate whether that poor performance is inherent to the

particular matchmaking algorithm or has to be attributed to an unoptimized proof-of-concept implementation of the algorithm. It is hoped that participants of the contest are investigating the causes for encountered performance issues and will report on corresponding improvements in subsequent editions of the contest. It is worth noting that the S3 Contest evaluates the runtime performance and the correctness of the returned results, thereby allowing to put the runtime performance measures in relation to the achieved correctness.

The WS Challenge represents a very similar evaluation approach for composition instead of discovery algorithms. A testbed consisting of service descriptions, composition requests and an evaluation environment is provided to the participants. A composition requests specifies the available inputs and the desired outputs of a service. The task is to compose the provided available component services into a WS-BPEL process such that the process requires only available inputs and provides all desired outputs. The algorithms need to assess the composability of services using type inheritance relationships of the service's interfaces. Credit is given to the systems that solve the task best (see *Correctness*) and fastest. Apart of the different scope (composition versus discovery), the main difference between the WS Challenge and the S3 Contest is the origin of the test data used. While the S3 Contest relies on manually manufactured service descriptions, the WS Challenge uses a configurable, but fully automated test data generator.

Discussion and Suggestions for Improvements

It is obvious that runtime performance measures are highly dependent on the test data used. Unfortunately, no standard test collection for the evaluation of SWS exists yet. To make experimental performance evaluations possible the test collections OWLS-TC[14] and SAWSDL-TC[15] have been developed. These are the only sizeable ones currently available and employed by the S3 Contest. Due to the tremendous effort involved and in order to reflect different views and different perspectives, standard test collections can only be built by the community as a whole. The organizers of the S3 Contest therefore invite the community to help the ongoing efforts across different institutions to further extend and improve the test collections OWLS-TC and SAWSDL-TC. Since the evaluation of retrieval performance bases on the availability of such test collections, the first three editions of the S3 Contest could only focus on matchmakers for OWL-S and SAWSDL services. Unfortunately, as of now, there is still no public test collection of WSML services available which is hoped to change soon. For the future, large standard test collections of the same set of services in at least all three major formalisms, that are OWL-S, WSML and the standard SAWSDL, need to be developed.

Another viable approach of using generated test data is the one taken by the WS-Challenge. However, generating test data that reliably resembles the characteristics of real world data is a continuous challenge. Furthermore, the automatic synthesis of test data is the more difficult, the more expressive and general the used formalisms are. More research on reliable test data generators is clearly desirable here.

Scalability is not yet explicitly evaluated, neither by the S3 Contest nor the WS Challenge. However, this could be done with limited additional effort. It requires splitting the test collections in subcollections of different sizes and exploring the degradation of the runtime performance with increasing size of the test data. Obviously the remarks about sensitivity towards the composition of the employed test collections apply in the same way as discussed above.

Conclusions

Performance and scalability measures and their associated potential pitfalls are very well understood and have been used in all areas of software engineering for decades. Their application in the area of SWS is currently primarily hampered by practical issues. In contrast to a variety of theoretic work in the area of SWS matchmaking for instance, only few implementations of the proposed matchmaking algorithms are readily available. This is particularly true for the more sophisticated algorithms proposing the use of more expressive formalisms. The lack of readily downloadable tools is a blocker for better evaluations also with respect to other criteria.

Additionally, the lack of test collections of SWS has proven to be difficult to overcome. The effects of the properties and composition of the test collections on the evaluation results need to be studied carefully. This will allow building standard test collections or standard data generators that are diverse and balanced, ensuring reliable evaluations.

Usability / Effort

Status

An initial attempt to evaluate the usability of a framework has been made within the DIANE Benchmark. The approach is based on evaluating the initial effort to create the necessary ontologies and the continuous effort to update and maintain these. The initial effort is evaluated by measuring the time it takes an experienced developer to formalize an ontology given as a UML model in the language of the target framework. The continuous effort to maintain a framework is estimated by the DIANE Benchmark via a questionnaire that tries to assess the quality of the available tool support and documentation.

Besides the approach of the DIANE Benchmark, significant effort has been devoted to develop a methodology to assess the flexibility of solutions within the SWS-Challenge. The approach is based on evaluating the effort necessary to adapt a solution for a given complete problem scenario to variations of that base scenario. Notably, approaches based on SWS as well as more traditional software engineering technologies participate in the SWS-Challenge. This allows to investigate not only the relative advantage of one SWS approach over another, but also to compare them with traditional technologies. A detailed description of the methodology employed by the SWS-Challenge and the difficulties encountered is available as a W3C Incubator Group Report (Petrie et al., 2008a).

Discussion and Suggestions for Improvement

While the SWS-Challenge relies on complete natural language descriptions of scenarios, the DIANE Benchmark follows a much more restricted approach. It is thus easier to implement and involves less effort for participants. However, the task of formalizing an ontology given as a UML model prescribes the level of detail to be formalized. Lightweight frameworks, which do not exploit many details from the descriptions of services during the matchmaking, might be penalized with the effort of formalizing aspects which are of no use to them.

Generally, the choice of the right level of detail for a formalization of a problem still constitutes one of the core research problems in the area and should not be dictated by the testbed for an evaluation. Though experience with natural language scenario descriptions within the SWS-Challenge showed that these descriptions were ambiguous in several cases, such ambiguities were discovered by the participants and could subsequently be resolved. This way even scenarios described in natural language only become sufficiently well-defined over time.

It thus seems appropriate to combine both approaches, provide complete natural language descriptions of use cases (as the SWS-Challenge does) and evaluate the time necessary to implement these with a framework (in the spirit of the DIANE Benchmark). This setup reflects the strengths and weaknesses of the frameworks more adequately. A lightweight framework, for instance, might benefit from a reduced modelling effort but later suffer from poorer measures regarding the correctness of the achieved results.

Notably, this approach has not been taken so far. Because of the amount of work involved in implementing such an approach, the SWS-Challenge has resorted to evaluating the effort of implementing changes on top of existing solutions instead of evaluating the effort of creating the initial solutions in the first place. Furthermore, there were concerns that measuring the time needed to perform the necessary adaptations would lead to an unwanted competitive atmosphere and would be overly sensitive towards the personal performance of the programmer implementing the changes. As a consequence, the current approach is to measure the amount of code that needs to be changed instead of the time needed to implement those changes. Unfortunately, this change-based approach proved to be very difficult to implement in cases where code is not written as textual instructions but by assembling processes graphically in a GUI. A satisfying solution to this issue has still to be found. Similarly, the investigation of other compromises is still an open issue. It should be possible to develop scenarios with a sufficiently limited scope to make an evaluation of the overall effort of implementing them feasible.

Regarding the complementary questionnaire approach of the DIANE benchmark it is felt that a questionnaire is a good since lightweight starting point. However, the current implementation has several problems: The answering scheme (*yes - partially - no*) is too coarse-grained, some answers cannot be verified objectively and the weighting of the single questions in the total result is not based on experimental evidence.

Conclusions

Overall, it seems that efforts regarding the evaluation of the usability and ultimately the increase in programmer productivity achieved through SWS frameworks are in their infancy and have not received appropriate attention so far. One of the problems currently hindering more extensive usability evaluations is the already mentioned lack of implementations and tools for the proposed algorithms. This lack of ready-to-use, well documented downloadable tools needs to be overcome by the community.

The lack of ready-to-use tools might also explain the fact that current evaluations have focused on usability on a technical level, e.g. investigated how long it takes to update an ontology. However, ontologies and their management are just a means and technology to achieve higher level goals. Therefore, such evaluation efforts need to be complemented by evaluations of the increase in productivity on a higher, more goal-oriented level. Such evaluations would also improve the comparability of SWS technology with traditional software engineering technologies, a crucial factor for the adoption of SWS by industry. The attempts of the SWS-Challenge to measure the flexibility of solutions are a promising step in this direction, but also illustrate that the question how to reliably and objectively measure an increase in productivity achieved by using different SWS approaches is a still unsolved research problem. Much more effort is needed here.

Correctness

Status

Prior to the establishment of the S3 Contest in 2007, there have not been comparative correctness evaluations of different SWS matchmaking approaches at all. To get started, the S3 Contest borrowed the well-established evaluation approach from the series of TREC conferences[16] in information retrieval (IR) using the previously discussed OWLS-TC and SAWSDL-TC. Correctness of service matchmaking is evaluated by means of the traditional IR measures precision and recall. Precision measures the proportion of retrieved services, which are indeed relevant, and recall measures the proportion of relevant services, that are correctly retrieved. Until 2008, the contest relied on binary relevance judgments, i.e. service offers are judged as either relevant or irrelevant to a request, but no further ranking is considered. In 2009 graded relevance judgments will be introduced to the Contest.

The WS-Challenge investigates the correctness of service composition algorithms and gives extra credits to algorithms that return better (e.g., shorter) solutions. However, problems are defined such that finding good correct solutions is not difficult in principle, but algorithms are forced to traverse a very large search space. This way, the primary focus of the challenge is on evaluating the speed rather than the correctness of composition algorithms.

The SWS-Challenge focuses on functional coverage of frameworks (see below) and currently does not aim at providing quantitative measures for the correctness achieved by participating approaches. An entry to the challenge is usually developed until it correctly solves a scenario and not submitted otherwise.

The DIANE Benchmark presents two approaches to evaluate correctness. The first is similar to the approach of the S3 Contest but focuses on whether correct results can be achieved in an explicitly decoupled setting. It will be covered in the following Section. The other approach complements the S3 Contest in that it focuses on how well the real world semantics of services can be captured in the formalism used by a framework. It therefore attempts to evaluate correctness by experimentally evaluating the expressivity of the employed formalism. To define the benchmark, a group of test subjects not familiar with semantic web technology were asked to formulate service requests for two different application domains. The queries the test subjects devised were formulated in natural language. This resulted in about 200 requests. Additionally, domain experts developed ontologies they deemed necessary to handle the two domains. The evaluation approach of the benchmark is to measure the proportion of the 200 requests which can be formalized in a given framework correctly. Each request can be rated green (the request can be directly formalized), yellow (the request could be formalized with extensions to the domain ontologies) or red (the request cannot be appropriately expressed using the language constructs provided by the framework).

Discussion and Suggestions for Improvement

The adoption of the well-established correctness measures precision and recall from IR is a self-evident first approach towards correctness measures in the field of SWS retrieval. Obviously, the general remarks about the sensitivity of evaluation results towards the composition of the employed test collection and the discussion about the lack of standard test collections across formalisms made in Section apply here, too.

However, as argued in (Küster et al., 2007b, Küster and König-Ries, 2009), traditional IR and SWS retrieval differ in that the former typically operates directly on the original resources, whereas the latter is based on formal semantics that are explicitly manually attached to the resources to support their precise and correct retrieval. Following the TREC evaluation approach the S3 Contest presets the semantic descriptions used for the retrieval. The major benefit of this approach is twofold: it mimics real world environments, where SWS descriptions are not formalized by the developers of a SWS matchmaker (see Sec-

tion on Coupling) and it limits the effort involved in participation in the Contest. It does have the drawback, however, that recall and precision alone in such a setting can only be of limited significance. The problem is, that the question whether a semantic service description matches a semantic request description should be determinable unambiguously based on the formal semantics of the employed description formalism. In this aspect, it is unclear to what extent false results of the matchmaking (and thus a low precision and recall) should be attributed to inapt service and request formalizations or to shortcomings of the evaluated matchmaking algorithms.

Thus, an ideal evaluation of SWS retrieval correctness needs to cover two aspects: First, how well the real world semantics of services can be captured in the formalism used by a framework. Second, how effectively the framework's matchmaker can then exploit this information during the matchmaking.

An evaluation where the descriptions are preset is by design restricted to evaluating only the second aspect. On an implementation level, diverse test collections that contain service descriptions at various levels of detail and with varying complexity are required to evaluate this aspect reliably. Such collections are only partially available.

With respect to the first aspect, i.e. how to experimentally measure the quality of the formalization of a service's semantics possible in a framework, the DIANE Benchmark that relies on natural language service descriptions constitutes an important first achievement. Despite of that, an analysis of the evaluation of DSD performed with the DIANE Benchmark sheds light on two problems in the current setup of this part of the benchmark. First, the distinction between green and yellow ratings seems arbitrary in many cases. It remains unclear, why certain concepts were included in the initial ontologies (leading to green ratings) while others were not (leading to yellow ratings) and why this is a relevant measure for the expressivity of a framework. It seems more appropriate to evaluate the effort necessary to implement required extensions to the ontology and use this as a measure for the usability and effort of a framework. A framework whose formalism is expressive enough to support a flexible and elegant modelling would consequently benefit from a high score on this metric. The second problem is a lack of objectivity regarding green ratings. Green ratings are supported by providing formalizations of these requests in the target formalism. However, the judgment that these formalizations fully capture the semantics of the service (justifying a green rating) is made by the subjective estimate of the expert formalizing the requests. Such estimates need to be supported by an additional recall/precision analysis.

Conclusions

Until recently, there have not been any comparative evaluations of the correctness achieved by different SWS framework at all. It is very promising that this important issue is starting to receive the attention it deserves. However, as can be seen from the discussion above a meaningful correctness evaluation is far from trivial and the above mentioned problems illustrate the need for further research in this direction:

First, current evaluations have either focused on the correctness of the matchmaking, or the correctness (or expressivity) of the formalization, but not on both. It needs to be investigated how this can be improved to achieve more reliable and comprehensive results. To this end, an alternate new track will be implemented in the 2009 edition of the S3 Contest where participants formalize given services themselves and the effects of different annotation styles to the matchmaker performance will be studied.

Second, current evaluations of correctness via recall and precision rely on binary relevance judgments. This approach has been a natural starting point, but does not reflect that virtually all SWS matchmakers support multi-valued matchmaking

degrees and does not allow evaluating the important aspect of the quality of the ranking performed by SWS matchmakers. Necessary research on better measures, e.g. based on graded instead of binary relevance, has started and is ongoing (Tsetsos et al., 2006, Küster and König-Ries, 2008a). In fact, the 2009 edition will initially introduce the usage of such measures in the S3 Contest.

Third, the previously mentioned lack of standard test collections of SWS is even more critical for correctness evaluations than for performance evaluations. Reliable and meaningful correctness evaluations require diverse and realistic test data which cannot be generated automatically. This test data needs to be available in natural language to experimentally evaluate the expressivity of a formalism employed by a framework. Additionally, complete and high quality semantic descriptions for a common set of services are required in different formalisms to effectively compare the correctness achieved by the various algorithms. Generally, the desirable properties of test collections need to be investigated more thoroughly and procedures how to obtain the necessary data and ensure its quality need to be developed (Küster and König-Ries, 2008c). It should be stressed that the indispensable standard test collections can only be built by the community as a whole. Everybody interested is thus invited to join the corresponding efforts.

Coupling

Status

An evaluation of the level of coupling was so far not in the scope of the SWS-Challenge. Within the participating teams the same developers typically formalize all goal and offer descriptions. The WS-Challenge uses generated test data using one common schema type hierarchy. An investigation of the effects of decoupled creation of service annotations is not within its scope. Similarly it has not been explicitly in the focus of the S3 Contest so far.

The DIANE Benchmark presents an experimental setup to evaluate the degradation of delivered correctness in an explicitly decoupled setting. A number of inexperienced users are given an introduction to a framework and description formalism to be used. Subsequently they are divided into two groups that are not allowed to communicate with each other. A number of natural language service descriptions are provided as test data to the groups. The first group is asked to formalize them as offer descriptions, the second as request descriptions. Afterwards, the framework is used to match the resulting offer and request descriptions and precision and recall of the matchmaking are determined by considering request and goal descriptions relevant to each other if and only if they originate from the same natural language service description.

Discussion and Suggestions for Improvements

The experience from applying this experimental setup to DIANE/DSD highlights an important issue: in practice, even using predefined ontologies, a high correctness is not easy to achieve in a decoupled setting. In the experiment a service that books a train ticket has been formalized as a service after whose execution a ticket is *reserved* by the first group. In contrast, the second group formalized the same service as a service after whose execution a ticket is *owned*. Subsequently, these different formalizations of the same real world semantics resulted in a false fail when the two descriptions were matched. This emphasizes the negative effects of variance in possible ways to formalize the real world semantics of a service. Such variance will inevitably be encountered in real world environments. It can be assumed that formalisms differ with respect to the likelihood of such modelling differences and that frameworks differ in how well they are able to handle them.

Thus, a corresponding evaluation provides important clues about the performance of a framework in real world settings.

On a practical level, the DIANE Benchmark experiment needs to be considered preliminary. First, the remarks about binary relevance judgments in the context of SWS matchmaking made above apply here, too. Second, the test data defined by the DIANE Benchmark for this experiment (ten services) is currently much too small to support reliable results in practice. Further work is required to address both issues. To this end an improved implementation of the experiment based upon graded relevance measures and a much larger realistic testbed will be implemented as part of the 2009 edition of the S3 Contest[17].

Conclusions

The importance of evaluating the level of coupling and its effects within SWS frameworks is illustrated by the experience from the preliminary experiment in the context of DIANE/DSD. Yet, this aspect has received much too little attention so far. Typically, research, development, and evaluation of a given SWS framework is performed within a single research team and thus in a tightly coupled setting. In contrast, the envisioned use cases for SWS target strongly decoupled settings. It is essential to start investigating the issues which may result from this discrepancy and to research methodologies to evaluate the tolerance of SWS frameworks towards these.

Scope and Automation

Status

It is the main evaluation goal of the SWS-Challenge to evaluate the functional scope of participating frameworks. The approach is to define a set of problem scenarios, which consist of increasingly complex problem levels. This may be illustrated by an example from one of the discovery scenarios. The shipping scenario deals with discovering, binding and invoking a suitable shipping service for a given concrete shipment request. Five services with different pricing models and different functional restrictions, e.g. on the operation range, are specified. The various problem levels are defined by concrete requests that require taking more and more aspects of a service into consideration during the matchmaking. The first level requires to discover a shipper based on operation range, the second level requires to take restrictions regarding the weight of the parcel into account, the third level includes price restrictions, which in the case of one service requires to dynamically inquire price information at the service's endpoint, the fourth level requires basic composition capability to support shipping of multiple packages and the fifth level requires to reason about temporal constraints regarding pickup times and shipping durations. Participating solutions are certified at the Challenge workshops with respect to whether they are able to solve a particular problem level correctly. A review of the code during the workshop ensures that frameworks actually solve the problems by reasoning about the formalized problem semantics and not hard-wiring the correct solution.

An evaluation of the scope of frameworks is neither performed by the S3 Contest or the WS Challenge nor within the scope of the DIANE Benchmark. The S3 Contest is limited to static discovery of services, i.e. discovery which identifies relevant services based on static descriptions only. The WS Challenge is (since the discontinuation of the discovery track in 2007) concerned with fully automated service composition exclusively. The DIANE Benchmark assumes support for dynamic discovery, ranking, selection and invocation and does not provide a fine-grained evaluation of frameworks, which only support some of these tasks.

Conclusions

The evaluation and certification of the functional scope of SWS frameworks is at the focus of the main SWS evaluation initiative and has been subject of a corresponding W3C Incubator Group[18]. It therefore does not come as a surprise that the underlying methodology is quite mature meanwhile. However, the SWS-Challenge comprises only five scenarios so far which cover only parts of the problem space yet. Many more scenarios are needed to provide a more complete coverage of the problem space. More scenarios would also bring in the different perspectives and assumptions of different research groups in the area and thus help to confirm or revise the existing evaluation results. A continuous call for submission of scenario proposals is thus part of the SWS-Challenge[19]. More community response is still desired here. Fundamentally, also more research on methodologies that help ensuring the relevance and a certain completeness and balance of the testbed of scenarios is required. Experience from building similar testbeds in other fields of computer science may serve as important input here.

SUMMARY AND DIRECTIONS FOR FUTURE RESEARCH

Doing science means producing reproducible results that can be independently evaluated. This is an indispensable requirement for scientific progress and industrial adoption of research results. In the area of SWS, only three years ago, it was impossible to evaluate and compare different approaches by different groups across formalisms in a fair and objective way. The meanwhile formation of international open evaluation campaigns like the SWS-Challenge, the S3 Contest and the WS Challenge is a very promising and significant achievement towards reproducibility and third-party verification of results and thus, ultimately, towards the vision of bringing semantic web services to reality. These campaigns have been possible only by community participation.

In this section, we summarize once more the main conclusions from the last sections and suggest a research agenda to further improve the existing evaluation initiatives and SWS evaluations in general. Like the work already achieved, these further steps can only be realized collaboratively and require even more help and participation from the community. After all, evaluations become the more objective, reliable, and meaningful the more groups contribute to the testbeds and participate in the evaluation events. You are therefore invited to join now to participate in the further evolution of the SWS evaluation campaigns with respect to the issues listed below and others that you may bring in.

Summary of the Status

Here is a very brief summary of the status in SWS evaluation as discussed in the previous section:

- With respect to *performance and scalability* on the one hand more and better implementations of matchmakers are needed, on the other hand, standard SWS test collections need to be build.
- To meaningfully evaluate SWS frameworks' *usability and amount of effort* more fundamental work is needed, in particular, suitable measures on a high level of abstraction need to be identified.
- Concerning *correctness* what is lacking is a unified approach to evaluating correctness of matchmakers and formalisms, fine grained criteria that are suitable to measure correctness more precisely, and sufficiently large standard test collections.
- *Decoupling* has not been regarded in depth yet, so reliable measures need to be defined. A foundation of those would be, again, standard test collections.
- *Functional Scope and Level of Automation*

is probably the most thoroughly investigated of all the criteria. Nevertheless, to reach meaningful results, a more diverse set of scenarios and a closer analysis of the dependence between scenario, approach, and performance are needed.

Overall, SWS evaluation is an emerging field. Much more research is necessary to develop measures that are sufficiently mature to become standard. Below, we suggest the most important activities towards such standard measures. Closely related areas of computer science have many years of experience in developing their evaluations. Among many others, there are TREC, NTCIR[20] and INEX[21] from information retrieval, the ICAPS Competitions[22] from the planning community, the Trading Agent Competitions[23] from the agent community, or the series of EON workshops[24] from the ontology evaluation community. These initiatives have succeeded to set approved standards in their communities. They provide valuable experience and input to the SWS evaluation domain that obviously should be taken into account in any further activities. Successful such examples are the collaboration of the SWS-Challenge with the last EON workshop[24] or the proposed adoption of retrieval evaluation measures from INEX and NTCIR to the SWS evaluation domain (Küster and König-Ries, 2008a).

Building Standard SWS Test Collections

We have outlined above that one major, still lacking prerequisite for meaningful evaluation of SWS frameworks with respect to virtually all criteria are standardized SWS test collections. Research on how to build such collections is required. In our opinion, they need to:

- support several formalisms to make comparisons across approaches feasible,
- be diverse with respect to use cases, their

complexity, domains covered etc.,
- contain realistic services that are described in sufficient detail to take advantage of the power of semantic approaches,
- provide natural language descriptions of the services to simplify usability and cross-formalism evaluation,
- be sufficiently large to support a statistically significant number of tests,
- contain offers and requests that were developed independent of each other to allow testing for decoupling,
- and contain services contributed by as many different groups as possible to avoid an unintended bias towards a particular approach.

Such test collections cannot be provided by an individual group, not only because that would violate the last requirement, but also because the effort involved in building such a collection is tremendous. Therefore, the community has to work together to create these collections. In order to support community involvement, suitable tools are needed. These had been lacking, but improvements in this respect were recently achieved with the releases of the OPOSSum Portal[25] (Küster and König-Ries, 2008b).

Making Evaluations More Reliable

Current approaches build on a limited number of services as well as a limited number of scenarios. In order to overcome the first, we already identified the need for standard test collections. These alone will not suffice, though. What is also needed is a more systematic investigation of the context parameters of SWS usage scenarios. Testbeds should contain different types of scenarios and somewhat redundant similar scenarios. Once these scenarios have been developed, it will become possible to investigate how results change in different scenarios, whether this change is due to the type of scenario or change, and which influence

different assumptions (about the degree of automation desired, the complexity of choreography, the diversity of underlying services etc.) have on the outcome of the evaluation.

Only such research will allow controlling the influence of context parameters on the evaluations. This will make them not only more reliable, but also more useful in providing potential users with the guidance they wish to have for their decisions regarding which approach to use for a particular task.

Unifying Existing Evaluation Approaches

As outlined in the section on evaluation criteria, evaluations are much more significant, if they cover all dimensions of evaluation conjointly. As can be seen from Table 1 this is not yet the case. Existing testbeds and evaluations need to be integrated more closely.

Further Activities

Up to now, we have listed a number of activities that must come from inside the semantic web services community to improve the situation with regard to evaluation of their research results. To support such activities, here, we list measures that could be taken more from the outside or more on a meta-level to help with this:

First, funding agencies should put more emphasis on proper evaluations. They should both make sure that evaluations promised in the proposals really take place and should explicitly fund research geared towards evaluation.

Second, the relevant conferences in the field should think about adding evaluation tracks comparable to the one the VLDB conferences has started in its 2008 edition. Together, these measures will ensure that evaluation gets more visibility and a higher priority - something that our field is in dire need of.

ACKNOWLEDGMENT

The authors would like to acknowledge the contributions of Dr. Charles Petrie, who co-authored a prior version of this article.

REFERENCES

Balzer, S., Liebig, T., & Wagner, M. (2004). Pitfalls of OWL-S: a practical semantic web use case. In *Proceedings of the Second International Conference on Service-Oriented Computing* (IC-SOC2004), New York, NY, USA.

Bansal, A., Blake, M. B., Kona, S., Bleul, S., Weise, T., & Jaeger, M. C. (2008). WSC-08: Continuing the web services challenge. In *Proceedings of the 10th IEEE International Conference on E-Commerce Technology (CEC2008) / 5th IEEE International Conference on Enterprise Computing, E-Commerce and E-Services (EEE2008)* (pp. 351–354). Washington, DC, USA.

BasiliV. R. (1992). *Software modeling and measurement: the goal/question/metric paradigm.* Technical report. College Park, MD, USA: University of Maryland at College Park.

Berners-Lee, T., Hendler, J., & Lassila, O. (2001). The semantic web. *Scientific American,* 5.

Blake, M. B., Cheung, W., Jaeger, M. C., & Wombacher, A. (2006). WSC-06: the web service challenge. In *Proceedings of the Eighth IEEE International Conference on E-Commerce Technology (CEC 2006) and Third IEEE International Conference on Enterprise Computing, E-Commerce and E-Services (EEE 2006),* Palo Alto, California, USA.

Blake, M. B., Cheung, W. K.-W., Jaeger, M. C., & Wombacher, A. (2007). WSC-07: evolving the web services challenge. In *Proceedings of the 9th IEEE International Conference on E-Commerce Technology (CEC 2007),* Tokyo, Japan.

Bleul, S., Weise, T., & Geihs, K. (2009). The web service challenge - a review on semantic web service composition. In *Proceedings of the Workshop on Service-Oriented Computing at KIVS 2009,* Kassel, Germany.

Cobo, J. M. L., Losada, S., Corcho, Ó., Benjamins, V. R., Niño, M., & Contreras, J. (2004). SWS for financial overdrawn alerting. In *Proceedings of the Third International Semantic Web Conference (ISWC2004),* Hiroshima, Japan.

Colucci, S., Noia, T. D., Sciascio, E. D., Donini, F. M., & Mongiello, M. (2005). Concept abduction and contraction for semantic-based discovery of matches and negotiation spaces in an e-marketplace. *Electronic Commerce Research and Applications, 4*(4), 345–361. doi:10.1016/j.elerap.2005.06.004

Fischer, T. (2005). *Entwicklung einer Evaluationsmethodik für Semantic Web Services und Anwendung auf die DIANE Service Descriptions* (in German). Master's thesis, IPD, University Karlsruhe.

Friesen, A. & Grimm, S. (2005). *DIP deliverable D4.8: Discovery specification.* Technical report.

Friesen, A., & Namiri, K. (2006). Towards semantic service selection for B2B integration. In *Proceedings of the Joint Workshop on Web Services Modeling and Implementation using Sound Web Engineering Practices and Methods, Architectures and Technologies for e-service Engineering (SMIWEP-MATeS'06) at the Sixth International Conference on Web Engineering (ICWE06),* Palo Alto, CA, USA.

Gugliotta, A., Tanasescu, V., Domingue, J., Davies, R., Gutiérrez-Villarías, L., Rowlatt, M., Richardson, M., & Stinčić, S. (2006). *Benefits and challenges of applying semantic web services in the e-government domain.* Semantics 2006.

Harman, D. (1992). Overview of the first Text REtrieval Conference (TREC-1). In *Proceedings of the first Text REtrieval Conference (TREC-1)*, Gaithersbury, MD, USA.

Klein, M., König-Ries, B., & Müssig, M. (2005). What is needed for semantic service descriptions - a proposal for suitable language constructs. [IJWGS]. *International Journal on Web and Grid Services*, *1*(3/4), 328–364. doi:10.1504/IJWGS.2005.008393

KluschM. (2008a). Semantic web service coordination. In SchumacherH. H. M. (Ed.), CASCOM - Intelligent Service Coordination in the Semantic Web. Springer.

Klusch, M. (2008b). Semantic web service description. In M. Schumacher, H. H., editor, CASCOM - Intelligent Service Coordination in the Semantic Web, chapter 3. Springer.

Klusch, M., & Zhing, X. (2008). Deployed semantic services for the common user of the web: A reality check. In *Proceedings of the 2nd IEEE International Conference on Semantic Computing (ICSC2008)*, Santa Clara, CA, USA.

Küster, U., & König-Ries, B. (2007). Supporting dynamics in service descriptions - the key to automatic service usage. In *Proceedings of the Fifth International Conference on Service Oriented Computing (ICSOC07)*, Vienna, Austria.

Küster, U., & König-Ries, B. (2008a). Evaluating semantic web service matchmaking effectiveness based on graded relevance. In *Proceedings of the 2nd International Workshop SMR² on Service Matchmaking and Resource Retrieval in the Semantic Web at the 7th International Semantic Web Conference (ISWC08)*, Karlsruhe, Germany.

Küster, U., & König-Ries, B. (2008b). On the empirical evaluation of semantic web service approaches: Towards common SWS test collections. In *Proceedings of the 2nd IEEE International Conference on Semantic Computing (ICSC2008)*, Santa Clara, CA, USA.

Küster, U., & König-Ries, B. (2008c). Towards standard test collections for the empirical evaluation of semantic web service approaches. *International Journal of Semantic Computing*, *2*(3), 381–402. doi:10.1142/S1793351X0800052X

Küster, U., & König-Ries, B. (2009). Relevance judgments for web services retrieval - a methodology and test collection for sws discovery evaluation. In *Proceedings of the 7th IEEE European Conference on Web Services (ECOWS09)*, Einhoven, The Netherlands.

Küster, U., König-Ries, B., Klein, M., & Stern, M. (2007a). DIANE - a matchmaking-centered framework for automated service discovery, composition, binding, and invocation on the web. *International Journal of Electronic Commerce (IJEC) - . Special Issue: Semantic Matchmaking and Resource Retrieval on the Web*, *12*(2), 41–68.

Küster, U., Lausen, H., & König-Ries, B. (2007b). Evaluation of semantic service discovery - a survey and directions for future research. In *Proceedings of the 2nd Workshop on Emerging Web Services Technology (WEWST07) at the 5th IEEE European Conference on Web Services (ECOWS07)*, Halle (Saale), Germany.

Lausen, H., Petrie, C., & Zaremba, M. (2007). W3C SWS testbed incubator group charter. Available online at http://www.w3.org/2005/Incubator/swsc/charter.

Li, L., & Horrocks, I. (2003). A software framework for matchmaking based on semantic web technology. In *Proceedings of the 12th World Wide Web Conference (WWW2003)*, Budapest, Hungary.

McIlraith, S. A., Son, T. C., & Zeng, H. (2001). Semantic web services. *IEEE Intelligent Systems, 16*(2), 46–53. doi:10.1109/5254.920599

Petrie, C., Küster, U., & Margaria-Steffen, T. (2008a). W3C SWS challenge testbed incubator methodology report. *W3C incubator report, W3C.* Retrieved from http://www.w3.org/2005/Incubator/swsc/XGR-SWSC/

PetrieC.LausenH.ZarembaM.MargariaT. (Eds.). (2008b). Semantic Web Service Challenge - Results from the First Year. *Semantic Web and Beyond* (Vol. 8). Springer.

Preist, C. (2004). *A conceptual architecture for semantic web services (extended version).* Technical Report HPL-2004-215, HP Laboratories Bristol.

Preist, C. (2007). Goals and vision: Combining web services with semantic web technology. In *Semantic Web Services: Concepts, Technologies, and Applications* (pp. 159–178). Springer-Verlag New York, Inc.

Preist, C., Cuadrado, J. E., Battle, S. A., Grimm, S., & Williams, S. K. (2005). Automated business-to-business integration of a logistics supply chain using semantic web services technology. In *Proceedings of the Fourth International Semantic Web Conference, Galway, Ireland.*

Ragone, A., Straccia, U., Noia, T. D., Sciascio, E. D., & Donini, F. M. (2007). Vague knowledge bases for matchmaking in P2P e-marketplaces. *In Proceedings of the 4th European Semantic Web Conference (ESWC2007),* Innsbruck, Austria.

Sim, S. E., Easterbrook, S. M., & Holt, R. C. (2003). Using benchmarking to advance research: A challenge to software engineering. In *Proceedings of the 25th International Conference on Software Engineering (ICSE2003)*, Portland, Oregon, USA.

Sîrbu, A. (2006). *DIP deliverable D4.14: Discovery module prototype.* Technical report.

Sîrbu, A., Toma, I., & Roman, D. (2006). A logic based approach for service discovery with composition support. In *Proceedings of the ECOWS06 Workshop on Emerging Web Services Technology, Zürich, Switzerland.*

Stollberg, M. (2004). SWF use case. *WSMO working draft D3.5.* Retrieved from http://swf.deri.at/usecase/20041019/SWFUseCase-20041019.pdf.

Toma, I., Iqbal, K., Roman, D., Strang, T., Fensel, D., & Sapkota, B. (2007). Discovery in grid and web services environments: A survey and evaluation. *International Journal on Multiagent and Grid Systems, 3*(3).

Tsetsos, V., Anagnostopoulos, C., & Hadjiefthymiades, S. (2006). On the evaluation of semantic web service matchmaking systems. In *Proceedings of the 4th IEEE European Conference on Web Services (ECOWS2006)*, Zürich, Switzerland.

Unspecified (2006). *RW2 project deliverable D2.3: Prototype implementation of the discovery component.* Technical report.

ENDNOTES

[1]   http://cordis.europa.eu/fp6/projects.htm
[2]   http://trec.nist.gov/
[3]   https://www.goldpractices.com/practices/gqm/
[4]   http://www.dfki.de/~klusch/s3/

5   http://projects.semwebcentral.org/projects/sme2/

6   http://dfki.de/~klusch/s3/html/2008.html

7   http://sws-challenge.org/

8   http://www.w3.org/2005/Incubator/swsc/

9   http://www.ws-challenge.org/

10 http://hnsp.inf-bb.uni-jena.de/DIANE/

11 http://hnsp.inf-bb.uni-jena.de/Diane/benchmark/

12 http://rw2.deri.at/

13 http://seals-project.eu

14 http://projects.semwebcentral.org/projects/owls-tc/

15 http://www.semwebcentral.org/projects/sawsdl-tc/

16 http://trec.nist.gov/

17 http://fusion.cs.uni-jena.de/professur/jgdeval

18 http://www.w3.org/2005/Incubator/swsc/

19 http://sws-challenge.org/wiki/index.php/Scenarios

20 http://research.nii.ac.jp/ntcir/

21 http://inex.is.informatik.uni-duisburg.de/

22 http://icaps-conference.org/index.php/Main/Competitions

23 http://www.sics.se/tac/

24 http://sws-challenge.org/wiki/index.php/EON-SWSC2008

25 http://fusion.cs.uni-jena.de/OPOSSum/

Chapter 2
Semantic Web Services and Mobile Agents Integration for Efficient Mobile Services

Vasileios Baousis
University of Athens, Greece

Vassilis Spiliopoulos
University of the Aegean and National Centre of Scientific Research "Demokritos", Greece

Elias Zavitsanos
University of the Aegean and National Centre of Scientific Research "Demokritos", Greece

Stathes Hadjiefthymiades
University of Athens, Greece

Lazaros Merakos
University of Athens, Greece

ABSTRACT

The requirement for ubiquitous service access in wireless environments presents a great challenge in light of well-known problems like high error rate and frequent disconnections. In order to satisfy this requirement, we propose the integration of two modern service technologies: Web Services and Mobile Agents. This integration allows wireless users to access and invoke semantically enriched Web Services without the need for simultaneous, online presence of the service requestor. Moreover, in order to improve the capabilities of Service registries, we exploit the advantages offered by the Semantic Web framework. Specifically, we use enhanced registries enriched with semantic information that provide semantic matching to service queries and published service descriptions. Finally, we discuss the implementation of the proposed framework and present our performance assessment findings

Copyright © 2010, IGI Global, distributing in print or electronic forms without written permission of IGI Global is prohibited.

INTRODUCTION

Efficient execution of wireless applications is of paramount importance due to the highly dynamic wireless network conditions. Link outages occur in a near-stochastic pattern, thus, rendering the execution of applications quite tedious and uncertain. Research on mobile computing has for a long time focused on this specific aspect of wireless application engineering (Pour, 2006). In this article, we adopt the mobile agent paradigm in order to overcome the difficulties discussed above. Surely, this is not the first time that mobile agents are proposed as the vehicle for the implementation of wireless/mobile applications. Their autonomic nature and wide spectrum of characteristics render the specific technological platform a great enabler for the emerging ubiquitous computing paradigm.

Mobile computing is not the only development that significantly impacts the computer industry nowadays. Service-oriented architectures (SOA) are gradually changing the contemporary structure of the Internet and become a key facilitator for electronic commerce applications and related application domains. We try to incorporate both the discussed technologies into our wireless/mobile computing framework. Mobile agents are dispatched by mobile terminals in order to efficiently and safely satisfy the specific computing needs of their nomadic owner. After securing the autonomicity characteristic in order to progress the required task without the need for the mobile terminal to be constantly online, we try to minimize the service-related tasks. Our prime concern lies on the exact identification of the services to be executed at the demand of the user and minimize potential waste of time on unwanted invocations. The accuracy of the service inquiry mechanism has to be improved to really boost the mobile agent and service-oriented architecture. To expedite the service querying procedure and simplify the querying semantics, we employ a semantically enriched service registry. A precise

definition of the user's requirement is mapped to existing services through a semantically enriched registrar.

In this article, we introduce a novel framework for dynamic discovery and integration of semantically enriched Web Services (WS) with Mobile Agents (MA). The proposed framework is mostly intended for wireless environments where users access Semantic Web Services (SWS) in the fixed network (the terms Web Service (WS) and Semantic Web Service (SWS) are used interchangeably within this article). This framework enhances the fixed network with the intelligence needed to dispatch the service requests of the wireless user in an efficient, reliable and transparent manner. The proposed approach enables users to execute multiple services with minimum interaction, without the requirement of being online during their entire session. Additionally, the proposed framework provides better fixed network utilization since unnecessary communication overhead is avoided and reliable delivery of the service results is provided.

The rest of this article is structured as follows. In section 2, we provide some background knowledge about the implemented technologies, whereas section 3, we discuss relevant prior work. In section 4, we present an overview of the proposed architecture. Section 5 studies the performance of the proposed framework and presents the results. Finally, section 6 concludes the article.

BACKGROUND KNOWLEDGE

In this section, we briefly describe the two technologies that are integrated in our proposed framework, namely Web Services and Mobile Agents.

Web services (WS) provide a loosely coupled infrastructure for service description, discovery and execution. In the traditional WS model, service requestors find the appropriate service by placing a request to the service registry, often implemented with universal description, discovery and integration (UDDI), obtain the result(s)—public interfaces of the chosen service(s) (expressed in Web services description language - WSDL) and, finally, send simple object access protocol (SOAP) messages to WS provider(s).

The main problems experienced in these interactions are:

- UDDI guarantees syntactic interoperability, and does not provide a semantic description of its content. UDDI is characterised for its lack of semantic description mechanisms, such as semantic interoperability, explicit semantic models to understand the queries and inference capabilities. UDDI service discovery is performed primarily by service name (keyword matching), but not by service attributes/capabilities. UDDI tModels may be regarded as a vocabulary where service descriptions are unstructured and intended for human comprehension. Different services with the same capabilities can thus be categorized in different business categories.
- WSDL is XML-based and used to specify the interface of a WS. It describes the information being exchanged (structure of the SOAP messages), how this information is being exchanged via interactions with the WS (transport protocols) and where the WS is located. However, WSDL does not contain any information about the capabilities of the described service and as such service discovery based on service capabilities or semantics cannot be performed.

Several efforts have been made to address the lack of expressiveness in WSDL in terms of semantic description that fall into the area of the Semantic Web (SW). SW is a vision in which Web pages are augmented with semantic information and data expressed in an unambiguous manner and can be understood and interpreted by

machine applications and humans alike (Berners-Lee, 2001). This requires means to represent the semantics of the exchanged data so that it could be automatically processed. This requirement is met with the use of ontologies. Ontologies facilitate knowledge sharing among heterogeneous systems, through explicit formal specifications of the terms used in a knowledge domain and relations among them (Gruber, 1993). Ontologies are machine-understandable and, as such, a computer can process data, annotated with references to ontologies. Through the knowledge encapsulated in the ontology, a computer can deduce facts from the originally provided data. The use of ontologies enables systems to share common understanding of the structure of information and reuse of domain knowledge, make domain assumptions explicit and separate domain knowledge from the operational knowledge.

Currently, several upper ontologies (terminology in the form of an ontology) have been proposed for Web Service description. The first was DAML-S (McIlraith, 2003), which was based on DAML+OIL ontology language. When DAML+OIL evolved to the widely accepted OWL (Web Ontology Language) family of languages, DAML-S was replaced by OWL-S (OWL-S, 2007). Still, OWL-S does not constitute a commonly accepted description language; there are also other languages proposed such as WSDL-S (Verma, 2006), WSMO (Roman, 2005) and SWSO (SWSL Committee, 2007). All these languages differ in terms of expressiveness, complexity and tool support.

OWL-S, which is adopted in our work, has well-defined specifications by the W3C (World Wide Web) consortium (OWL-S, 2007) and is widely accepted by the scientific community. OWL-S ontology implicitly defines message types (as input/output types of processes) in terms of OWL classes, which allows for a rich, class-hierarchical semantic foundation. Specifically, OWL-S models the Web services via a three-part ontology: (i) a service profile describes what the service requires from users and what it gives them; (ii) a service model specifies how the service works; and (iii) a service grounding provides information on how to use the service.

With OWL-S, SWS are described in an unambiguous manner allowing for a potential service requestor to place a capability search in a service registry rather than a keyword search in UDDI registries. Registries that offer such capability search functionalities are called Semantic Web Registries (SWR).

The most representative matching techniques used are detailed in Tsetsos (2007) and are summarised below:

- **Semantic capability matching:** The basic idea is that an advertised service matches a requested one, when all the inputs (respectively outputs) of a requested service are matched by the inputs (respectively outputs) of the advertised service. For this purpose, description logics (DL) reasoning services are exploited for inferring relations between ontology concepts.
- **Multi-level mapping:** Matching is performed in many levels, not only between input and output descriptions. Service categories or other custom service parameters (e.g., OoS) may be exploited. The result is a more efficient ranking of the matched services.
- **DL matching with service profile ontologies:** Each service and query is represented as ontologies following the DL formalization. Hence, a DL reasoner is utilized for placing the query concept in its proper position in each service ontology description (e.g., as a sub-concept). Then specific rules are applied for computing the degree of relevance between the query and each service description.
- **Information-retrieval-based:** In this category, vector space techniques (Raghavan,

1986) are utilized for locating the most related service to a provided query.

- **Graph-based approaches:** Ontologies representing services are transformed into directed graphs and various algorithms accomplish the matching between such graphs.

There is a plethora of tools that provide Semantic Web Services functionalities (e.g., OWLS-MX (OWLS-MX, 2007) and TUB OWLSM (OWLSM, 2007), each one implementing a portion of the above matching techniques. In our work, we adopted the OWL-S/UDDI Matchmaker tool (Paolucci, 2002; Srinivasan, 2004; OWL-S/UDDI Matchmaker Web Interface, 2007), which mainly implements techniques from the first aforementioned matching technique.

Mobile agent technology is one of the most promising technologies for communicating and managing functional components comprising a mobile service (Lange, 1998; Wooldridge, 2002). A MA has the unique ability to autonomously transport itself from one system to another. The ability to travel allows a MA to move to a system that contains an entity (-ies) with which the agent wishes to interact and take advantage of being in the same host or network with the collaborating entity. MAs can operate synchronously and asynchronously, and are equipped with the appropriate intelligence and knowledge to dynamically accomplish their task without user interaction. MAs are not trying to replace traditional ways of communication but to enhance the functionality and operation of the involved service entities. Researchers agree that MAs are not always the best solution and a combination of the MA, client-server and remote execution paradigms delivers the best performance with respect to network operation metrics like bandwidth, response time, and scalability.

RELATED WORK

In this section, we provide an overview of the related work performed in the areas of semantic WS and multi-agent systems and, especially, on research activities that integrate these two technologies.

In Ishikawa (2004; 2004b), BPEL (business process execution language) is used to form simple rules to describe MA physical behaviours (e.g., migration and cloning). Such simple rules are separated from the integration logic, allowing for addition or change of physical behaviours without modification of the BPEL description. This separation is considered helpful in dealing with the dynamic environment of WS, however, the discussed framework supports actions only in case of predefined events. The implemented rules do not consider dynamic events that might be generated during WS invocation and MA roaming. Moreover, and importantly, directory services and multicast protocols are assumed pre-existing and not discussed. The discussed framework refers only to interactions occurring among MA and WS without considering the interactions of the MA and service registries that have equal importance in such a system. Finally, the system description does not include any implementation, hence benchmarking is not considered.

There are several proposed models that adopt BPEL4WS (Business Process Execution Language for Web Services) as a specification language for expressing the social behaviour of multi-agent systems and adapt to changing environment conditions (Bulher, 2003;2004). Moreover, in Montanari (2003; 2003b), the authors propose a policy-based framework for flexible management and dynamic configurability of agent mobility behaviour in order to reduce code mobility concerns and support rapid mobile code-based service provisioning. Policies specify when, where, how and the parts of the agent that will perform a given task (e.g., migrating to a host and invoke a service). However, these models do not provide for the semantic description of the WS involved in their systems. Other proposed frameworks adopt DAML-S for describing the WS, thus, allowing for service capability search and matching (Kagal, 2002; Gibbins, 2004). However, the proposed systems are intended for fixed networks, and problems related to the wireless environments are not considered.

An agent-based approach for composite mobile WS is proposed in Zahreddine (2005), where three methods for compositions are discussed: parallel, sequential and a hybrid of these two. The service composition scenario is that a user with a wireless device places a request to execute a WS and a MA executes the service on behalf of the user by moving to the service registry, query the registry, get service description (in WSDL), and finally invoke the service. Service execution, depending on the WS itself, is performed with one of the aforementioned composition methods. This approach does not consider semantic information describing the involved WS, thus services are selected by simple keyword queries to the UDDI registry. Additionally, it does not include mechanisms to decide which composition approach to follow. Integration depends upon the nature of the WS (if the service is a composition of other services it must be accessed sequentially, if not, then in parallel). A similar approach is proposed in Cheng (2002), with the difference that a personal and a service agent are used to perform the task of the MA described in the previously mentioned approach.

Moreover, in the research literature, it has proposed the use of Asynchronous Web Services (AWS) in order to access WS with asynchronous interaction. AWS can be used where the standard Web Service Business Model has some limitations, as described in Brambilla (2004): a. when service time is expected to be too long, b. when response time is not predictable, and c. when users may not be continuously online. The most common way to achieve asynchronous calls to Web Services is by using a correlation or con-

Figure 1. Service implementation scenario

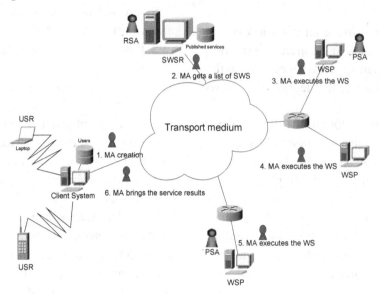

versation ID (Huang, 2003; Brambilla, 2004). This unique ID is assigned initially by the Web Service providers to each Web service transaction and it is passed in each exchanged message between the conversational parties. This way, the client is able to perform correlation and to retrieve application data related to current conversation. The drawback though of such an approach is the production of possible mismatches. Specifically, if multiple asynchronous Web Service calls happen in the context of a single conversation, responses might not be able to be unambiguously related to their requests (Brambilla, 2004).

FRAMEWORK ARCHITECTURE

The proposed framework consists of the mobile user that uses SWS, the MA representing the user in the fixed network, the service registry and the SWS provider. The last two entities are implemented as stationary agents. According to the service implementation scenario (Figure 1), a mobile user accesses the proposed system and places service requests specifying some criteria. Subsequently, the system creates a MA (step

1) that migrates to the registry to find the WS that best meets the user requirements (step 2). Service registry allows for a capability search to be performed, since it is enriched with semantic information. The MA, after acquiring the WS listing and technical details, migrates to service provider(s), invokes the WS, collects the results (steps 3-5) and returns to the service requestor to deliver the results to the mobile user (step 6). In the presented scenario, the SWS that matched the service request were three thus MA migrates and invokes these three services (steps 3-5). If the service request matched more than three services during the step 2, the MA would migrate to all these matched WS (Figure 1 would include more steps). The advantages of this scenario is that the MA has the necessary intelligence to invoke only the best matched service(s) and unnecessary service invocations are avoided leading to better network utilization, and the wireless user is not required to be online and may obtain the results on future time.

In the proposed framework, the route of the agent may vary, depending on the service requestor preferences and the network topology. As explained below, the user may dynamically force his MA to send its clones to the providers, invoking the services in parallel, rather than serially migrate to each one. Moreover, the user may force the MA to implement different service execution strategies (e.g., execute all services locally or remotely, change timeout limit), during its itinerary and execution of service(s).

Our framework consists of the following functional components: (1) User service requestor (USR) who is the user that invokes a SWS, and the client system, the system in the fixed network that provides user access to the SWS, (2) mobile agent which is the representative of the user in the fixed network (3) provider stationary agent (PSA) which is a stationary agent that resides in the host offering a certain WS (its implementation is optional), (4) registry stationary agent (RSA) which is a stationary agent that acts as a broker between the MA and the service registry (its implementation is optional), (5) Semantic Web services registry (SWSR), the registry where the service providers advertise their services, and (6) Web service provider (WSP) which provides the WS to interested users. Their structure and functionalities are described below. In the end of this section, we provide a service implementation scenario presenting all possible supported service invocation alternatives.

User Service Requestor (USR)

USR is the client that invokes a WS. USR logs into the client system, which communicates with the agent platform using IIOP (Internet Inter-ORB Protocol). The agent platform is responsible for creating and handling MA, according to user specifications. The client system is implemented in JSP/Servlet technology, and many users can be accommodated without having java runtime environment (JRE) or the MA platform (MAP) installed on their device. The only requirement is a browser to access the client system.

The client system offers services to clients like: account creation, user login/logout, service

invocation policies profile editing, and control of existing agents. Moreover, the administrator is allowed to add/remove/edit user properties/profiles. Finally, users' service invocation policy profiles are serialised and stored into the server's database that enables the seamless and transparent provision of services.

The proposed framework is in addition able to communicate with mobile devices that are capable of hosting JADE/LEAP (Lightweight Extensible Agent Platform) (JADE, 2007). LEAP is an extension of JADE that enables MAs to be executed on wireless devices with limited processing capabilities. In such a case the MA is spawned on the mobile device, gathers the user preferences/specifications either from this device or from the client system. The behaviour of the system and of the device created the MA is exactly the same.

Mobile Agent (MA)

The MA is the representative of the user in the fixed network and is capable of roaming, finding and executing services and delivering results to the user. The MA may also spawn clones that execute the selected WS in parallel to minimize the total processing time. Clones can migrate and invoke simultaneously the chosen WS and return to the service requestor with the results. The MA has the following components: (1) data state, (2) code, (3) migration and cloning policies, (4) matching engine, and, (5) policy management component (Figure 2).

The proposed MA architecture is based on that the logic of the MA has to be separated from its implementation, enabling the modelling of the MA to be platform independent. That is to say, the physical behaviours of the MA are portable to any MAP (Jade, Grasshopper, etc.). Below, we describe the components of a MA.

The data component contains the information collected by the MA from the SWS invocations. Several compression algorithms may be applied in

Figure 2. Mobile agent structure

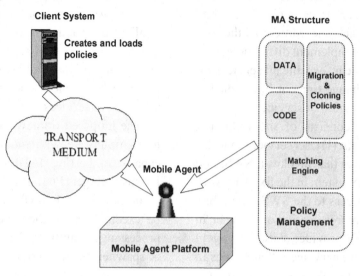

Figure 3. MA policy management component

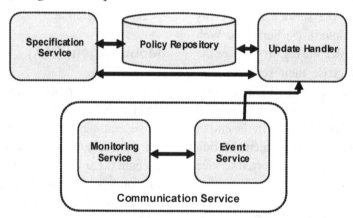

order to reduce the size of the collected information. The migration and cloning policies component specifies the autonomous behaviour of the MA. It should be noted that the social behaviour of the MA (migration, cloning) is separated from integration logic and code implementation. This separation is accomplished with user's specified invocation policies that govern the behaviour of the MA, being external and independent of its code and integration with the WS. Moreover, the matching engine component is responsible for post-processing the service registry query results,

that is, confirm the availability of the service providers prior to agent migration.

The policy management component is responsible for the MA external communication and the transparent installation of policies into the agent's repository.

As shown in Figure 3, the policy management component provides four services, namely communication, update handler, specification and policy repository. Policy repository contains the user preferences and policies that govern the behaviour of the MA. Communication service

Table 1. Policy names and their respective meaning

Policy name	Type	Description
<Migrating> and <Cloning>	Boolean	MA's ability to migrate to another host and spawn clones, respectively.
<retryTimes>	Numerical	The number of attempts that MA will perform when a WS is unavailable.
<timeBetweenReattempts>	Numerical	The time that MA will wait between consecutive reattempts.
<suspendWhenFinished>	Boolean	States if the user wishes (dis)-connected operation and what the MA should do when it returns to the client system (suspend its state and wait for user to connect back or to deliver immediately the service results).
<rollBackBehaviour>	Boolean	Specifies in a case of failure if a roll back solution will be followed.
<maxNumberOfHits>	Numerical	The maximum number of services to be invoked.
<minNumberOfResults>	Numerical	The minimum number of results when searching the semantically enriched service registry (it is accomplished through the similarity level that is returned from the semantic engine that enables the system to always return a result, even though it does not always satisfy completely the request).
<pingServer>	Boolean	States that the MA should check if the targeted service provider is alive, before MA starts the migrating process to this host.
<migrateToServer>	Boolean	Specifies if the service will be invoked locally or remotely.
<remoteCall>	Boolean	MA invokes the chosen services using SOAP/RPC (remotely from other host) without migrating to each provider.
<callThroughStationary>	Boolean	Indicates if communication between WS and MA will take place with or without the Provider's Stationary Agent (PSA).
<HitAllServices>	Boolean	Forces the MA to invoke all retrieved services from service registry.
<cloneToServer>	Boolean	Enables the agent to decide whether to serially migrate to each located service provider or sent clones to accomplish the task in parallel and return service results to their parent agent and then are self-destroyed.
<UserDisconnectedOperation>	Boolean	States that user wishes to retrieve results in a future time, by reconnecting to the client system.
<timeBetweenReattempts>	Numerical	The time that MA will wait between consecutive reattempts.

enables the MA to interact with the client and other network entities. Such functionality is achieved through the monitoring service which filters the messages coming from the client system and through the event service which handles events concerning policy changes. When a policy change occurs, the update handler is notified to update the policy repository. Specification service is responsible for fulfilling this task.

The agent's policies determine its physical behaviour while roaming in the network and executing WS. Currently, the MA considers the policies (Table 1), which are Boolean and numerical variables. Agent policies are expressed in XML and stored in a serialised format into the client system database. For each registered user there is an associated policies file, to provide personalized WS access.

Provider Stationary Agent (PSA)

PSA is a stationary agent that resides in the host offering a certain WS. Its purpose is to wrap the functionality of the WS. The PSA is created and maintained by the service provider. PSA communicates with the service providers through protocols

Figure 4. Provider stationary agent logic

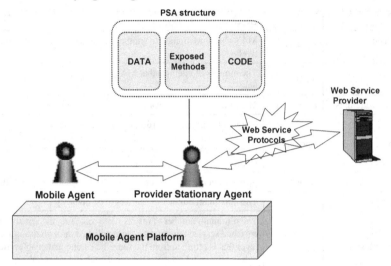

specified for WS invocation and interaction (e.g., SOAP). When the MA migrates to a host offering a WS with a PSA, it obtains the results through the PSA. This communication is performed with agent-to-agent protocols (either Remote Method Invocation or exchanging FIPA/ACL messages using a FIPA/Message Transport Protocol-MTP (FIPA, 2007)), instead of the resource consuming SOAP. In this approach, the MA need not be SOAP fluent, thus leading to a lightweight implementation. It should be noted that this implementation maintains the platform independence as far as it concerns the SWS provider. This is due to the fact that the PSA wraps the SWS functionality, and is also SOAP fluent and exposes the same SWS's functionality in a native form to the MA.

Figure 4 presents the structure of a PSA. PSA interface exposes the available methods of the SWS as they are described in OWL-S. PSA consists of two parts: (1) its data state, and, (2) its code. PSA methods are multi-threaded to accommodate and simultaneously serve multiple MAs.

Registry Stationary Agent (RSA)

RSA is a stationary agent that acts as a broker between the MA and the service registry (Figure

5). RSA implements part of the registry's functionality and serves MA's requests. By using a RSA in the WS registry, MA does not have to be aware of the implementation-specific functionalities of the registry. Thus, different service registries can be used as long as RSA acts between WS registry and MA. The proposed framework can be used with different registries that are currently available (e.g., ebXML (ebXML, 2007), OWLS-MX (OWLS-MX, 2007), and TUB OWLSM (OWLSM, 2007)).

Semantic Web Services Registry (SWSR)

The SWSR (Figure 5) consists of the RSA, the matchmaking tool and the UDDI registry. The matchmaker (OWL-S/UDDI Matchmaker Web Interface, 2007) is a tool which enhances the UDDI server by adding capability-based discovery. In combination with Racer (RACER, 2007), it processes the ontologies expressed in OWL. Service advertisements are first processed by the UDDI server, and if any semantic information is contained by them, they are passed to the OWL-S matchmaking engine. Finally, the engine processes service queries and returns the results

Figure 5. Semantic WS registry

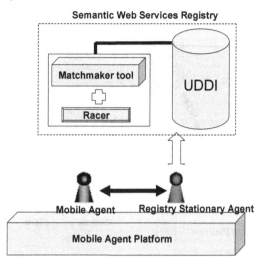

to the UDDI server, which in turn, communicated with the requesting service client.

The matching algorithm used by Matchmaker to match a service request to a service advertisement is based on matching all the outputs of the first to the outputs of the latter, and all the inputs of the latter to the inputs of the first. The matching degree (between I/O of a request and I/O of an advertisement) depends on the correlation of the domain ontology concepts associated with these I/O. Matchmaker specifies four matching degrees (in decreasing order of matching importance): Exact, plugin, subsumes, and fail. The query language used in the registry is the standard query language of Racer that has its basis on LISP. It is powerful and has more functionalities than standard OWL query languages.

Matchmaker is a tool that integrates seamlessly with registries such as UDDI. In our system, we used a local implementation of UDDI, called jUDDI (jUDDI, 2007). JUDDI is a Web application for Apache Tomcat. The matchmaker tool is responsible for the mapping of the OWL-S service description to JUDDI. Matchmaker is plugged in JUDDI and is available in two versions, a Web-based and a standalone version. The standalone version provides a matching engine and a client API for invoking this engine. In our framework,

we used the standalone version of Matchmaker. An extensive description of matchmaker can be found in Paolucci (2002) and Sycara (2004).

Web Service Provider (WSP)

The WSP provides the WS to interested clients. It maintains a description of the WS expressed in WSDL and OWL-S. Figure 6 depicts the WSP and their supported functionalities. Service invocation by the MA depends on the OWL-S description of the service. In our framework, service invocation by MA is performed either directly or through the PSA. In the direct access case, the agent has to be SOAP fluent, a fact that increases the size of the MA when moving over the network. Inside the OWL-S description of the WS, it is indicated if a PSA wraps the functionality of the service to allow the roaming MA to interact with the PSA instead of the SWS.

As mentioned above, OWL-S is used to enhance the expressiveness of WSDL in terms of semantic information. For this reason, in our framework, WS are described both in WSDL and OWL-S. WSDL is used to describe the technical details (information included in the service grounding) and OWL-S is used to specify the input and output ontologies, thus, enabling an

Figure 6. Web service provider

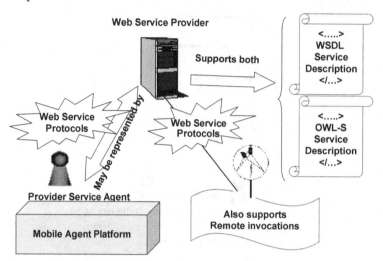

advanced service capability search (service profile and model). Upon retrieval of the desired services from the registry, the WSDL description is used to find the necessary definitions for its successful invocation.

As already mentioned, the SWS provider can expose a PSA to act as his delegate and interact with the user's MA. This is revealed to the MA through the OWL-S description. If this is not the case, the MA infers that no PSA is offered and the service should be accessed directly.

Service Usage Description

In this section, a functional description of the proposed framework is provided, through a service scenario. According to this scenario, a USR needs to find and invoke a certain WS by using a mobile device. Therefore, he/she connects to the client system, the platform front-end. After a successful registration, the USR sets the desired criteria for the WS. The user also defines the MA service invocation policies and forces the MA to follow a certain policy while roaming throughout the network. Subsequently, a MA is created, equipped with the user's unique ID, service invocation and agent behavioural policies, to represent the user in the fixed network and dispatch his service re-

quests. The aforementioned policies are passed to the MA in XML format and stored into its policy repository, which remind the update handler that he has the authority to change these policies, according to the messages that the event service may receive from the USR or other network entities. The MA, after creation, migrates to the SWSR. The SWSR provides SWS descriptions and allows service capability search. When the MA arrives at the service registry, it communicates with the RSA, which queries the registry on behalf of the MA. RSA finds the service(s) that meet the user needs and delivers them to the MA, which decides on the next step according to its specified service invocation and agent behavioural policies.

The MA may follow several WS invocation alternatives and these are listed below:

1.   Poll the servers where the services are located to check their availability, in order to migrate only to those that are alive. In this way, the MA is released from the burden of migrating to a malfunctioning remote server. This strategy improves the overall performance of the framework by avoiding unnecessary migrations.

2.   Try to invoke the services from remote and not migrate to the provider. Remote invoca-

tion or migration of MA is specified in the MA policies. Specifically, depending on the size of the MA or the distance between its current location and the location of the provider, it might be preferable not to migrate, but remotely invoke the WS.

3. Migrate to the WSP and collaborate with the PSA. The MA invokes the service and obtains the results through the PSA.

4. Migrate to the WSP and directly invoke the WS. This option requires the MA to carry additional code libraries. The implementation of the WSP is much simpler and straightforward since there is no change in the traditional WS implementation model.

5. Finally, to send clones to each WSP, instead of migrating serially to each one. This scenario results to a parallel invocation of WSs where each MA clone invokes one WS. In this way, the overall service invocation time is reduced in comparison to the previous service invocation alternatives.

All these service invocation alternatives are decided at runtime through the user's specified service invocation and agent behavioural policies. When the MA(s) have collected the results, there are two options depending on the selected policies:

1. When the MA invokes all the services, it migrates back to the client system. If the user is logged in the system, the MA passes the results to the user. Otherwise, the MA waits for the user to login and ask for the service results.

2. When the MA clones have been used for service invocation, they return to the client system and deliver service results to the father MA. After this interaction, the MA clones are destroyed. Consequently, the father MA delivers the services results to the user in a similar way to the previous case.

When the USR obtains the results, he may ask the MA to repeat one of the above scenarios by changing, if necessary, its policies, or he may cancel the execution of the agent. The USR may also, at any time, search for the agent, instruct him to return or cancel its execution at runtime.

A practical example of the proposed framework usage could be to book a trip from a place A to a place B and probably specifying some preferences on each action (e.g., the flight to have an intermediate stop to location C). The user requests this service by specifying his preferences and a MA fulfils this request. The MA has the intelligence to query the Semantic Web Service Registry and with the help of the semantic matchmaking capability of the registry to retrieve the most accurate service (that meets the requirements of the user), to invoke this service and provide synchronously or asynchronously the results to the user without his/her on-line presence. The semantic expression of the WS to the registry and the unambiguous matching of the user's criteria with the capabilities of the available SWS, leads to as many accurate results as possible, as well as maximization of the recall.

Maximization of the matching performance is of paramount importance, since it might be possible that the exact service does not exist in the registry catalogue, but still the most accurate result has to be retrieved. The matching algorithm that is used in the registry ensures this fact: it defines a flexible matching mechanism based on the OWL's subsumption mechanism. The degree of match between the request and the available services depends on the match between the concepts of the two ontologies. Specifically, the matching mechanism relies on a semantic matching between concepts, rather than a syntactic one. Let us consider the practical example mentioned above. The user wants to book a "flight" from location A to location B, and the registry contains a service that does not match exactly with the user's request in the sense that in the service advertisement the output is specified as "trip",

Figure 7. Semantic matching

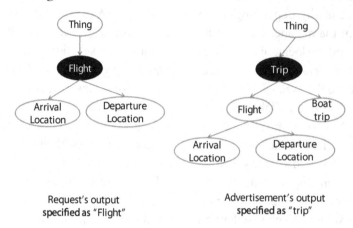

Request's output
specified as "Flight"

Advertisement's output
specified as "trip"

Figure 8. Web service retrieval

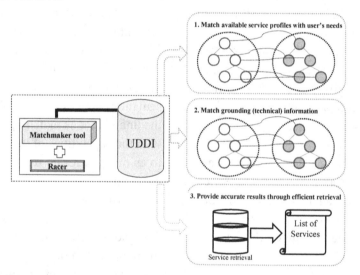

as shown in Figure 7. Although there is no exact match between the output of the request and the advertisement, the matching algorithm recognizes a match, since "trip" subsumes "flight". This is a clear advantage over a simple string matching-based UDDI registry.

Figure 8 illustrates the semantic matching process that ensures efficient service retrieval since compares concepts that are unambiguous specified on three levels, service profile, model, and grounding.

If traditional methods of WS invocation are followed, this booking would be performed as

follows: the user would browse to a UDDI registry, request all the WSs that provide a flight booking service and get the results. Due to the lack of semantics in the service registry (UDDI does not supports for WS semantic annotation) and to keyword search that is performed in such registries, the user would obtain WSs that provide booking services, probably either irrelevant WSs or services that are not classified according to the relevance of the query. As a result, the user would need to sequentially or randomly invoke each service till he finds a service that best meets his requirements. This interaction requires the online presence of the user during the whole interaction.

PERFORMANCE EVALUATION

In this section, we discuss the performance evaluation and present the results of the proposed system. Specifically, we compare the performance of our framework against the traditional business model of WS provision. In the following description, the term "conventional WS Business Model" (WSBM), refers to the model where a user requests a service to be executed and the system dispatches (either automatically or with user intervention) the request by discovering the appropriate service(s) from the service registry, and then, sequentially, invokes these WS, receives and forwards/presents to the user the service results. All communication among the involved network entities is performed with SOAP. Moreover, in our framework the mobile agents are implemented on JADE (JADE, 2007) MA platform. We have developed and tested the following system:

a. A WS system implemented with the "Conventional WS Business Model" (WSBM).
b. Our framework (Semantic Web services and mobile agents) (SWS& MA)

The SWS logic implemented in our experiments is as follows: the SWS have an extensive service description, stating unambiguously their capabilities in OWL-S. This description is published in the registry (SWSR). However, the SWS internal functionality is fairly simple, returning a pre-specified data volume subject to the service request. In our trials, these service results are 1 KB, 10 KB, 100KB and 1 MB. Moreover, six SWS have been implemented and distributed in the testing network.

In the performance evaluation scenario, a user requests a service, specifies his/her preferences and each of the above systems dispatches this re-

quest to the service registry. The service registry in the WSBM is a simple local UDDI providing a keyword service search on each service request, whereas in the SWS&MA system the registry is offering a service capability search to the placed service requests. In our evaluation, the description of SWS had small differences in the OWL-S descriptions. As a result, in the WSBM system, the service search to the UDDI registry had an average of three matches per service search/request. Contrary to WSBM system, in the SWS&MA system the MA had the necessary intelligence and knowledge to filter the results from the semantic registry and invoke only a SWS where its semantic description matched the service request and user's preferences. Consequently, in the WSBM system, we considered the average time this system requires to execute a service and we multiplied that by three (the average service results from the registry), whereas in SWS&MA system we consider the average time that is needed to invoke only a SWS. Moreover, in the SWS&MA system, the average time need was used from all the system variations to execute a SWS. These system variations are: (a) a system that uses MA cloning, (b) a system that uses PSA, and (c) a system that uses both MA cloning and PSA.

The testing platform we used is depicted in Figure 9. The system is a LAN that is composed of two workstations and a portable PC, all connected to the Internet through University's MAN.

Below, we elaborate on the metrics that we adopted in order to assess the performance of the two systems. In Equation (1), total service time (TST_{MA}) (for the SWS&MA platform) is the sum of registry interaction time (RIT), migration of MA to a service provider time (MSPT) and the interaction time with this service provider (ITSP):

$$TST_{MA} = RIT + MSPT + ITSP \qquad (1)$$

In the WSBM system, Equation (1) has the form:

Figure 9. Performance evaluation network topology

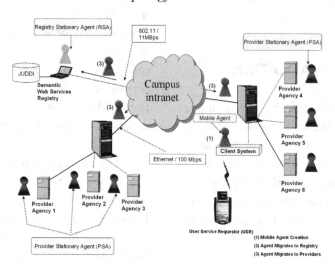

Figure 10. Total service time (TST) vs. service result size

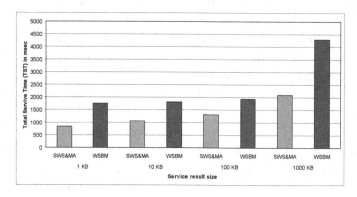

$$TST_{WSBM} = RIT + \left\lfloor \frac{N}{2} \right\rfloor * \overline{ITSP} \qquad (2)$$

where the $\overline{ITSP}$ is defined as:

$$\overline{ITSP} = N^{-1} * \sum_{i=1}^{N} ITSP_i \qquad (3)$$

In (2) $ITSP_i$ is the time between service request submission and service results reception.

In Figure 10, the results of the proposed system performance evaluation and comparison against a system implemented using the Conventional WS Business Model are presented. More specifically, the average time needed to execute three services

for the WSBM, is plotted against the time required to invoke only one SWS in the SWS&MA for each service result size (1 KB, 10 KB, 100KB and 1 MB). We observe that the TST in the SWS&MA system is approximately half the TST in the WSBM system, irrespective of the service results size. It should be noted that the RIT in our system is considerably greater than the WSBM system, and this explains that the TST of the SWS&MA is half and not the one third (or even smaller) of the TST of the WSBM system. The high RIT of the proposed SWS&MA framework is attributed to the specific semantic registry implementation and might be less if other semantic registry is used (e.g., OWLS-MX (OWLS-MX, 2007), and TUB OWLSM (OWLSM, 2007).

CONCLUSION

In this article, we presented a framework that provides wireless access to WS using MA to find and execute WS in the fixed segment. The WS are semantically enriched and are expressed in OWL-S. Furthermore, the proposed system adopts an enhanced WS registry enriched with semantic information that provides semantic matching between service requests submitted and the service description published to them. The advantages of the presented system are: (1) users may invoke a set of services with only one interaction with the fixed network (post the request and receive the results), (2) users do not have to be connected during service discovery and invocation; the results of such operations are downloaded to their mobile devices after their network session re-establishment, (3) service invocations are performed locally or according to the user's specified policies, and unnecessary information is not transmitted over the network leading to better resource utilization, (4) the framework ensures the delivery of the service results to the user, (5) the MA dynamic behaviour improves system robustness and fault tolerance, (6) new services, agents, users and service registries can be easily integrated to the framework, thus, providing an expandable, open system.

Future work includes the study of agent mobility for SWS dynamic invocation and composition that takes network events into account. Network events (e.g., node failures, overloading) occurring while the service invocation is underway, may force the MA to dynamically reschedule its itinerary. The MA will implement routing algorithms that generate itineraries by considering network information published in the WS description, network status and topology.

REFERENCES

Berners-Lee, T., Hendler, J., & Lassila, O. (2001). The semantic Web. *Scientific American,* 2001.

Buhler, P., et al. (2003). Adaptive workflow = Web services + agents. *Proceedings of the International Conference on Web Services (ICWS03).* Las Vegas, NV.

Buhler, P., & Vidal, J. (2004). Enacting BPEL4WS specified workflows with multi-agent systems. *Proceedings of the Workshop on Web Services and Agent-Based Engineering (WSABE04).* New York, NY.

Brambilla, M., Ceri, S., Passamani, M., & Riccio, A. (2004). Managing asynchronous Web services interactions. *Proceedings of the IEEE International Conference on Web Services (ICWS).*

Cheng, S., et al. (2002). A new framework for mobile Web services. *Proceedings of the Symposium on Applications and the Internet (SAINT'02w).* Nara City, Japan.

ebXML. (2007). Retrieved June 1, 2007 from http://www.ebxml.org

FIPA. (2007). *Foundation for the intelligent physical agents.* Retrieved June 1, 2007 from http://www.fipa.org.

Gibbins, N., Harris, S., & Shadbolt, N. (2004). Agent-based Semantic Web services. *Journal of Web Semantics, 1.*

Gruber, T. (1993). A translation approach to portable ontology specification. *Knowledge Acquisition, 5.*

Huang, Y., & Chung, J. (2003). A Web services-based framework for business integration solutions. *Electronic Commerce Research and Applications, 2*(1), 15-26.

Ishikawa, F., Tahara, Y., Yoshioka, N., & Honiden, S. (2004b). Behavior descriptions of mobile agents for Web services integration. *Proceedings of the IEEE International Conference on Web Services* (ICWS) (pp. 342-349). San-Diego, CA.

Ishikawa, F., Yoshioka, N., Tahara, Y., & Honiden, S. (2004). Mobile agent system for Web services integration in pervasive networks. *Proceedings of the International Workshop on Ubiquitous Computing* (IWUC) (pp. 38-47). Porto, Portugal.

JADE. (2007). *Java agent development environment.* Retrieved June 1, 2007 from http://jade.tilab.com

jUDDI. (2007). *Open source Java implementation of the universal description, discovery, and integration (UDDI) specification for Web services.* Retrieved June 1, 2007 from http://ws.apache.org/juddi/

Kagal, L., et al. (2002). Agents making sense of the semantic Web. *Proceedings of the First International Workshop on Radical Agent Concepts, (WRAC).* McLean, VA.

Lange, D., & Oshima, M. (1998). *Programming and deploying Java mobile agents with aglets.* Addison-Wesley.

Li, K., Verma, K., Mulye, R., Rabbani, R., Miller, J., & Sheth, A. (2006). Designing semantic Web processes: The WSDL-S approach. In: J. Cardoso & A. Sheth (Eds.), *Semantic Web services, processes and applications.* Springer-Verlag.

McIlraith, S., & Martin, D. (2003). Bringing semantics to Web services. *IEEE Intelligent Systems, 18*(1), 90-93.

Montanari, R., Tonti, G., & Stefanelli, C. (2003). A policy-based mobile agent infrastructure. *Proceedings of the 3rd IEEE International Symposium on Applications and the Internet Workshops (SAINT03) IEEE Computer Society Press.* Orlando, FL.

Montanari, R., Tonti, G., & Stefanelli. C. (2003). Policy-based separation of concerns for dynamic code mobility management. Proceedings of the 27th International Computer Software and Applications Conference, (COMPSAC'03). Dallas, TX: IEEE Computer Society Press.

OWL-S. (2007). *OWL Web ontology language for services (OWL-S).* Retrieved June 1, 2007 from http://www.w3.org/Submission/2004/07/

OWLSM. (2007). *The TUB OWL-S Matcher.* Retrieved June 1, 2007 from http://kbs.cs.tu-berlin.de/ivs/Projekte/owlsmatcher/index.html

OWLS-MX. (2007). *Hybrid OWL-S Web Service Matchmaker.* Retrieved June 1, 2007 from http://www.dfki.de/~klusch/owls-mx/

OWL-S/UDDI Matchmaker Web Interface. (2007). Retrieved June 1, 2007 http://www.daml.ri.cmu.edu/ matchmaker/

Paolucci, M., Kawamura, T., Payne, T., & Sycara, K. (2002). Semantic matching of Web services capabilities. *Proceedings of the International Semantic Web Conference (ISWC).* Sardinia, Italy.

Pour, G., & Laad, N. (2006). Enhancing the horizons of mobile computing with mobile agent components. *Proceedings of the 5th IEEE/ACIS International Conference on Computer and Information Science and 1st IEEE/ACIS International Workshop on Component-Based Software Engineering, Software Architecture and Reuse (ICIS-COMSAR'06)* (pp. 225-230).

RACER. (2007). *DL reasoner.* Retrieved June 1, 2007 from http://www.racer-systems.com

Raghavan, V., & Wong, S. (1986). A critical analysis of vector space model for information retrieval. *JASIS, 37*(5), 279-287.

Roman, D., Keller, U., Lausen, H., de Bruijn, J., Lara, R., Stollberg, M., et al. (2005). Web service modeling ontology. *Applied Ontology, 1*(1), 77-106.

Srinivasan, N., Paolucci, M., & Sycara, K. (2004). Adding OWL-S to UDDI, implementation and throughput. *Proceedings of the First International Workshop on Semantic Web Services and Web Process Composition (SWSWPC).* San Diego, CA.

SWSL Committee. (2007). *Semantic Web services framework (SWSF).* Retrieved June 1, 2007 from http://www.daml.org/services/swsf

Sycara, K., Paolucci, M., Ankolekar, A., & Srinivasan, N. (2004). Automated discovery, interaction and composition of semantic Web services. *Journal of Web Semantics, 1.*

Tsetsos, V., Anagnostopoulos, C., & Hadjiefthymiades, S. (2007). Semantic Web service discovery: Methods, algorithms and tools. In: J. Cardoso (Ed.), *Semantic Web services: Theory, tools and applications.* Hershey, PA: IGI Publishing.

Wooldridge, M. (2002). *An introduction to multi-agent systems.* John Wiley & Sons.

Zahreddine, W., & Mahmoud, Q. (2005). An agent-based approach to composite mobile Web services. *Proceedings of the 19th IEEE International Conference on Advanced Information Networking and Applications (AINA05).* Taipei, Taiwan.

This work was previously published in International Journal on Semantic Web & Information Systems, Vol. 4, Issue 1 , edited by A. Sheth, pp. 1-19, copyright 2008 by IGI Publishing (an imprint of IGI Global).

Chapter 3
Mobile Ontologies:
Concept, Development, Usage, and Business Potential

Jari Veijalainen
University of Jyvaskyla, Finland

ABSTRACT

The number of mobile subscribers in the world is soon reaching the three billion mark. According to the newest estimates, majority of the subscribers are already in the developing countries, whereas the number of subscribers in the industrialized countries is about to stagnate around one billion. Because especially in the developing countries the only access to Internet are mobile devices, developing high quality services based on them grows in importance. Ontologies are an important ingredient towards more complicated mobile services and wider usage of mobile terminals. In this article, we first discuss ontology and epistemology concepts in general. After that, we review ontologies in the computer science field and introduce mobile ontologies as a special category of them. It seems reasonable to distinguish between two orthogonal categories, mobile domain ontologies and flowing ontologies. The domain of the former one is in some sense related with mobility, whereas the latter ones are able to flow from computer to computer in the network. We then discuss the creation issues, business aspects, and intellectual property rights (IPR), including patentability of mobile ontologies. We also discuss some basic requirements for computer systems architectures that would be needed to support the usage of mobile ontologies.

INTRODUCTION

The mobile subscriber base in the world is growing fast. The industry itself estimates that at the end of 2006, the number of subscribers reached 2.7 billion and it is expected that the number of subscribers will grow with 480 million during 2007 (Umsoy, 2007). The biggest growth will be in the developing countries, like India and China. There are over 130 3G WCDMA networks in 60 countries with 100 million subscribers. The latter number will grow to 170 million during 2007.

Copyright © 2010, IGI Global, distributing in print or electronic forms without written permission of IGI Global is prohibited.

Low-cost WCDMA terminals (65 € a piece) are coming to the market. High Speed Packet Access (HSPA) with 3.6 Mbps downlink capacity is deployed in 51 countries in 93 networks and there were 128 devices on the market supporting HSDPA in March 2007 (Umsoy, 2007).

Digital convergence is tearing apart the old barriers between entertainment, media, telecom and computer industries, and all these industries are melting together into one huge industry. At the same time, the wireless operators are pondering their position on this market. They want to be more than bit pipes providing access to Internet for wireless terminals. Many operators think that they must provide better and more appealing services to the subscribers. How can appealing services be offered to mobile users both in developed and developing countries? These can be location-based or context-aware in a wider sense, or other services adapted to mobile Internet.

At the same time, the top models of mobile wireless terminals have reached capabilities of a laptop computer a few years ago with gigabytes of memory, programmability, fast processors, GPS receivers, text editors, calendars, e-mail clients, browsers, and so forth. Many have cameras and can record images and video with sound. Thus, users have begun to generate multimedia contents using these devices. Assuming that a user takes, for example, 2,000 digital photographs and some video clips in a year, there will be a substantial number, tens of thousands, even hundred thousand of these kinds of objects after 30-50 years. These are mostly relevant for the person himself or herself and for his friends and family members. Managing reasonably these emerging digital archives requires semantic metadata that cannot be generated fully automatically. Rather, user's help is needed (Sarvas, 2006). Also, storage space (approaching terabyte range for a life-time archive) is a problem and the stability of the formats used. Who guarantees that for example, the currently so popular JPEG-format would be supported in 2060? If the format originally used to store the

images or video clips is not any more supported, what kind of automatic means are there to transform the contents into newer formats?

YouTube (Youtube, 2007) is currently one of the most known sites in the world where people can upload their video clips and other users can download them. Many of those videos have been produced by mobile handsets. Flickr (Flickr, 2007) offers sharing of photographs and a simple annotation in the form of tags. Not all material is suitable for distribution all over the world, though, for moral, legal, cultural, or privacy reasons. For instance, Flickr site does not allow sexually-oriented contents beyond a certain limit, although the tags "sex" and "sexy" are in use.

The above needs of individuals while managing and sharing digital contents are rather different from those of the companies offering various kinds of *mobile services*. Both can be satisfied in several ways. Perhaps the most sophisticated approach is to use *ontologies* in all these contexts. Because terminals are becoming more and more powerful over time, they can also be used to run complex computations, for example, inferences, required while using *formal ontologies* for various purposes. This is the main motivation behind this article.

In section 2, we discuss the concept of ontology and epistemology in general and in section 3, we discuss the concept of ontology in computer science field. In section 4, we discuss what should be understood by mobile ontologies. In section 5, we will turn our attention to the ontology creation issues in general and the peculiarities when creating mobile ontologies. In section 6, we discuss so-far largely ignored business and IPR issues related to mobile ontologies. Section 7 concludes the article.

ONTOLOGY AND EPISTEMOLOGY

"What is there? What exists?" This could be understood as the basic question of ontology, that is, *study of being* or existence in philosophy. Different answers to this question were given over the course of history. One fundamental issue is, whether the deepest reality is ever changing and moving or whether it is stable and movement is just a human illusion After the Renaissance in Europe, one began to explore the nature in order to find the explanations from it itself by the methods of natural science. The starting point of the scientific inquiry is that there are no reasons or causes external to the nature and that the causes and true explanations can be found by interacting with the nature. Another starting point is that human perception of the nature is different from the nature itself, because otherwise we would know the essence of nature without further interactions and its exploration would be unnecessary. We adhere to the view that there are two different realities, one within the individual human *consciousness* and the other outside of it. Further, change and movement are real and change is actually the ultimate attribute of the realities. Stability is just transient.

The modern thinking and the concrete exploration of the nature have radically changed the answer to the ontological question and also the structure of modern societies. It has brought up such *concepts* as electrons, neutrons and other particles, atoms consisting of them and possibility to split atoms to gain energy, molecules and chemical industry, DNA, living cells, bio-industry and modern medicine, electro-magnetism, electronics and electrical industry including computer industry, relativity theory, galaxies, black holes, and so forth. In mathematics, one has developed axiomatic mathematics, formal logic and formal languages, paving the way to computing and formal ontologies.

The modern thinking has further divided the external reality into *physical* and *social* reality. Physical reality exists also without people, that is, it existed before any human being existed and will exist after human beings have vanished from the universe with their concepts and ideas, such

as stability, gods, good life, good and bad, right and wrong. That is, physical reality is more fundamental than social reality, although admittedly also other views on the structure of physical reality and its relationship with the social reality have existed in the consciousness of the individuals and collectives over history.

Already the great Greek philosophers Plato and Aristotle posed the *epistemological* questions "What can we humans know of the reality?", "What is truth?", "What is knowledge?" These questions are always related with the basic ontological *world view that* covers all the elements considered basic by a certain group of people, such as nature or matter, human beings and perhaps various kinds of spirits or souls. *Concepts* and their relationships, *theories,* form the knowledge part of the contents of the consciousness and thus the above epistemological questions can be rephrased in terms of concepts and utterances about their relationship with the physical and social external reality. Which concepts refer to something existing and which relationships can be confirmed in the reality?

Coming back to the fundamental questions of ontology and epistemology and their relationships, our view is the following. A plausible solution to a consistent ontology and epistemology is that human beings develop their concepts using their mental, creative capabilities, while *interacting* with the physical reality and communicating with other people in a society, that is, while being part of the social reality. The *individual and collective needs* to develop and adopt new *concepts* emerge always in a certain social context. This means that the answer to the basic ontological question, "what is there", changes over time, represented in new concepts and their relationships. The concepts are developed by various groups of people in interaction with themselves and with the physical reality. During the modern times, these kind of activities produce ontology that is based on the methods of natural and other sciences and explain the nature from and within itself, whereas in the past various kinds of spirits or gods were often included into the ontologies supported by various groups. Another object of the studies is the social reality, that is, human societies. In our view, macro- and microeconomic theories, as well as concepts of politics and social sciences belong to this sphere. The modern concepts and theories describing these are evidently widely different from those describing physical reality. Individuals adopt the views developed by previous generations and mediated by oral and/or written means and only some develop them further. In current societies different groups of people and even a single individual can have different ontological views that can be also contradictory.

In the modern separation of physical and social reality, the *artifacts* developed by human beings, such as houses, cars, fashion, mobile networks and terminals belong clearly to the physical reality created by human beings. But their existence or development cannot be explained in a similar manner from nature as development of, for example, mountains or oceans. Rather they are at the same time also results of human social activity. This duality should be reflected in the specific ontology describing them. There is an extensive discussion on a suitable ontology for these kind artifacts, that is, in Pohjola (2007). These kinds of discussions about the "true essence" of artifacts are relevant for ontologies in computer science, because they also are socially created artifacts that exist in the physical (digital) reality. What is a suitable "artifact ontology" for computerized ontologies is an interesting question, but beyond the scope of this article.

The general questions and issues above are relevant also for ontology development in the computer field. We point to them below at appropriate places.

ONTOLOGIES IN COMPUTER SCIENCE

In the computer science field, McCarthy introduced in 1980 the concept *environment's ontology* that contained a list of concepts involved in a problem (environment) and their meanings (Sanchez, 2007). Since then, the term has been associated with the representation of concepts and the usage has spread out to many fields of computer science. The often cited definition by Gruber reads "ontology is an explicit conceptualization of a domain", although in the abstract of the same paper it reads "A specification of a representational vocabulary for a shared domain of discourse — definitions of classes, relations, functions, and other objects — is called an ontology" (Gruber, 1993). The definition does not explicitly relate ontology to a specific group of people or its validity period. It has also been pointed out, for example, by Smith (2004) that "conceptualization" remains undefined in the definition.

In the sequel, we mean by ontology *a conceptualization of a domain created and shared by a group of human beings. The domain can also be called a possible world.* This definition stresses that an ontology must be understood by a group of people in the same way as far as it is possible; must be representable in an interpersonal form (using natural or formal language, pictures, etc.), and must refer to a common domain that the group agrees upon. The domain or possible world does not need to exist in the current physical or social reality, only in the consciousness of the group members, and as the corresponding externalized representation. Most often, though, an ontology is established with the goal of claiming that the domain indeed has had, has, or will have the structure, relationships and properties the ontology referring to the domain claims it to have. In this narrower sense, an ontology can be understood as a *body of knowledge describing some domain and as a representation vocabulary for it.* In this capacity, it also makes sharing of knowledge among individuals and groups possible (Chandrasekaran, 1999). This view on ontology is narrower than the general definition above because knowledge should be truthful, that is, refer to reality it is to the best of our knowledge. One cannot say the same of an arbitrary possible world, or even about a possible future world. The fitness of an ontology as a carrier of knowledge is discussed, for example, in Smith (2006b) and more general discussion on the various aspects on ontologies can be found in Brewster (2007) and in the special issue of the International Journal of Human-Computer Studies.

Conceptualizations we have in mind are *terms* with natural and/or formal language definitions that *refer* to universals or instances in the physical or social reality or human consciousness, and the relationships between the terms. A fairly general way to construct ontology is expressed in LOA (2007): "ontology is assumed here as a semiotic object, including at least three objects: a graph (information object), a conceptualization (description), a semantic space (abstract). The semantic space refers to the 'formal' semantics of an ontology graph, while the conceptualization refers to its 'cognitive' semantics". For instance, "VW is-a car" means that there is a collection of physical artifacts called cars on Earth and some of them are manufactured by Volkswagen. The semantic space contains the set of cars and VW-cars are a subset of it. These can be represented by set-theoretic, inter-subjective notations, but the notations can only again refer to the real collection of physical cars by human mental act—or by computerized version thereof. The cognitive "car" refers to the culturally given connotations of a car as an artifact, vehicle, status symbol, and so forth, as individuals perceive them. Depending on the goal of the ontology, certain relationships with other concepts are included into the ontology graph, but not necessarily all. For example, the concept of car can only be related with vehicle (as a subclass), but other culturally relevant concepts are not included into the ontology. Thus, an ontology can be understood in the same way by different people, as concerns the concepts (signs), but these can have different connotations and thus the ontology is not understood in the same way by the people (Mancini, 2006).

Ontologies in computer science have been classified in several ways. The authors of vHeijst (1997) classify ontologies, according to their use, in *terminological, information, and knowledge modeling* ontologies, whereas Guarino (1998) divides them into *top-level, domain/task,* and *application* ontologies, based on their generality. The authors in Gomez-Perez (2003) classify ontologies into *lightweight* and *heavyweight* ontologies. The former include concepts, concept taxonomies, relationships between concepts, and properties describing the concepts. The latter enhance the former with axioms and constraints. D. Fensel introduces five categories differentiating between *metadata, domain, generic, representational,* and *method/task* ontologies (Fensel, 2004). Thus, we see that currently there is no commonly accepted single classification for ontologies.

Ontology development is an activity performed by a group of people. At the beginning of the development process, humans usually rely on written and spoken natural language and informal schemata and the end result can even remain in this informal form. The process of developing ontology can be from bottom-up or top-down, although both directions are usually mixed. The mixed version, where both directions are used simultaneously, is often called middle-out. In the bottom-up approach, the existing terms and concepts of a domain are taken as a starting point, definitions given and relationships between concepts established that reflect the relations in the domain. In the top-down approach, one can start from an existing upper ontology and refine and enhance it with the concepts of the domain. Of course, the process of developing ontologies is rather complex. For instance, the borders of the domain can be unclear and the domain understood in a different way by participants at the beginning. Thus, as part of the ontology development, the exact domain can emerge and become shared by the people.

In general, the external representation of ontology is composed of symbols of one or several languages. It is a representation of the shared understanding of the group members of what the domain is and what is essential or interesting for the domain. As such, it is just a finite (information) object, carrying meanings to people, and it can be encoded into a bit string and stored on a computer. It means something only for those people who understand the languages used. A computer "understands" an ontology or part of it, if there is a portion represented with a formal enough language that can be interpreted by the computer. In other words, programs must run that use this portion as input and that compute results using it. Such ontologies that are composed using a formal language or contain a formal language portion are called *formal ontologies,* others are called informal *ontologies.*

The formal languages used are usually subsets of first-order predicate logic, such as description logic or frame logic (Staab, 2004), but also (extended) UML and ER-notation have been proposed to be used as a formal ontology language (Sanchez, 2007). *Automatic reasoning* in computers based on the axioms and inference rule(s) of the logic become thus possible. Generally, any formal language that can be given an operational, computable semantics would be a possible candidate for an ontology description language, as long as it is easy for a human being to represent concepts and their relationships, as well as restrictions that are typical of the domain. In Smith (2006), it is stated that such a resulting ontology should be *intelligible*, that is, understandable by other persons that did not develop it, with a reasonable effort. Often, formal ontologies are not especially intelligible; check the proposed ontologies, for example, at WSMO (2007) or LOA (2007). Therefore, formal ontologies usually contain also portions that contain descriptions of the concepts and relationships

in natural language. Based on the informal and formal parts one can also ask, whether on ontology is internally *coheren*t, that is, do the informal and formal part specifies the same domain, the same relationships and axioms.

Another set of requirements presented by Smith (2006a) requires *openness:* "ontology should be open and available to be used by all potential users without any constraint, other than (1) its origin must be acknowledged and (2) it should not to be altered and subsequently redistributed except under a new name... In addition the ontology should be (3) explained in ways which make its content intelligible to human beings, and (4) implemented in ways which make this content accessible to computers." It is rather clear that open ontologies in the above sense would be usable by anybody and those who develop them could not sell them and thus directly take the benefit. Indirectly, it might be possible, though. The last point (4) would namely mean that all ontologies should be flowing (or native) and thus mobile in one sense (see below). In this form, they could possibly be integrated or downloaded into larger computer systems and used by software. A business opportunity might exist here both for the developers of the ontology or for the third parties (see the next section).

MOBILE ONTOLOGIES

What would then be mobile ontologies? While answering this question, we are actually constructing a further classification of ontologies. The term mobile could be added to almost any class above, obtaining such terms as mobile top-level, mobile domain, mobile application, mobile metadata, or mobile terminological ontology. But what would they mean? We gave a tentative characterization for the term mobile ontology in Veijalainen (2006), and refined it in the preliminary version of this article (Veijalainen, 2007). According to it, a mobile ontology can conceptualize a mobile domain, that is, the possible world the ontology is conceptualizing must be related with mobility. On the other hand, an ontology can itself be mobile, that is, its digital representation can move from one node to another among networked computers, or it can move physically with the terminal. These two aspects are largely orthogonal.

What should be understood by a mobile domain in this context? Let us start from bottom up. In the current business practice and also in the scientific literature, the term mobile is used in many different ways. One speaks, for example, about mobile networks, mobile applications, mobile users, mobile terminals, and so forth. Often, the term mobile refers only indirectly to physical movement, and the reference is primarily to wireless and other technologies that make physical movement possible or that can be used while on the move. In some contexts, the term mobile could be replaced with the term wireless to emphasize that the central issue dealt with is wireless communication technology that facilitates physical movement of the terminal during service delivery. Seen from the service accessibility point of view, mobility in service delivery refers to the possibility to *deliver the services anytime anywhere.* Where the user happens to be and whether the user moves or not or is not of importance for the service delivery.

How should "mobile" or by "mobility" be defined in the context of the mobile ontology? If we think that these terms are somehow directly or indirectly related with the physical movement of the human user or movement of the ontology representation either from one computer to another or within the computer around, we can conceptualize the movement as *context change.* We can ask, what a user or ontology would need in a *new context* and in which cases she/it would need (portions of) her existing context? In general, a context can always be related with a particular physical place, but there can be different relevant contexts attached to a place. The context can change even if the user sits in her chair in the of-

fice, once speaking to (VoIP) phone, once having a face-to-face meeting with some people in her office, once wanting to concentrate alone on her work. The context usually changes, though, if the user is roaming to another country, and it could change as a result of the micro-mobility, at least from the network infrastructure perspective.

The user context and its management can be taken care of mainly by the terminal with the help of the user, but it often requires support also from the network infrastructure. From the network infrastructure point of view, "mobility" of a terminal or person can refer to at least five different aspects (cf. (Puttonen, 2006)):

1. A person changes the terminal in use (often as a result of physical movement, or context change)
2. A terminal changes its point of attachment to the network (often as a result of the physical movement with its owner; cf. hand-over)
3. Application is migrated from one network node to another (cf. mobile agents)
4. An on-going session is moved from one terminal to another (cf. 1)
5. Services available for a subscriber at one network location are offered at a new location the subscriber physically moves to (cf. 2; context transfer)

The above view on mobile domain and mobility is mainly a context change issue from the network infrastructure point of view. Although this is an important domain, it does not cover all mobile domains. Keeping this in mind, we can refine the concept of mobile ontologies further. We introduce the shorthand notion *md-ontology* for mobile *domain ontology,* where the domain is related with mobility (see below). On the other hand, if ontology (representation) can move from one computer network node to another, such ontology is called *flowing or fl-ontology.* Those ontologies that are stored (by manufacturers or operators, etc.) into terminals or other devices and move physically with them, but cannot flow into them from the network, are called *native* or *nt-ontologies*. Notice that we allow the native ontologies to be read, that is, flow out, from the terminal or other wireless device. In addition, all mobile ontologies can be divided into formal and informal ontologies as discussed above. These two aspects are orthogonal and thus, informal-formal and flowing-native divide the set of mobile ontologies into pair-wise disjoint subsets. Are there any ontologies that are not mobile in any sense? Yes, those whose domain is not mobile (say bioinformatics (OBO, 2007)) and which are neither installed into terminals by manufacturers nor can be downloaded into them later for whatever reason.

All the aspects, 1-5 above, seen from the network infrastructure's point of view, can be a domain of a md-ontology. In addition, there can be further md-ontologies that model, for example, physical movements of objects on earth. In that case, the ontology would support, for example, tracking applications where the physically moving objects are not primarily users, but physical objects that are tracked, such as trucks or parcels—or terminals or RFID chips mounted on them. Ontologies describing essential concepts for this application domain (such as tracking, positioning, trace, trajectory, velocity, etc.) can also be regarded as mobile domain ontologies.

Ontologies that help in anywhere/anytime service delivery to mobile terminals are also typical md-ontologies. They do not need to be installed at the terminals, but can reside also at other network components, like servers providing the anywhere/anytime services. This subcategory might contain md-ontologies that support content format transformations and mobile Web service descriptions. Another case is described in Massimo (2007) where the mobile device accesses a tag in its vicinity to which information and/or a Web service is provided from a server. The (ontology-based) service description is dynamically loaded into the device and, for example, information on movies or a movie ticket can be provided to the device as a result of the service invocation.

Fl-ontologies are a special case of 3 if we consider ontologies to be a special kind of software or belonging to a software package moving in the network from one node to another. They have many commonalities with mobile agents, and one might argue that such ontologies are as such actually pieces of software moving around in the network. This view is valid, if the ontology can be directly interpreted or compiled at the receiving node and appropriate actions taken by the computer. An example of this is presented in Khusraj (2005), where a user interface for a Web service is generated from a semantic description at a mobile device. The ontologies might also be carried by mobile agents as part of their state. Another possible scenario is software package that is downloaded from the network and is installed at the terminal. Its functionality might be guided by an ontology component that travels with it or that is downloaded separately.

Any ontology that is stored at a home location or by manufacturer into a device can be considered an nt-ontology. The significance of this concept is that such an ontology could have been designed to a certain environment or context (e.g., by an operator or a manufacturer) and it might not work properly in other environments or contexts the terminal roams to. But it might also be upper-level ontology that works everywhere and does not need to be changed, based on the location. Some nt-ontologies might be invisible to the outside world, but some of them might flow out, that is, they might be readable from outside. This might a possibility for future digital tags that can tell what to store and how to access it.

Point 5 above is challenging from the usage and development point of view of such services that are based on ontologies. Challenge concerning point 3 is heterogeneity and autonomy, but also the applicable business model that makes transfer of (formal) ontologies profitable, or at least possible.

What is the relationship between informal-formal and flowing-native ontologies? Informal ontologies can flow "more easily" than formal ones, because they are only based on natural language and perhaps on some commonly available drawing tool or text editor formats, including XML-based ones, whereas the formal ontologies need rigorous execution (reasoning) environment and in a heterogeneous environment in addition powerful mediators that translate from one formal language to another (Roman, 2005; Euzenat, 2007). The formal ontologies usually also have an XML encoding for transmission purposes, so that at this basic level they can be transported in computer networks or over a wireless short-range link from node to node. In these cases, the enhancement of an ontology with another might happen and the consistency issues are of importance.

DEVELOPING MOBILE ONTOLOGIES

Developing ontologies can be performed by various actors. Known alternatives are research groups, research projects, and larger organizations who have hired specialists to do the work for themselves, or coordinate the work paid by large companies and government organizations. Further, developer communities can engage in the development of ontologies, in a similar fashion as some groups develop free software. ISO is an example of a large international organization that has developed a standard ISO 15926 (ISO, 2003) that could be used as an upper ontology. Barry Smith has checked the quality of the ontology, though, and comes to the conclusion that it is not an ontology at all due to many flaws (Smith, 2006b). Because it can be downloaded from the ISO site as a pdf-file, it would be an fl-ontology, but not a formal one.

Another example of an existing ontology is, for example, "high-level mobile ontology" developed by the SPICE project (Zhanova, 2006). It is developed for the mutual understanding of the project. It is also exploiting many other existing ontologies and related specifications, such OMA's UAp (OMA, 2006) and FOAF vocabulary (FOAF, 2007). The ontology specifies the concept of service and subtypes thereof, device and subtypes thereof, mobile access network and subtypes thereof, person (a physical thing), user groups, configuration, location, context, contents and contents types, and so forth. It is an md-ontology in our classification that can be used to describe mobile infrastructures. It is a formal upper-level ontology that could be used by various terminals and by the service delivery sites. It is developed by a research consortium.

Is developing mobile ontologies any different from other ontologies? If it is question of md-ontologies, the same challenges are encountered as while developing ontologies for other domains. The only difference might be that some md-ontologies are inherently related with changes in the domain, and change is a general challenge for ontologies. As concerns methodologies, Sanchez (2007) reviews shortly several proposed ontology development methodologies. It seems that any of them could be used, but it is too early to say whether various md-ontologies would have specialties that would require modifications to the methodologies, or perhaps new developing methodologies to be developed. In any case, Fl-ontologies, especially formal ones, present additional challenges, both organizational and technical. When an ontology crosses an organizational border, the receiving organization should understand and accept the world view its developers had and also *trust* the sending side. Neither is by no means generally given between autonomous organizations. Detecting the discrepancies between different world views is easy in the case of intelligible ontologies (cf. above), because they explicate the views of the developers for other humans. Perceiving the world view is more difficult in the case of usual software, because any piece of software crossing an organizational border carries with it a world view of the developers, but it is often represented only in the code and detected only when using the software. The same might be true for large formal ontologies that cannot be understood by humans without a big effort and high technical skills. And of course, if the ontology comes as data part of mobile agent or software package, the problem is essentially the same as for any moving software. If we think that pure ontologies or mobile agents would be downloaded by ordinary mobile users, without special technical skills, the problem is aggravated. They could not check the quality of the ontology, mobile agent or piece of software, but rather they could only trust the provider.

The technical challenges are mostly software engineering challenges in the mobile environment for the flowing ontologies. They are similar to downloading software from the network. There must be a platform support for correctly installing and interpreting the ontology. What the support exactly looks like depends at least partially on the formalism used to represent the ontology and the nature of the ontology (top-level vs. application, lightweight vs. heavyweight, etc.). A requirement peculiar to ontologies is that if the ontology is to be integrated with an existing one, or existing ones, then the resulting ontology should be at least *consistent*. This means that no contradictions can be inferred from valid input definitions (Gomez-Perez, 2004). There should be tools to check this at least at the provider site, but perhaps also at the terminal. Like in the case of other software entities, there should be versioning mechanisms and valid configuration schemes for mobile ontologies. Using them, compatibility relationships could be expressed between different ontologies and their versions.

According to Gomez-Perez (2004), ontologies should also be evaluated for *completeness* (everything meant to be there is explicit or can be inferred, and each definition is complete), *conciseness* (no redundancy), *expandability* (how easy is it to add new definitions and knowledge without altering the set of already guaranteed proper-

ties), and *sensitiveness* (how small changes alter the well-defined properties already guaranteed). All these are relevant attributes for md- and fl-ontologies and should be taken into consideration when developing and updating them.

There are many emerging formal ontologies in various domains, such as biomedicine, law, software engineering, and so forth, (LOA, 2007; OBO, 2007; Ontomed, 2006). Some of these could be perhaps used as part of mobile ontologies.

The problem of generating metadata for private photographs taken by camera phones has been investigated in Sarvas (2006). The author concluded that this area is a special domain and requires metadata—or ontology—that is different from the commercial multimedia material. He also discovered in user tests that people are not willing to insert the metadata at spot (who are on the picture, what was the social situation the picture was taken in, etc.), because it tends to disturb the photographing act.

In jpg-metadata there is already some information, such as camera type, shutter, date, and so forth, but coordinates where the picture was taken should be added. This would require GPS or other satellite receiver to be integrated to or accessible for the terminal. Currently, the trend is that high-end terminals begin to include a GPS receiver. To the coordinates, one could attach the name of the place automatically when precise enough geographic information was made available. Automatic face recognition might be possible for acquainted people in the picture, if once done and the resulting meta-information stored at the terminal. The hard parts are the semantically high level concepts, like "situation" or "social context" where the picture was taken. This should be described by the user textually or orally and transformed into text by speech recognition. Speech recognition could be also used to identify people in the picture if they happened to speak when the picture was taken. In Khusraj (2005), the concept of semantic cache was proposed that keeps track of the places that the user has visited lately. These can be directly included into the metadata and used by the inference engine.

A general solution to ontology development is to reuse existing pieces of ontology. In Salminen (2005) the authors present an architecture that allows a mobile terminal user to develop, organize, and share the digital contents and the associated metadata. The device manufacturer would provide a software that is able to store and interpret the metadata, and evidently, a native (meta)ontology. The user can then enhance this with flowing components or develop himself or herself new ontologies.

Although the ontologies conceptualizing low-level mobile protocol layers or device characteristics are important for the end-to-end service delivery, still modeling the service, context, and contents domains is the key for the proliferation of nice services. Could the vast end-user population help here? What are the minimal skills and minimal knowledge required? If we are speaking of informal taxonomies, such as folksonomies (Koivunen, 2006; Wikipedia, 2007), the requirements are not so high. They can be generated by ordinary users and are used to tag all kinds of digital objects. A collection of such tags is usually not a genuine conceptualization of a domain, that is, an ontology in a strict sense. This is because tagging can be contradictory and usually lacks hierarchical relationships, such as "is a", "part-of", and so forth. Collectively, generated tags can still be used to organize private photographs either at Web sites like Flickr (Flick, 2007) or on private devices. What kind of tools would be needed at the mobile terminals to support generation of remote tags? It seems that inserting photos to the above Flickr site directly from camera phones and tagging them is possible already now.

Folksnomies are developed by a user community. The approach bears resemblance to the development of open source software. Whereas open software cannot be developed by unskilled people, folksnomies can be developed by people who cannot write code. How big is the distance from folksonomies to ontologies and further to proper formal ontologies that could be used by programs as input? Folksonomies can be used at least as some kind of starting point to develop ontologies for certain domains bottom up, but it is evident that developing even an informal ontology and especially a formal ontology requires expert work. For instance, the Flickr tags are just a collection of individual words and the frequency they occur in metadata of the photographs reflects the frequency of the situations the pictures were taken in. A rather common tag is for instance "Canon" referring to the camera manufacturer, and "Wedding" referring to a situation the picture was taken in. One might argue that not even every person who is able to write, for example, Java programs would be able to compile a formal ontology. The latter requires different skills than programming.

ONTOLOGY SHOPPING

The organization or a group of individuals that develops an ontology, or fraction of it, primarily owns it. Some capable experts might be interested in developing ontologies in the same spirit as they are ready to write articles to Wikipedia or open source software. Still, if formal ontologies would become directly usable by mobile terminals, then it would make sense to develop them as commercial activity and pay for the work. This is currently hardly envisaged in the research literature. Probably, because developing ontologies, especially formal ones, requires high skills and is currently still research activity.

What legal status would ontologies have? They are scientific or technical works and fall under the Berne Convention that also regulates software ownership and rights (WIPO, 2007). According to Berne convention, a copyright holder is inherently the creator of the work. The rights cover economic and moral rights and the creator has thus the right to demand economic compensation when the work is performed or distributed to audience. The creator can also sell his or her rights to another person or company totally or in part. Those countries that have joined the Berne Convention treat the rights uniformly, although the convention allows exceptions. The local legislation may, for instance, automatically move the copyrights of an employee to the employer in some cases. For instance, the rights to (production) software, if produced by employees as part of their normal duties at a Finnish university, are moved by the law to the university without further action and without additional compensation. The copyright protection holds of course to original enough works, not works that would infringe the rights of other copyright owners. Another question is whether ontologies would be software or other scientific of technical works. The informal ontologies could hardly be considered as software, but the formal ones could be interpreted as software if they can be executed in a computer like any other program. Some formal ontologies have been copyrighted as software, such as Ontomed ontology (Ontomed, 2006). This can be inferred from the fact that the ontology includes a GPL-like license at the beginning and categorizes the contents as "software". In any case, all kind of ontologies are material that is protected by copyright if developed in a country that has joined Berne Convention (cf. WIPO, 2007).

Whereas copyright grants legal and moral rights to the owner, it does not protect the ideas presented in the work. That is, if somebody buys a book, where a construction of a machine a process, a business model, and so forth, is presented, the copyright owner neither can prohibit the buyer to construct the machine or implement the process or business model, nor can demand any economic compensation for the possible yield. *Patents* protect the innovations and give the exclusive rights to the patent owner to reap the economic benefits from the innovation for a limited period of time (e.g., 20 years) in the jurisdiction the patent has been granted in (e.g.,

USA, EU, Japan). A patent is a public document. After the patent has expired, the innovation can be copied and developed further by others and economic benefits reaped freely.

Could ontologies be *patented?* In this case, there is evidently a difference between informal and formal ontologies. The former cannot be patented, only copyrighted and usage perhaps licensed in some cases. If formal ontologies are considered to be software, then in some countries (such as USA) they might be patentable even as such, or at least as part of some larger software system or other technical context. The patentability seems to be largely open, though, because the exact nature of them as creative work is not established yet.

Digital music, videos and software can be bought and used in the mobile terminals. Full-fledged formal ontologies are also machine-process able and could become at least in theory, separate objects of trade. Their behavior and usage is quite close to a of piece software. They need some kind of interpreter in order to be usable, in a similar fashion as Java byte code. But can formal ontologies be considered as software in the legal sense? Or are they treated rather like other digital contents? This is largely open, but in both cases ontologies could become intangible goods—or information society services as the EU jargon proposes.

There are not many examples of ontology shopping. ISO has developed an international standard ISO 15926 (IS, 2003) that is also considered by some groups to be an upper-level ontology (cf. above). As a standard, it has a price tag of CHF 258 (EUR 156). It is protected by copyright that denies its further distribution. Thus, it evidently could not be used in computerized ontology applications without licensing—if somebody managed to make it executable in computers, that is, to formalize it properly.

In order for ontology market to be economically viable, several conditions must be met. They are rather similar as those for the other mobile contents or mobile application software. Some device manufacturers could, for example, implement some functionality of the devices using ontology-based technology and thus increase the attractiveness of the devices. The devices could have an ontology (reasoner) engine installed by the manufacturer, in a similar manner as some now have a Java virtual machine or a media player. This engine could then be used to process ontologies in various contexts. The engine could also be licensed and installed later, and necessary ontologies could then be downloaded and processed using it.

The manufacturer could install some nt-ontologies into the device that would not need to be md-ontologies. A typical example would be an ontology for digital pictures that would make their indexing and retrieval possible for the user or other digital contents (Salminen, 2005).

Mobile md-ontologies might also come with the device, but the user could order various md-ontologies as he or she needs, over the network or on a memory stick/memory card. So, those md-ontologies that are bought during the usage should be designed as fl-ontologies. Technical problems are similar to those of downloading software from the network. Perhaps it makes sense to develop "source code form" and some kind of "byte code" for the mobile ontologies as well, in analogy to Java, or one could also develop the interpreter in Java. Source code format should have XML encoding, like OWL-S and WSML (WSMO, 2007) have.

While selling or otherwise distributing private contents, privacy becomes an issue. The actual contents, but also metadata can contain information that a person might not want to share with a larger audience, although this would be shareable within, for example, family. This has been addressed, for example,. in Sarvas (2006) and Salminen (2005).

CONCLUSION

We have discussed in this article mobile ontologies; what should be understood by them, how they could be used, who would develop them, and why. The concept is still under development and the term "mobile" can refer to two rather different aspects. On one hand, the domain of the ontology can be related to mobility (md-ontology), on the other hand the interpersonal representation of the ontology can move (flow) from node another in the network (fl-ontology) or move with the terminal (native or n-ontology). In the latter cases, the domain of the ontology can be anything. The definition of mobile ontology should address these aspects. We suggest the following definition: *If the domain of an ontology is related with mobility or it can be mounted or downloaded to and used at a mobile terminal, or both, th*en *it is a mobile ontology.* Informal ontologies can flow more easily, as far as technical constraints are considered, whereas formal ontologies that have usually a portion consisting of first-order logic expressions have more difficulties in crossing heterogeneous and autonomous system borders. The latter kind of ontologies facilitate formal reasoning, and further automatic processing, whereas informal ontologies can only be applied by humans. Organizational autonomy is also an important issue in the scenario, where ontologies are dynamically downloaded to mobile terminals or incorporated into the ICT infrastructure of an organization. Because ontologies are difficult to understand and inspect, an organization, not to speak about a usual user, must trust the ontology provider.

Mobile formal ontologies might become objects of trade, if they turn out to be useful enough to justify the investment in developing a software infrastructure and terminal and ontology base for them. Business models for these might look similar to those of the mobile software and both native and flowing ontologies could be used. Free ontologies are also possible, in a similar manner as free software, and in analogy, open mobile ontologies are also possible.

Quality of ontologies is an emerging theme and the identified attributes like consistency, completeness, conciseness, expandability, and sensitiveness are important to evaluate for mobile ontologies. It is evident that if ontologies are downloaded to a terminal, the providers should indicate with which earlier versions of which other ontologies a certain ontology is compatible. Compatibility statements must evidently consider all quality attributes above.

Intellectual property rights in the context of ontologies seem similar to scientific pieces of work or software and are thus primarily governed by copyright laws. Only formal ontologies could be viewed as software and as patentable is some countries, but the entire area of intellectual property rights in the context of ontologies is largely open. The solution might have some ramifications to the possible mobile ontology market, though, as we have seen in software business in the context of free/open software.

ACKNOWLEDGMENT

The author wishes to thank the reviewers of this article and those of the preliminary version (Veijalainen, 2007) that appeared in Proceedings of the MoSO2007 workshop, available at IEEE Digital Library.

REFERENCES

Brewster, C., & O'Hara, K. (2007). Knowledge representation with ontologies: Present challenges—Future possibilities. *International Journal of Human-Computer Studies 65,* 563-568.

Chandrasekaran, B., Josephson, J., & Benjamins, V. (1999). What are ontologies, and why do we need them?. *IEEE Intelligent Systems, 14,*(Jan.-Feb.), 20-26,

Euzenat, J., & Shvaiko, P. (2007). *Ontology matching.* Berlin/Heidelberg: Springer-Verlag.

Fensel, D. (2004). *Ontologies, a silver-bullet for knowledge management and electronic commerce,* 2nd ed. Berlin: Springer Verlag.

Flickr Virtual Community. (2007). www.flickr.com.

Friend-of-Friend Virtual Community. (2007). www.foaf-project.org

Folksonomies. (2007). www.wikipedia.org/folksonomy

General Formal Ontology. (2007). Retrieved May 30, 2007 from http://www.onto-med.de/ontologies/gfo.owl

Gomez-Perez, A. (2004). *Ontology evaluation.* Ch. 13 in [StSt2004].

Gomez-Perez, A., Fernadez-Lopez, M., & Corcho, O. (2003). *Ontological engineering.* London: Springer Verlag.

Gruber, T. (1993). A translation approach to portable ontology specification. *Knowledge Acquisition, 5*(2), 199-220. Retrieved October 14, 2007 from http://tomgruber.org/writing/ontolingua-kaj-1993.pdf

Guarino, N. (1998). Formal ontology and information systems. In: N. Guarino (Ed.), *Formal ontology in information systems. Proceedings of FOIS'98* (pp. 3-15). Trento, Italy, Amsterdam: IOS Press. http://www.loa-cnr.it/Papers/FOIS98.pdf

Herre, H., Heller, B., Burek, P., Hoehndorf, R., Loebe, F., & Michalek, H. (2007). *General formal ontology (GFO); A foundational ontology integrating objects and processes. Part I, v.1.0.1.* Retrieved May 30, 2007 from http://www.onto-med.de/en/theories/gfo/part1-drafts/gfo-part1-v1-0-1.pdf

ISO. (2003). *Industrial automation systems and integration — Integration of life-cycledata for process plants including oil and gas production facilities —Part 2: Data Model.* International standard, 1ST ed. www.iso.org

Khusraj, D., & Lassila, O. (2005). Ontological approach to generating personalized user interfaces for Web services. In: Y. Gil, et al. (Eds.), *ISWC 2005, LNCS 3729* (pp. 916-927). Berlin/ Heidelberg: Springer.

Koivunen, M-R. (2006). Annotea and semantic-Web-supported collaboration. Retrieved October 31, 2007 from http://kmi.open.ac.uk/events/usersweb/papers/01_koivunen_final.pdf

Laboratory for Applied Ontologies. (2007). *LOA site.* Retrieved October 31, 2007 from http://wiki.loa-cnr.it/index.php/Main_Page; http://www.loa-cnr.it/ontologies/EVAL/oQual.owl

The OBO foundry. (2007). Retrieved October 31, 2007 from http://obofoundry.org/

Ontomed. (2006). *Ontomed ontology.* Retrieved October 31, 2007 from http://www.onto-med.de/ontologies/gfo.owl

Open Mobile Alliance. (2006). *User Agent profile ,Version 2.* Retrieved February 28, 2007 from http://www.openmobilealliance.org/release_program/docs/UAProf/V2_0-20060206-A/OMA-TS-UAProf-V2_0-20060206-A.pdf

Peterson, E. (2006). Beneath the metadata; Some philosophical problems with folksonomy. *D-Lib Magazine 12*(11). Retrieved May 31, 2007 from http://www.dlib.org/dlib/november06/peterson/11peterson.html

Pohjola, P. (2007). *Technical artefacts, an ontological investgation of arfacts.* Jyväskylä Studies in Education, Psychology and Social Research, Report No. 300. Retrieved October 14, 2007 from http://dissertations.jyu.fi/studeduc/9789513927561.pdf

Paoluccci, M., Broll, G., Hamard, J., Rukzio, E., Wagner, M., & Schmidt, A. (2008). *Bringing semantic services to real-world objects.* In this issue.

Puttonen, J. (2006). *Mobility management in wireless networks.* Doctoral Thesis. Jyväskylä Studies in Computing # 69, University of Jyvaskylä, Jyväskylä, Finland.

Roman, D., Keller, U., Lausen, H., deBruijn, J., Lara, R., Stollberg, M., et al. (2005). Web service modeling ontology. Applied Ontology, *1*(1), 77-106.

Sanchez, D., Cavero, J., & Martinez, E. (2007). The road towards ontologies. Ch. 1. in *Ontologies: A handbook of principles, concepts and applications in information systems.* New York, NY: Springer Verlag.

Salminen, I., Lehikoinen, J., Huuskonen, P. (2005). Developing and extensible metadata ontology. In: W. Tsai & M. Hamza (Eds.), *Proceedings of the 9th IASTED Intl. Conference on Software Engineering and Applications (SEA)* (pp. 266-272). .Phoenix, AZ: ACTA Press.

Sarvas, R. (2006). *Designing user-centric metadata for digital snapshot photography.* Doctoral Dissertation, Helsinki University of Technology, Department of Computer Science and Engineering/Soberit, and Helsinki Institute for Information Technology (HIIT)/HUT. http://lib.tkk.fi/Diss/2006/isbn9512284448/isbn9512284448.pdf

Zhanova, A. (Ed.). (2006). *Deliverable 3.1, Ontology definition for the DCS and DCS resource description, User rules. EU-IST SPICE project.* Retrieved February 28, 2007 from http://www.ist-spice.org/documents/D3.1_061017_v1_final_bis.pdf

Smith, B. (2004). Beyond concepts, or: Ontology as reality representation systems. In: A. Varzi & L.Vieu (Eds.), *Proceedings of the 3rd International Conference on Formal Ontology in Information, Systems, Turin 4-6 (FOIS 2004)* (pp. 73-84). Amsterdam: IOS Press. Retrieved May 29, 2007 from http://ontology.buffalo.edu/bfo/BeyondConcepts.pdf

Smith, B. (2006a). Against fantology. In: M. Reicher & J. Marek (Eds.), *Experience and analysis (pp. 153-170).*

Smith, B. (2006b). Against idiosyncrasy in ontology development. In: B. Bennett & C. Fellbaum (Eds.), *Formal ontology in information systems: Proceedings of the 4th International Conference (FOIS 2006). Frontiers in Artificial Intelligence and Application, 150.* New York, NY: IOS Press. Retrieved October 14, 2007 from http://ontology.buffalo.edu/bfo/west.pdf

Staab, S., & Studer, R. (Eds.). (2004). *Handbook on ontologies.* Berlin-Heidelberg, Germany, New York, NY: Springer Verlag.

Umsoy, M. (2007). *3GSM Congress 2007 Notes.* Retrieved February 27, 2007 from http://cartagena-capital.com/pdfs/3gsm_congress_2007_notes.pdf

van Heijst, G., Schreiber, A., & Wielinga, B. (1997). Using explicit ontologies in KBS development. *International Journal of Human-Computer Studies, 46*(2-3), 183-292.

Veijalainen, J., Nikitin, S., & Törmälä, V. (2006). Ontology-based semantic Web service platform in mobile environments. *Proceedings of Mobile Ontologies Workshop.* Nara, Japan. http://csdl2.computer.org/persagen/DLPublication.jsp?pubtype=p&acronym=MDM

Veijalainen, J. (2007). Developing mobile ontologies; who, why, where, and how?. *Mobile Services-oriented Architectures and Ontologies Workshop (MoSO 2007).* Mannheim, Germany.

World Intellectual Property Organisation. (2007). *Berne convention.* Retrieved April 3, 2007 from http://www.wipo.int/treaties/en/ip/berne/

Web Services Modeling Ontology. (2007). http://www.wsmo.org/

Youtube Virtual Community. (2007). www.youtube.com

This work was previously published in International Journal on Semantic Web & Information Systems, Vol. 4, Issue 1, edited by A. Sheth, pp. 20-34, copyright 2008 by IGI Publishing (an imprint of IGI Global).

Chapter 4
Service Provisioning through Real World Objects

Massimo Paolucci
DoCoMo Communications Laboratories Europe GmbH, Germany

Gregor Broll
Medieninformatik, Ludwig-Maximilians-Universität, Germany

John Hamard
DoCoMo Communications Laboratories Europe GmbH, Germany

Enrico Rukzio
Computing Department, Lancaster University, UK

Matthias Wagner
DoCoMo Communications Laboratories Europe GmbH, Germany

Albrecht Schmidt
Fraunhofer IAIS, University of Bonn, Germany

ABSTRACT

The last few years have seen two parallel trends emerge. The first of such trends is set by technologies such as Near Field Communication, 2D Bar codes, RFID and others that support the association of digital information with virtually every object. Using these technologies ordinary objects such as coffee mugs or advertisement posters can provide information that is easily processed. The second trend is set by (semantic) Web services that provide a way to automatically invoke functionalities across the Internet lowering interoperability barriers. The PERCI system, discussed in the chapter, provides a way to bridge between these two technologies allowing the invocation of Web services using the information gathered from the tags effectively transforming every object in a service proxy.

DOI: 10.4018/978-1-60566-992-2.ch004

Copyright © 2010, IGI Global. Copying or distributing in print or electronic forms without written permission of IGI Global is prohibited.

INTRODUCTION

In recent years, tagging technologies, such as Near Field Communication (hereafter NFC) (ECMA 2006), Radio Frequency Identification (RFID) (EPC Global 2006) and 2-dimensional bar codes (Adams, 2007) have received a great deal of attention because of their ability to associate digital information with arbitrary objects. In principle everything can be cheaply tagged, from coffee mugs to advertisement posters, and applications can be invoked on the basis of the information that is gathered from the tags on the object.

Japan has seen initial commercial deployments of these technologies. There 2D tagging of advertisements is quite common as shown by the banner in Figure 1. By taking a picture of the tag, a mobile user would immediately gain access to an airline Web page and there buy tickets to fly anywhere in the world. NFC tagging in combination with mobile phones is also widely used in Japan through iMode-FeliCa (Yoshinaga, 2003). Tagging technologies are also becoming increasingly common in Europe and the US. For example, the German railroad operator Deutsche Bahn uses 2D bar codes to store train tickets directly on the phone (Deutsche Bahn, 2007). Furthermore, tagging is also widely used in B2B solutions to monitor stock inventory, logistics and transport to track moving goods (Meloan, 2003). By tagging containers as well as single products, companies can easily manage their inventory, keep track of the goods that have been received and monitor their position during the delivery process (IDTechEx, 2007)(Tohamy, 2005).

Whereas tagging is entering the computer science main stream, it also provides new challenges. The first one is that tags, by and large, do not have any processing abilities, rather they always passively return the same value. Even when active tags exists, as in the case of NFC and RFID, their cost is approximately 100 times higher than the corresponding passive tags making the broad use of active tags very costly. The second

Figure 1. A banner with a 2D bar code in Tokyo

challenge is that tags have very limited memory storage, which ranges from a few bytes to a few Kbytes. The third challenge is that the range of the "network" to read a tag is also very limited, spanning from a few centimeters in the case of NFC tags, to a few meters in the case of RFID tags. The fourth challenge, which is important for this chapter, is that tags break the traditional structure of SOA-based applications which assumes that services are always available and discoverable through a registry.

In this chapter, we attempt to tackle the challenge of providing a general Web service infrastructure to support the user to interact with advertisement posters (UsingRFID.com, 2007). Through the chapter, we will use the movie poster displayed in Figure 2 as our main example. The goal of the poster is to advertise movies that are playing in town. But the poster achieves more than that, the little squares on the side of the

Figure 2. PERCI movie poster

poster specify additional information such as: the movie theaters where the movies are played (on the upper left side), the show times (on the upper right), and the number of tickets that the user may be able to buy (on the bottom left), public transport tickets to go to the theater (on the bottom right).). Crucially, each one of the little boxes is associated with an NFC tag that can be read with any mobile phone with an appropriate reader. A mobile user swiping her phone on the tags should be able to purchase a ticket to a showing of the desired movie, and a public transport ticket to go to the movie. Ultimately, the poster becomes the interface of a ticket selling services.

To exploit tagged objects such as the poster displayed in Figure 2 we introduce the PERCI system (Broll et al., 2007; PERCI, 2005). PERCI (PERvasive serviCe Interaction) provides an infrastructure that supports users to perform complex interactions with arbitrary objects. The basic idea

behind PERCI is to use Semantic Web service technology to associate the object to the corresponding service. Using Semantic Web services, PERCI establishes on the fly a service client on the basis of the information read from the tags on the object, exposing to the user an interface to interact with the service.

In the rest of the chapter, we will discuss the ideas behind PERCI in more detail. In Section 2 we will review existing literature and applications using tags on objects; in Section 3, we discuss the PERCI system and implementation; in Section 4, we will discuss the properties and relevance of the system, and finally in Section 5 we conclude. Throughout the chapter we will assume familiarity with the basic Web services standards, such as WSDL (Chinnici, 2006), and with the main ideas of OWL-S (Martin et al., 2007).

RELATED WORK

There are multiple ways to connect services and tags. In 1999, Want et al. presented some of the first examples by linking everyday objects (e.g. books, documents, business cards) and digital resources (e.g. electronic documents, URLs, email-addresses) through RFID-tags (Want et al., 1999). Since then, Ubicomp applications have used various enabling technologies to implement the tagging of physical objects and the interaction with them. Among them are NFC (Want, 2006), Bluetooth, infrared beacons (Kindberg et al., 2002), laser-pointer (Rukzio et al., 2006), GPS or the recognition of visual markers (Rohs and Gfeller, 2004) which will eventually be displaced by marker-less image recognition (Quack et al., 2008).

In the case of NFC/RFID-based interaction, the tag may consist of an active reader that is connected to the service, and the user holds a passive card or a phone with a card embedded in it. To trigger the service, the user swipes a card in front of the reader which reads known location on the card and then communicates the data directly to a service. Eventually, information may be sent back from the service and written on the card as a response. This solution is used in a number of applications from public transport to building access, as well as in location aware systems (Hazas, 2004). But the problem is that this approach is also very rigid when used for service provisioning. Since cards are associated with services, in the worst case, the user needs a different card for each service she uses. Even when the card is shared across applications, as in the case of FeliCa cards on Japanese phones (Yoshinaga, 2003), the memory on the card should be managed carefully to prevent clobbering information across services.

An alternative common way to associate (passive) tags to services is by linking them to web pages. An example of such tags is shown in Figure 1 where a 2D bar code is used to encode the URL of an airline. The mobile phone decodes the image to extract the URL and it displays the corresponding Web page on the browser. The association of tags with URLs has been widely proposed in the academic literature. Most prominently, the Cooltown project (Kindberg and Barton, 2001) (Kindberg et al, 2002) advocated the use of web links to connect tags in the environment to information about different objects. The problem with this approach is that it does not easily support the type of interaction that is required by the poster displayed in Figure 2, because in this case the content of the page would depend on a number of different tags, rather than one single reading. The second problem of this approach is associated with the lack of semantics of HTML. Specifically, while the user can buy the movie ticket from an HTML page, the ticket should be stored on the service site, as it is done for all e-commerce applications running on the Web, instead of being stored on the phone. Therefore the ticket could not be used to relate different services and applications; for instance, it could not be used to tell the user's calendar that a given time is blocked for the movie.

A number of projects propose a direct access to the service assuming that service clients have been delivered to the phone before the tag has been read. These solutions include iMode-FeliCa that requires an i-appli stub to access any service (Yoshinaga, 2003). A similar approach is adopted by Riekki et al (Riekki, Salminen and Alakärppä, 2006) who describe how to access local printing and calling services. The ActivePrint project (ActivePrint 2007) also adopts preloaded clients to connect users to services which have been tagged with 2D bar codes. In this case the user takes a picture of the bar code and then she may initiate a Web download, or send an SMS or make a call or get contact data about some product. In this solution, a service middleware engine loaded in the phone activates a service stub corresponding to the tag selected. In the case of these solutions, when no i-appli or no service stub is available on the phone, no service is invoked.

The solutions highlighted above, and others that adopt pre-loaded clients to connect services to tags suffer from the fact that services can be used only when a client is actually present in the phone. To the extent that the services are well known and persistent, as in the case of accessing a bank statement or a transportation system with iMode-FeliCa, or known printing services, or SMS services with ActivePrint, the system works fine and may be extremely secure also. But in the case of advertisement posters like the one described in Figure 2 the service may be specific for the poster. In turn each poster may refer to a different service. It is unfeasible to expect that users will have all possible clients for all possible posters. Instead, we need to find a new way to provision the services associated with the posters that can flexibly connect the poster with the service without any requirement of pre-loaded clients.

A final way to connect services and tags is provided by Kerer et al. in (Kerer et al., 2007). Here RFID is used to identify objects or people that are present in a room, while Web services are used to offer services. Potentially, such a system may take advantage of the full power of SOA solutions to connect services with tags. But, despite the fact that Web services and RFID are used in the same system they perform two very different tasks and they never work together. RFID is only used for identification of people and objects in the environment. On the other side, services are invoked through the infrastructure described by the Service Oriented Architecture (SOA) (Papazoglou and Heuvel, 2007). At no time during the interaction with Web services the RFID tags are used for any other purpose than provide identification information on the objects and people in the environment. Whereas this system uses SOA, the only use of the tags is for security and permission of using services, they are not used to provision the services as would be required by an interaction with the poster in Figure 2.

In addition to the problem of the connection with services, another dimension is defined by the interaction between users and the objects. Normally, the user needs to do only one action such as swiping the phone or the card in front of a tag, or take a picture of a visual marker. The action invokes the service and sends the appropriate data to the service. This user interaction paradigm is not enough to address the problem described above in relation with the poster in Figure 2, where multiple actions are required to invoke a service. To our knowledge, this problem has not been addressed in the academic literature and we are not aware of any industrial applications that exploit this interaction mechanism.

Similar work on more complex interactions with tagged objects has been done by several researchers: Reilly et al., have augmented maps with RFID-tags, turning them into interactive surfaces that support complex selection techniques like path-, lasso- or menu-select on the mobile device (Reilly et al., 2005). Rukzio et al. have compared the interaction techniques Touching (based on NFC), Pointing (based on a laser-pointer) and Scanning (using Bluetooth) for interaction with smart-home appliances (Rukzio et al., 2006).

Ultimately these works are orthogonal to ours since we aim at using long sequences of single gestures, while they use only single (although complex) interactions. Future work may aim at combining the different approaches.

Next to technical aspects, several studies have also explored the usability and accessibility of mobile interaction with tagged objects: O'Neill et al. have compared NFC to two-dimensional barcodes and showed that although untrained users were faster using the latter, trained users could significantly improve their performance with the NFC-tags (O'Neill et al., 2007). Other studies, e.g. (Geven et al., 2007) or (Mäkelä et al., 2007), have also investigated how novice users interact with NFC-tags or visual markers. Most of them were not familiar with these new technologies, did not know how to initiate the interaction with them and struggled with various technical constraints. In this context, Broll et al. have evaluated different cues to improve the learnability of NFC/RFID-based mobile interaction and found that an explicit start-tag provided effective help for novice users to initiate the interaction with tagged objects (Broll et al., 2009).

In conclusion none of the works proposed in the literature provide a way to address the problem posed by the poster shown in Figure 2. On the service side, the proposals to connect services to tags prove to be too rigid and do not support automatic service provisioning. On the user interface side, the theories on the actions to be performed are still inadequate. The main contribution of this chapter will be to overcome both limitations by providing a way to connect tags to services that support on-line service provisioning and on the user side by providing a way to support multiple actions.

The PERCI System

The diagram in Figure 3 provides an abstract representation of the PERCI system and its relations with the different components. As a starting

Figure 3. An abstract description of the problem

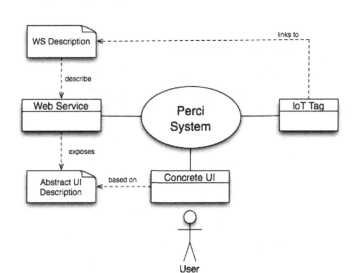

point, there are three information sources: (1) a service, (2) a set of tags on the poster that refer to the service, and (3) the user who wants to take advantage of poster. To solve the interaction problem, PERCI requires a basic infrastructure which enables the interaction with these three information sources to be already present on the phone[1]. Specifically, the first component required by PERCI is the *(OWL-S) Web services stack*: a set of libraries that supports the processing of OWL-S descriptions and the automatic creation of service clients on the basis of their OWL-S specification. The second component is a *Tag Reader*, i.e. the hardware and the software that transforms the signal from the tag in digital information that the rest of the system can use. The third component is a *Rendering Engine* that transforms the abstract UI description into a concrete UI that is displayed to the user.

A crucial problem of a system like PERCI is that it mediates between the user and the service without assuming any direct relation between the reading of the tag and the invocation of the service. The problem emerges from the fact that the service follows a very well defined protocol in which the invocation of a process on the service side may require information coming from different tags; on the other hand, the user is not aware of the requirements of the service, therefore she may read the tags following a very different order. In such a case, the service and the user may loose synchronization. For example, the service may expect information in a very strict order, such as the movie theater before the movie title, whereas the user may select the movie title before selecting the theater.

To address the synchronization problem, PERCI needs to de-couple the tag reading from the service invocation to reconcile the service and the users. The resulting architecture is shown in Figure 4, which highlights the main components of the PERCI system and the main data and control flow within the system. The Tag Reader is responsible for reading the tag and extracting the information. Since there are many different types of tags, such as 2D-bar codes and NFC, the Tag reader employs the PMIF framework (Rukzio, Wetzstein and Schmidt 2005) to abstract from the specific type of tag to the content of the tag which can be used within the system.

Figure 4. PERCI infrastructure

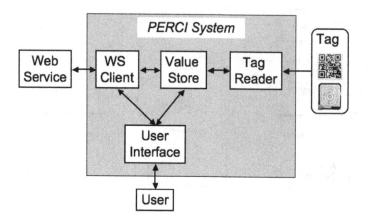

The content of the tag is then stored in the *Value Store* which is responsible to act as a buffer between the tag and the service invocation. Tags refer to the service that can process them, therefore the tag is used to instantiate the Web Service Client and the User Interface. Specifically, upon reading the tag, the service description is downloaded and used by the web services stack to configure on the fly the Web Service Client, and by the Rendering Engine is used to instantiate the User interface.

The centrality of the Value Store is crucial in PERCI since it guarantees the decupling between the tag reading and the service and the user interface. In broad strokes, the service client waits until all data that it expects is read by the user and put on the Value Store and only when this condition is satisfied the service is invoked. In the following three subsections we will analyze this process in greater details. Specifically we will look at the form of tags that are required, and at the interaction with the services and the user interface.

Representing the Service

In order to instantiate a service client, PERCI needs to know the interaction protocol of the service, and specifically, what messages does the service does accept and in which order. In OWL-S the service interface is represented as a workflow of processes, named Process Model, in which each process is described by the input/output messages that the service exchanges with the client, and precondition/effect transformations that result from those messages. In turn the inputs and outputs are grounded into messages described using the WSDL description of the service.

In a system like PERCI, the representation of the interaction protocol is not enough, since it is crucial to interleave the interaction with the service with the interactions with the user. Users need to be sure that the phone understood their selections: that the movie that they desire is selected and that the ticket applies to the show of their choice. Furthermore, users need reassurance that the phone and the service are progressing toward a completion of the transaction. Finally, the user needs to react to failures that may occur during the interaction. For all these reasons it is essential to display a user interface that communicates to the user the status of the interaction.

The solution that we adopted to generate a user interface is to derive an abstract user interface directly from the service description (Khushraj and Lassila, 2007). Specifically, as shown

Figure 5. The extended OWL-S model

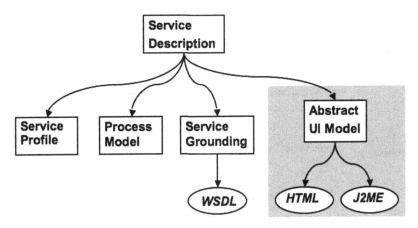

in Figure 5, we extended OWL-S with a new model, which we named "Abstract UI Model", which is to be thought a parallel of the OWL-S Grounding to WSDL, but rather than mapping OWL-S processes into WSDL it maps them in a user interface. To map a process description into a user interface, the OWL-S Abstract UI Model specifies how input and output parameters map to graphic widgets, furthermore it maps the data input by the user into data that can be processed by the service. Symmetrically, it transforms output data from the service in a way that it can be exposed to the user.

One problem of associating a user interface to a mobile application like PERCI is that there is no telling on which terminal the interface will be displayed. A bottom line approach that can be adopted in this case is to assume that every mobile phone supporting data connection has a browser, so the interface is rendered in HTML. The resulting interface can be displayed on every terminal, irrespective of its capabilities; but this assumption effectively pushes the interface to the minimum lower denominator, so that it will waste the capabilities of high-end terminals or display badly on low-end terminals. The solution adopted within the PERCI system is different.

Instead of committing to a technology at design and service description time, PERCI commits at execution time when the terminal to be used is known. Therefore, the graphic widgets used in the User Groundings specify how the information is presented to the user, but they do not commit to a specific technology to display the widget (Broll et al., 2007). The set of abstract widgets used in the PERCI system is shown in Figure 6. Of these widgets, Direct input widget provides an arbitrary input, e.g. via a text field; Single Select Input provides a single value from a given choice, such as a drop down or radio button menu; Multiple Selection Input widget provides several values from a given choice, e.g. from a checkbox; Single Selection and Multiple Selection widgets allow a loose interpretation of the widget, meaning that a widget may be rendered as direct input or selection input; Plain Output parameter widget will usually be rendered as a simple textual message.

The concrete rendering is decided when the service is delivered and the terminal of the user is known. If the user terminal supports the graphic libraries of J2ME, and the terminal has sufficient resources to display a user interface, the user interface is displayed using the java graphic widgets; otherwise it is displayed using HTML.

Figure 6. Types of widgets used in the abstract user interface

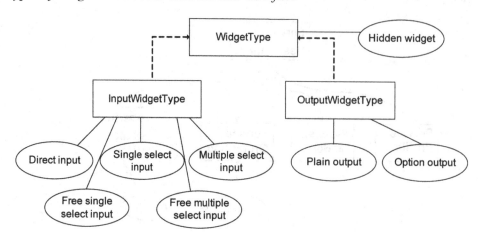

Content of the Tags

The tags on a poster like the one shown in Figure 2 essentially provide two types of information. First, they describe the values to be assigned to the parameters. For example they say whether the movie is "Geisha" or "The Da Vinci Code". Second, they specify the function to be applied to the parameter; in other words whether the user wants to buy the ticket or whether she wants information about the movie. For this reason, PERCI distinguishes between the three types of tags.

1. *Action Tags* that are associated with processes performed by the service, such as reserving a ticket or purchasing goods. Action tags uniquely identify uniquely the process to be performed.
2. *Value Tags* that are associated with a value. For example the tags associated with the title of a movie or with the showing time. These tags contain three pieces of information: (a) the value of the data, (b) the type of the data, (c) an id which can be used to associate the data to both the information to send to the service and the information to display to the user, and (d) a URI of the service to which the data will be sent.

3. *Hybrid tags* that combine the previous two types by expressing both an action to be performed as well as a value.

The different types of tags also play a different role in the interaction with the service since action tags explicitly specify that the user wants to perform a function, such as buying tickets; while parameters tags specify the different value selections of the user. Finally, the role of hybrid tags is to provide a shortcut where the service is invoked on a given value.

Managing the Interaction with the Service

Upon reading a tag, the PERCI system has to make two decisions: the first one is whether to invoke a process on the service side; the second one is whether to display a user interface.

The decision of which process to perform next is driven by the Process Model of the OWL-S service description that describes the workflow of the interaction with the service. But the decision of which process to invoke depends also on the action tags that are activated by the user and by the data that is available to send to the service. Specifically, there are three simple conditions that specify whether a process can be executed at a given time.

1. It is the next process in the order described by the protocol language;
2. The process has been selected by the user through an action tag;
3. All the input data required by the process has been provided. Such input data is provided either by the user selection of a value tag or through user input, and it should be available in the Value Store.

The third condition has an important consequence: the invocation of a process on the service is conditioned on having all data from the user. In turn, this rule prioritizes the user interface over the invocation of processes: whenever a process depends on some user data, the user interface should be displayed first. Displaying the abstract UI includes:

1. Selecting the display action to perform. This operation will result in either displaying the data, or displaying error and warning messages;
2. Selecting the data to display to the user. This selection is based on the data available in the Value Store and on the requirements of the user interface;
3. Displaying the data consistently with the Abstract User Interface specification;
4. Possibly read inputs from the user if this is required by the user interface. User inputs are then stored in the value-store.

Once all data required by the process is available in the Value Store, the Service Client is responsible for identifying which data to send to the service. Such an invocation, which is performed by the Service Client component, results in using the OWL-S Grounding to select the WSDL operation to perform and performing the data translation required to invoke the operation.

Upon completing a process invocation, the Interaction Manager waits for the results of the process. When the process completes and all the results have been received, they are added to the Value Store and possibly displayed to the user if an abstract interface is specified for that process. Finally, the Service Client moves on to the next process to execute. When the last process of the Service Process Model has been performed, the interaction with the service is completed.

Implementation

We implemented the PERCI system in a running prototype using two posters, the first one is a movie poster, the second one is a transportation poster for the Munich public transport system. In the implementation we used two types of tags. The first one based on the 2d bar codes using the Semacode toolkit (Semacode.org, 2007) running on a Nokia N70; the second one based on NFC running on a Nokia 3220 with the NFC shell. The abstraction from the tagging technology is based on PMIF (Rukzio, Wetzstein and Schmidt 2005). The Web services stack used in the implementation is based on Axis, and the Mindswap OWL-S API (Sirin, 2004) was used to execute the OWL-S description of services. We extended the OWL-S API to handle the abstract interface definition through. XML transformations were implemented on the Cocoon framework.

Given the amount of code that was involved in the implementation of PERCI, it was impossible to run the complete application on the mobile phones, therefore we had to move most of the computational load onto a proxy running on a public server. In the implementation the phone is responsible for the rendering of the concrete interface, while the proxy is responsible for the invocation of the services and the management of interaction proxies; while the communication between the phone and the proxy was based on synchronous http calls. While the use of a proxy in mobile applications is often considered as a "necessary evil" to go around limitations of mobile phones, three important issues need to be considered. The first one is that the synchronous http calls could be easily replaced by function calls on more powerful phones; the second issue is that many advanced service applications in the research arena require proxies, which suggest that mobile operators may devise new business models around the hosting of proxies to increase their revenue streams while supporting increasingly complex services.

DISCUSSION

Currently, the PERCI system is unique in its aim and technical nature. As discussed above, at this point, no other system features similar capabilities and functionalities in combining NFC technology with Semantic Services. In this discussion section we analyze PERCI's properties and we provide an initial evaluation of the system.

Properties of PERCI

The first property is that PERCI supports *long sequences of actions that are performed by the user*. Namely, with the different actions the user selects the movie, the theater, the time of the desired show, and the number of tickets to buy. Long sequences of actions are supported by storing the values read by the user and by passing them to the service on the bases of its needs.

The second property of PERCI is the support of *automatic invocation with arbitrary services*. This property is crucial since users of advertisement posters will not have any client specialized to interact with each poster. The process described in section 3.3 does not require any user intervention at the system level. Rather it is completely driven by the service description and by the user's reading of the tags read. Furthermore, the decoupling of tag reading and process invocation supports the separation between the user's process and the service protocol.

The third property of PERCI is the ability to *mirror the choices proposed by the poster on the mobile phone*. As a consequence the mobile phone user has the choice to either continue the interaction with the physical object, or to leave the object and continue the interaction to the screen of the phone. This feature may be very useful in case the user needs to interrupt the interaction with the object before it is concluded. Significantly, this property shows that PERCI can display the same of opening a Web page in Cooltown, ActivePrint, and 2D bar codes with iMode. The difference is that whereas in these systems, applications are designed to remove the interaction from the object pushing it to the browser. In our case, we provide two interfaces to the same object: one physical through the tags, the other virtual through the mobile's screen. The decision of which one is best is left to the user and the condition in which she is working. The user studies discussed in (Siorpaes, 2006; Broll et al., 2007) and summarized in Section 4.2, compare the usage of the two interaction modalities showing that by and large users prefer to interact with the object rather than shift their attention to the mobile screen.

Usability and User Experience

PERCI involves different aspects from the user interface and usability issues. To this end, we have performed two user studies (Broll et al. 2006; Broll et al. 2007; Siorpaes, 2006): the first one was a low fidelity mock-up evaluation (Nielsen, 2003) (Snyder 2003) to understand the expectations of the potential users before proceeding with the implementation. In the second study, 10 subjects were asked to use the implemented system to buy movie and transport tickets from the posters. In this study, the subjects were asked to solve the same problem under 3 different conditions. In the first condition the subjects interacted with the posters using only NFC tags; in the second

Table 1. Results of the experiment

		Applies	Not Applies	Unsure
NFC	Easy	10	0	0
	Fun	8	1	1
	Reliable	9	1	0
Direct Input	Easy	8	0	2
	Fun	0	3	7
	Reliable	10	0	0
2D bar codes	Easy	0	9	1
	Fun	3	7	0
	Reliable	4	5	1

condition the subjects were required to use only direct input on the phone through menus and by typing implementing the interaction mechanism employed by systems such as iMode, Active Print and Cooltown described above; in the third condition, the subjects were required to use 2D bar codes instead of NFC tags.

In summary, the results of both studies have been positive and promising especially given that most European mobile users are not yet used to NFC and tagging technology in general. The detailed results of the second experiment are shown in Table 1. The table is organized in three rows describing the three conditions (namely: the use of NFC tags, the use of Direct Input to simulate existing systems, and the use of 2D bar codes). The users were asked to evaluate whether they found the system *easy* to use, *fun* and appealing, and whether they had the feeling that it was *reliable* and they would trust such a system. As shows the subjects found the NFC and Direct Input versions of the system easy and reliable. This result is quite interesting since the subjects had great familiarity with the use of menus and forms on the Web and other applications therefore they were very familiar of the "direct input" condition, on the opposite of the NFC condition since they used NFC for the first time. This suggests that NFC

can be easy to use in practice. On the other side, the NFC was found more fun and appealing of the use of "direct input" because of its novelty. 2D bar codes scored quite badly in the experiment because their use is more cumbersome of NFC tags which resulted in a negative impression of the users. In conclusion, the experiment revealed that systems based on the multiple touch ideas presented in this chapter may be very appealing to mobile users, and that the PERCI system results in very usable applications.

While the PERCI system provides an initial solution to the problem of interaction with advertisement posters, and potentially with arbitrary objects, it also raises a number of problems that were unseen before. On the user side, the user interface is split between the poster and the mobile phone, which inevitably means that the user needs to shift attention between the two interfaces. The reduction and possibly the management of such attention shifts is crucial for the success of this technology since it entails a cognitive overload that may vanish the advantages of the technology. Furthermore the design of the poster and of the object in general becomes crucial since the object needs to achieve different goals in the same time and satisfy very different constraints. For example, an advertisement poster should be appealing to

Figure 7. A PERCI poster and an equivalent ticketing machine

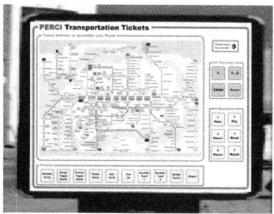

entice users to buy from it, but also easy to use with the tags placed in a convenient and intuitive way, and it should satisfy geometric constraints on the size of the icons to be presented: typically if the icons become too small and too close two or more icons may be served by the same tag making them indistinguishable. An additional problem is the management of wrong or inconsistent user actions, such as double selections of the same tag, or missed selections of tags, such as missed selection of the movie theater, or showing time.

CONCLUSION

Tagging technology is bound to become a common part of our life. In a short while many usual actions, from opening a door, to paying for a bus ride will be performed using tags and possibly our mobile phone. Virtually every object then will become a source of electronic information. Although, this vision may sound very futuristic, the transformation is already happening as shown by the poster in Figure 1 and by the growing applications of NFC and 2D bar codes that are emerging on the market. Somewhat surprisingly, within the Semantic Web there has been no ap-

preciation of these events and virtually no work toward the semantic annotation of tags.

To our knowledge, PERCI is the first attempt to bring semantics to tags and to use them to invoke web services. As a result PERCI opens new opportunities that go beyond what has been deployed as existing services such as the linking of 2D bar codes and basic Internet-based i-mode services in Japan and existing ticketing solutions. Specifically, PERCI shows how exploiting semantic web service technology it is possible to explore new types of relations between objects and services on one side and more complex interactions between users and services.

The impact of PERCI-like systems is potentially huge. Consider the poster displayed on the left side of Figure 7; it has the same functionalities of the ticketing machine displayed on the right side of the same figure, but with two striking differences. First, the cost of the poster is much lower (approximately 50 €) with virtually no maintenance costs; second, additional information can be loaded on the phone that cannot be loaded on a ticket, as for example the way to go to a given station.

From the SOA point of view, PERCI opens a new way to provision services to users, and therefore also a new way to think about service composition. The traditional SOA-based composition assumes universal availability of services through the network, but PERCI shows that there are other ways to provisions services that break that assumption. Indeed services are not universally available, but only available in the short range of the tags that are reachable by the user. Semantics is going to play a pivotal role in the provisioning of this type of pervasive services

The fundamental question raised by the chapter is how to combine services offered to the user, keeping into account that pervasive services are deployed in different places with different modalities and their provisioning to the user is necessarily spread over a long time. In such a case, the tag read by a poster may be used in new and unexpected ways to work with a service for which they were not designed. The solution of this problem requires semantic annotation both in the abstraction of the content of the tags to find the most appropriate service to process them, as well as in the invocation of those services. PERCI is a first step toward this new model of opportunistic service composition in which services may be combined on the fly depending on the users' needs, and her context.

REFERENCES

ActivePrint. (2007). *Active Print Web Site*. Retrieved Sept 13, 2007, from http://www.active-print.org/

Adams, R. (2007, April 04) *2-D Bar Code Page*. Retrieved September 11, 2007, from http://www. adams1.com/pub/russadam/stack.html

Broll, G., Keck, S., Holleis, P., & Butz, A. (2009). Improving the Accessibility of NFC/RFID-based Mobile Interaction through Learnability and Guidance. In Proc. of MobileHCI'09. Bonn, Germany, September 15 - 18, 2009.

Broll, G., Siorpaes, S., Rukzio, E., Paolucci, M., Hamard, J., Wagner, M., & Schmidt, A. (2006) Supporting Service Interaction in the Real World. Permid Workshop in conjunction with Pervasive 2006, Dublin, Ireland, May 7 2006.

Broll, G., Siorpaes, S., Rukzio, E., Paolucci, M., Hamard, J., Wagner, M., & Schmidt, A. (2007). *Supporting Mobile Service Usage through Physical Mobile Interaction.* In Proc. of PERCOM'07 (pp. 262-271). IEEE Computer Society, Washington, DC.

Chinnici, R., Moreau, J., & Ryman, A. *Web Services Description Language (WSDL) Version 2.0 Part 1: Core Language.* W3C Candidate Recommendation 27 March 2006; http://www.w3.org/TR/2006/CR-wsdl20-20060327

Deutsche Bahn, A. G. (2007). *Handy-Ticket.* Retrieved Sept 11, 2007; www.bahn.de/p/view/planen/reiseplanung/mobileservices/handy_ticket.shtml.

ECMA International. (Sept. 2006). *Near Field Communication White paper*; Ecma/TC32-TG19/2004/1 EPCGlobal *RFID Implementation Cookbook, 2nd Release.* Retrieved September 11, 2007, from http://www.epcglobalinc.org/what/cookbook/

Geven, A., Strassl, P., Ferro, B., Tscheligi, M., & Schwab, H. (2007) Experiencing real-world interaction: results from a NFC user experience field trial. In Proc. of MobileHCI '07, vol. 309 (pp. 234-237). ACM, New York, NY.

Hazas, M., Scott, J., & Krumm, J. (2004). Location-aware computing comes of age. *Computer, 37*(2), 95–97. doi:10.1109/MC.2004.1266301

IDTechEx. (2007); *RFID Logistics Case Studies: Thirty detailed RFID logistics case studies.* From. http://www.idtechex.com/products/en/view.asp?productcategoryid=49. Retrieved September 22, 2007, Kerer, C., Dustdar, S., Jazayeri, M, Gomes, D., Szego, A., & Burgos Caja, J.A. (2004). *Presence-Aware Infrastructure using Web services and RFID technologies.* 2nd European Workshop on Object Orientation and Web Services, ECOOP Workshop, 14 June 2004, Oslo, Norway, Springer LNCS

Khushraj, D., & Lassila, O. (2005) *Ontological Approach to Generating Personalized User Interfaces for Web Services.* 4th International Semantic Web Conference (ISWC 2005)

Kindberg, T., & Barton, J. (2001). A Web-based nomadic computing system. *Computer Networks, 35*(4), 443–456. doi:10.1016/S1389-1286(00)00181-X

Kindberg, T., Barton, J.J., Morgan, J., Becker, G., Caswell, D., Debaty, P., Gopal, G., Frid, M., Krishnan, V., Morris, H., Schettino, J., Serra, B., & Spasojevic, M. (2002). People, Places, Things: Web Presence for the Real World. *MONET, 7*(5).

Mäkelä, K., Belt, S., Greenblatt, D., & Häkkilä, J. (2007). *Mobile interaction with visual and RFID tags: a field study on user perceptions.* In *Proc. of CHI '07*(pp. 991-994). New York: ACM.

Martin, D., Burstein, M., McDermott, D., McIlraith, S., Paolucci, M., & Sycara, K. (2007). Bringing Semantics to Web Services with OWL-S. *World Wide Web (Bussum), 10*(3). doi:10.1007/s11280-007-0033-x

Meloan, S. (2003). *Toward a Global "Internet of Things".* Sun Developers Network. November 11, 2003. Retrieved on September 22, 2007 from http://java.sun.com/developer/technicalArticles/Ecommerce/rfid/

Nielsen, J. (2003). *Paper Prototyping: Getting User Data Before You Code.* Retrieved on September 22, 2007 from http://www.useit.com/alertbox/20030414.html

O'Neill, E., Thompson, P., Garzonis, S., & Warr, A. (2007). Reach out and touch: Using nfc and 2d barcodes for service discovery and interaction with mobile devices. In Proc. of Pervasive'07 (LNCS 4480, pp. 19-36).

Papazoglou, M., & Heuvel, W. (2007). Service oriented architectures: approaches, technologies and research issues. *The VLDB Journal, 16*(3). doi:10.1007/s00778-007-0044-3

PERCI. (PERvasive ServiCe Interaction) website (2005). Retrieved on July 15, 2009 from http://www.hcilab.org/projects/perci

Quack, T., Bay, H., & Van Gool, L. J. (2008). Object Recognition for the Internet of Things. *IOT, 2008,* 230–246.

Reilly, D., Dearman, D., Welsman-Dinelle, M., & Inkpen, K. M. (2005, October-December). Evaluating Early Prototypes in Context: Trade-offs, Challenges, and Successes. *IEEE Pervasive Computing / IEEE Computer Society [and] IEEE Communications Society, 4*(4), 10–18. doi:10.1109/MPRV.2005.76

Riekki, J., Salminen, T., & Alakärppä, I. (2006). Requesting Pervasive Services by Touching RFID Tags. *IEEE Pervasive computing.*

Rohs, M., & Gfeller, B. (2004). Using Camera-Equipped Mobile Phones for Interacting with Real-World Objects. In Advances in Pervasive Computing, Austrian Computer Society (OCG) (pp. 265-271).

Rukzio, E., Leichtenstern, K., Callaghan, V., Holleis, P., Schmidt, A., & Shiaw-Yuan Chin, J. (2006). *An Experimental Comparison of Physical Mobile Interaction Techniques: Touching, Pointing and Scanning* (pp. 87–104). Proc. of Ubicomp.

Rukzio, E., Wetzstein, S., & Schmidt, A. (2005). *A Framework for Mobile Interactions with the Physical World*. Wireless Personal Multimedia Communication (WPMC'05). Aalborg, Denmark, 2005.

Semacode.org. (2007). *Semacode SDK technical paper*. Retrieved September 21, 2007, from http://semacode.org/about/technical/

Siorpaes, S. (2006). *A Physical Mobile Interactions Framework based on Semantic Descriptions*. Diploma Thesis, Institut für Informatik, Ludwig-Maximilans-Universität München; July 2006.

Sirin E. (2004). OWL-S API. Retrieved on Sept 22, 2007, from hwww.mindswap.org/2004/owl-s/api/

Snyder, C. (2003). *Paper Prototyping: The Fast and Easy Way to Design and Refine User Interfaces*. The Morgan Kaufmann Series in Interactive Technologies.

Tohamy, N. (2005). *The Present and Future of RFID in Logistics*. Forrester Research. Retrieved November 16, 2005 from http://www.rfidupdate.com/articles/?id=998

Toye, E. (2007, January). Interacting with mobile services: an evaluation of camera-phones and visual tags. *Personal and Ubiquitous Computing, 11*(2), 97–106. doi:10.1007/s00779-006-0064-9

Using, R. F. I. D. com (2007). *UK-based NFC smart poster marketing system launched*. Retrieved May 14, 2007 from http://www.usingrfid.com/news/read.asp?lc=h33830ax1078zd

Want, R. (2006). An Introduction to RFID Technology. *IEEE Pervasive Computing / IEEE Computer Society [and] IEEE Communications Society, 5*, 25–33. doi:10.1109/MPRV.2006.2

Want, R., Fishkin, K. P., Gujar, A., & Harrison, B. L. (1999). Bridging physical and virtual worlds with electronic tags. In *Proc. of CHI 1999* (pp. 370-377). New York: ACM.

Yoshinaga, H., Hattari, Y., Sato, T., Yoschida, M., & Washio, S. (2003). i-Mode FeliCa. *NTT DoCoMo Technical Journal, 6*(3).

ENDNOTE

[1]   For simplicity, in this chapter we use the term "phone" in a broad sense to mean the user's computational infrastructure. As discussed more in details in the implementation section, this infrastructure may include proxies running on the network. From the point of view of the user's experience there will be no difference between running code on the phone or running it on the network proxies.

Chapter 5
Semantic–Based Bluetooth–RFID Interaction for Advanced Resource Discovery in Pervasive Contexts

Tommaso Di Noia
Politecnico di Bari, Italy

Michele Ruta
Politecnico di Bari, Italy

Eugenio Di Sciascio
Politecnico di Bari, Italy

Floriano Scioscia
Politecnico di Bari, Italy

Francesco Maria Donini
Università della Tuscia, Italy

Eufemia Tinelli
Politecnico di Bari and Università degli Studi di Bari, Italy

ABSTRACT

We propose a novel object discovery framework integrating the application layer of Bluetooth and RFID standards. The approach is motivated and illustrated in an innovative u-commerce setting. Given a request, it allows an advanced discovery process, exploiting semantically annotated descriptions of goods available in the u-marketplace. The RFID data exchange protocol and the Bluetooth service discovery protocol have been modified and enhanced to enable support for such semantic annotation of products. Modifications to the standards have been conceived to be backward compatible, thus allowing the smooth coexistence of the legacy discovery and/or identification features. Also noteworthy is the introduction of a dedicated compression tool to reduce storage/transmission problems due to the verbosity of XML-based semantic languages.

Copyright © 2010, IGI Global, distributing in print or electronic forms without written permission of IGI Global is prohibited.

INTRODUCTION AND MOTIVATION

Radio-frequency identification (RFID) is an increasingly widespread and promising wireless technology interconnecting via radio a transponder carrying data (*tag*) located on an object, and an interrogator (*reader*) able to receive the transmitted data. Tags usually contain a unique identification code, which can be used by readers to identify the associated object. Since low-cost tags can be fastened to objects unobtrusively, preserving their common functions, RFID de facto increases the "pervasiveness" of a computing environment. Current RFID applications focus on retrieving relevant attributes of the object the tag is clung to, via a networked infrastructure from a fixed information server. This identification process involves the code associated to the transponder exploited as index key. Nowadays, tags with larger memory capacity and on-board sensors enable new scenarios and further applications, not yet explored.

We believe that in the era of semantic technologies and mobile computing, there is room for more advanced and significant applications of RFIDs extended with structured descriptions, so that a good equipped with an RFID can semantically describe itself along its whole life-cycle. We therefore conceived a unified framework where a semantic-enhanced RFID-based infrastructure and an advanced Bluetooth service discovery—also endowed of semantic-based discovery features—are virtually "interconnected" at the application layer permitting innovative services in u-environments. In our mobile framework, tagged objects expose to a reader not simply a string code but a semantically annotated description. Such objects may hence describe themselves in a variety of scenarios (e.g., during supply chain management, shipment, storing, sale and post-sale), without depending on a centralized database. The exploitation of these annotations calls for discovery/interaction protocols that are able to effectively deal with rich and articulated descriptions. Therefore, a novel multi-protocol and interactive discovery mechanism has been designed. In this effort, we borrowed from ideas and technologies devised for the semantic Web initiative. To simply illustrate our proposal, we set our stage in a *u-marketplace* context[1], where objects endowed with RFID tags are dipped into an enhanced Bluetooth framework.

In particular, building on previous works that enhanced the basic discovery features of Bluetooth with semantic-based discovery capabilities (Ruta et al., 2006a), we propose an extension of EPC-global specifications for RFID tag data standards, providing semantic-based value-added services. Coping with limited storage and computational capabilities of mobile and embedded devices, and with reduced bandwidth provided by wireless links, issues related to the verbosity of semantic annotation languages cannot be neglected. Compression techniques become essential to enable storage and transmission of semantically annotated information on mobile devices. We hence devised and exploited a novel efficient XML compression algorithm, specifically targeted for DIG 1.1 (Bechhofer et al., 2003) document instances. Benefits of compression apply to the whole ubiquitous computing environment, as decreasing data size means shorter communication delays, efficient usage of bandwidth and reduced battery drain for mobile devices in a Mobile ad hoc NETwork (MANET).

The remainder of the article is structured as follows. In the next section, relevant technological bricks of the proposed framework are surveyed. Section 3 outlines the framework, explaining the discovery process as well as proposed semantic-based enhancements to RFID standards. The compression algorithm for semantic annotations is outlined in section 4. Section 5 exemplifies the approach in a u-commerce scenario. Results on key performance measures to assess the feasibility of the proposed approach, are provided in section 6. Conclusion closes the article.

Semantic-Based Bluetooth-RFID Interaction for Advanced Resource Discovery in Pervasive Contexts

Basics

In this section, we survey relevant aspects of languages, technologies and protocols we use and adapt, concentrating on key features our proposal is based on. We assume the reader is familiar with at least basic elements of Semantic Web and ontologies (Berners-Lee et al., 2001; Horrocks et al., 2001; Martin et al., 2002; McGuinness et al., 2002; Shadbolt et al., 2006), of OWL (http://www.w3.org/TR/owl-features/) and related languages, such as Description Logics (DLs) (Borgida, 1995; Donini et al., 1996). We therefore move straightforwardly to analyze issues closely related to our proposal.

Exploiting Semantically Annotated Descriptions

Given a domain ontology $\mathcal{T}$, DL-based systems usually provide at least two basic reasoning services: *Concept satisfiability* and *concept subsumption*. Using subsumption, it is possible to establish if a description C is more specific than a description D, $\mathcal{T} \models C \sqsubseteq D$. If the previous relation holds, then we may say that information C associated to a given resource completely satisfies what has been requested in D, that is, a *full match* occurs. With concept satisfiability, the discovery of incompatible resources with respect to a request can be performed. If $D \sqcap C$ is not satisfiable with regards to the ontology $\mathcal{T}$, then C is not compatible with the request. Obviously, *full matches* cannot be deemed the one only useful, as they will be probably rare in a variety of contexts. Given a request and a set of resources, usually $C \not\sqsubseteq D$ and $D \sqcap C$ is satisfiable with regards to $\mathcal{T}$. That is, the resource does not completely satisfy the request but it is compatible with it. Hence, a metric is needed to establish "how much" the resource C is compatible with the request D or, equivalently, "how much" it is not specified in C to completely satisfy D, in order to make the subsumption relation $C \sqsubseteq D$ true. In Di Noia

et al. (2004) *rankPotential* algorithm was proposed to evaluate this measure. Given an $\mathcal{ALN}$ (attributive language with number restrictions) ontology $\mathcal{T}$ and two $\mathcal{ALN}$ concepts C and D both satisfiable in $\mathcal{T}$, *rankPotential*($C, D, \mathcal{T}$) computes a *semantic distance* of C from D with respect to the ontology $\mathcal{T}$.

If some requirements in the request D are in conflict with the resource C, *rankPotential* cannot be applied. Nevertheless, in looking for "not so much" unsatisfactory matches when recovering from an initial "no match", a partial match could still be useful. In Di Noia et al. (2004) the *rankPartial* algorithm was proposed for ranking incoherent pairs of descriptions. Given an ontology $\mathcal{T}$ and two concept expressions D and C, both satisfiable with respect to $\mathcal{T}$, if D is not compatible with C, that is, their conjunction is not satisfiable with respect to $\mathcal{T}$, then *rankPartial* returns a score measuring the semantic incompatibility of D and C.

Semantic-Based Bluetooth Service Discovery

Usually, resource discovery protocols involve a requester, a lookup or directory server and finally a resource provider. As a MANET is a volatile environment, a flexible resource discovery paradigm is needed to overcome difficulties due to the host mobility. Nevertheless, existing protocols for mobile applications use a simple string-matching, which is largely inefficient in advanced scenarios (Ruta et al., 2006b). With specific reference to the Bluetooth service discovery protocol (SDP), it is based on a 128 bit universally unique IDentifier (UUID) associated to single service classes. Resource matching in Bluetooth is hence strictly syntactic, and SDP manages only exact matches. In Ruta et al. (2006a) a framework has been proposed that allows the management of both syntactic and semantic discovery of resources, by integrating a semantic layer within the OSI Bluetooth stack at application level. The Bluetooth

Table 1. Select command structure in RFID protocol

Opcode	Target	Action	MemBank	Pointer	Length	Mask	Truncate	CRC
1010_2	3 bits	3 bits	2 bits	bit vector	8 bits	1-255 bits	1 bit	16 bits

standard has been enriched by new functionalities which permitted to maintain a backward compatibility (handheld device connectivity), adding the support to discovery of semantically annotated resources. Unused classes of 128 bit UUIDs in the original Bluetooth standard were exploited to mark each specific ontology thus calling this identifier *OUUID* (ontology universally unique IDentifier). By means of the OUUID matching the context was identified and a preliminary selection of resource referring to the same request's ontology was performed. The fundamental assumption is that each resource is semantically annotated. A service provider stores annotations within resource records, labelled with unique 32-bit identifiers. Each record contains general information about a single semantic-enabled resource and it entirely consists of a list of resource attributes. In addition to the OUUID attribute, there are a *ResourceName* (a human-readable name for the resource), a *ResourceDescription* (expressed using DIG syntax) and a variable number of *ResourceUtilityAttr_i* attributes, that is, numerical values used according to specific applications. In Ruta et al. (2006a), by adding four SDP Protocol Data Units (PDUs) *SDP_OntologySearch* (request and response) and *SDP_SemanticServiceSearch* (request and response) to the original standard (exploiting not used PDU ID), together with the original SDP capabilities, further semantic-enabled discovery functionalities were introduced. The overall interaction was based on the original SDP in Bluetooth. No modifications were made to the original structure of transactions. In fact, a semantic-based micro-layer has been built over the standard SDP recycling its basic parameters, data structures and functions, just differently using the basic framework.

RFID Features

In our framework, we refer to RFID transponders compliant with EPCglobal standard for Class 1-Generation 2 UHF tags (Traub et al., 2005). Tag memory is divided in four logical banks (EPCglobal Inc., 2005a): **(1)** *Reserved*. It is optional; if present, it stores 32-bit kill and access to passwords; **(2)** *Electronic product code (EPC)*. It stores, starting from address 0: (i) 16 bits for a cyclic redundancy check (CRC) code; (ii) a 16-bit protocol control (PC) field, composed of 5 bits for identification code length, 2 bits reserved for future use and 9 bits of numbering system identification; (iii) an EPC field for the identification code; **(3)** *Tag IDentification (TID)*. It stores at least tag manufacturer and model identification codes. This bank may be enlarged to store other manufacturer or model-specific data (e.g., a tag serial number); **(4)** *User*. An optional bank that stores data defined by the user application. Memory organization is user-defined. EPCglobal air interface protocol is an *Interrogator-Talks-First* (ITF) protocol: tags only reply to reader commands. Here, we briefly outline basic protocol features.

An RFID reader can preselect a subset of the tag population currently in range, according to user-defined criteria, by means of a sequence of *Select* commands.

Select command sends a bit string to all tags in range. Each tag will compare it with the content of a memory area specified by the reader, then it will assert/de-assert one of its status flags according to the comparison result (match/no-match). Command structure is shown in Table 1; parameters are as follows: (i) *Target* determines which tag status flag will be modified by the Select command; (ii) *Action* tells how a tag is required

Table 2. Read command structure in RFID protocol

Opcode	MemBank	WordPtr	WordCount	RN	CRC
11000010_2	2 bits	bit vector	8 bits	16 bits	16 bits

Table 3. Write command structure in RFID protocol

Opcode	MemBank	WordPtr	Data	RN	CRC
11000011_2	2 bits	bit vector	16 bits	16 bits	16 bits

to modify the flag (assert, de-assert, do nothing) for either positive or negative match outcome (a three-bit field is thus required to encode the six cases); (iii) *MemBank* indicates what memory bank must be compared; (iv) *Pointer* is the address of the first bit of MemBank tag memory area that must be compared; (v) *Length* is the length of the bit string to be compared; (vi) *Mask* is the bit string to be compared with the content of the memory area selected by MemBank, Pointer and Length values; (vii) *Truncate* tells the tag to send only part of its EPC code in the following protocol step; (viii) *CRC*, used for command data integrity protection.

After this phase, the inventory loop begins. In each iteration, the reader isolates one tag in range, reads its EPC code and can access its memory content. Among available commands, only *Read* and *Write* are relevant for our purposes.

Read command allows reading from one of the four tag memory banks. Command structure is shown in Table 2; parameters are as follows: (i) *MemBank* indicates the bank data must be read from; (ii) *WordPtr* points to the first 16-bit memory word to be read; (iii) *WordCount* is the number of consecutive 16-bit memory words that must be read (if it is 0, then the tag will send data stored up to the end of the memory bank); (iv) *RN*, random number used as access transaction identifier between reader and tag; (v) *CRC*.

Write command allows a reader to write a 16-bit word to one of the four tag memory banks.

Command structure is similar to *Read*, as shown in Table 3.

Together with tag data and air interface protocol, the EPCglobal standard defines a support infrastructure for RFID applications, where a key role is played by *object naming service (ONS)* (EPCglobal Inc., 2005b). It is based on the domain name system adopted to solve symbolic Internet addresses. ONS allows retrieval of services related to a specific object using the EPC code stored within the tag as a URI. *EPCglobal network protocol parameter registry* is maintained by EPCglobal consortium and contains suffixes identifying all valid service types (e.g., *ws* for a Web service, *html* for a Web page of the manufacturer, *epcis* for a EPCglobal information service providing authoritative information about the object associated with an EPC code).

FRAMEWORK AND APPROACH

We designed a unified semantic-aware framework, comprising modified RFID- and Bluetooth- based infrastructures that are virtually "interconnected" at the application layer permitting innovative services in u-environments. Our framework introduces a proposed extension of EPCglobal standard, allowing a semantic-based object discovery. Protocols to read/write tags have been preserved maintaining original code-based access (so keeping a compatibility with legacy applica-

Figure 1. Infrastructure elements: semantic-enhanced RFID tags; air-interface EPCglobal RFID protocol; middleware stratum; Bluetooth SD protocol, hotspot enriched with semantic matchmaking capabilities.

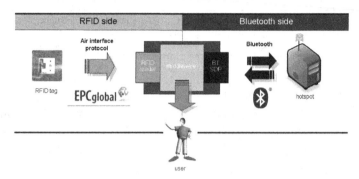

tions practically without modifications). A good can be easily and thoroughly described by means of a semantic annotated description stored within the tag it is associated with. Main elements of the proposed framework (see Figure 1) are: 1) goods equipped with semantic-enhanced RFID tags, 2) a middle tier component provided with an RFID reader and Bluetooth connectivity, 3) a hotspot enriched with semantic matchmaking capabilities. Two identification/discovery paradigms are involved: EPCglobal air interface protocol for RFID tags and semantic-enhanced Bluetooth Service Discovery Protocol. Interaction can be triggered by the user by means of either an implicit or an explicit request. The simplest—though not trivial, as obviously requests may change over time and during the product life-cycle—form of interaction is querying the tag (of the good) for some information, exploiting user's mobile handheld device. In implicit requests, the framework can be used to recognize choices the user performed so intercepting and interpreting them as a preliminary interaction aimed at discovery of goods similar or to be combined with the chosen one. In the first case, the user can directly interact with the hotspot, issuing requests to it via the semantic-enhanced Bluetooth SDP and waiting for replies. In the latter one, the user plays a more passive role as the "Environment" (in the sense of a pervasive and intelligent context, a

marketplace in our example scenario) is able to perceive modifications with regards to an earlier situation. RFID tags are required for hosting product features and to set a link between the *real* and the *digital* world, whereas the middle tier is a double-faced component. It listens for descriptions directly coming from the objects (by reading the tag memory content), issues requests to the service provider and finally records and displays results to the user. The RFID reader, scanning characteristics of a selected product, enables the further discovery phase which is aimed at identifying resources similar to the chosen one or to be combined with it. Via the semantic-based Bluetooth SDP and exploiting non-standard inference services outlined above, best matching resources of the marketplace will be discovered and returned to the user. Hence, the middleware integrates RFID and Bluetooth environments at the application layer: data coming from RFID tags are extracted, processed and reformatted. Furthermore, they are arranged to enable the interaction with the service provider (*hotspot*) via the semantic-enhanced Bluetooth SDP. The hotspot keeps track of resources within the marketplace and replies to a submitted request with the best matching products for similarity and association. To this aim, it is equipped with a DL reasoner able to provide previously introduced services. Such an approach may provide several benefits. Informa-

Table 4. Select command parameters to detect semantic-enabled tags

Parameter	Target	Action	MemBank	Pointer	Length	Mask
Value	100_2	000_2	01_2	00010101_2	00000010_2	11_2
Description	SL flag	assert in case of match, deassert otherwise	EPC memory bank	initial address	number of bits to compare	bit mask

tion about a product is structured and complete; it accurately follows the product history within the supply chain, being progressively built or updated during the good life cycle. This improves traceability of production and distribution, facilitates sales and post-sale services thanks to an advanced and selective discovery infrastructure.

Semantic-Enhanced EPCGlobal RFID Standard

In this subsection, we outline the proposed backward-compatible extensions to EPCglobal RFID standards enabling the framework described above. It is noteworthy that our semantic-enabled descriptions are expressed in DIG formalism (Bechhofer et al., 2003), a more compact syntactic variant of OWL.

Two reserved bits in the EPC area within each tag memory are exploited. The first one—at 15_h (10101_2) address—is exploited to indicate if the tag has a user memory (bit set) or not (bit cleared). The next one—at 16_h address—is asserted to mark semantic-enabled tags. In this manner, by means of a *Select* command (see Table 4), a reader can easily distinguish semantic-based tags. In particular, target and action parameters have the effect to assert the SL tag status flag only for semantic-enabled tags and de-assert it for remaining ones. The following inventory step will skip tags having SL flag de-asserted, thus allowing a reader to identify only semantic-enabled tags (protocol commands belonging to the inventory step have not been described, because they are used in the standard fashion).

The EPC standard for UHF-Class 1 tags impose the content of TID memory up to $1F_h$ bit is fixed. As said above, optional information could be stored in the TID memory. We use the TID memory area starting from 100000_2 address. There we store the identifier of the ontology (OUUID) with regards to the description contained within the tag is expressed. In order to make RFID systems compliant with the ontology support system proposed in Ruta et al. (2006a), we define a bidirectional correspondence of OUUIDs stored in RFID transponders with those managed by Bluetooth devices. To retrieve the OUUID value stored within a tag, a reader will exploit a *Read* command with parameters as in Table 5.

Within the user memory bank, together with the semantically annotated description of the good the tag is clung to (opportunely compressed), there will be stored also contextual parameters (whose meaning depends on the specific application).

The extraction or the storing of a description within a tag can be performed by a reader through one or more read or write commands, respectively. Both commands are used in compliance with the standard air interface protocol. In Table 6, parameters of the read command for extracting a compressed description are reported.

In our approach, the ONS mechanism is considered as a supplementary system able to grant the ontology support. In case the reader does not manage the ontology the description within the tag refers to, it may need an Internet connection in order to retrieve the related DIG file, which will then remain stored for further usage on other goods of the same category. For this purpose, we use the ONS service and we hypothesize to register

Table 5. Read command parameters to extract OUUID from TID memory bank

Parameter	MemBank	WordPtr	WordCount
Value	10_2	000000010_2	00001000_2
Description	TID memory bank	initial address	read up to 8 words (128 bits)

Table 6. Read command parameters to extract semantic annotations from the user bank

Parameter	MemBank	WordPtr	WordCount
Value	11_2	000000000_2	00000000_2
Description	User memory bank	initial address	read up to the end

within the *EPCglobal Network Protocol Parameter Registry* a new service suffix, the *dig* one, that will contain the URL of the DIG file ontology. Of course the same can be done for OWL.

In case of EPC code families derived from the GS1 standard (formerly EAN.UCC) for barcode product identification, we assume that the pair of fields used for ONS requests—which refers to the manufacturer and to the merchandise class of the good—will correspond to a specific ontology. In fact, that pair exactly identifies the product category. Two goods with the same value for that field parameter will be surely homogeneous or even equal. Note that the vice versa is not verified, but this is not a concern for our purposes because ONS searches proceed only from the EPC code toward the ontology. Hence we can surely have an unambiguous correspondence.

Deploying the Approach

In our case study framework, we hypothesize a "smart shopping cart" is equipped with a sensor and a tablet computer, which integrates an RFID reader and Bluetooth connectivity. When a customer picks up a product, the system assists him/her in discovering additional items, either similar or to be combined with the selected one. To this aim, a two-step discovery is performed,

exploiting two different but related ontologies. In the first step, *rankPotential* algorithm is exploited to retrieve correspondences with the request. Resources analogous to the one selected by the user are identified, but at the same time, semantically incompatible goods are recognized. Their descriptions are submitted to the second matchmaking step. It exploits *rankPartial* over a differently modeled ontology allowing the discovery of products to be associated with the chosen one. The hotspot will return two different lists of resource records, respectively, for objects in a potential correspondence with the request and in a partial one.

In advanced mobile scenarios, usually the match between a request and a provided resource involves not only the description of the resource itself but also data-oriented contextual properties. In fact, it would be quite strange to have a mobile commerce application without taking into account, for example, price or delivery time, among others. Hence, the overall match value should depend not only on the semantic distance between the description of the demand and of the resource, but also on those subsidiary values. An overall *utility function* has to combine them with semantic matchmaking results, in order to give a concrete match measure (Ruta et al., 2006b). In the proposed case study—referred to a u-commerce electronic product store—the utility function

Table 7. Product category contextual parameter

Product category	phones	computers	photo	audio/video	hobbies
Value	1	2	3	4	5

adopts three contextual parameters: price (in U.S. dollars), estimated delivery time (in days), and product category, as shown in Table 7. They are exploited in a post-processing phase following the semantic-based matchmaking and aimed to better match discovery results with user needs.

The proposed utility function (whose formulation derives from common sense considerations) has two expressions, for potential and partial matches respectively:

$$f_{POT}(\cdot) = \frac{pot\_match}{2} + \frac{\tanh(\frac{t_R - t_O}{\beta})}{3} u(t_R - t_O)$$
$$+ (\frac{p_O}{p_R} - 0.5)\frac{(1+\alpha)p_R - p_O}{3(1+\alpha)p_R}$$

$$f_{PAR}(\cdot) = \frac{par\_match}{2} + \frac{\tanh(\frac{t_R - t_O}{\beta})}{6} u(t_R - t_O)$$
$$+ \frac{1 - \gamma|c_R - c_O|}{3(2 + |c_R - c_O|)}$$

where *pot_match* and *par_match* are the potential and partial match values, p is price, t is delivery time and c is product category. The index R is referred to the request whereas the O one is referred to the supply and $u(\cdot)$ is the Heaviside step function. Parameters α, β, γ can be used to fine tune the utility function. Values we experimentally experienced with good results were $\alpha = 0.1$, $\beta = 10$, $\gamma = 0.2$. They have been determined by means of empirical tests through the comparison of system results with human users' judgment. The higher the utility value the better the obtained match. In both formulas, the leading term is represented by the semantic match.

The second term depends on the estimated delivery time and it is differently weighted in proposed formulas. In the first one (discovery of goods similar to the request), a late delivery is more penalized. On the other hand, partial matches refer to items that can be used together with the selected one (such as accessories or complements); therefore, a delay is less of a concern.

The last term is different in the two formulas. For potential matches, it is related to product price. The price imposed by the requester is increased with a factor α on the assumption that usually, the demander is willing to pay up to some more than what s/he originally specified, on the condition that s/he finds the requested item or something very similar. Supplies with a much lower price than requested (less than 50%) are penalized since they likely represent items in a different market segment. In the formula for partial matches, the last addend considers product category. Products in the same category are favored because they are presumably more suitable to be used together with the one selected by the user.

Coping with Verbose Descriptions

Languages at the heart of Semantic Web are based upon XML, whose known drawback is verbosity. Usually, this is not a concern for Internet-based applications (because link bandwidth and host memory capacity are enough for most practical purposes), but surely reduces efficiency of data storage and communication in mobile environments. Adapting ideas and techniques from the Semantic Web vision to ubiquitous scenarios requires coping with the limited storage and computational capabilities of mobile and embedded devices and with reduced bandwidth provided by wireless links. Here, we provide details about a novel efficient XML compression algorithm devised for the purposes of the framework pre-

Figure 2. Structure of the proposed DIG compression tool

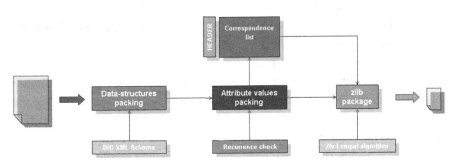

sented in this article. It is specifically oriented to the packing of standard DIG 1.1 syntax. The XML Schema for DIG format contains 40 tags at most. A DIG is an XML document exposing specific characteristics. That is, no value is set for any tag; the value of tag attributes is within a well-defined finite set of values.

A basic distinction among various encoding techniques is in *fixed length* and *variable length* algorithms (Hamming, 1986). In the first case, having a specified alphabet, a fixed bit number is used to encode each symbol: in particular, we need $n = \log_2 k$ bits, with k alphabet symbols. A DIG file is encoded by means of `ISO 8859-1` or `UTF-8` encoding. In particular, each allowed character can be associated to 1 byte (special characters needing more than 1 byte in `UTF-8` do not belong to the symbol set of DIG). Hence, in order to obtain a good compression rate, we must recur to a variable length coding algorithm: in this case the most efficient algorithm is the *Huffman* one (Huffman, 1952; Cover & Thomas, 1991). It requires having a *dictionary* containing the correspondences between each symbol and the bits sequence encoding it. This dictionary obviously varies according to the document. Although the Huffman algorithm could seem like a good choice to compress an ontology in DIG syntax, it does not work well with short semantically annotated DIG descriptions as the ones referred to resource metadata annotation. A resource description is usually a few hundred bytes long, so the Huffman

compression is sometimes inadequate because a description could be smaller than the dictionary itself. We propose a different DIG compression solution, particularly suitable for pervasive applications, whose structure is shown in Figure 2. We exploit the peculiarity of the DIG format having few, well-defined and limited tag elements and being mostly composed of empty XML elements. Three fundamental phases can be identified: **(1)** *data-structures packing*; **(2)** *attribute-values packing*; **(3)** *zlib packing*.

1. *Data-structures packing.* The proposed compression algorithm is based on two fundamental principles. First of all, pure data have to be divided from data structures; furthermore, data and data structures have to be separately encoded in order to obtain a more effective compression rate. Data structures are basically XML elements with possible related attributes, whereas data simply are attribute values. Recall that data structures in DIG syntax are fixed and well defined by means of the DIG XML Schema, whereas data are different from document to document. XML elements are encoded by associating an unambiguous 8-bit code to each structure in a static fashion. Consider that DIG files adopt an encoding which exploits one byte for each character: so an early size saving is performed. Note that the association between XML structures and

corresponding code is fixed and invariable. This is a further benefit because it is unnecessary to integrate within the compressed file a header containing the decoding table.

2. *Attribute-values packing.* In order to pack the attribute values, in the proposed approach, a further phase is introduced. Most recurrent words are identified in the previously distinguished data section. They will be encoded with a 16-bit sequence. The second compression stage allows to obtain a further size-saving especially in ontologies with recurrent concepts and roles. The second packing phase needs to build and maintain a header of the compressed file containing correspondences between each text string and the related 16-bit code. It is dynamically created and exclusively belongs to a specific DIG document instance. The provided header will be exploited in the decompression steps. Notice that assigned codes differ for the second byte, because the first octet is adopted as padding in order to distinguish the attribute value coding from the ASCII one. The use of this header could compromise compression performances for short files: recall that the size consumption for the header reduces saving obtained with compression. Hence, the encoding of all the string values of a DIG file without any a priori distinction must be avoided. Care has to be taken in the choice of attribute-value strings to encode. A correct compression procedure should properly take into account both the length of an attribute string and its number of occurrences within the file. The minimum length of strings to encode can be trivially established by comparing the size consumption needed to store correspondences *string–code* and the saving obtained with the encoding: in the proposed approach only text attributes with a length of at least three characters will be processed. Furthermore, in order to establish what at-

tribute values (among remaining ones) have to be encoded, we must evaluate the number of occurrences of each attribute i (from now on $nr\_occurences\_i$). We fix a minimum optimum value $nr\_occurences\_min$ and we will encode only i attribute values where $nr\_occurences\_i > nr\_occurences\_min$. We have performed statistical evaluations trying the compression of 72 sample ontologies and evaluating obtained compression rates varying $nr\_occurences\_min$. Results that show the best compression rates are produced by $nr\_occurences\_min$ values within the range [2–8] with an average of 4.03 and a standard deviation in the range [0–0.3]. In the proposed approach, we set $nr\_occurences\_min = 4$, so we will encode only attribute strings with at least three characters recurring at least four times.

3. *Zlib packing.* The third and final compression step exploits *zlib* library. Although the *zlib* algorithm does not work well when it has to compress a partially encoded input (it is difficult to find more occurrences of the same sequence), the use of *zlib* in our approach resulted however useful especially for large files, where it produces the compression of words excluded by the previous compression steps and of the file header.

PROTOTYPE FRAMEWORK

U-commerce was chosen as a reference scenario for evaluating the effectiveness and feasibility of our object discovery framework and architecture.

A central role is played by the user interface component equipped with an integrated RFID reader as well as Bluetooth connectivity. The above logical framework can be adapted to different real scenarios with various physical devices involved. It will now be clarified and motivated in a consumer electronics store case study, where

Figure 3. Sequence diagram of a basic use case in our reference scenario

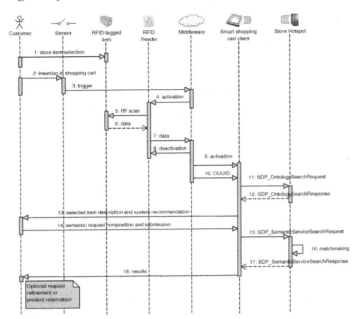

a "smart shopping cart" equipped with a tablet touchscreen, RFID reader and Bluetooth transceiver interacts with the store the hotspot at SDP level. The UML sequence diagram in Figure 3 shows the role played by these logical elements in a basic use case. We hypothesize that hotspot maintains semantic annotations and context values. Annotations of products in the marketplace refer to a consumer electronics ontology, marked with a specific identifier we indicate as $OUUID_E$. Interaction is triggered by inserting an item into the shopping cart, which is detected by a pressure sensor (also simulated in our current environment) and identified by the integrated RFID reader.

In the proposed object discovery framework, a session starts after the submission from client to server of the ontology identifier $OUUID_E$, in order to agree on the resource category to be adopted in upcoming requests. Semantic annotation describing the selected item will be exploited as basic user request to be adapted or updated for discovering further resources. Feature selection is performed by an intentional navigation of the reference ontology, represented as a hierarchy of

elements. A tabbed panel allows easy navigation even in large ontologies. The user can concentrate on his/her current focus and at the same time freely change the entry point through the upper tabs which record navigation history (Colucci et al., 2006). Pop-up menus and drag-and-drop are supported to further simplify user interaction.

Simulation Test Bed

A prototypical scenario was developed to validate the theoretical framework and to evaluate the feasibility and effectiveness of the proposed solution. IBM WebSphere RFID Tracking Kit (Chamberlain et al., 2006) was adopted as a development and simulation platform. It is a message-based service-oriented middleware for the integration of RFID systems and other mobile and embedded technologies in enterprise applications. It is based on OSGi (Open Service Gateway Initiative) Alliance open standard for platform-neutral, network-managed SOAs (Service Oriented Architectures) (OSGi Alliance, 2005).

Figure 4. Test bed: HW?SW nodes and components

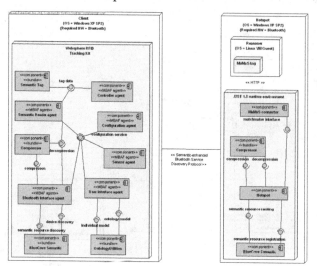

The OSGi basic building block is the *bundle*, a self-contained software module whose lifecycle (install/start/update/restart/stop/uninstall) can be managed dynamically through a network. Bundle implementing EPCglobal RFID tag standards has been extended with support to semantic-based product descriptions: RFID tags and readers are software-simulated in our test bed.

Upon this infrastructure, WebSphere RFID Tracking Kit provides MBAF (MicroBroker application framework), a framework for event-based notification among software components. It adopts WebSphere MQTT (Message Queue Telemetry Transport), a lightweight publish-subscribe protocol for asynchronous message exchange. Components developed within MBAF are called *agents*. MBAF agents comply to OSGi bundle specifications and an agent behaves like a black box: it subscribes to messages representing events of interest. Upon message receipt, the agent processes its content and publishes zero or more new messages as a result. Overall application behavior is determined by the message flow among agents.

This service and message-oriented design fits well into ubiquitous computer paradigms, as it is aimed at maximizing modularity, flexibility

and scalability. Such properties are essential in volatile and resource-constrained mobile environments, and benefits were noticeable in prototype testing and evolution. Simulation sessions with our prototype platform evidenced that semantic-enhanced object discovery services can coexist with traditional RF identification and tracking applications. Test bed deployment and system components are represented in the UML diagram depicted in Figure 4 and the main elements are highlighted here. Both client and hotspot were deployed on notebook PCs running Microsoft Windows XP. WebSphere RFID Tracking Kit runs on client machine, integrating a Bluetooth communication interface with simulated RFID reader, sensors and an user interface by means of dedicated MBAF agents. Controller and configuration agents are added for supervising the application execution and managing system operating parameters, respectively. Hotspot hosts a J2SE runtime environment for running the service provider and a Linux Virtual Machine for running MAMAS-tng reasoner (Di Noia et al., 2004). The compression library implementing the algorithm described in the above section is included in both hosts as well as BlueCove[2], an open source Java Bluetooth library which

Figure 5. Product details are read via RFID and shown to the user

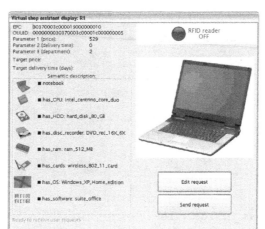

was extended with support for semantic-based resource discovery. Both these components are deployed as standard Java archives in the hotspot, whereas they are encapsulated in OSGi bundles on the client node.

Example Scenario

Let us suppose Mary is looking for a new laptop computer. She notices a quite cheap notebook model, bundled with an office productivity suite. She puts it into the smart shopping cart. A sensor detects the event and the RFID reader is triggered. It reads data stored within the tag attached to the laptop package, then it is deactivated again. Extracted tag data consists of product EPC, ontology identifier $OUUID_E$, semantic-annotated description (stored as a compressed DIG expression) and contextual parameters. Let us suppose that tagged description corresponds to a notebook with Intel Centrino Core Duo CPU, 1 GB RAM, 80 GB hard disk drive, DVD writer and wireless LAN connectivity; it includes Microsoft Windows XP Home Edition OS and an office software suite. The price is $550, delivery time is 0 days and product category is 2. The equivalent expression in DL formalism with regards to $OUUID_E$ reference ontology is:

```
R:  notebook ⊓∀has_CPU.Intel_centri-
    no_core_duo ⊓∀has_HDD.hard_
    disk_80_GB ⊓∀has_disc_recorder.
    DVD_rec_16X_6X ⊓∀has_ram.ram_1_
    GB ⊓∀has_cards.wireless_802_11 card
    ⊓∀has_OS.Windows_XP_Home_edition
    ⊓∀has_software.suite_office
```

As reported in Figure 5, the tablet touch screen shows the received product details for building further semantic-based requests. Let us suppose Mary likes her choice. Now she would like to find some basic accessories.

She confirms the system-recommended request (shown in Figure 6), which is submitted via the semantic-enhanced Bluetooth SDP from the smart shopping cart to the hotspot.

Let us suppose the following products are available in the store knowledge base:

S1: notebook with AMD Athlon XP-M CPU, 1 GB RAM, 80 GB hard disk drive, DVD writer and wireless LAN connectivity. It is bundled with Windows XP Professional and antivirus software. Price is $599; delivery time is 0 days; product category is 2:

```
notebook ⊓∀has_CPU.AMD_Athlon_
XP_M ⊓∀has_HDD.hard_disk_80_
GB ⊓∀has_disc_recorder.DVD_
```

Figure 6. Graphical user interface for semantic request composition

```
rec _ 16X _ 6X  ⊓∀has _ cards.wire-
less _ 802 _ 11 _ card  ⊓∀has _ ram.
ram _ 1 _ GB  ⊓∀has _ OS.Windows _
XP _ Professional ⊓∀has _ software.
antivirus
```

S2: notebook with Intel Centrino Core Duo CPU, 1 GB RAM, 80 GB hard disk drive, DVD writer and wireless LAN connectivity. It is bundled with Linux and an office suite. Price is $529; estimated delivery time is 1 day; product category is 2:

```
notebook   ⊓∀has _ CPU.Intel _ cen-
trino _ core _ duo ⊓∀has _ HDD.hard _
disk _ 80 _ GB ⊓∀has _ disc _ record-
er.DVD _ rec _ 16X _ 6X ⊓∀has _ cards.
wireless _ 802 _ 11 _ card  ⊓∀has _
ram.ram _ 1 _ GB 6 ...has _ OS.Linux
⊓∀has _ software.suite _ office
```

S3: a desktop computer with Intel Pentium 4 CPU, 1 GB RAM, 250 GB hard disk drive, DVD writer, wireless LAN connectivity and an LCD display. It is bundled with Windows XP Home Edition and an office suite. Price is $499; delivery time is 0 days; product category is 2:

```
desktop _ computer  6 ...has _ CPU.
Intel _ Pentium _ 4 6 ...has _ HDD.
hard _ disk _ 250 _ GB  6 ...has _
display.LCD _ display  6 ...has _
disc _ recorder.DVD _ rec _ 16X _ 6X
6 ...has _ ram.ram _ 1 _ GB 6 ...has _
cards.wireless _ 802 _ 11 _ card  6
```

```
¼has _ OS.Windows _ XP _ Home _ edi-
tion 6 ...has _ software.suite _ of-
fice
```

S4: a blue notebook bag. Price is $19; delivery time is 0 days; product category is 2:

```
notebook _ bag ⊓∀has _ color.blue
```

S5: a silver-colored UMTS mobile phone with dual display and miniSD memory card support. Price is $169; delivery time is 0 days; product category is 1:

```
mobile phone ⊓∀has _ connectivity.
UMTS ⊓ =2 has _ display ⊓∀has _ dis-
play.LCD _ display ⊓∀has _ memory _
card.mini _ sd
```

Hotspot performs the discovery and matchmaking processes as described in section 3 and returns results via Bluetooth SDP. Matchmaking results for this example are presented in Table 8. The second column shows whether each retrieved resource is compatible with request **R**. If so, the *rankPotential* computed result is shown, otherwise the *rankPartial* computed result is presented. In the last column, results of the overall utility function are reported. Note that **S2** is ranked as the best supply for similarity match, despite a longer delivery time than **S1**. This is due to a better *rankPotential* outcome. Among candidate resources for combination, category affinity favors **S4** over **S5**, while **S3** has a clearly poorer match. For each retrieved resource, a picture is returned

Table 8. Matchmaking results

Supply	Compatibility (Y/N)	*rankPotential* score	*rankPartial* score	$f(\cdot)$
S1: notebook with antivirus	Y	6		0.001
S2: notebook with office suite	Y	3		0.236
S3: desktop computer	N		79	0.166
S4: notebook bag	N		26	0.502
S5: UMTS phone	N		23	0.443

Figure 7. Retrieved results are shown to the user

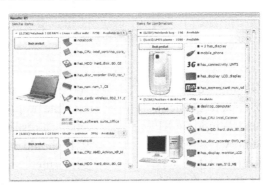

along with matchmaking score, price and description, as displayed in Figure 7.

EXPERIMENTAL RESULTS

A thorough and significant experimental evaluation of all aspects of system performance requires a complete implementation of our framework into a testbed with real semantic-enabled RFID devices. That would only be possible through partnership agreements with device manufacturers/integrators. Therefore, analysis with our current PC-based simulation test bed focused on four groups of performance measures, that can provide valuable and reliable information about practical feasibility and efficiency of the proposed approach: 1) performance of the compression algorithm as a stand-alone tool; 2) impact of compression over Bluetooth system performance; 3) preliminary evaluation of access time of compressed seman-tic annotations on RFID tags with regards to tag scanning performance of EPCglobal RFID systems; 4) estimation of semantic matchmaking processing time.

The following subsections cover methods, results and discussion for each of the four analyses.

Compression Algorithm

Performance evaluation of the proposed algorithm has been carried out estimating three fundamental parameters: **(1)** compression rate; **(2)** turnaround time; **(3)** memory usage.

Two stand-alone tools were developed in C language implementing our compression and decompression algorithms, named *DIG Compressor* and *DIG Decompressor*, respectively. Currently, Windows and Linux platforms are supported, leveraging the freely available *zlib* compression library. Tests for compression rate and running

Figure 8. Compression rates obtained by the proposed algorithm

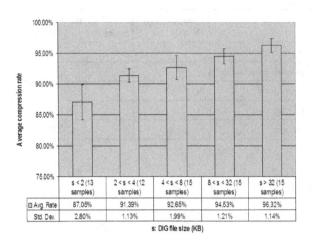

	s < 2 (13 samples)	2 < s < 4 (12 samples)	4 < s < 8 (15 samples)	8 < s < 32 (15 samples)	s > 32 (15 samples)
□ Avg. Rate	87.05%	91.39%	92.65%	94.53%	96.32%
Std. Dev.	2.80%	1.13%	1.99%	1.21%	1.14%

s: DIG file size (KB)

time were performed using a PC equipped with an Intel Pentium 4 CPU (3.06 GHz clock frequency), 512 MB RAM at 266 MHz and Windows XP operating system. Tests for memory usage were performed on a PC running Gentoo GNU/Linux with 2.6.19 kernel version and *Valgrind* profiling toolkit (Nethercote & Seward, 2007). This second PC was equipped with a Pentium M CPU (2.00 GHz clock frequency) and 1 GB RAM at 533 MHz.

1. The compression rates achieved by the proposed algorithm were tested with 70-DIG documents of various size. Our aim was to evaluate them for both smaller instance descriptions and larger ontologies. Figure 8 shows average compression rates and standard deviations for different size ranges of DIG input data. Overall, the average compression rate is 92.58±3.58%. As expected, higher compression rates were achieved for larger documents. Even for very short DIG files (less than 2 KB), however, average compression rate is 87.05±2.80, which is surely satisfactory for our purposes. A comparative evaluation was carried out using *XMill* general purpose XML compressor (Liefke & Suciu, 2000) and *gzip* generic compres-

sor[3] as benchmarks. Testing the compression rate, the proposed tool allowed to obtain the smallest resulting files, as shown in Figure 9. It should be noticed that our algorithm performed significantly better for small DIG documents. This is a very encouraging result, since mobile scenarios usually deal with small XML annotations of available resources.

2. In order to evaluate turnaround time, each test was run ten times consecutively, and the average of the last eight runs was taken. Results are presented in Figure 10. It can be noticed that processing times are comparable for documents up to 80 kB. For larger documents DIG Compressor has higher turnaround times than other tools, though absolute values are still quite acceptable. Such an outcome suggests further work should be put into optimizing the implementation for execution speed.

3. Finally, memory usage analysis was performed using *Massif* tool of *Valgrind* debugging/profiling toolkit. Massif measures stack and heap memory profile throughout the life of a process. For our comparison, only the memory occupancy peak was considered. Results are reported in Table 9.

Figure 9. Compression rates in gzip, XMill and DIG compressor

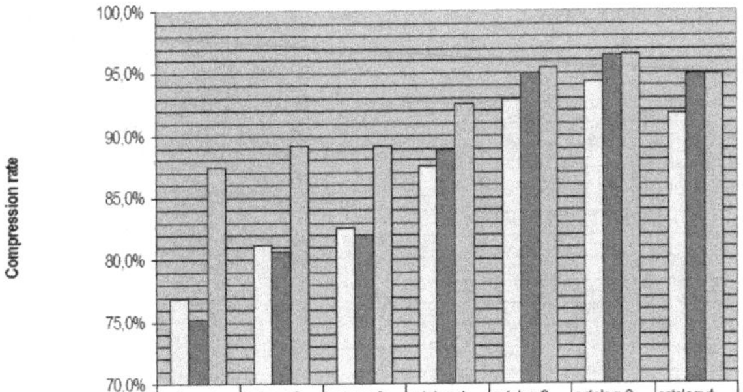

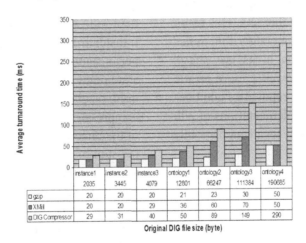

	instance1 2035	instance2 3445	instance3 4079	ontology1 12801	ontology2 66247	ontology3 111384	ontology4 190685
☐ gzip	76,9%	81,2%	82,6%	87,6%	92,9%	94,3%	91,7%
▣ XMill	75,2%	80,7%	82,0%	88,9%	95,0%	96,4%	94,9%
☐ DIG Compressor	87,5%	89,2%	89,2%	92,5%	95,5%	96,5%	94,9%

Original DIG file size (byte)

Figure 10. Turnaround time in gzip, XMill and DIG compressor

	instance1 2035	instance2 3445	instance3 4079	ontology1 12801	ontology2 66247	ontology3 111384	ontology4 190685
☐ gzip	20	20	20	21	23	30	50
▣ XMill	20	20	29	36	60	70	50
☐ DIG Compressor	29	31	40	50	89	149	290

Original DIG file size (byte)

Table 9 Memory usage peak (kB) in gzip, XMill and DIG compressor

DIG document	Original size (B)	gzip	XMill	DigCompressor
Playstation_2_Slim.dig	2035	220	2700	290
Kodak_P880_camera.dig	3445	200	4500	250
Asus_A3FP_Notebook.dig	4079	200	6500	250
Toy_ontology.dig	12801	200	4000	240
Rent_ontology.dig	66247	200	6500	250
clothing_ontology.dig	111384	202	4500	250
electronic_products_ontology.dig	190685	210	4000	260

Figure 11. Ontology transfer time via Bluetooth (data compression disabled and enabled)

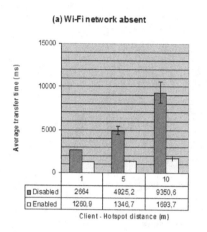

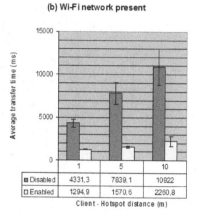

DIG compressor memory usage is only slightly higher than the one of gzip, with high correlation ($r = 0.96$) between the two value sets. This result could be expected, since our algorithm relies on Ziv-Lempel compression in its last phase. On the contrary, XMill showed a more erratic behavior. Outcomes can be reputed as good because memory-efficient implementations of zlib library are currently available for all major mobile platforms.

Impact of Compression Over Bluetooth Performance

Like other wireless networking technologies, throughput of data transfer between two Bluetooth nodes is influenced mostly by: (1) fading due to obstacles and physical distance between nodes (Zanella et al., 2002), and (2) interference from other electromagnetic sources in range (Haartsen & Zürbes, 1999). In particular, Bluetooth operates in the unlicensed 2.45 GHz band also used by IEEE 802.11 wireless LANs, which are widespread in home and business environments. It is therefore important to take the above two factors into proper account when investigating the impact of data compression on Bluetooth application performance in ubiquitous computing scenarios.

Since, in our approach a domain ontology is typically two or three orders of magnitude larger than individual resource annotations, ontology transfer from hotspot to a client was chosen as performance measure. The consumer electronics store ontology developed for the case study was used: original document size is 187 kB, whereas compressed size is 9.5 kB. Bluetooth transfer time of the uncompressed ontology was compared to the sum of (i) hotspot compression, (ii) transfer and (iii) client decompression time for the same resource. Tests were repeated at three client/hotspot distances (1 m, 5 m and 10 m) and both with and without a 802.11b/g WLAN (composed of an access point and a terminal) actively operating in the same room, for six different environmental conditions. Each ontology transfer test was run ten times consecutively; average values and standard deviations were then calculated.

Figure 11 summarizes results. Reported transfer time when compression is enabled, comprises the time spent in encoding and decoding of ontological data. Compression produces a significant speedup in all cases. At the same time, when compression is enabled, the system is much more resilient to performance degradation due to longer communication distance and interference by an active Wi-Fi network.

Figure 12. Hotspot encoding, Bluetooth transmission and client decoding times for a compressed ontology in various environmental conditions

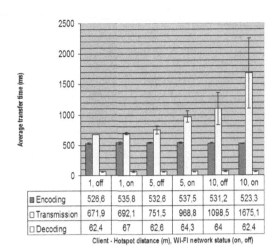

	1, off	1, on	5, off	5, on	10, off	10, on
■ Encoding	526,6	535,8	532,6	537,5	531,2	523,3
☐ Transmission	671,9	692,1	751,5	968,8	1098,5	1675,1
☐ Decoding	62,4	67	62,6	64,3	64	62,4

In Figure 12, the overall transfer time is dissected into its three components. Note that data compression occupies a significant share of total time (23.1% to 41.8%), while decompression is almost negligible. As expected, transmission time accounts for much of total variability and is affected by environmental conditions, while compression and decompression times are substantially constant.

Access Time of Simulated Semantic-Enhanced RFID Tag

This evaluation has been performed with the aim of providing a preliminary judgment of the impact that our approach may have on RFID system performance. Compressed semantic annotations of 40 different marketplace items created for the above case study were used. Their mean size is 266±104 B (range 91-440 B). Simulated RFID data access from each tagged item was repeated 100 times, recording the sum of reading and decompression time. For each item, the mean value was then considered.

Results are reported in Figure 13. The average access time is 2.02±0.36 ms, corresponding to a theoretical tag read rate of approximately 500 tags/s. Since tests were run on a software-simulated RFID platform, exact numerical values are not as significant as their order of magnitude. The latter can be sensibly compared to performance of RFID systems compliant with EPCglobal standards for Class 1 Generation 2 UHF RFID systems.

RFID performance in the field highly depends on the application, environmental conditions (electromagnetic noise, RFID reader density) and local regulations affecting the available bandwidth. Alien Technology RFID equipment manufacturer claimed maximum tag read rates of 1000 tags/s in environments with good insulation from electromagnetic noise and 50-100 tags/s in noisy environments (Alien Technology, 2005). Early simulations and tests by universities and independent laboratories estimated read rates ranging from 7 to approximately 100 tags/s in typical application conditions (Kawakita & Mistugi, 2006; Ramakrishnan & Deavours, 2006). Our simulation results are fully compatible with such data, thus providing very preliminary evidence that adoption of compressed semantic resource annotations on RFID tags does not impair performance of

Figure 13. RFID tag reading and decompression time for 40 resource descriptions

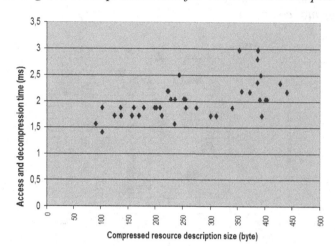

Figure 14. Performance evaluation of semantic matchmaking

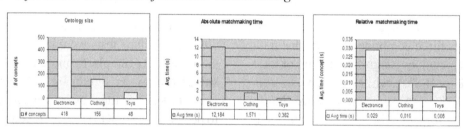

semantic-based RFID applications in the field with regards to to traditional ones. The latter, in turn, will not suffer any direct performance degradation from the newly introduced features, as they will read the EPC only. Finally, access time showed a moderate positive correlation (r = 0.60) with annotation size. This may suggest that structure of a DIG annotation also has an impact over the decompression.

Semantic Matchmaking Processing Computation

A semantic-enhanced Bluetooth simulated test bed embedded in *ns-2 Network Simulator*[4] has been used to assess semantic matchmaking processing times. Three ontologies of different levels of complexity were examined, and five different demands for each one were submitted to

MAMAS-tng reasoning engine. Average response times were recorded. Figure 14 shows the average response time, the number of concepts and the ratio of these two values for each ontology.

It can be noticed that, for the most complex ontologies, semantic matchmaking time dominates the other system performance measures shown in previous subsections. This problem was also pointed out by Ben Mokhtar et al. (2006), who devised optimizations to reduce online reasoning time in a semantic-based mobile service discovery protocol. The main proposed optimizations were offline pre-classification of ontology concepts and concept encoding: both solutions, however, are viable in matchmaking schemes based on pure subsumption (and therefore able to provide only binary yes/no answers), but are not directly applicable to our matchmaking scheme. Also note that, due to the large amount of time required by the matchmaker computation, RFID reading times have a relative importance within the overall performance evaluation. From this point of view, the differences between tag reading time interval in a practical deployment of the system and in the simulated one are un-influential in an extensive evaluation of the approach.

RELATED WORK

Smart identification technologies and techniques have been discussed in many recent research proposals in the field of ubiquitous computing. In De et al. (2004), a pervasive architecture for tracking mobile objects in real time is presented, aimed at supply chain and B2B transaction management. A global and persistent IT infrastructure is necessary in order to interface RFID systems within partner organizations through the Internet. These requirements make the approach less suitable for B2C and C2C scenarios especially in MANET contexts. An XML formalism named Physical Markup Language (PML) is used to describe objects and processes. However, it does not exploit any semantics of resource descriptions and only allows string-matching discovery.

Römer et al. (2004) present two frameworks (respectively based on Jini and UDDI service discovery protocols) for ubiquitous computing applications using smart identification technologies. Core design abstractions such as object location, neighborhood, composition, history and context make them flexible. Nevertheless, as admitted by the authors, scalability issues are present. A further limitation is that semantics of object properties and capabilities is not explicit, but it is encapsulated in either Java classes or Web services.

A key usability issue of mobile and ubiquitous computing solutions is to assist the user in timely and unobtrusive ways, without either being inappropriate or altering his/her habits. In our framework, interaction is started implicitly, that is, by user actions in the real world. Schmidt et al. (2000) focus on implicit *Human-Computer Interaction* (HCI) in pervasive computing. The authors introduce a wearable RFID solution enabling operations on an information system simply by picking up or using an operation-related tagged object. The proposed system has been also integrated with SAP R/3 in a case study. Since no semantic information is associated to tags, however, RFID is used merely as a bridge towards the centralized information infrastructure. Interaction patterns are quite unnatural in some cases, because real-world objects are used to start even those tasks that need explicit HCI (e.g., editing a document in a word processor).

In Siegemund and Florkemeier (2003), interaction patterns between users endowed with GSM phones and everyday objects are investigated. Exploited objects are augmented through active RFID transponders equipped with on-board sensors, modest computing capabilities and Bluetooth connectivity. An infrastructure enabling a hybrid implicit-explicit HCI model is implemented. In order to minimize user involvement, an "invisible" pre-selection based on contextual conditions is performed. Elected objects send *interaction stubs* to the GSM terminal of the user. Basically, stubs are SMS templates to issue commands to objects or to ask their status. Authors claim that proposed interaction patterns are perceived as natural, nevertheless sending SMS messages to special objects requires too much user attention, thus altering normal relationships between people and everyday things. The need for a costly communication link such as GSM is an open issue.

In Kawakita et al. (2004), a support system aimed at enhancing information exchange within a conference room is presented. RFID-enabled badges are given to the meeting attendants, everyone having a remotely stored profile. Each room has an RFID reader. A location- and time-aware middleware tracks participants while entering or exiting meetings. Upon this basic infrastructure, location-based instant messaging and file sharing services are provided. This is a good example of implicit HCI in ubiquitous computing, even though the applicability is somewhat limited by the preliminary explicit profiling of both users and conference events.

Data compression of XML-based ontological languages is another major problem tackled in our proposal. Gzip (along with its library version *zlib*) is perhaps the most popular universal compression tool. It is based on a variant of the LZ77 algorithm (Ziv & Lempel, 1977). Among general purpose compression algorithms and tools, the *PAQ* family (Mahoney, 2005) shows the best compression rates. It is based on two fundamental ideas which evolve upon classic Huffman encoding algorithm: *context mixing* and *arithmetic coding*. A major drawback of PAQ algorithms is their huge processing and memory requirements, which currently are far beyond the capabilities of mobile computing devices.

By exploiting structural peculiarities of XML, better compression rates can be achieved than most general purpose tools. *XMill* (Liefke & Suciu, 2000) is an efficient XML compressor. Its approach is based upon the separation of XML content into different *containers*, which are stored sequentially in the output file. Each container is compressed by a specialized module. XMill performances are better than generic compressors only for medium and large XML documents.

CONCLUSION AND FUTURE WORK

In this article, we proposed a fully unified framework integrating RFID technologies with enhanced Bluetooth SDP supporting formal semantics. Objects tagged with RFID transponders carry a semantically annotated description so permitting to implement an advanced object discovery. Thanks to the semantic-enhanced SDP in Bluetooth, it is possible to exploit reasoning services from everywhere in the marketplace also in case of the lack of dependable and stable network links. The proposed approach aims to avoid the need for stable Internet connections in order to make the framework really "mobile", as a Bluetooth infrastructure is deeply different from a fixed one in terms of resource consumption and required support, therefore more suitable for giving a *non-invasive* structure to fully decentralized volatile environments. This is a good feature in sight of a future work in the mobility direction aimed to make the reasoner resident on mobile devices. Some slight modifications to the EPCglobal standard have allowed to support ontology-based data as well as non-standard inference services, while keeping total compatibility with legacy applications. The framework includes a compression tool based on an efficient algorithm specifically aiming at size reduction of document instances expressed in various ontological languages. The complete framework has been implemented within a message-oriented commercial middleware in order to test the feasibility and the usability of the proposed solutions.

Current limits of the proposed approach and tool emerge because the time spent in performing the overall discovery and ranking procedure is still somewhat high to be definitively acceptable (even if it has to be traded off with a far higher quality of the discovery with regards to traditional approaches). Future work is aimed to an optimization of the reasoner features for a dedicated utilization in pervasive and ubiquitous applications.

A real-world, practical application of the proposed framework has to face concrete difficulties of the modification of a closed standard as the EPCglobal currently is, and furthermore exhaustive preliminary studies have to be performed in order to test the feasibility of the approach in case of multiple readings (in those cases the collision phenomenon must be taken into account, although it is not expected to be a real problem). Finally, privacy and security issues have to be faced in order to make the proposed approach ready for a real-world commercial exploitation.

REFERENCES

Alien Technology. (2005). *EPC global Class 1 Gen 2 RFID Specification*. Whitepaper. Morgan Hill, CA: Alien Technology Corporation.

Baader, F., Horrocks, I., & Sattler, U. (2003). Description logics as ontology languages for the semantic Web. *Lecture Notes in Artificial Intelligence*. Springer.

Bechhofer, S., Möller, R., & Crowther, P. (2003). The DIG description logic interface. *Proceedings of the 16th International Workshop on Description Logics (DL'03)*.

Ben Mokhtar, S., Kaul, A., Georgantas, N., & Issarny, V. (2006). Efficient semantic service discovery in pervasive computing environments. *Proceedings of the ACM/IFIP/USENIX 7th International Middleware Conference, Middleware '06*.

Berners-Lee, T., Hendler, J., & Lassila, O. (2001). The semantic Web. *Scientific American, 248*(4), 34-43.

Borgida, A. (1995). Description logics in data management. *IEEE Transactions on Knowledge and Data Engineering, 7*(5), 671-682.

Brachman, R., & Levesque, H. (1984). The tractability of subsumption in Frame-based description languages. *4th National Conference on Artificial Intelligence – AAAI-84* (pp. 34-37).

Chamberlain, J., Blanchard, C., Burlingame, S., Chandramohan, S., Forestier, E., Griffith, G, et al. (2006). *IBM WebSphere RFID handbook: A solution guide*, 1st ed. IBM International Technical Support Organization.

Colucci, S., Di Noia, T., Di Sciascio, E., Donini, F., Ragone, A., & Rizzi, R. (2006). A semantic-based fully visual application for matchmaking and query refinement in b2c e-marketplaces. *8th International conference on Electronic Commerce, ICEC 06* (pp. 174-184).

Cover, T., & Thomas, J. (1991). *Elements of information theory*. John Wiley and Sons Inc.

De, P., Basu, K., & Das, S. (2004). An ubiquitous architectural framework and protocol for object tracking using RFID tags. *The First Annual International Conference on Mobile and Ubiquitous Systems, Networking and Services, MOBIQUITOUS 2004* (pp. 174-182).

Di Noia, T., Di Sciascio, E., Donini, F., & Mongiello, M. (2004). A system for principled matchmaking in an electronic marketplace. *International Journal of Electronic Commerce, 8*(4), 9-37.

Donini, F., Lenzerini, M., Nardi, D., & Schaerf, A. (1996). Reasoning in description logics. In: G. Brewka (Ed.), *Principles of knowledge representation: Studies in logic, language and information* (pp. 191-236). CSLI Publications.

EPCglobal Inc. (2005a). *EPC Radio-Frequency Identity Protocols Class-1 Generation-2 UHF RFID Protocol for Communications at 860 MHz-960 MHz*. January 2005.

EPCglobal Inc. (2005b). *Object Naming Service (ONS - ver. 1.0)*. October 2005.

Haartsen, J., & Zürbes, S. (1999). *Bluetooth voice and data performance in 802.11 DS WLAN environment*. Ericsson Sig Publication.

Hamming, R. (1986). *Coding and information theory*. Prentice Hall.

Horrocks, I., van Harmelen, F., Patel-Schneider, P., Berners-Lee, T., Brickley, D. (2001). *DAML+OIL specifications*. Retrieved May 01, 2007 from http://www.daml.org/2001/03/daml+oil-index.html.

Huffman, D. (1952). A method for the construction of Minimum Redundancy Codes. *IRE*, 1098-1101.

Kawakita, Y., Wakayama, S., Hada, H., Nakamura, O., & Murai, J. (2004). Rendezvous enhancement for conference support system based on RFID. *International Symposium on Applications and the Internet Workshops, SAINT2004* (pp. 280-286).

Kawakita, Y., & Mistugi, J. (2006). Anti-collision performance of Gen2 Air Protocol in Random Error Communication Link. *International Symposium on Applications and the Internet Workshops, SAINTW'06* (pp. 68-71).

Liefke, H., & Suciu D. (2000). XMill: An efficient compressor for XML data. *SIGMOD Rec., 29*(2), 153-164.

Mahoney, M. (2005). *Adaptive weighing of context models for lossless data compression*. Florida Tech. Technical Report, CS-2005-16.

Martin, D., Burstein, M., Hobbs, J., Lassila, O., McDermott, D. (n.d.). *OWL-S: Semantic markup for Web services*. Retrieved May 01, 2007 from http://www.daml.org/services/owl-s/1.1/overview/.

McGuinness, D., Fikes, R., Hendler, J., & Stein, L. (2002). DAML+OIL: An ontology language for the semantic Web. *IEEE Intelligent Systems, 17*(5), 72-80.

Nethercote, N., & Seward J. (2007). Valgrind: A framework for heavyweight dynamic binary instrumentation. *Conference on Programming Language Design and Implementation - PLDI 07*. ACM SIGPLAN.

OSGi Alliance. (2005). *About the OSGi service platform* (rev. 4.1). San Ramon, CA: OSGi Alliance.

Ramakrishnan, K., & Deavours, D. (2006). Performance benchmarks for passive UHF RFID tags. *Proceedings of the 13th GI/ITG Conference on Measurement, Modeling, and Evaluation of Computer and Communication Systems*. Nurenberg, Germany.

Römer, K., Schoch, T., Mattern, F., & Dübendorfer, T. (2004). Smart identification frameworks for ubiquitous computing applications. *Wireless Networks, 10*(6), 689-700.

Ruta, M., Di Noia, T., Di Sciascio, E., & Donini, F. (2006a). Semantic-enhanced Bluetooth discovery protocol for M-Commerce applications. *International Journal of Web and Grid Services, 2*(4), 424-452.

Ruta, M., Di Noia, T., Di Sciascio, E., Donini, F., & Piscitelli, G. (2006b). Advanced resource discovery protocol for semantic-enabled M-commerce. *Encyclopaedia of Mobile Computing and Commerce (EMCC)*. Hershey, PA: Idea Group.

Schmidt, A., Gellersen, H., & Merz, C. (2000). Enabling implicit human computer interaction: A wearable RFID tag reader. *The 4th International Symposium on Wearable Computers* (pp. 193-194).

Siegemund, F., & Florkemeier, C. (2003). Interaction in pervasive computing settings using Bluetooth-enabled active tags and passive RFID technology together with mobile phones. *Proceedings of the 1st IEEE International Conference on Pervasive Computing and Communications, PerCom 2003* (pp. 378-387).

Shadbolt, N., Hall, W., & Berners-Lee, T. (2006). The semantic Web revisited. *IEEE Intelligent Systems, 21*(3), 96-101.

Traub, K., Allgair, G., Barthel, H., Bustein, L., Garrett, J., et al. (2005). *EPCglobal architecture framework*. Technical report, EPCglobal Inc., July 2005.

Zanella, A., Tonello, A., & Pupolin S. (2002). On the impact of fading and inter-piconet interference on Bluetooth performance. *The 5th International Symposium on Wireless Personal Multimedia Communications, 1*, 218-222.

Ziv, J., & Lempel, A. (1977). A universal algorithm for sequential data compression. *IEEE Transactions on Information Theory, 23*(3), 337-343.

ENDNOTES

[1]   *i.e.,* an ubiquitous environment where mobile peer users—both buyers and sellers—can submit their advertisements, browse through available ads and be assisted in finding the best available counterparts to meet their needs so beginning a commercial transaction.

[2]   http://sourceforge.net/projects/bluecove/

[3]   http://www.gzip.org/

[4]   http://www.isi.edu/nsnam/ns/

This work was previously published in International Journal on Semantic Web & Information Systems, Vol. 4, Issue 1, edited by A. Sheth, pp. 50-74, copyright 2008 by IGI Publishing (an imprint of IGI Global).

Chapter 6
In Defense of Ambiguity Redux

Patrick J. Hayes
Institute for Human and Machine Cognition, USA

Harry Halpin
School of Informatics, University of Edinburgh, UK

ABSTRACT

URIs, a universal identification scheme, are different from human names insofar as they can provide the ability to reliably access the thing identified. URIs also can function to reference a non-accessible thing in a similar manner to how names function in natural language. There are two distinctly different relationships between names and things: access and reference. To confuse the two relations leads to underlying problems with Web architecture. Reference is by nature ambiguous in any language. So any attempts by Web architecture to make reference completely unambiguous will fail on the Web. Despite popular belief otherwise, making further ontological distinctions often leads to more ambiguity, not less. Contrary to appeals to Kripke for some sort of eternal and unique identification, reference on the Web uses descriptions and therefore there is no unambiguous resolution of reference. On the Web, what is needed is not just a simple redirection, but a uniform and logically consistent manner of associating descriptions with URIs that can be done in a number of practical ways that should be made consistent.

THE IDENTITY CRISIS ON THE WEB

One might imagine that there would be no problems of identification on the Web. After all, the Web seems to be about identifying and accessing web pages. Yet the Web's ambition goes beyond normal hypertext systems content with accessing documents, for it wishes to use its identification system to identify objects that aren't even accessible via the Web. The ongoing problems and confusion that plague Web architecture follow from this goal. This is because there are two distinct relationships between names and things—reference and access.

The idea of a resource on the Web was from its outset universal: "A common feature of almost all the data models of past and proposed systems is something which can be mapped onto a concept of 'object' and some kind of name, address, or identi-

DOI: 10.4018/978-1-60566-992-2.ch006

Copyright © 2010, IGI Global. Copying or distributing in print or electronic forms without written permission of IGI Global is prohibited.

fier for that object. One can therefore define a set of name spaces in which these objects can be said to exist. In order to abstract the idea of a generic object, the web needs the concept of the universal set of objects, and of the universal set of names or addresses of objects" (Berners-Lee, 1994). The claim is that a URI can identify anything, not just a Web page. If the Web is to fulfill its ambition of being a universal information space, then the Web naturally has to stretch across to other information systems to objects one might want to access, like files through File Transfer Protocol or e-mail addresses through a *mailto:* URI scheme. These pose no philosophical problems as they are all streams of bits that happen to conform to different protocols.

Later, Berners-Lee and others attempted to define a *resource* as "anything that has identity" in RFC 2396 (1998). Even in this definition, a resource was defined as broader than just things that are accessible via the Web, since resources may be "electronic documents" and "images" but also "not all resources are network retrievable; e.g., human beings, corporations, and bound books in a library" (Berners-Lee et al., 1998). In the latest version, RFC 3986, the definition of resource is updated to state that "abstract concepts can be resources, such as the operators and operands of a mathematical equation, the types of a relationship (e.g., "parent" or "employee"), or numeric values (e.g., zero, one, and infinity)" (Berners-Lee et. al, 2005). So a resource is anything someone might want to identify with a URI, including things far outside the reach of the Web.

Most previous hypertext systems assumed that "resource" meant an accessible thing. This corresponds fairly accurately to the English meaning of resource, which is just a thing that can be used for support or help. Although Berners-Lee has always supported a wider role for URIs as "Universal Resource Identifiers," at first he could only get through IETF standards track a specification for "Uniform Resource Locators" that was for a "resource available via the Inter-

net" (Berners-Lee et al., 1994). When the idea became more prominent that things that were not accessible via the Web needed to be given some sort of Web name, a new scheme called Uniform Resource Names (URNs) was invented "to serve as persistent, location-independent, resource identifiers" (Moats, 1997). URNs do not have to access anything, although they could possibly, since unlike URLs they were centralized through a registry and through this registry had experimental resolution services (Mealling and Daniels, 1999). URNs are more like natural language names like "Eiffel Tower" rather than an address like "Tour Eiffel Champ de Mars 75007 Paris." With a name one can talk about the Eiffel Tower without actually having any idea how to get there, but with a location one can go up and bump a toe against the Eiffel Tower. A URN lets one refer to some thing, while a URL would let one access some bits on the Web. However, both URNs and URLs were subsumed under the single idea of a URI in RFC 3986, since a URL was just a URI that "in addition to identifying a resource" specifies a method "of locating the resource by describing its primary access mechanism (e.g., its network location)" while URNs are just another URI scheme, albeit a centralized one without an agreed-upon access mechanism (Berners-Lee et al., 2005).

The end result of this saga of URNs and URLs merging into URIs is that on the Web there is a single universal identification scheme for both identifying accessible and non-accessible resources. In this regard the Web is radically different from previous identification schemes. In programming languages, an identifier translates into the identity of some block of memory, even if there is no code that runs at that location. In other hypertext systems, one assumed that the unique identifiers were allowing links between accessible documents or some sort of file. Yet on the Web one can have a URI for the "Eiffel Tower in itself," such as http://www.example. dingansich.org/EiffelTower. This brings up a new type of problem for users, for if they access that URI, how do they know it identifies the Eiffel Tower itself and not just a Web page about the Eiffel Tower? Assuming it is useful to identify non-accessible things on the Web using URIs, should we distinguish between these two types of things and if so, how? Should a URI for "The Eiffel Tower itself" bear some special marking that makes it different from a URI that lets one access Web pages about the Eiffel Tower?

REFERENCE AND ACCESS

There are two distinct relationships between names and things: reference and access. The architecture of the Web determines access, but has no direct influence on reference. Identifiers like URIs can be considered types of names. It is important to distinguish these two possible different relationships between a name and a thing.

1. *accesses,* meaning that the name provides a causal pathway to the thing, perhaps mediated by the Web.
2. *refers to*, meaning that the name is being used to mention the thing.

Current practice in Web Architecture uses "identifies" to mean both or either of these, apparently in the belief that they are synonyms. They are not, and to think of them as being the same is to be profoundly confused. For example, when uttering the name "Eiffel Tower" one does not in anyway get magically transported to the Eiffel Tower. One can talk about it, have beliefs, plan a trip there, and otherwise have intentions about the Eiffel Tower, but the name has no causal path to the Eiffel Tower itself. In contrast, the URI http://www.tour-eiffel.fr/ offers us access to a group of Web pages via an HTTP-compliant agent. A great deal of the muddle Web architecture finds itself in can be directly traced to this confusion between access and reference.

If one understands "access" as inclusively as possible, it includes uses of a URI to access a Web site, that is, an HTTP endpoint that produces a "representation" (in the REST sense) of a resource such as a Web page, a file, a mailbox, a webcam, a Coke machine connected to the Internet in Australia, and so on endlessly: anything at all that can receive, send or be directly influenced by, or indeed itself be, any piece of information that can be transferred by a transfer protocol, either now or in the foreseeable future. Cast this net as broadly as you like, the accessible things will always be an extremely small subset of the set of all things that can be referred to. Even in the possible world where every single thing that we normally consider a physical item was somehow given a URI and attached via some sort of chip that allowed the thing to send a byte back and forth across the Web, there would still be imaginary things and things in the future or past, and this class would be larger than the class of accessible things. Moreover, although one can of course refer to accessible things, most acts of reference will be to things that are not accessible, because most of the world's business is concerned with things other than the architecture of the Web, like the weather in Oaxaca. Most of the things in the world do not have a URI and are not accessible over the Web. Reference is not a secondary phenomenon, but a primary one.

Reference has to do with the semantics of language; *access* has to do with network architecture. Successful reference is part of a communicative act between cognitive agents capable of using language. Successful access requires neither cognition nor linguistic communication; it is a purely causal interaction, not necessarily informational. Access is mediated by transmission over a network, and uses energy. The act of reference and its referent do not have a physical relationship at the time of use of a name. Although reference is built on top of robustly physical acts like uttering a name and some sort of neural processing, the cone of reference far outstrips local physical causation. One can use a very physical mouth and lips to communicate about a distant referent by uttering words such as "The Eiffel Tower is in France" when one is in Boston.

Reference is grounded in our physical orientation towards the world. However, it is still not scientifically or even philosophically understood how reference is established and communicated. In the classical analysis of Russell, reference can be established by acquaintance or by description (1911). A theory where a name directly refers to its referent is called a "direct theory of reference." Russell states that "patches of sense-data" known through "direct acquaintance" allow one to ground the use of a name by attaching it to the physical world through the use of demonstratives. This grounding can be signaled by pointing or the use of demonstratives in natural language, such as when one approaches the Eiffel Tower, points at it and says "That is the Eiffel Tower." According to Russell, a person has then identified the Eiffel Tower with that particular patch of sense-data, and so has directly "named" the Eiffel Tower. After that, the person can refer to the Eiffel Tower even if they are no longer in direct physical contact with it.

In contrast, description is inherently ambiguous. If a person is trying to identify the Eiffel Tower to a friend, then the person may attempt to communicate their thought about the Eiffel Tower by uttering a description such as "the monument in Paris." Yet even the friend may think they are talking about the Arc de Triomphe without further information. If the person tries to give more descriptions, such as "the steel tower," then the hearer might think of the Eiffel Tower, but there are no guarantees. The hearer may also think of the steel dome of Galeries Lafayette. Even if the person said, "the structure made by Gustave Eiffel," the hearer may think of a lesser-known structure like La Ruche. One can imagine that with enough descriptions a person could uniquely pick out the referent for the hearer. Even with an infinite amount of descriptions this may be impossible,

since it involves the large presumption that the hearer shares our same ontology of things in the world. The hearer may simply have no conception that the Eiffel Tower even exists, and so may be unable to grasp the referent regardless of the number of descriptions given. Surprisingly, adding more descriptions may even make the referent more ambiguous.

Reference by acquaintance can be done only to accessible entities. How can anyone directly refer to things they are not acquainted with, such as imaginary or historical objects? Many possible referents one may wish to refer to, one is not acquainted with by the constraints of life. One may simply not be able to afford a plane ticket to visit the Eiffel Tower, or it may not be possible to live long enough to visit a distant galaxy or survive visiting the edge of a black hole. References to non-accessible entities must be by description, and hence must be ambiguous.

Since URIs are used to refer to things, and reference is ambiguous, there is a problem with the slogan "a URI identifies one thing." For the Semantic Web to work, URIs will have to refer to things by description, so a URI can not universally and unambiguously identify one thing. Or can it? Kripke's "causal theory of naming" states that at least some proper names may be unambiguous (1980). This is precisely the account appealed to by some members of the W3C Technical Architecture Group such as Dan Connolly (2006). Kripke claims that proper names have the same referent regardless of description and in every possible world. Gustave Eiffel is not equivalent to the "architect of the Eiffel Tower" because he would still be Gustave Eiffel even in the possible world where he did not create the Eiffel Tower. To briefly outline Kripke's theory, a historical causal chain between a current user of the proper name and past users allows the referent of a name to be transmitted unambiguously through time. The meaning of any sentence can then supposedly be dependent in an unambiguous manner on the referents of the names used in the sentence.

The historical chain is established by a name being given its original referent through a process Kripke calls "baptism." *Baptism* is a combination of direct acquaintance with the referent and the action of naming the referent. Baptism is often quite literal. Gustave Eiffel got his name via an actual baptism.

Kripke's account of unambiguous names can then be transposed to the Web with a few minor variations (1980). In this story, a URI is like a proper name and baptism is given by the registration of the domain name, which gives a legally binding owner to a URI. The referent of a URI is established by fiat by the owner, and then can be communicated to others in a causal chain in the form of publishing documents at the URI (or a redirection thereof) or by creating Semantic Web data about the URI. In this manner, the owner of the URI can thereby determine the meaning of the URI. So, if one got a URI like http://www.example.dingansich.org/EiffelTower and one wanted to know what the URI referred to, one could use a service such as *whois* to look up the owner of the URI, and then simply call them and ask them what the URI referred to.

So Kripke leaves us an important insight, that naming is a social act, although Kripke himself would be unlikely to endorse this view. Even Kripke himself says "a name refers to an object if there exists a chain of communication, stretching back to baptism, at each stage of which there was a successful intention to preserve reference" (1980), and communication is a social phenomenon. Yet baptizing then cannot function purely causally, since the naming convention requires communication between more than one person. The only way an act of naming could be purely causal would be if every person using the name had some form of direct acquaintance with the referent. The chain between the act of naming and the use of the name depends on reference. Ambiguities and errors can happen. For example, Gareth Evans pointed out that African natives may have used the word "Madagascar" to refer to the African mainland but when Marco Polo heard it, he thought it referred to an island off of Africa. What should be clear is that the ambiguity remains. The notion of success is undefined, but it is clear that the chain is not just one of causation, but communication and so subject to ambiguity since communication is often due to description.

The social nature of naming applies to URIs on the Web as much as it does to proper names in natural language. The use of domain name registration to "own" a URI is just a social act with a technical infrastructure that happens to support it. It is possible to argue that the domain name system somehow builds the referents of URIs into the social contract implicit in buying a top-level domain name, so that if one is using the Web, then one is in effect part of a name-using community. Under this assumption, if a user were given the URI http://www.example.dingansich.org/EiffelTower then the user would be part of the community of the Web and the user is then forced to buy into the owner's claim that the URI refers to the Eiffel Tower. This argument is trivially not true on the Web. The owner cannot communicate via telepathy what the URI refers to. In a decentralized system such as the Web, a user of the URI can usually tell what a URI is supposed to refer to by accessing Web pages through the URI, and Web pages are another form of description for things and so subject to ambiguity. Even if the owner of the URI somehow "knows" what the URI is supposed to refer to, the referent of the URI cannot be communicated unambiguously, for the owner must communicate the referent using descriptions in either natural language or Web pages. The owner of the URI has even further problems, for most of the things they will want to refer to they cannot know through direct acquaintance, and so their own understanding is ambiguous. Practically, many people use URIs where they do not own the top-level domain, and so most people do not "control" what their URI refers to on the domain-name level.

Interestingly, the use of URIs as referring mechanisms reveals a fatal flaw in assuming that any naming convention is universal. One reason that examples used in declaring that naming is unambiguous use famous names like "Cicero" or "Gustave Eiffel" is because the reader of the example is already in the naming-using community of that particular name. For names of not well-known people like "Kavita Thomas" or URIs like http://www.example.dingansich.org/EiffelTower the famous name convention does not hold, and so it becomes evident that a universal naming convention cannot be assumed. Furthermore, for people there is a clear and legal process of baptism. For things like the "Eiffel Tower" or "the integers" it becomes much harder to find a clear baptism. Any naming convention must be established, not assumed.

REFERENCE IS INHERENTLY AMBIGUOUS

Access is dependent on architecture. It is precisely by providing a space of names for access that Web architecture is useful. In order to be useful, access should be unambiguous. In contrast, reference to natural entities is inherently ambiguous. In this manner, reference on the Web is the same as reference off the Web. This is simply obvious. The Web is a transport mechanism for (what are in the REST sense) representations such as web pages. What a representation represents, and how the names in it refer, has nothing particularly to do with how the representations are transported. In the words of Korzybsky, "the map is not the territory" (1931). Web architecture does not determine what any names, including URIs, refer to. It only determines what they access.

The relationship between access and reference is essentially arbitrary; it is ours to decide and cannot be decided by Web architecture. Since most of the things referred to by names are not accessible, references to them can only be determined by description, perhaps based on other preexisting naming conventions. If a URI is intended to refer to Gustave Eiffel, this reference cannot be established by acquaintance, since Gustave Eiffel isn't accessible today. It has to be done by description and descriptions can never pin down a referent exactly. There will always be some slack, some possible doubt about what exactly is being referred to. As said before, reference by description is inherently ambiguous. This claim may seem to fly in the face of common sense, for it seems clear that language does use names successfully to refer. What we need is a criterion for what "success" in communicating what a name refers to could be.

A name refers successfully when a use of the name is sufficient to communicate a thought about the referent during an act of communication. The actual processes which constitute having a thought about a referent in human communication are mysterious. The best formal account we have, which also applies to the Semantic Web, says that this is a process of inference. The same considerations apply whether the agents involved are humans speaking English or Web agents drawing conclusions in OWL. It is difficult, perhaps impossible, to make enough inferences so as to be sure that what the recipient understands a name to refer to is exactly the same thing as what the sender had in mind since communication using referring names is always hostage to slips of reference. A formal version of this claim is based on Gödel's theorem: as long as the language used for communication is sufficient to express arithmetic, it will have "nonstandard" models. The point is made better informally by looking at normal human communication. Take the most direct and unambiguous kind of name, a famous proper name of a public entity such as "Paris." This might refer to the central part of greater Paris defined by the arrondissements or to the larger metropolitan area. It might refer to the state of the city now, or it might refer to the entire history of the city. In the right context, it can be used to refer to the inhabitants of Paris, the buildings in Paris, the customs of Paris, and so forth. Another example: "Everest." How much does Everest weigh? Where are its edges? In most instances it appears that communication can be successful without the details of precisely what referent is being referred to being resolved.

We have left unanswered the question how successful reference is achieved using names. The problem with any direct theory of reference lies precisely in the assumption that reference must be resolved for reference to be meaningful. There is an alternative to both the direct theory of reference and the causal theory of naming that allows for ambiguous names to have meaning and be used successfully while maintaining the ambiguity of reference. The key idea lies in the observation made by Frege that the meaning of any term, including names, is determined by what Frege calls the "sense" of the sentences that use the term (1892). According to Frege, two sentences could be the same only if they shared the same *sense*. His example uses the two statements "Hesperus is the Evening Star" and "Phosphorus is the Morning Star." To the ancient Greeks these two sentences have different senses even if they had the same referent, the planet Venus, since the ancient Greeks did not know that the referent was the same, for they did not know that "Hesperus is Phosphorus" (Frege, 1892).

Previously we have presupposed that the meaning of a name is determined by whatever thing the name refers to. The meaning of sentence "Dan Connolly works for the World Wide Web Consortium" would be determined by first figuring out what person "Dan Connolly" refers to, and then figuring out what organization the "World Wide Web Consortium" refers to. Only after calculating the referents of the names can one build up a meaning of the sentence, which would then theoretically be precise and unambiguous. We have to be careful precisely because the word "meaning" is one of the most ambiguous, confusing, and debated terms in the English language. From here on out, it would be better to think of

the "meaning" of a name to be defined by the "meaning" of sentences that use the name (Luntley, 1999). So in contrast to our previous example, the meaning of the sentence "Dan Connolly works for the World Wide Web Consortium" determines the meaning of "Dan Connolly" and "the World Wide Web Consortium." After someone utters that sentence, we can reasonably believe that "Dan Connolly" in that sentence is not the same "Dan Connolly" that plays football for the New England Patriots. If we hear enough sentences about "Dan Connolly" we can get a better sense of what "Dan Connolly" means. The meaning of the name "Dan Connolly" is not determined by the meaning of a single sentence or set of descriptions, but the normative use of all the sentences in the language that bear upon "Dan Connolly." Assuming that the meaning of a sentence is determined by simply identifying the referents of the terms gets the picture backwards. The possible referents of a name are always ambiguous, but are defined as much as they need to be by the use of the name in sentences. Names simply make no sense by themselves. We don't even need to be directly acquainted with something to give it a name. We can just use the name in sentences, and the meaning is created by the name-using community that shares those sentences. We can also understand "sentences" to mean not just natural language sentences but also Semantic Web statements and the non-linguistic dimensions of communication. Uttering "Dan Connolly!" in exasperation after a discussion means something different from yelling his name while trying to get his attention in a busy airport. What determines the meaning of sentences is the "sense" of the sentences, which is constructed from the patterns of use of sentences in a language and the behavior those sentences engender. This includes the inferences one can draw from a sentence.

The wrong picture of meaning on the Semantic Web would be that of a giant decentralized dictionary that listed a URI and its referent. Since a URI can refer to non-accessible things, we cannot have the complete list of URIs and their referents. The URI http://www.example.dingansich.org/ EiffelTower can not give us the Eiffel Tower itself. A URI could be given a "definition" in natural language like the English words "The Eiffel Tower." However, looking up a URI and getting natural language terms or sentences is just not too much help if one was translating a language one does not already know, such as "the language of a hitherto untouched people" or a hitherto unused form of computing language like the Semantic Web (Quine, 1960). How does one know if the URI would reference only the monument itself or copies of the monument like the one in Paris, Texas? So the translator can never "really" know unambiguously what the term means. This is Quine's radical indeterminacy of translation, and it defeats any attempt to think of a language as a simple dictionary (1960).

How would we really know what a URI meant? One plausible solution to this problem is to employ the argument of "radical interpretation" from Davidson (1973). Davidson constructs his notion of radical interpretation as a semantic version of Quine's argument of radical translation. Davidson notes that radical translation "deals with the wrong topic, the relation between two languages, where what is wanted is an interpretation of one" (1973). Unlike a dictionary theory of meaning, which is merely the translation of representations (syntactic languages) from one to another, the construction of the meaning of those representations (a meta-theory) is what in turn lets a translation be possible. Some of the construction of this meta-theory, which should take the form of the ability to assign Tarski-style truth conditions to statements, can rely on the grammar of language. "Dan Connolly works for the World Wide Web Consortium and lives in Kansas" can be explained by analysis of the connective "and" and the two sub-sentences. However, at some point we bottom out in sentences that have meaning by themselves even if the referents of each term therein is ambiguous. The main point again is that it is impossible for

a single name by itself to mean anything except in its relationship to other names and its use in sentences. So, the meaning does not lie purely in the terms, but in the language itself, where a language consists of both the rules of grammatical construction, which can be formalized, and the meaning of sentences. The only way to learn a language is to be competent in it, to participate in its usage, and to assume other speakers share a rational point of view on the world. In order to have radical interpretation of the language of a visiting alien we must assign "truth conditions to alien sentences that make native speakers right when plausibly possible, according, of course, to our own view of the right. What justifies the procedure is the fact that disagreement and agreement alike are intelligible only against a background of massive agreement" (Davidson, 1973).

The social aspect of naming means accepting a background of massive agreement when understanding names and sentences and accepting the norms of the community in using those names and sentences. If someone said "Dan Connolly thinks that data types in XML should be context independent," one assumes that this is the same Dan Connolly that works at the World Wide Web Consortium. If someone said, "Dan Connolly is Spiderman," one might assume that the background assumptions that you and that speaker share are radically different. When you use a language successfully we can usually assume other people share agreement without relying on the impossible task of unambiguously connecting names to referents. The question is: How much background agreement is necessary for success?

Ordinary discourse is full of ambiguities which are rarely noted because they have no practical importance, but which are rendered vivid by trying to agree about "common sense" well enough to write it down in a formal notation. One example is a disagreement about whether or not a fitted carpet was "in" an office or "part of" the office. Two competent, intelligent adult native speakers of English each discovered, to their mutual amazement, that the other would believe what they thought was an obviously false claim. Over an hour of discussion it gradually emerged, by a process of induction from many examples, that they understood the meaning of "office" differently. For one it meant, roughly, an inhabitable place; for the other, something like a volume of space defined by the architectural walls. These two people never knew, until this event, that they had different mental meanings for "office" and more generally, for "room." Presumably this was possible because they had never previously engaged in a communicative act in which their conceptual differences made any difference to the communication. Their success notwithstanding, each of them had, in fact, been understanding the English word "office" differently. In this example, "office" is ambiguous, and this can equally apply to other words in natural language. No doubt the same logic can be applied to any language on the Web that uses reference.

Saying more can make reference by description even more ambiguous. Adding richer formal ontologies to a notion does not reduce ambiguity of reference, but increases it by providing for finer ontological distinctions. If all one wants to say about persons is that they have mailboxes and friends, then one can treat "person" as a simple category. Even when a stable situation of mutual reference has been reached it can be upset by the addition of new vocabulary. If one wishes to include persons in a comprehensive upper-level ontology, then more arcane questions about personhood and how it relates to existence must be answered. Suppose two agents agree that "Tim Berners-Lee" refers to a particular person. Still, they might have divergent notions of what it means to be a person. Such divergences are already found in "standard" ontologies. For example, DOLCE requires a high-level distinction to be made between continuants and occurrents, and a person would naturally be classed as a continuant; but other ontologies reject this contrast and subsume all temporal entities under one heading (Gangemi

et al., 2002). So are all names of persons rendered ambiguous by the presence of this high-level ontological divergence of opinion, so that we have to distinguish Tim Berners-Lee the continuant from Tim Berners-Lee the four dimensional history? For formal purposes, the difference is important, and indeed confusion between these concepts can produce immediate logical contradictions, such as inferring that Berners-Lee is both 52 years old and 7 years old. This error can arise because Berners-Lee was once seven years old, and a continuant retains its identity through time. Do we need Tim Berners-Lee Lite? Do we really want to require all reasoners to agree on the most abstract of philosophical distinctions in order to have successful inference? Many reasoners are simply not concerned with this distinction.

One disturbing result of this is that we may need different versions of the concept of a "person." This question is not just a question of technically determining what the proper ontological description of a "person" is. If one wants to reason about people's lifestyles, travel plans, medical histories and legal rights, then one is obliged to distinguish finer categories of personhood that in turn rely on social and legal constructions with many infamously difficult and even contested distinctions. The more one is able to say and is obliged to reason about, the more possible distinctions there are to be made. As the knowledge increases in scope, the more possibilities arise for making distinctions that were formerly impossible.

What makes this kind of consideration particularly acute is the view that URIs should be global and eternal in scope. This makes things worse. It means that if there is any possibility of some such ontological distinction being made by anyone, anywhere, at any time, then in order to avoid ambiguity of reference, the URI must make all the potentially disambiguating decisions ahead of time. This is of course manifestly impossible, because there is always the possibility of some new distinction being made later. It is impossible to achieve unambiguous universal reference of names by using descriptions. So we should not set out to attempt unambiguous reference, nor pose it as a goal or a "good practice."

IF AMBIGUITY IS INEVITABLE, LET'S MAKE LEMONADE

Since reference by description is inherently ambiguous, it might be better to set out to utilize the inevitable rather than try to minimize it. The "Identity Crisis" is said to result from phenomena of using the same URI to refer to Tim Berners-Lee and his Web site, the Eiffel Tower and a picture of the Eiffel Tower, the weather and the weather report. These are all examples of *overloading*, using a single name to refer to multiple referents. Overloading isn't always as bad as it is rumored to be, since it is a way of using names efficiently. Natural language is rife with lexical ambiguity which does not hinder normal communication, as the multiple meanings of even common words like "rose" and "bank" show. Even programming languages routinely do it, as for example many programming languages use "+" to mean both integer and real addition. Using overloading does not violate any principle of formal semantics, as Common Logic allows a single name to denote an individual, a function and a relation (Delugach, 2007). In general, overloading is harmless when it is possible to figure out from the information available at the time which of the various referents is intended by that particular use of the name. Often this is easy when the referents are in different ontological categories, as with a person and a web page. On a social networking site to befriend a Web page is odd, but not to befriend a "person." One way to think about overloading is that an overloaded term denotes a single "complex thing" which has all the usual referents as parts or facets, selected by implicit selectors. This often works surprisingly well. The syntax of logic is enough to select the appropriate referent in the Common Logic formal semantics when a single name could

be used to refer to an individual, a function, or a relation. For people and Web sites it seems to work, for usually Berners-Lee is not affected by an attempt to HTTP GET him instead of his Web site, and his Web site isn't going to spend his salary. The normal infrastructures of interaction with people and Web sites are sufficiently robust to disambiguate this kind of overloading when they need to be disambiguated by humans.

As pointed out by Connolly, there can be problems in inference due to ambiguity (2006). While there is not room to go through the details of his example here, we will reconstruct a similar example. Imagine an ontology where one defines Web pages and people to be disjoint. However, because of the decentralized nature of the Web, a person can use the URI that accesses their Web page to make statements about themselves using an ontology for people. Let's assume that Dan Connolly has two URIs. The first http://www.w3.org/People/Connolly/ accesses his Web page. The second http://www.example.org/Dan_Connolly# refers to Dan Connolly as a person. Dan Connolly then carefully makes statements about his Web page like "http://www.w3.org/People/Connolly/ was created in 1994." He also makes statements about himself, like "http://www.example.org/Dan_Connolly# works for the W3C." However, because the Web is a decentralized system and there is no way to tell what http://www.example.org/Dan_Connolly# refers to, someone makes a statement on the Web like "http://www.w3.org/People/Connolly/ lives in Kansas." Since earlier it was defined that Web pages and people are disjoint, and "lives" is a predicate that applies to living people and not Web pages, we get a contradiction when we run an OWL reasoner. While humans can sort out this ambiguity of reference machines cannot. However, is this is a problem for inference? It actually isn't a problem with inference per se, it's a problem with stating ahead of time two things are disjoint, a sort of sneaky use of the Law of the Excluded Middle on the Web. However, assuming one wants to keep that sort of statement possible in Web languages like OWL, then one could claim that the problem is some person is stating incorrectly and implicitly that http://www.w3.org/People/Connolly/ is a person instead of a Web page. Yet what if Dan Connolly himself attempted to state that http://www.w3.org/People/Connolly/ lives in Kansas? Who could stop him?

A Web site accessible from a URI could allow the owner to describe how they want their URI to be used. This would be using the one advantage the Web has over previous languages, the ability to access representations via URIs. One can reconsider the issue of radical interpretation. Given a URI, how can one tell what the owner thinks the URI is supposed to refer to? The answer of Davidson is to look at its systematic and normative use in the entire language, including Web languages like Web pages and Semantic Web statements (1973). Of course one is only going to observe a small portion of its use, so ambiguity remains. One way the owner of the URI can help clarify the situation is by making representations for both humans and machines accessible from the URI itself. If the user of the URI gets these representations that are accessible from the URI itself, they may have a better idea of how the owner of the URI at least intends their URI to be used. If the owner intends the URI to be used for reference to a non-accessible thing, the same URI can be used for both reference to a non-accessible things and hosting accessible representations about the non-accessible thing. Yet in order to communicate about a non-accessible thing, the fundamental confusion between reference and access returns.

The Technical Architecture Group (TAG) of the W3C took on the "identity crisis," calling it the *httpRange-14* problem. They phrased it as the question "What is the range of the HTTP dereference function?" In their solution, they define a class of resources on the Web called "information resources," which they specify as a resource "whose essential characteristics can be conveyed in a message." (Jacobs and Walsh, 2004). This definition is unclear at best. While a Web page is clearly an information resource, is the text of Moby Dick an information resource? Is the World Wide Web Consortium itself an information resource? Yet what the term "information resource" seems to be groping towards is that some things are accessible on the Web and others are not. It would be better for things that are accessible on the Web to be called by a term like "Web resources." It is possible that the term "information resource" was chosen to define something that in some possible world could be accessible on the Web. "The text of Moby Dick" could be an information resource, because even if the complete text of Moby Dick isn't on the Web, one day it might be. However, a "particular collector's edition of Moby Dick" could not be, since after all, the part that is collectible isn't the text, but the physical book itself. The actual hackers and webmasters on the streets need a term like "Web resource" that they can use to mean something like "accessible via the Web" (such as by being an HTTP end point) without arguing metaphysics about the "essential nature" of Moby Dick every time they want to add a URI to the Semantic Web.

Despite their invention of new terminology, the TAG's solution has two desiderata, both of which are respectable. Even if overloading is harmless most of the time, there should be some mechanism that is able to distinguish between the use of a URI to access a thing and the intended use of a URI to refer to a non-accessible thing. Furthermore, even for URIs that are intended to refer to non-accessible things, there should be a way to access descriptions to help users of the URI make sense of the resource. What the TAG resolves is less than ideal. In the case of a non-information resource, a non-accessible thing that is referred to using a URI, an agent should not get any sort of representation without a redirection to another URI resource. This disambiguation is done through the "303 See Other" HTTP header.

So the official resolution to "Identity Crisis" is given in terms of HTTP response headers:

1. If an HTTP resource responds to a GET request with a 2xx response, then the resource identified by that URI is an information resource;
2. If an HTTP resource responds to a GET request with a 303 (See Other) response, then the resource identified by that URI could be any resource;
3. If an HTTP resource responds to a GET request with a 4xx (error) response, then the nature of the resource is unknown.

To give an example, let's say our user is trying to access a URI that is "supposed to" refer to the Eiffel Tower like http://www.example.dingansich.org/EiffelTower. Upon attempting to access that resource with an *HTTP* GET request, since the Eiffel Tower itself can not be an HTTP endpoint, one should not host any representations there. Instead, the user gets a 303 response code that says "See Other" that in turn redirects them to another URI that hosts Web pages about the Eiffel Tower such as our trustworthy http://www.tour-eiffel.fr/. When this URI returns the 200 status code in response to an HTTP GET request, we know that http://www.tour-eiffel.fr/ is actually an "information resource." The URI used to refer, http://www.example.dingansich.org/EiffelTower, could be any kind of resource. That is, we know what we did before the 303 redirection, namely that http://www.tour-eiffel.fr/ can be used to access a web page. The agent knows nothing about the original URI, http://www.example.dingansich.org/EiffelTower. So this method fails actually to deliver on any sort of distinction between those things that are information resources and those that aren't. The reason that the use of the 303 status code cannot possibly tell us that the resource redirected from was used for referring, arises because the 303 status code was specified as "See Other" before

the "Identity Crisis" was even noticed. There is no reason why it can't be used to simply to redirect from one "information resource" to another "information resource."

In practice, web architecture does not determine what any names, including URIs, refer to. It only determines what they access. The relationship of reference is determined by the users of the URI. The use of 303 redirection seems to presume that if a URI accesses something directly (not through an HTTP redirect) then the URI must refer to what it accesses. This presumes, wrongly, that the distinction between access and reference is based on the distinction between accessible and inaccessible referents. There is no law of the universe that prevents a URI that accesses one referent, such as "http://www.amazon.com," from also being used to refer to a particular company in everyday speech. It places the responsibility for deciding the relationship between referring and accessing at the wrong end of the communication channel, that of the person who hosts representations accessible at the URI, not the user of the URI. While everyone could do precisely what the TAG recommends by using 303 redirection, there is no architectural way to enforce this doctrine, so instead people will do what is convenient and works in practice, and 303 redirection is far from convenient.

Pragmatically, there are problems with the TAG's suggested redirection. It uses a distinction in how a text is delivered (an HTTP code) to disambiguate the accessible Web page itself; a category mistake analogous to requiring the postman dance a jig when delivering an official letter. Since the vast majority of names, even on the Web, refer to things which are not accessible, this requires referring URIs to perform a act of redirection with doubtful benefit. As shown earlier, since the URI bears no trace of its delivery to the majority of human Web users that do not monitor or understand HTTP status codes, no disambiguation is achieved for the human. The TAG is correct in noticing this solution could solve the problem of inference brought up by Connolly (2006), but it does so in such a manner that not only makes normally harmless overloading illegal but that does not even make the distinction between access and reference clear. The particular solution requires the use of an arcane redirection technique that most people actually hosting URIs are not familiar with and cannot even deploy, since deploying 303 redirection requires access to the web server many users may not have. It also produces harmful effects by misusing HTTP codes for an alien purpose. The particular code, 303, is only valid for HTTP 1.1 and was originally introduced to solve a completely different problem. As put by the specification, "this method exists primarily to allow the output of a POST-activated script to redirect the user agent to a selected resource," not to distinguish access and reference (Fielding et al., 1999). The 303 status code was invented due to the over-use of the HTTP 1.0 302 status code to redirect both temporarily and permanently. The 307 and 303 status codes in HTTP 1.1 could disambiguate between the two cases of redirection, with the 303 status code having future requests to that URI being automatically redirected by the browser unlike the 307 status code, which is only a "temporary" redirection. Given this history, it is unclear why 303 is suitable for distinguishing between access and reference. Why not just invent a new HTTP status code? Of course, forcing agents to implement a new HTTP status code also has a high cost, so perhaps it is better to re-use an older code, albeit using it somewhat strangely.

The main alternative to using HTTP 303 is to have a fragment identifier—the hash—attached to a URI to get redirection for free. So, if one wanted a URI that referred to the Eiffel Tower itself without the hassle of a 303 redirection, one would use the URI http://www.tour-eiffel.fr/# to refer to the Eiffel Tower and the URI http://www.tour-eiffel.fr/ to access a Web page about the Eiffel Tower. Since browsers think the "#" at the end

of the URI means a fragment of a document or some other representation, if a user tries to access via HTTP GET a "hash URI" it will not return a "404 Not Found" status code, but instead simply resolve to the URI before the hash. In this way machine reasoners can keep the URI that refers to the Eiffel Tower and a Web page about the Eiffel Tower separate, while a human can access the URI "about" the Eiffel Tower and receive some information about it, in essence by taking advantage of some predefined behavior in web browsers. This solution would solve the inference problem where monuments and Web pages are defined in OWL as disjoint. This is valid because according to the W3C TAG's "Architecture of the Web," using a fragment identifier technically also identifies a separate and distinct "secondary resource" (Jacobs and Walsh, 2004). Further, the TAG states that "primary and secondary simply indicate that there is a relationship between the resources for the purposes of one URI: the URI with a fragment identifier. Any resource can be identified as a secondary resource" (Jacobs and Walsh, 2004). Yet using hash URIs has the exact same problem as 303 redirection, since it doesn't normatively define any sort of relationship between the two URIs, much less distinguish between access and reference.

It appears that the W3C may very well be contradicting the relevant IETF specification by supporting hash URIs. The URI specification says "the semantics of a fragment identifier are defined by the set of representations that might result from a retrieval action on the primary resource. The fragment's format and resolution is therefore dependent on the media type of a potentially retrieved representation, even though such a retrieval is only performed if the URI is dereferenced" (Berners-Lee et al., 2005). If the media type explicitly defines what fragment identifiers do, then the user should obey the standard of the media type. Only "if no such representation exists, then the semantics of the fragment are considered unknown and are effectively unconstrained" (Berners-Lee et al., 2005). In other words, only if you get a 404 from http://www.tour-eiffel.fr/ can http://www.tour-eiffel.fr/# mean anything you want. However, if a Web page with the "text/html" media type is returned by accessing the primary (no hash) URI, then according to the HTML specification, "for documents labeled as text/html, the fragment identifier designates the correspondingly named element; any element may be named with the *id* attribute" (Connolly, 2000). In other words, fragment identifiers should be used for named elements in the document, not as a shortcut for distinguishing URIs used for reference and access. This defeats the entire purpose of using hash URIs, since the supposed benefit is that a human can "follow-their-nose" by accessing the primary URI and thereby access some human readable HTML about the URI. In the case where the "application/rdf+xml" media type is returned by the accessible URI, things are different. "In RDF, the thing identified by a URI with fragment identifier does not necessarily bear any particular relationship to the thing identified by the URI alone" so the hash convention can legitimately identify anything, including non-accessible resources (Schwartz, 2004). This seems to defeat the point of returning representations, since unlike rendered HTML, RDF/XML is much more easily used by machines than humans. If people accessed http://www.tour-eiffel.fr/ and received RDF/XML most would have no idea what to do with it. It is most useful for machine processing, not informing humans.

Strangely enough, the very idea that a media type determines the semantics of the fragment identifier is in conflict with other statements from the W3C. Even if one accepted the "URI identifies one thing" slogan, by using content negotiation, if both the "application/rdf+xml" and "text/html" media types were available for a URI, then the meaning of the URI with fragment identifier would be interpreted two different ways depending on

the media type received, and so the URI would not identify a single resource with a global scope. This fundamentally breaks the orthogonality of the specifications, as a single resource can return different kinds of representations, so how a "hash URI" can be used is dependent on media types. The URI specification explicitly says one should not do this, for "whatever is identified by the fragment should be consistent across all those representations" (Berners-Lee et al., 2005). One could imagine the hash somehow being consistent across representations, but if the fragment identifier exists in a RDF document *and* in the HTML document, the meaning of the fragment identifier will be muddled since it will identify both a portion of a document in HTML and possibly some non-Web accessible thing. In cases where the fragment identifier exists in RDF and not in HTML, it will be a broken fragment identifier for an HTML document and perhaps specified by the RDF, and so inconsistent. If the fragment identifier is non-existent in both the RDF and HTML documents, in RDF the fragment identifier can identify a non-Web accessible resource but not so in the HTML document, where it will just be a broken fragment identifier for a particular document. Regardless, there needs to be a mechanism in HTML for saying that either the given use of a fragment identifier is for non-Web accessible things or that fragment identifiers that are not given by the HTML representation can be anything, including non-Web accessible things. So, this use of fragment identifiers to identify non Web-accessible things, while convenient and much more practical than 303 redirection, is as far from "a URI identifies one thing" as one can get. One can assume that at some point the W3C will fix the relevant specifications to be more inline with their proposed solutions, but the hash URI is no panacea for distinguishing access and reference. While easier for users to deploy than 303 redirection, it still does not distinguish access and reference any better than 303 redirection.

DISTINGUISHING BETWEEN REFERENCE AND ACCESS ON THE WEB

We should first examine our presumptions. Using the same URI to refer to the Eiffel Tower and to access a Web site about the Eiffel Tower isn't even an example of overloading. It only becomes that if we assume that the name which accesses the Web site therefore also refers to the Web site. Why do we make this assumption? It would be possible to lose the assumption that access means reference on the Web. One could state that URIs only refer to accessible things just when the accessible thing is actually assigned that name; and assigning a name is done only by an explicit naming convention, the Web equivalent of pointing to the thing and giving it a name. There are two ways to attach a name to a thing: by being it or by naming a URI that accesses it. The two kinds of naming convention this makes possible are similar, respectively, to wearing a name badge and to having someone point at you and say, "I will call you Spiderman." Unlike reference by description, this kind of naming can be unambiguous under certain conditions. In particular, that the naming convention should be shared and the accessible entity itself has the naming convention attached. In that case, assigning the name to an accessible entity inside the entity itself makes the name "permanent" and global in scope. Named graphs fulfill this, as do properties in the header of HTML document, and both are under the control of the owner of the document. However, we are still dodging the fundamental question, since the class of referable things far outweighs the class of accessible things, and these things may need to be distinguished, we need some actual mechanism for assigning referents to names. Right now there aren't any, because access isn't the same thing as reference.

The solution would be just to have some sort of statement that explicitly stated a URI was being used for reference and associated descriptions with that URI. This "naming convention" needs to unambiguous, easily deployed, and allow access to representations. In theory, the solution can be solved on a number of levels by allowing the URI, in the HTTP header status codes, or in the representation itself. The basic naming convention could be a RDF predicate called *ex:refersTo* whose subject was the URI that had accessible descriptions of the thing and whose object was the URI being used as a referring name for a thing. The natural inverse would be an RDF predicate *ex:describedBy* whose subject would be a URI used as a name for a thing and whose object would be the URI that had accessible descriptions. It seems intuitively obvious the subject of *ex:refersTo* and the object of *ex:describedBy* should be Web-accessible resources like Web pages, what the TAG might call "information resources." It is not clear if the reverse should apply. Should the object of *ex:refersTo* and subject of *ex:describedBy* be non-Web-accessible things, or what the TAG might call "non-information resources?" While at first this may seem to be the right choice, it would be a premature slicing of the Web into two classes of things. After all, there is nothing to prevent a URI for a Web page from being used as a referring term, or for a Web page to be described by another Web page. In other words, in order to allow flexibility of reference, the object of *ex:refersTo* and the subject of *ex:describedBy* should be anything, whether that thing is Web-accessible or not. The question then might return about how we specify that a referent is non-accessible. The obvious solution is to create a class, *ex:nonAccessible*, for non-Web-accessible things. This class can then be applied as needed to particular objects of *ex:refersTo* and particular subjects of *ex:describedBy*.

Interestingly enough, the definition of these predicates would be weaker than *owl:sameAs* but more powerful than *rdfs:seeAlso,* The proposed *ex:refersTo* and *ex:describedBy* are somewhat similar to *foaf:topic* and *foaf:page,* respectively. The obvious advantage of having an explicit RDF predicate is that distinguishing between access and reference would almost always be a distinction only made on the Semantic Web, so RDF is a much more natural technology than HTTP response headers for making the distinction. Furthermore, this sort of RDF predicate can then be easily embedded in HTML documents using techniques such as RDFa and GRDDL. This allows accessible representations such as Web pages to say what "thing" they describe if the "thing" they refer to happens to have a separate URI without violating any existing specifications. Unlike both the hash URIs and 303 redirection, this resource specifies precisely when a URI is used for access and when a URI is used for reference. Further, since there is no reason to define these classes as disjoint, it will not cause any ad hoc problems in inference but will merely enrich the results.

So, we can now outline how we would in a disciplined manner solve our problem about distinguishing referring to the Eiffel Tower and accessing a Web page with representations of the Eiffel Tower. First, this distinction would be necessary if one was building a directory of tourist attraction Web sites. Since there are multiple Web sites about the Eiffel Tower, one could connect them by having in RDF that all of these Web sites refer to the same tourist attraction, so there is a concrete need to both refer to the Eiffel Tower itself and to refer to the Web page(s) about the Eiffel Tower. This distinction could even be clarified in an ontology that classifies Web pages and monuments as disjoint. In the tourist directory, the Web sites would be grouped by URIs about particular attractions, such as the Eiffel Tower. One mints http://www.example.tourism.org/EiffelTower/# to refer to the Eiffel Tower. At http://www.example.tourism.org/EiffelTower would be hosted a RDF/XML document that contained the statement "http://www.example.tourism.org/EiffelTower#*ex:describedBy*http://www.tour-eiffel.fr/." This single statement allows the Semantic Web to distinguish reference and access in a manner at least unambiguous to RDF.

Furthermore, by hosting an RDF/XML document at http://www.example.tourism.org/EiffelTower/ we keep the semantics of the fragment identifier of http://www.example.tourism.org/EiffelTower# unconstrained. We can then ask for "back-link" from the various Eiffel Tower–describing Web sites, which then using RDFa can embed their inverse statement, for example: "http://www.tour-eiffel.fr*ex:refersTo*http://www.example.tourism.org/EiffelTower#."

One argument against this solution is that people may not have access to the representation itself. There is no reason why something semantically identical with *ex:describedBy* cannot be using other formats. For example, one could imagine the use of a "link" element in the header of a HTML document to specify *ex:refersTo*. One could also use a revived "Link" HTTP header, as was included in an earlier version of HTTP, IETF RFC 2068 (Fielding et al., 1997). but was left out of the latest version, IETF RC 2616 (Fielding et al., 1999). So reintroducing the "Link" header would not be adding anything new to HTTP, merely using a neglected feature. The main issue with the "Link" header is that it would lack the semantics to distinguish reference and access. In other words, it's just a link from one resource to another, and makes no statement about whether one resource is accessible or not. The use of a "Link" header could be given proper semantics if it could be used in combination with a profile header or link relations that allowed the type of the "link" to be specified as either for reference or access. The URI for reference and access used in the profile header could be as simple as reusing URIs from the RDF as the profile value or link relation such as *ex:refersTo* and *ex:describedBy*. If we are beginning to edit specifications, one could also dictate that a URI ending in just a fragment identifier indicates that the URI should be used for reference regardless of the media type, thus legalizing the use of hash URIs for reference in RDF. After all, in HTML it's a reference to a point in the HTML document! There are cases where accessing and actually editing a representation for adding in the proper RDF statement could be difficult, and so the use of a combination of a "Link" header and link relations with URIs could be crucial.

Imagine the organization in charge of http://www.tour-eiffel.fr/ may not want to disturb their delicate HTML by inserting RDFa statements inside of it. Perhaps their Web page is made by a Web designer who specializes in graphics. However, they have been swayed by their technical engineer that making their Web page part of the Semantic Web would make their site be more useful and popular. The tourist attraction directory is having difficulty attracting visitors, since the visitors cannot make heads or tails of the RDF/XML documents accessible from http://www.example.tourism.org/EiffelTower/. Assuming a world where "Link" and URIs with link relations are now valid parts of HTTP, we can fix this problem without altering any representation. We can have a HTML Web page accessible from http://www.example.tourism.org/EiffelTower/ by having the "Link" header use the URI http://www.example.tourism.org/EiffelTower/index.html, which is just a human-readable Web page, and by using http://www.example.org/describedBy in the link relation. Then a human user could be redirected to the human-readable Web page via a 303 redirection and it would be possible for them to know why they are being redirected there. Likewise, the webmaster of the Eiffel Tower site can then have a link to the Semantic Web URI by using the "Link" header to specify http://www.example.tourism.org/EiffelTower/# and then specifying its semantics by: the use of the http://www.example.org/refersTo as the link relation. In this way, no HTML has to be changed but the links are still there. A machine could follow this links to discover more information while keeping the URIs for access and reference distinct, while a human could always get a human-readable version. It is interesting that after the initial version of this paper was brought out, the W3C POWDER Recommendation is

now deploying a *wdrs:describedBy* relationship. Furthermore, the proposed IRW (Identity, Reference, and the Web) ontology separates out *irw:accesses* and *irw:refersTo* relationships and models many of the distinctions explored here (Halpin and Presutti, 2009).

Regardless of the details, the use of any technology in Web architecture to distinguish between access and reference, including our proposed *ex:refersTo* and *ex:describedBy*, does nothing more than allow the author of a URI to explain how they would like the URI to be used. Ultimately, there is nothing that Web architecture can do to prevent a URI from being used to refer to some thing non-accessible. However, at least having a clear and coherent device, such as a few RDF predicates, would allow the distinction to be made so the author could give guidance on what they believe best practice for their URI would be. This would vastly improve the situation from where it is today, where this distinction is impossible. The philosophical case for the distinction between reference and access is clear. The main advantage of Web architecture is that there is now a *de facto* universal identification scheme for accessing networked resources. With the Semantic Web, we can now extend this scheme to the wide world outside the Web by use of reference. By keeping the distinction between reference and access clear, the lemons of ambiguity can be turned into lemonade. Reference is inherently ambiguous, and ambiguity is not an error of communication, but fundamental to the success of communication both on and off the Web.

AMBIGUITY REDUX WITH LINKED DATA

When the issues of access versus reference were first raised, they seemed to be a mere academic argument about the philosophy of Web architecture (Halpin et al., 2006). Today we can now tell that these issues are not merely academic, but have serious consequences for the real-world deployment of the Semantic Web. This is exemplified by the rise of **Linked Data**, the use of Web architecture to deploy the Semantic Web (Bizer et al., 2007). In particular, with the explosion of Linked Data, there are now claims of billions of URIs for real world non-Web accessible entities being out there. Before the advent of Linked Data, our work came to the conclusion that there was nothing special about knowledge representation *per se* that would somehow guarantee the success of the Semantic Web, so that the success of the Semantic Web would require taking advantage of Web architecture. This is precisely what Linked Data does: Linked Data requires the separation of URIs for Web-accessible resources and URIs for things not accessible from the Web. Furthermore, a URI for a non-Web accessible thing like the Eiffel Tower connects to these "associated descriptions" via the use of the 303 redirection (Bizer et al., 2007). Furthermore, Linked Data uses content negotiation to determine whether machine-usable RDF or human-readable HTML is returned, and these two kinds of associated descriptions are given different URIs. So, for one non-Web accessible thing like Paris you get three separate URIs on Linked Data: http://dbpedia.org/resource/Paris for the non-information resource, http://dbpedia.org/data/Paris for the RDF description, and http://dbpedia.org/page/Paris for the human-readable HTML. To some extent, this is a vindication of earlier viewpoint that access and reference are separable. Thus in Linked Data, ambiguity is in theory reduced, and separate URIs for access and reference are given, with the various pitfalls around media-types avoided. Despite the complexity of using 303 redirection and content negotiation, Linked Data appears to be a success.

Currently, the problem is a sheer overload of Linked Data URIs – there are simply too many URIs for what appears to be "one thing" such as the Eiffel Tower. Most of Linked Data consists of exports from already existing sources, usually relational databases or non-RDF web sources.

Therefore, each identifier in the already existing source is kept and given a new URI form. For example, http://www.dbpedia.org/resource/Paris is given as as the export of the identifier for Paris in DBPedia, an RDF export of Wikipedia (Auer et al. 2007). This URI is given via *owl:sameAs* as the same as http://sws.geonames.org/2988507/, the URI of of an RDF export of the location of Paris from Geonames, since both URIs identify the "same thing." However, the *owl:sameAs* predicate is not an innocent term with no consequence, but it has consequences for inference. In particular, it would mean that since, in description logic terms, the two URIs identify the same individual, then all inferences and descriptions that apply to one individual apply to the other individual. This is usually not what is implied by those that apply the *owl:sameAs* predicate. Is Paris really identified by the precise latitude and longitude given by geonames? Again, we return to the questions posed earlier: Does the Geonames URI include in its definition of Paris the arrondissements or to the larger metropolitan area? Linking the Geonames URI with DBPedia might be viewed as problematic, as the Wikipedia article refers not just to the state of the city now, but the entire history of the city, including such ephemeral aspects of Paris such as the inhabitants of Paris, the buildings in Paris, the customs of Paris, and the like. Do we *really* want to say that this broad view of Paris is logically the same as its latitude and longitude? Other W3C specifications like SKOS (Simple Knowledge Organization System) have put forward new predicates like *skos:exactMatch,* which would seem like a more suitable version of *owl:sameAs* but without any logical repercussions, but to no avail. Therefore, many have viewed the proliferation of the use of *owl:sameAs* to interlink data-sets as a massive collective error, a danger that must be corrected. After all, with the use of *owl:sameAs*, ambiguity is leaking irreversibly into the actual Semantic Web.

There have been two notable attempts to solve this issue. The first practical system to heroically tackle this issue is, the *Consistent Reference Service* that automatically finds *owl:sameAs* statements and inverse functional properties and then calculates their closure (Glaser et al., 2008). Implemented in *RKBExplorer.com* over bibliographic data and WordNet, their consistent reference service stores the result of the closure in its own as RDF using its own Semantic Web co-reference vocabulary. These co-reference closures are given their own URI and their own associated descriptions in RDF leading to an explosion of new URIs. So, with the Consistent Reference Service each URI now has a double for any co-referenced URI. None of associated descriptions of each co-referential URI are checked for consistency, much less validity. While a useful service for determining what other URIs have been declared to be about the same thing, it does not solve the problem of determining co-reference but merely points out when some user somewhere thinks two URIs are co-referential. Furthermore, without the necessary provenance, it is unclear by what criteria that these two URIs are determined to refer to the same thing.

A more ambitious attempt is the OKKAM project, which is directly inspired by the exposition of Kripke and Berners-Lee given in an earlier version of this exposition, OKKAM takes its name from the famous principle of OKKAM's razor, rephrasing the famous maxim to "entity identifiers should not be multiplied beyond necessity" (Bouquet, 2007). The first point that we made earlier that OKKAM project took on board was that there is more likelihood to be substantial agreement on concrete entities than on higher-level abstractions. From this valid point, OKKAM attempts to build a system that maintains an index of URIs, called OKKAM IDs for every conceivable *entity*, where an entity is taken to be some concrete 'thing' such as "electronic documents to bound books, from people to cars, from conferences to unicorns" as opposed to a more 'abstract concept' such as ``predicates, relations, assertions" (Bouquet, 2007). Roughly speaking, the distinction is equivalent to the distinction in description

logics between entities as individuals in an *ABox* and concepts in a *TBox* in description logics. Furthermore, as a consequence of their endorsement of Kripke's causal theory of names, OKKAM lets the only information accessible via these URIs to be non-logical: collections of pictures, text from other web-pages which mentions the same referent, and the like. OKKAM stores "untyped data for the reason that typing an entity's attributes would require us to classify the entity" because any logical description could lead to disagreement and thus harm re-use of the URIs (Bouquet, 2007). While the future is still unwritten for the OKKAM project, it seems by forcibly denying themselves the use of descriptions in RDF due to the fear of ambiguity, OKKAM may be limiting the utility of OKKAM IDs. Linked Data, despite its ambiguous and controversial descriptions and often controversial use of *owl:sameAs*, is taking off.

If anything, the success of Linked Data has demonstrated some minimal agreement on conventions for deploying data using URIs was necessary. Indeed, while it may seem that the use of content negotiation and the 303 HTTP status code is to some extent as inconsequential as having the postman dance a jig before delivering a letter, it appears that this jig so far has been a popular hit. However, the real question should be: Has Linked Data, by deploying separate URIs for the thing described and the associated descriptions somehow dispelled ambiguity from the Web? Of course not, and the very controversy around the epidemic use of *owl:sameAs* shows that ambiguity is still rife on the Linked Data. Indeed, the problem is *not* ambiguity on the level of URIs. The use of *owl:sameAs,* far from being a bug, is a feature. If anything, Linked Data will profit more from the use of techniques from artificial intelligence and machine-learning that take advantage of massive statistics to determine when two things are more or less close enough to be the same.

The elimination of ambiguity is often falsely viewed as some sort of ideal goal, such that somehow creating knowledge representations in terms of logic like RDF, OWL, or even first-order predicate logic would somehow magically dispel ambiguity. This is simply untrue: far from eliminating ambiguity, formal logic is just one well-understood model that takes ambiguity into account. There are always *multiple* interpretations that satisfy the model-theoretic semantics of a knowledge representation language, and it is in this way that logic does justice to the ambiguity inherent in our descriptions of the world. The model-theoretic semantics of RDF are fairly unconstrained, and even when constrained by inference, ranging from the relatively simplistic inferential capabilities of RDF(S) to OWL to full first-order predicate logic, it is impossible to constrain logically almost any network of formal statements to a *single* interpretation, although inferences can eliminate *some* interpretations. To believe that somehow logic can magically banish ambiguity so a name can refer to a single thing is a misunderstanding of logic. Although the Web may require new and different kinds of logic, it is far more likely that these will be new kinds of logic that are even more tolerant of inconsistency, decentralization, and ambiguity. Representations can only be models of reality. Even the most expressive logic or the most elaborate knowledge representation can only be a partial account of the actual world. It is the great strength of logical theory that it faces up to this inescapable limitation of our models, and replaces the illusion of certainty with a defense of ambiguity.

REFERENCES

Auer, S., Bizer, C., Lehmann, J., Kobilarov, G., Cyganiak, R., & Ives, Z. (2007). DBpedia: A nucleus for a web of open data. In *Proceedings of the International and Asian Semantic Web Conference (ISWC/ASWC2007)* (pp. 718–728). Busan, Korea.

Berners-Lee. Fielding, R., & McCahill, M. (1994). *IETF RFC (Obsolete) 1738 Uniform Resource Locators (URL)*. http://www.ietf.org/rfc/rfc1738.txt.

Berners-Lee, T. (1994). *IETF RFC (Informational) 1630 Universal Resource Identifier (URI)*. http://www.ietf.org/rfc/rfc1630.txt.

Berners-Lee, T., Fielding, R., & Masinter, L. (1998). *IETF RFC (Obsolete) 2396 Uniform Resource Identifier (URI): Generic Syntax*. http://www.ietf.org/rfc/rfc2396.txt.

Berners-Lee, T., Fielding, R., & Masinter, L. (2005). *IETF RFC 3986 Uniform Resource Identifier (URI): Generic Syntax*. http://www.ietf.org/rfc/rfc3986.txt.

Bizer, C., Cygniak, R., & Heath, T. (2007). *How to Publish Linked Data on the Web*. http://www4.wiwiss.fu-berlin.de/bizer/pub/LinkedDataTutorial/

Bouquet, P., Stoermer, H., & Giacomuzzi, D. (2007). OKKAM: Enabling a Web of Entities. In *Proceedings of I3: Identity, Identifiers, Identification. Proceedings of the WWW2007 Workshop on Entity-Centric Approaches to Information and Knowledge Management on the Web*, Banff, Canada, May 8, 2007., CEUR Workshop Proceedings.

Connolly, D. (2000). *IETF RFC (Informational) 2854 The 'text/html' Media Type*. http://www.ietf.org/rfc/rfc2854.txt.

Connolly, D. (2006). A Pragmatic Theory of Reference for the Web. Proceedings of the Identity, Reference, and the Web (IRW2006) Workshop at the World Wide Web Conference (WWW2006). Edinburgh, United Kingdom. May 22nd 2006.

Davidson, D. (1973). Radical Interpretation. *Dialectica, 27*, 314–328. doi:10.1111/j.1746-8361.1973.tb00623.x

Delugach, H. (2007). *Common Logic (CL): a framework for a family of logic-based languages. ISO/IEC 24707.* http://www.iso.org/iso/iso_catalogue/catalogue_tc/catalogue_detail.htm?csnumber=39175

Fielding, R., Gettys, J., Mogul, J., Frystyk, H., & Berners-Lee, T. (1997). *IETF RFC 2068 - Hypertext Transfer Protocol – HTTP/1.1.* http://www.ietf.org/rfc/rfc2068.txt.

Fielding, R., Gettys, J., Mogul, J., Frystyk, H., Masinter, L., Leach, P., & Berners-Lee, T. (1999). *IETF RFC 2616 - Hypertext Transfer Protocol – HTTP/1.1.* http://www.ietf.org/rfc/rfc2616.txt.

Frege, G. (1892). Uber sinn und bedeutung. Zeitshrift fur Philosophie and philosophie. *Kritic, 100,* 25–50.

Gangemi, A., Guarino, N., Masolo, C., Oltramari, A., & Schneider, L. (2002). Sweetening Ontologies with DOLCE. In *Proceedings of International Conference on Knowledge Engineering and Knowledge Management. Ontologies and the Semantic Web.* Siguenza, Spain. 1-4 October 2002 (pp. 166-181). London: Springer-Verlag.

Glaser, H., Millard, I., & Jaffri, A. (2008). RKBExplorer.com: A knowledge driven infrastructure for Linked Data providers. In *Proceedings of European Semantic Web Conference (ESWC),* Tenerife, Spain. (pp. 797–801).

Halpin, H., Hayes, P., & Thompson, H. S. (Eds.). (2006). *Proceedings of the WWW2006 Workshop on Identity, Reference, and the Web,* Edinburgh, United Kingdom, May 23, 2008, CEUR Workshop Proceedings. http://www.ibiblio.org/hhalpin/irw2006.

Halpin, H., & Presutti, V. (2009). An Ontology of Resources: Solving the Identity Crisis. In *Proceedings of European Semantic Web Conference (ESWC),* Heraklion, Greece (pp. 521-534).

Hayes, P., & Halpin, H. (2008). In defense of ambiguity. *International Journal on Semantic Web and Information Systems, 4*(3), 1–18.

Jacobs, I., & Walsh, N. (2004). *Architecture of the World Wide Web. W3C Recommendation.* http://www.w3.org/TR/webarch/.

Korzybski, A. (1931). A Non-Aristotelian System and Its Necessity for Rigour in Mathematics. In *Proceedings of the American Mathematical Society.* New Orleans, Louisiana. December 28 1931 (pp. 747-761). Providence, RI: American Mathematical Society.

Kripke, S. (1980). *Naming and Necessity.* Cambridge, MA: Harvard University Press.

Luntley, M. (1999). *Contemporary Philosophy of Thought.* Oxford, UK: Blackwell.

Mealling, M., & Daniel, R. (1999). *IETF RFC (Experimental) 2483 URI Resolution Services Necessary for URN Resolution.* http://www.ietf.org/rfc/rfc2483.txt.

Moats, R. (1997). *IETF RFC (Proposed) 2141 Uniform Resource Names.* http://www.ietf.org/rfc/rfc2141.txt.

Quine, W. (1960). *Word and Object.* Cambridge, MA: MIT Press.

Russell, B. (1911). Knowledge by acquaintance, knowledge by description. In . *Proceedings of the Aristotelian Society, 11,* 197–218.

Schwatrz, A. (2004). IETF RFC 3870 application/rdf+xml Media Type Registration. http://www.ietf.org/rfc/rfc3870.txt

Chapter 7
Identity of Resources and Entities on the Web

Valentina Presutti
ISTC National Research Council (CNR), Italy

Aldo Gangemi
ISTC National Research Council (CNR), Italy

ABSTRACT

One of the main strengths of the Web is that it allows any party of its global community to share information with any other party. This goal has been achieved by making use of a unique and uniform mechanism of identification, the uniform resource identifiers (URI). Although URIs succeed when used for retrieving resources on the Web, their suitability for identifying any kind of thing, for example, resources that are not on the Web, is not guaranteed. In this article we investigate the meaning of the identity of a Web resource, and how the current situation, as well as existing and possible future improvements, can be modeled and implemented on the Web. In particular, we propose an ontology, IRE, that provides a formal way to model both the problem and the solution spaces. IRE describes the concept of resource from the viewpoint of the Web, by reusing an ontology of information objects, built on top of DOLCE+ and its extensions. In particular, we formalize the concept of Web resource, as distinguished from the concept of a generic entity, and how those and other concepts are related, for example, by different proxy for relations. Based on the analysis formalized in IRE, we propose a formal pattern for modeling and comparing different solutions to the problems of the identity of resources.

Copyright © 2010, IGI Global, distributing in print or electronic forms without written permission of IGI Global is prohibited.

INTRODUCTION

The Web is an information space realized by computationally accessible resources, each embedding some information, which is encoded in some language, and expresses some meaning. One of the successful achievements of the Web is allowing different parties of its global communities to share information (Jacobs & Walsh, 2004). Typically, typing an address in a Web browser is enough to visualize or download an object, the meaning of which can be then understood by a human agent. The Web address is a uniform resource identifier, a URI (Berners-Lee, Fielding, & Masinter, 2005). The URI mechanism is key to the Web success. However, another ambitious goal of the Web is that of referencing *things* in general. For example, consider the World Wide Web Consortium (W3C)'s URI http://www.w3.org: it should be possible to distinguish (on the Web) the reference to the organization from that to its Web site.

The simple association of a URI to a thing or real world entity is very powerful. On one hand, it has already demonstrated its effectiveness with regard to the identification of objects that are accessible through the Web, for example, Web pages. On the other hand, there is no complete consensus on how to manage identification of things that are not on the Web. Reducing the ambiguity of identifying the entities a Web resource refers to is essential for information sharing, interoperability, and reasoning on the Web (Berners-Lee et al., 2006). In order to propose solutions to this issue, it is crucial to analyze and properly describe the problem space.

The problem space can be expressed in terms of the impact that identification of (generalized) resources has on the Web. In this article we analyze the state of art related to this problem, and from this analysis we show how five distinct issues emerge. We propose that in order to describe these issues and to compare the respective solutions, we need to analyze the reason why a URI can be associated with an entity. We carry out this analysis based on an ontology called *identity of resources and entities on the Web (IRE)*.

IRE focuses on four main classes: *URI, Web resource, information object*, and *entity*, which encompass the things in the domain of discourse of the Web referencing problem.

Once the problem domain has been analyzed, the solution domain can be approached. We discuss how the current evolution of Web science from the confluence of the Web, the Web 2.0, and the Semantic Web has affected the solution domain. We also consider some proposed and envisaged solutions, and discuss them in terms of IRE.

The rest of the article is organized into sections as follows: "history" tells a story about the existing literature on the problem of identifying a Web resource. "Issues in the problem space" discusses how the problem of resource identification impacts on the Web. "The IRE Metamodel" informally presents the IRE ontology. We then deal with the "solution space," and we also present an extension of IRE in order to represent it. "Conclusion and remarks" summarizes the main arguments presented. Finally, the appendix contains a first-order logic formalization of IRE. The OWL version of IRE can be downloaded from http://wiki.loacnr.it/index.php/LoaWiki:IRE.

HISTORY

The identification of resources is an important task to use them on the Web (Berners-Lee et al., 2006). Currently, there is a diffuse feeling that resource identification procedures suffer from a lack of consensus about how to handle them. This lack of consensus partially finds its root from normative documents where the concept "resource" has been defined in the context of the Web. However there are also other motivations underlying the identification problem, which we discuss in this article.

The term "resource" is generally used for all things that might be identified by a URI (Jacobs et al., 2004). In the literature, we find several definitions for the term "resource" used in the context of world wide Web. In particular we quote here three normative documents, IETF RFC 2396 (Berners-Lee et al., 1998), IETF RFC 3986 (Berners-Lee et al., 2005), the W3C's "Architecture of the World Wide Web" (Jacobs et al., 2004)1 and discuss the way and consequences of the definition they provide for "resource." In IETF RFC 2396 the concept of resource is defined as follows (Berners-Lee et al., 1998):

A resource can be anything that has identity. Familiar examples include an electronic document, an image, a service (e.g., "today's weather report for Los Angeles"), and a collection of other resources. Not all resources are network retrievable: human beings, corporations, and bound books in a library can also be considered resources. The resource is the conceptual mapping to an entity or set of entities, not necessarily the entity that corresponds to that mapping at any particular instance in time. Thus a resource can remain constant even when its content—the entities to which it currently corresponds—changes over time, provided that the conceptual mapping is not changed in the process.

The following definition of "resource" is given by IETF RFC 3986 (Berners-Lee et al., 2005), which updates IETF RFC 2396:

This specification does not limit the scope of what might be a resource; rather, the term "resource" is used in a general sense for whatever might be identified by a URI. Familiar examples include an electronic document, an image, a source of information with a consistent purpose (e.g., "today's weather report for Los Angeles"), a service (e.g., an HTTP-to-SMS gateway), and a collection of other resources. A resource is not necessarily accessible via the Internet; for example, human

beings, corporations, and bound books in a library can also be resources. Likewise, abstract concepts can be resources, such as the operators and operands of a mathematical equation, the types of a relationship (e.g., "parent" or "employee"), or numeric values (e.g., zero, one, and infinity).

In W3C's "Architecture of the World Wide Web" the concept of resource is used with a twofold meaning: either whatever might be identified by a URI, or anything that can be the subject of a discourse, such as cars, people, etc (Jacobs et al., 2004). Furthermore, the concept of *information resource* is defined as a resource whose essential characteristics can be conveyed in a message. The W3C also defines the principle of *opacity* of a URI, which promotes the independence between an identifier and the state of the identified resource (Jacobs et al., 2004).[2]

Given that, at least four (possibly conflicting) interpretations of the term "resource" can be singled out:

- **Computational object:** A resource can be a computational object, an electronic document for example (Berners-Lee et al., 2005). In this context we define "computational object" as both (i) the physical realization of an information object and (ii) something that can participate in a computational process. Examples of computational objects are a database, a digital document, and a software application. The identity of a computational object is not reducible to a region in an abstract space, because a computational object is a physical entity and is the support for a certain information object, while abstract spaces are not physical, and do not have temporal or spatial properties. Information objects are not regions in an abstract space either, because they can change while remaining the same object, whereas abstract objects have no lifecycle. As a practical consequence, in the context of the Web, either computational or information objects cannot be regions in an abstract space if that space should be uniquely identifiable through URIs. For example, the personal home page of Aldo Gangemi is a document that exists on the Web, and is reachable through the dereferencing of its URI, but it does continue to exist also if it changes its location or if the server it is stored in goes offline.

- **Conceptual mapping:** If a resource is intended as a "conceptual mapping" (Berners-Lee et al., 1998). then its identity cannot be also intended as a "computational object." As a conceptual mapping, a resource can be characterized as a location in the abstract space of the combinatorial regions that are identified by the URIs. Consequently, the identity of a resource in this sense is equivalent to a localization in that space. As a matter of fact, without that space, it would not exist, and its URI is sufficient to identify it unambiguously.

- **Proxy:** Considering the principle of *opacity* (Jacobs et al., 2004), the sense of a resource can be that of a "proxy," which is a localized in a region of the abstract space identified by the URI. In this case, the resource is actually intended as a computational object, and its identity is given by the set of elements composing the proxy. For example, an English text, a picture, a metadata schema, would be a proxy. According to this meaning of "resource," its identity goes beyond its location. A resource does exist beyond its location, and its identity holds over its presence on the Web.

- **Entity:** The definition of "resource" as an entity, being either a computational object or not, is problematic because the relationship that holds between a resource and a URI would be the same for addressing computational objects as well as non-computational physical or abstract objects.

However, besides these interpretations, the identity of entities referenced on the Web is de facto implemented as the location at which a resource is placed. This implicit assumption is very confusing when we want to use a URI to reference entities that are not Web resources. In other words, there is a need for an explicit distinction between the identity of entities, the reference of a resource, and its identifier. For example, the http://www.w3.org URI has its own identity as an identifier (a string), the Web location it is associated to has its own identity as an abstract place, the Web document has its own identity as a computational object (a file), and the subject of the document has its own identity (the W3C organization as a social object). Now, a question like the following can arise: when used in a resource, does the URI "http://www.w3.org" turn up identifying the Web document that is placed at that Web location, or the W3C organization?

There have been many proposals suggesting different approaches to the aim of addressing the issue. A brief summary of some significant ones is presented here.

Alistar Miles describes his perception of the problem by identifying a possible obstacle: the creation of a same URI for representing different concepts (2005). This has also been named *URI collision* (Jacobs & Walsh, 2004). Miles proposes an interesting low-level approach as a best practice, that of using HTTP URIs to address entities that are not accessible on the Web. He proposes to manage the problem at the server side by means of a negotiation on how to resolve the URI. For example, if one creates the URI http://foo.com/me to describe himself or herself, then it could be resolved by the server as the URI http://foo.com/me.html or http://foo.com/me.xml or other, depending on a sort of configuration of the browser.

Pepper expresses a similar difficulty about the use of URIs for identifying all kinds of entities (Pepper & Schwab, 2003). In particular, he proposes to associate a resource to a document, whose content describes the subject of the resource (i.e., a subject indicator) (Pepper, 2006). Nevertheless, this solution leaves the responsibility of interpreting the identity of a resource to a human agent, and there is no way to ensure that the subject indicator refers to a single subject.

Clark discusses the "tidiness" of Web specifications, and the importance to clarify the conceptual assumptions upon which the Web is built, and the semantic Web is being built (2002).

Booth proposes an informal categorization of what can be identified by a URI, suggesting the definition of different conventions for each of the many uses he has identified (2003).

Black suggests to create a sort of machine-oriented Wikipedia, in order to create stable URIs and share knowledge through the construction of Web sites such as http://del.icio.us (2006).

Parsia and Patel-Schneider formally analyze the issue of defining meaning in the semantic Web (2006). They propose to determine the meaning of a document as the result of an entailment. In this sense, "only documents explicitly mentioned in constructs like the OWL importing mechanism contribute to the meaning of that document" (Parsia et al., 2006).

Bouquet, Stoermer, Mancioppi, and Giacomuzzi propose to build a system, "OkkaM," to implement a catalog of URIs that reference arbitrary entities in a "one-to-one" manner (2006). Those URIs should be reused as much as possible, supported by tools, and advised as a good practice to refer to entities.

Another good suggestion comes from Pat Hayes who underlines the difference between *access* and *reference* (2006). Both are relationships between names and things, but they are inherently different and the fact that W3C does not distinguish between the two contributes to cause confusion (Jacobs et al., 2004).

Recently, in the context of a W3C working group, an effort on how to embed RDF triples in HTML has produced a working draft with a proposal for a syntax, RDFa, for typing html links (Adida & Birbeck, 2006).

All the previous proposals are important contributions to solve the "identity" problem. However, none of them provides a comprehensive analysis of the aspects involved in the "identification of resources" problem domain, and how they impact on the Web. What is more, no proposal contains a formal semantic model that describes a common ground to situate solutions at either the syntactic or operational levels. Our goal is to cover this lack while doing justice to the existing solutions that have been devised for the Web identity problem.

ISSUES IN THE PROBLEM SPACE

The story we have told shows that the problem of Web resource identification has been approached from different perspectives. In this section we want to answer the following question: what issues and needs are involved in the identification of resources? How do they impact on Web science? From a critical analysis of the state of the art previously presented, and the preliminary distinctions drawn between URIs, Web resources, and entities, at least five different issues emerge:

1. **Web semantics:** How to clarify the semantics of the Web: what are its basic notions, and how can we formalize them (Gangemi & Presutti, 2006)?

2. **Sense of referencing:** How to clarify what it is meant by *referencing things* (Hayes, 2006)?

3. **Multiplicity of referencing:** How to clarify whether (or when) a reference to something is unique or multiple? This is related to the so-called *uniqueness* principle (Kent, Ahmed, Albert, Ketabchi, & Shan, 1992) Another aspect is whether only one identifier is admitted for the reference, which is

Figure 1. The URI-entity relation

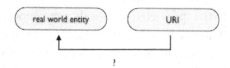

in turn related to the *singularity* principle (Kent et al., 1992).

4. **Coupling between the Web and the real world:** How to make explicit the relations between Web elements and objects in the real world (Gangemi et al., 2006)?

5. **Resolvability of references:** How to clarify when and how a reference is resolvable (Booth, 2003)?

In order to understand the previous issues, which characterize our problem space, and possibly to improve on the current situation, we need to analyze the reason why a URI can be associated with an entity. In other words, we need to understand the nature of the apparently simple relation that is informally depicted in Figure 1.

The next section presents an ontology named *identity of resources and entities on the Web (IRE)*. IRE allows us to formally describe the nature of the relation between a URI and (one or more) entities, as well as to express the five issues characterizing the space of the Web referencing problem.

THE IRE METAMODEL

We firstly provide an informal description of the rationale behind the IRE metamodel.

The relation in Figure 1 is directly connected to a general assumption of computer science, and in Web science too: *the virtual world is made of symbols while the real world is made of things*.3 This makes it impossible for machines to recognize (or "resolve," or "refer to") entities

as such, unless they are symbols as well.4 Typically, computational reference to entities implies either that humans will interpret it, like when a Web page includes the string "W3C" or an image of downtown Prague, or that computational simulations of those entities substitute real world entities, such as when dice are thrown in a virtual casino application.

Most problems of Web referencing are due to this assumption; therefore we need to analyze in more detail how URIs can be interpreted as references to entities.

Referencing is analyzed in the IRE design by assuming four layers. These layers distinguish the types of things in the domain of the Web referencing problem: *URI, Web resource, information object*, and *entity*, as shown in Figure 2. This layering reflects generic assumptions that hold in the traditional domains of philosophy of language, and semiotics. Whenever an assumption taken goes beyond common sense, it will be commented and introduced briefly. The ontology of Constructive Descriptions and Situations (Gangemi, 2008) covers most of the assumptions in some detail.

An example of layering is the following: the URI http://www.w3.org identifies a file (a Web resource), stored on a W3C server that is accessed when the above URI is resolved; the file is made up of ;linguistic or XHTML information (a set of information objects); that information is about the actual W3C organization (a real world entity).

The general assumption previously mentioned (in the context of Web science) can be now re-phrased: *the Web is made up of URIs and Web resources. The real world is made up of entities in general, including information objects, humans, substances, cables, etc. The real world can only be processed by agents that have adequate recognition and processing capabilities. The topmost problem is then how to encode the real world parts on the Web, and in a way that approximates intelligent agents' recognition and processing of those parts.?* Answering this question is part of

Figure 2. Four layers of Web referencing

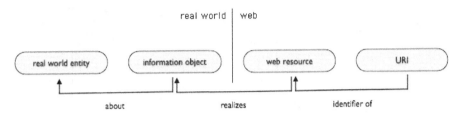

the solution space (see next section), while in the rest of this section we detail the IRE layers and their formalization.

Each layer can be related to the next one as follows (see Figure 2).

URIs identify Web resources. The URI mechanism creates a combinatorial space made of what we call *abstract Web locations*. Each abstract Web location (e.g., the one localized by http://www.w3.org, can "contain" a computational object at a certain time), such as a digital file stored on a W3C server. If it is accessible through the Web, that is, the URI is resolvable, then the computational object is a *Web resource*.

This first step enables us to reduce the problem space from analyzing the nature of relations between URIs and the real world entities to that of analyzing the relations between Web resources and entities.

Web resources contain information that has been produced and has entered a life-cycle, such as the information encoded in English or XHTML within the W3C Web resource. We say that **a Web resource realizes some information object**. The *realizes* relation is the same that holds for example between a poem (an information object) and the printed book containing it (its realization). Consider also that same poem as realized by a Web document: it would be a different occurrence of the realizes relation for that same information object. Realization holds also for resources different from typical documents in Web pages: computed Web resources, non-propositional Web resources (e.g., MP3, JPG, MPEG), time-varying Web resources, etc. This work does not analyze all

possible solutions for all possible Web resources, but IRE provides the basic patterns to talk about those solutions and resources. For example, an MP3 of Charlie Parker's recording of "Lover Man" from July 29, 1946, can be said to realize the sonic information object that has been first recorded on the master copy. Moreover, it also realizes the "Lover Man" musical composition, written by Jimmy Davis, Roger Ramirez, and Jimmy Sherman in 1942. Similar entrenchments between composition, copies, reproduction, and performances hold for all multimedia resources, as well as for resources that get computed (the so-called deep Web), and for those that vary over time according to external input. The *realizes* relation crosses the line between the Web and the real world. Now, if we accept the *opacity* principle (Web resources can change for the same URI) *for all URIs*, the uniqueness of reference would be already broken at this point. On the contrary, if we admit that at least some URIs are unique, our problem space is reduced to analyzing the nature of the relations between information objects and the real world entities.

The assumption that certain URIs are unique lets us go out of the computational world and enter areas that are traditionally covered by philosophy of language, linguistics, semiotics and logic. In this article we do not enter the details of the literature from those domains, but we use some results of those disciplines, in order to provide a rationale that gives room to a formal description of the problem space that is addressed by solutions like the Semantic Web and several Web 2.0 applications.

Figure 3. The IRE basic model

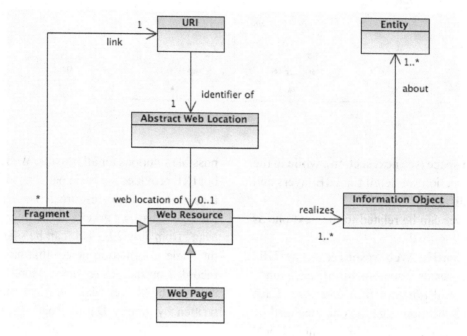

We generalize the relations between information objects and the real world entities as "being about": **an information object is about some real world entity.** For example, the linguistic description of W3C from the W3C pages *is about* W3C (as well as about many other things). The being about relation requires that information objects are interpreted by someone that is able to conceive a "reference" from information objects (either those contained in a resource, or others that can be associated with them), to a set of circumstances, in which real world entities are "situated" (Gangemi, 2008; Gangemi & Mika, 2003).

How can we express and operationalize the being about relation, so analyzed, on the Web? In order to answer this question we need to enter the solution domain, which will be done in the next section.

Figure 3 depicts a UML (The unified modeling language, http://www.omg.org/uml) class diagram containing the basic elements and relations of the IRE model. In the remainder of this section, we still concentrate on the problem domain and on the formalization of IRE, which is summarized as follows.

- **URIs identify abstract Web locations:** A *URI* is the *identifier of* an *abstract Web location. Abstract Web locations* are regions in a dimensional space, and they are not "created" or "changed" over time or in space. *URIs* are *identifiers* for those locations. On the other hand, URIs can be "bought" and "owned" (therefore they seem to have a spatio-temporal identity), but in this case what is bought or owned is a legal right to have a name dereferenced into a Web resource, not a region in an abstract space.

- **Abstract Web locations are locations of Web resources:** Each *abstract Web location* can be the *Web location of* at most one *Web resource*. On the contrary, a *Web resource* can be placed in one or more *abstract Web location*(s). This means that the identity of a Web resource is something that goes beyond its location. An abstract Web location is a region in the combinatorial space that is

Figure 4. The IRE basic taxonomy

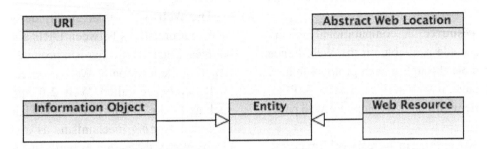

created by the URI addressing mechanism (i.e., each URI identifies one and only one abstract Web location). To this aim, the data-type relation *identifier of* and its inverse are functional (have a one-to-one cardinality).

- **Links relate fragments of Web tesources to URIs:** Link relations are said (Raggett, Le Hors, & Jacobs, 1999) to relate different Web resources, which include Web pages, fragments of Web pages, etc. "A link has two ends–called anchors–and a direction. The link starts at the "source" anchor and points to the "destination" anchor, which may be any Web resource." As we explained in the section "history," URIs and Web locations are not the same type of entities as Web resources, therefore we need to look at links in more detail. What a link actually does is to relate a special fragment of a Web resource, such as a piece of text enclosed into the <a> syntax (the so-called source anchor),5 to a URI (the so-called destination anchor). The reason why the common intuition (included W3C specifications) claims that a link relates two resources is probably due to the typical intention of the link creator, which amounts to relating information from within two Web resources.

On the other hand, if something changes in the destination resource, for example the URI cannot be resolved anymore, or if the resource does not contain anymore the original information that the link creator intended to be reachable through the link, the link still holds.6 Links are therefore tools for "approximate" and "temporally bound" references that are used as (shortcuts for) relations between resources.

- **Web resources realize information objects that are about entities:** A *Web resource realizes* one or more *information objects*, which in turn are *about* some real world *entity.*

In order to make the model clearer, Figure 4 depicts the IRE basic taxonomy. We give a prose description for each element that has been introduced:

- **URI:** A string that satisfies syntactical rules defined in IETF RFC 3986 (Berners-Lee et Al., 2005).
- **Abstract Weblocation:** A point in the combinatorial space identified by the URI mechanism.
- **Information object:** An information unit that has been created by some agent at some time for some reason, independently from its rendering, materialization, etc. Information objects range from texts to pictures, from poems to logical formulas, from diagrams to musical compositions, and are independent from their physical realization, which can take any form that is technologically

practicable (printed texts, digital pictures, formulas on a whiteboard, performed songs, etc.).

- **Web resource:** A computational object7 that is made available on the Web, hence accessible through a Web protocol (e.g., a Web page, a Web service, a MP3, MPEG, JPG file with a URI, a computed Web page, etc.).
- **Entity:** Anything in the real world (material, social, cognitive, etc.).

With regard to the five issues listed in the previous section, they can be now redescribed in terms of the following IRE model elements:

- **I:** Web resource, URI, and link provide the basic primitives for expressing the issues raised by Web semantics.
- **II:** These four layers and the three corresponding relations allow one to model the Web referencing problem.
- **III:** The issue of multiple referencing can be represented as a path thorugh IRE relations (and cardinalities), as constructed from the class URI to the class entity.
- **IV:** The IRE ontology describes elements and relations that are both in the Web and in the real world, hence providing what is needed in order to express the "coupling" issue.
- **V:** URI and Web resource are the primitives involved in the resolvability issue.

Moreover, not only does IRE allow one to formally model the problem space of Web referencing issues, but it also provides means to understand the relations between those issues.

THE SOLUTION SPACE

In the previous sections, we have analyzed the problem space of Web referencing. In this section, we discuss how the solution space is populated by existing technology.

The **Web** as it was originally designed only deals with relations between URIs and Web resources. The URI mechanism provides a tool for denoting the location of Web resources.

Recently, so-called **Web 2.0** applications, such as Flickr, Wikipedia, and del.icio.us, have exploited *tagging* mechanisms as a solution to clarify Web referencing. Actually, it was possible since early versions of HTML to add "meta" tags to the header part of Web pages. They were intended mainly as an aid to search engines, and only very experienced users used them to annotate Web pages.

Web 2.0 applications allow users to *tag* Web resources, and are usually associated with a social community that share a common interest. Tags are used as hints on the intended meaning that is assigned by a user to the information contained in a Web resource.8 For example, consider the Flickr community Web site. Each Flickr user has his or her own Web space to put pictures in, thereby sharing them with the Flickr community of users. Each picture can be commented and users can *tag* them either by creating a new tag, or by using so called *machine tags*. On the Flickr Web site (http://www.flickr.com) you can find the following suggestions about *tags*: "You can give your photos a "tag", which is like a keyword or category label. Tags help you find photos which have something in common. You can assign up to 70 tags to each photo."

Following IRE, tags are information objects that "are about" entities, types of entities, or even relations between entities that are also referenced by the tagged information objects. In other words, the Web 2.0 adds new information objects to the Web, in order to suggest useful hints on how the information contained in Web resources (Web pages, images, videos, bookmarks) can be classified and retrieved.

Lately, the Web 2.0 trend has turned to the use of controlled vocabularies for structuring

Figure 5. An example of tagging (1)

tags (e.g., with Flickr "machine tags" or with "microformats"). However, the interpretation of tags still relies entirely on humans; therefore tagging remains within the Web 1.0 metamodel, and is not sufficient to clarify the *about* relation between information objects and entities.

Figure 5 shows a typical example of tags associated with a picture on the Flickr Web site. The picture shows Gangemi during his visit in Prague. The first two tags are about the picture's content. The second two are about the technical details on the picture seen as a Web resource, the camera with which it has been taken, and its resolution. Furthermore, there are also two machine tags taken from the namespace identified by the prefix geo:. They are about the relation between the picture and the place at which it has been taken. The first indicates its longitude, while the second indicated the latitude.

Figure 6 shows another example of Flickr-style tagging. The picture depicts a view of Prague that is referred by the machine tag geo:locality, and by the czechrepubliccapital tag. There is no way to relate the geo:lon and geo:lat to the geo:locality machine tags, as well as Prague, and czechrepubliccapital appear to be unrelated to a machine.

Additional solutions have been introduced by the Semantic Web initiative. The Semantic Web provides a stack of languages that allows to express Web referencing in more explicit and sophisticated ways. RDF9 allows us to create graphs of URIs with a relational syntax, and RDF Schema allows us the declaration of explicit schemas (Brickley & Guha, 2004) to create those graphs with reference to the names included in the schemas. OWL allows us to add a real first-order *formal semantics* to those graphs and names,10 which become ontology elements. The formal semantics used for OWL is *set-theoretic semantics*.

In this article, we create a correspondence between those names and *tags* used in Web 2.0 applications, assuming that tags can be given a formal interpretation similarly to11 names used for OWL ontology elements.

Formal semantics allows a rigorous interpretation of the names included in an *ontology*. An ontology is a logical theory, which is composed of (briefly and informally speaking): predicate (e.g., OWL classes and properties) names, individual

Figure 6. An example of tagging (2)

(e.g., OWL individuals) names, and axioms (what is asserted in a particular ontology (e.g., OWL class subsumption and disjointness), *rdf:type* assertions, relationships between OWL individuals).

Predicate and individual names are identified by URIs in Web ontologies. On the contrary, Web 2.0 tags are not usually identified by URIs. This is important from the viewpoint of Web semantics, but it is less important when we consider tags as potential names for ontology elements, once they are given a formal semantics. However, this difference is not crucial in the rest of this section.

In this article, we are interested in how ontology element names (and their context, provided by the axioms within an ontology) help make Web referencing more precise, and possibly more precise than in Web 2.0 applications. In order to do that, we need to know firstly how the names used in ontologies refer to real world entities. This is straightforward: within set-theoretic semantics, individual names are assumed to refer to individuals in the real world (Notice that we are using "real world entity" here to mean any entity except the symbols used on the Web), while predicate names are assumed to refer to sets of individuals or to sets of relationships between individuals in the real world. Individuals and their relationships are

assumed as the basic elements from the *domain of interpretation* of an ontology.

Therefore, in IRE we can assume that OWL ontologies introduce new names for either individuals or predicates, which are the formal counterpart of real world entities (respectively sets of entities).

Figure 7 depicts, by using a graph notation, three simple OWL ontologies. White ovals are used for OWL classes; yellow ovals are used for OWL individuals; rectangles are used for datatypes values (strings, float, etc.); and arrows are used for object and datatype properties. The "multimedia" ontology contains classes and properties for describing multimedia objects like, photos, videos, digital cameras, etc. The "location" ontology addresses the description of geographical places and their characteristics. Finally, the "MyFriends" ontology is about people that are friends of the ontology author. Notice that we re-use here the class *foaf:Person*. By instantiating these simple ontologies, the pictures of Figure 5 and 6 can be tagged with OWL individuals and "property values." In this way, it is possible to formally express what we are referencing, and, say, to relate the two pictures, even in the case where different tagging terms are used. For ex-

Figure 7. An example of tagging with OWL

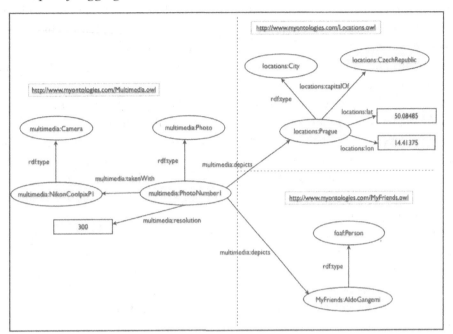

ample, consider the case of the photo of Figure 5 that is represented by the OWL individual multimedia:PhotoNumber1 of Figure 7. With only this assertion— multimedia:PhotoNumber1 rdf:type multimedia:Photo—we are saying something about it, namely,., it is a photo. Moreover, we can relate the photo to the camera we used to take it, which is represented by an OWL individual with a specific type as well (multimedia:MyNikonCoolpixP1 rdf:type multimedia:Camera). The photo is then related to (multimedia:depicts) MyFriends:AldoGangemi, which is a Person, and to locations:Prague, which is formally introduced as a city, capital of the Czech republic in the Location ontology. Of course, analogously to having different Web 2.0 tags with the same sense, we could have different ontologies for the same domain, defining individuals and predicates that have the same sense in those different ontologies. However, in this last case there are other formal constructs that can express these equivalences.

Currently, the semantic Web provides the best approach for addressing Web referencing (Issue II), because it allows to create specific URIs, usable within any Web resource, which are associated with both information objects (OWL names) and real world entities (by means of their formal counterparts: individuals, relationships, and sets, which are assigned to OWL names through a formal interpretation function).

In practice, the semantic Web provides languages to create new URIs for information objects (individuals and predicate names), which can help ensure uniqueness of reference (called "denotation" by logicians) by providing a formal interpretation over a well-defined domain that includes counterparts of the individuals and concepts that exist in the real world. OWL names and constructs are in fact additional Web resources, which are available to a machine in order to "recognize" entities, thus gathering a more explicit processing of Web reference. For the sake of clarity, we call "semantic" those URIs that identify these additional Web resources.

There is something that is still missing from the picture. While formal semantics allows us to establish a unique relation between semantic URIs and (counterparts of) entities, the *reason* why those entities are referenced is not addressed by formal semantics alone, since it has to do with the motivations, goals, and rationales of the humans, communities, and agents that use the Web and the semantic Web. Those motivations can be extremely varied, and while formal semantics ensures the uniqueness of reference within a formal domain of discourse, it cannot ensure that the structural context provided by an ontology (its axioms) is enough to unambiguously reference an entity (i.e., that the domain of interpretation actually reflects the world as intended by a human interpreter). Ontologies can make different assumptions (different axioms) with respect to the same set of real world entities, so that their domains of interpretation may need to be mapped in non-trivial ways. Indeed, this is already the case with the so-called matching problem over decentralized ontologies.

This last observation makes us move from the problem of the *sense* of Web referencing (Issue II) to the problem of the *multiplicity* of referencing (Issue III), which is another way to deal with the resource *identity* problem.

According to Kent et al., in order to have an effective "object identification mechanism," identifiers have to satisfy the following principles (1992):

- **Immutability:** An object's identifier should be the same at any point in time and everywhere (globally recognizable)
- **Uniqueness:** Two objects cannot be represented by the same identifier
- **Singularity:** Two different identifiers cannot represent the same object.

Assuming URIs as identifiers (immutable by definition) and entities as objects, a specific Web ontology (by which reference is unique and singular, as explained above) can satisfy the previous principles.12 This could be effective if

it was reasonable to assume that ontologies are univocal in referencing real world entities. But we know this is not reasonable.

The names of logical elements are useful to give hints on how (the URI of) a tagged Web resource references entities, but this hint is obtained by putting those names in the namespace of a specific ontology, therefore the same entity can appear in different namespaces with either the same or different names. For example, most Web users know that Italy is an existing entity, whatever existing may mean for them and whatever interpretations those users may want to attach to Italy as an existing entity. When we put Italy in the domain of interpretation of some ontology, the result is that Italy is being assumed as a new entity, and an *owl:sameAs* axiom is required to assert the identity of Italy in the domain of ontology *A* as the same as that of Italy in the domain of ontology *B*.13

Moreover, our Web referencing problems deal with how URIs of *any* Web resource reference entities, not only with how Web 2.0 tags or the names of Web ontologies reference those entities. Consequently, even the fact that URI references can be unique and singular does not ensure that the reference of (the URI of) the Web resources tagged with those URIs will be unique and singular as well. For example, we can use the following axioms in order to tag the photo from the previous example, which then appear to have heterogeneous real world references:

1. mm:PhotoNumberI rdf:type mm:Photo
2. mm:UGolemaAd rdf:type ad:Advertisement
3. mm:PhotoNumberI mm:depicts MyFriends:AldoGangemi
4. mm:UGolemaAd ad:testimonial golemLovers:AldoGangemi

Now, we can intuitively know that a photo *can be used as* an advertisement, and that a person *can play the role of* a testimonial, but these relations must be reconstructed, and semantics alone is not able to do that; again, we need additional mapping effort, with or without assistance from tools.

The earlier example of Italy suggests us a workaround that can lead us to a new breed of solutions that can fit very well in an evolving space of Web ontologies.

Consider the possibility that there exists a collection of entities in the real world, each element of which can be assigned a unique and singular URI on the Web, and with no dependence on any specific context. Let's call the resulting URI collection: *Web catalog of entities.*

An example of such a catalog is Okkam, which presents an application for "identity management support" (Bouquet et al., 2006). The authors propose a catalog of URIs that uniquely and singularly reference entities. Those URIs should be reused as much as possible, supported by tools, and advised as a good practice to refer to entities.

Now, if we fill such a catalog with semantic URIs, those URIs will identify semantic Web resources, for instance, OWL individuals corresponding to entities. The semantic catalog workaround consists then in relaxing the interpretation of referencing to the point of having an ontology with an (almost) empty set of predicate names, but with as many individual names as possible.

Contrary to current practices for ontology design and exploitation, which firstly create predicate names and axioms, and then populate the namespace with individual names, the semantic catalog approach suggests to populate an ontology with individual names, and then to add axioms for the entities that are assigned to those names. Each ontology could provide a view on the same set of individuals, thus avoiding the difficult and arbitrary practice of introducing *owl:sameAs* axioms in order to map differently viewed individuals.

The potential advantages of reusing URIs in different ontologies is intuitive, as well as the fact that Kent et al.'s principles applied to such URIs would allow their easy reuse, and provide a solu-

tion to the identification of entities as referenced on the Web (1992).

Solving the identity problem by means of a catalog is quite simple, because it seems to rely on the appeal of natural language terms, but it's a matter of fact that our social behavior makes a lot of assumptions of existence just based on names and conventional practices to "dereference" them when needed. Also the reason we assume existence is often accepted without revision, or the assumption is so shared and relevant to most of us that we can do without asking about it. Examples include countries, geographic locations, institutions, organizations, persons, well-known objects (buildings, roads), and historical facts..

Although it is true that assertions of existence for entities are dependent on a specific context, which is characterized by certain motivations, goals, and rationales, there are entities whose existential conditions are *socially recognized,* that is, their existence is a social statement. In order to understand those conditions, the usage of the Web needs to be observed.

The Web is growing as a virtual simulation of social processes. It is not much related to physical processes as instead it is the case with "the Internet of things" (Dolin, 2006).14

It is reasonable to assume that the criteria by which entities should be included in the catalog are the same that govern the social agreement over the way entities are publicly shared. A similar intuition is described by Mika, where the relations between social networks and semantics are discussed (2005). Gangemi et al. also discuss the contextual nature of identity conditions for entities (2003). Social agreement on what should be assumed in a universe of discourse seems much more powerful than philosophical discussions on what should be assumed to exist.

For example, many entities that physically exist in the real world (say, a stone) only acquire value for the Web when they are put in a specific context (say,, collaborative geological cataloging) This is in line with the fact that associations

Figure 8. The procedure for creating the Web catalog of entities.

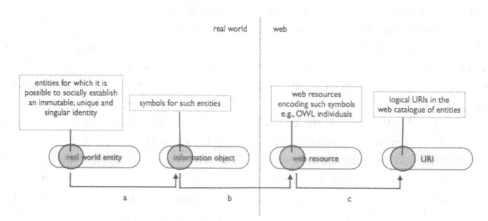

between URIs and entities depend on a given context. On the other hand, there are entities that have no physical existence, but whose existence is universally recognized because they satisfy well-known social conditions: large organizations (e.g., United Nations), corporations (e.g., Daimler Benz), famous fiction characters (e.g., Mickey Mouse, Jupiter), concepts (e.g., force, beauty, being a friend), etc.

Figure 8 informally depicts the procedure by which a Web catalog of entities is built from the perspective of the four layers from IRE (see previous section). Relation *a* associates an entity, whose identity is socially recognized regardless to any specific interpretation, with an information object that is about it, complying for example to the semantics of an OWL individual name. Relation *b* holds between the information object and its realization on the Web, that is, a (semantic) Web resource for that name. Finally, relation *c* represents the association of that Web resource with a Web location, hence with a URI.

The catalog idea can be strengthened, in order to cover associations too. An association catalog can also be built if the semantics of association between entities is also relaxed and based on evidence coming for example from statistical methods (such as those currently used by search engines), from NLP techniques (e.g., named-

entity recognition and relation extraction), and from existing association repositories (factbooks, organizational thesauri, etc.). An additional merit of these ideas is to disclose a new strategy to integrate top-down work from ontology engineering and the Semantic Web, with bottom-up work from NLP, information retrieval and extraction, and folksonomy-based Web applications. A formal model of the association catalog idea is presented in the next section.

The Solution Domain in Terms of IRE

In this section, we present the IRE model extended in order to cover the needed expressivity for representing the solution domain. Although on the Web we cannot resolve the reference to an entity of the real world that is not a computational object, we need to be able to assert facts about an entity on the Web. As mentioned above, we can approach this issue in different ways depending on the technology we use.

In general we say that a Web resource *works as a proxy for* an entity, at a given time. This association between a Web resource and an entity means that the Web resource realizes an information object, which is about some entities at a given time.

Figure 9. The IRE model for identification of resources on the Web

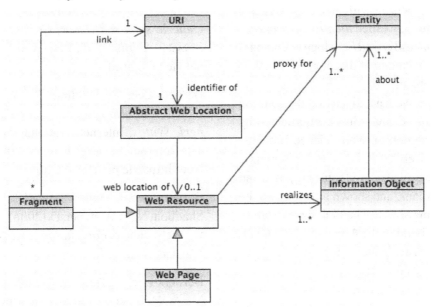

Figure 9 depicts the IRE diagram, which includes the relation *proxy for* between a Web resource and an entity.

A Web resource can be a proxy for one or more than one entity. This aspect suggests a categorization for the *proxy for* relation. Notice that each specialization of *proxy for* can correspond to a different computational approach, or more specifically to a different operational semantics associated with the resolution of the Web resource's URI.

The kinds of *proxy for* relations can be described informally as follows:

- **Approximate proxy for:** Is a relationship between a Web resource and more than one entity at a given time, where the Web resource realizes some information objects, which are about those entities. In this case the Web resource *approximately* represents those entities.
- **Exact proxy for:** A relationship between a semantic resource and one entity at a given time, where the semantic resource realizes an information object, which is about only that

entity, and describes it through a semantic structure. For example, an individual from an OWL ontology.

For example, consider the Web catalog of entities we have discussed in the previous section. It contains, among the others, two OWL individual names: one for "Prague," the other for "Aldo Gangemi." These two individuals are *exact proxy for* the city of Prague and the person Aldo Gangemi, respectively, while the photo shown in Figure 5 is an *approximate proxy for* them.

CONCLUSION AND REMARKS

The *identification of resources on the Web* has been mentioned as one of the essential issues to be addressed by Web science in order to successfully perform information sharing, interoperability, and reasoning on the Web. In this article we have firstly analyzed the state of the art related to this problem and from this analysis we made it emerge five distinct issues. We have described these issues and compared the respective solutions through the investigation of the reason why a URI can be associated with an entity. We have proposed an ontology called *identity of resources and entities on the Web (IRE)*, which encompass the things in the domain of discourse of the Web referencing problem.

Furthermore, we have discussed the solution domain in terms of how it has been affected by the current evolution of Web Science from the Web 1.0 to the Web 2.0 and then to the Semantic Web. We have also considered some proposed and envisaged solutions, and shown how they can be modeled in terms of IRE. The FOL formalization of IRE can be found in the Appendix. The OWL version of IRE is available at http://wiki.loa-cnr. it/index.php/LoaWiki:IRE.

ACKNOWLEDGMENT

We are grateful to the members of the NeOn consortium who contributed to the NeOn vision being funded by the European Commission 6th IST Framework Programme. Further information on NeOn is available on http://www.neon-project. org. We also the anonymous reviewers, that have substantially helped us debugging the article.

REFERENCES

Adida, B., & Birbeck, M. (2006). *RDFa Primer 1.0 Embedding RDF in XHTML*. Technical report, World Wide Web Consortium. Retrieved from http://www.w3.org/TR/xhtml/rdfa/primer/

Behrendt, W., Gangemi, A., Maass, W., & Westen-thaler, R. (2005). Towards an ontology based distributed architecture for paid content. *Proceedings of the European Semantic Web Conference (ESWC 2005)* (pp. 257-271). Herakion, Greece. May 29 - June 1, 2005. London: Springer-Verlag.

Berners-Lee, T., Fielding, R., & Masinter, L. (1998). *Uniform resource identifier (URI): Generic syntax. IETF RFC 2396*, The Internet Society, August 1998. Retrieved from http://rfc. net/rfc2396.html

Berners-Lee, T., Fielding, R., & Masinter, L. (2005). *Uniform resource identifier (URI): Generic syntax*. Internet Draft standard RFC3986, The Internet Society, January 2005. Retrieved from http://rfc.net/rfc3986.html

Berners-Lee, T., Hall, W., Hendler, J., O'Hara, K., Shadbolt, N., & Weitzner, D. (2006). A framework for Web science. *Foundations and Trends in Web Science, 1*(1).

Berners-Lee, T., Hall, W., Hendler, J., Shadbolt, M., & Weitzner, D. (2006). Creating a science of the Web. *Science, 313*(11), 771.

Black, J. (2006). Creating a common ground for URI meaning using socially constructed Web sites. *Proceedings of Identity, Reference, and the Web (IRW2006), WWW2006 Workshop*. Edinburgh, United Kingdom. May, 22nd 2006. http://www.ibiblio.org/hhalpin/irw2006/jblack.pdf.

Booth, D. (2003). *Four uses of a URL: Name, concept, web location, and document instance*. Retrieved from http://www.w3.org/2002/11/dbooth-names/dbooth-names_clean.htm

Bouquet, P, Stoermer, H., Mancioppi, M., & Giacomuzzi, D. (2006). OkkaM: Towards a solution to the "identity crisis" on the semantic Web. *Proceedings of the Italian Semantic Web Workshop (SWAP 2006)*. Pisa, Italy, December 18-20, 2006.

Brickley, D., & Guha, R. (2004). *RDF Vocabulary Description Language 1.0: RDF Schema*. W3C Recommendation. Retrieved from http://www. w3.org/TR/2004/REC-rdf-schema-20040210/

Clark, K. (2002). Identity crisis. Retrieved from http://www.xml.com/pub/a/2002/09/11/deviant. html

Dolin, R. (2006). Deploying the Internet of things. *Proceedings of the International Symposium on Applications on Internet (SAINT 2006)* (pp. 216-219). Phoenix, USA. Los Alamitos, CA: IEEE Computer Society.

Duerst, M., & Signard, M. (2005). *Internationalized resource identifiers (IRIs). RFC 3987*, Internet Society, January 2005. Retrieved from http://www.ietf.org/rfc/rfc3987.txt

Gangemi, A. (2008). Norms and plans as unification criteria for social collectives. *Journal of Autonomous Agents and Multi-Agent Systems, 16*(3).

Gangemi, A., & Mika, P. (2003). Understanding the semantic Web through descriptions and situations. *Proceedings of International Conference of Ontologies, Databases, and Applications of Semantics (ODBASE2003)* (pp. 689-706). Catalina, Italy. November 3-7th 2003. London: Springer-Verlag.

Gangemi, A., & Presutti, V. (2006). The bourne identity of a Web resource. *Proceedings of the Identity, Reference, and the Web (IRW2006) Workshop at the World Wide Web Conference (WWW2006)*. Edinburgh, United Kingdom. May, 23rd 2006. http://www.ibiblio.org/hhalpin/irw2006/presentations/-vpresutti.pdf.

Gangemi, A., Borgo, S., Catenacci, C., & Lehmann, J. (2005) *Task taxonomies for knowledge content*. Deliverable D07 of the Metokis Project. Retrieved from http://www.loa-cnr.it/Papers/D07_v21a.pdf

Gruber, T. (2007). Ontology of folksonomy: A mash-up of apples and oranges. *Journal on Semantic Web & Information Systems, 3*(2).

Hayes, P. (2006). In defense of ambiguity. *Proceedings of the Identity, Reference, and the Web (IRW2006), WWW2006 Workshop*. Edinburgh, United Kingdom. May, 23rd 2006. http://www.ibiblio.org/hhalpin/irw2006/presentations/-HayesSlides.pdf.

Jacobs, I., & Walsh, N. (2004). *Architecture of the World Wide Web*. W3C Recommendation. Retrieved from http://www.w3.org/TR/Webarch

Kawamura, T., Ueno, K., Nagano, S., Hasegawa, T., & Ohsuga, A. (2004). Ubiquitous service finder discovery of services semantically derived from metadata in ubiquitous computing. *Proceedings of International Semantic Web Conference (ISWC 2005)* (pp 909-915). Galway, Ireland. November 6-10th 2004. London: Springer-Verlag.

Kent, W., Ahmed, R., Albert, J., Ketabchi, M., & Shan, M. (1992). Object identification in multidatabase systems. *Proceedings of Conference on Semantics of Interoperable Databases* (pp. 313-330). Lorne, Australia. November 16-20th 1992. Amsterdam: Elsevier.

Masolo, C., Gangemi, A., Guarino, N., Oltramari, A., & Schneider, L. (2004). *WonderWeb EU project deliverable D18: The WonderWeb Library of Foundational Ontologies*. Retrieved from http://wonderWeb.semanticWeb.org/deliverables/documents/D18.pdf

Mika, P. (2005). Ontologies are us: A unified model of social networks and semantics. *Proceedings of International Semantic Web Conference (ISWC 2005)* (pp. 522-536). Galway, Ireland. November 6-10th 2004. London: Springer-Verlag.

Miles, A. (2005). *Working around the identity crisis*. Retrieved from http://esw.w3.org/topic/SkosDev/IdentityCrisis

Parsia, B., & Patel-Schneider, P. F. (2006). *Meaning and the semantic Web. Proceedings of Identity, Reference, and the Web (IRW2006), WWW2006 Workshop.* Edinburgh, United Kingdom. May, 23rd 2006. http://www.ibiblio.org/hhalpin/irw2006/bparsia.pdf.

Pepper, S. (2006). The case for published subjects. *Proceedings of Identity, Reference, and the Web (IRW2006), WWW2006 Workshop.* Edinburgh, United Kingdom. May, 23rd 2006. http://www.ibiblio.org/hhalpin/irw2006/spepper2.pdf.

Pepper, S., & Schwab, S. (2003). *Curing the Web's identity crisis: Subject indicators for RDF.* Technical report, Ontopia, 2003. Retrieved from http://www.ontopia.net/topicmaps/materials/identitycrisis.html

Raggett, D., Le Hors, A., & Jacobs, I. (1999). *HTML 4.01 Specification.* W3C Recommendation 24 December 1999. Retrieved from http://www.w3.org/TR/html401/

ENDNOTES

[1] Note that RFC 2396 (Berners-Lee et al., 1998) has been replaced by RFC 3986 (Berners-Lee et al., 2005), however we decided to quote and discuss it because it helps in understanding the historical motivations why there is confusion on the sense of "resource" on the Web.

[2] Notice that IRIs (Internationalized Resource Identifier) are supposed to replace URIs in the future (Duerst and Signard, 2005). Modulo that replacement, IRIs involvement in the IRE model is the same that URIs have.

[3] Whatever we assume to exist in the real world: either physical or social, mental or abstract, possibly including symbols themselves.

[4] For example, some bits in the database on the computer at my bank are not a simulation of my bank balance, but exactly that balance as a computational object. On the other hand, the balance as a social object reflects my economic power, not just some calculations.

[5] By *fragment* we mean here any part of a Web page, either code or text, either linked or not. A fragment can be associated with a URI e.g., by means of either the "id" or "name" attribute in HTML documents. A fragment can also be the source anchor to a URI e.g., by means of the "href" attribute in HTML documents. The following links include examples of special fragments that are used within links:

```
<p id="FirstParagraph">This is the first paragraph of
    the document</p>
<a name="Label">
<a href="http://www.myWebpage.com">go to my
    Web page</a>This is the text associated with
    Label</a>
<a name="LinkToMyWebPage" href="http://www.
    myWebpage.com">go to my Web page</a>
```

See Appendix for a formal characterization of Web pages, fragments, etc..

[6] This potential violation of the integrity of Web references is anyway one the main reasons for the success of the WWW.

[7] In this context, we define "computational object" as (i) the physical realization of an information object, (ii) something that can participate in a computational process. Examples of computational objects are: a database, a digital document, a software application.

[8] Tom Gruber (2007) has characterized the formal relation implied by tagging: an agent uses a tag to describe a Web resource at some time, with a judgment polarity (positive-negative). In terms of IRE and Gruber's tagging relation, we have characterized elsewhere (http://www.loa-cnr.it/codeps/

owl/tagging.owl) tagging as a linguistic act that an agent performs by using (at a time) an information object that expresses an intended *meaning* about an entity that a resource is able to reference. That meaning can be based on a *referential* function, such as "cat" used for a photo depicting a cat, or on an *expressive* function, such as "cool" used for that photo, etc.

9   The relevant W3C specifications are at http://www.w3.org/RDF/.

10 RDF has a formal semantics, but it is defined by reifying its syntactic constructs, not as an actual theory about the domain (entities and relationships) described by those constructs.

11 The term *ontology* has been used also to refer to many data structures: thesauri, lexicons, folksonomies, database schemas, logical theories, etc., independently from how they are encoded, but we focus here on its use within the Semantic Web, where ontology indicates either RDF schema or OWL models).

12 Notice that this only holds for one specific ontology, because decentralized ontologies can easily violate the singularity principle. Furthermore, that violation can even be an advantage when trying to learn mappings between different ontologies.

13 The problem is even worse: the same entity can be referenced by two names even within a same namespace—*Prague, Praha, CzechRepublicCapital*—and an *owl:sameAs* axiom is required to assert their identity. Other solutions include multiple labelling or functional properties that make a reasoner infer the identity.

14 The internet of things could be an additional component to be exploited on the Web for supporting identification of entities; for example, to realize so-called ubiquitous computing (Kawamura et al., 2005). Nevertheless, this aspect is out of scope for this article.

APPENDIX: FOL FORMALIZATION OF IRE

The IRE model specializes the DOLCE+ (in the Ultralite variety, abbreviated as DUL) reference ontology, and some of its modular extensions, namely Information Objects (IOLite) and Knowledge Content Objects (KCO) modules, the last two have been developed in the EU Metokis project (Gangemi et al., 2005). All modules are available in OWL as described at http://wiki.loa-cnr.it/index.php/LoaWiki:Ontologies. For a rather complete FOL ontology that includes most of the theory underlying DOLCE+ and IRE, please refer to Gangemi, (2008).

The IRE ontology specializes or reuses the following predicates (classes have capitalized names. We use the prefixes *dul:*, *iol:*, *kco:*, and *xsd:* for predicates imported from DUL, IOLite, KCO, and XML Schema, respectively.

IRE uses the following predicates:

{*dul:Entity, dul:Region, dul:AbstractRegion,*
dul:InformationObject,
dul:InformationRealization,
dul:TimeInterval, dul:Method,
dul:describes, dul:isRegionFor, dul:realizes, dul:isComponentOf,
dul:isConstituentOf.
dul:isAbout, iol:FormalLanguage,
iol:Text, iol:Code, iol:hasRepresentationLanguage, kco:ComputationalObject,
URI, AbstractWebLocation, ResolutionMethod, WebResource,
link, hasIdentifier, WebLocationOf,
ProxyFor,
ApproximateProxyFor, SemanticResource, ExactProxyFor.}

The following axioms either characterize or define the above predicates.

$$hasIdentifer(x,y) \rightarrow dul:Region(x) \wedge xsd:Datatype(y) \tag{1}$$

Axiom (1) introduces a relation between identifiers (specializing the class *Region* from DOLCE) and datatypes as encoded in XSD. In OWL, this is a so-called DatatypeProperty.

$$URI(x) \rightarrow xsd:Datatype(x) \tag{2}$$

A URI is characterized in (2) as an XSD datatype, since this is the current practice for xml-based languages like OWL. The possible integration between DOLCE regions and datatypes consists in assuming a datatype structure as a metric for DOLCE regions; for example, *xsd:Date* can be assumed as a metric for a subset of 'time intervals,' which are regions in DOLCE.

$$AbstractWebLocation(x) =_{df} dul:SpaceRegion(x) \wedge$$
$$\exists y(URI(y) \wedge hasIdentifier(x,y) \wedge$$
$$\neg \exists z(URI(z) \wedge y \neq z \wedge hasIdentifier(x,z)) \tag{3}$$

Abstract Web locations are defined in (3) as DOLCE abstract regions that have exactly one URI as an identifier. Furthermore, in (4), we state that no URI can identify more than one abstract region. This ensures the isomorphism between URI-like encoding and the abstract Web space generated by it (the abstract Web space being the maximal sum of all abstract Web locations).

$$
\begin{aligned}
& AbstractWebLocation(x) \rightarrow \neg\exists(y,z) \\
& (URI(y) \wedge AbstractWebLocation(z) \wedge x \neq z \wedge \\
& hasIdentifier(x,y) \wedge hasIdentifier(z,y))
\end{aligned}
\tag{4}
$$

(5) defines a relation between an abstract Web location and a computational object at a time interval. The definition specializes the relation *eAbstractLocationOf* (imported from the Spatial Relations ontology) for abstract Web locations and computational objects. *eAbstractLocationOf* is a generic relation holding between regions and physical objects.

$$
\begin{aligned}
& WebLocationOf(x,y,t) =_{df} dul{:}isRegionFor(x,y,t) \wedge \\
& AbstractWebLocation(x) \wedge \\
& kco{:}ComputationalObject(y) \wedge dul{:}TimeInterval(t)
\end{aligned}
\tag{5}
$$

Notice that being a Web location of a computational object does not imply the successful resolution of the URI for the abstract Web location into the computational object (see (7) below), but only the assignment of an address to the resource.

$$
ResolutionMethod(x) \rightarrow dul{:}Method(x)
\tag{6}
$$

$$
Web\,Resource(x) =_{df} kco{:}ComputationalObject(x) \wedge \exists(m,y,t)(ResolutionMethod(m) \wedge dul{:}TimeInterval(t) \wedge
$$

$$
(WebLocationOf(y,x,t) \wedge dul{:}describes(m,x,t)))
\tag{7}
$$

(7) defines Web resources as computational objects that have an assigned abstract Web location. In operational terms, Web resources have been here restricted to those computational objects that are involved in a computational method that ensures the resolution of a URI, given certain circumstances (e.g., an abstract Web location is an assigned Web location of the resource, the server is switched on, the connection is active, etc).

$$
\begin{aligned}
& WebPage(x) \rightarrow WebResource(x) \ni \exists(y,z,t)(Code(y) \ni \\
& iol{:}Text(z) \wedge dul{:}TimeInterval(t) \ni dul{:}isConstituentOf(y,x,t) \wedge dul{:}isConstituentOf(z,x,t)
\end{aligned}
\tag{8}
$$

$$
Fragment(x) \rightarrow WebResource(x)\,) \ni \neg WebPage(x)
\tag{9}
$$

$$
Fragment(x) \leftrightarrow \exists(y,t)(WebPage(y) \ni dul{:}TimeInterval(t) \ni dul{:}isComponentOf(x,y,t)
\tag{10}
$$

(8) and (9) state that both *WebPage*s and *Fragment*s are *WebResource*s. (8) also states that *WebPages* are constituted by both code and text at some time. (9) also says that *Fragments* are *WebResources*, but not *WebPages*. Finally, (10) says that *Fragments* are equivalent to components of some *WebPage* at some

time. In practice, a *Fragment* is intended here as any piece of a *WebPage*; some types of fragments are relevant for IRE, for example. a source anchor of a link, which is enclosed within a href or name statement, or an "html fragment," which is addressed by a hash href.

$$link(x,y,t) \rightarrow Fragment(x) \ni URI(y) \ni dul:TimeInterval(t) \tag{11}$$

(11) defines the *link* relation between a *Fragment* (the source anchor) and a *URI* (the identifier of the location of the destination anchor) at a given time, e.g., the HTML attribute *href.*

$$kco:ComputationalObject(x) \rightarrow dul:InformationRealization(x) \tag{12}$$

The KCO ontology specializes the Information Objects ontology in order to build a conceptual schema for digital and analog content. The concept *ComputationalObject* specializes *InformationRealization* for the computational world, and includes any physical document, electronic service, file, application, etc.

$$dul:InformationObject(x) \rightarrow dul:Entity \tag{13}$$

$$dul:realizes(x,y,t) \rightarrow$$
$$WebResource(x) \ni dul:InformationObject(y) \ni$$
$$dul:TimeInterval(t) \tag{14}$$

A *WebResource* is the realization of an *InformationObject* (13) at a given time, as formalized by axiom (14).

$$dul:about(x,y,t) \rightarrow$$
$$dul:InformationObject(x) \ni dul:Entity(y) \ni dul:TimeInterval(t) \tag{15}$$

Finally, axiom 15 formalizes the reference relation between information objects and entities at a time.

Below we report the formalization of the *proxy* relations. We introduce the following predicates:

$$proxyFor(x,y,z) =_{df} WebResource(x) \wedge dul:Entity(y) \ni$$
$$dul:TimeInterval(t) \ni \exists z(dul:InformationObject(z) \ni$$
$$dul:realizes(x,y,t) \ni dul:about(z,y,t)) \tag{16}$$

(16) defines a relation between a *WebResource* x and any *Entity* y the *WebResource* can be a proxy for, at a time interval *t*. The definition says that for x to be a *proxy for y*, it must *realize* an information object that is *about y.*

In the following definitions, we introduce a typology of proxy relations, independently from the available technology.

$$approximateProxyFor(x,y,t) =_{df} proxyFor(x,y,t) \land \exists z(dul:Entity(z) \land y \neq z \land$$
$$proxyFor(x,z,t)) \tag{17}$$

A resource is an *approximateProxyFor* an *Entity* (17) when it is a proxy for at least two entities; for example, an HTML page can contain more than one link, or a document (text, image, etc.) can refer to several entities, either computational or not.

$$SemanticResource(x) = WebResource(x) \land$$
$$\exists(y,t,z,w)(proxyFor(x,y,t) \land dul:InformationObject(z) \land$$
$$iol:FormalLanguage(w) \land dul:realizes(x,z,t) \land$$
$$dul:about(z,y,t) \land iol:hasRepresentationLanguage(z,w)) \tag{18}$$

(18) introduces *SemanticResources*, that is, the *WebResources* that realize *InformationObjects* that are represented by means of a formal language--one of the Semantic Web languages such as OWL or RDF.

$$exactProxyFor(x,y,t) = SemanticResource(x) \land proxyFor(x,y,t) \land$$
$$\neg\exists z(dul:Entity(z) \land y \neq z \land proxyFor(x,z,t)) \tag{19}$$

A resource is an *exactProxyFor* an *Entity* (19) when it is a *SemanticResource* that works as a proxy for only one *Entity*. For example, the URI-referenced entry of an Italian legal ontology: http://www.loa-cnr.it/ontologies/CLO/LegalILI.owl#Controparte is a formal *exactProxyFor* the concept *Controparte* in the Italian Law.

This work was previously published in International Journal on Semantic Web & Information Systems, Vol. 4, Issue 2, edited by A. Sheth; M. Lytras, pp. 49-72, copyright 2008 by IGI Publishing (an imprint of IGI Global).

Chapter 8

Ontological Indeterminacy and the Semantic Web or Why the Controversy Over Same–Sex Marriage Poses A Fundamental Problem for Current Semantic Web Architecture

Allen Ginsberg
Consultant, USA

ABSTRACT

The expected utility of the Semantic Web (SW) hinges upon the idea that machines, just like humans, can make and interpret statements about "real world" objects, properties, and relations. A cornerstone of this idea is the notion that Uniform Resource Identifiers (URIs) can be used to refer to entities existing independently of the web and to convey meanings. In this chapter, when a URI is used in this manner we will say that it is used declaratively, or that it is an R-URI. The key question is this: when an R-URI is used declaratively on the SW how is an agent, especially a non-human one, supposed to "understand" or "know" what it is intended to refer to or mean? Within the broad community of computational on-tologists and SW practitioners there seems to be a widespread understanding that to provide a meaning/referent for an R-URI the responsible "web-presence" should return (or provide reference to) a formal ontology, or some set of formal "core assertions," that can be used to "establish" the "denotation" of the R-URI. This view, which we will call the Ontology-Mediated (OM) view of SW reference/meaning, presupposes that terms can be given precise conditions for their applicability, and that the latter can be used to "pick out" the intended real world referent/meaning of terms. This chapter argues that the

DOI: 10.4018/978-1-60566-992-2.ch008

Copyright © 2010, IGI Global. Copying or distributing in print or electronic forms without written permission of IGI Global is prohibited.

presuppositions of the OM view are incompatible with the requirement that SW terms/statements should be identical or analogous in meaning to corresponding natural language terms/statements. Natural language is a rule-governed activity, but the rules for using a term or uttering a statement are typically not fully determinate. This phenomenon is a consequence of Ontological Indeterminacy: the inescapable fact that two or more incompatible conceptual systems can often be applied to a domain of interest with equal empirical adequacy. This chapter presents a detailed "real world" example - based upon the currently controversial topic of same-sex marriage - and develops a use-case to buttress the claim that this phenomenon causes problems for the OM view. It seems, therefore, that SW developers/users are faced with a dilemma. If, on the one hand, formal semantic methods, like ontologies, are essential for "picking out" the meaning of SW terms, then those terms will not, in many cases, have the same meaning as their natural language counterparts. If, on the other hand, formal methods are not used to define SW terms, then how is it possible to provide them with meanings that can be interpreted by machines? In this chapter, we will see that this dilemma is based on the mistaken presupposition that the meanings of SW terms must always be determined by giving precise applicability conditions in order for the goals of the SW to be achieved. We show that this presupposition is bound up with the philosophical view that reference and meaning are a function of correspondence of language to reality. We will see that an alternative philosophical account, namely, a "meaning as use" point of view, can be the basis for an account of the meaning of SW terms that avoids the problems of the OM view. The key insight we draw from this account is that there is a distinction between the intention to use a term in some customary manner and the decision to adopt a formal theory that explains or explicates that usage. Formal methods provide a means of explicating the intended senses of SW terms so those senses can be processed by machines for use in certain applications. The intention to use a term according to a certain known natural language community usage, however, can be communicated and processed independently of the decision to accept a particular theory that explicates the intended sense. This account satisfies the goals of the SW and avoids the problems associated with the OM view.

INTRODUCTION

According to the World Wide Web Consortium's (W3C) page on Semantic Web Activity (http://www.w3.org/2001/sw/), the Semantic Web (SW) is "about two things:"

... common formats for interchange of data... Also it is about language for recording how the data relates to real world objects. That allows a person, or a machine, to start off in one database, and then move through an unending set of databases which are connected not by wires but by being about the same thing. (Italics added.)

Though couched in terms of databases, this paragraph implies that the SW should make it possible for machines to interpret and make *statements* about "real world objects" that would be direct analogues to human-generated statements about the same things. In order for the formal language used by a machine to have the same kind of utility as a natural language used by a human, there must be a way for the reference/meaning of SW terms to be established. A key idea behind the SW is to use *Uniform Resource Identifiers* (URIs) to play this role by allowing them to be used to "identify" real world objects, properties, and relations. Although there has been some controversy concerning technical details (Clark 2002; Pepper 2003) it seems clear that schemes allowing URIs to be used to *refer to things* (while still allowing them to be used as addresses in URLs) is compatible with established protocols (Halpin and Thompson 2005; Pepper 2003; Ginsberg 2006).

All relevant accounts, beginning with IETF RFC 2396 (Berners-Lee et. al. 1998), and up to and including recent web architecture work in W3C TAG (Lewis ed., 2007) and most recently (Booth 2009), accept and utilize the fundamental idea that URIs can be used to *refer* to ("identify") things ("resources"), whether these be web pages, or objects, properties, relations, etc. existing independently of the web. Thus, in contrast to the *Uniform Resource Locators* (URLs) of the original web, which can be thought of as being "addresses" for "locations" in a virtual space (the web), the SW requires that URIs also be used *linguistically* by agents in various contexts to make certain statements, just as *words* uttered by humans in various contexts can be used to do the same. In this chapter, when a URI is used in this manner we will say that it is used *declaratively*; we will also use the term "referential-URI" (*R-URI* for short) to designate this type of SW usage.

For a *Uniform Resource Locator* (URL) there is no question about what it "refers to" or "means:" a URL is simply a kind of address, and one can only use it to attempt to retrieve whatever item (if any) is stored at the corresponding location. If it "identifies" anything, it identifies a virtual location, *not* the *contents* of the location; see (Ginsberg 2006) for a detailed discussion of this point. But when a URI is used declaratively on the SW, how is an agent, especially a non-human one, supposed to "understand" or "know" what its intended referent or meaning is? Given that R-URIs can be used as subjects, predicates, and objects in statements in RDF and other SW languages, it is vital that a SW agent be able to determine when they are being used to refer to the same entity or mean the same thing. While syntactic identity of R-URIs is a sufficient condition for resource-identity, it is not a necessary one. Syntactically different R-URIs can refer to the same resource. This issue has been the concern of recent research (Bouquet et. al., 2008). The concern of

this chapter is, however, of a more fundamental, and admittedly, philosophical, nature. The key question we address here is the following: *what exactly must be the case for it to be true to say that a machine has succeeded in using an R-URI to refer to some extra-web entity or to mean the same as some natural language term?*

According to what we will call "received dereferencing practice" for using R-URIs, as outlined in, for example, (Lewis ed., 2007) and most recently in (Booth 2009), the intended meaning or referent of an R-URI is given by using the R-URI as a URL for a "web-presence" that is capable or providing *some* kind of formal, machine-processable, information – Booth (2009) calls this a "URI Declaration" - which in turn can be used to establish an intended referent or meaning, i.e., a "denotation". The approach advocated in (Lewis ed., 2007) is to set up the web presence to return an HTTP 303 response code ("See Other"). This lets the retrieving agent know that the URI identifies a resource "whose essence is not information," to use the language of (Lewis ed., 2007). According to the practice given in (Lewis ed., 2007), the response can also contain another URI that would be used to access information associated with the resource. Presumably this associated information would help the retrieving agent to determine what the intended referent/meaning of the original R-URI is.

The exact protocol and/or mechanism by which this information is conveyed is immaterial to this chapter. What is important for our discussion is that depending upon the kind of information provided and what one means by "establishing" an intended referent/meaning, there are potentially many different ways of understanding and implementing this practice.

The Ontology-Mediated View of Semantic Web Reference/Meaning

Within the broad community of computational ontologists and SW practitioners, there seems to be a widespread way of understanding the afore-mentioned received dereferencing practice for R-URIs. It amounts to the following: to provide a meaning/referent for an R-URI the responsible web-presence should return (or provide reference to) a formal ontology that includes (or imports) a precise definition for the resource (object, property, or relation) the R-URI is intended to pick out. By a "precise definition" we do not necessarily mean a set of necessary and sufficient conditions for something's being (or being an instance of) the resource in question. Rather, by "precise definition" we mean a set of formal expressions that are held to be unambiguously true or false in any given applicable case and that can help a SW agent determine the intended referent/meaning of the term, i.e., a SW agent in possession of this ontology can, *ipso facto*, correctly use the term to designate its intended referent or with the intended meaning. Thus, for example, as stated in (Booth 2009), the determination of the "denotation" of an R-URI involves the processing of a "URI dec-laration" that specifies a "set of core assertions," which assertions typically include formal state-ments such as those contained in an ontology. We will refer to this view as the *Ontology-Mediated* view of reference/meaning for SW terms, or the *OM* view for short.

In order to understand the OM view better it will be helpful to use a concrete example. Consider the natural language statement

```
All employees are persons. (1)
```

This statement could be rendered in OWL using

```
<owl:Class rdf:ID="Employee">
<rdfs:subClassOf>
<owl:Class rdf:ID="Person"/>
</rdfs:subClassOf>
</owl:Class>. (2)
```

Assume that these expressions are part of an OWL ontology defined in a larger file named *employment.owl*, and assume that it has the web address http://www.example.org/employment. owl. Then the URI

```
http://www.example.org/employ-
ment.owl#Employee (3)
```

is a pointer to the declaration of the RDF identifier "Employee" in that file. When used as an R-URI, a SW agent would determine the referent of (3) by processing the entire *employment.owl* file (and any imports). If we think of the *concept of an employee* as a "resource" then the *employment. owl* ontology provides a definition of that resource (and possibly others as well). If the definition in *employment.owl* is an adequate representation of the employee concept, then (3) is an R-URI whose referent (meaning) is the same as what natural language speakers refer to (mean by) that term. This discussion is summarized visually in figure 1 below.

While the OM view may seem to be "com-mon sense," it is important to understand that its power as an explanation of how terms can refer or have meaning rests upon deep philosophical assumptions that need, at the very least, to be made explicit. In brief these assumptions are as follows. Natural language terms like 'employee' or 'person' refer or have meaning because there are real world entities (*employees*, *persons*, the *properties* of being an employee or person) that these terms designate or correspond to. These enti-ties are, in a sense to be elaborated on below, "fully determinate:" they have precise distinguishable (in principle) characteristics that make them what they are. By analyzing the nature of the entities to which these terms correspond, i.e., determining their essential characteristics, precise definitions of the terms can be constructed in a formal ontology. In a more philosophically sophisticated version of this account, these definitions are held to be representations of *concepts*, and the mapping from linguistic-term to corresponding bit of reality is actually mediated by an intervening concept. We

Figure 1. The ontology-mediated view of semantic web reference

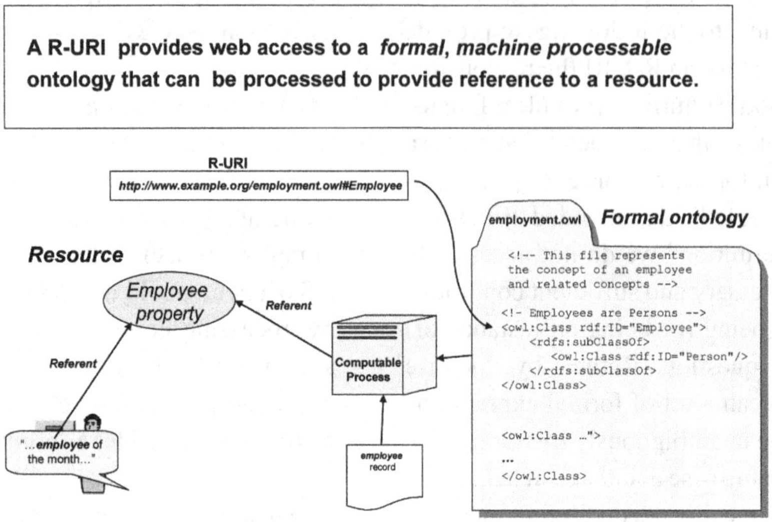

will elaborate on that model below. If an agent uses a term in a manner consistent with these definitions (has possession of the correct concept) then that agent can also, *ipso facto*, use the terms to refer to or mean the same as a natural language speaker using them.

Precisely because the aforementioned assumptions are so deeply embedded, it is difficult to find a general explicit statement of their usc in the technical literature. However if one looks at the work of ontology practitioners, for example, one can see this assumption being used. For example, Smith and Ceusters state that ontology will "provide us with a *common reference framework* which mirrors the structures of those entities in reality" (2007, p. 5). The authors go on to say that "the coding systems used in electronic healthcare records should be associated with a precise and formally rigorous ontology that is coherent with the ontology of the healthcare record as well as with those dimensions of the real world that are described therein" (p.10). The unstated assumption is: because the common reference ontology

"mirrors" reality, a system (in our case, a SW agent) in possession of that ontology can use the ontology's terms to refer to the corresponding real world entities.

Overview of the Chapter

The explanatory power of the OM view rests, as we have seen, upon certain assumptions concerning the relationship between language and reality. We will elaborate on those assumptions below by exploring a philosophical theory that we dub "the correspondence vision/view" of linguistic reference/meaning. We will see that there is good reason to doubt that the correspondence vision is an adequate account of meaning for natural languages. *A fortiori* it is therefore unlikely that the OM view, which presupposes correspondence, can adequately explain how machines and humans can use language in the same way.

The next section of this chapter presents an alternative philosophical vision of the relationship between language and reality that we dub "the holistic vision." This vision is associated with a view of linguistic meaning known by the slogan "meaning as use." A meaning-as-use account seems to have more promise as an account of the meaning of natural language terms than a correspondence view, but, unlike the latter, seems to be unsuited to giving an account of the semantics of formal languages. This leaves SW developers with a dilemma. If, on the one hand, formal semantic methods (typically presupposing correspondence) are used to define meaning and reference for SW terms, then those terms will not, in many cases, have the same meanings as their natural language counterparts. If, on the other hand, formal methods are not used to define SW terms, then how is it possible to provide them with meanings that can be interpreted by a machine?

In the section titled "Towards A Meaning-As-Use Model" below we will see that this dilemma is based on the mistaken presupposition that the *meanings/referents* of SW terms must always be given by precise *definitions* in order for the goals of the SW to be achieved. We will see that a meaning-as-use point of view can be integrated into an account of the meaning/reference of R-URIs that advocates the use of formal methods to help *explicate* the intended senses of SW terms rather than as a means of providing a precise definition of their meaning. Not only does such an account satisfy the goals of the SW, but it also enables SW technology to represent situations where diverse communities of users having substantive disagreements lay claim to having the correct understanding of the use of a term, something that seems to be problematic for the OM view.

The Marriage Use-Case in a Nutshell

In order to give the reader a sense of what the argument is all about, it will be helpful to give a preview of the key example used to develop the discussion. Suppose agent A defines *marriage* in such a way that the very idea of same-sex marriage

is logically incompatible with that definition and suppose agent B's definition is compatible with the idea of same-sex marriage. Suppose that it is true that the denotation of the concept of *marriage* is determined by the definition (or theory) an agent has concerning the concept (this is just the OM view). Cleary A's definition of the concept is incompatible with B's and therefore they cannot (on the OM view) have the same denotation (either extensionally or intensionally). When A and B use the vocabulary of marriage they are, by the OM view, talking about two entirely different things. They are "talking past" each other. Hence, it is not even possible for them to express any substantive disagreement using that vocabulary.

This conclusion violates common-sense. Many people have very strong conflicting views about what marriage is, others may take more neutral stances, but surely all these people can talk to each other and communicate using the same vocabulary. When one person says "marriage is only between one man and one woman" and another responds "two people of the same sex can be married to each other" they are in substantive disagreement with each other, not talking past each other. To the extent that current semantic web practice using the precepts of the OM view does not account for that fact, to that extent current semantic web practice is flawed.

Motivation

It is important to understand that the point of this chapter is not to advocate meaning-as-use over correspondence as a philosophy of language (or to deny the utility of formal semantic methods in SW practice). Both of these views accord well with *certain* intuitions concerning the way language works. The point is rather that the correspondence vision seems to be an unquestioned presupposition in much ontology-oriented SW practice. Historically this might arise from the fact that the correspondence vision has been an unquestioned presupposition of much work in the

AI community. However that may be, the goals of the SW clearly involve bridging the gap between formal languages and the natural languages of ordinary life in a way, and on a scale, that has never happened before in the history of computing. For this reason, issues and problems arising from the existence of that gap are bound to become more visible and important in the future. The goal of this chapter is to anticipate some of those problems, analyze them, and provide a principled way to handle them.

CORRESPONDENCE VERSUS HOLISM

Two Philosophical Visions of the Relationship between Language and Reality

Before describing the two visions it should be noted that these views are not necessarily attributable to any particular philosopher or philosophical school. Rather, the two visions described in this chapter are composite sketches based on the author's understanding of pertinent trends in the history of philosophy. The author's claim to some degree of competence in this realm arises from his having earned a Ph.D. in philosophy (Ginsberg 1983).

The essence of the correspondence vision is that it sees linguistic truth, reference, and meaning as being derived via a mapping to a fully determinate reality. *That* reality exists independently of thought/belief and language, and the aforementioned mapping of the latter to it. Statements are meaningful because their constituent non-logical terms correspond to pieces of reality, whether concrete objects, e.g., "The Moon," or properties, e.g. "being a person." When someone utters a statement what they have said is true, or false, depending on whether or not the intended mappings of the statement's constituent terms is, or is not, exemplified by the structure of reality. This appears to be, more or less, the view put forth by

"the early" Wittgenstein in (Wittgenstein, 1921), a view that he latter rejected in (Wittgenstein, 1963). Putting it in less picturesque terms, a statement's meaning is given by its "truth-conditions," which are determinate non-linguistic entities, and a statement is true if and only if its truth-conditions obtain. (Note that this is not to say that truth-conditions can be *expressed* independently of any language, only that their *existence* does not depend on language.)

On the holistic view, the meaning of a statement and its constituent terms is not a function of some mapping to an independent fully determinate reality. To quote Wittgenstein "...the meaning of a word is its use in the language game (Wittgenstein, 1963)." In other words, the meaning of a linguistic expression in a language is determined by how it is used by a community of competent rational speakers of the language. For our purposes we focus on the declarative use of language, i.e., statements. On the holistic view, the meaning of a statement and its constituent terms involves a complicated "web" of inferential, evidential, and behavioral connections to other statements and beliefs, as well as to actions that speakers of the language are disposed to take under various circumstances. Since meaning and truth are intimately related, this view has important consequences for the latter notion as well. Whereas the correspondence view tends to see language as something that we can use to render or represent an independent realm of truth "piece-by-piece", on the holistic view language and belief are interwoven into a total system that we use to structure the world we experience. To quote Quine: "Any statement can be held true come what may, if we make drastic enough adjustments elsewhere in the system (Quine, 1951)."

Fully Determinate Reality versus Ontological Indeterminacy

In order to better understand the correspondence vision we need to have some account of the notion of something's being "fully determinate," a notion which we have used without discussion thus far.

We can say that a concrete object O is *fully determinate* if and only if for any property P (or any relation involving other objects) it is either the case that has O has P or O does not have P. This seems like the ultimate tautology. Ignoring vagueness (when is someone "bald"?), and quantum-level reality (a quantum system in a "superposition" for an observable operator – *position*, for example - does not have a value for the corresponding property), isn't every concrete object fully determinate in this sense?

From the holistic point of view this question is misguided because it presupposes a clear-cut distinction between reality and the language used to talk about it, a distinction that a holist finds objectionable. For a holist, whether or not a *statement* of the form "O has P" (object O has property P) is true is not something that is determined solely by the "way things are" in some ultimate sense (i.e., without regard to a total system of language and belief). Consider two communities of rational speakers of a language such that in one community "O has P" is accepted and in the other "O does *not* have P" is accepted. Suppose that these two communities have taken account of all existing evidence in their system of belief, and that they have constructed their overall systems so that any future piece of evidence could in principle be accommodated while still holding onto their respective assent to or dissent from "O has P." By construction of the scenario, there *is* nothing more that anyone could *know* that would force one of these communities to change its world view on pain of otherwise falling into irrationality. Such scenarios are rather commonplace, in philosophy, e.g., Descartes' "evil genius" conjecture, in scientific theorizing, e.g., Poincare's conventionalist position regarding whether physical space is Euclidean or non-Euclidean, as well as in everyday life, e.g., whether or not the US constitution includes a right to privacy.

One of the novel aspects of twentieth century analytic philosophy, as represented by "the latter" Wittgenstein (1963) and Quine (1951, 1969), is the idea that such situations can be seen as involving *indeterminacy* rather than an epistemological quandary. In other words, the suggestion is that given two or more conflicting "total theories" of the world, or some domain, all of which are equally good in terms of their predictive power and other observable attributes, *there is no truth to the matter* as to which one is "correct." In this chapter we use the term *ontological indeterminacy* to describe situations in which two or more incompatible conceptual systems can be applied to structuring a domain of interest with equal empirical adequacy.

So far we have talked about full determinacy for concrete objects. What about properties and relations? What does it mean for a property, such as *being a person*, to be "fully determinate?" We may divide properties into two categories. The first type can be thought of as *primitive* in the sense that an object's having such a property is not reducible to anything else. Properties such as *being red* or *being blue* might fall into that category. Then a primitive property P is fully determinate if and only if every concrete object either is or is not an instance of P. Properties that are not primitive are, in some sense, composed out of logical combinations of other properties. For example the property of *being colored* would be a disjunctive composition of the properties *being red*, *being blue*, etc. This suggests the following *recursive* definition: a property is fully determinate if and only if it is either a fully determinate primitive property or is composed out of fully determinate properties.

As mentioned above, there is a more sophisticated version of the correspondence picture that introduces a layer of concepts that mediate the mapping from language to reality. As shown in Figure 2 below, it is the concepts that are in turn directly mapped to a fully determinate non-linguistic (and non-conceptual) reality. There are

Figure 2. The correspondence vision

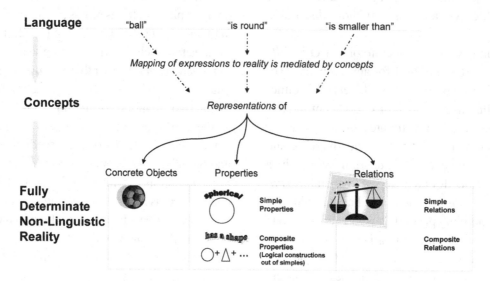

a number of reasons for introducing that layer, not least of which is a certain reluctance to posit the existence of composite properties as "first class" entities. Thus *being colored*, for example, would not have the same ontological status as the primitive *being red*. Moreover, introducing the concept layer also makes it easier for a correspondence theorist to explain how statements about non-existent entities are nonetheless meaningful (e.g., "The current king of France is bald"), and it also makes for a cleaner account of *analytic truth* as we shall now see.

For every fully determinate object, property, and relation we assume that the correspondence view postulates a corresponding fully determinate concept. (The reverse does not hold: the concept of a *round square*, for example, represents a composition of properties that does not exist, i.e., there is no property *being a round square*..) By the above definitions, statements formed by combining expressions referring to fully determinate concepts using standard logical operators must have a truth value, i.e., are either true or false. For example, given that *Employee* and *Person* are fully determinate concepts it follows that (1) above must be either true or false. Moreover, any

concept that represents a non-primitive fully determinate property will have certain *analytically* true statements associated with it, i.e., statements that are true by definition. For example, any statement of the form "If x is red then x is colored" must be true: the concept *red* represents the property *being red*, the concept *colored* represents the property *being colored*, and since the latter is a disjunctive property including the former, a determinate object that is red but not colored cannot exist.

To represent a fully determinate concept in some formal language one must formulate both its analytic and significant empirical relationships to other concepts as statements in that language. While the latter generally involve specialized knowledge gleaned by experience with the world, the former, being true by definition, should be accessible to anyone versed in the meanings of the concepts. The set of such statements is, by construction, guaranteed to include the "real world" as one of its models, in the sense of formal semantics. The more statements contained in the set, the more restrictive the set of models satisfying it. So eventually, for most intents and purposes, the set of statements can be said to pick out or refer to real world objects, properties, and relations, by virtue of its singling out the real world as its only model (*modulo* any isomorphic models).

Critique of Correspondence and the OM view

What is wrong with the OM view? There are two answers to this question, one that focuses on the correspondence presuppositions of the OM view, and one that focuses on the problems that adherence to it causes for SW practice. First let's look at the problems caused by the correspondence view.

Again we consider the *Employee* discussed above. On the correspondence view, statement (1) is meaningful and true because there exist two fully determinate concepts which are the referents of the terms "employee" and "person" and these concepts represent fully determinate composite properties such that being one necessarily involves being the other. (If statement (1) does not strike the reader as a good example of analytic truth, then another example, such as "Cats are animals" can be used instead.)

Now ask yourself if there are no realistic circumstances under which you might come to question the truth of (1). Is it possible that someday computers or dogs or cats might become employees but still not be persons? Imagine a world in which the cause of animal-rights gains so much momentum that an "animal bill of rights" becomes legally binding in some region. This bill of rights might accord animals a legal status below that of personhood, but high enough that animals used for certain "jobs," e.g., bomb-sniffing dogs, must be treated as legal employees.

An adherent of the correspondence view might say that those are circumstances in which people might decide to use words differently, but that (1) would still be true under the original mapping to reality. After all, the concepts that make (1) true represent fully determinate entities that have an existence independent of any particular language.

Looking at this from the holistic view, one could argue that a term such as "employee" is a clear example of one that should not be viewed as getting its meaning primarily from a correspondence mapping to an external reality. On this view, not only were there large stretches of human history in which no employees existed, there were also times when neither the concept *Employee* nor the property *being an employee* existed – or at least there was no truth to the matter as to whether or not the latter existed. The *Employee* concept/property is a creation of our culture. The exact specification of this concept is never irrevocably fixed because our system of concepts, our language, is a highly interconnected web of statements and beliefs that is capable of being adjusted in the face of our ongoing experience. If we started to admit computers and other non-persons as employees, then they would *be* employees. To argue about whether this would amount to a change in our language versus a change in reality is to argue about nothing. There simply would be no truth to the matter as to whether the class of things that *really are employees* had been discovered to be larger than previously thought, or that the word "employee" no longer referred to the concept *Employee* but to some other concept.

The holistic view seems to be a better account to this extent: natural language is a rule-governed activity, but the rules for using a term or uttering a statement are typically not fully determinate, i.e., competent rational speakers of a language can disagree about whether or not the use of a term is applicable in a given circumstance. Maintaining that there really is a "truth to the matter" in such cases goes beyond the linguistic evidence and could put ontological engineers in the position of being "philosopher kings" when it comes to representing human knowledge.

It is important to be clear about what we are using the holist critique to say. We are *emphatically not* saying that formal ontologies and their formal semantic foundations are useless or always somehow flawed as representations on the SW. We *are* saying that when they are useful and good as SW representations it is in virtue of their being in good alignment with the current norms and rules of usage for the corresponding natural language terms within the community of interest, and *not* because they somehow are in correspondence with a fully determinate language-independent reality.

The OM view and Semantic Web Practice

Whatever one thinks of holism as a philosophical theory, SW practice must take the lesson of ontological indeterminacy to heart. If rational competent speakers of a natural language cannot "close ranks" on whether a dog can be an employee, or whether Pluto is a planet (Ginsberg, 2006), or whether a "same-sex marriage" *is* a marriage, should SW technology force a SW agent to infer one or the other view in order to use SW versions of those terms? If someone, even after Pluto's official demotion to non-planetary status, insists that Pluto *is* a planet, we understand what that person is saying, even if we endorse the official position., or have no position on the matter. However, on the OM view, it does not seem possible for a SW agent to be able to exercise this "ontological tolerance," so to speak. As we shall see shortly, the OM view, taken together with the standard first-order model theory used as the semantics for SW languages such as OWL, makes no provision for such disagreements to be represented *as substantive disagreements* in a machine interpretable manner at all.

We will use the term *Ontological Overdetermination* to designate situations in which the use of a formally defined SW term *ipso facto* commits a SW agent to accepting or drawing certain implications or consequences that one could refrain from accepting or drawing in natural language while still using the term in the same way. This is similar to, if not the same as, the issue of "social meaning"

(Clark, 2003). We now explore, in depth, a real world example of this situation.

Two Ontologies of Marriage

The statement that two people are a married couple is normally held to be a matter of fact that can be established by certain well-defined evidence. However, because the concept of *marriage* is tied to legal, religious, moral and cultural systems of language and belief, the question as to whether two people are *really* a married couple is one that can be answered differently in different communities even in the face of identical evidence, i.e., *marriage* is ontologically indeterminate. This is especially true in contemporary society as regards the "validity" of same-sex marriage. Indeed, it is entirely possible, if not probable, that developments in this area will lead to a world in which certain geopolitical entities recognize same sex unions as valid marriages whereas others explicitly prohibit such marriages. Appendix 1 below contains two OWL ontologies in XML syntax that formalize two incompatible understandings of the concept of marriage: MarriageA.owl formalizes the "marriage is between one man and one woman" idea and MarriageB.owl allows for same sex couples to be married couples. We will present a more readable summary of the highlights of these ontologies in the ensuing discussion.

As can be seen from Figure 3 above and Figure 4 below, both ontologies contain a notion of *Couple* that is defined in the same way: something belongs to the class *Couple* if it has exactly 2 values for the property *hasMember*, both of which belong to the class *Person*. The ontology MarriageA, posits *MaleCouple*, *FemaleCouple*, and *OppositeSexCouple*, as subclasses of *Couple*. A *MaleCouple*, in addition to meeting the restrictions of *Couple*, must also meet the more specific constraint that only entities belonging to class *MalePerson* (an entity belonging to class *Person* with value *Male* for property *hasGender*) are allowed as values of the *hasMember* property. The class *FemaleCouple*

Figure 3. Marriage defined in MarriageA ontology

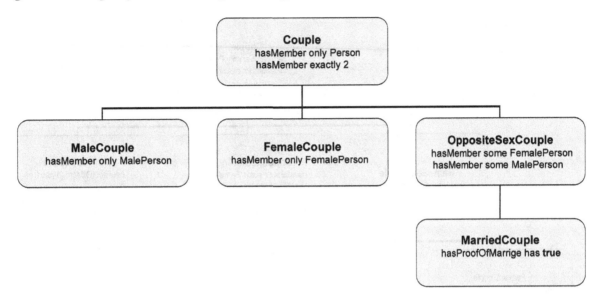

is similarly defined in terms of *FemalePerson*. *OppositeSexCouple* requires one *FemalePerson* as a value of *hasMember* and one MalePerson as a value of *hasMember*.

Finally a *MarriedCouple* is defined as an *OppositeSexCouple* for which the boolean-valued property *hasProofOfMarriage* has the value *true*. Intuitively the latter property should be interpreted to mean that the couple in question is known to have completed some process that is legally sanctioned to constitute marriage in *some* recognized geopolitical entity. The key point is that, according to MarriageA, no *MaleCouple* or *FemaleCouple* can be a *MarriedCouple* regardless of the corresponding value of that property, because no such couple can be an *OppositeSexCouple*.

The ontology MarriageB, posits *SameSexCouple*, *OppositeSexCouple*, and *MarriedCouple* as subclasses of *Couple*. The *SameSexCouple* subclass is essentially a union of *FemaleCouple* and *MaleCouple* as defined in MarriageA. Ideally one would like to define *SameSexCouple* as a *Couple* such that the gender values of its *hasMember* items are the *same*. This would seem to be require the use of individual variables which are

not available in OWL. *OppositeSexCouple* is also defined as in MarriageA. The key difference is that *MarriedCouple* is defined as a direct subclass of *Couple*, so that any couple with *hasProofOfMarriage* value *true* is a *MarriedCouple*.

Certain statements about individual persons and couples are not shown in the figures, but are included in the specification of these ontologies in Appendix 1. This is done in order to allow the reader to verify the inferential properties of the two ontologies. Thus MarriageA contains the following:

```
<MalePerson rdf:ID="Jack"/>
 <owl:AllDifferent>
  <owl:distinctMembers
rdf:parseType="Collection">
   <MalePerson rdf:ID="George"/>
   <MalePerson
rdf:about="#Jack"/>
  </owl:distinctMembers>
 </owl:AllDifferent>
<Couple rdf:ID="Couple_3">
 <hasMember
rdf:resource="#Jack"/>
```

Figure 4. Marriage defined in MarriageB ontology

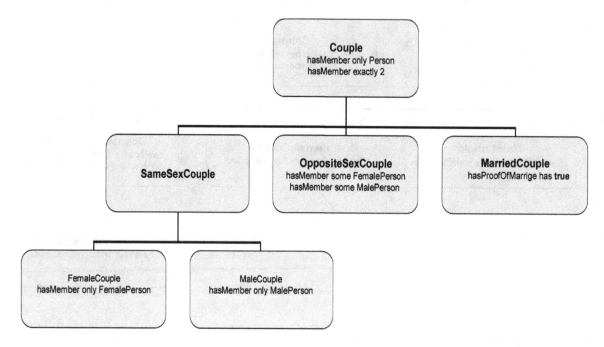

```
<hasMember
rdf:resource="#George"/>
 <rdf:type
rdf:resource="#MarriedCouple"/>
      </Couple>
```

These statements assert the existence of an instance of *MarriedCouple* consisting of distinct individuals *MalePerson* Jack and *MalePerson* George. Using a reasoner like Pellet (obtained at http://pellet.owldl.com/), it is easy to verify that MarriageA is inconsistent due to the presence of these statements. To be precise, Pellet (as configured for SWOOP version 2.3, obtained via http://www.mindswap.org/2004/SWOOP/) will say that one of either Jack or George is forced to be both a *FemalePerson* and a *MalePerson*, which is not possible, and therefore the ontology is inconsistent.

MarriageB contains the following:

```
<MalePerson rdf:ID="George"/>
<MalePerson rdf:ID="Jack"/>
<owl:AllDifferent>
  <owl:distinctMembers
rdf:parseType="Collection">
   <MalePerson
rdf:about="#George"/>
   <MalePerson
rdf:about="#Jack"/>
  </owl:distinctMembers>
 </owl:AllDifferent>
 <Couple rdf:ID="Couple_1">
    <hasMember
rdf:resource="#Jack"/>
    <hasProofOfMarriage
rdf:datatype="http://www.
w3.org/2001/XMLSchema#boolean">
      true</hasProofOfMarriage>
    <hasMember
rdf:resource="#George"/>
 </Couple>
```

These statements assert the existence of a *Couple,* Couple_1, consisting of distinct individuals *MalePerson* Jack and *MalePerson* George having the value *true* for *hasProofOfMarriage*. In this case a reasoner like Pellet will not only verify the consistency of the ontology but will also reach the valid conclusion that Couple_1 is an instance of *MarriedCouple* since all the restrictions on the latter are satisfied by Couple_1.

In order to see how the OM view leads to *ontological overdetermination* with respect to this property and to set the stage for future discussion we need to add a few more details. First, for the sake of brevity we define the following two prefixes:

```
mA = http://www.ontologies.net/
marriageA.owl
mB = http://www.ontologies.net/
marriageB.owl
```

so *mA:MarriedCouple* is the R-URI for the property *married couple* in ontology MarriageA and *mB:MarriedCouple* is the R-URI for the property *married couple* in ontology MarriageB. Secondly, let us suppose that the following instance data constitutes information that is to be asserted to two independent applications each utilizing one of these two ontologies:

```
<owl:AllDifferent>
 <owl:distinctMembers
rdf:parseType="Collection">
  <FemalePerson
rdf:about="#Jane"/>
  <FemalePerson
rdf:about="#Sally"/>
 </owl:distinctMembers>
</owl:AllDifferent>
<Couple rdf:ID="Couple_X">
  <hasMember
rdf:resource="#Jane"/>
  <hasMember
rdf:resource="#Sally"/>
```

```
<hasProofOfMarriage
rdf:datatype="http://www.
w3.org/2001/XMLSchema#boolean">
    true</hasProofOfMarriage>
</Couple>.                    (4)
```

That is, Couple_X has members Sally and Jane, two distinct female persons, with value *true* for *hasProofOfMarriage*. We refer to (4) as the "instance input data" of the scenario. Finally consider the following two statements:

```
Couple_X rdf:type
mA:MarriedCouple            (5)
Couple_X rdf:type
mB:MarriedCouple            (6).
```

(To be completely precise, all class, property, and individual terms used here should have a prefix to make it clear which ontology is being referenced. However, since the definition of these other terms is the same in both ontologies we can avoid that complication.) From our discussion it is clear that (5) is not only false, but also leads to an inconsistency relative to MarriageA (augmented with the instance input data). Statement (6) is true and can indeed be inferred from MarriageB and the instance input data.

Problem in Representing Substantive Conflict

While it *seems* that MarriageA and MarriageB are in disagreement over the implications of the instance input data, the fact is that, *given the OM view*, the problem is rather that *there is literally no disagreement*. The reason is that under the OM view mA:MarriedCouple and mB:MarriedCouple *cannot possibly be referring to the same property*. Under the OM view the properties identified by mA:MarriedCouple/mB:MarriedCouple are determined by the information encoded in MarriageA.owl/MarriageB.owl. But as we have seen, MarriageA.owl represents *married couple* in such a way that Couple_X *cannot possibly* be in the extension of that property, while MarriageB.owl is consistent with that fact. If these two R-URIs referred to the same property, then Couple_X would *both* be *and* not be an instance of that property, which is impossible. This is just another way of saying that there is no model for the theory formed by merging the class definitions of MarriageA.owl with MarriageB.owl *if* the two R-URIs are constrained to have the same interpretation. The bottom line is that, since the two R-URIs must refer to different "resources" (bits of fully determinate reality), statements (5) and (6) really do not represent a disagreement about anything.

Ontological Overdetermination

To see how this relates to the issue of ontological overdetermination we first note that a competent speaker of English can use terms like "marriage" or "married couple" correctly without necessarily having a firm view one way or the other as to whether or not a same sex couple can *really* be married. We also note that competent speakers of English on opposing sides of this issue see the question as to whether Couple_X in our example is a married couple as a *substantive* argument that cannot be resolved by saying that the two groups are referring to different properties when using the terminology in question.

On the OM view using an R-URI like mA:MarriedCouple to say something essentially commits a SW agent to the entire theory encoded in the defining ontology. There is no way for the agent to "say" something like "well, I am using the term in much the same way as the usage dictated in this ontology, but I don't necessarily accept all the implications of the ontology." If MarriageA and MarriageB are the two possible choices for a SW developer to use in an application, then once the choice is made certain facts follow irrevocably. If MarriageA is used then a SW agent based on this application will not be able to "deal with" the

possibility of same sex marriage, in the following sense: if it somehow is required to interpret an OWL or RDF statement using mB:MarriedCouple it will not be able to conclude that the statement in question is about marriage. Depending on the context and the application design it might conclude that the statement in question has nothing to do with marriage (mA:MarriedCouple) or it might conclude that it is invalid input or something of that nature. If MarriageB is chosen then, the application will have similar difficulties when presented with a statement couched in terms of MarriageA. There is no way for a SW developer to write an application which, like a competent speaker of English, can use the term *married couple* correctly without somehow giving the appearance that a definitive position on the question of same sex marriage has been adopted.

Use Case

Aside from the general desire to have the Semantic Web mirror human use of language, there are compelling design goals for requiring an application to have a way of separating the intention to use a term in a certain way from the commitment to a precise theory defining the meaning of that term. In order to see this, we present a use case that builds upon the scenario we have discussed.

Suppose that geopolitical entity A does not allow same sex marriage and geopolitical entity B does. That is, we may assume that ontology MarriageA/MarriageB captures the legally sanctioned meaning of *Married Couple* in A/B. Suppose that Jane and Sally are a legally married same sex couple from B traveling to A. A may not allow its own citizens to engage in same sex marriage, but it is legally bound to recognize certain of B's laws as they pertain to B's citizens traveling within its borders (including those governing marriage). (At the current time this scenario seems to exactly the case if one takes A as being the state of New York and B as being the state of Massachusetts.) If relevant software applications in A were based on MarriageA and worked according to the current SW practice, they would probably simply not allow information about Jane and Sally to be entered due to inconsistency. Or if it did accept the information it would not be able to appropriately process it in terms of the laws regarding marriage. That could be exactly the right behavior if Jane and Sally were citizens of A applying for a marriage license, but it is clearly not acceptable if, for example, some issue involving spousal rights arises while Jane and Sally are in A.

Any proposed solution needs to accept that there is no way that any authority can force A to adopt the more permissive MarriageB as the "correct" definition of the relevant concepts. However, it is in all parties' interests to make the software work correctly and do that as efficiently as possible.

TOWARDS A MEANING-AS-USE MODEL

Suppose we accept a meaning-as-use point of view, and accept the implication that the meanings of natural language terms cannot in general be precisely defined using formal ontologies. We are then faced with the second horn of the dilemma mentioned above, namely, how can machine-useable versions of these terms be constructed?

The way out of the dilemma is to recognize that it is not necessary for the meanings of natural language terms to be precisely definable in order for *people* to communicate "matters of fact" using those terms. Moreover, as we have seen, even when terms are precisely definable in alternate ways, and people are aware of those definitions, it is not always necessary for people to agree on a particular definition in order to communicate using those terms. In the same way, it should be possible to design SW applications to use terms in ways that communicate facts among themselves (and with humans) without requiring a SW agent to embrace a particular theory as to the definitive

meaning of those terms. A related design goal is the ability for applications using different theories involving the same term to communicate using that term despite differences in those theories.

Both of these goals can be achieved by allowing machines to link formal ontologies to terms as a means of *explicating* (explaining or providing a formal guide to) *the intended usage of a SW term* (so other machines can "understand" how the term is being used). Two machines might link two different, possibly incompatible, ontologies to the *same* intended usage of a term. Moreover, this idea can be extended to allow the problem of ontological overdetermination to be handled. Anyone developing an application that is required to remain "neutral" with respect to an SW term with two or more competing incompatible explications could do so in at least two ways: they could link the term in question to the intended usage without providing any explication, or they could indicate that their use of the term is *partially explicated* by two or more of the conflicting explications in question, where an understanding of the latter option will be provided below.

In this section we discuss some of the requirements of this meaning-as-use approach in more detail and show how it can handle the marriage use case.

Labeling Terms and Their Uses

In order to drive the wedge between *usage* and *explication* that the meaning-as-use model assumes, a standard way of labeling natural language terms and labeling the ways they are used in various domains or communities of interest is required. This could be thought of as a dictionary of usage similar to existing dictionaries or online resources such as WordNet (see http://wordnet.princeton. edu). The main requirements for the meaning-as-use model are: 1) it must be possible for an application developer to search the dictionary by term in order to determine what usages exist, 2) there should be enough natural language content (which can take the form of pointers to entries in established dictionaries) provided for each usage so that a developer can determine which one is best for the application at hand, and 3) each recorded usage must be machine-readable and uniquely labeled.

```
<http://www.umo.org/useage-
dict.owl#Usage-101.1>  rdf:type
umo:Usage ;
        umo:ID "101.1"^^xsd:string
;
        umo:hasLanguageTermPair
                umo:English-Java,
umo:German-Java, umo:Indonesian-
Java ;
        umo:hasDictionaryEntry
                "wordnet-sensekey:
java%1:18:00::"^^xsd:string ;
        umo:hasUsageComment
                "The Java program-
ming language"^^xsd:string .
<http://www.umo.org/useage-
dict.owl#Usage-101.2> rdf:type
umo:Usage ;
        umo:ID "101.2"^^xsd:string
;
        umo:hasLanguageTermPair
                umo:English-Java,
umo:German-Java, umo:Indonesian-
Jawa ;
        umo:hasDictionaryEntry
                "wordnet-sense-
key: java%1:15:00::"^^xsd:string
;
        umo:hasUsageComment
                "An island of
Indonesia"^^xsd:string .
```

The details of how a usage dictionary that meets these requirements is designed, implemented, and maintained, are issues beyond the scope of this chapter. Above should suffice as a concrete example of what two usages might look like written

in an OWL/RDF language (Turtle). The classes and properties used in above are also formalized by means of OWL/RDF and may be viewed in Appendix 2 below. Each usage portrayed in above is an individual in the ontology http://www.umo.org/useagedict.owl (a fictional ontology maintained by the fictional "Usage Maintenance Organization (UMO)"). The first entry, with usage label (ID) 101.1 corresponds to the English (German, Indonesian) use of the word 'Java' to talk about the well-known programming language, while the entry labeled 101.2 relates to the usage of that term to talk about the island in Indonesia in the same languages. Information that a developer would use to select one of these usages is, in this scheme, is conveyed by both the hasUsageComment and hasDictionaryEntry properties. In this ontology the latter is a string that contains information pointing to a word-sense in WordNet. (Another way of supplying such information would be to provide links to entries in well-known portals such as Wikipedia.) An interesting possibility shown in the schema of above is the use of multiple hasLanguageTermPair property values to provide multilingual capability. (Thus note that the Indonesian term for the island of Java is 'Jawa.') In other words, a single usage dictionary based on the schema of in Appendix 2 could accommodate as many natural languages as desired.

Although there are advantages in assuming a *single* standard usage dictionary, the meaning-as-use model does not impose that as a requirement, and we do not make that assumption here. That is why the link from intended usage records to usages is specified by a URL formed by combining the URI for a usage dictionary with the code assigned to the usage by that dictionary, e.g., http://www.umo.org/useagedict.owl#Usage-101.1, and not by a presumed globally unique usage code.

Intended Usage Records

Assuming the existence of a usage dictionary meeting the requirements outlined above, there are several issues that need to be addressed: 1) how does a SW developer link an application's use of a SW term to the desired usage, 2) how does a SW developer link that intended usage to a formal explication of it, and 3) how does an arbitrary SW agent or application figure out what usage and explication has been associated with a SW term by the developer?

It is clear that in order to successfully address these issues *some* well-publicized format with "clear semantics" must be available for developers to use in addressing (1) and (2). SW agents and applications could then easily be designed to deal with issue (3) by making them able to handle the same format. We will call this format an *Intended Usage Record* (IUR) specification. In this chapter we present a simple outline of such a specification. However, given the importance of R-URIs to the SW, it would be reasonable to suppose that at some point such a specification would be proposed and maintained by an appropriate organization. For now we imagine a "Semantic-Web-Term Maintenance Organization" is responsible. Therefore we use the prefix "swm" in our specification to designate a namespace developed by that organization. Appendix 3 below contains an OWL/RDF specification for the entities and properties to be introduced below. The schema in Appendix 3 formalizes three types of IURs: a "basic" type and two subtypes which are subclasses of the basic type. In this chapter we are mostly concerned with the two subtypes.

Below is an OWL/RDF version of an IUR subtype1 instance (see Appendix 3). The value of the property hasSemanticWebTerm, is the SW term for which the IUR is intended. The value of the hasUsageURI property contains a URL for the desired usage record in the usage dictionary. In the scheme shown here this URL is formed by combining the URI for the usage dictionary with the latter's code for the intended usage. Finally the value for the hasExplication property contains a reference to an ontology (or other machine-readable specification using a SW standard) that provides a formal theory concerning that usage.

```
<http://www.program-
ming.com/iur-java> rdf:type
swm:IntendedUsageRecord ;
  swm:hasUsageURI "http://
www.umo.org/useagedict.
owl#101.1"^^xsd:anyURI ;
  swm:hasSemanticWebTerm
"Java"^^xsd:string ;
      swm:hasExplication
"http://www.ontologies.org/pro-
gramming.owl"^^xsd:anyURI .
```

Now assume that www.programming.com is a URI that has a web-presence and that its owners would like to use http://www.programming.com/Java as an R-URI intended to refer to the Java programming language. How would they accomplish that? Assuming that something like the HTTP dereferencing scheme outlined in (Lewis ed., 2007) has been adopted as standard practice, the mechanism would work as follows. The owners of the web-presence would make sure that http://www.programming.com/Java returns an HTTP 303 response code ("see other") which would also include a URL for the IUR shown in above. . The fact that an HTTP 303 response code is returned tells the application that the identifier in question is indeed an R-URI. The redirected response to the IUR allows the application to access the intended usage via the information encoded therein. For example, the value of the hasUsageURI property, in itself, would enable a machine (or human) to know that two or more occurrences of a term in various RDF or OWL files are intended to be used in the same way. The URL in the hasExplication field could be used to retrieve the ontology that is intended to provide a formal explication of the usage of the SW term.

Use Case Revisited

We return to the example of marriage use case to show how the meaning-as-use model can address the design goals illustrated therein. Below is an OWL/RDF specification for a possible usage entry for the natural language term "married couple."

```
<http://www.umo.org/useage-
dict.owl#Usage-503.1> rdf:type
umo:Usage ;
        umo:ID
"503.1"^^xsd:string ;

umo:hasLanguageTermPair
              umo:English-Mar-
ried_Couple ;
        umo:hasDictionaryEntry
              "word-
net-sense-key: married_
couple%1:14:00::"^^xsd:string ;
    umo:hasUsageComment
              "Two people who
are legally married to each
other."^^xsd:string .
```

Shown below are two IURs of subtype1 for 'married couple' corresponding to the two competing theories of geopolitical entities A and B, where the ontologies referenced by the hasExplication property are the two ontologies MarriageA and MarriageB.

```
<http://www.GeoPolEnt-A.gov/
iur-MarriedCouple> rdf:type
swm:IntendedUsageRecord ;
      swm:hasUsageURI "http://
www.umo.org/useagedict.
owl#503.1"^^xsd:anyURI ;
      swm:hasSemanticWebTerm
"MarriedCouple"^^xsd:string ;
      swm:hasExplication
"http://www.GeoPolEnt-A.gov/Mar-
riageA.owl"^^xsd:anyURI .
```

```
<http://www.GeoPolEnt-B.gov/
iur-MarriedCouple> rdf:type
swm:IntendedUsageRecord ;
      swm:hasUsageURI "http://
www.umo.org/useagedict.
owl#503.1"^^xsd:anyURI ;
      swm:hasSemanticWebTerm
"MarriedCouple"^^xsd:string ;
      swm:hasExplication
"http://www.GeoPolEnt-B.gov/Mar-
riageB.owl"^^xsd:anyURI .
```

Let the following two prefixes be defined (and assume the existence of corresponding web-presences):

```
GEO-A = http://www.GeoPolEnt-A.
gov/
GEO-B = http://www.GeoPolEnt-B.
gov/
```

so that GEO-A:MarriedCouple and GEO-B:MarriedCouple would be dereferenced to the IURs shown above.

The instance input statements (4) described in the section titled "Two Ontologies of Marriage" above are also assumed to be given. Corresponding to statements (5) and (6) in that section we now consider

```
Couple_X rdf:type GEO-
A:MarriedCouple (8)
Couple_X rdf:type GEO-
B:MarriedCouple (9).
```

The IURs retrieved from dereferencing the SW terms in these statements have the same usage URI (http://www.umo.org/useagedict.owl#503.1). That makes it easy to see that the usage of those terms is intended to be the same. Using the given instance data and the two ontologies a machine can determine that (8) is false and (9) is true. But since the machine also knows that both statements are intended to be about the *same* couple and the *same* use of the term "married couple," the machine knows that the situation is one in which a substantive disagreement exists.

However, the crux of the use case concerns how A can accommodate legally married same sex couples from B without compromising its own legal position on same sex marriage. For the purposes of this discussion we may make the assumption, which may in fact be warranted, that for any application involved in managing and administrating common public services it can be known in advance whether or not that service involves considerations related to the *conferring* of marital status according to the laws of A. For example, the service of providing a marriage license to a couple is an example of the latter, while any service that references spousal rights based upon a pre-existing marriage, such as probating a will, is not. In that case, developer's of A's applications could safely use GEO-A:MarriedCouple in the former type of applications, and GEO-B:MarriedCouple (or something equivalent) in the latter type. A couple applying for a marriage license in A would have to be of opposite gender in order to satisfy GEO-A:MarriedCouple, while a couple claiming spousal visitation rights in a hospital, for example, would have to satisfy GEO-B:MarriedCouple and could therefore be a same sex couple.

Avoiding Ontological Overdetermination

Continuing with this example, we show how the mechanism of IURs can be used to avoid ontological overdetermination. Using GEO-A:MarriedCouple or GEO-B:MarriedCouple to make statements could be seen as taking one view or the other concerning marriage by virtue of implications of the explicating theory. Suppose an application developer, or a user, wants to avoid giving that appearance. One way of doing so is to create an IUR that has no value for the hasExplication property. That could have some utility as far as human communication is concerned, since the

usage given in the IUR would give other users the intended sense. Obviously, that strategy would be unsatisfactory it the user wanted an application to reason using the term.

```
<http://www.example.org/
iur-MarriedCouple> rdf:type
swm:IntendedUsageRecord ;
    swm:hasUsageURI "http://
www.umo.org/useagedict.
owl#503.1"^^xsd:anyURI ;
    swm:hasSemanticWebTerm
"MarriedCouple"^^xsd:string ;
    swm:hasCompetingExplication
"http://www.GeoPolEnt-A.gov/Mar-
riageA.owl"^^xsd:anyURI ;
    swm:hasCompetingExplication
"http://www.GeoPolEnt-B.gov/Mar-
riageB.owl"^^xsd:anyURI .
```

By way of showing the flexibility that arises by drawing the distinction between *usage* and *explication*, we now present a way of achieving the desired neutrality without sacrificing machine-processing capability. To see how, assume that http://www.example.org is another web-presence, and consider the IUR of subtype2 (see Appendix 3) shown above.

In contrast to the previously shown IURs, the one in above has multiple values for the property hasCompetingExplication instead of any for the hasExplication property. Links to the two competing ontologies we have presented are present in that field.

This shows a way for a user to use the term in question with the same intended usage, 503.1, but that avoids taking sides on the issue of same sex marriage. Let EXP be the prefix http://www.example.org, and assume that EXP:MarriedCouple has been set up as an R-URI dereferenced to the IUR in above. Then to evaluate the truth-value of a statement of the form

```
Couple_X rdf:type
EXP:MarriedCouple (10)
```

a SW agent would consider *all* the competing theories listed in the hasCompetingExplication. If the evaluation comes out with the *same* result in all cases, e.g., *true*, then the application can use that result. If, on the other hand, the statement evaluates to different results depending on the theory used, the application can judge the statement to have no truth value. Thus, with respect to Couple_X as defined by (4) in the earlier section, statement (10) would fail to have a truth value. This idea is reminiscent of van Fraassen's (1969) notion of a supervaluation.

DISCUSSION

The IUR types presented here are one way in which the basic idea of separating intended usage from formal explication of a usage can be operationalized for the SW. Indeed the specification given in Appendix 3 could be improved upon in a number of ways. For example, in the case of subtype2 there should be some way of specifying the "semantics" of competing explications. We have talked about one method - supervaluations - but others are certainly possible.

However, the main goal of this chapter has been to make the basic argument that insightful and useful aspects of the meaning-as-use philosophy of language can be successfully integrated into the formal machinery of the SW. The chapter illustrates how doing so leads to solutions to problems encountered by the OM view. The specifications provided here are sufficient for that purpose.

To conclude, therefore, let us review and clarify some of the main points. First, the reasoning of this chapter is not an argument against the use of formal semantic methods vis-à-vis the SW. It is rather an argument against the idea that natural language terms (and therefore their SW counterparts) can be defined by formal methods in any more than

an approximate way. That is not to say that there is some other methodology that can yield *exact* definitions of such terms, it is rather an acknowledgment that no such definitions exist.

It is therefore central to the philosophical health of the SW vision that a more satisfying approach to SW reference/meaning than the OM view be found and integrated into SW architecture. If it currently seems there is no urgent need to convert into practice something like the solution expressed in this chapter, that is not because the problems addressed by this solution are not real. Rather it is because the SW is in its infancy. Understandably, at this stage researchers tend to be more concerned with high-profile issues that are likely to lead to immediate progress, such as establishing a workable regime whereby the whole idea of creating and maintaining global identifiers for entities can actually be realized, as in (Bouquet et. al., 2008). However, as the vision of the SW web gains currency, as developers and users alike come to appreciate the benefits of that vision, the demand for SW-enabled applications and services will grow. The ability to support semantically-rich interactions among SW applications which have no *a priori* knowledge of each other whatsoever will be a crucial requirement of the underlying architectures that will make it possible to fuel that demand. Without some principled approach to the problems caused by what we have termed "ontological indeterminacy" in this chapter, that requirement will not be met.

ACKNOWLEDGMENT

An earlier version of this chapter (Ginsberg 2006) was presented at the WWW2006 workshop on Identity, Reference, and the Web. I would like to thank the chairs of that workshop (Pat Hayes, Harry Halpin, and Henry Thompson) for providing a venue for the discussion of these issues and encouraging ongoing work in this area. Harry Halpin also offered useful suggestions on a version of this chapter, and I also thank him for the role he played in bringing a special issue of JSWIS into being in which that version of the chapter appeared (Ginsberg 2008). I also thank the editors and the anonymous reviewers of that chapter for their comments and suggestions. Finally, I am grateful to Leo Obrst of MITRE for providing encouragement and suggestions on the first version of this chapter.

REFERENCES

Berners-Lee, T. (2002). *What do HTTP URIs Identify?* http://www.w3.org/DesignIssues/HTTP-URI.html.

Berners-Lee, T., et al. (1998). *RFC 2396: Uniform Resource Identifiers (URI): Generic Syntax.* http://www.ietf.org/rfc/rfc2396.txt.

Booth, D. (2009). *Denotation as a Two-Step Mapping in Semantic Web Architecture.* Paper presented at IJCAI-2009, Pasadena, California. Retrieved from http://dbooth.org/2009/denotation/

Bouquet, P., Stoermer, H., Niederee, C., & Mana, A. (2008). Entity Name System: The Backbone of an Open and Scalable Web of Data. In *Proceedings of the IEEE International Conference on Semantic Computing.* Retrieved from http://www.okkam.org/publications/stoermer-EntityNameSystem.pdf

Clark, K. G. (2002). *Identity Crisis.* http://www.xml.com/pub/a/2002/09/11/deviant.html.

Clark, K. G. (2003). *The Social Meaning of RDF.* http://www.xml.com/pub/a/2003/03/05/social.html

Ginsberg, A. (1983). *Quantum Statistics, Quantum Field Theory, and The Interpretation Problem.* Ph.D. dissertation.

Ginsberg, A. (2006). *The Big Schema of Things: Two Philosophical Visions of the Relationship Between Language and Reality and Their Implications for the Semantic Web.* Paper presented at WWW 2006, Edinburg, Scotland. Retrieved from http://www.ibiblio.org/hhalpin/irw2006/aginsberg.pdf.

Ginsberg, A. (2008). Ontological Indeterminacy and The Semantic Web. *International Journal on Semantic Web and Information Systems*, *4*(2), 19–48.

Halpin, H., & Thompson, H. (2005). *Web Proper Names: Naming Referents on the Web.* Chiba, Japan: The Semantic Computing Initiative Workshop.

Lewis, R. (Ed.). (2007). *Dereferencing HTTP URIs, Draft Tag Finding.* Retrieved from http://www.w3.org/2001/tag/doc/httpRange-14/2007-08-31/HttpRange-14.html.

Pepper, S. (2003). *Curing the Web's Identity Crisis.* http://www.ontopia.net/topicmaps/materials/identitycrisis.html.

Quine, W. V. O. (1951). Two Dogmas Of Empiricism. *The Philosophical Review*, *60*, 20–43. doi:10.2307/2181906

Quine, W. V. O. (1969). Ontological Relativity . In *Ontological Relativity and Other Essays*. Columbia University Press.

Smith, B., & Ceusters, W. (2007). Ontology as the Core Discipline of Biomedical Informatics . In Crnkovic, G. D., & Stuart, S. (Eds.), *Computing, Information, Cognition* (pp. 104–122). Newcastle: Cambridge Scholars Press.

van Fraassen, B. (1969). Presuppositions, Supervaluations, and Free Logic . In Lambert, K. (Ed.), *The Logical Way of Doing Things* (pp. 67–91). New Haven: Yale University Press.

Wittgenstein, L. (1921) *Tractatus Logico-Philosophicus*. Retrieved from http://www.gutenberg.org/etext/5740.

Wittgenstein, L. (1963). *Philosophical Investigations*. New York: The Macmillan Company.

APPENDIX A: TWO ONTOLOGIES

MarriageA.owl

```
<?xml version="1.0"?>
<rdf:RDF
    xmlns="http://wwwontologies.net/marriageA.owl#"
    xmlns:rdf="http://www.w3.org/1999/02/22-rdf-syntax-ns#"
    xmlns:xsd="http://www.w3.org/2001/XMLSchema#"
    xmlns:rdfs="http://www.w3.org/2000/01/rdf-schema#"
    xmlns:owl="http://www.w3.org/2002/07/owl#"
  xml:base="http://wwwontologies.net/marriageA.owl">
  <owl:Ontology rdf:about=""/>
  <owl:Class rdf:ID="MarriedCouple">
    <owl:equivalentClass>
      <owl:Restriction>
        <owl:onProperty>
          <owl:DatatypeProperty rdf:ID="hasProofOfMarriage"/>
        </owl:onProperty>
        <owl:hasValue rdf:datatype="http://www.w3.org/2001/
XMLSchema#boolean"
        >true</owl:hasValue>
      </owl:Restriction>
    </owl:equivalentClass>
    <rdfs:subClassOf>
      <owl:Class rdf:ID="OppositeSexCouple"/>
    </rdfs:subClassOf>
  </owl:Class>
  <owl:Class rdf:ID="MaleCouple">
    <rdfs:subClassOf>
      <owl:Class rdf:ID="Couple"/>
    </rdfs:subClassOf>
    <owl:equivalentClass>
      <owl:Restriction>
        <owl:onProperty>
          <owl:ObjectProperty rdf:ID="hasMember"/>
        </owl:onProperty>
        <owl:allValuesFrom>
          <owl:Class rdf:ID="MalePerson"/>
        </owl:allValuesFrom>
      </owl:Restriction>
    </owl:equivalentClass>
  </owl:Class>
  <owl:Class rdf:about="#MalePerson">
```

171

```
  <owl:disjointWith>
    <owl:Class rdf:ID="FemalePerson"/>
  </owl:disjointWith>
  <rdfs:subClassOf>
    <owl:Class rdf:ID="Person"/>
  </rdfs:subClassOf>
  <owl:equivalentClass>
    <owl:Restriction>
      <owl:onProperty>
        <owl:ObjectProperty rdf:ID="hasGender"/>
      </owl:onProperty>
      <owl:hasValue>
        <Gender rdf:ID="MALE"/>
      </owl:hasValue>
    </owl:Restriction>
  </owl:equivalentClass>
</owl:Class>
<owl:Class rdf:about="#Couple">
  <rdfs:subClassOf rdf:resource="http://www.w3.org/2002/07/
owl#Thing"/>
  <rdfs:subClassOf>
    <owl:Restriction>
      <owl:onProperty>
        <owl:ObjectProperty rdf:about="#hasMember"/>
      </owl:onProperty>
      <owl:allValuesFrom>
        <owl:Class rdf:about="#Person"/>
      </owl:allValuesFrom>
    </owl:Restriction>
  </rdfs:subClassOf>
  <rdfs:subClassOf>
    <owl:Restriction>
      <owl:cardinality rdf:datatype="http://www.w3.org/2001/
XMLSchema#int"
      >2</owl:cardinality>
      <owl:onProperty>
        <owl:ObjectProperty rdf:about="#hasMember"/>
      </owl:onProperty>
    </owl:Restriction>
  </rdfs:subClassOf>
</owl:Class>
<owl:Class rdf:about="#OppositeSexCouple">
  <owl:equivalentClass>
    <owl:Class>
```

```
      <owl:intersectionOf rdf:parseType="Collection">
        <owl:Restriction>
          <owl:onProperty>
            <owl:ObjectProperty rdf:about="#hasMember"/>
          </owl:onProperty>
          <owl:someValuesFrom rdf:resource="#MalePerson"/>
        </owl:Restriction>
        <owl:Restriction>
          <owl:someValuesFrom>
            <owl:Class rdf:about="#FemalePerson"/>
          </owl:someValuesFrom>
          <owl:onProperty>
            <owl:ObjectProperty rdf:about="#hasMember"/>
          </owl:onProperty>
        </owl:Restriction>
      </owl:intersectionOf>
    </owl:Class>
  </owl:equivalentClass>
  <rdfs:subClassOf rdf:resource="#Couple"/>
</owl:Class>
<owl:Class rdf:about="#Person">
  <rdfs:subClassOf>
    <owl:Restriction>
      <owl:cardinality rdf:datatype="http://www.w3.org/2001/
XMLSchema#int"
      >1</owl:cardinality>
      <owl:onProperty>
        <owl:ObjectProperty rdf:about="#hasGender"/>
      </owl:onProperty>
    </owl:Restriction>
  </rdfs:subClassOf>
  <rdfs:subClassOf rdf:resource="http://www.w3.org/2002/07/
owl#Thing"/>
</owl:Class>
<owl:Class rdf:about="#FemalePerson">
  <owl:equivalentClass>
    <owl:Restriction>
      <owl:hasValue>
        <Gender rdf:ID="FEMALE"/>
      </owl:hasValue>
      <owl:onProperty>
        <owl:ObjectProperty rdf:about="#hasGender"/>
      </owl:onProperty>
    </owl:Restriction>
```

```
    </owl:equivalentClass>
    <owl:disjointWith rdf:resource="#MalePerson"/>
    <rdfs:subClassOf rdf:resource="#Person"/>
  </owl:Class>
  <owl:Class rdf:ID="Gender"/>
  <owl:Class rdf:ID="FemaleCouple">
    <owl:equivalentClass>
      <owl:Restriction>
        <owl:allValuesFrom rdf:resource="#FemalePerson"/>
        <owl:onProperty>
          <owl:ObjectProperty rdf:about="#hasMember"/>
        </owl:onProperty>
      </owl:Restriction>
    </owl:equivalentClass>
    <rdfs:subClassOf rdf:resource="#Couple"/>
  </owl:Class>
  <owl:ObjectProperty rdf:about="#hasGender">
    <rdfs:domain rdf:resource="#Person"/>
    <rdfs:range rdf:resource="#Gender"/>
  </owl:ObjectProperty>
  <owl:ObjectProperty rdf:about="#hasMember">
    <rdfs:range rdf:resource="#Person"/>
    <rdfs:domain rdf:resource="#Couple"/>
  </owl:ObjectProperty>
  <owl:DatatypeProperty rdf:about="#hasProofOfMarriage">
    <rdfs:domain rdf:resource="#Couple"/>
    <rdfs:range>
      <owl:DataRange>
        <owl:oneOf rdf:parseType="Resource">
          <rdf:first rdf:datatype="http://www.w3.org/2001/
XMLSchema#boolean"
          >false</rdf:first>
          <rdf:rest rdf:parseType="Resource">
            <rdf:first rdf:datatype="http://www.w3.org/2001/
XMLSchema#boolean"
            >true</rdf:first>
            <rdf:rest rdf:resource="http://www.w3.org/1999/02/22-
rdf-syntax-ns#nil"/>
          </rdf:rest>
        </owl:oneOf>
      </owl:DataRange>
    </rdfs:range>
  </owl:DatatypeProperty>
  <MalePerson rdf:ID="Jack"/>
```

```
  <owl:AllDifferent>
    <owl:distinctMembers rdf:parseType="Collection">
      <MalePerson rdf:ID="George"/>
      <MalePerson rdf:about="#Jack"/>
    </owl:distinctMembers>
  </owl:AllDifferent>
  <Couple rdf:ID="Couple_3">
    <hasMember rdf:resource="#Jack"/>
    <hasMember rdf:resource="#George"/>
    <rdf:type rdf:resource="#MarriedCouple"/>
  </Couple>
</rdf:RDF>
```

MarriageB.owl

```
<?xml version="1.0"?>
<rdf:RDF
    xmlns="http://www.ontologies.net/marriageB.owl#"
    xmlns:rdf="http://www.w3.org/1999/02/22-rdf-syntax-ns#"
    xmlns:xsd="http://www.w3.org/2001/XMLSchema#"
    xmlns:rdfs="http://www.w3.org/2000/01/rdf-schema#"
    xmlns:owl="http://www.w3.org/2002/07/owl#"
  xml:base="http://www.ontologies.net/marriageB.owl">
  <owl:Ontology rdf:about=""/>
  <owl:Class rdf:ID="MarriedCouple">
    <rdfs:subClassOf>
      <owl:Class rdf:ID="Couple"/>
    </rdfs:subClassOf>
    <owl:equivalentClass>
      <owl:Restriction>
        <owl:onProperty>
          <owl:DatatypeProperty rdf:ID="hasProofOfMarriage"/>
        </owl:onProperty>
        <owl:hasValue rdf:datatype="http://www.w3.org/2001/
XMLSchema#boolean"
        >true</owl:hasValue>
      </owl:Restriction>
    </owl:equivalentClass>
  </owl:Class>
  <owl:Class rdf:ID="Gender"/>
  <owl:Class rdf:ID="SameSexCouple">
    <rdfs:subClassOf>
      <owl:Class rdf:about="#Couple"/>
    </rdfs:subClassOf>
```

```
</owl:Class>
<owl:Class rdf:ID="FemalePerson">
  <rdfs:subClassOf>
    <owl:Class rdf:ID="Person"/>
  </rdfs:subClassOf>
  <owl:equivalentClass>
    <owl:Restriction>
      <owl:onProperty>
        <owl:ObjectProperty rdf:ID="hasGender"/>
      </owl:onProperty>
      <owl:hasValue>
        <Gender rdf:ID="FEMALE"/>
      </owl:hasValue>
    </owl:Restriction>
  </owl:equivalentClass>
</owl:Class>
<owl:Class rdf:ID="FemaleCouple">
  <rdfs:subClassOf rdf:resource="#SameSexCouple"/>
  <owl:equivalentClass>
    <owl:Restriction>
      <owl:onProperty>
        <owl:ObjectProperty rdf:ID="hasMember"/>
      </owl:onProperty>
      <owl:allValuesFrom rdf:resource="#FemalePerson"/>
    </owl:Restriction>
  </owl:equivalentClass>
</owl:Class>
<owl:Class rdf:ID="MaleCouple">
  <rdfs:subClassOf rdf:resource="#SameSexCouple"/>
  <owl:equivalentClass>
    <owl:Restriction>
      <owl:allValuesFrom>
        <owl:Class rdf:ID="MalePerson"/>
      </owl:allValuesFrom>
      <owl:onProperty>
        <owl:ObjectProperty rdf:about="#hasMember"/>
      </owl:onProperty>
    </owl:Restriction>
  </owl:equivalentClass>
</owl:Class>
<owl:Class rdf:about="#Person">
  <rdfs:subClassOf rdf:resource="http://www.w3.org/2002/07/
owl#Thing"/>
  <rdfs:subClassOf>
```

```
      <owl:Restriction>
        <owl:onProperty>
          <owl:ObjectProperty rdf:about="#hasGender"/>
        </owl:onProperty>
        <owl:cardinality rdf:datatype="http://www.w3.org/2001/
XMLSchema#int"
          >1</owl:cardinality>
      </owl:Restriction>
    </rdfs:subClassOf>
  </owl:Class>
  <owl:Class rdf:ID="OppositeSexCouple">
    <owl:equivalentClass>
      <owl:Class>
        <owl:intersectionOf rdf:parseType="Collection">
          <owl:Restriction>
            <owl:onProperty>
              <owl:ObjectProperty rdf:about="#hasMember"/>
            </owl:onProperty>
            <owl:someValuesFrom>
              <owl:Class rdf:about="#MalePerson"/>
            </owl:someValuesFrom>
          </owl:Restriction>
          <owl:Restriction>
            <owl:onProperty>
              <owl:ObjectProperty rdf:about="#hasMember"/>
            </owl:onProperty>
            <owl:someValuesFrom rdf:resource="#FemalePerson"/>
          </owl:Restriction>
        </owl:intersectionOf>
      </owl:Class>
    </owl:equivalentClass>
    <rdfs:subClassOf>
      <owl:Class rdf:about="#Couple"/>
    </rdfs:subClassOf>
  </owl:Class>
  <owl:Class rdf:about="#Couple">
    <rdfs:subClassOf rdf:resource="http://www.w3.org/2002/07/
owl#Thing"/>
    <rdfs:subClassOf>
      <owl:Restriction>
        <owl:cardinality rdf:datatype="http://www.w3.org/2001/
XMLSchema#int"
          >2</owl:cardinality>
        <owl:onProperty>
```

```
              <owl:ObjectProperty rdf:about="#hasMember"/>
          </owl:onProperty>
        </owl:Restriction>
    </rdfs:subClassOf>
    <rdfs:subClassOf>
      <owl:Restriction>
        <owl:allValuesFrom rdf:resource="#Person"/>
        <owl:onProperty>
          <owl:ObjectProperty rdf:about="#hasMember"/>
        </owl:onProperty>
      </owl:Restriction>
    </rdfs:subClassOf>
  </owl:Class>
  <owl:Class rdf:about="#MalePerson">
    <rdfs:subClassOf rdf:resource="#Person"/>
    <owl:equivalentClass>
      <owl:Restriction>
        <owl:hasValue>
          <Gender rdf:ID="MALE"/>
        </owl:hasValue>
        <owl:onProperty>
          <owl:ObjectProperty rdf:about="#hasGender"/>
        </owl:onProperty>
      </owl:Restriction>
    </owl:equivalentClass>
  </owl:Class>
  <owl:ObjectProperty rdf:about="#hasMember">
    <rdfs:range rdf:resource="#Person"/>
    <rdfs:domain rdf:resource="#Couple"/>
  </owl:ObjectProperty>
  <owl:ObjectProperty rdf:about="#hasGender">
    <rdfs:domain rdf:resource="#Person"/>
    <rdfs:range rdf:resource="#Gender"/>
  </owl:ObjectProperty>
  <owl:DatatypeProperty rdf:about="#hasProofOfMarriage">
    <rdfs:domain rdf:resource="#Couple"/>
    <rdfs:range>
      <owl:DataRange>
        <owl:oneOf rdf:parseType="Resource">
          <rdf:rest rdf:parseType="Resource">
            <rdf:first rdf:datatype="http://www.w3.org/2001/
XMLSchema#boolean"
              >true</rdf:first>
            <rdf:rest rdf:resource="http://www.w3.org/1999/02/22-
```

```
rdf-syntax-ns#nil"/>
        </rdf:rest>
        <rdf:first rdf:datatype="http://www.w3.org/2001/
XMLSchema#boolean"
        >false</rdf:first>
      </owl:oneOf>
    </owl:DataRange>
  </rdfs:range>
</owl:DatatypeProperty>
<MalePerson rdf:ID="George"/>
<MalePerson rdf:ID="Jack"/>
<owl:AllDifferent>
  <owl:distinctMembers rdf:parseType="Collection">
    <MalePerson rdf:about="#George"/>
    <MalePerson rdf:about="#Jack"/>
  </owl:distinctMembers>
</owl:AllDifferent>
<Couple rdf:ID="Couple_1">
  <hasMember rdf:resource="#Jack"/>
  <hasProofOfMarriage rdf:datatype="http://www.w3.org/2001/
XMLSchema#boolean"
  >true</hasProofOfMarriage>
  <hasMember rdf:resource="#George"/>
</Couple>
</rdf:RDF>
```

APPENDIX B: EXAMPLE USAGE-DICTIONARY SCHEMA

```
# Base: http://www.umo.org/useagedict.owl#
@prefix xsd: <http://www.w3.org/2001/XMLSchema#> .
@prefix default: <http://www.umo.org/useagedict.owl#> .
@prefix rdfs: <http://www.w3.org/2000/01/rdf-schema#> .
@prefix rdf: <http://www.w3.org/1999/02/22-rdf-syntax-ns#> .
@prefix owl: <http://www.w3.org/2002/07/owl#> .

###### CLASSES AND PROPERTIES ######

<http://www.umo.org/useagedict.owl>
      rdf:type owl:Ontology .
umo:Language
      rdf:type owl:Class .
umo:Term
      rdf:type owl:Class .
umo:Usage
      rdf:type owl:Class ;
      rdfs:subClassOf owl:Thing ;
      rdfs:subClassOf
            [ rdf:type owl:Restriction ;
              owl:minCardinality "1"^^xsd:int ;
              owl:onProperty umo:hasUsageComment
            ] ;
      rdfs:subClassOf
            [ rdf:type owl:Restriction ;
              owl:minCardinality "1"^^xsd:int ;
              owl:onProperty umo:hasLanguageTermPair
            ] ;
      rdfs:subClassOf
            [ rdf:type owl:Restriction ;
              owl:cardinality "1"^^xsd:int ;
              owl:onProperty umo:ID
            ] ;
      rdfs:subClassOf
            [ rdf:type owl:Restriction ;
              owl:minCardinality "1"^^xsd:int ;
              owl:onProperty umo:hasDictionaryEntry
            ] .
umo:LanguageTermPair
      rdf:type owl:Class ;
      rdfs:subClassOf owl:Thing ;
      rdfs:subClassOf
```

```
                              [ rdf:type owl:Restriction ;
                                owl:allValuesFrom umo:Term ;
                                owl:onProperty umo:hasTerm
                              ] ;
            rdfs:subClassOf
                              [ rdf:type owl:Restriction ;
                                owl:cardinality "1"^^xsd:int ;
                                owl:onProperty umo:hasLanguage
                              ] ;
            rdfs:subClassOf
                              [ rdf:type owl:Restriction ;
                                owl:allValuesFrom umo:Language ;
                                owl:onProperty umo:hasLanguage
                              ] ;
            rdfs:subClassOf
                              [ rdf:type owl:Restriction ;
                                owl:cardinality "1"^^xsd:int ;
                                owl:onProperty umo:hasTerm
                              ] .


    # Properties

umo:hasTerm
      rdf:type owl:ObjectProperty ;
      rdfs:domain umo:LanguageTermPair ;
      rdfs:range umo:Term .
umo:ID
      rdf:type owl:DatatypeProperty, owl:FunctionalProperty ;
      rdfs:domain umo:Usage ;
      rdfs:range xsd:string .
umo:hasLanguage
      rdf:type owl:ObjectProperty ;
      rdfs:domain umo:LanguageTermPair ;
      rdfs:range umo:Language .
umo:hasLanguageTermPair
      rdf:type owl:ObjectProperty ;
      rdfs:domain umo:Usage ;
      rdfs:range umo:LanguageTermPair .
umo:hasUsageComment
      rdf:type owl:DatatypeProperty ;
      rdfs:domain umo:Usage ;
      rdfs:range xsd:string .
umo:hasDictionaryEntry
      rdf:type owl:DatatypeProperty ;
```

```
      rdfs:domain umo:Usage ;
      rdfs:range xsd:string .
```

INDIVIDUALS
Languages

```
umo:English
      rdf:type umo:Language .
umo:Indonesian
      rdf:type umo:Language .
umo:German
      rdf:type umo:Language .
```

Terms

```
umo:Java
      rdf:type umo:Term .
umo:Jawa
      rdf:type umo:Term .
```

Language-Term pairs

```
umo:Indonesian-Jawa
      rdf:type umo:LanguageTermPair .
   umo:hasLanguage umo:Indonesian ;
      umo:hasTerm umo:Jawa .
umo:English-Java
      rdf:type umo:LanguageTermPair ;
      umo:hasLanguage umo:English ;
      umo:hasTerm umo:Java .
umo:German-Java
      rdf:type umo:LanguageTermPair ;
      umo:hasLanguage umo:German ;
      umo:hasTerm umo:Java .
umo:Indonesian-Java
      rdf:type umo:LanguageTermPair ;
      umo:hasLanguage umo:Indonesian ;
      umo:hasTerm umo:Java .
```

Usages

```
<http://www.umo.org/useagedict.owl#Usage-101.1>
      rdf:type umo:Usage ;
      umo:ID "101.1"^^xsd:string ;
```

```
       umo:hasDictionaryEntry
             "wordnet-sensekey: employee%1:18:00::"^^xsd:string ;
       umo:hasLanguageTermPair
             umo:English-Java, umo:German-Java, umo:Indonesian-Java
;
       umo:hasUsageComment
             "The Java programming language"^^xsd:string .
<http://www.umo.org/useagedict.owl#Usage-101.2>
       rdf:type umo:Usage ;
       umo:ID "101.2"^^xsd:string ;
       umo:hasDictionaryEntry
             "wordnet-sense-key: java%1:15:00::"^^xsd:string ;
       umo:hasLanguageTermPair
             umo:English-Java, umo:German-Java, umo:Indonesian-Jawa
;
       umo:hasUsageComment
             "An island of Indonesia"^^xsd:string .
```

APPENDIX C: EXAMPLE INTENDED USAGE RECORD SPECIFICATION

```
swm:hasUsageURI
      rdf:type owl:DatatypeProperty ;
      rdfs:domain swm:IntendedUsageRecord ;
      rdfs:range xsd:anyURI .
swm:hasSemanticWebTerm
      rdf:type owl:DatatypeProperty, owl:FunctionalProperty ;
      rdfs:domain swm:IntendedUsageRecord ;
      rdfs:range xsd:string .
swm:hasExplication
      rdf:type owl:DatatypeProperty ;
      rdfs:domain swm:IntendedUsageRecord ;
      rdfs:range xsd:anyURI .
swm:hasCompetingExplication
      rdf:type owl:DatatypeProperty ;
      rdfs:domain swm:IntendedUsageRecord ;
      rdfs:range xsd:anyURI .
swm:IntendedUsageRecord-Basic
      rdf:type owl:Class ;
      rdfs:subClassOf owl:Thing ;
      rdfs:subClassOf
            [ rdf:type owl:Restriction ;
              owl:cardinality "1"^^xsd:int ;
              owl:onProperty default:hasUsageURI
            ] ;
      rdfs:subClassOf
            [ rdf:type owl:Restriction ;
              owl:cardinality "1"^^xsd:int ;
              owl:onProperty swm:hasSemanticWebTerm
            ] .
swm:IntendedUsageRecord-Subtype1
      rdf:type owl:Class ;
      rdfs:subClassOf swm:IntendedUsageRecord-Basic ;
      rdfs:subClassOf
            [ rdf:type owl:Restriction ;
              owl:cardinality "1"^^xsd:int ;
              owl:onProperty swm:hasExplication
            ] .
swm:IntendedUsageRecord-Subtype2
      rdf:type owl:Class ;
      rdfs:subClassOf swm:IntendedUsageRecord-Basic ;
      rdfs:subClassOf
            [ rdf:type owl:Restriction ;
```

```
owl:minCardinality "2"^^xsd:int ;
owl:onProperty swm:hasCompetingExplication
] .
```

Chapter 9
Ontology Driven Document Identification in Semantic Web

Marek Reformat
thinkS²: thinking software and system laboratory, Electrical and Computer Engineering, University of Alberta, Canada

Ronald R. Yager
Machine Intelligence Institute, Iona College, USA

Zhan Li
thinkS²: thinking software and system laboratory, Electrical and Computer Engineering, University of Alberta, Canada

ABSTRACT

The concept of Semantic Web (Berners, 2001) introduces a new form of knowledge representation – an ontology. An ontology is a partially ordered set of words and concepts of a specific domain, and allows for defining different kinds of relationships existing among concepts. Such approach promises formation of an environment where information is easily accessible and understandable for any system, application and/or human. Hierarchy of concepts (Yager, 2000) is a different and very interesting form of knowledge representation. A graph-like structure of the hierarchy provides a user with a suitable tool for identifying variety of different associations among concepts. These associations express user's perceptions of relations among concepts, and lead to representing definitions of concepts in a human-like way. The Internet becomes an overwhelming repository of documents. This enormous storage of information will be effectively used when users will be equipped with systems capable of finding related documents quickly and correctly. The proposed work addresses that issue. It offers an approach that combines a hierarchy of concepts and ontology for the task of identifying web documents in the environment of the Semantic Web. A user provides a simple query in the form a hierarchy that only partially "describes" documents (s)he wants to retrieve from the web. The hierarchy is treated as a "seed" representing user's initial knowledge about concepts covered by required documents. Ontologies are treated as supplementary knowledge bases. They are used to instantiate the hierarchy with concrete information, as well as to enhance it with new concepts initially unknown to the user. The proposed approach is used to design a prototype system for document identification in the web environment. The description of the system and the results of preliminary experiments are presented.

DOI: 10.4018/978-1-60566-992-2.ch009

Copyright © 2010, IGI Global. Copying or distributing in print or electronic forms without written permission of IGI Global is prohibited.

INTRODUCTION

Amount of information available on the Internet creates a number of challenges for the text identification processes. Users should be able to find web pages containing text/documents that belong to a category of interest without missing too many of them. Development of effortless and efficient ways of finding such documents is of critical importance.

A number of methods addressing the issue of identifying relevant documents have been developed recently. Majority of them are built based on different Machine Learning techniques. Those methods "see" documents as vectors of weighted terms (words). Many systems constructed for text categorization purposes induce vectors that are characteristic for each category. In a nutshell, a categorization process takes place via comparison of those characteristic vectors with vectors representing documents.

For a person, identification of documents that belong to a specific category, as well as documents that are related to it, is an everyday activity. A person finds a document based on concepts related to their category of interest. The set of concepts is like a network. Individual concepts are linked among themselves, and the links represent different relationships that can exist between those concepts. Some of possible relationships are: *meronymy* – when a concept C' is part of C'', *holonymy* – a concept C' has C'' as a part, *hyponymy* (*troponymy*) – in the case when C' is subordinate of C'', or *synonymy* – if C' denotes the same as C''. A document identification process is performed via exploration of concepts and links between them. If one concept is found in a document, it "activates" concepts linked to it, and the document is checked if it contains those activated concepts. Eventually, more and more evidence is collected towards the statement that the document belongs to a category of interest. When some threshold value is reached the identification

process is stopped. The idea of mimicking such an identification process is explored in the paper.

Introduced in May 2001, the concept of Semantic Web (Berners, 2001), seen as an extension of the current web, defines an environment in which information is given a well-defined meaning. The Semantic Web is a place where machines can analyze all the data on the Web (Fensel, 2003) (Antoniou, 2004). A common element of all of those definitions is a reference to a new method of representing data. A new representation of resources on the web is based on usage of ontology. An ontology is a formal, explicit specification of a shared conceptualization (Gruber, 1993). It is a set of well-defined classes that describe data models in a specific domain. (The term *class* will be used in this work to represent a concept defined in ontologies. Therefore, the term *concept* as used in hierarchies of concepts, and the term *class* as used in ontologies mean the same thing – a concept. The term *category* represents a set of entities – web pages in this work – that are grouped together due to their relevance to the same concept.) Together with their individuals (instances of classes), ontologies work as knowledge vehicles to express individual facts (Scott, 2002). This new representation of knowledge introduced to the web environment brings new possibilities of utilization of information (Marin, 2004; Sanchez, 2006).

A different format of knowledge representation has been proposed in (Yager, 2000). The format, called hierarchy of concepts (HOFC), represents concepts with atomic attributes, words or other concepts. As the result a graph-like structure is established where each vertex is a concept, and terminal vertices are attributes. The edges of the hierarchy represent any relationships that help defining concepts with other concepts and/or attributes. These edges (connections) are of significant importance to the whole idea of hierarchy of concepts. Another important element of HOFC is an indication how "existence" of more complex concepts depends on existence of lower level concepts. This is controlled using linguistic quantifiers translated into the Ordered Weighted Averaging (OWA) operator. Hierarchies of concepts can be used for representing any human-like structures of concepts, for example queries (Yager, 2000).

As it has been stated earlier, the paper investigates a method suitable for imitating a human-like process of identification of documents. In a nutshell, the idea is based on utilization of concept hierarchies that are populated and enhanced with the help of ontologies. A user provides a simple hierarchy describing contents of text/documents of interest. This hierarchy contains the most obvious concepts for the user. The concepts of HOFC are linked together. The links indicate different types of relationships that can exist between those concepts. The concepts that constitute the hierarchy are generic ones – they are just definitions of concepts. The specific pieces of information are extracted form ontologies and "attached" to the concepts of hierarchy – in other words ontologies are used to populate the hierarchy. Additionally, relations existing between ontology classes are used to find new concepts that are added to the HOFC. This provides a mechanism for dynamic enhancement of HOFCs.

The paper outline is following. Section RELATED WORK brings a short description of related work in the area of text categorization. The necessary background knowledge is presented in Section BACKGROUND. It starts with a very brief introduction to aggregation mechanism and in particular to an ordered weighted aggregating operator. An idea of hierarchy of concepts is presented in Section Hierarchy of Concepts. The last part of Section BACKGROUND is dedicated to ontology. Section CONCEPT HIERARCHY AS CATEGORY IDENTIFIERS is a description of application of hierarchy of concepts as representation of a category. The idea is further developed in Section HIERARCHY OF CONCEPTS AND ONTOLOGY. Application of ontology to enhance concept hierarchies is included there. An example of application of the approach to the identifica-

tion of soccer web pages is shown in Section SEMANTIC WEB APPLICATION. The paper ends with a set of conclusions and indications related to future work.

RELATED WORK

The onset of text categorization research can be traced back to the early '60s. However, it gained popularity in the early '90s thanks to increased applicative interest and to the availability of powerful hardware (Sebastiani, 2002).

Until the '80s, the most popular approach for document categorization was based on manual construction of an expert system capable of categorizing text. Such a system would contain a set of manually defined if-then rules. A document was categorized under a category if it satisfied the "if" part of a rule. The most famous example of this approach is the CONSTRUE system (Hayes, 1990), built by Carnegie Group for the Reuters news agency.

Since the early '90s, the Machine Learning approach has gained popularity and become the most common one (see (Mitchell, 1996) for a comprehensive introduction to Machine Learning). In this approach, an inductive process is used for construction of a categorization system for a category C_i. This process requires a set of documents that are categorized as belonging to C_i, as well as documents that are not classified as belonging to C_i. In this approach, a classifier gleans characteristics of documents that belong to a given category and is able to categorize a new unseen document. Such categorization problem is an example of supervised learning. (Learning process is supervised what means that the knowledge of the categories and of the training instances that belong to them are required for a classifier construction process.) Application of Machine Learning techniques requires pre-processing of documents. In general, a document d_j is represented as a vector of term weights

$$d_j = <w_{1j}, w_{2j}, ..., w_{|T|j}>$$

where T is the set of terms (sometimes called features, in practical applications terms are words) that occur at least once in at least one document; w_{kj} (in the range $[0,1]$) represents, loosely speaking, how much term (word) k contributes to the document d_j.

A number of different Machine Learning techniques have been applied to the text categorization applications. Probabilistic classifiers (Lewis, 1998) see classification as a probability that a document represented by a vector of words belongs to a given category. Examples of Naïve Bayesian classifiers can be found in (Lewis, 1992; Koller, 1997; Larkey, 1996). In 1994, Apte, et al. (Apte, 1994), have used decision rules to build an automated system for text categorization. Decision tree text classifiers have been used either as the main classification tool (Fuhr, 1991) (Lewis, 1994), as baseline classifiers (Cohen, 1999), or as members of classifier committees (Li, 1998). In (Vidulin, 2007), decision trees and bagging approaches are used to train "genre" classifiers for identifying web documents. Each "genre" was representing a concept to be recognized.

In 1998, Joachims (Joachims, 1998) uses Support Vector Machine (SVM) as learning text classifiers, and shows that the SVM outperforms other regular classifiers, such as k-NN, C4.5 and Naïve Bayesian. Aphinynyanaphongs, et al. (Aphinya, 2005) apply multiple models like Naïve Bayes, a specialized AdaBoost algorithm, and SVM to classify medical papers in the areas of etiology, prognosis, diagnosis, and treatment. As a conclusion, they state that using machine-learning methods, it is possible to automatically build models for retrieving high-quality, content-specific articles. Anagnostopoulous, et al. (Anagnost, 2008) combine an SVM model with a search engine model to classify document into different categories, where documents are indexed and described by fewer than 10 terms.

Yang (Yang, 1994) develops an expert network for a categorization process. This network sets the input nodes as the terms in the training text, and output nodes as categories. The links between nodes are computed based on statistics of the word distribution and the categorization distribution over the training set. This method is close to the regular k-NN method.

Other techniques used for text classification problems are: regression methods (Ittner, 1995), neural networks (Schutze, 1995), Bayesian inference networks (Dumais, 1998), genetic algorithms (Clack, 1997), and maximum entropy modeling (Manning, 1999).

In 2004, Shen, et al. (Shen, 2004) compare Latent Semantic Analysis (LSA) as a web document summarization method with two classical text classifiers, which are Naïve Bayes Classifier and SVM. They argue that the classifiers built based on the summaries produced by the human editors are significantly better than ones built using only the text of web documents. Choi and Peng (Choi, 2004) postulate that the manual classification could hardly "keep up with the growth of the web". Based on that, they have built their own automatic classification system that can dynamically add new categories. The proposed system improved classification. The idea is very interesting but in the real world application, a number of categories could be too large to process.

Since categories are represented as sets of concepts, more attention is being put on identifying text documents based on their contents of category-related concepts. This means that systems require more knowledge about categories they have to recognize. Many researchers are working on constructing background concept structures as knowledge bases for concept definitions.

One of the possible options is application of synonym thesauri. The thesauri help define keywords of the query by expanding them with their synonyms. Anick (Anick, 1994) proposes a system, which automatically generates synonym-extended Boolean conditions in the following way:

"a Boolean expression is composed by ORing each query term with any stored synonyms and then ANDing these clusters together (Anick, 1994)." This means, that each keyword of a query is ORed with its synonyms from an online thesaurus. This method increases chances that useful information is found in the retrieved documents, but it increases the amount of the retrieved documents as well. Moreover, since it is normal that one term has multiple synonyms with possibly different meanings, the extension with right synonyms is a challenge.

Another option is application of conceptual taxonomy as a hierarchical organization of concepts. Each concept in conceptual taxonomy is connected with its super-concepts and its sub-concepts. Therefore, it provides a topological structure for efficient conceptual search and retrieval. In the project initiated by Sun Microsystems, a conceptual indexing technique is proposed to automatically generate conceptual taxonomies (Woods, 1997).

In many semantic-enhanced systems for information retrieval, a large lexical dictionary *WordNet* plays an important role as a linguistic ontology (Miller, 1995). The knowledge embedded in *WordNet*, including explanations of terms, relations between terms (synonym, antonym, etc.), is used to expand queries with semantically related terms. Voorhees (Voorhees, 1994) expands queries with lexical semantic relations in *WordNet*. Gong, et al. (Gong, 2005) utilize *WordNet* to expand queries in three dimensions using hypernym, hyponymy, and synonym relations. Du, et al. (Du, 2008) introduce an information retrieval system that uses *WordNet* as the source of corpus independent knowledge and Latent Semantic Indexing (LSI) as the source of corpus dependent knowledge. However, the systems that apply *WordNet* "suffer" from Word Sense Disambiguation (WSD) due to polysemy. Baziz, et al. (Baziz, 2005) use co-occurrence and semantic relatedness as two criteria to eliminate WSD in *WordNet*. Kolte (Kolte, 2008) also proposes an

approach for dealing with WSD. This approach is based on an unsupervised learning technique used for determining the domain that keywords belong to. Kim, et al. (Kim, 2008) transform *WordNet* into a matrix with terms as vectors. They apply singular value decomposition (SVD) to reduce the size of matrix, which in the end helps to relieve WSD. However, researchers report difficulties in applying linguistic-based ontology into non-linguistic applications (Guarino, 1999).

The introduction of the concept of Semantic Web has triggered a lot of interests in utilization of ontology to enhance systems dedicated to information retrieval. The term ontology (Gruber, 1993) is originated from philosophy, in the branch of metaphysics. It represents the study of existence or being, i.e., the kinds of things that actually exist, and how to describe them. The Semantic Web defined a "novel" view of ontology – ontology is a representation of a set of concepts and relations between those concepts in a given domain of interest (see Section Ontology for some short description). Ontologies are used in a number of different ways, and are objects of numerous research activities, for example, development of fuzzy ontologies (Sanchez, 2006), (Tho, 2006). The most relevant are applications supporting users in finding more accurate information on the web. Domain ontology describes vocabulary – terms and relations – related to a specific domain. This helps eliminating vagueness of linguistic terms. Guarino, et al. (Guarino, 1999) propose an information retrieval system called OntoSeek. The system uses Sensus ontology built from online yellow pages and product catalogs. In the OntoSeek project, the authors link conceptual graphs, which are transferred from queries, to the Sensus ontology using lexical conceptual graphs. In (Kalfo, 2001) the authors have proposed an ontology-based profiling tool that allows users to specify their interests (search criteria). The tool is used to search for relevant news items. The authors also target issues of ontology maintenance and population.

In (Maed, 2002), the authors present an interesting approach for bootstrapping an ontology-based information extraction system with the help of machine learning. The approach allows for fast creation of an ontology-based information extraction system relying on several basic components, viz. a core information extraction system, an ontology-engineering environment and an inference engine. The paper contains the description of a comprehensive system that semi-automatically extends an ontology by an ontology learning process. The system semi-automatically maps free text, like web pages, onto ontology-based target knowledge structures.

An interesting work related to applications of ontology for categorization of web pages is presented in (Stuck, 2002). The authors described a system for categorizing individual pages on the basis of their syntactic structure. Their categorization procedure requires classification rules that relate characteristic page structures to each category. They use ontology as a model of the contents of a web site – each ontology class represents a single category. The authors explain how to learn those rules using Inductive Logic Programming.

Vallet, et al. (Vallet, 2005) develop another ontology based information retrieval system. Once the terms and concepts are connected through ontology-driven annotation of documents, a classic vector-space model is utilized to evaluate the relevance between documents and queries. The structure of the system is very practical. However an ontology has a hierarchical structure, while query does not have one – in a classical vector-space model, a query is a vector. Therefore, a full utilization of knowledge embedded in the ontology is difficult in such a case.

Dridi, et al. (Dridi, 2008) propose a ontology-based framework for semantic information retrieval using GATE (Cunningham, 2009) as information extraction module. GATE annotates documents via extracting breast cancer ontology concepts from documents. In this way, the

concepts are indexed, and used for retrieving relevant documents. However, based on the description of the system it may have difficulties with handling multiple domain ontologies and large corpus – indexing of concepts instead of terms is more intense.

Another ontology-based system for extracting news items related to specific concepts of interest is presented in (Borsje, 2008). The authors propose a framework that supports a categorization process using an ontology-based knowledge base that stores information about news domain and *Wordnet*. The categorization process requires concept identifiers that are composed based on a concept acquired from the news ontology, and its synonyms and words denoting the concept extracted from *Wordnet*.

BACKGROUND

Aggregation Mechanism

Ordered Weighted Averaging (OWA): Aggregation of different pieces of information is a common aspect of any system that has to infer a single outcome from multiple facts. A very interesting class of aggression operators is called the Ordered Weighted Averaging (*OWA*) (Yager, 1988). In the simplest possible statement, this operator is a weighted sum over ordered pieces of information.

In a formal representation, the *OWA* operator, defined on the unit interval I and having dimension n (n arguments), is a mapping $F_w: I^n \rightarrow I$ such that:

$$F_w(a_1, \ldots, a_n) = \sum_{j=1}^{n} (w_j * b_j) \qquad (1)$$

where b_j is the jth largest of all arguments $a_1, a_2, \ldots, a_n$, and w_j is a weight such that w_j is in *[0, 1]* and

Figure 1. Linguistic quantifiers: for all (a), some (b), and most (c)

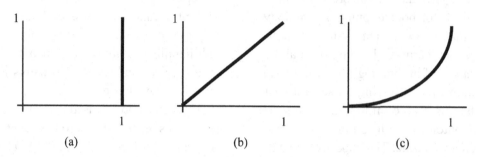

(a) (b) (c)

$\sum_{j=1}^{n} w_j = 1$. If $id(j)$ is the index of the jth largest of a_i then $a_{id(j)} = b_j$ and $F_w(a_1,\ldots,a_n) = \sum_{j=1}^{n} (w_j * a_{id(j)})$.

If W is an n-dimensional vector whose j^{th} component is w_j and B is an n-dimensional vector whose j^{th} component is b_j then $F_w(a_1, a_2,\ldots, a_n)$ $=W^T B$. In this formulation W is referred to as the *OWA* weighing vector and B is called the ordered argument vector.

The OWA operator is parameterized by the weighing vector W. A number of interesting observations can be done when different W are considered. For example, if $W=W_*$ where $w_n = 1$ and $w_j = 0$ for $j \neq n$ then $F_w(a_1, a_2,\ldots, a_n) = Min_j[a_j]$. If $W=W^*$ where $w_1 = 1$ and $w_j = 0$ for $j \neq 1$ then $F_w(a_1, a_2,\ldots, a_n) = Max_j[a_j]$. If $W=W_N$ where $w_n = \dfrac{1}{n}$ then $F_w(a_1,\ldots,a_n) = \dfrac{1}{n}\sum_{j=1}^{n} a_j$, what represents an arithmetic mean (average). Various other forms can be described. In general, it can be said that different values of weights w_j control the level of contribution of single pieces of information towards the final outcome.

At the beginning of eighties, Zadeh has introduced the concept of linguistic quantifiers (Zadeh, 1983). Those quantifiers describe a proportion of objects. According to Zadeh, a person knows a vast array of terms that are used to express information about proportions. Some examples are *most*, *at least half*, *all*, and *about 1/3*. The important issue is to formally represent those quantifiers.

In the mid-nineties, Yager showed how we can use a linguistic quantifier to obtain a weighing vector associated with an OWA aggregation. In (Yager, 1993), he has introduced parameterized families of the Regular Increasing Monotone (RIM) quantifiers. These quantifiers are able to guide aggregation procedures by verbally expressed concepts in a description independent dimension. A RIM quantifier is a fuzzy subset Q over I = [0, 1] in which for any proportion $r \in I$, Q(r) indicates the degree to which r satisfies the concept indicated by the quantifier Q (Yager, 1996). A fuzzy subset Q represents a RIM quantifier if:

1) $Q(0) = 0$
2) $Q(1) = 1$
3) if $r1 > r2$ then $Q(r1) > Q(r2)$ (monotonic)

For example, let us take a look at the parameterized family $Q(r) = r^p$, where $p \in [0,\infty)$. Here if $p=0$ we obtain the *existential (max)* quantifier; when $p \to \infty$ we have the quantifier *for all (min)*, and when $p=1$ we have $Q(r) = r$ and we deal with the quantifier *some*. In addition for the case $p=2$, $Q(r) = r^2$, we obtain one possible interpretation of the quantifier *most*. These quantifiers are shown in Figure 1.

An interesting quantifier is shown in Figure 2. It is the quantifier *at least α*. For this quantifier $w_j=1$ for j such that $\dfrac{j-1}{n} < \alpha < \dfrac{j}{n}$ and $w_j=0$ for all other js.

Figure 2. Linguistic quantifier at least α

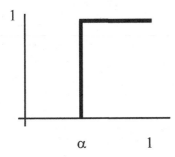

Figure 3. Obtaining weights from a quantifier

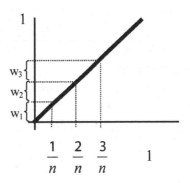

Assuming a RIM quantifier, we can associate with Q an OWA weighing vector W such that for $j=1$ to n

$$w_j = Q(\frac{j}{n}) - Q(\frac{j-1}{n}) \qquad (2)$$

where n is a number of pieces of information to be aggregated. This expression indicates that the weighing vector W is a manifestation of the quantifier underlying the aggregation process, and $Q(k) = \sum_{j=1}^{k} w_j$, where $k \leq n$. (The relations between a quantifier Q and a weighing vector can be illustrated by the following observation: *Q(O) = 0* if a decision-maker is absolutely not satisfied (no criteria satisfied); *Q(n) = 1* if he is completely satisfied, i.e., if all criteria are satisfied.) Using this expression the values of the weighing vector can be obtained directly from the expression representing the quantifier. For example, the quantifier *some* can be expressed by the formula *Q(r) = r*. For this quantifier we have

$$w_j = \frac{j}{n} - \frac{j-1}{n} = \frac{1}{n}$$

and this gives us a simple average. Such process is illustrated in Figure 3.

The concept that is associated with OWA operator is the measure of its "orness". If we have W_* (see above for explanation of W_*) then an OWA opearator F is a pure "and" operator, while if we have W^*, then F is a pure "or" operator. We can further observe the closer the total weight is to being in w_1, the closer the F function is to being a pure "or" operator, while the closer it is to being in w_n, the function is closer to an "and." The formal definition of "orness" is presented below:

Assume F is an OWA aggregation operator with weighing vector $W = [\, w_1, w_2, \ldots, w_n]$. The degree of "orness" associated with this operator is defined as

$$orness(W) = \frac{1}{n-1} * \sum_{i=1}^{n}((n-i) * w_i)$$

The "orness" of the parameterized family $Q(r) = r^p$, where $p \in [0, \infty)$ is approximated by $1/(p+1)$. So, for the quantifiers *for all*, *some*, and *most* "orness" is equal to *0*, *1/2*, and *1/3* respectively.

OWA with Argument Importance: Earlier, we have shown how a quantifier Q indicating interaction between pieces of information can be used to calculate an OWA weighing vector W. However, not all pieces of information are of the same importance. A user may desire to ascribe different weights (importance) to the different arguments (pieces of information).

Let $m_i \in [0,1]$ be a value associated with an argument a_i indicating its importance. In such a case, let M be a n-dimensional importance vector

$[m_1, m_2, \ldots, m_n]$, and the weighing vector W has to be calculated based upon both Q and M.

The first step is to calculate the ordered argument vector B (see Eq. (1)), such that b_j is the jth largest of all arguments $a_1, a_2, \ldots, a_n$. Furthermore, we assume μ_j to denote the importance weight associated with the attribute that has the jt^h largest value. Thus if $a5$ is the largest value, then $b1\_a5$ and $\mu_1 = _m5$. The next step is to calculate the OWA weighing vector W *u*sing a modified version of the Eq. (2):

$$w_j = Q(\frac{S_j}{T}) - Q(\frac{S_{j-1}}{T}) \qquad (3)$$

where

$$S_j = \sum_{k=1}^{j} \mu_k \text{ and } S_j = \sum_{k=1n}^{j} \mu_k$$
$$T = S_n = \sum_{k=1}^{n} \mu_k \text{ and } T = S_n = \sum_{k=1}^{n} \mu_k .$$

So, S_j is the sum of the importances of the jth largest arguments, and T is the sum of all importances. When all arguments have the same importance, the Eq. (3) simplifies to the Eq. (2).

Example: Let us assume that there are three pieces of information (arguments) a_1, a_2, and a_3. The value of these arguments are $a_1=0.3$, $a_2=0.2$, and $a_3=0.5$. The importances associated with these arguments are $m_1=0.6$, $m_2=1.0$, and $m_3=0.4$. From this we obtain $T = \sum_{k=1}^{3} m_k = 2$. We shall assume the quantifier guiding this aggregation is *most*, which is defined by $Q(r)=r^2$.

Our objective is to aggregate all three pieces of information. We start with ordering of arguments in Table 1.

Then the weights are:

$$w_1 = Q(\frac{0.4}{2}) - Q(\frac{0}{2}) = 0.04$$

Table 1.

	b_j	μ_j
a_3	0.5	0.4
a_1	0.3	1
a_2	0.2	0.6

$$w_2 = Q(\frac{1.4}{2}) - Q(\frac{0.4}{2}) = 0.45$$

$$w_3 = Q(\frac{2.0}{2}) - Q(\frac{1.4}{2}) = 0.51$$

In such a case, the aggregated information value is:

$F(a_1, a_2, a_3) = 0.04*0.5 + 0.45*0.3 + 0.51*0.2 = 0.257$

Hierarchy of Concepts

The approach of representing concepts as a hierarchy has been introduced by Yager (Yager, 2000). In a nutshell, the idea uses a notion of representing concepts with atomic attributes, words or other concepts. As the result a graph-like structure is established where each vertex is a concept, and terminal vertices are attributes. The edges of the hierarchy of concepts (HOFC) represent relationships that help defining concepts with other concepts and/or attributes. These edges (connections) are of significant importance to the whole idea of HOFC. If we assume that a concept C_1 is defined by other two concepts C_2 and C_3, then the hierarchy will have two edges connecting C_2 with C_1, and C_3 with C_1. The concept C_1 is called a super-concept, and C_2 and C_3 are sub-concepts. This also means that "activation" of concepts C_2 and C_3 leads to activation of C_1.

The HOFC proposed by Yager introduces a very important element – the process of activation of super-concept by active sub-concepts is fully controlled by a user. There are two controlling components: importance vector M and linguistic

Figure 4. Example of a simple hierarchy of concepts (HOFC)

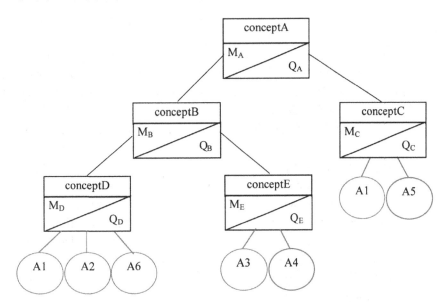

quantifier Q. The vector M is an indicator of significance of each sub-concept in defining a super-concept. In other words, M determines a weight of each of the participating (sub-) concepts in a process of identifying an activation level of the super-concept. The linguistic quantifier Q is guiding the aggregation of sub-concept activations. Both M and Q determine how activation levels of sub-concepts should be combined using the OWA operator (Section Aggregation Mechanism).

A simple example of HOFC is shown in Figure 4. According to the hierarchy, the *conceptA* is defined in the following way:

conceptA=(conceptB, conceptC, M_A,Q_A)

This means that the *conceptA* is defined by two other concepts *conceptB* and *conceptC*. M_A determines importance of both of these concepts towards "defining" *conceptA*. It is a two-value vector $M_A=[M_{A-B}, M_{A-C}]$ that implies importance of activations of both sub-concepts during calculation of activation level of the *conceptA*. The quantifier Q_A can be of any type, for example *most* or

some, and identifies a mechanism of combining activation levels of sub-concepts. The rest of the concepts are defined in the following way:

conceptB=(conceptD, conceptE, M_BQ_B)

conceptD=A1,A2,A6, $M_{D_i}Q_D$)

conceptE=(A3,A4, $M_{E_i}Q_E$)

conceptC=(A1,A5, $M_{c_i}Q_C$)

As we can see the *conceptD, conceptE,* and *conceptC* are defined by attributes only. Activation levels of these concepts are calculated by aggregating activations of attributes. Activation of an attribute means that the attribute is present, for example, on a web page. The aggregation process for each concept is controlled via M and Q associated with that concept. For the concept *conceptD* aggregation of activations of attributes *A1, A2,* and *A6* is based on the OWA operator with a weighing vector determined by M_D and Q_D. For more details regarding HOFCs see (Yager, 2000).

Ontology

The term ontology is used in two different ways. In its first usage – *Philosophical Ontology* – an ontology is a description of reality in terms of classification of reality (Smith, 2003). In its second usage defined by the Semantic Web – *Ontology and Information Systems* – an ontology deals with a taxonomy of terms that describe a certain area of knowledge. In this context, the most popular definition says "an ontology is a specification of a conceptualization" (Gruber, 1993). This definition indicates that ontology can be used for building conceptual nets equipped with a structure representing mutual relationships among the concepts (Sheth, 2004). Because ontologies do more than just control a vocabulary, they are thought of as knowledge representations.

The most important aspect of the ontology used for semantic web applications is related to identifying two ontology layers: the ontology definition layer, and the ontology instance layer. (According to the terminology adopted by the Semantic Web community, the term "instance" has been replaced by the term "individual". For the purpose of clarity, the term instance – similar to the term *instantiated* – is used throughout the work.)

The *ontology definition layer* represents a framework used for establishing a structure of ontology and for defining classes (concepts) existing in a given domain. A structure of ontology is built based on a relation *is-a* between classes. This relation represents a *subClassOf* connection between a superclass and a subclass. In such a way, a hierarchy of classes is built. This hierarchy is a partially ordered set of classes, and the resulted ontology is a directed acyclic graph.

Additionally, the ontology definition contains detailed descriptions of all classes of the ontology. These classes are defined using two types of the properties: datatype properties, and object properties. Both of them provide a way for an accurate

and complete description of a class. The details of both types of properties are presented below:

- *datatype property* – this type of property focuses on describing features of a class; datatype properties are used to represent attributes that can be expressed as values of such data types as boolean, float, integer, string, and many more (for example, byte, date, decimal, time);
- *object property* – this property defines other than *is-a* relationships among classes (nodes); these relationships follow the notion of Resource Description Framework (RDF) that is based on a triple *subject-predicate-object*, where: *subject* identifies what object the triple is describing; *predicate* (property) defines the piece of data in the object a value is given to; and *object* is the actual value of the property; for example, the triple "John likes books" has "John" as subject, "likes" as predicate and "books" as object.

Both types of properties are very important for defining ontology. The possibility of defining class attributes and any relations between classes creates a very versatile framework capable of expressing complex situations with sophisticated classes and multiple relationships of different kinds existing among them.

Once the ontology definition is constructed, its instances can be built. The properties of classes are filled out with real data – values are assigned to datatype properties, and links to instances of other classes are assigned to object properties.

An example of an object property, the critical element in the approach proposed in the paper, is shown in Figure 5. It represents a very simple and intuitive relation *liveIn*. The triple defining the relation is <*subject = person, property = liveIn, object = city*>. The domain of the relation is the class *person*, and its range is *city*. Any instance of the class *person* can have the object property *liveIn*

Figure 5. Definition of the class person with object property liveIn "binding" it with the class city

that links it with an instance of the class *city*, for example *John liveIn New York*, Figure 6.

CONCEPT HIERARCHY AS CATEGORY IDENTIFIERS

Structure of Concepts as Category Description

Any category of interest can be described by a set of keywords. Such an approach is taken in many solutions to text categorization. A new document is checked against keywords and if all or fraction of words (depending of the applied text categorization technique) are found in a given document then the document is considered as belonging to a category described by the keywords. Usually, keywords are associated with weights identifying their importance. The keywords are represented as a flat structure, and there is no indication that they are "related" to each other, and that some of them depend on others.

A human looks at a document and "searches" for keywords related to a given category. However, for a human all keywords are interconnected. They constitute a network of keywords representing concepts. (A concept can be defined, in a sort of a bottom-up approach (extensional), as an abstract or general idea derived from specific instances. We turn over that definition, making a top-down version of it (intensional), and define a concept as a set of attributes that describe a group of individuals. From now on, we will use the term

concepts instead of keywords.) Activation of one concept initiates activation of related concepts. Relations between concepts can be of different nature: some can "point" to more *specific* concepts, some can relate to concepts that are *parts of* the original concept, and some can relate to concepts that *contain* the original one. Human sees the document, and its content activates a number of concepts, as well as prompts a user to "check" if a document contains other, related, concepts. More connected concepts are found in the document more support is collected towards assigning this document to a category described by the keywords/concepts.

Example: Let us take a look at a simple scenario representing such a situation and consider the category *soccer*. What first comes to mind when we think about soccer is a small set of well-known concepts: *player*, *team*, and *event*. These concepts and their links are shown in Figure 7. The connections are simple and intuitive. (The orientation of arrows indicates a direction of activation.) When we go further, each of the concepts can be described by a set of other concepts and/or attributes. Structures describing concepts *team* and *event* are presented in Figure 8. It can be observed that the concept *team* is colligated with three other concepts. These concepts described *team* in three different ways: via indication what it possesses – a *team's name*, via indication what it consists of – *player*, and via indication of its association with *official*. Similarly, such a situation occurs for the concept *event* – it is defined by a number of (sub-)concepts.

The structures presented in Figures 7 and 8 can be used for recognizing if a document is related to the category *soccer*. This can be done via exploitation of activated concepts and links in a "bottom-up approach". Activations of a number of lower-level concepts – *team's name, forward, mid-fielder, defender*, or *doctor, coach, manager* contribute to activation of higher-level concepts – *player, official*, and eventually *team*. In general, a

Figure 6. Instances of the classes person and city with object property liveIn

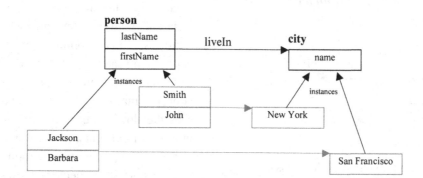

Figure 7. A simple structure of concepts representing the category soccer

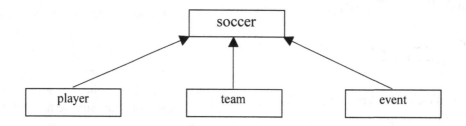

different number of lower-level concepts is needed for activation of different higher-level concepts.

The above example is a good illustration of scenario how the structure of concepts implicates a categorization process. Very important aspects of the structure are:

- different types of relationships existing among concepts; *is-a* relationship – represents sub- or super-ordinate relationship between concepts, for example, *players->forward*; *part of* relationship – represents a scenario where one concept is a part of another, for example, *players<-team*; *consist of* relationship – indicates a relationship where one concept includes another one, for example *match->action_of_match;*
- activation of concepts; a number of active concepts and their importance has a significant impact on activation of higher-level

concepts. (In this section activation process refers to concepts, however in the proposed approach the activation is being referred to instances of concepts. See Section System Description for details)

Category Identifiers

The HOFC (Section Hierarchy of Concepts) and the aspects mentioned above lead to an observation that HOFCs can be used as "implementations" of structures of concepts described in the previous section. The rules governing construction of hierarchies do not impose any restrictions on a type of relationships identified between concepts. Activation of higher-level concepts is "controlled" using an aggregation operator defined with a linguistic quantifier (Q) and an importance vector (M) what provides flexibility in merging activations of lower-level concepts.

Figure 8. More detailed structures for concepts team (a) and event (b)

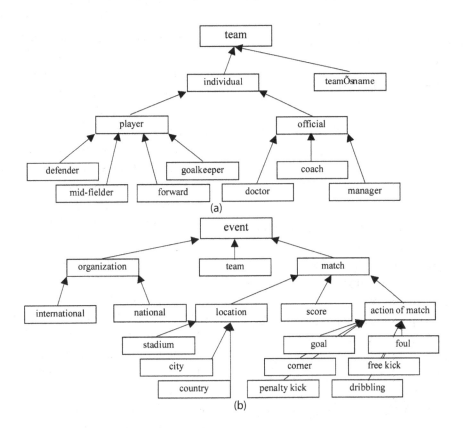

The Q associated with a concept represents a linguistic quantifier that is used at the time of aggregation of activation levels of attributes and sub-concepts describing the concept. It is possible to have such quantifiers as *some, most, at least half, about 1/3,* or *for all*. The notion of linguistic quantifiers plays an important role in representing different ways of combining activation levels.

The M part indicates importance of each sub-concept and attribute that has to be taken into consideration during an aggregation process. Figure 8 contains a number of cases where a single concept is defined by a set of sub-concepts. In general, it can be said that not all sub-concepts and attributes "contribute" uniformly to the activation of the super-ordinate concept. Introduction of importance brings ability to express identification power of individual concepts/attributes.

Example: Figure 9 represents a single element of HOFCs. The concept *forward* is defined by three attributes. The Q defines how the concept *forward* can be identified (activated) based on existence (activation) of the attributes. If Q is *for all* – all attributes have to be present in a document, if Q is *at least one* – then one of attributes is required, and if Q is *most* – then the majority of attributes should be present. The M is a vector with three values, and each value indicates importance of each attribute. If M=[1,1,1] then all attributes are equally important for activation of the *forward* (player) concept, if M=[0.5, 1, 0.75] the *last name* is the most important, the *nick name* is second, and the *first name* is the least important.

Two hierarchies representing the concepts *team* and *event* are shown in Figure 10. It is easy to identify that a Q/M section has been added to

Figure 9. A single concept forward

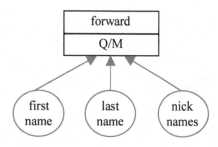

each concept. Additionally, some nodes represent attributes that define concepts.

Concepts and attributes shown in Figure 10 are generic. Looking at the graphs it is difficult to say that these HOFCs refer to soccer related concepts. All concepts and attributes are nonrepresentational, and almost any kind of a team could fit these HOFCs.

Overall, HOFC provides us with a representation framework that gives ability to articulate variety of relationships among concepts for evaluation purposes. Presented above, notion of Q/M and generic character of hierarchy are very important for the proposed idea of using HOFC as category identifiers. Q/M components are an essential element in identifying which sub-concepts and attributes are important, and activation of how many of them leads to activation of higher-level concepts.

HIERARCHY OF CONCEPTS AND ONTOLOGY

An ontology as proposed by the Semantic Web community (Section Ontology) represents a very attractive and powerful approach for knowledge representation. In particular an ontology is suitable for representing:

- detailed description of concepts/nodes in the sense of attributes identifying concepts' features (as indicated earlier, we will use the term class to distinguish ontology concepts from HOFC concepts);
- variety of relationships among classes which are additional to the basic *is-a* relationship;
- detailed hierarchy of classes based on principles of specialization/generalization (top-down/bottom-up);
- concrete information as instances of definitions of ontology classes;

This richness of information that can be included in an ontology triggers an idea that an ontology can be used to provide concrete and additional information for HOFC. In the first case, we talk about instantiation of HOFCs, and about enrichment of hierarchies in the second case.

In this section we describe details of the proposed idea, that is, what steps are used to enhance a HOFC with ontology. In the Section SEMANTIC WEB APPLICATION we provide a description how a categorization process with an ontology-enhanced HOFC is preformed.

Instantiation of Hierarchy of Concepts

HOFCs presented in Figure 10 are nonspecific. As we indicated earlier they can fit a description of any team. At this point we illustrate how ontology can be used to "instantiate" a HOFC with specific information related to the *soccer* category (see Appendix for its short description). Any concept that has only attributes as its description (for example, concepts *defender*, *coach*, in Figure 10a) undergoes an instantiation process. Each of the attributes is assigned a value taken from an ontology. In other words, an ontology is being queried and the result of that query is used to create instances of concept.

Figure 10. (a) HOFC for the concept team (b) HOFC for the concept event (fragment)

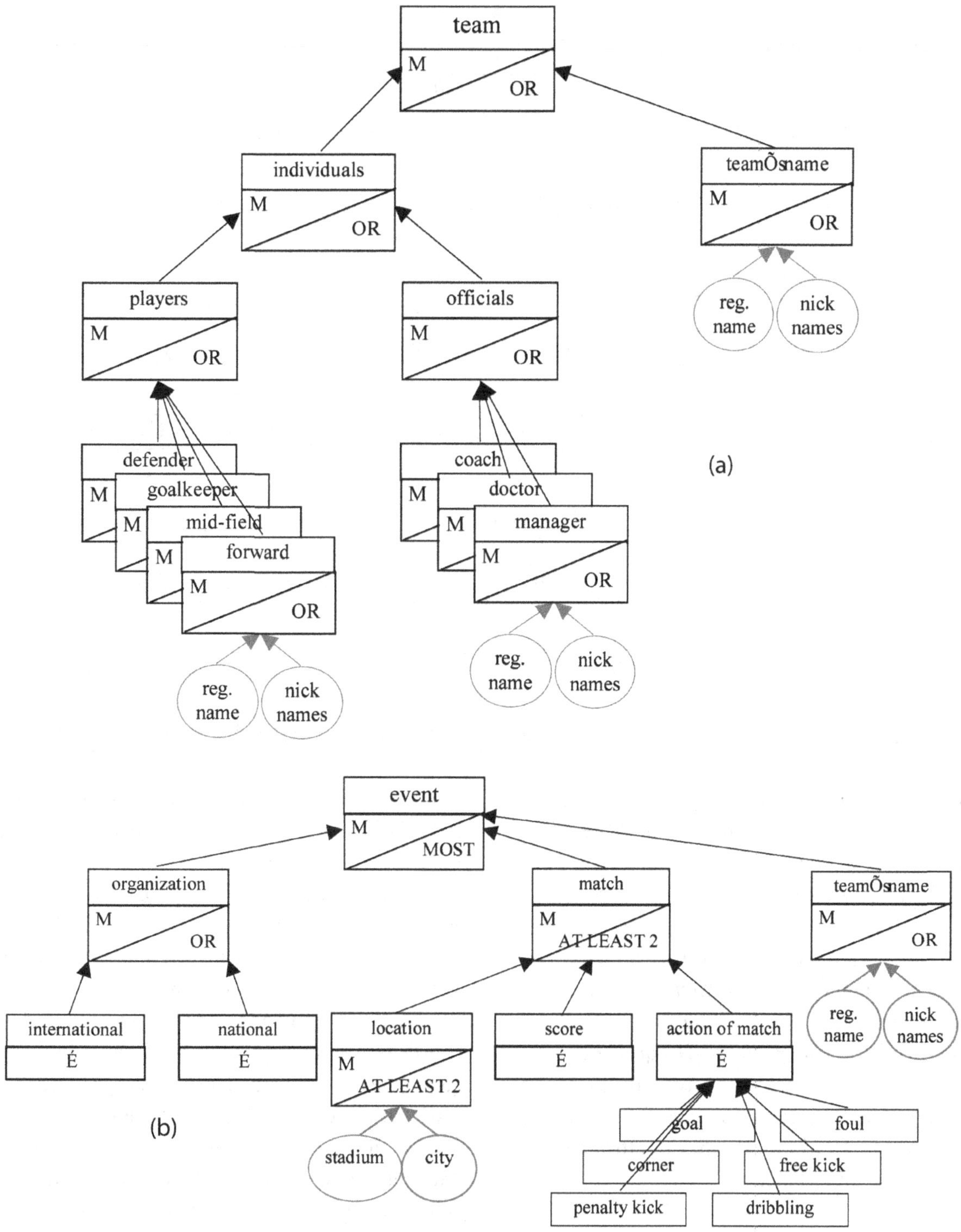

Figure 11. The concept forward (a) and its four instances (b)

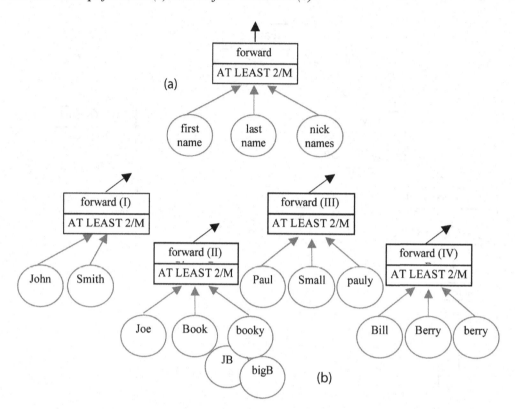

An example of that is presented in Figure 11. The *soccer* ontology is queried about the concept *forward*, Figure 11a). It is anticipated that each player has at least two attributes: *first name*, *last name*, and a number (including 0) of the attributes *nick name*. The result – four players – is presented in Figure 11b). For example, the first forward player is identified with the first and second name only: *John Smith*. However, the second player has, besides the first and second name, a couple of nicknames. The quantifier "AT LEAST 2" means that two words have to be in a document to indicate that a player is mentioned, while *M=[1 1 1]* indicates that all attributes are of the same importance.

Enriching Hierarchy of Concepts

Ontology can also be treated as a knowledge repository for providing new concepts that can enhance concepts already existing in a HOFC. This enhancement can be twofold: in the form of more specific (lower-level) concepts, and in the form of concepts that are in different relationships with concepts held in a hierarchy.

Concepts included in a hierarchy provided by a user do not have to be fully defined by other (lower-level) concepts. The user can provide only basic (high-level) concepts. These concepts are used to find corresponding classes in an ontology. The sub-classes of these classes are taken from this ontology and attached to the concepts of HOFC as new sub-concepts. The quantifiers and importance vectors of these sub-concepts are equal to the quantifier and the importance vector of the original concept. An example of such scenario is shown in Figure 12.

Classes defined in an ontology possess object properties (Section Ontology). Object properties are definitions of "non-trivial" relations that exist between pairs of ontology classes. For example, the ontology class *soccer_FORWARD* (see Appendix, see Figure 22) has an object property *playsFor* that is capable of "binding" any instance of *soccer_FORWARD* with an instance of the soccer ontology class *soccer_TEAM*. For example, let us assume that there is an instance of the class *soccer_FORWARD* called *Joe_Book*. *Joe_Book* has an object property *playsFor* that binds *Joe_Book* with an instance of the class *soccer_TEAM - FC_Creek*. This means that we can affiliate the instance *Joe_Book* of the HOFC concept *forward* with the instance *FC_Creek*, Figure 13. The quantifier Q and the importance vector M for *FC_Creek* are taken from the concept *forward*.

SEMANTIC WEB APPLICATION

System Description

The proposed approach of using hierarchies of concepts for document identification can be implemented in the environment of the Semantic Web. According to its core definition, the Semantic Web provides access to many ontologies defined in different domains. The exact localization of ontologies is not important. According to the Semantic Web paradigm these ontologies are always accessible on the web no matter where they are physically located. When ontologies are specified using a specification language OWL each definition and instance of ontology is uniquely identified and can be easily accessed locally or remotely. With such assumption, a prototype of a document identification system has been design and developed. Its architecture is presented in Figure 14.

Figure 12. Addition of new sub-concepts extracted from a relevant ontology: (a) the original concept, and (b) the concept after addition

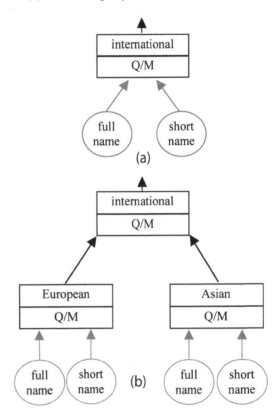

The main piece of information required by the system is a hierarchy of concepts. The hierarchy is provided by a user and built with a set of basic concepts. The assumption here is that these concepts are ontology nodes, and all of them have IDs of nodes from definition layers of different ontologies (Section Ontology). (The assumption that IDs of HOFC concepts are the same as IDS of ontology classes is made to simplify explanation and implementation of the proposed approach. In the real life applications, ontology mapping techniques have to be used. The ontology mapping is an interesting and challenging research topic.) This also means that the ontology specification language OWL is used to represent the hierarchy.

Figure 13. The instance FC_Creek is being affiliated with the instance Joe_Book

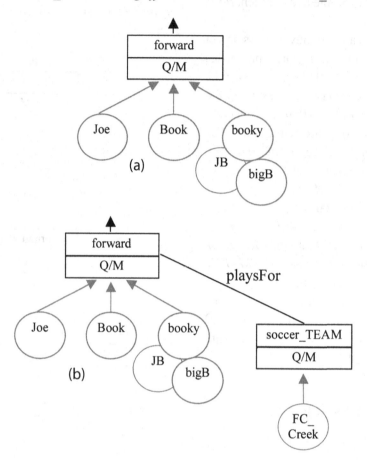

Figure 14. Architecture of a prototype system for document identification using hierarchy of concepts

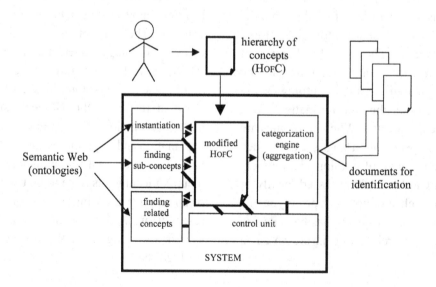

The first activity of the system is instantiation of the provided hierarchy. All terminal nodes of HOFC are "associated" with instances from ontologies. This process uses node IDs to identify information relevant to those nodes and extract it from ontologies.

Once the HOFC is instantiated the system starts recursively "travel" along paths of the hierarchy. Every time the system reaches a terminal node (concept) it performs checking of a document. The document is checked against all (it could be one or more) instances associated with this node. Each instance contains a set (or subset) of attributes, and the document is checked if it contains these attributes. This is equivalent to checking if the attributes (that is the instance) are activated by this document. Activations of attributes are weighted based on the importance vector M defined for this node, and then aggregated using OWA operator determined by the linguistic quantifier Q of this node. The result is a value representing a level of activation of the instance by the considered document. This process is repeated for every instance associated with this node. This leads to a set of activation values that are further aggregated using "OR" based OWA operator with the same importance for all values. The final result indicates up to what level the concept (identified by the terminal node) is activated by the considered document.

The activation of concepts is propagated upwards verifying if higher-level (super-) concepts are activated. If a concept is not activated, the system tries to enhance the HOFC. The first step in this process is to find more (sub-)concepts of the concept that cannot be found in the document. This is accomplished via interaction with ontologies. New sub-concepts are found and attached to the HOFC concept that is not present in the document. This process resembles a simple scenario presented in Figure 12. Next, all these new concepts are instantiated. The process of checking if the instances of new sub-concepts are activated by the considered document is performed.

When the extension of the HOFC with new sub-concepts does not lead to activation, a process of finding related concepts begins. The ID of the concept that cannot be activated is used to find object properties of the ontology class that is corresponding to the non-activated concept. Collected object properties contain IDs of classes that are in relationships with the corresponding class. Those relationships are defined in ontologies and a user has no prior knowledge about their existence. The definitions of object properties are used to "bring" new concepts. These concepts are affiliated with the concept that the system failed to activate due to non-existence of its instances in the document, see Figure 13. (The affiliation is done only for the time of checking of a single document. HOFC is modified only via addition of sub-concepts. The affiliation ensures a dynamic character of the enhancement process of HOFC.) The instances of new concepts are checked against the document.

The above presented activities are being repeated as long as there is no activation of a root concept, or both enhancing processes: extension and finding related concepts, can not be executed anymore. If all possibilities are explored and the root concept is not activated then the document being tested does not belong to the category described by the HOFC. Otherwise, if the highest concept is activated the document belongs to the category associated with the hierarchy of concepts.

Values of Importance Vector M

Importance vectors Ms are critical elements necessary for determining levels of activation of concepts based on activation of attributes and sub-concepts. Each node of the HOFC is associated with the vector M, and its values are indicators of levels of contributions of attributes and sub-concepts towards activation of a concept. Values of M, together with Q, are used for calculating OWA weights. In order to determine the values of importance vectors for different concepts, we use a special *Adaptive Assignment of Term Importance* (*AATI*) schema introduced in (Zhan, 2009). This schema is capable of "calculating" term importance values in an unsupervised manner using a stream of web documents. (The expression "term", used in AATI schema, represents an attribute, sub-concept or keyword that appears in a document.) The process of updating the importance values is being preformed all the time, as long as there is an incoming stream of documents.

The *AATI* schema consists of definitions of two measures: *term weight* (*TW*) representing importance of a single term (keyword) and *page value (PV)* which is a sum of term weights of terms found on a page, relations between them, as well as an iterative algorithm for calculating *TW* values based on web documents.

The AATI has a number of important features which make it appropriate for defining term importance for concept, and identification of concepts in web documents:

- terms (keywords) are taken from an ontology for a specific domain;
- *TW* values are determine on-line according to discrimination power of terms, i.e., if a term appears often in documents containing a concept this term is related to, its *TW* value increases, on the other hand, a term that occurs not so often have its *TW* value decreased; this process is fully "controlled" by a stream of upcoming web documents;
- *TW*s are updated at the same time when *PV*s of web documents are evaluated without any prior knowledge about concepts included in those web documents; this eliminates a need for training data sets which are required for constructing a classifier model;
- *TW* are calculated based on *PV*s, and *PV*s based on *TW*s; *TW* values are initialized with random numbers.

The ability of the AATI schema to adapt *TW* values to changes in the contents of web documents, and to deal with variety of different web documents makes this schema an ideal tool for determining values of importance vectors *M* associated with HOFC nodes. For more details related to the AATI schema and its evaluation, see (Zhan, 2009).

Sample Execution

A prototype of the system has been developed in Java. The Protégé API is used to access ontology classes, their properties and instances. (Protégé is a free, open source ontology editor and knowledge-based framework – http://protege.stanford.edu/.) API functions allow for creating a new enhanced hierarchy of concepts based on classes and individuals obtained from the domain ontology and the hierarchy of concepts given by a user.

A simple example that illustrates application of the prototype system is presented. The HOFC used in the experiment is shown in Figure 15. It is a very simple hierarchy representing the category *soccer*. A user is a novice to this category, and the only concepts that define soccer are *players*, and *match* with two sub-concepts *score* and *location*. All attributes are of the same importance. The linguistic quantifiers are shown in Figure 15 as well. This HOFC can be translated into the following statement:

The concept soccer is 'activated' if there are "MOST" of players and match. The concept players is activated if there exists regular_name "OR" nick_name. The concept match is activated if there are active "SOME" of score and location. The concept score is active when there exists first_half_score "OR" final_score. The concept location is active if there are active "SOME" city_name and stadium_name.

This simple HOFC is used to identify documents related to soccer.

Figure 15. A simple HOFC representing the category soccer

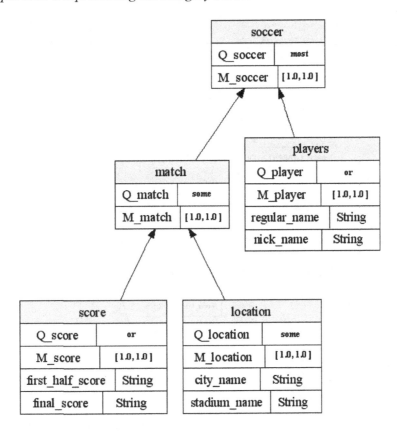

Instantiation of HOFC: The first step of the identification process is related to instantiation of the hierarchy and its extension with new sub-concepts. The automatic process of extracting instances from the *soccer* ontology as well as sub-concepts of the concept *players* is invoked first. The *soccer* ontology contains a number of sub-concepts of the concept *players*. All of them are extracted from the ontology and added to the user's hierarchy of concepts. The soccer ontology has eleven individuals of the concept *players* and its sub-concepts representing the players. All these players (instances) are extracted from the ontology and attached to the HOFC. For concepts *match*, *score* and *location* the *soccer* ontology does not have any additional sub-classes. Only five instances of the concept *location* are extracted from the ontology and attached to the hierarchy. As

the result of this instantiation phase the enhanced HOFC is created, Figure 16.

The instantiated HOFC is "ready" to perform a categorization process. An example of a page is shown in Figure 17. The page contains attributes of three different concepts *soccer_MIDFIELDER*, *soccer_DEFENDER*, and *location*:

- Guti is the attribute *nick_name* activated for *soccer_MIDFIELDER*
- Pepe is the attribute *nick_name* activated for *soccer_DEFENDER*
- Santiago_Bernabeu is the attribute *stadium_name* for *location*

This means that three concepts are being "activated". The levels of activation of these concepts are calculated using OWA operator defined

Figure 16. The instantiated HOFC with individuals of categories players (a) and location (b) (shaded boxes represent the original HOFC)

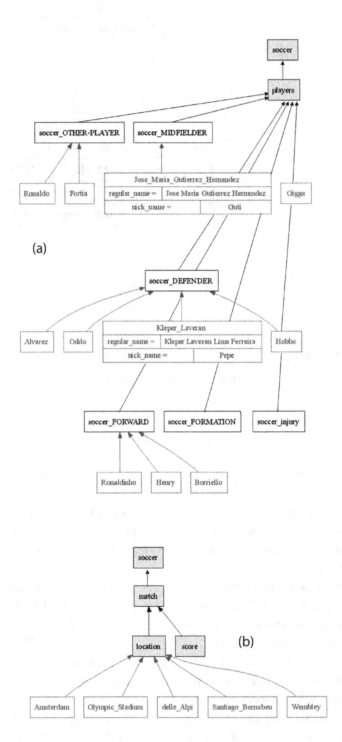

Figure 17. A web page with activated attributes: Guti, Pepe, and Snatiago Bernabeu

individually for each concept – "OR" for both *soccer_MIDFIELDER* and *soccer_DEFENDER*, and "SOME" for *location*. Assuming the attribute activation is 1.0 the activation levels obtained for the concepts are – 1.0 and 1.0 for *soccer_MIDFIELDER* and *soccer_DEFENDER*, and 0.5 for *location*. Moving to the higher levels in the HOFC the activation levels for concepts *players* and *match* are 1.0 and 0.25 respectively. Finally, the activation level for the concept *soccer*, associated with the quantifier "MOST", is 0.4375.

If a user changes the linguistic quantifier associated with the concept *soccer* from "MOST" to the quantifier "AT LEAST ONE" the activation of the concept *soccer* will change to 1.0. This reflects the fact that a user identifies a soccer page based on information about *players* or about *matches*. The scenario with the quantifier "MOST" indicates that a user has to have information about *players* and *matches* to classify a page as soccer one.

Enhancement of HOFC: An interesting example of the proposed categorization process is obtained for a document that belongs to the category *soccer* but does not have any words related to the *players* or *match* concepts. In such a case the second phase of identification is invoked – finding related concepts (Section System Description). The class *soccer_PLAYER* in the *soccer* ontology has an object property *playsFor* that links a player with a soccer team he plays for. The prototype system is able to detect this and extract from the ontology names of teams for which players play. Figure 18 represents instances of the concept *players* with affiliated instances of the ontology class *soccer_TEAM* identified by the object property *playsFor*.

Figure 19 represents a sample web page that is related to the *soccer* category but does not contain any instances (their attributes in particular) of concepts of the HOFC shown in Figure 16. However, the described enhancement process provides new instances to the HOFC. In this particular case we have instances of the category class *soccer_TEAM*, Figure 18. In such case the page in Figure 19 "activates" one of these instances – *FC Barcelona*. This leads to

Figure 18. Instances of the four sub-concepts of the concept players together with affiliated instances (shaded boxes) of the ontology class soccer_TEAM

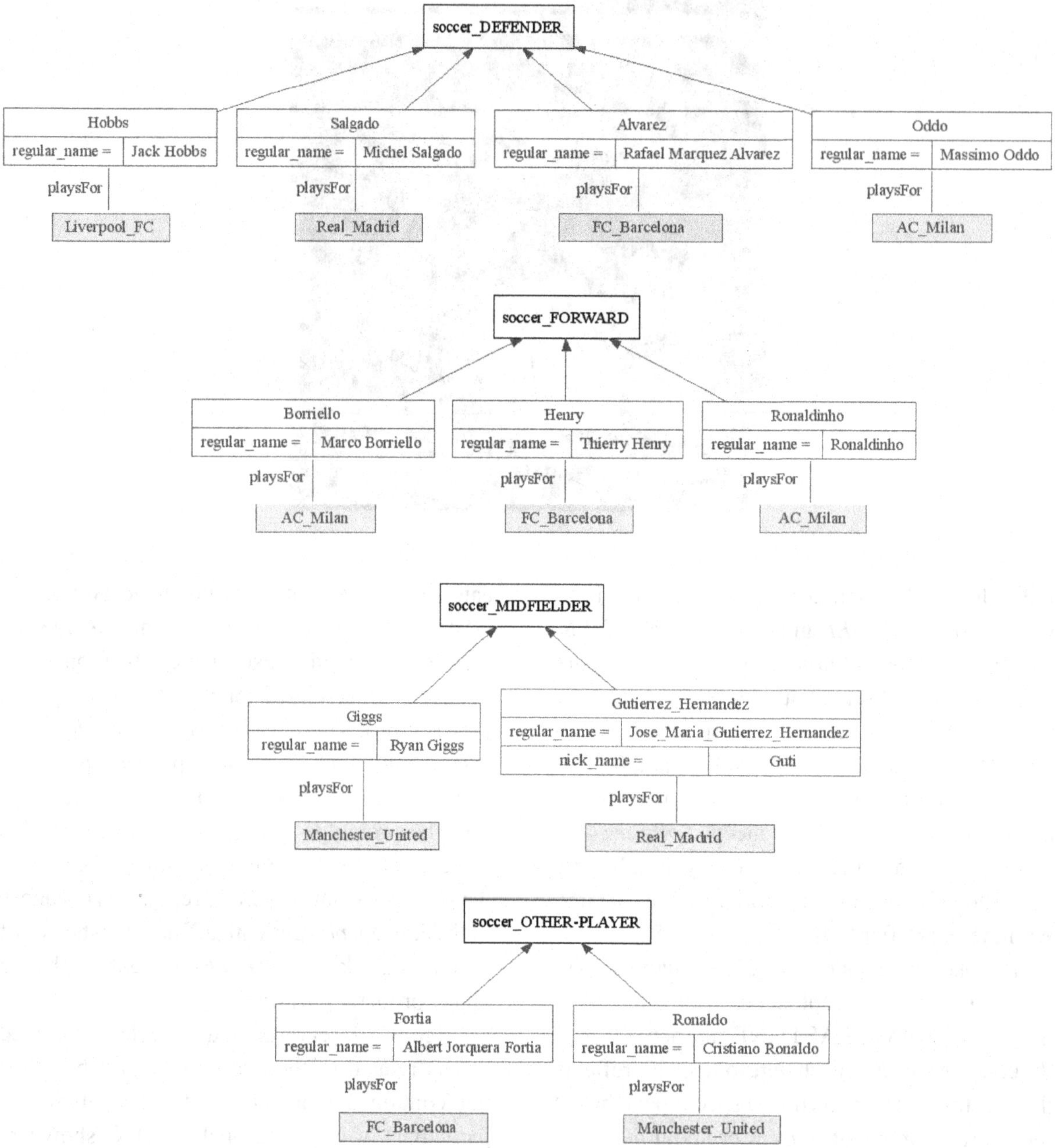

the activation level of 1.0 for the concept *soccer* when the quantifier "AT LEAST ONE" is used, and 0.25 with the quantifier "MOST". As in the previous example case, the level of activation of the HOFC concept *soccer* by the web page depends on user's categorization criteria.

Figure 19. A Web page that is related to the soccer concept that does not contain any attributers of concepts players and match

Identification of Documents: Web-Based Experiments

Description: An additional set of experiments has been performed in order to do a thorough examination of the proposed document identification method, evaluate usefulness of HOFCs as category identifiers, and compare obtained results with other approaches. The experiments are run on a local repository of web documents with a simple category identifier (presented below).

A local repository contains documents that have been crawled from BBC News web site (http://www.bbc.co.uk). BBC News editors labeled all those documents, therefore it is known which pages are related to "soccer" (they have been stored in the "football" folder of the web site), and which ones are not. In total, 16856 web pages have been collected. Among them, there are 4173 documents relevant to soccer, and 12683 are no-soccer documents.

The evaluation of experimental results is based on *TopN* schema, which has been widely used to evaluate information retrieval (IR) systems (Baziz, 2005; Vallet, 2005; Chang, 2006), especially the web based systems. Kobayashi, et al. (Kobayashi, 2000) argued that in IR systems for "finding'" web documents, "there is little hope of actually measuring the recall rate, ..., pages retrieved in the top 10 or 20 ranked documents (rather than all related pages)" are more important for evaluation. After all, most users do not have the patience to read all identified/found documents. *TopN* schema is focused on the top N documents ranked by IR systems. For example, if N is 10, the 10 documents with the highest ranks are considered and studied using a variety of metrics. Here, we perform evaluation based on the top 50, 100, 200, 250, 300, 350, 400, 450 and 500 ranked web documents. The metric we use is very simple – a percentage of related documents in the N documents.

The category identifier (a user's query) used in the experiments presented below is the HOFC presented in Figure 20.

This HOFC reflects user's associations with the concept *soccer*. Analyzing Figure 20 we can say that in the user's opinion the concept *soccer* is "defined" with two other concepts – *team* and *player*. Further, the concept *player* is "not defined" by any other concepts, while the concept *team* is

Figure 20. HOFC used in web-based experiments

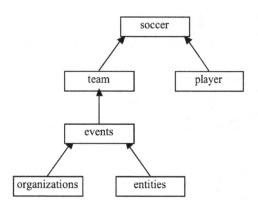

"defined" by the concept *events*, and this concept is "defined" by two other concepts: *organizations* and *entities*.

In order to compare the proposed method, four different sets of experiments are done with four different forms of the above presented category identifier. These experiments can be described in the following way:

The *first experiment* is performed using an ordinary keyword-matching approach. Extracted documents are ranked using the classical vector space approach (Manning, 2008). For our identifier, the relevant documents are those containing five individual, not connected in any way, words "team", "player", "events", "organizations" and "entities".

The *second experiment* uses an enhanced keyword-matching approach. A simple keyword-based identifier, like the one from the first experiment, is enhanced with additional keywords. That is, we use a domain ontology and "add" more keywords to the identifier. For example, for the term "player" we add the following terms: "Beckham", "David", "AC Milan" (see Appendix for *soccer* ontology). The rest of concepts are enhanced in the similar way.

The *third experiment* uses an identifier exactly as in the form presented above, i.e., it is a structure

of simple keywords. No enhancement of any form is performed.

The *fourth experiment* represents the proposed method. The identifier is represented as a structure instead of unstructured lists of concepts, and additionally all concepts are enhanced with concepts from a domain ontology.

It has to be mentioned that all four experiments use a linguistic quantifier to aggregate occurrences of words in documents, and compute a single value indicating relevance of a document to the domain.

Results: The results of all previously described experiments are shown in Tables 2 and 3. The values included in the tables represent how many documents (percentage wise) are soccer related in the top N documents.

The first table reports results of four sets of experiments performed with the linguistic quantifier *most*. Let us take a look at some *TopN* values. At *Top50*, the queries without enrichment – simple keywords and HOFC (the first and third columns in Table 1) – have not found any soccer-related documents. These results have been anticipated – the keywords used here (Figure 20) are very generic, and their "discrimination" abilities are minimal. The process of enrichment helps a lot. For enriched keyword query (second column, Table 1), 33 documents out of top 50 (66%) are related to the soccer category. For HOFC, all top 50 documents are soccer ones – it seems that HOFC combined with enrichment has very good identification abilities.

For experiments without enhancement (columns one and three), the percentage of related documents is increasing with the increasing value of N. The application of HOFC provides slightly better results. The increase of soccer related documents in top N is somehow related to the fact that more and more documents are taken into consideration. For experiments with enrichment (second and fourth columns), the percentage decreases with increasing N. The experiment with enriched keywords (third column) never identifies

Table 2. The document ranking with linguistic quantifier most

	Keywords: non-enriched (first column)	Keywords: enriched (second column)	HofC: non-enriched (third column)	HofC: enriched (fourth column)
Top 50	0.00%	66.00%	0.00%	100.00%
Top 100	0.00%	50.00%	2.00%	100.00%
Top 150	1.33%	43.33%	9.33%	99.33%
Top 200	10.00%	48.50%	17.00%	95.00%
Top 250	15.20%	54.40%	22.40%	92.00%
Top 300	18.67%	54.00%	24.00%	85.70%
Top 350	21.71%	49.14%	25.71%	80.30%
Top 400	26.00%	48.50%	31.50%	82.25%
Top 450	26.89%	47.56%	32.00%	83.33%
Top 500	30.60%	48.40%	32.00%	84.80%

Table 3. The document ranking with linguistic quantifier some

	Keywords: non-enriched (first column)	Keywords: enriched (second column)	HofC: non-enriched (third column)	HofC: enriched (fourth column)
Top 50	8.00%	100.00%	8.00%	100.00%
Top 100	11.00%	100.00%	11.00%	100.00%
Top 150	16.67%	75.33%	16.67%	75.33%
Top 200	18.50%	70.50%	18.50%	70.50%
Top 250	21.60%	75.20%	21.60%	75.20%
Top 300	18.00%	76.00%	18.00%	76.00%
Top 350	17.14%	75.43%	17.14%	75.43%
Top 400	21.25%	74.25%	21.25%	74.25%
Top 450	21.11%	73.78%	21.11%	73.78%
Top 500	23.00%	74.20%	23.00%	74.20%

full N number of documents. The first overlooked document for the experiment with enriched HOFC appears in *Top150*, for *Top500* the HOFC enriched queries identifies 424 relevant documents. The decrease in soccer related documents for experiments with enriched queries (columns two and four) are related to the fact that the highest "rated" documents are already found and less relevant documents are more difficult do distinguished from non-soccer related ones.

Overall, it is obvious that queries based on HOFC with enrichment consistently provide the best results.

The results of experiments are different when the linguistic quantifier *some* is used. For the experiments with non-enriched queries – keywords and HOFC (first and third columns, Table 2) – the results are identical, and worse than for the experiments with enriched queries. The experiments with enriched keywords and HOFC (second and third column) provide better results. It is interesting to see that both sets of experiments – columns one and three, and columns two and four in Table 2 – have the same results. The reason for that is applied linguistic quantifier. The quantifier *some* (Figure 1b) "flattens" the HOFC hierarchies, and they have the same discriminative power as queries with keywords only. The aggregation process is changed due to the application of *some* quantifier: it improves the performance of non-enriched queries (compare the first and third columns of Table 1 with the same columns of Table 2) and non- HOFC queries (column two of both tables); and slightly degrades the performance of queries that use enriched HOFC. This means that the linguistic quantifier *most* leads to a better selection of documents that are related to soccer when enriched HOFC is used. If we think about it, it is logically sound to see more confidence in the identification process when documents are evaluated using enriched hierarchies of concepts where most of keywords defining concepts have to be present in the related documents.

CONCLUSION

The paper investigates an approach for development of a concept-based structure suitable for text categorization. The method uses hierarchies of concepts as category identifiers. The hierarchies are graph-like structures of interconnected concepts that represent relationships between sub- and super- concepts. The hierarchies use OWA operators with argument importance to control conditions that have to be satisfied by sub-concepts in order to "activate" super-concept.

Application of hierarchies of concepts brings two important elements to a process of categorization:

- ability to utilize dependencies between concepts, in particular, levels of contributions of sub-concepts in defining a super-concept; linguistic quantifiers (translated into weights of OWA operators) are used to defined these dependencies;

- ability to express different levels of importance of sub-concepts in defining super-concepts; this is achieved by utilization of importance levels (also translated into weights of OWA operators).

Both these elements provide some aspects of human-like ways of identifying activated concepts, and bring new and interesting facets to a text categorization process.

Hierarchies of concepts used to represent a category identifier can be expanded using new concepts pull out from ontologies. The methodology presented here shows how this can be accomplished. An ontology is used to add new concepts (sub-concepts) to hierarchies of concepts, as well as to alternate them via introduction of related concepts. An ontology allows for defining different types of relations between classes, and these connections are fully utilized in a process of enhancing hierarchies of concepts.

A prototype of the system that is an application of the proposed approach is described in the paper. Some results of experiments are reported.

Promising results obtained during experiments with a prototype have triggered investigations in the following areas:

- automatic determination of importance levels of sub-concepts (so far it has been assumed that the importance levels are the same for all sub-concepts);
- linguistic quantifiers that reflect different ways of determining activated concepts;
- ontology mapping approaches suitable for a process of enhancing hierarchies of concepts with concepts form different ontolgoies;
- design and development of a full-scaled application that implements all aspects of the proposed approach.

REFERENCES

Anagnostopoulos, A., Broder, A., & Punera, K. (2008). Effective and efficient classification on a search-engine modeling. *Knowledge and Information Systems, 16*(2), 129–154. doi:10.1007/s10115-007-0102-6

Anick, P. (1994). Adapting a full-text information retrieval system to the computer troubleshooting domain. *17th Annual International ACM SIGIR Conference on Research and Development in Information Retrieval* (pp. 349-358).

Antoniou, G., & van Harmelen, F. (2004). *A Semantic Web Primer*. Cambridge, MA: The MIT Press.

Aphinyanaphongs, Y., Tsamardinos, I., Statnikov, A., Hardin, D., & Aliferis, C. F. (2005). Text categorization models for high-quality article retrieval in internal medicine. *Journal of the American Medical Informatics Association, 12*(2), 207–216. doi:10.1197/jamia.M1641

Apte, C., Damerau, F., & Weiss, S. (1994). Automated Learning of Decision Rules for Text Categorization. *ACM Transactions on Information Systems, 12*, 233–251. doi:10.1145/183422.183423

Baziz, M., Boughanem, M., Aussenac-Gilles, N., & Chrisment, C. (2005). Semantic cores for representing documents in IR. *ACM Symposium on Applied Computing, Santa Fe, New Mexico* (pp. 1011-1017).

Berners-Lee, T., Hendler, J., & Lassila, O. (2001). The Semantic Web. *Scientific American, 284*, 34–43. doi:10.1038/scientificamerican0501-34

Borsje, J., Levering, L., & Frasincar, F. (2008). Hermes: a Semantic Web-Based News Decision Support System. *23rd Annual ACM Symposium on Applied Computing (SAC 2008)* (pp. 2415-2420).

Chang, Y.-C., & Chen, S.-M. (2006). A new query reweighting method for document retrieval based on genetic algorithms. *IEEE Transactions on Evolutionary Computation, 10*(5), 617–622. doi:10.1109/TEVC.2005.863130

Choi, B., & Peng, X. (2004). Dynamic and hierarchical classification of web pages. *Online Information Review, 28*(2), 139–147. doi:10.1108/14684520410531673

Clack, C., Farringdon, J., Lidwell, P., & Yu, T. (1997). Autonomous document classification for business. *1st International Conference on Autonomous Agents, MarinadelRey, CA* (pp. 201-208).

Cohen, W. W., & Singer, Y. (1999). Context-sensitive learning methods for text categorization. *ACM Transactions on Information Systems, 17*(2), 141–173. doi:10.1145/306686.306688

Cunningham, H., Maynard, D., Bontcheva, K., Tablan, V., Ursu, C., Dimitrov, M., et al. (2009). *Developing language processing components with GATE*. Retrieved from http://gate.ac.uk/sale/tao

Dridi, O., & Ahmed, M. B. (2008). Building an ontology-based framework for semantic information retrieval: application to breast cancer. *3rd International Conference on Information and Communication Technologies: From Theory to Applications, ICTTA 2008, v2* (pp. 1-6).

Du, L., Jin, H., de Vel, O., & Liu, N. (2008). A latent semantic indexing and WordNet based information retrieval model for digital forensics. *IEEE International Conference on Intelligence and Security Informatics, ISI 2008* (pp. 70-75).

Dumais, S. T., Platt, J., Heckerman, D., & Sahami, M. (1998). Inductive learning algorithms and representations for text categorization. 7th ACM International Conference on Information and Knowledge Management CIKM-98, Bethesda, MD (pp. 148-155).

Fensel, D., Hendler, J., Lieberman, H., & Wahlster, W. (2003). *Spinning the Semantic Web.* Cambridge, MA: MIT Press.

Fuhr, N., Hartmann, S., Knorz, G., Lustig, G., Schwantner, M., & Tzeras, K. (1991). AIR/X—a rule-based multistage indexing system for large subject fields. *3rd International Conference "Recherche d'Information Assistee par Ordinateur" RIAO-91, Barcelona, Spain* (pp. 606-623).

Gong, Z., Cheang, C., & L. H. U., (2005). Web query expansion by WordNet (LNCS 3588, pp. 166-17).

Gruber, T. E. (1993). A translation approach to portable ontology specifications. *Knowledge Acquisition, 5*, 199–220. doi:10.1006/knac.1993.1008

Guarino, N., Masolo, C., & Vetere, G., Ontoseek. (1999). Content-based access to the web. *IEEE Intelligent Systems, 14*(3), 70–80. doi:10.1109/5254.769887

Hayes, P. J., Andersen, P. M., Nirengurg, I. B., & Schmandt, L. M. (1990). Tcs: a shell for content-based text categorization. *6th IEEE Conference on Artificial Intelligence Applications CAIA-90, Santa Barbara, CA* (pp. 320-326).

Ittner, D. J., Lewis, D. D., & Ahn, D. D. (1995). Text categorization of low quality images. In *Proceedings of SDAIR-95, 4th Annual Symposium on Document Analysis and Information Retrieval, Las Vegas, NV* (pp. 301-315).

Joachims, T. (1988). Text Categorization with Support Vector Machines: Learning with Many Relevant Features. *Machine Learning, ECML-98,* 137–142.

Kalfoglou, Y., Domingue, J., Motta, E., Vargas-Vera, M., & Shum, S. B. (2001). myPlanet: An Ontology-Driven Web-Based Personalized News Service. *Workshop on Ontologies and Information Sharing - IJCAI 2001* (pp. 44-52).

Kim, Y.-B., & Kim, Y.-S. (2008). Latent semantic kernels for WordNet: Transforming a tree-like structure into a matrix. *IEEE International Conference on Advanced Language Processing and Web Information Technology, ALPIT '08, Dalian Liaoning* (pp. 76-80).

Kobayashi, M., & Takeda, K. (2000). Information retrieval on the web. *ACM Computing Surveys, 32*, 144–173. doi:10.1145/358923.358934

Koller, D., & Sahami, M. (1997). Hierarchically classifying documents using very few words. *14th International Conference on Machine Learning ICML-97, Nashville, TN* (pp. 70-178).

Kolte, S., & Bhirud, S. (2008). Word sense disambiguation using WordNet domains. *1st IEEE International Conference on Emerging Trends in Engineering and Technology, ICETET '08, Nagpur, Maharashtra* (pp. 1187-1191).

Larkey, L. S., & Croft, W. B. (1996). Combining classifiers in text categorization. *19th ACM International Conference on Research and Development in Information Retrieval SIGIR-96, Zurich, Switzerland* (pp. 289-297).

Lewis, D. D. (1992). *Feature selection and feature extraction for text categorization* (pp. 212–217). San Francisco, USA: Speech and Natural Language Workshop.

Lewis, D. D. (1998). Naïve (Bayes) at forty: The independence assumption in information retrieval. *10th European Conference on Machine Learning ECML-98, Chemnitz, Germany* (pp. 4-15).

Lewis, D. D., & Ringuette, M. (1994). A comparison of two learning algorithms for text categorization. *3rd Annual Symposium on Document Analysis and Information Retrieval SDAIR-94, Las Vegas, NV* (pp. 81-93).

Li, Y. H., & Jain, A. K. (1998). Classification of text documents. *The Computer Journal, 41*(8), 537–546. doi:10.1093/comjnl/41.8.537

Maedche, A., Naumann, G., & Staab, S. (2002). *Bootstrapping an Ontology-based Information Extraction System for the Web. Intelligent Exploration of the Web, Series - Studies in Fuzziness and Soft Computing*. Springer/Physica-Verlag.

Manning, C. D., Raghavan, P., & Schutze, H. (2008). *Introduction to information retrieval*. New York: Cambridge University Press.

Manning, C. D., & Schutze, H. (1999). *Foundations of Statistical Natural Language Processing*. Cambridge, MA: MIT Press.

Martin, T. (2004). Searching and smushing on the semantic web-challenges for soft computing . In Nikravesh, M., Azvine, B., Yager, R. R., & Zadeh, L. A. (Eds.), *Enhancing the Power of the Web* (pp. 167–188). Heidelberg: Springer.

Miller, G. A. (1995). WordNet: a lexical database for English. *Communications of the ACM, 38*(11), 39–41. doi:10.1145/219717.219748

Mitchell, T. M. (1996). *Machine Learning*. New York: McGraw Hill.

Sanchez, E. (2006). *Fuzzy Logic and the Semantic Web*. Amsterdam: Elsevier.

Sanchez, E., & Yamanoi, T. (2006). Fuzzy Ontologies for the Semantic Web. *Flexible Query Answering Systems* (. *LNCS, 4027*, 691–699.

Schutze, H., Hull, D. A., & Pedersen, J. O. (1995). A comparison of classifiers and document representations for the routing problem. *18th ACM International Conference on Research and Development in Information Retrieval SIGIR-95, Seattle, WA* (pp. 229-237).

Scott, F., Lewis, W. D., & Langendoen, D. T. (2002). An ontology for Linguistic Annotaion 1-2. *14th Innovative Applications of AI Conference, Edmonton, Canada* (pp. 11-19).

Sebastiani, F. (2002). Machine Learning in Automated Text Categorization. *ACM Computing Surveys, 34*(1), 1–47. doi:10.1145/505282.505283

Shen, D., Chen, Z., Zeng, H.-J., Zhang, B., Yang, W.-Y., Ma, Q., & Lu, Y. (2004). Web-page classification through summarization. *27th Annual International ACM SIGIR Conference on Research and development in information retrieval, Sheffield, United Kingdom* (pp. 242–249).

Sheth, A., Arpinar, I. B., & Kashyap, V. (2004). Relationships at the heart of Semantic Web: modeling, discovering and exploiting complex semantic relationships. In Nikravesh, M., Azvine, B., Yager, R. R., & Zadeh, L. A. (Eds.), *Enhancing the Power of the Web* (pp. 63–94). Heidelberg: Springer.

Smith, B. (2003). Ontology. An Introduction . In Floridi, L. (Ed.), *Blackwell Guide to the Philosophy of Computing and Information* (pp. 155–166). Oxford: Blackwell.

Stuckenschmidt, H., Hartmann, J., & van Harmelen, F. (2002). Learning Structural Classification Rules for Web-Page Categorization. *FLAIRS Conference* (pp. 440-444).

Tho, Q. T., Hui, S. C., Fong, A. C. M., & Tru Hoang, C. (2006). Automatic Fuzzy Ontology Generation for Semantic Web. *IEEE Transactions on Knowledge and Data Engineering, 18*, 842–856. doi:10.1109/TKDE.2006.87

Vallet, D., Fernandez, M., & Castells, P. (2005). An ontology-based information retrieval model. *2nd European Semantic Web Conference, ESWC 2005, Springer, Grete, Greece* (pp. 455-470).

Vidulin, V., Lustrek, M., & Gams, M. (2007). Training a genre classifier for automatic classification of web pages. *Journal of Computing and Information Technology, 15*(4), 305–311.

Voorhees, E. M. (1994). *Query expansion using lexical-semantic relations. 17th Annual ACM SIGIR conference on research and development in information retrieval* (pp. 61–69). Springer-Verlag.

Woods, W. A. (1997). *Conceptual indexing: a better way to organize knowledge*. Retrieved from http://research.sun.com/techrep/1997/abstract- 61.html.

Yager, R. R. (1988). On ordered weighted averaging aggregation operators in multi-criteria decision making. *IEEE Transactions on Systems, Man, and Cybernetics, 18*, 183–190. doi:10.1109/21.87068

Yager, R. R. (1993). Families of OWA operators. *Fuzzy Sets and Systems, 59*, 125–148. doi:10.1016/0165-0114(93)90194-M

Yager, R. R. (2000). A Hierarchical Document Retrieval Language. *Information Retrieval, 3*, 357–377. doi:10.1023/A:1009911900286

Yang, Y. (1994). Expert Network: Effective and Efficient Learning from Human Decisions in Text Categorization and Retrieval. *17th Annual International ACM-SIGIR Conference on Research and Development in Information Retrieval, Dublin, Ireland* (pp. 3-6). ACM/Springer.

APPENDIX: SOCCER ONTOLOGY

All examples of the paper are related to the soccer ontology. A special ontology has been developed for that purpose. Of course, this is one of possible soccer ontolgoies and the fact of using this particular one does not introduce any limitations. A very generic drawing representing basic classes is included in Figure 21.

Figure 21. The soccer ontology (the highlighted term owl:Thing represents the root)

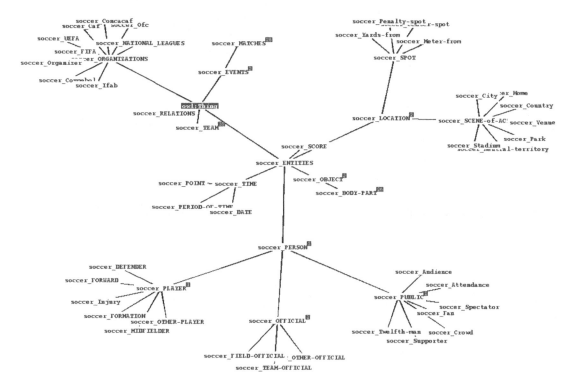

The highest-level classes are presented in Figure 22. All of them are sub-classes of the main class *Thing*. For some of them, the *is-a* hierarchy goes even further (a solid triangular indicates sub-concept). For example, the class *soccer_ENTITIES* has five sub-classes, and four of them have their own sub-classes.

Another important aspect of the soccer ontology is existence of a variety of relationships among ontology classes. Figure 23 represents a definition of the relation *playsFor* that is an object property of the class *soccer_PLAYER*. In the window PROPERTY EDITOR, it is seen that its domain is the concept *soccer_PLAYER* and its range the concept *soccer_TEAM*. This relation has also an inverse relation *hasPlayer*. An additional constrain imposed on this relation is *cardinality 1*. This indicates that a player can only play for one team.

Figure 22. The basic four concepts of the category soccer together with their sub-concepts

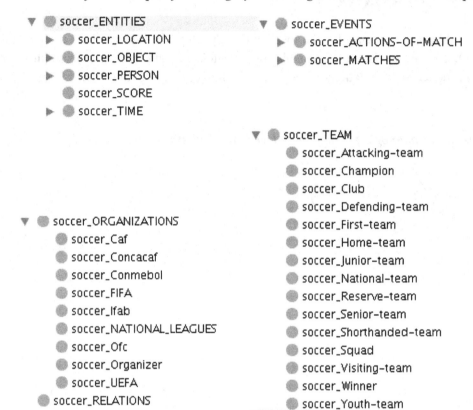

Figure 23. The snapshot of the tool Protégé during editing of the soccer ontology shows the object property playsFor of the class soccer_PLAYER

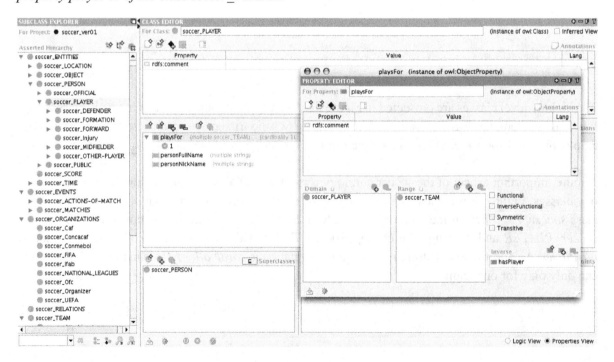

Chapter 10
A Fuzzy Ontology Generation Framework from Fuzzy Relational Databases

Z.M. Ma
Northeastern University, China

Yanhui Lv
Northeastern University, China

Li Yan
Northeastern University, China

ABSTRACT

Ontology is an important part of the W3C standards for the Semantic Web used to specify standard conceptual vocabularies to exchange data among systems, provide reusable knowledge bases, and facilitate interoperability across multiple heterogeneous systems and databases. However, current ontology is not sufficient for handling vague information that is commonly found in many application domains. A feasible solution is to import the fuzzy ability to extend the classical ontology. In this article, we propose a fuzzy ontology generation framework from the fuzzy relational databases, in which the fuzzy ontology consists of fuzzy ontology structure and instances. We simultaneously consider the schema and instances of the fuzzy relational databases, and respectively transform them to fuzzy ontology structure and fuzzy RDF data model. This can ensure the integrality of the original structure as well as the completeness and consistency of the original instances in the fuzzy relational databases.

Copyright © 2010, IGI Global, distributing in print or electronic forms without written permission of IGI Global is prohibited.

INTRODUCTION

The Semantic Web (Berners-Lee, Hendler, & Lassila, 2001) is a vision of the next generation Web, which specifies how to display Web resources for human consumption, that will be enhanced with semantic markups (often called annotations), which will specify the meaning of Web resources so as to make them more accessible to automatic processes. Ontology, as a representation of a shared conceptualization of a specific domain, plays an important role in the Semantic Web. Ontology defines a set of representational primitives with which to model a domain of knowledge or discourse. The representational primitives are typically classes (or entities), attributes (or properties), and relationships (or relations among class members). The definitions of the representational primitives include information about their meaning and constraints on their logically consistent application.

Ontology can be generated from various data resources such as textual data, dictionary, knowledge-based, semistructured schemata, and database schemata. Compared to other types of data, ontology generation from relational data has increasingly attracted the most attention because most formatted data on the Web are still stored in relational databases and are not published as an open Web of inter-referring resources (Berners-Lee, Hall, Hendler, Shadbolt, & Weitzner, 2006). To be able to use the data in a semantic context to achieve interoperability, an effective way is to extract the information from relational databases to build ontology (Mukhopadhyay, Banik, & Mukherjee, 2007; Trinh, Barker, & Alhajj, 2006). Although relational databases are based on closed-world assumption, while ontology uses open-world semantics, there exist some approximate correspondences between them. Database schema, for instance, describes a collection of domain entities and their relationships which are analogous to the concepts and their relationships in the ontology. For this reason, database schema

has become the dominant source for acquiring knowledge for ontology development. In fact, relational databases can be formalized by First Order Logic (FOL); while the logical foundation for ontology is Description Logic (DL) (Baader, McGuinness, Nardi, & Patel-Schneider, 2003), which is a subset of FOL. So it is feasible to generate ontology utilizing the data in relational databases.

It should be noted that the classical ontology is limited to crisp concepts and may not be sufficient for handling imprecise information that is commonly found in many application domains. In order to present and reason imprecise information in ontology, a possible solution is to incorporate fuzzy logic into ontology, that is, fuzzy ontology. More recently some efforts have been made to propose fuzzy ontology. Lam (2006) introduces a fuzzy ontology map (FOM) based on fuzzy theory and graph theory for fuzzy extension of the hard-constraint ontology. Abulaish and Dey (2007) describes a fuzzy ontology framework in which a concept descriptor is represented as a fuzzy relation that encodes the degree of a property value using a fuzzy membership function. Calegari and Ciucci (2007) develops a suited plug-in of the KAON Project in order to introduce fuzziness in ontology. A schema structure is presented to store ontologies and their instances in a FORDBMS capable of handling fuzzy datatypes in Barranco, Campana, Medina, and Pons (2007). In addition, Sanchez and Yamanoi (2006) introduces a fuzzy ontology structure from the aspects of lexicon and knowledge base. Just like the generation of classical ontology, fuzzy ontology can be generated from various fuzzy data resources. In Quan, Hui, Fong, and Cao (2006), a fuzzy ontology generation framework (FOGA) is proposed for fuzzy ontology generation on uncertainty information. The framework is based on the idea of fuzzy theory and formal concept analysis. Nevertheless, less research has been done in the construction of fuzzy ontology. It is particularly true in using the fuzzy databases for generating fuzzy ontology. To our best knowledge, so far, there are not any reports on fuzzy ontology generation from fuzzy databases.

In this article, we present a framework for the construction of fuzzy ontology from fuzzy relational databases. The article makes the following main contributions:

1. We identify that the fuzzy ontology consists of ontology structure and its instances. The fuzzy ontology is generated from the fuzzy relational databases through simultaneously considering fuzzy relational schema and fuzzy relational instances.
2. The fuzzy ontology structure is generated by the mapping of fuzzy relational schema, which preserves the structural semantics of the fuzzy relational database.
3. We use the fuzzy RDF data model to represent the instances of fuzzy ontology and generate the fuzzy RDF data model by the mapping of fuzzy relational instances.

The rest of the article is organized as follows. First, we introduce the basic concepts of fuzzy set theory and fuzzy relational databases. Second, we build the fuzzy ontology structure by mapping the fuzzy relational schema after identifying the semantics of fuzzy database schema. Third, we construct the fuzzy RDF data model, which is used to represents the instances of fuzzy ontology, by mapping the fuzzy relational instances. Finally, we conclude this article and present some topics for further research.

PRELIMINARIES

This section first gives some definitions of fuzzy set theory before introducing the basic knowledge of fuzzy relational databases.

Fuzzy Sets

Fuzzy sets theory, introduced by L. A. Zadeh (Zadeh, 1965), allows dealing with imprecise and vague data. Here, we only give some basic definitions of fuzzy set theory.

Definition 1 (Fuzzy set). A fuzzy set F with respect to a universe of discourse U is characterized by a membership function $\mu_F\colon U{\rightarrow}[0, 1]$, assigning a membership degree $\mu_F(u)$ to each $u{\in}U$. Membership function $\mu_F(u)$ provides a measure of the degree of the belonging of u to F.

Typically, if $\mu_F(u) = 1$ then u definitely belongs to F. For example, $\mu_F(u) = 0.7$ means that u is "likely" to be an element of F by a degree of 0.7. For ease of representation, a fuzzy set F over universe U is organized into a set of ordered pairs:

$$F = \{(u\,/\mu_F(u))|u{\in}U\} \qquad (1)$$

If U is not a discrete set, the fuzzy set F can be represented by

$$F = \int_{u{\in}U} u\,/\,\mu_F(u) \qquad (2)$$

When the $\mu_F(u)$ above is explained to be a measure of the possibility that a variable X has the value u, where X takes values in U, a fuzzy value is described by a possibility distribution π_X (Zadeh, 1978).

$$\pi_X = \{\ u_1/\pi_X(u_1),\ u_2/\pi_X(u_2),\ldots,\ u_n/\pi_X(u_n)\} \qquad (3)$$

Here, $\pi_X(u_i)$, $u_i{\in}U$, denotes the possibility that u_i is true. A fuzzy set is a representation of a concept while possibility distribution relates with the possibility of occurring a value within a distribution. Let π_X and F be the possibility distribution representation and the fuzzy set representation for a fuzzy value, respectively. It is clear that $\pi_X = F$ is true (Raju & Majumdar, 1988). By means of fuzzy sets and possibility distributions, a fuzzy value on U can be characterized by a fuzzy set or a possibility distribution in U.

Definition 2 (Fuzzy relation). A fuzzy relation has degree of membership whose value lies in [0, 1].

$$\mu_R: A \times B \rightarrow [0, 1]$$

$$R = \{((x, y), \mu_R(x, y))| \mu_R(x, y)| \mu_R(x, y) \geq 0, x \in A, y \in B\} \quad (4)$$

Here R denotes a fuzzy relation from fuzzy set A to fuzzy set B, and $\mu_R(x, y)$ is interpreted as the strength of relation between x and y. When $\mu_R(x, y) \geq \mu_R(x', y')$, (x, y) is more strongly related than (x', y'). When a fuzzy relation $R \subseteq A \times B$ is given, R can be regarded as a fuzzy set in the space $A \times B$.

Assume a Cartesian product space $X_1 \times X_2$ composed of two sets X_1 and X_2. This space makes a set of pairs (x_1, x_2) for all $x_1 \in X_1, x_2 \in X_2$. Given a fuzzy relation R between two sets X_1 and X_2, this relation is a set of pairs $(x_1, x_2) \in R$. Consequently, this fuzzy relation can be presumed to be a fuzzy restriction to the set $X_1 \times X_2$. Therefore, $R \subseteq X_1 \times X_2$.

Fuzzy binary relation can be extended to n-ary relation. If we assume $X_1, X_2, ..., X_n$ to be fuzzy sets, fuzzy relation $R \subseteq X_1 \times X_2 \times ... \times X_n$ can be said to be a fuzzy set of tuple elements $(x_1, x_2, ..., x_n)$, where $x_1 \in X_1, x_2 \in X_2, ... , x_n \in X_n$.

Fuzzy Relational Databases

A relation instance r on a relational schema $R(A_1, A_2, ..., A_n)$ is a subset of the Cartesian product of Dom $(A_1) \times$ Dom $(A_2) \times ... \times$ Dom (A_n), in which Dom (A_i) is the domain of attribute A_i. Therefore, a relation instance can be viewed as a table whose rows and columns are called the *tuples* and *attributes* of the relation, respectively. Fuzzy set and possibility distribution theories have been used to extend relational database model and this has resulted in several fuzzy relational database models. One of the fuzzy relational database models is

based on fuzzy relation (Raju & Majumdar, 1988), and similarity relation (Buckles & Petry, 1982). The other one is based on possibility distribution (Prade & Testemale, 1984), which can further be classified into two categories: tuples associated with possibilities and attribute values represented by possibility distributions.

Now let us look at the tuples of fuzzy relational databases in order to understand the fuzzy relational database models. The form of an n-tuple in each of the above-mentioned fuzzy relational models can be expressed, respectively, as follows.

$t = <p_1, p_2, ..., p_i, ..., p_n>$ (for *type 1* fuzzy relational model)

Here $p_i \subseteq$ Dom (A_i) with Dom (A_i) being the domain of attribute A_i. For each Dom (A_i), there exists a similarity (or proximity and resemblance) relation.

$t = <a_1, a_2, ..., a_i, ..., a_n, d>$ (for *type 2* fuzzy relational model) and

$t = <\pi_{A1}, \pi_{A2}, ..., \pi_{Ai}, ..., \pi_{An}>$ (for *type 3* fuzzy relational model),

Here $a_i \in$ Dom (A_i), $d \in (0, 1]$, π_{Ai} is the possibility distribution of attribute A_i on its domain Dom (A_i), and $\pi_{Ai}(x)$, $x \in$ Dom (A_i), denotes the possibility that x is the actual value of $t[A_i]$.

Based on the above-mentioned basic fuzzy relational database models, there are several extended fuzzy relational database models. Clearly one can combine two kinds of fuzziness in possibility-based fuzzy relational databases where attribute values may be possibility distributions, and tuples are connected with membership degrees. Such fuzzy relational databases are called possibility-distribution-fuzzy relational models in Umano and Fukami (1994). Another possible extension is to combine possibility distribution and similarity (proximity or resemblance) relation, and the extended possibility-based fuzzy relational databases proposed in Ma and Mili (2002), where possibility distribution and resemblance relation arise in a relational database simultaneously. For

Table 1. Example of fuzzy database schema

Relation list	Attribute list	Foreign key and referenced relation
Client	clientID, cName, age, salary, e-mail, state, city, street, code, dept_ID, μ	dept_ID(Department(deptID))
PrClient	clientID, PrDept_ID, discount, μ	PrDept_ID(PrDept(deptID)), clientID(Client(clientID))
Department	deptID, dName, μ	No
PrDept	deptID, pName, μ	deptID(Department(deptID))
Service	serID, μ	No
CONTRACT	contractID, client_ID, dept_ID, ser_ID, μ	client_ID(Client(clientID)), dept_ID(Department(deptID)), ser_ID(Service(serID))

a comprehensive review of fuzzy relational databases, one can refer to Ma and Yan (2008).

This article focuses on the fuzzy relational databases where n-tuples have the following form:

$$t = <\pi_{A1}, \pi_{A2}, ..., \pi_{Ai}, ..., \pi_{An}, d>$$

Here each tuple may be associated with a possibility degree, and its attribute values may be fuzzy ones represented by possibility distributions. The formal definition of this kind of fuzzy relational database is given as follows:

Definition 3 (Fuzzy relation). A fuzzy relation r on a relational schema R $(A_1, A_2, ..., A_n, \mu_R)$ is a subset of the Cartesian product of Dom (A_1) × Dom (A_2) × ... × Dom (A_n) × Dom (μ_R), where Dom (A_i) $(1 \leq i \leq n)$ may be a fuzzy subset or even a set of fuzzy subset and Dom (μ_R) is (0, 1].

FUZZY ONTOLOGY STRUCTURE

This section presents the transformation of fuzzy database schema to fuzzy ontology structure. It goes through two steps: extracting the semantics of fuzzy database schema and mapping to the fuzzy ontology structure.

Identifying the Structure of Fuzzy Relational Schema

The relational schema defines a set of relation names, attribute names, and the constraints that should hold for every instance, that is, it describes a collection of domain entities and their relationships. Identifying the constructs of fuzzy database schema may refer to some approaches in reverse engineering (Andersson, 1994; Chiang, Barron, & Storey, 1994; Ramanathan & Hodges, 1997), which includes two phases: identifying entity and identifying relationships. Now, we use an example to illustrate the identification of the structure of fuzzy relational schema.

Table 1 shows the fuzzy database schema information about contracts between customers and departments for services and about registration of customers at departments. Some customers may be registered at "promotion departments." In Table 1, the attributes underlined stand for primary key. The foreign key is followed by the parenthesized relation named referenced relation, in which the foreign key is the primary key. Also, some representative data of two relations are listed in Table 2 and Table 3, respectively.

To the purpose of identifying entities, a relation can qualify to be mapped to an entity in two cases. First, the relation with only one attribute in the primary key corresponds to an entity. Second, if a relation's key has more than one attribute and at

Table 2. Sample data of relation client

clien-tID	cName	age	salary	e-mail	state	city	street	code	dept_ID	μ
11001	John Smith	{35/0.8, 36/0.9}	4000-6000	{J_S@yahoo.com/0.9, J_Smith@msn.com/0.8}	Hawaii	Oahu	1501	01370	D_001	0.9

Table 3. Sample data of relation department

deptID	dName	μ
D_001	Dept1	0.8

least one of them is not a foreign key, the relation corresponds to an entity.

To the purpose of identifying relationships, we distinguish three types of relationships between relations (or entities), which are association, inheritance, and aggregation.

1. Association between the entities is connected via foreign key. Existence of foreign key between two entities implicates existence of some kind of semantic relationships between them. Establish an association between an entity and the entity corresponding to each foreign key, unless it also happens to be a part of the primary key which is actually an aggregation relationship mentioned below. Three types of cardinalities of association are 1-1 association, 1-many association, and many-many association.

   - Identifying 1-1 association. Consider an association A (ET1, ET2) between two entities ET1 and ET2. If ET1 has more than one candidate key and the foreign key is one of the candidate key referring to ET2, then the association between ET1 and ET2 may be involved in 1-1 association.
   - Identifying 1-many association. If in an association A (ET1, ET2), entity ET2 contains a foreign key corresponding to ET1 but ET1 does not contain a foreign key corresponding to ET2, then more

than one instance of ET2 may be associated with each instance of ET1.
   - Identifying many-many association. A relation whose primary key has more than one attribute and is entirely composed of foreign key represents an association between all the entities corresponding to the foreign keys. The association is actually many-many association. If the many-many association has its own attribute, it is also an entity.

2. A pair of entities (ET1, ET2) that has the same primary key may be involved in an inheritance relationship. The inheritance relationships ET1 "is-a" ET2 exists if the primary key of ET1 is also a foreign key that refers to ET2.

3. Consider an entity ET1 whose primary key has more than one attribute and at least one of them is not a foreign key. If ET1 whose foreign key corresponds to the primary key of entity ET2, then ET1 "is-part-of" ET2 exists, which recognizes aggregation relationships of association entities ET1 and ET2.

Let us look at the example in the Table 1. In Table 1, each relation is an entity. The 1-many associations exist in entities Client and Department as well as PrClient and PrDept, respectively called REG-AT and PROMOTION. A 3-ary many-many association (called CONTRACT) is established among entities Client, Department, and Service. In addition, there are the inheritance relationships PrClient "is-a" Client and PrDept "is-a" Department.

Transformation to Fuzzy Ontology Structure

Definition 4 (Fuzzy ontology). A fuzzy ontology is a couple $O = (O_s, I)$ where O_s is a fuzzy ontology structure and I is a set of instances of concepts and relationships associated with the fuzzy ontology structure, which are represented by fuzzy RDF data model (being illustrated in the next section). A fuzzy ontology structure is defined as the tuple $O_s = (C, A^C, R, X)$, where:

- C is the set of concepts (or classes). Each concept $c \in C$ is a fuzzy set on the domain of instances $c: I \rightarrow [0, 1]$
- A^C is a collection of attributes sets in concept set C. Each concept c can be described by a set of attributes denoted by $A^C(c)$ and the attribute values of concept can be a fuzzy set.
- $R = (R_N, R_T)$ is the set of relations, which consists of two elements: R_N is a set of n-ary nontaxonomy fuzzy relation on the domain of concepts: $C^n \rightarrow [0, 1]$. R_T is a set of taxonomy relationships: $C^2 \rightarrow [0, 1]$.
- X is the set of axioms. Each axiom in X is a constraint on the concept's and relationship's attribute values or a constraint on the relationships between concept objects. The constraints can be described by using the first-order logic format.

The definition of fuzzy ontology here in also introduced in Barranco et al. (2007) and Quan et al. (2006).

Based on the given fuzzy ontology structure, now we apply the example in Table 1 to illustrate how $O_s = (C, A^C, R, X)$ corresponds to the fuzzy database schema.

C = {"Client," "PrClient," "Department," "PrDept," "Service"}

A^C("Client")={"clientID," "cName," "age," "salary," "e-mail," "state," "city," "street," "code," "dept_ID," "μ"}

A^C("PrClient")={"clientID," "PrDept_ID," "discount," "μ"}

A^C("Department")={"deptID," "dName," "μ"}

A^C("PrDept")={"deptID," "pName," "μ"}

A^C("Service")={"serID," "μ"}

R_N = {CONTRACT("Client," "Department," "Service"), PROMOTION("PrClient," "PrDept"), REG-AT("Client," "Department")}

R_T = {subC("PrClient," "Client"), superC("Client," "PrClient"), subC("PrDept," "Department"), superC("Department," "PrDept"), subP("PROMOTION," "REG-AT"), superP("REG-AT," "PROMOTION")}

X = {$\forall x \exists y \exists z$ CONTRACT$(x, y, z) \Rightarrow$ REG-AT(y, z), $\forall x \exists y$ PrClient$(x) \Rightarrow$ Client(y), $\forall x \forall y \exists z$ PROMOTION$(x, y) \Rightarrow$ REG-AT(x, z), $\forall x \forall y$ Client.clientID(x)=Client.clientID(y) $\Rightarrow x=y$,...}

Here the fuzzy ontology structure contains five concepts (classes), which are Client, PrClient, Department, Service, and PrDept. The attributes of these concepts are denoted as A^C("Client"), A^C("PrClient"), A^C("Department"), A^C("PrDept"), and A^C("Service"), respectively. Furthermore, relation set R_N defines a 3-ary relation CONTRACT, and two 2-ary relations REG-AT and PROMOTION. The set R_T defines three hierarchical relations, namely, "PrClient" is a subclass of "Client," "PrDept" is a subclass of "Department," and "PROMOTION" is a subproperty of "REG-AT." The axiom sets X contains some basic rules that imply the defined relations.

After establishing the correspondence from the fuzzy database schema to the fuzzy ontology structure, we need to export the fuzzy ontology file by encoding the constructs of fuzzy relational schema into the fuzzy OWL format. Here we use "fowl" as namespace of fuzzy ontology. The encoding of fuzzy constructors, axioms, and

Figure 1. Mapping 1-1 association to fuzzy ontology

```
<fowl:ObjectProperty rdf:ID="REGToDepartment">
    <rdfs:domain rdf:resource="#Client">
    <rdfs:range rdf:resource="#Department">
    <rdf:type rdf:resource="&owl;FunctionalProperty"/>
</fowl:ObjectProperty>

<fowl:ObjectProperty rdf:ID="REGToClient">
    <rdfs:domain rdf:resource="#Department">
    <rdfs:range rdf:resource="#Client">
    <rdf:type rdf:resource="&owl;FunctionalProperty"/>
</fowl:ObjectProperty>
```

constraints can be referred to Stoilos, Stamou, Tzouvaras, Pan, and Horrocks (2005). According to the characteristics of fuzzy database schema, we propose the following five process steps.

Step 1: Encoding entities

The concepts of entities in fuzzy relational schema are similar to the concepts of classes in fuzzy ontology (or owl:Class in OWL). So the mapping of entities into OWL class is straightforward. After this step the fuzzy ontology is populated with basic classes that represent its core, and every entity from the fuzzy relational schema has its counterpart in the fuzzy ontology. The snippet <fowl:Class rdf:ID= "Client"/>, for example, declares the entity Client to be the name of an OWL class.

Step 2: Encoding binary relationships

In this step, we need to distinguish three types of binary relationships and then respectively encode them.

1.   Encoding 1-1 association

The 1-1 association means that each instance from one side of the relationship is connected with one instance from the opposite side of the relationship. The functional property owl:FunctionalProperty

in OWL is equivalent to the concept of 1-1 association in fuzzy relational schema. Suppose entities Client and Department have 1-1 association, and the mapping result is presented in Figure 1.

In the mapping above, the 1-1 association is composed from two inverse properties, REG-ToDepartment and REGToClient. Every property represents one side of the relationship. Properties REGToDepartment and REGToClient are mapped to object properties owl:ObjectProperty. Object properties are used to identify a property whose value is a reference to an individual as opposed to a datatype value. The value of an object property is a resource rather than a string literal. Domain and range tags inside object property denote source and target for relationships. Property REGToDepartment connects Client with Department, and Client hereby becomes a domain in which Department is the range for this property. Property REGToDepartment is inverse property to REGToClient. Relationship cardinality is represented through functional properties.

2.   Encoding 1-many association

Rules for mapping 1-many association are similar to the rules for mapping 1-1 association except for the definition of cardinality. The relationship REG-AT between Department and Client is a 1-many association and the mapping is represented in Figure 2. Cardinality of REGToDepartment

Figure 2. Mapping 1-many association to fuzzy ontology

```
<fowl:ObjectProperty rdf:ID="REGToDepartment">
  <rdfs:domain rdf:resource="#Client">
  <rdfs:range rdf:resource="#Department">
  <rdf:type rdf:resource="&owl;FunctionalProperty"/>
</fowl:ObjectProperty>

<fowl:ObjectProperty rdf:ID="REGToClient">
  <rdfs:domain rdf:resource="#Department">
  <rdfs:range rdf:resource="#Client">
  <rdf:type rdf:resource="&owl;InverseFunctionalProperty"/>
</fowl:ObjectProperty>
```

Figure 3. Mapping inheritance relationships to fuzzy ontology

```
<fowl:Class rdf:ID="Client"/>
<fowl:Class rdf:ID="PrClient">
  <rdfs:subClassOf rdf resource="#Client"/>
</fowl:Class>
```

Figure 4. Mapping subproperty relationships to fuzzy ontology

```
<fowl:ObjectProperty rdf:ID="PROMOTION">
  <rdfs:subPropertyOf rdf:resource="REG-AT"/>
</fowl:ObjectProperty>
```

property is 1 and the property is marked as functional. Property REGToClient is marked as inverse functional property because many clients can be registered in one department.

3.   Encoding many-many association

Each many-many association can be transformed into two corresponding 1-many relationships in fuzzy relational schema. It needs to create a new entity that semantically represents the name of many-many relationships. The entity is composed from foreign keys with reference to every entity that participates in creation of many-many relationships.

Step 3: Encoding inheritance relationships and subproperty relationships

In OWL, the construct rdfs:subClassOf means that the class extension of a class description is a subset of the class extension of another class description. The relationship between PrClient and Client declared in Figure 3 is **a** subclass relation.

Also, the property extension is in similar fashion to class extension. The construct rdfs:subPropertyOf defines that the property is a subproperty of some other property. The property PROMOTION declared in Figure 4 is a subproperty of REG-AT.

Step 4: Encoding constraints

In the relational schema, the general constraints include UNIQUE, NULL, primary key, and foreign key. UNIQUE and NULL are attribute constraints. The former is mapped to an inverse functional property and the latter is mapped to a minimum cardinality of 1. As to primary key constraint, it is unique and not null. So the primary key constraint is simultaneously mapped to an inverse functional property and a minimum cardinality of 1. In Figure 5, clientID is declared as a primary key.

The characteristic of foreign key can be described using object properties, which define a property with the restriction that its values should be individuals. The mapping result of foreign key dept_ID is shown in Figure 6.

Figure 5. Mapping primary key constraint to fuzzy ontology

```
<fowl:DatatypeProperty rdf:ID="clientID"/>
 <rdfs:domain rdf:resource="#Client">
 <rdfs:range rdf:resource="&xsd;string">
 <rdf:type rdf:resource="&owl;InverseFunctionalProperty">
<fowl:Restriction>
   <fowl:onProperty rdf:resource="#clientID"/>
   <fowl:minCardinality rdf:datatype="&xsd;nonNegativeInteger" 1/>
</fowl:Restriction>
</fowl:DatatypeProperty>
```

Figure 6. Mapping foreign key constraint to fuzzy ontology

```
<fowl:ObjectProperty rdf:ID="dept_ID"/>
 <rdfs:domain rdf:resource="#Client">
 <rdfs:range rdf:resource="#Department">
</fowl:ObjectProperty>
```

Figure 7. Mapping SQL data type to XSD

```
<owl:DatatypeProperty rdf:ID="clientID">
  <rdfs:domain rdf:resource="#Client"/>
  <rdfs:range rdf:resource="&xsd;integer"/>
</owl:DatatypeProperty>
```

Step 5: Encoding data types

Unlike SQL, OWL does not have any built-in data types. Instead, it uses XML Schema Data types (XSD). Most of the mapping of attributes has to do with mapping data types from SQL to XSD. Figure 7 shows attribute clientID uses integer (XML schema data type) as its range.

Note that a fuzzy ontology may not support all constructs of fuzzy relational databases. As a result, some of the semantics will necessarily be lost in transformation (e.g., a constraint DEFAULT has no correspondence in the ontological model). So, we need to analyze the loss of semantics caused by the transformation. One way to do this is to retransform the generated fuzzy ontology to a fuzzy relational database and see if the transformation is reversible.

Let T_1 be the transformation of a fuzzy relational schema S_1 to the fuzzy ontology structure

O_s. Let T_2 be the reverse transformation of the fuzzy ontology structure O_s to a fuzzy relational schema S_2. Formally, T_1 is said to be reversible if S_2 is equivalent to S_1. That is, $T_1(S_1) = O_s \wedge T_2(O_s) = S_2 \Rightarrow S_1 \equiv S_2$. Then, S_2 is said to be equivalent to S_1 if a lexical overlap measure denoted as $L(S_1, S_2)$ takes a value of 1 (Sabou, 2004), namely, $L(S_1, S_2) = 1 \Rightarrow S_1 \equiv S_2$. The lexical overlap measure is calculated with $L(S_1, S_2) = |L_1 \cap L_2|/|L_1|$, where L_1 is a set of all constructs in S_1 and L_2 is a set of all constructs in S_2.

FUZZY RDF DATA MODEL

The relational instances are the content of databases and reflect the values of the schema. To be able to use the data in relational databases in a semantic context, one needs to map the relational instances to RDF, the data format of the Semantic Web. The data model behind RDF is a directed labeled graph, which consists of nodes and labeled directed arcs linking pairs of nodes (i.e., a set of RDF triples). For the purpose of mapping, the relational instances should be mapped to the graph-based RDF data model. In addition to the graph-based RDF data model, the XML syntax for RDF called RDF/XML (Beckett, 2004) is also a very suitable format for expressing relational database information.

An RDF triple containing predicate, subject, and object can describe a simple fact such as a relationship between two things, in which the predicate names the relationship, and the subject and object denote the two things. In the relational database, however, a relation is generally permitted to have an arbitrary number of attributes and a tuple of which expresses information corresponding to a unique instance of the subject of the relation. Furthermore, in a pure relational database, a relation has a primary key whose value is used to uniquely identify every tuple. To map the relational tuples into the RDF triples, the tuples have to be decomposed. In addition, we use a tuple ID or take the primary key as the center in RDF triples. The formal mapping from a relational tuple to RDF triples is summarized as follows:

- The primary key value corresponds to the common subject of a collection of triples and the subject has an rdf:type property whose value is the relation name,
- The attribute name of each relation corresponds to the predicate, and
- The value in the cell corresponds to the object.

After the mapping above, a more complex fact in the relational instances can be expressed in RDF using a conjunction of simple binary relationships. Through the use of extensible URI-based vocabularies, RDF provides for expression of facts about arbitrary subjects, that is, assertions of named properties about specific named things. A URI can be constructed for any thing that can be named, so RDF facts can be about any such things.

It should be pointed out, however, that the information described in RDF is assumed precise and there is not any uncertainty. As a result, the relational instances cannot be directly mapped into the RDF data model because of fuzzy information in the fuzzy relational instances. In order to construct the fuzzy ontology instance from the fuzzy relational instances, we need to use fuzzy extended RDF data model. Currently, little work has been carried out on the fuzzy extension of

RDF (Mazzieri & Dragoni, 2005; Vaneková, Bella, Gurský, & Horváth, 2005). In Lv, Ma, and Yan (2008), a comprehensive fuzzy RDF data model, including its syntax and semantics, is presented. In the following, we briefly describe the fuzzy RDF data model based on the RDF graph.

Consider a set v of vocabulary partitioned in three pairwise disjoint sets: a set $\mathcal{U}$ of URI references (or URIrefs), a set ß of blank nodes, and a set £ of literals (itself partitioned into two disjoint sets, the set $\mathcal{L}_p$ of plain literals and the set $\mathcal{L}_T$ of typed literals). The abstract representation of fuzzy RDF data model in graph is defined as follows.

Definition 5: *(Fuzzy RDF triple). A fuzzy RDF triple is of the form (s p o)/n where the triple (s p o) is an element of $(\mathcal{U} \cup \mathcal{B}) \times \mathcal{U} \times \mathcal{V}$ and n $\in$ [0, 1] denotes the fuzzy truth value of the triple.*

Definition 6: *(Fuzzy RDF graph). A fuzzy RDF graph is a set of fuzzy RDF triples. A subgraph of a fuzzy RDF graph is a fuzzy subset of triples in the fuzzy RDF graph.*

Definition 7: *(Instance of fuzzy RDF graph). Consider a fuzzy RDF graph G and a mapping i: $\mathcal{B}' \rightarrow \mathcal{V}$ mapping each blank node $\mathcal{B}'$ in G to the set of vocabulary $\mathcal{V}$, and each URIrefs or literal to itself. The RDF tripleset $G_i = \{(i(s) p i(o))/n \mid (s p o)/n \in G\}$ is called an instance of G.*

Let us look at the fuzzy relational instances given in Table 2. In Table 2, the values of the attributes *age* and *e-mail address* for John Smith are fuzzy. Here, the value of attribute age is a unique nonnegative integer. Assume that the age for John Smith is unknown so far, and we only know his age is 35 with possibility 0.80 or 36 with possibility 0.90, denoted by a disjunctive possibility distribution: {35/0.8, 36/0.9}. In contrast, the e-mail address for John Smith is multiple character strings because he has several e-mail addresses simultaneously available, and we do not have complete knowledge of his e-mail address. We may say that the e-mail address is "J_S@

Figure 8. An example of fuzzy RDF graph

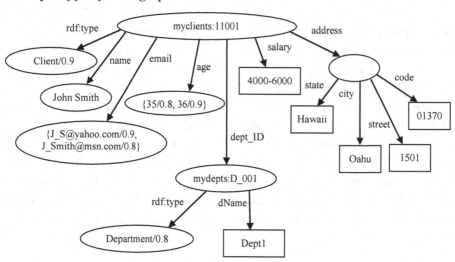

yahoo.com" with possibility 0.9 and "J_Smith@ msn.com with possibility 0.8, denoted by a conjunctive possibility distribution: {J_S@yahoo. com/0.9, J_Smith@msn.com /0.8.}.

Using the above-mentioned mapping from a relational tuple to RDF triples, a fuzzy RDF graph corresponding to Table 2 and Table 3 is given in Figure 8. In Figure 8, the value of primary key clientID, say 11001, is taken as the center in RDF triples and it has an rdf:type property. The value of this property is the relation name Client with a membership degree, say 0.9, indicating to what extent the tuple represented by the primary key value 11001 belongs to the fuzzy relation Client. Similarly, the value D_001 of primary key deptID also has an rdf:type property, whose value is Department/0.8, indicating that the tuple with primary key value D_001 may belong to the fuzzy relation Department with membership degree 0.8. The value of the attribute *age* is fuzzy and it is represented by a possibility distribution. For the address containing four components of state, city, street, and code, we introduce a blank node in fuzzy RDF graph. Also the blank nodes in the fuzzy RDF graph can represent *n*-ary relationships although the classical RDF graph can only represent binary relationships directly. Moreover,

the foreign key dept_ID of relation Client points to the referenced relation Department in Figure 8.

In addition to the graph-based representation of fuzzy RDF, we can also choose the XML syntax for fuzzy RDF. At this point, a fuzzy XML model is needed because the classical XML model cannot represent imprecise and uncertain information. In Ma and Yan (2007), a fuzzy XML data model is proposed by introducing fuzzy constructs Val and Dist as well as fuzzy attribute Poss to accommodate the fuzziness of elements and attribute values of elements in XML documents. Val is to specify the membership degree of a given element existing in the RDF/XML document, and Dist is to specify a possibility distribution, disjunctive or conjunctive. Typically, a Dist element has multiple Val elements as its children. Using the fuzzy XML model in Ma and Yan (2007), it is not difficult to give the fuzzy RDF/XML corresponding to Table 2 and Table 3. This article does not present the details.

BRIEF DISCUSSION

Generally speaking, the transformation of fuzzy relational databases to fuzzy ontology should consider and handle the following problems:

- Loss of data: The result of the transformation should adequately describe the original data with incorporation of (fuzzy) data types.
- Loss of semantics: In some cases, the transformation is not really lossless in the sense that not all constructs in a fuzzy relational database can be mapped to fuzzy ontology. Therefore, the quality of the transformation should be analyzed.
- Correctness: The transformation should have provable correctness.

To achieve the transformation of fuzzy relational databases to fuzzy ontology, this article proposes an approach that respectively considers the fuzzy relational schema and instances, and can hereby guarantee the integrality of both structure and data of the fuzzy relational databases.

For the fuzzy relational databases being transformed, the transformation allows only for the fuzzy relational databases which schema is at least in third normal form (3NF) in the article. Of course, such a requirement may not be applied in practical situations. At this point, the transformation suffers from the applicability problem. But in some cases, the transformation is not really general in the sense that its application is rather restricted. In fact, most of the databases in the real applications are highly likely to satisfy the 3NF requirement, and the restriction of 3NF on the proposed transformation in the article should be acceptable and satisfiable. It is identified that there may be two main reasons for a database not to be in 3NF: performance reasons or poor database design. For the latter, the databases can be normalized to improve its design and satisfy the 3NF requirement. The normalization of fuzzy database schema concerns eliminating fuzzy transitive and functional dependencies. This issue is beyond the scope of this article.

The evaluation of the proposed transformation from the fuzzy relational databases to the fuzzy ontology depends on the evaluation of the constructed fuzzy ontology. The evaluation of

constructing, mapping, and merging ontology is an important and central issue, but it is also a difficult task. Currently, there are still not any frameworks/metrics that are widely adopted for ontology evaluation. Some research often chose some measures to evaluate ontology according to own requirements. Here, we suggest using the standard information retrieval metrics (Van Rijsbergen, 1986) to assess the quality of the proposed approach in our work, which are *Precision*, *Recall*, and *F-measure*, which are defined as follows:

$$Precision = \frac{\#correct\_identified\_constructs}{\#identified\_constructs} \qquad (5)$$

$$Recall = \frac{\#correct\_identified\_constructs}{\#all\_need\_identified\_constructs} \qquad (6)$$

$$F\text{-measure} = \frac{2 \times Precision \times Recall}{Precision + Recall} \qquad (7)$$

For the transformation from the fuzzy relational databases to the fuzzy ontology, correct identification of the fuzzy database constructs is the key precondition, and we need to consider the evaluation of identification of fuzzy database constructs. The simulation and quantitative evaluation of the proposed transformation will be investigated in our future development.

CONCLUSION AND OUTLOOK

Fuzzy ontology with fuzzy concepts and fuzzy relations is an extension of the classical ontology, which is more suitable to describe the domain knowledge for solving the uncertainty representation and reasoning problems. In this article, we propose a framework that can generate the fuzzy ontology from the fuzzy relational databases. For the given fuzzy relational databases, we consider the fuzzy relational schema and fuzzy relational instances which are respectively transformed to the fuzzy ontology structure and fuzzy RDF data model. This can ensure the integrality of the original structure, as well as the completeness and consistency of the original instances in the fuzzy relational databases. The fuzzy ontology structure generated from the fuzzy relational schema is encoded. The fuzzy ontology instances are represented by the fuzzy RDF model, which is generated from the fuzzy relational instances.

It should be pointed out that there are some problems to be resolved in the future. One research direction involves further analyzing the problem of semantic loss accompanied by the construction of the fuzzy ontology from the fuzzy databases. Another direction is how to quantitatively evaluate the generated fuzzy ontology. These two problems are also common bottlenecks associated with many current classical ontology generation systems. Besides, in order to lay a solid foundation for the Semantic Web, efficient management and usage of large fuzzy RDF/OWL data obtained from the fuzzy relational databases is in high demand.

ACKNOWLEDGMENT

The authors wish to thank the anonymous referees for their valuable comments and suggestions, which improved the technical content and the presentation of the article. Work is supported by the Program for New Century Excellent Talents in University (NCET-05-0288) and in part by the National Natural Science Foundation of China (60873010) and MOE Funds for Doctoral Programs (20050145024).

REFERENCES

Abulaish, M., & Dey, L. (2007). A fuzzy ontology generation framework for handling uncertainties and non-uniformity in domain knowledge description. In *Proceedings of the International Conference on Computing: Theory and Applications*, Kolkata, India (pp. 287-293).

Andersson, M. (1994). Extracting an entity relationship schema from a relational database through reverse engineering. In *Proceedings of the 13rd International Conference of the Entity-Relationship Approach*, Manchester, UK (LNCS 881, pp. 403-419).

Baader, F., McGuinness, D. L., Nardi, D., & Patel-Schneider, P. F. (2003). *The description logic handbook: Theory, implementation, and applications*. Cambridge University Press.

Barranco, C. D., Campana, J. R., Medina, J. M., & Pons, O. (2007). On storing ontologies including fuzzy datatypes in relational databases. In *Proceedings of the 16th IEEE International Conference on Fuzzy Systems*, London, UK (pp. 1-6).

Beckett, D. (2004). *RDF/XML syntax specification* (revised). Retrieved September 24, 2008, from http://www.w3.org/TR/2004/REC-rdf-syntax-grammar-20040210/

Berners-Lee, T., Hall, W., Hendler, J., Shadbolt, N., & Weitzner, D. J. (2006). Creating a science of the Web. *Science, 313*(11), 769-771.

Berners-Lee, T., Hendler, J., & Lassila, O. (2001). The Semantic Web. *The Scientific American, 284*(5), 33-43.

Buckles, B. P., & Petry, F. E. (1982). A fuzzy representation of data for relational database. *Fuzzy Sets and Systems, 7*(3), 213-226.

Calegari, S., & Ciucci, D. (2007). Fuzzy ontology, fuzzy description logics and fuzzy-OWL. In *Proceedings of the 7th International Workshop on Fuzzy Logic and Applications*, Camogli, Italy (LNAI 4578, pp. 118-126).

Chiang, R. H. L., Barron, T. M., & Storey, V. C. (1994). Reverse engineering of relational databases: Extraction of an EER model from a relational database. *Journal of Data and Knowledge Engineering, 12*(2), 107-142.

Lam, T. H. W. (2006). Fuzzy ontology map—a fuzzy extension of the hard-constraint ontology. In *Proceedings of the 5th IEEE/WIC/ACM International Conference on Web Intelligence*, Hong Kong, China (pp. 506-509).

Lv, Y., Ma, Z. M., & Yan, L. (2008). Fuzzy RDF: A data model to represent fuzzy metadata. In *Proceedings of the 17th IEEE International Conference on Fuzzy Systems*, Hong Kong, China (pp. 1439-1445).

Ma, Z. M., & Mili, F. (2002). Handling fuzzy information in extended possibility-based fuzzy relational databases. *International Journal of Intelligent Systems, 17*(10), 925-942.

Ma, Z. M., & Yan, L. (2007). Fuzzy XML data modeling with the UML and relational data models. *Data & Knowledge Engineering, 63*(3), 970-994.

Ma, Z. M., & Yan, Li (2008). A literature overview of fuzzy database models. *Journal of Information Science and Engineering, 24*(1), 189-202.

Mazzieri, M., & Dragoni, A. F. (2005). A fuzzy semantics for Semantic Web languages. In *Proceedings of the 4th ISWC2005 Workshop on Uncertainty Reasoning for the Semantic Web*, Galway, Ireland (pp. 12-22).

Mukhopadhyay, D., Banik, A., & Mukherjee, S. (2007). A technique for automatic construction of ontology from existing database to facilitate Semantic Web. In *Proceedings of the 10th International Conference on Information Technology*, Rourkela, India (pp. 246-251).

Prade, H., & Testemale, C. (1984). Generalizing database relational algebra for the treatment of incomplete or uncertain information and vague queries. *Information Sciences, 34*, 115-143.

Quan, T. T., Hui, S. C., Fong, A. C. M., & Cao, T. H. (2006). Automatic fuzzy ontology generation for Semantic Web. *IEEE Transaction on Knowledge and Data Engineering, 18*(6), 842-856.

Raju, K. V. S. V. N., & Majumdar, A. K. (1988). Fuzzy functional dependencies and lossless join decomposition of fuzzy relational database systems. *ACM Transactions on Database Systems, 13*(2), 129-166.

Ramanathan, S., & Hodges, J. (1997). Extraction of object-oriented structures from existing relational databases. *ACM SIGMOD Record, 26*(1), 59-64.

Sabou, M. (2004). Extracting ontologies from software documentation: A semi-automatic method and its evaluation. In *Proceedings of the 16th European Conference on Artificial Intelligence Workshop on Ontology Learning and Population*, Valencia, Spain.

Sanchez, E., & Yamanoi, T. (2006). Fuzzy ontologies for the Semantic Web. In *Proceedings of the 7th International Conference on Flexible Query Answering Systems*, Milan, Italy (pp. 691-699).

Stoilos, G., Stamou, G., Tzouvaras, V., Pan, J. Z., & Horrocks, I. (2005). Fuzzy OWL: Uncertainty and the Semantic Web. In *Proceedings of the 1st International Workshop of OWL: Experiences and Directions*, Galway, Ireland.

Trinh, Q., Barker, K., & Alhajj, R. (2006). RDB2ONT: A tool for generating OWL ontologies from relational database systems. In *Proceedings of the 2nd Advanced International Conference on Telecommunications and International Conference on Internet and Web Applications and Services*, Guadeloupe, French Caribbean (pp. 170-178).

Umano, M., & Fukami, S. (1994). Fuzzy relational algebra for possibility-distribution-fuzzy-relational model of fuzzy data. *Journal of Intelligent Information Systems, 3*, 7-27.

Van Rijsbergen, C. J. (1986). A new theoretical framework for information retrieval. In *Proceedings of the 9th Annual International ACM SIGIR Conference on Research and Development in Information Retrieval*, Pisa, Italy (pp. 194-200).

Vaneková, V., Bella, J., Gurský, P., & Horváth, T. (2005). Fuzzy RDF in the Semantic Web: Deduction and induction. In *Proceedings of the 6th Workshop on Data Analysis*, Abaujszanto, Hungary (pp. 16-29).

Zadeh, L. A. (1965). Fuzzy sets. *Information and Control, 8*(3), 338-353.

Zadeh, L. A. (1978). Fuzzy sets as a basis for a theory of possibility. *Fuzzy Sets and Systems, 1*(1), 3-28.

This work was previously published in International Journal on Semantic Web & Information Systems, Vol. 4, Issue 3, edited by A. Sheth, pp. 1-15, copyright 2008 by IGI Publishing (an imprint of IGI Global).

Chapter 11
Tightly Coupled Fuzzy Description Logic Programs under the Answer Set Semantics for the Semantic Web

Thomas Lukasiewicz
Computing Laboratory, University of Oxford, UK

Umberto Straccia
ISTI-CNR, Italy

ABSTRACT

This chapter presents a novel approach to fuzzy description logic programs (or simply fuzzy dl-programs) under the answer set semantics, which is a tight integration of fuzzy disjunctive logic programs under the answer set semantics with fuzzy description logics. From a different perspective, it is a generalization of tightly coupled disjunctive dl-programs by fuzzy vagueness in both the description logic and the logic program component. The authors show that the new formalism faithfully extends both fuzzy disjunctive logic programs and fuzzy description logics, and that under suitable assumptions, reasoning in the new formalism is decidable. The authors present a polynomial reduction of certain fuzzy dl-programs to tightly coupled disjunctive dl-programs, and we analyze the complexity of consistency checking and query processing for certain fuzzy dl-programs. Furthermore, the authors provide a special case of fuzzy dl-programs for which deciding consistency and query processing can both be done in polynomial time in the data complexity.

INTRODUCTION

The *Semantic Web* (Berners-Lee, 1999; Fensel et al., 2002) aims at an extension of the current World Wide Web by standards and technologies that help machines to understand the information on the Web so that they can support richer discovery, data integration, navigation, and automation of tasks. The main ideas behind it are to add a machine-readable meaning to Web pages, to use ontologies for a precise definition of shared terms in Web resources, to use KR technology for automated reasoning from Web

DOI: 10.4018/978-1-60566-992-2.ch011

Copyright © 2010, IGI Global. Copying or distributing in print or electronic forms without written permission of IGI Global is prohibited.

resources, and to apply cooperative agent technology for processing the information of the Web.

The Semantic Web consists of several hierarchical layers, where the *Ontology layer*, in form of the *OWL Web Ontology Language* (W3C, 2004; Horrocks et al., 2003), is currently the highest layer of sufficient maturity. OWL consists of three increasingly expressive sublanguages, namely, *OWL Lite*, *OWL DL*, and *OWL Full*. OWL Lite and OWL DL are essentially very expressive description logics with an RDF syntax (Horrocks et al., 2003). As shown in (Horrocks & Patel-Schneider, 2004), ontology entailment in OWL Lite (resp., OWL DL) reduces to knowledge base (un)satisfiability in the description logic SHIF(**D**) (resp., SHOIN(**D**)). As a next step in the development of the Semantic Web, one aims especially at sophisticated representation and reasoning capabilities for the *Rules*, *Logic*, and *Proof layers* of the Semantic Web.

In particular, there is a large body of work on integrating rules and ontologies, which is a key requirement of the layered architecture of the Semantic Web. Significant research efforts focus on hybrid integrations of rules and ontologies, called *description logic programs* (or *dl-programs*), which are of the form $KB=(L,P)$, where L is a description logic knowledge base, and P is a finite set of rules involving either queries to L in a loose integration (see especially (Eiter et al., 2008; Eiter et al., 2004; Eiter et al., 2006)) or concepts and roles from L as unary resp. binary predicates in a tight integration (see especially (Lukasiewicz, 2007a; Rosati, 2006)).

Other works explore formalisms for *handling uncertainty and vagueness / imprecision* in the Semantic Web. In particular, formalisms for dealing with uncertainty and vagueness in ontologies have been applied in ontology mapping and information retrieval. Vagueness and imprecision also abound in multimedia information processing and retrieval. Moreover, handling vagueness is an important aspect of natural language interfaces to the Web. There are several recent extensions of description logics, ontology languages, and dl-programs for the Semantic Web by probabilistic uncertainty and by fuzzy vagueness. In particular, dl-programs under probabilistic uncertainty and under fuzzy vagueness have been proposed in (Lukasiewicz, 2005; Lukasiewicz, 2006b) and (Straccia, 2006c; Straccia, 2006b; Lukasiewicz, 2006a), respectively.

In this paper, we continue this line of research. We present *tightly coupled fuzzy description logic programs* (or simply *fuzzy dl-programs*) *under the answer set semantics*, which are a tight integration of fuzzy disjunctive programs under the answer set semantics with fuzzy generalizations of SHIF(**D**) and SHOIN(**D**). Even though there has been previous work on fuzzy positive dl-programs (Straccia, 2006c; Straccia, 2006b) and on loosely coupled fuzzy normal dl-programs (Lukasiewicz, 2006a), to our knowledge, this is the first approach to tightly coupled fuzzy disjunctive dl-programs (with default negation in rule bodies). The main contributions of this paper can be briefly summarized as follows:

- We present a novel approach to fuzzy dl-programs, which tightly integrates fuzzy disjunctive programs under the answer set semantics with fuzzy description logics. It generalizes the tightly coupled disjunctive dl-programs in (Lukasiewicz, 2007a) by fuzzy vagueness in both the ontological and the rule component.

- We show that the new fuzzy dl-programs have nice semantic features. In particular, all their answer sets are also minimal models, and the cautious answer set semantics faithfully extends both fuzzy disjunctive programs and fuzzy description logics. The new approach also does not need the unique name assumption.

- As an important property, in the large class of fuzzy dl-programs that are defined over a finite number of truth values, the problems of deciding consistency, cautious

Table 1. Axioms for conjunction and disjunction strategies

Axiom Name	Conjunction Strategy	Disjunction Strategy
Tautology / Contradiction	$a \otimes 0 = 0$	$a \oplus 1 = 1$
Identity	$a \otimes 1 = a$	$a \oplus 0 = a$
Commutativity	$a \otimes b = b \otimes a$	$a \oplus b = b \oplus a$
Associativity	$(a \otimes b) \otimes c = a \otimes (b \otimes c)$	$(a \oplus b) \oplus c = a \oplus (b \oplus c)$
Monotonicity	if $b \leqslant c$, then $a \otimes b \leqslant a \otimes c$	if $b \leqslant c$, then $a \oplus b \leqslant a \oplus c$

Table 2. Axioms for implication and negation strategies

Axiom Name	Implication Strategy	Negation Strategy
Tautology / Contradiction	$0 \triangleright b = 1$, $a \triangleright 1 = 1$, $1 \triangleright 0 = 0$	$\ominus 0 = 1$, $\ominus 1 = 0$
Antitonicity	if $a \leqslant b$, then $a \triangleright c \geqslant b \triangleright c$	if $a \leqslant b$, then $\ominus a \geqslant \ominus b$
Monotonicity	if $b \leqslant c$, then $a \triangleright b \leqslant a \triangleright c$	

consequence, and brave consequence are all decidable.

- We present a polynomial reduction for certain fuzzy dl-programs to the tightly coupled disjunctive dl-programs in (Lukasiewicz, 2007a), and analyze the complexity of consistency checking and query processing for certain fuzzy dl-programs.

- Furthermore, we delineate a special case of fuzzy dl-programs where deciding consistency and query processing are both data tractable.

COMBINATION STRATEGIES

Rather than being restricted to an ordinary binary truth value among **false** and **true**, *vague propositions* may also have a truth value strictly between **false** and **true**. In the sequel, we use the unit interval $[0,1]$ as the set of all possible truth values, where 0 and 1 represent the ordinary binary truth values **false** and **true**, respectively. For example, the vague proposition "John is a tall man" may be more or less true, and it is thus associated with a truth value in $[0,1]$, depending on the body height of John.

In order to combine and modify the truth values in $[0,1]$, we assume *combination strategies*, namely, *conjunction, disjunction, implication*, and *negation strategies*, denoted $\otimes$, $\oplus$, $\triangleright$, and $\ominus$, respectively, which are functions $\otimes$, $\oplus$, $\triangleright$:$[0,1] \times [0,1] \to [0,1]$ and $\ominus$:$[0,1] \to [0,1]$ that generalize the ordinary Boolean operators $\wedge$, $\vee$, $\to$, and $\neg$, respectively, to the set of truth values $[0,1]$. For $a, b \in [0,1]$, we then call $a \otimes b$ (resp., $a \oplus b$, $a \triangleright b$) the *conjunction* (resp., *disjunction, implication*) of a and b, and we call $\ominus a$ the *negation* of a.

As usual, we assume that combination strategies have some natural algebraic properties, namely, the ones shown in Tables 1 and 2. Note that conjunction and disjunction strategies (with the properties in Table 1) are also called *triangular norms* (or *t-norms*) and *triangular co-norms* (or *s-norms*) (Hájek, 1998), respectively. We do not assume properties that relate the combination strategies to each other (such as de Morgan's law); although one may additionally assume such properties, they are not required here.

Table 3. Combination strategies of various fuzzy logics

	Łukasiewicz Logic	Gödel Logic	Product Logic	Zadeh Logic
$a \otimes b$	$\max(a+b-1,0)$	$\min(a,b)$	a,b	$\min(a,b)$
$a \oplus b$	$\min(a+b,1)$	$\max(a,b)$	$a+b-a\cdot b$	$\max(a,b)$
$a \triangleright b$	$\min(1-a+b,1)$	$\begin{cases} 1 & \text{if } a \leqslant b \\ b & \text{otherwise} \end{cases}$	$\min(1,b/a)$	$\max(1-a,b)$
$\ominus a$	$1-a$	$\begin{cases} 1 & \text{if } a = 0 \\ 0 & \text{otherwise} \end{cases}$	$\begin{cases} 1 & \text{if } a = 0 \\ 0 & \text{otherwise} \end{cases}$	$1-a$

Example 1. The combination strategies of various fuzzy logics are shown in Table 3. Some of their further properties are highlighted in Table 4. Note that we cannot enforce that a choice of the combination strategies satisfies all these properties, because then the fuzzy logic would collapse to classical Boolean propositional logic.

FUZZY DESCRIPTION LOGICS

We assume fuzzy generalizations of the expressive crisp description logics SHIF(**D**) and SHOIN(**D**), which stand behind OWL Lite and OWL DL, respectively. We now recall the syntax and the semantics of fuzzy SHIF(**D**) and fuzzy SHOIN(**D**) (Straccia, 2005; Straccia, 2006a) (see also (Stoilos et al., 2005)). For further details and background, see (Lukasiewicz & Straccia, 2008). There also exists an implementation of fuzzy SHIF(**D**) under Zadeh, Łukasiewicz, and classical semantics, called the *fuzzyDL* system, see (fuzzyDL, 2008; Bobillo & Straccia, 2008a).

Intuitively, description logics model a domain of interest in terms of concepts and roles, which represent classes of individuals and binary relations between individuals, respectively. A description logic knowledge base encodes in particular subset relationships between classes of individuals, subset relationships between binary relations, the membership of individuals to classes, and the membership of pairs of individuals to binary relations. In fuzzy description logics, these relationships and memberships then have a degree of truth in [0,1].

Syntax

We first define the syntax of fuzzy SHOIN(**D**). The elementary ingredients are similar to the ones of crisp SHOIN(**D**), except that we now also have fuzzy datatypes and fuzzy modifiers. We assume a set of *data values*, a set of *elementary datatypes*, and a set of *datatype predicates* (each with a pre-defined arity $n \geqslant 1$). A *datatype* is an elementary datatype or a finite set of data values. A *fuzzy datatype theory* **D**=$(\Delta^{\mathbf{D}},\cdot^{\mathbf{D}})$ consists of a datatype domain $\Delta^{\mathbf{D}}$ and a mapping $\cdot^{\mathbf{D}}$ that assigns to each data value an element of $\Delta^{\mathbf{D}}$, to each elementary datatype a subset of $\Delta^{\mathbf{D}}$, and to each datatype predicate of arity n a fuzzy relation over $\Delta^{\mathbf{D}}$ of arity n (that is, a mapping $(\Delta^{\mathbf{D}})^n \rightarrow [0,1]$). We extend $\cdot^{\mathbf{D}}$ to all datatypes by $\{v_1,\ldots,v_n\}^{\mathbf{D}} = \{v_1^{\mathbf{D}},\ldots,v_n^{\mathbf{D}}\}$.

Example 2. A crisp unary datatype predicate $\leqslant_{18}$ over the natural numbers denoting the integers of at most 18 may be defined by $\leqslant_{18}(x)=1$, if $x \leqslant 18$, and $\leqslant_{18}(x)=0$, otherwise. Then, $Minor = Person \wedge \exists age. \leqslant_{18}$ defines a person of age at most 18.

Non-crisp predicates are usually defined by functions for specifying fuzzy set membership degrees, such as the well-known trapezoidal,

Table 4. Further properties of the combination strategies of various fuzzy logics

Property	Łukasiewicz Logic	Gödel Logic	Product Logic	Zadeh Logic
$a \otimes \ominus a = 0$	•	•	•	
$a \oplus \ominus a = 1$	•			
$a \otimes a = a$		•		•
$a \oplus a = a$		•		•
$\ominus \ominus a = a$	•			•
$a \triangleright b = \ominus a \oplus b$	•			•
$\ominus(a \triangleright b) = a \otimes \ominus b$	•			•
$\ominus(a \otimes b) = \ominus a \oplus \ominus b$	•	•	•	•
$\ominus(a \oplus b) = \ominus a \otimes \ominus b$	•	•	•	•

Figure 1. (a) Trapezoidal function trz(x;a,b,c,d), (b) triangular function tri(x;a,b,c), (c) left-shoulder function ls(x;a,b), and (d) right-shoulder function rs(x;a,b)

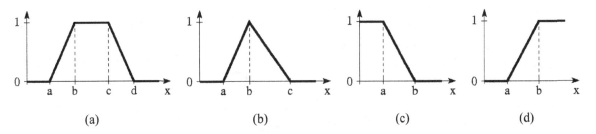

(a)   (b)   (c)   (d)

triangular, left-shoulder, and right-shoulder functions (see Fig. 1).

Example 3. A fuzzy unary datatype predicate *Young* over the natural numbers denoting the degree of youngness of a person's age may be defined by $Young(x)=ls(x;10,30)$. Then, $YoungPerson=Person \wedge \exists age,Young$ denotes a young person.

Let $\mathbf{A}, \mathbf{R}_A, \mathbf{R}_D, \mathbf{I}$, and $\mathbf{M}$ be pairwise disjoint sets of *atomic concepts, abstract roles, datatype roles, individuals*, and *fuzzy modifiers*, respectively. Here, a *fuzzy modifier m* (Hölldobler et al., 2004; Tresp & Molitor, 1998) represents a function f_m on [0,1], which changes the membership function of a fuzzy set.

Example 4. The fuzzy modifiers *very* resp. *slightly* may represent the two functions $very(x)=x^2$ resp. $slightly(x) = \sqrt{x}$. Then, the concept of

sports cars may be defined as $SportsCar=Car \wedge \exists speed,very(High)$, where *High* is a fuzzy datatype predicate over the domain of speed in km/h, which may be defined as $High(x)=rs(x;80,250)$.

Roles and concepts in fuzzy SHOIN(**D**) are defined in nearly the same way as concepts in SHOIN(**D**), except that we now also allow fuzzy modifiers from **M** as unary operators on concepts. A *role* is any element of $\mathbf{R}_A \cup \mathbf{R}_A^- \cup \mathbf{R}_D$ (where $\mathbf{R}_A^-$ is the set of *inverses* R^- of all $R \in \mathbf{R}_A$). We define *concepts* inductively as follows. Each $A \in \mathbf{A}$ is a concept, $\perp$ and T are concepts, and if $a_1,...,a_n \in \mathbf{I}$, then $\{a_1,...,a_n\}$ is a concept (called *oneOf*). If C, C_1, C_2 are concepts, $R \in \mathbf{R}_A \cup \mathbf{R}_A^-$, and $m \in \mathbf{M}$, then $(C_1 \sqcap C_2), (C_1 \sqcup C_2), \neg C$, and $m(C)$ are concepts (called *conjunction, disjunction, negation*, and *fuzzy modification*, respectively), as well as $\exists R.C, \forall R.C, \geqslant nR$, and $\leqslant nR$ (called *existential, value, atleast,* and *atmost restriction,* respectively) for an integer $n \geqslant 0$. If *D* is a datatype and $T, T_1, \ldots, T_n \in \mathbf{R}_D$, then $\exists T_1, \ldots, T_n.D$, $\forall T_1, \ldots, T_n.D$, $\geqslant nT$, and $\leqslant nT$ are concepts (called *datatype existential, value, atleast,* and *atmost restriction,* respectively) for an integer $n \geqslant 0$. We eliminate parentheses as usual.

A *crisp axiom* has one of the following forms:

1. $C \sqsubseteq D$ (called *concept inclusion axiom*), where *C* and *D* are concepts (note that concept inclusion axioms $C \sqsubseteq D$ involve fully general concepts *C* and *D*);
2. $R \sqsubseteq S$ (called *role inclusion axiom*), where either $R, S \in \mathbf{R}_A \cup \mathbf{R}_A^-$ or $R, S \in \mathbf{R}_D$;
3. **Trans**(*R*) (called *transitivity axiom*), where $R \in \mathbf{R}_A$;
4. $C(a)$ (called *concept assertion axiom*), where *C* is a concept and $a \in \mathbf{I}$;
5. $R(a,b)$ (resp., $T(a,v)$) (called *role assertion axiom*), where $R \in \mathbf{R}_A$ (resp., $T \in \mathbf{R}_D$) and $a, b \in \mathbf{I}$ (resp., $a \in \mathbf{I}$ and *v* is a data value); and
6. $A = b$ (resp., $a \neq b$) (*equality* (resp., *inequality*) *axiom*), where $a, b \in \mathbf{I}$ (note that the equality (resp., inequality) in equality (resp., inequality) axioms is crisp).

We define *fuzzy axioms* as follows: A *fuzzy concept inclusion* (resp., *fuzzy role inclusion, fuzzy concept assertion, fuzzy role assertion*) *axiom* is of the form $\alpha \theta n$, where α *is* a concept inclusion (resp., role inclusion, concept assertion, role assertion) axiom, $\theta \in \{\leqslant, =, \geqslant\}$, and $n \in [0,1]$. Informally, $\alpha \leqslant n$ (resp., $\alpha = n$, $\alpha \geqslant n$) encodes that the truth value of α is at most (resp., equal to, at least) n. We often use α *to* abbreviate $\alpha = 1$. A fuzzy *(description logic) knowledge base L is* a finite set of fuzzy axioms, transitivity axioms, and equality and inequality axioms. For decidability, number restrictions in L are restricted to simple abstract roles; informally, such roles are

abstract roles with no transitive subroles, where sub*role is* the reflexive and transitive closure of "$\sqsubseteq$" between roles (see (Horrocks et al., 1999) for details). Notice that L may contain fuzzy concept inclusion axioms (between general concepts).

Fuzzy SHIF(D) **h**as the same syntax as fuzzy SHOIN(D), but without the oneOf constructor and with the atleast and atmost constructors limited to 0 and 1.

Example 5 (Shopping Agent). A fuzzy description logic knowledge base L encoding a car selling Web site (such as, e.g., the one at http://www.autos.com) may contain in particular the following axioms:

$$Cars \sqcup Trucks \sqcup Vans \sqcup SUVs \sqsubseteq Vehicls; \qquad (1)$$

$$PassengerCars \sqcup LuxuryCars \sqsubseteq Cars; \qquad (2)$$

$$CompactCars \sqcup MidSizeCars \sqcup SportyCars \sqsubseteq PassengerCars \qquad (3)$$

$$Cars \sqsubseteq (\exists hasReview.Integer) \sqcap (\exists hasInvoice.Integer)$$

$$\sqcap (\exists hasResellValue.Integer) \sqcap (\exists hasMaxSpeed.Integer)$$

$$\sqcap (\exists hasHorsePower.Integer) \sqcap \ldots; \qquad (4)$$

$$MazdaMX5Miata : SportyCars \sqcap (\exists hasInvoice.18883)$$

$$\sqcap (\exists hasHorsePower.166) \sqcap \ldots; \qquad (5)$$

$$MitsubishiExlipseSpyder : SportyCars \sqcap (\exists hasInvoice.24029)$$

$$\sqcap (\exists hasHorsePower.166) \sqcap \ldots \qquad (6)$$

Eqs. 1-3 describe the concept taxonomy of the site, while Eq. 4 describes the datatype attributes of the cars sold in the site. For example, all cars, trucks, vans, and SUVs are vehicles, and every car is related via the datatype role *hasReview* to an integer value. Furthermore, Eqs. 5-6 describe the properties of some sold cars. For example, the *MazdaMX5Miata* is a sports car, costs 18883 €, and has a power of 166 HP.

We may then encode "costs at most about 22000 €" and "has a power of around 150 HP" in a buyer's request through the following concepts *c* and *D*, respectively:

$$C = \exists hasInvoice.LegAbout22000 \text{ and }$$
$$D = \exists hasHorsePower.Around150$$

where *LegAbout22000* and *Around150* are fuzzy datatype predicates for "at most about 22000 €" and "around 150 HP", which are defined by *LegAbout22000(x)=ls(x; 22000.25000)* and *Around150(x)=tri(x; 125,150.175)* (see Fig. 1), respectively. The former is modeled as a left shoulder function stating that if the prize is less than 22000 €, then the degree of truth (degree of buyer's satisfaction) is 1, else the truth is linearly decreasing to 0, reached at 25000 €. In fact, we are modeling a case were the buyer would like to pay less than 22000 €, though may still accept a higher price, up to 25000 €, to a lesser degree. Similarly, the latter models the fuzzy concept "around 150 HP" as a triangular function with vertice in 150 HP.

Semantics

We now define the semantics of fuzzy SHIF(**D**) and fuzzy SHOIN(**D**). The main idea behind it is that concepts and roles are interpreted as fuzzy subsets of an interpretation's domain. Therefore, rather than being satisfied (true) or unsatisfied (false) in an interpretation, axioms are associated with a degree of truth in [0,1]. In the following, let $\otimes, \oplus, \triangleright$, and $\ominus$ be arbitrary but fixed conjunction, disjunction, implication, and negation strategies (see Table 3), respectively.

A *fuzzy interpretation* I-$(\Delta^I, \cdot^I)$ relative to a fuzzy datatype theory **D**=$(\Delta^D, \cdot^D)$ consists of a nonempty set Δ^I (called the *domain*), disjoint from Δ^D, and of a *fuzzy interpretation function* $\cdot^I$ that coincides with $\cdot^D$ on every data value, datatype, and fuzzy datatype predicate, and it assigns

- to each individual $a \in \mathbf{I}$ an element $a^I \in \Delta^I$;
- to each atomic concept $A \in \mathbf{A}$ a function $A^I : \Delta^I \to [0,1]$;
- to each abstract role $R \in \mathbf{R}_A$ a function $R^I : \Delta^I \times \Delta^I \to [0,1]$;
- to each datatype role $T \in \mathbf{R}_D$ a function $T^I : \Delta^I \times \Delta^D \to [0,1]$;
- to each fuzzy modifier $m \in \mathbf{M}$ the modifier function $m^I = f_m : [0,1] \to [0,1]$. For properties of such modifier functions, we refer the reader to (Hájek, 1998).

The mapping $\cdot^I$ is extended to all roles and concepts as follows (where $x, y \in \Delta^I$):

$$(R^-)^I(x,y) = R^I(y,x);$$
$$T^I(x) = 1;$$
$$\perp^I(x) = 0;$$
$$\{a_1,...,a_n\}^I(x) = \begin{cases} 1 & \text{if } x \in \{a_1^I,...,a_n^I\}; \\ 0 & \text{otherwise}; \end{cases}$$
$$(C_1 \sqcap C_2)^I(x) = C_1^I(x) \otimes C_2^I(x);$$
$$(C_1 \sqcup C_2)^I(x) = C_1^I(x) \oplus C_2^I(x);$$
$$(\neg C)^I(x) = \ominus C^I(x);$$
$$(m(C))^I(x) = m^I(C^I(x));$$
$$(\exists R.C)^I(x) = \sup_{y \in \Delta^I} R^I(x,y) \otimes C^I(y);$$
$$(\forall R.C)^I(x) = \inf_{y \in \Delta^I} R^I(x,y) \triangleright C^I(y);$$
$$(\geqslant nR)^I(x) = \sup_{y_1,...,y_n \in \Delta^I, |\{y_1,...,y_n\}|=n} \bigotimes_{i=1}^{n} R^I(x,y_i);$$
$$(\leqslant nR)^I(x) = \inf_{y_1,...,y_{n+1} \in \Delta^I, |\{y_1,...,y_{n+1}\}|=n+1} (\bigotimes_{i=1}^{n+1} R^I(x,y_i)) \triangleright 0;$$
$$(\exists T_1,...,T_n.D)^I(x) = \sup_{y_1,...,y_n \in \Delta^D} (\bigotimes_{i=1}^{n} T_i^I(x,y_i)) \otimes D^D(y_1,...,y_n);$$
$$(\forall T_1,...,T_n.D)^I(x) = \inf_{y_1,...,y_n \in \Delta^D} (\bigotimes_{i=1}^{n} T_i^I(x,y_i)) \triangleright D^D(y_1,...,y_n);$$
$$(\geqslant nT)^I(x) = \sup_{y_1,...,y_n \in \Delta^D, |\{y_1,...,y_n\}|=n} \bigotimes_{i=1}^{n} T^I(x,y_i);$$
$$(\leqslant nT)^I(x) = \inf_{y_1,...,y_{n+1} \in \Delta^D, |\{y_1,...,y_{n+1}\}|=n+1} (\bigotimes_{i=1}^{n+1} T^I(x,y_i)) \triangleright 0.$$

The mapping $\cdot^{\top}$ is extended to concept inclusion, role inclusion, concept assertion, and role assertion axioms as $\top$ follows (where $a, b \in \mathbf{I}$ and $v \in \Delta^{\mathbf{D}}$):

$$
\begin{aligned}
(C \sqsubseteq D)^{\mathcal{I}} &= \inf_{x \in \Delta^{\mathcal{I}}} C^{\mathcal{I}}(x) \triangleright D^{\mathcal{I}}(x); \\
(R \sqsubseteq S)^{\mathcal{I}} &= \inf_{x,y \in \Delta^{\mathcal{I}}} R^{\mathcal{I}}(x,y) \triangleright S^{\mathcal{I}}(x,y); \\
(T \sqsubseteq U)^{\mathcal{I}} &= \inf_{(x,y) \in \Delta^{\mathcal{I}} \times \Delta^{\mathbf{D}}} T^{\mathcal{I}}(x,y) \triangleright U^{\mathcal{I}}(x,y); \\
(C(a))^{\mathcal{I}} &= C^{\mathcal{I}}(a^{\mathcal{I}}); \\
(R(a,b))^{\mathcal{I}} &= R^{\mathcal{I}}(a^{\mathcal{I}}, b^{\mathcal{I}}); \\
(T(a,v))^{\mathcal{I}} &= T^{\mathcal{I}}(a^{\mathcal{I}}, v^{\mathbf{D}}).
\end{aligned}
$$

The notion of a fuzzy interpretation I *satisfying* a transitivity, equality, inequality, or fuzzy axiom E, or I being a *model* of E, denoted $I \models E$, is defined as follows:

- $I \models \mathrm{Trans}\,®$ iff $R^{\mathcal{I}}(x,y) \geqslant \sup_{z \in \Delta^{\mathcal{I}}} R^{\mathcal{I}}(x,z) \otimes R^{\mathcal{I}}(z,y)$ for all $x, y \in \Delta^{\mathrm{I}}$;
- $I \models a = b$ iff $a^{\mathrm{I}} = b^{\mathrm{I}}$, and $I \models a \neq b$ iff $a^{\mathrm{I}} \neq b^{\mathrm{I}}$; and
- $I \models \alpha\theta n$ iff $\alpha I \theta n$

A concept C i*s* sat*isfiable if*f there exists an interpretation I and an individual $x \in \Delta I$ s^{u}ch that $CI(x) > 0$. We say I sa*tisfies a* fuzzy description logic knowledge base L, *or* I is a mod*el of* L, *d*enoted $I \models L$, *if*f I satisfies every $E \in L$. *W*e say L is sat*isfiable if*f there exists a model of L. *A* fuzzy axiom E i*s* a log*ical consequence of* L, *d*enoted $L \models E$, *if*f every model of L s*a*tisfies E.

Example 6 (Shopping Agent cont'd). Consider again the fuzzy description logic knowledge base L i*n* Example 5. It is not difficult to verify that L *i*s satisfiable, and that the crisp axioms P*assenger*Cars$\sqsubseteq$*Vehicles a*nd S*porty*Cars*(MazdaMX5Miata)* are logical consequences of L. Informally, all passenger cars are vehicles, and the M*azda*MX5*Miata i*s a sports car, respectively. The following fuzzy axioms are some other logical consequences of L *(*under the Zadeh semantics of the connectives):

$$C\textit{(MazdaMX5Miata)}=1.0;$$
$$C\textit{(MitsubishiExlipseSpyder)}=0.32;$$

$$D\textit{(MazdaMX5Miata)}=0.36;$$
$$D\textit{(MitsubishiExlipseSpyder)}=0.52$$

Informally, the two cars *MazdaMX5Miata* and *MitsubishiEclipseSpyder* cost at most about 22000 € to the degrees of truth 1.0 and 0.32, respectively, and they have a power of around 150 HP to the degrees of truth 0.36 and 0.52, respectively.

FUZZY DESCRIPTION LOGIC PROGRAMS

In this section, we present a tightly coupled approach to *fuzzy disjunctive description logic programs* (or simply *fuzzy dl-programs*) under the answer set semantics. We extend the tightly coupled disjunctive description logic programs in (Lukasiewicz, 2007a), which have very nice features compared to other tightly coupled description logic programs; see (Lukasiewicz, 2007a) for more details on these crisp programs and a comparison to related works in the literature. Note that differently from (Lukasiewicz, 2006a) (in addition to being a tightly coupled approach to fuzzy dl-programs), the fuzzy dl-programs here additionally allow for disjunctions in rule heads. We first introduce the syntax of fuzzy dl-programs and then their answer set semantics.

The basic idea behind the tightly coupled approach in this section is as follows. Suppose that we have a fuzzy disjunctive program P. Under the answer set semantics, P is equivalent to its grounding *ground(P)*. Suppose now that some of the ground atoms in *ground(P)* are additionally related to each other by a fuzzy description logic knowledge base L. That is, some of the ground atoms in *ground(P)* actually represent concept and role memberships relative to L. Thus, when processing *ground*(P), we also have to consider L. However, we only want to do it to the extent that we actually need for processing *ground*(P). Hence, when taking a fuzzy Herbrand interpretation $I \subseteq HB_\Phi$, we have to ensure that I represents a valid truth value assignment relative to L. In other words, the main idea behind the semantics is to interpret P relative to Herbrand interpretations that also satisfy L, while L is interpreted relative to general interpretations over a first-order domain. Thus, we modularly combine the standard semantics of fuzzy disjunctive programs and of fuzzy description logics as in (Lukasiewicz, 2006a), which allows for building on the standard techniques and the results of both areas. However, our new approach here allows for a much tighter integration of L and P.

Syntax

We assume a function-free first-order vocabulary Φ with nonempty finite sets of constant and predicate symbols. We use Φ_c to denote the set of all constant symbols in Φ. We also assume pairwise disjoint denumerable sets $\mathbf{A}$, $\mathbf{R}_A$, $\mathbf{R}_D$, $\mathbf{I}$, and $\mathbf{M}$ of *atomic concepts*, *abstract roles*, *datatype roles*, *individuals*, and *fuzzy modifiers*, respectively, as in the previous section. We assume that Φ_c is a subset of $\mathbf{I}$. This assumption guarantees that every ground atom constructed from atomic concepts, abstract roles, datatype roles, and constants in Φ_c can be interpreted in the description logic component. We do not assume any other restriction on the vocabularies, that is, Φ and $\mathbf{A}$ (resp., $\mathbf{R}_A \cup \mathbf{R}_D$) may have unary (resp., binary) predicate symbols in common.

Let X be a set of variables. A *term* is either a variable from X or a constant symbol from Φ. An *atom* is of the form $p(t_1, \ldots, t_n)$, where p is a predicate symbol of arity $n \geqslant 0$ from Φ, and $t_1, \ldots, t_n$ are terms. A *literal l* is an atom p or a default-negated atom *notp*. Note that the default-negated atom *notp*

refers to the lack of evidence about the truth of the atom p, and thus has a different meaning than the classically negated atom $\neg p$, which refers to the presence of knowledge asserting the falsehood of the atom p. A *disjunctive fuzzy rule* (or simply *fuzzy rule*) r is of the form

$$a_1 \vee_{\oplus_1} \cdots \vee_{\oplus_{l-1}} a_l \leftarrow_{\otimes_0} b_1 \wedge_{\otimes_1} b_2 \wedge_{\otimes_2} \cdots \wedge_{\otimes_{k-1}} b_k \wedge_{\otimes_k}$$
$$not_{\ominus_{k+1}} b_{k+1} \wedge_{\otimes_{k+1}} \cdots \wedge_{\otimes_{m-1}} not_{\ominus_m} b_m \geqslant v,$$

$$(7)$$

where $l \geqslant 1$, $m \geqslant k \geqslant 0$, $a_1, \ldots, a_l$ $b_{k+1}, \ldots, b_m$ are atoms, $b_1, \ldots, b_k$ are either atoms or truth values from $[0,1]$, $\oplus_1, \ldots, \oplus_{l-1}$ are disjunction strategies, $\otimes_0, \ldots, \otimes_{m-1}$ are conjunction strategies, $\ominus_{k+1}, \ldots, \ominus_m$ are negation strategies, and $v \in [0,1]$. We refer to $a_1 \vee_{\oplus_1} \cdots \vee_{\oplus_{l-1}} a_l$ as the *head* of r, while the conjunction $b_1 \wedge_{\otimes_1} \cdots \wedge_{\otimes_{m-1}} not_{\ominus_m} b_m$ is the *body* of r. We define $H(r) = \{a_1, \ldots, a_l\}$ and $B(r) = B^+(r) \cup B^-(r)$, where $B^+(r) = \{b_1, \ldots, b_k\}$ and $B^-(r) = \{b_{k+1}, \ldots, b_m\}$. A *disjunctive fuzzy program* (or simply *fuzzy program*) P is a finite set of fuzzy rules of the form (7). We say P is a *normal fuzzy program* iff $l=1$ for all fuzzy rules (7) in P. We say P is a *positive fuzzy program* iff $l=1$ and $m=k$ for all fuzzy rules (7) in P.

A *disjunctive fuzzy description logic program* (or simply *fuzzy dl-program*) $KB=(L,P)$ consists of a fuzzy description logic knowledge base L and a disjunctive fuzzy program P. It is called a *normal fuzzy dl-program* iff P is a normal fuzzy program. It is called a *positive fuzzy dl-program* iff P is a positive fuzzy program.

Example 7 (Shopping Agent cont'd). A fuzzy dl-program $KB=(L,P)$ is given by the fuzzy description logic knowledge base L in Example 5 and the set of fuzzy rules P, which contains only the following fuzzy rule (where $x \otimes y = \min(x,y)$):

$query(x) \leftarrow_\otimes SportyCar(x) \wedge_\otimes hasInvoice(x,y_1) \wedge_\otimes hasHorsePower(x,y_2) \wedge_\otimes$
$LeqAbout22000(y_1) \wedge_\otimes Around150(y_2) \geqslant 1.$

Informally, the predicate *query* collects all sports cars, and ranks them according to whether they cost at most around 22000 € and have around 150 HP (such a car may be requested by a car buyer with economic needs). Another fuzzy rule is given as follows (where $\ominus x=1\text{-}x$ and *Around300=tri(x; 250,300.350)*):

$$query'(x) \leftarrow_\otimes SportyCar(x) \wedge_\otimes hasInvoice(x,y_1) \wedge_\otimes hasMaxSpeed(x,y_2) \wedge_\otimes not_\ominus LeqAbout22000(y_1) \wedge_\otimes Around300(y_2) \geqslant 1.$$

Informally, this rule collects all sports cars, and ranks them according to whether they cost at least around 22000 € and have a maximum speed of around 300 km/h (such a car may be requested by a car buyer with luxurious needs). Another fuzzy rule involving also a disjunction in its head is given as follows (where $x\oplus y=\max(x,y)$ and *GeqAbout15000(x)=rs(x; 12000.15000)*):

$$Small(x) \vee_\oplus Old(x) \leftarrow_\otimes Car(x) \wedge_\otimes hasInvoice(x,y) \wedge_\otimes not_\ominus GeqAbout15000(y) \geqslant 0.7.$$

This rule says that a car costing at most around 15000 € is either small or old. Observe here that *Small* and *Old* may be two concepts in the fuzzy description logic knowledge base *L*. That is, the tightly coupled approach to fuzzy dl-programs under the answer set semantics also allows for using the rules in *P* to express relationships between the concepts and roles in *L*. This is not possible in the loosely coupled approach to fuzzy dl-programs under the answer set semantics in (Lukasiewicz, 2006a), since the dl-queries of that framework can only occur in rule bodies, but not in rule heads.

Semantics

We now define the answer set semantics of fuzzy dl-programs via a generalization of the standard Gelfond-Lifschitz transformation (Gelfond & Lifschitz, 1991).

In the sequel, let $KB=(L,P)$ be a fuzzy dl-program. A *ground instance* of a rule $r\in P$ is obtained from *r* by replacing every variable that occurs in *r* by a constant symbol from Φ_c. We denote by *ground(P)* the set of all ground instances of rules in *P*. The *Herbrand base* relative to Φ, denoted HB_Φ, is the set of all ground atoms constructed with constant and predicate symbols from Φ. Observe that we define the Herbrand base relative to Φ and not relative to *P*. This allows for reasoning about ground atoms from the description logic component that do not necessarily occur in *P*. Observe, however, that the extension from *P* to Φ is only a notational simplification, since we can always make constant and predicate symbols from Φ occur in *P* by "dummy" rules such as $constant(c)\leftarrow$ and $p(\mathbf{c})\leftarrow p(\mathbf{c})$, respectively. We denote by DL_Φ the set of all ground atoms in HB_Φ that are constructed from atomic concepts in **A**, abstract roles in $\mathbf{R}_A$, concrete roles in $\mathbf{R}_D$, and constant symbols in Φ_c.

We define Herbrand interpretations and the truth of fuzzy dl-programs in them as follows. An *interpretation I* is a mapping $I{:}HB_{\Phi\rightarrow[0,1]}$. We write $\mathbf{HB}_\Phi$ to denote the interpretation *I* such that $I(a)=1$ for all $a\in HB_\Phi$. For interpretations *I* and *J*, we write $I\subseteq J$ iff $I(a)\leqslant J(a)$ for all $a\in HB_\Phi$, and we define the *intersection* of *I* and *J*, denoted $I\cap J$, by $(I\cap J)(a)=\min(I(a),J(a))$ for all $a\in HB_\Phi$. Observe that $I\subseteq\mathbf{HB}_\Phi$ for all interpretations *I*. We say that *I* is a *model* of a ground fuzzy rule *r* of the form (7), denoted $I\models r$, iff

$$I(a_1)\oplus_1\cdots\oplus_{i-1}I(a_i) \geqslant \begin{cases} I(b_1)\otimes_1\cdots\otimes_{k-1}I(b_k)\otimes_k\ominus_{k+1}I(b_{k+1}) & \text{if } m\geqslant 1; \\ \otimes_{k+1}\cdots\otimes_{m-1}\ominus_m I(b_m)\otimes_0 v & \\ v & \text{otherwise.} \end{cases}$$

(8)

Here, we implicitly assume that the disjunction strategies $\oplus_1,\ldots,\oplus_{i-1}$ and the conjunction strategies $\otimes_1,\ldots,\otimes_{m-1},\otimes_0$ are evaluated from left to right (as they may not coincide). Notice also that the above definition implicitly assumes an implication strategy $\triangleright$ that is defined by $a \triangleright b = \sup\{c \in [0,1] \mid a \otimes_0 c \leqslant b\}$ for all $a,b \in [0,1]$ (and thus for $n,m \in [0,1]$ and $a=n$, it holds that $a \triangleright b \geqslant m$ iff $b \geqslant n \otimes_0 m$, if we assume that the conjunction strategy $\otimes_0$ is continuous). Observe that such a relationship between the implication strategy $\triangleright$ and the conjunction strategy $\otimes$ (including also the continuity of $\otimes$) holds in Łukasiewicz, Gödel, and Product Logic (see Table 3).

We say that I is a *model* of a fuzzy program P, denoted $I \models P$, iff $I \models r$ for all $r \in ground(P)$. We say I is a *model* of a fuzzy description logic knowledge base L, denoted $I \models L$, iff $L \cup \{a=I(a) \mid a \in HB_\Phi\}$ is satisfiable. Intuitively, I is compatible with L. An interpretation $I \subseteq \mathbf{HB}_\Phi$ is a *model* of a fuzzy dl-program $KB=(L,P)$, denoted $I \models KB$, iff $I \models L$ and $I \models P$. We say KB is *satisfiable* iff it has a model.

The *Gelfond-Lifschitz transform* of a fuzzy dl-program $KB=(L,P)$ relative to an interpretation $I \subseteq \mathbf{HB}_\Phi$, denoted KB^I, is defined as the fuzzy dl-program (L,P^I), where P^I is the set of all fuzzy rules obtained from $ground(P)$ by replacing all default-negated atoms $not_{\ominus_j} b_j$ by the truth value $\ominus_j I(b_j)$. We are now ready to define the answer set semantics of fuzzy dl-programs as follows.

Definition 8. Let $KB=(L,P)$ be a fuzzy dl-program. An interpretation $I \subseteq \mathbf{HB}_\Phi$ is an *answer set* of KB iff I is a minimal model of KB^I. We say that KB is *consistent* (resp., *inconsistent*) iff KB has an (resp., no) answer set.

Example 9 (Shopping Agent cont'd). Consider again the fuzzy dl-program $KB=(L,P)$ of Example 7. It is not difficult to verify that KB has an answer set, and so is consistent. In fact, KB has a unique answer set M, and the following holds for M:

$M(query(MazdaMX5Miata))$=0.36; $M(query(MitsubishiEclipseSpyder))$=0.32

For example, the first value follows from

min(min(min(min(min(1,1),1),*ls*(18883; 22000,25000)),*tri*(166; 125,150,175)).1)=0.36

We finally define the notions of *cautious* (resp., *brave*) *reasoning* from fuzzy dl-programs under the answer set semantics as follows.

Definition 10. Let $KB=(L,P)$ be a fuzzy dl-program. Let $a \in HB_\Phi$ and $n \in [0,1]$. Then, $a \geqslant n$ is a *cautious* (resp., *brave*) *consequence* of a fuzzy dl-program KB under the answer set semantics iff $I(a) \geqslant n$ for every (resp., some) answer set I of KB.

Example 11 (Shopping Agent cont'd). Consider again the fuzzy dl-program KB of Example 7. By Example 9, $query(MazdaMX5Miata) \geqslant 0.36$ and $query(MitsubishiEclipseSpyder) \geqslant 0.32$ are both cautious and brave consequences of KB.

SEMANTIC PROPERTIES

In this section, we summarize some important semantic properties of fuzzy dl-programs under the above answer set semantics.

Minimal Models

The following theorem shows that, like for ordinary disjunctive programs, every answer set of a fuzzy dl-program KB is also a minimal model of KB, and the answer sets of a positive fuzzy dl-program KB are the minimal models of KB.

Theorem 12. *Let $KB=(L,P)$ be a fuzzy dl-program. Then, (a) every answer set of KB is a minimal model of KB, and (b) if KB is positive, then the set of all answer sets of KB is given by the set of all minimal models of KB.*

Faithfulness

An important property of integrations of rules and ontologies for the Semantic Web is that they are a faithful (Motik et al., 2006) extension of both rules and ontologies.

The following theorem shows that the answer set semantics of fuzzy dl-programs faithfully extends its counterpart for fuzzy programs. That is, the answer set semantics of a fuzzy dl-program $KB=(L,P)$ with empty fuzzy description logic knowledge base L coincides with the answer set semantics of its fuzzy program P.

Theorem 13. *Let $KB=(L,P)$ be a fuzzy dl-program such that $L=\varnothing$. Then, the set of all answer sets of KB coincides with the set of all answer sets of the fuzzy program P.*

The next theorem shows that the answer set semantics of fuzzy dl-programs also faithfully extends the first-order semantics of fuzzy description logic knowledge bases. That is, for $a \in HB_\Phi$ and $n \in [0,1]$, it holds that $a \geq n$ is true in all answer sets of a positive fuzzy dl-program $KB=(L,P)$ iff $a \geq n$ is true in all fuzzy first-order models of $L \cup ground(P)$. The theorem holds also when a is a ground formula constructed from HB_Φ using $\wedge$ and $\vee$, along with conjunction and disjunction strategies $\otimes$ resp. $\oplus$.

Theorem 14. *Let $KB=(L,P)$ be a positive fuzzy dl-program, and let $a \in HB_\Phi$ and $n \in [0,1]$. Then, $a \geq n$ is true in all answer sets of KB iff $a \geq n$ is true in all fuzzy first-order models of $L \cup ground(P)$.*

As an immediate corollary, we obtain that $a \geq n$ is true in all answer sets of a fuzzy dl-program $KB=(L,\varnothing)$ iff $a \geq n$ is true in all fuzzy first-order models of L.

Corollary 15. *Let $KB=(L,P)$ be a fuzzy dl-program with $P=\varnothing$, and let $a \in HB_\Phi$ and $n \in [0,1]$. Then, $a \geq n$ is true in all answer sets of KB iff $a \geq n$ is true in all fuzzy first-order models of L.*

Unique Name Assumption

Another aspect that may not be very desirable in the Semantic Web (Horrocks & Patel-Schneider, 2006) is the *unique name assumption* (which says that any two distinct constant symbols in Φ_c repre-

sent two distinct domain objects). It turns out that we actually do not have to make this assumption, since the fuzzy description logic knowledge base of a fuzzy dl-program may very well contain or imply equalities between individuals. Intuitively, since we have no unique name assumption in L, we also do not have to make the unique name assumption in P.

Example 16. The unique answer set of the fuzzy dl-program $KB = (L,P) = (\{a = b\}, \{p(a) \geq 0.7\})$, where $a,b \in \Phi_c \cap \mathbf{I}$ and $p \in \Phi \cap \mathbf{A}$, associates with both ground atoms $p(a)$ and $p(b)$ the value 0.7, since L contains the equality axiom $a=b$, and P contains the fuzzy fact $p(a) \geq 0.7$.

This result is included in the following theorem, which shows an alternative characterization of the satisfaction of L in $I \subseteq \mathbf{HB}_\Phi$: Rather than being enlarged by a set of axioms of exponential size, L is enlarged by a set of axioms of polynomial size. This characterization essentially shows that the satisfaction of L in I corresponds to checking that (i) I restricted to DL_Φ satisfies L, and (ii) I restricted to HB_Φ-DL_Φ does not violate any equality axioms that follow from L. In the theorem, an equivalence relation $\sim$ on Φ_c is *admissible* with an interpretation $I \subseteq \mathbf{HB}_\Phi$ iff $I(p(c_1,\ldots,c_n))=I(p(c_1,\ldots,c_n))$ for all n-ary predicate symbols p, where $n>0$, and constant symbols $c_1,\ldots,c_n, c_1,\ldots,c_n \in \Phi_c$ such that $c_i \sim c_i$ for all $i \in \{1,\ldots,n\}$.

Theorem 17. *Let L be a fuzzy description logic knowledge base, and let $I \subseteq \mathbf{HB}_\Phi$. Then, $L \cup \{a=I(a) | a \in HB_\Phi\}$ is satisfiable iff $L \cup \{a=I(a) | a \in DL_\Phi\} \cup \{c \neq c' | c \not\sim c'\}$ is satisfiable for some equivalence relation $\sim$ on Φ_c admissible with I.*

REDUCTION OF FUZZY DL-PROGRAMS TO DL-PROGRAMS

In this section, we present a polynomial reduction of fuzzy dl-programs to the tightly coupled dl-programs in (Lukasiewicz, 2007a). Hence, reasoning in fuzzy dl-programs under the answer set semantics can be reduced to

1. reasoning in tightly coupled dl-programs under the answer set semantics, and
2. reasoning in fuzzy description logics.

Similarly, reasoning in fuzzy description logics is additionally reduced to reasoning in crisp description logics, as shown in (Bobillo et al., 2006; Bobillo & Straccia, 2008b; Bobillo et al., 2008; Straccia, 2004).

The reduction applies to all fuzzy dl-programs *KB* that

1. are closed under $TV_n = \{0, 1/n, ..., n/n\}$ for some $n > 0$, and
2. contain only combination strategies from Zadeh Logic.

Here, *KB* is *closed* under TV_n iff

1. every datatype predicate in *KB* is interpreted by a mapping to TV_n,
2. every fuzzy modifier *m* in *KB* is interpreted by a mapping $f_m: TV_n \to TV_n$,
3. every truth value in *KB* is from TV_n, and
4. every combination strategy in *KB* is closed under TV_n (which holds, e.g., for the combination strategies of Łukasiewicz, Gödel, and Zadeh Logic).

Note that for fuzzy dl-programs *KB* that are closed under TV_n, the problems of deciding consistency, cautious consequences, and brave consequences are all decidable, since we only have to consider the finite number of interpretations $I \subseteq \mathbf{HB}_\Phi$ to TV_n.

We first give some preparative definitions as follows. We denote by Φ^n the alphabet that is obtained from the alphabet Φ by replacing every predicate symbol *p* by the new predicate sym-

bols p^α with $\alpha \in TV_n^+ = TV_n \setminus \{0\}$. For atoms $a = p(t_1, ..., t_k)$ and $\alpha \in TV_n^+$, the atom a^α over Φ^n is defined by $a\alpha = p\alpha(t^1, ... t_k)$. Every fuzzy interpretation $I \subseteq HB\Phi$ is associated with the binary interpretation $t(I) = \{a^\alpha \mid a \in HB_\Phi, \alpha \in TV_n^+, I(a) \geqslant \alpha\}$.

We are now ready to define the polynomial reduction of fuzzy dl-programs to the tightly coupled dl-programs in (Lukasiewicz, 2007a). The *crisp transform* of a fuzzy dl-program $KB=(L,P)$ is the crisp dl-program $t(KB)=(t(L),t(P))$, where $t(L)$ is the crisp transformation of L according to (Bobillo et al., 2008) and $t(P)$ is the set (i) of all rules $p^\beta(*1, ..., xk) \leftarrow p^\alpha(x1, ... xk)$ such that p is a k-ary predicate symbol from Φ, $x1, ... xk$ are distinct variables, $\alpha \in TV_n^+ \setminus \{1/n\}$, and $\beta = \alpha - 1/n$, and (ii) of all rules $a_1^\alpha \vee \cdots \vee a_l^\alpha \leftarrow b_1^\alpha \wedge \cdots \wedge b_k^\alpha \wedge not\ b_{k+1}^\gamma \wedge \cdots \wedge not\ b_m^\gamma$ such that a rule of the form (7) belongs to P, $\alpha \in TV_n^+$, $\alpha \leqslant v$, and $\gamma = 1 - \alpha + 1/n$. Note here that the generated crisp description logic component $t(L)$ and the generated crisp logic program component $t(P)$ have both a polynomial size in KB and TV_n^+ (assuming a unary number encoding for the truth values).

Example 18 (Shopping Agent cont'd). The last fuzzy dl-rule of Example 7 is translated into the following dl-rules in the crisp transform (for $TV1_0 = \{0, 0.1, ..., 1\}$):

$$
\begin{aligned}
Small^{0.1}(x) \vee Old^{0.1}(x) &\leftarrow Car^{0.1}(x) \wedge hasInvoice^{0.1}(x,y) \wedge not\ GeqAbout15000^{1.0}(y), \\
Small^{0.2}(x) \vee Old^{0.2}(x) &\leftarrow Car^{0.2}(x) \wedge hasInvoice^{0.2}(x,y) \wedge not\ GeqAbout15000^{0.9}(y), \\
Small^{0.3}(x) \vee Old^{0.3}(x) &\leftarrow Car^{0.3}(x) \wedge hasInvoice^{0.3}(x,y) \wedge not\ GeqAbout15000^{0.8}(y), \\
Small^{0.4}(x) \vee Old^{0.4}(x) &\leftarrow Car^{0.4}(x) \wedge hasInvoice^{0.4}(x,y) \wedge not\ GeqAbout15000^{0.7}(y), \\
Small^{0.5}(x) \vee Old^{0.5}(x) &\leftarrow Car^{0.5}(x) \wedge hasInvoice^{0.5}(x,y) \wedge not\ GeqAbout15000^{0.6}(y), \\
Small^{0.6}(x) \vee Old^{0.6}(x) &\leftarrow Car^{0.6}(x) \wedge hasInvoice^{0.6}(x,y) \wedge not\ GeqAbout15000^{0.5}(y), \\
Small^{0.7}(x) \vee Old^{0.7}(x) &\leftarrow Car^{0.7}(x) \wedge hasInvoice^{0.7}(x,y) \wedge not\ GeqAbout15000^{0.4}(y).
\end{aligned}
$$

The following theorem shows that, for certain fuzzy dl-programs *KB*, the answer sets of *KB* correspond to the answer sets of the crisp transform of *KB*.

Theorem 19. *Let KB=(L,P) be a fuzzy dl-program that (i) is closed under $TV_n = \{0, 1/n, ..., n/n\}$*

*for some n>0 and (ii) contains only combination strategies from Zadeh Logic. Then, I⊆**HB**$_\Phi$ is an answer set of KB iff t(I) is an answer set of t(KB).*

COMPLEXITY

The following theorem shows that, for certain fuzzy dl-programs, consistency checking and cautious / brave reasoning are complete for NEXP^{NP} and co-NEXP^{NP} / NEXT^{NP}, respectively, and thus have the same complexity as consistency checking and cautious / brave reasoning for the tightly coupled disjunctive dl-programs in (Lukasiewicz, 2007a). These results follow from the complexity of consistency checking and cautious / brave reasoning for the tightly coupled disjunctive dl-programs in (Lukasiewicz, 2007a): the lower complexity bounds, because the tightly coupled disjunctive dl-programs in (Lukasiewicz, 2007a) are a special case of fuzzy dl-programs, and the upper complexity bounds, because of the polynomial reduction in Theorem 19.

Theorem 20. *Given (i) a finite set of truth values TV_n={0,1/n,...,n/n} with n>0, (ii) a fuzzy dl-program KB=(L,P) such that (ii.1) KB is closed under TV_n, (ii.2) KB has only combination strategies from Zadeh Logic, and (ii.3) L is in fuzzy SHIF(**D**) or fuzzy SHOIN(**D**), and (iii) a∈HB$_\Phi$ and v∈[0,1],*

(a) *deciding whether KB has an answer set is complete for NEXP^{NP}, and*

(b) *deciding whether $a \geqslant v$ is true in every (resp., some) answer set of KB is complete for co-NEXP^{NP} (resp., NEXP^{NP}).*

TRACTABILITY RESULTS

In this section, we present a special class of fuzzy dl-programs *KB* for which the problems of deciding consistency and of query processing are both data tractable. These fuzzy dl-programs are defined relative to *fuzzy DL-Lite* (Straccia, 2006b) (see also (DLMedia, 2008; Straccia & Visco, 2007)), which is a fuzzy generalization of the description logic *DL-Lite* (Calvanese et al., 2007). Note that *DL-Lite* and its variants are able to capture the main notions of both ontologies and conceptual modeling formalisms in databases and software engineering (Calvanese et al., 2007). By (Straccia, 2006b) (resp., (Calvanese et al., 2007)), deciding whether a knowledge base in *DL-Lite* (resp., *fuzzy DL-Lite*) is satisfiable can be done in polynomial time, and conjunctive query processing from a knowledge base in *DL-Lite* (resp., *fuzzy DL-Lite*) can also be done in polynomial time in the data complexity.

We first recall *DL-Lite* and *fuzzy DL-Lite*. Let **A**, **R**$_A$, and **I** be pairwise disjoint sets of atomic concepts, abstract roles, and individuals, respectively. A *basic concept in fuzzy DL-Lite* is either an atomic concept from **A** or an existential restriction on roles ∃R,**T** (abbreviated as ∃R), where $R \in \mathbf{R}_A \cup \mathbf{R}_A^-$. A *literal in DL-Lite* is either a basic concept *b* or the negation of a basic concept ¬*b*. *Concepts in DL-Lite* are defined by induction as follows. Every basic concept in *DL-Lite* is a concept in *DL-Lite*. If *b* is a basic concept in *DL-Lite*, and ϕ_1 and ϕ_2 are concepts in *DL-Lite*, then ¬b and $\phi_1 \sqcap \phi_2$ are also concepts in *DL-Lite*. An axiom in *DL-Lite* is either

1. a concept inclusion axiom b⊑φ, where b is a basic concept in *DL-Lite*, and φ is a concept in *DL-Lite*, or
2. a fu*nctionality axiom* (fu**nctR**), where $R \in \mathbf{R}_A \cup \mathbf{R}_A^-$, or
3. a concept assertion axiom *b(a)*, where *b* is a basic concept in *DL-Lite* and a∈**I**, or
4. a role assertion axiom *R(a,c)*, where R∈**R**$_A$ and a,c∈**I**.

A *fuzzy concept* (resp., *role*) *assertion axiom* is of the form $b(a) \geqslant n$ (resp., $R(a,c) \geqslant n$), where

$b(a)$ (resp., $R(a,c)$) is a concept (resp., role) assertion axiom in *DL-Lite*, and $n \in [0,1]$. A *fuzzy axiom in DL-Lite* is either a fuzzy concept assertion axiom or a fuzzy role assertion axiom. A *fuzzy knowledge base in DL-Lite L* is a finite set of concept inclusion, functionality, fuzzy concept assertion, and fuzzy role assertion axioms in *DL-Lite*.

We next define a preparative transformation on certain fuzzy dl-programs. For the conjunction strategies of Gödel and Zadeh Logic, every knowledge base in *fuzzy DL-Lite L* can be transformed into an equivalent one in *fuzzy DL-Lite trans(L)* in which every concept inclusion axiom is of form $b \sqsubseteq \ell$, where b (resp., ℓ) is a basic concept (resp., literal) in *DL-Lite*. For fuzzy dl-programs $KB=(L,P)$ with L in *DL-Lite*, we then define $trans(KB)=(L,trans(P))$ by $trans(P)=P \cup \{b'(X) \leftarrow b(X) | b \sqsubseteq b' \in trans(L), b'$ is a basic concept$\} \cup \{\exists R(X) \leftarrow R(X,Y) | R \in \mathbf{R}_A \cap \Phi\} \cup \{\exists R^-(Y) \leftarrow R(X,Y) | R \in \mathbf{R}_A \cap \Phi\}$.

We now define the notion of local stratification for disjunctive fuzzy programs. A *local stratification* of a disjunctive fuzzy program P is a mapping $\lambda: HB_\Phi \rightarrow \{0,1,\ldots,k\}$ such that $\lambda(\alpha) \geqslant \lambda(\beta)$ (resp., $\lambda(\alpha) > \lambda(\beta)$) for each $r \in ground(P)$, $\alpha \in H^®$, and $\beta \in B^+(r)$ (resp., $\beta \in B^-(r)$), where $k \geqslant 0$ is the *length* of λ. We say P is *locally stratified* iff it has a stratification λ of some length $k \geqslant 0$.

We are now ready to define fuzzy dl-programs in *DL-Lite* as follows. We say that a fuzzy dl-program $KB=(L,P)$ is defined in *DL-Lite* iff

1. L is in *fuzzy DL-Lite* and interpreted relative to the conjunction strategies of Gödel or Zadeh Logic,
2. *Trans(P)* is normal and locally stratified, and
3. KB is closed under $TV_n=\{0,1/n,\ldots,n/n\}$ for some $n>0$, where we assume a unary encoding of the numbers in TV_n.

Like for the crisp case (Lukasiewicz, 2007a), consistency checking and query processing for fuzzy dl-programs in *DL-Lite* are both data trac-table. This result follows from the fact that such programs have either no or a unique answer set, which can be computed by a finite sequence of fixpoint iterations.

Theorem 21.*Let KB be a fuzzy dl-program in DL-Lite. Then,*

(a) *deciding whether KB has an answer set, and*

(b) *computing the truth value of a ground atom $a \in HB_\Phi$ in the answer set of KB can both be done in polynomial time in the data complexity.*

Example 22 (Shopping Agent cont'd). Consider the fuzzy dl-program $KB=(L,P)$, where L is a finite set of concept and (abstract) role assertion axioms, with truth values from some $TV_n=\{0,1/n,\ldots,n/n\}$ with $n>0$, and P is the first rule of Example 7. Then, KB is defined in *DL-Lite*, KB is satisfiable, and the truth values of all *query©* in the answer set of KB can be computed in polynomial time in the data complexity.

RELATED WORK

Most closely related to the presented approach are other integrations of rules and ontologies that allow for handling fuzzy vagueness. Also related are integrations of rules and ontologies that allow for handling probabilistic uncertainty.

The earliest works on fuzzy dl-programs are (Straccia, 2006b) and (Lukasiewicz, 2006a), which propose tightly coupled positive fuzzy dl-programs under the canonical least model semantics and loosely coupled normal fuzzy dl-programs under the answer set semantics, respectively. Moreover, (Lukasiewicz & Straccia, 2007b) presents an efficient top-k retrieval technique in this context, while (Venetis et al., 2007) studies a fuzzy extension of the mapping between ontologies and rules in (Grosof et al., 2003).

The earliest work on probabilistic dl-programs (Lukasiewicz, 2005) is based on loosely coupled normal dl-programs under the answer set and the well-founded semantics. Recent extensions include especially a tractable variant (Lukasiewicz, 2007b), particularly for probabilistic data integration, a unified framework for handling both fuzzy vagueness and probabilistic uncertainty (Lukasiewicz & Straccia, 2007a), and a tightly coupled disjunctive version (Calì & Lukasiewicz, 2007; Calì et al., 2008), particularly for representing and reasoning with mappings between ontologies. A related (less expressive) approach is (Predoiu & Stuckenschmidt, 2007), which is based on Bayesian logic programs, combining dl-programs with Bayesian networks.

CONCLUSION

We have presented tightly coupled fuzzy dl-programs under the answer set semantics, which generalize the tightly coupled disjunctive dl-programs in (Lukasiewicz, 2007a) by fuzzy vagueness in both the description logic and the logic program component. We have shown that the new formalism faithfully extends both fuzzy disjunctive programs and fuzzy description logics, and that under suitable assumptions, reasoning in the new formalism is decidable. We have presented a polynomial reduction for certain fuzzy dl-programs to tightly coupled disjunctive dl-programs, and we have analyzed the complexity of consistency checking and query processing for certain fuzzy dl-programs. Finally, we have also provided a special case of fuzzy dl-programs for which deciding consistency and query processing are both data tractable.

An interesting issue for future work is the implementation of the presented framework and its experimental testing along applications in practice.

ACKNOWLEDGMENT

This work was partially supported by the German Research Foundation (DFG) under the Heisenberg Programme.

REFERENCES

W3C (2004). OWL Web Ontology Language Overview. W3C Recommendation (10 February 2004). Retrieved from www.w3.org/TR/2004/REC-owl-features-20040210/.

Berners-Lee, T. (1999). *Weaving the Web*. San Francisco: Harper.

Bobillo, F., Delgado, M., & Gómez-Romero, J. (2006). A crisp representation for fuzzy SHOIN with fuzzy nominals and general concept inclusions. In *Proc. URSW-2006, CEUR Workshop Proceedings* 218. CEUR-WS.org.

Bobillo, F., Delgado, M., & Gómez-Romero, J. (2008). Optimizing the crisp representation of the fuzzy description logic SROIQ. In *Proc. URSW-2007, CEUR Workshop Proceedings* 327. CEUR-WS.org.

Bobillo, F., & Straccia, U. (2008a). fuzzyDL: An expressive fuzzy description logic reasoner. In *Proc. FUZZ-IEEE-2008*, pp. 923-930. IEEE Computer Society.

Bobillo, F., & Straccia, U. (2008b). Towards a crisp representation of fuzzy description logics under Łukasiewicz semantics. In *Proc. ISMIS-2008*, (LNCS 4994, pp. 309-318).

Calì, A., & Lukasiewicz, T. (2007). Tightly integrated probabilistic description logic programs for the Semantic Web. In *Proc. ICLP-2007* (LNCS 4670, pp. 428-429).

Calì, A., Lukasiewicz, T., Predoiu, L., & Stuckenschmidt, H. (2008). Tightly integrated probabilistic description logic programs for representing ontology mappings. In Proc. FoIKS-2008 (LNCS 4932, pp. 178-198).

Calvanese, D., De Giacomo, G., Lembo, D., Lenzerini, M., & Rosati, R. (2007). Tractable reasoning and efficient query answering in description logics: The *DL-Lite* family. *Journal of Automated Reasoning, 39*(3), 385–429. doi:10.1007/s10817-007-9078-x

DLMedia. (2008). Retrieved from http://gaia.isti.cnr.it/ straccia/software/DLMedia/DLMedia.html.

Eiter, T., Ianni, G., Lukasiewicz, T., Schindlauer, R., & Tompits, H. (2008). Combining answer set programming with description logics for the Semantic Web. *Artificial Intelligence, 172*(12/13), 1495–1539. doi:10.1016/j.artint.2008.04.002

Eiter, T., Ianni, G., Schindlauer, R., & Tompits, H. (2006). Effective integration of declarative rules with external evaluations for Semantic Web reasoning. In *Proc. ESWC-2006* (LNCS 4011, pp. 273-287).

Eiter, T., Lukasiewicz, T., Schindlauer, R., & Tompits, H. (2004). Well-founded semantics for description logic programs in the Semantic Web. In Proc. RuleML-2004 (LNCS 3323, pp. 81-97).

Fensel, D., Wahlster, W., Lieberman, H., & Hendler, J. (Eds.). (2002). *Spinning the Semantic Web: Bringing the World Wide Web to Its Full Potential*. MIT Press. fuzzyDL (2008). Retrieved from http://gaia.isti.cnr.it/ straccia/software/fuzzyDL/fuzzyDL.html.

Gelfond, M., & Lifschitz, V. (1991). Classical negation in logic programs and disjunctive databases. *New Generation Comput., 9*(3/4), 365–386. doi:10.1007/BF03037169

Grosof, B. N., Horrocks, I., Volz, R., & Decker, S. (2003). Description logic programs: Combining logic programs with description logics. In *Proc. WWW-2003* (pp. 48-57). ACM Press.

Hájek, P. (1998). *Metamathematics of Fuzzy Logic*. Kluwer.

Hölldobler, S., Störr, H.-P., & Khang, T. D. (2004). The subsumption problem of the fuzzy description logic ALC_{FH}. In *Proc. IPMU-2004* (pp. 243-250).

Horrocks, I., & Patel-Schneider, P. F. (2004). Reducing OWL entailment to description logic satisfiability. *Journal of Web Semantics, 1*(4), 345–357. doi:10.1016/j.websem.2004.06.003

Horrocks, I., & Patel-Schneider, P. F. (2006). Position paper: A comparison of two modelling paradigms in the Semantic Web. In *Proc. WWW-2006* (pp. 3-12). ACM Press.

Horrocks, I., Patel-Schneider, P. F., & van Harmelen, F. (2003). From SHIQ and RDF to OWL: The making of a Web ontology language. *Journal of Web Semantics, 1*(1), 7–26. doi:10.1016/j.websem.2003.07.001

Horrocks, I., Sattler, U., & Tobies, S. (1999). Practical reasoning for expressive description logics. In *Proc. LPAR-1999*, LNCS (LNCS 1705, pp. 161-180). Springer.

Lukasiewicz, T. (2005). Probabilistic description logic programs. In *Proc. ECSQARU-2005* (LNCS 3571, pp. 737-749). Extended version: *Int. J. Approx. Reason., 45*(2), 288-307, 2007.

Lukasiewicz, T. (2006a). Fuzzy description logic programs under the answer set semantics for the Semantic Web. In Proc. RuleML-2006 (pp. 89-96). IEEE Computer Society. Extended version: Fundam. Inform., 82(3), 289-310, 2008.

Lukasiewicz, T. (2006b). Stratified probabilistic description logic programs. In *Proc. URSW-2005, CEUR Workshop Proceedings* 173. CEUR-WS. org.

Lukasiewicz, T. (2007a). A novel combination of answer set programming with description logics for the Semantic Web. In *Proc. ESWC-2007* (LNCS 4519, pp. 384-398).

Lukasiewicz, T. (2007b). Tractable probabilistic description logic programs. In *Proc. SUM-2007* (LNCS 4772, pp. 143-156).

Lukasiewicz, T., & Straccia, U. (2007a). Description logic programs under probabilistic uncertainty and fuzzy vagueness. In *Proc. ECSQARU-2007* (LNCS 4724, pp. 187-198). Springer.

Lukasiewicz, T., & Straccia, U. (2007b). Top-k retrieval in description logic programs under vagueness for the Semantic Web. In *Proc. SUM-2007* (LNCS 4772, pp. 16-30). Springer.

Lukasiewicz, T., & Straccia, U. (2008). Managing uncertainty and vagueness in description logics for the Semantic Web. *Journal of Web Semantics*, *6*(4), 291–308. doi:10.1016/j.websem.2008.04.001

Motik, B., Horrocks, I., Rosati, R., & Sattler, U. (2006). Can OWL and logic programming live together happily ever after? In *Proc. ISWC-2006* (LNCS 4273, pp. 501-514).

Predoiu, L., & Stuckenschmidt, H. (2007). A probabilistic framework for information integration and retrieval on the Semantic Web. In *Proc. InterDB-2007 Workshop on Database Interoperability*.

Rosati, R. (2006). DL+*log*: Tight integration of description logics and disjunctive Datalog. In *Proc. KR-2006* (pp. 68-78). AAAI Press.

Stoilos, G., Stamou, G., Tzouvaras, V., Pan, J., & Horrocks, I. (2005). Fuzzy OWL: Uncertainty and the Semantic Web. In *Proc. OWLED-2005, CEUR Workshop Proceedings* 188. CEUR-WS.org.

Straccia, U. (2004). Transforming fuzzy description logics into classical description logics. In *Proc. JELIA-2004*, (LNCS 3229, pp. 385-399). Springer.

Straccia, U. (2005). Towards a fuzzy description logic for the Semantic Web (preliminary report). In *Proc. ESWC-2005* (LNCS 3532, pp. 167-181).

Straccia, U. (2006a). A fuzzy description logic for the Semantic Web . In Sanchez, E. (Ed.), *Fuzzy Logic and the Semantic Web, Capturing Intelligence* (pp. 73–90). Elsevier.

Straccia, U. (2006b). Fuzzy description logic programs. In *Proc. IPMU-2006* (pp. 1818-1825).

Straccia, U. (2006c). Uncertainty and description logic programs over lattices . In Sanchez, E. (Ed.), *Fuzzy Logic and the Semantic Web, Capturing Intelligence* (pp. 115–133). Elsevier.

Straccia, U., & Visco, G. (2007). DLMedia: An ontology mediated multimedia information retrieval system. In *Proc. DL-2007, CEUR Workshop Proceedings* 250. CEUR-WS.org.

Tresp, C., & Molitor, R. (1998). A description logic for vague knowledge. In *Proc. ECAI-1998* (pp. 361-365). J. Wiley & Sons.

Venetis, T., Stoilos, G., Stamou, G. B., & Kollias, S. D. (2007). f-DLPs: Extending description logic programs with fuzzy sets and fuzzy logic. In *Proc. FUZZ-IEEE-2007* (pp. 1-6). IEEE Computer Society.

APPENDIX: PROOFS

Proof of Theorem 12. (a) Let $I{\subseteq}\mathbf{HB}_\Phi$ be any answer set of KB. That is, I is a minimal model of $KB^I{=}(L,P^I)$. In particular, (i) $I{\models}L$ and (ii) $I{\models}r$ for every $r{\in}P^I$. This is equivalent to (i) $I{\models}L$ and (ii) $I{\models}r$ for every $r{\in}ground(P)$. That is, I is a model of KB. We now show that I is also a minimal model of KB. Towards a contradiction, suppose that there exists a model $J{\subset}I$ of KB. That is, (i) $J{\models}L$ and (ii) $J{\models}r$ for every $r{\in}ground(P)$. By the monotonicity and antitonicity of conjunction and negation strategies, respectively, (i) $J{\models}L$ and (ii) $J{\models}r$ for every $r{\in}P^I$. That is, J is also a model of KB^I. But this contradicts I being a minimal model of KB^I. In summary, this shows that I is a minimal model of KB.

(b) Since $KB^I{=}(L,ground(P))$ for every positive fuzzy dl-program $KB{=}(L,P)$, it follows that the set of all answer sets of KB, that is, the set of all minimal models of KB^I, coincides with the set of all minimal models of KB. $\square$

Proof of Theorem 13. Observe first that $I{\subseteq}\mathbf{HB}_\Phi$ is a model of $KB^I{=}(L,P^I)$ iff (i) $I{\models}L$ and (ii) $I{\models}r$ for every $r{\in}P^I$. Since $L{=}\varnothing$, this is equivalent to $I{\models}r$ for every $r{\in}P^I$. Thus, $I{\subseteq}\mathbf{HB}_\Phi$ is a minimal model of KB^I iff I is a minimal model of P^I. That is, $I{\subseteq}\mathbf{HB}_\Phi$ is an answer set of KB iff I is an ordinary answer set of P. $\square$

Proof of Theorem 14. Observe first that, by Theorem 12, since P is positive, the set of all answer sets of KB is the set of all minimal models $I{\subseteq}\mathbf{HB}_\Phi$ of KB. Observe then that for $a{\in}HB_\Phi$, $a \geqslant n$ is true in all minimal models $I{\subseteq}\mathbf{HB}_\Phi$ of KB iff $a \geqslant n$ is true in all models $I{\subseteq}\mathbf{HB}_\Phi$ of KB. It thus remains to show that $a \geqslant n$ is true in all models $I{\subseteq}\mathbf{HB}_\Phi$ of KB iff $a \geqslant n$ is true in all first-order models of $L{\cup}gound(P)$:

($\Rightarrow$)Suppose $a \geqslant n$ is true in all models $I{\subseteq}\mathbf{HB}_\Phi$ of KB. Let I be any fuzzy first-order model of $L{\cup}gound(P)$. Let $I{\subseteq}\mathbf{HB}_\Phi$ be defined by $I(b){=}\mathrm{I}(b)$ for all $b{\in}HB_\Phi$. Then, I is a model of $L^* = L \cup \{a = I(a) \mid a \in HB_\Phi\}$, and thus L^* is satisfiable. Hence, I is a model of L. Since I is a model of $ground(P)$, also I is a model of $ground(P)$. In summary, I is a model of KB. Hence, $a \geqslant n$ is true in I, and thus $a \geqslant n$ is true in I. Overall, $a \geqslant n$ is true in all first-order models of $L{\cup}gound(P)$.

($\Leftarrow$)Suppose $a \geqslant n$ is true in all first-order models of $L{\cup}gound(P)$. Let $I{\subseteq}\mathbf{HB}_\Phi$ be any model of KB. Then, $L^* = L \cup \{a = I(a) \mid a \in HB_\Phi\}$ is satisfiable. Let I be a first-order model of L^*. Then, I is in particular a model of L. Furthermore, since I is a model of $ground(P)$, also I is a model of $ground(P)$. In summary, I is a model of $L{\cup}gound(P)$. It thus follows that $a \geqslant n$ is true in I, and thus $a \geqslant n$ is also true in I. Overall, $a \geqslant n$ is true in all models $I{\subseteq}\mathbf{HB}_\Phi$ of KB. $\square$

Proof of Theorem 17. ($\Rightarrow$)Let I be a first-order model of $L^* = L \cup \{a = I(a) \mid a \in HB_\Phi\}$. Let the equivalence relation $\sim$ on Φ_c be defined by $c{\sim}d$ iff $c^I{=}d^I$. Since I is a model of L^*, it follows that $\sim$ is admissible with I. Furthermore, it follows that I is a model of $L{\cup}\{a{=}I(a)|a{\in}DL_\Phi\}{\cup}\{c{\neq}c\,'|c{\sim}c\,'\}$.

($\Leftarrow$)Let I be a model of $L{\cup}\{a{=}I(a)|a{\in}DL_\Phi\}{\cup}\{c{\neq}c\,'|c{\sim}c\,'\}$ for some equivalence relation $\sim$ on Φ_c admissible with I. Thus, I can be extended to a model I' of $L{\cup}\{a{=}I(a)|a{\in}HB_\Phi\}$ by I'$(b){=}$I(b), for all $b{\in}HB_\Phi{-}DL_\Phi$. $\square$

Proof of Theorem 19. Recall that every fuzzy interpretation $I \subseteq \mathbf{HB}_\Phi$ (to TV_n) corresponds to the binary interpretation $t(I) = \{a^\alpha \mid a \in HB_\Phi, \alpha \in TV_n^+, I(a) \geqslant \alpha\}$. Hence, every a^α encodes that the truth value of a is at least α. Thus, the rules $p\beta(x^1, \dots xk) \leftarrow_p \alpha(x^1 \dots, xk)$ such that p is a k-ary predicate symbol from Φ, x1,...,xk are distinct variables, $\alpha \in TV_n^+ \setminus \{1/n\}$, and $\beta = \alpha - 1/n$ encode all the logical relationships between the $a\alpha$'s, while the other rules in t(P) encode the instances of every rule in P under every possible truth value combination of its body atoms. Then, for every fuzzy interpretation $I \subseteq HB\Phi$, **(i)** the Gelfond-Lifschitz transform of P relative to I directly corresponds to the Gelfond-Lifschitz transform of t(P) relative to t(I), and (ii) L directly corresponds to t(L) (*Bobillo et al., 2008; Straccia, 2004*). This then implies that the fuzzy interpretation $I \subseteq HB\Phi$ is $\mathbf{a}_n$ answer set of KB iff t(I) is an answer set of t(KB). □

Proof of Theorem 20. As for the lower bounds, fuzzy dl-programs generalize tightly coupled disjunctive dl-programs, and consistency checking and cautious / brave reasoning in the latter are hard for NEXPNP and co-NEXPNP / NEXPNP (Lukasiewicz, 2007a), respectively.

As for the upper bounds, to solve the three problems, we first transform KB=(*L*,P) into its crisp equivalent t(KB)=(t(L),t(P)), as described in the body of the paper. Note that both the crisp description logic component t(L) and the crisp logic program component t(P) have a polynomial size in KB and TV_n^+. By Theorem 19, KB has an answer set iff t(KB) has an answer set. As shown in (Lukasiewicz, 2007a), deciding the latter is in NEXPNP. By Theorem 19, $a \geqslant v$ is true in every / some answer set of KB iff av is true in every / some answer set of t(KB). As shown in (Lukasiewicz, 2007a), deciding the latter is in co-NEXPNP / NEXPNP □

Proof of Theorem 21 (sketch). Like for the crisp case (Lukasiewicz, 2007a), it can be shown that fuzzy dl-programs in *DL-Lite* have either no or a unique answer set, which can be computed by a finite sequence of fixpoint iterations, as usual. Hence, for such programs, consistency checking and query processing are both data tractable. □

Chapter 12
Evolutionary Conceptual Clustering Based on Induced Pseudo-Metrics

Nicola Fanizzi
Università degli studi di Bari, Italy

Claudia d'Amato
Università degli studi di Bari, Italy

Floriana Esposito
Università degli studi di Bari, Italy

ABSTRACT

We present a method based on clustering techniques to detect possible/probable novel concepts or concept drift in a Description Logics knowledge base. The method exploits a semi-distance measure defined for individuals, that is based on a finite number of dimensions corresponding to a committee of discriminating features (concept descriptions). A maximally discriminating group of features is obtained with a randomized optimization method. In the algorithm, the possible clusterings are represented as medoids (w.r.t. the given metric) of variable length. The number of clusters is not required as a parameter, the method is able to find an optimal choice by means of evolutionary operators and a proper fitness function. An experimentation proves the feasibility of our method and its effectiveness in terms of clustering validity indices. With a supervised learning phase, each cluster can be assigned with a refined or newly constructed intensional definition expressed in the adopted language.

Copyright © 2010, IGI Global, distributing in print or electronic forms without written permission of IGI Global is prohibited.

INTRODUCTION

In the context of the Semantic Web (henceforth SW) there is an extreme need of automatizing those activities which are more burdensome for the knowledge engineer, such as ontology construction, matching, and evolution. These phases can be assisted by specific learning methods, such as instance-based learning (and analogical reasoning) (Aarts, Korst, & Michiels, 2005), case-based reasoning (d'Aquin, Lieber, & Napoli, 2005), inductive generalization (Esposito, Fanizzi, Iannone, Palmisano, & Semeraro, 2004; Iannone, Palmisano, & Fanizzi, 2007; Lehmann & Hitzler, 2008) and unsupervised learning (clustering) (Fanizzi, Iannone, Palmisano, & Semeraro, 2004; Kietz & Morik, 1994), crafted for knowledge bases expressed in description logics (DLs) *The Description Logic Handbook, 2003* (that are the standard representations of the field) and complying with their semantics.

In this work, we investigate on unsupervised learning for DL knowledge bases. In particular, we focus on the problem of conceptual clustering of semantically annotated resources surveying recent work on metric induction and evolutionary methods (Fanizzi, d'Amato, & Esposito, 2007). Besides, we propose the exploitation of clustering in order to detect the evolution of the ontologies over time by detecting *concept drift* (Widmer & Kubat, 2006) or *novelties* (Spinosa, Ponce de Leon Ferreira de Carvalho, & Gama, 2007) arising from the newly acquired individuals and their related assertions. Indeed, these two phenomena are mainly due to the introduction of new (previously unknown) assertions of individuals as instances of one or more concepts.

The benefits of *conceptual clustering* (Stepp & Michalski, 1986) in the context of semantically annotated knowledge bases are manifold. Clustering annotated resources enables the definition of new emerging concepts (*concept formation*) on the grounds of the concepts defined in a knowledge base; supervised methods can exploit these clusters

to induce new concept definitions or to refining existing ones (*ontology evolution*); intensionally defined groupings may speed-up the task of search and *discovery* (Aarts et al., 2005; d'Amato, Staab, Fanizzi, & Esposito, 2007); a clustering may also suggest criteria for *ranking* the retrieved resources based on the distance from the centers.

Essentially, most of the clustering methods are based on the application of similarity (or density) measures defined over a fixed set of attributes of the domain objects. Classes of objects are taken as collections that exhibit low interclass similarity (density) and high intraclass similarity (density). These methods are rarely able to take into account some form of *background knowledge* that could characterize object configurations by means of global concepts and semantic relationships. This hinders the interpretation of the outcomes of these methods which is crucial in the SW perspective that enforces sharing and reusing the produced knowledge in order to enable forms of semantic interoperability across different knowledge bases and applications.

Conceptual clustering methods can answer these requirements since they have been specifically crafted for defining groups of objects through (simple) descriptions based on selected attributes (Stepp & Michalski, 1986). In the perspective, the expressiveness of the language adopted for describing objects and clusters (concepts) is extremely important. Related approaches, specifically designed for DLs representations, have recently been introduced (Fanizzi et al., 2004; Kietz & Morik, 1994). They pursue logic-based methods for attacking the problem of clustering with respect to some specific DL languages. The main drawback of these methods is that they are language-dependent, which prevents them from scaling to the standard SW representations that are mapped on complex DLs. Moreover, purely logic methods can hardly handle noisy data.

These problems motivate the investigation on similarity-based clustering methods which can be more noise-tolerant and language-independent.

Specifically, the extension of distance-based techniques able to cope with the standard SW representations is presented. The proposed method also profit by the benefits of a randomized search for optimal clusterings. Indeed, it is intended for grouping similar resources with respect to a notion of similarity, coded in a distance measure, which fully complies with the semantics knowledge bases expressed in DLs. The individuals are gathered around cluster centers according to their distances. The choice of the best centers (and their number) is performed through an evolutionary approach (Ghozeil & Fogel, 1996; Lee & Antonsson, 2000).

From a technical viewpoint, upgrading existing distance-based algorithms to work on (multi-) relational representations requires similarity measures that are suitable for such languages and their semantics. A theoretical problem is posed by the *Open World Assumption* (OWA) that is generally made on the semantics of DL knowledge bases, differently from the *Closed World Assumption* (CWA) which is standard in other contexts. This makes SW knowledge bases inherently incomplete (*The Description Logic Handbook, 2003*), which makes distance-based clustering harder than in the case of relational databases (Kirsten & Wrobel, 1998). Namely, proposed distance functions are ultimately based on the assessment of the cardinality of concept extensions which cannot be determined with certainty in the SW settings[1], yet it may evolve over time, as long as more assertions are acquired.

Moreover, as pointed out in a seminal paper on similarity measures for DLs (Borgida, Walsh, & Hirsh, 2005), most of the existing measures focus on the similarity of atomic concepts within hierarchies or simple ontologies.

Recently, dissimilarity measures have been proposed for some specific DLs (d'Amato, Fanizzi, & Esposito, 2006). Although they turned out to be quite effective for specific inductive tasks, they were still partly based on structural criteria which makes them fail to fully grasp the underlying semantics and hardly scale to more complex ontology languages. Moreover, they have been conceived for assessing *concept* similarity, whereas, for other tasks, a notion of similarity between *individuals* is required.

Therefore, a family of dissimilarity measures for semantically annotated resources has been devised, which can overcome the aforementioned limitations (Fanizzi, d'Amato, & Esposito, 2007). Following the criterion of semantic discernibility of individuals, a family of measures is derived that is suitable for a wide range of languages since it is merely based on the discernibility of the input individuals with respect to a fixed committee of features represented by a set of concept definitions. Hence, the new measures are not absolute. Rather, they depend on the knowledge base they are applied to. Thus, the choice of good feature sets also deserves a preliminary optimization phase, which can be performed by means of a well-known randomized search procedure such as *simulated annealing* or *genetic programming*.

As regards the clustering algorithm, in our setting, instead of the notion of *centroid* that characterizes many distance-based algorithms descending from k-means (Jain, Murty, & Flynn, 1999), one may resort to the notion of *medoids* (Kaufman & Rousseeuw, 1990) as central individuals in a cluster.

The proposed clustering algorithm employs genetic programming as a search schema. The evolutionary problem is modeled by considering populations made up of strings of medoids with different lengths. The medoids are computed according to the semantic measure induced with the methodology mentioned above. On each generation, the strings in the current population are evolved by mutation and cross-over operators, which are also able to change the number of medoids. Thus, this algorithm is also able to suggest autonomously a promising number of clusters. Accordingly, the fitness function is based both on the optimization of a cluster cohesion index and on the penalization of lengthy medoid strings.

Finally, we propose the exploitation of the outcomes of the clustering algorithm for detecting the phenomena of concept drift or novelty from the data in the knowledge base. This can be further exploited to induce new concepts or refine the definitions of the existing ones by means of the mentioned operators. As these are inductive learning methods, the outcomes are not to be considered as semantically valid, but as suggestion to the ontology engineer for new forms of concepts which inductively arise from the state of the world as coded by the current knowledge base.

The remainder of the article is organized as follows. The next section presents the basics of the target representation and the semantic similarity measure adopted with the clustering algorithm, which will then be presented and discussed. Then, we report an experiment aimed at assessing the validity of the method on some ontologies available in the Web. The utility of clustering in the logic of ontology evolution is then discussed. Finally, we give a survey of related work, followed by an examination of conclusions and extensions.

SEMANTIC DISTANCE MEASURES

Preliminaries

In the following, we assume that resources, concepts, and their relationship may be defined in terms of a generic ontology language that may be mapped to some DL language with the standard model-theoretic semantics see the (Description Logics Handbook, 2003) for a thorough reference. As mentioned in the previous section, one of the advantages of our method is that it does not depend on a specific language for semantic annotations.

In the intended framework setting, a *knowledge base* $\mathcal{K} = \langle \mathcal{T}, \mathcal{A} \rangle$ contains a *TBox* $\mathcal{T}$ and an *ABox* $\mathcal{A}$. $\mathcal{T}$ is a set of concept definitions. The complexity of such definitions depends on the specific DL language constructors. $\mathcal{A}$ contains *assertions*

(ground facts) on *individuals* (domain objects) concerning the current world state, namely:

$C(a)$, a, is an instance of concept C; and
$R(a, b)$, a is R-related to b.

The set of the individuals referenced in the assertions of the ABox $\mathcal{A}$ will be denoted with *Ind*($\mathcal{A}$). The *Unique Names Assumption* can be made on the ABox individuals[2] therein.

As regards the required inference services, like all other instance-based methods, the measure proposed in this section requires performing *instance-checking*, which amounts to determining whether an individual, say a, belongs to a concept extension, that is, whether $C(a)$ holds for a certain concept C. In the simplest cases (primitive concepts), this requires simple lookups, yet for defined concepts the reasoner may need to perform a number of inferences. Besides, differently from the standard DB settings, due to the OWA, the reasoner might be unable to provide a definite answer. For instance, consider the following very simple knowledge base $\mathcal{T} = \{$*Woman*, *Mother*$\}$ where *Woman* and *Mother* are primitive concepts and $\mathcal{A} = \{$*Woman*(*Jane*)$\}$, asking to a reasoner if *Jane* is an instance of the concept *Mother*, namely, if *Mother*(*Jane*) occurs, the reasoner cannot give us any reply since there are no information neither for asserting that *Jane* in instance of *Mother*, nor for asserting that *Jane* is not instance of the concept *Mother*, namely, for asserting that ¬*Mother*(*Jane*) occurs. Hence, one has to cope with this form of uncertainty.

SEMANTIC SIMILARITY BETWEEN INDIVIDUALS

For our purposes, we need a function for measuring the similarity of individuals. It can be observed that individuals do not have a syntactic structure that can be compared. This has led to lifting them to the concept description level before comparing them (recurring to the approximation of the *most specific concept* of an individual with respect to the ABox) (d'Amato et al., 2006).

For clustering procedures, such as the one specified in the next section, a new measure was developed whose definition totally depends on semantic aspects of the individuals in the knowledge base. On a semantic level, similar individuals should behave similarly with respect to the same concepts, which form a sort of *context*[3]. A novel measure is needed for assessing the similarity of individuals in a knowledge base. It is based on the idea of comparing their semantics along a number of dimensions represented by a committee of concept descriptions. As such the measure is not necessarily an absolute one. Rather, it must reflect a certain point of view which may be encoded through a context, that is here represented by a set of concepts that should be considered to discern the various individuals.

Following some techniques for distance induction in clausal spaces developed in ILP (Sebag, 1997), we propose the definition of totally semantic distance measures for individuals in the context of a knowledge base which is also able to cope with the OWA.

The rationale of the new measure is to compare individuals on the grounds of their behavior with respect to a given set of features, that is a collection of concept descriptions, say $F = \{F_1, F_2, ..., F_m\}$, which stands as a group of discriminating *features* expressed in the considered DL language.

A family of dissimilarity measures for individuals inspired to the Minkowski's distances (L_p) can be defined as follows:

Definition 2.1 (family of dissimilarity measures): *Let $\mathcal{K} = \langle \mathcal{T}, \mathcal{A} \rangle$ be a knowledge base. Given set of concept descriptions $F = \{F_1, F_2, ..., F_m\}$, a family of functions $\{d_p^F\}_{p \in \mathbb{N}}$ with*

$$d_p^F : Ind(\mathrm{A}) \times Ind(\mathrm{A}) \mapsto [0,1]$$

is defined as follows: $\forall a, b \in Ind(\mathcal{A})$

$$d_p^F(a,b) := \frac{L_p(\boldsymbol{\pi}(a), \boldsymbol{\pi}(b))}{m}$$

$$= \frac{1}{m}\left(\sum_{i=1}^{m} |\pi_i(a) - \pi_i(b)|^p\right)^{\frac{1}{p}}$$

where $p > 0$ and the *i-th projection function* π_i of vector $\boldsymbol{\pi}$, $i \in \{1, ..., m\}$, is defined by: $\forall a, b \in Ind(\mathcal{A})$

$$\pi_i(a) = \begin{cases} 1 & \mathrm{K} \models F_i(a) \\ 0 & \mathrm{K} \models \neg F_i(a) \\ 1/2 & otherwise \end{cases}$$

The superscript F will be omitted when the set of features is fixed.

The case of $\pi_i(a) = 1/2$ corresponds to the case when a reasoner cannot give the truth value for a certain membership query (it can build models both for the membership and nonmembership case[4]. This is due to the inherent incompleteness of the DL knowledge bases due to the OWA, which is normally made in this context.

To better cope with the uncertainty of this case, variable projection values have recently been proposed (d'Amato, Fanizzi, & Esposito, 2008), which reflect the probability of $\mathcal{K} \models F_i(a)$, based on an estimate of the entropy of feature F_i as elicited from the current knowledge base (Fanizzi et al., 2008). In the following, we will not adopt such a proposal, which would introduce some overhead in the computation of the measure.

DISCUSSION

Compared to other proposed distance (or dissimilarity) measures for individuals (d'Amato et al., 2006), the presented function does not depend on the constructors of a specific language, thus making it totally language independent. This represents one of the main advantages, since it can be applied to any DL knowledge bases. On the contrary, language-dependent measures can be applied only to knowledge bases described with the DL language supported by the measures (most of the time $\mathcal{ALC}$ or $\mathcal{ALCNR}$) and they cannot be applied to most expressive ontologies that typically occur in the SW scenario. The presented function requires only the instance-checking service, that is used for deciding whether an individual is asserted in the knowledge base to belong to a concept extension or, alternatively, if this could be derived as a logical consequence.

It is easy to see that the functions $\{d_p^F\}_{p \in \mathbb{N}}$ are dissimilarity measures. Even more so, the standard properties for semidistances can be proven (Fanizzi et al., 2007):

Proposition 2.1 (semidistance): *For a fixed feature set* F *and p > 0, given any three individuals a, b* $\in$ *Ind($\mathcal{A}$). it holds that:*

1. $d_p^F(a,b) \geq 0$

2. $d_p^F(a,b) = d_p^F(b,a)$

3. $d_p^F(a,c) \leq d_p^F(a,b) + d_p^F(b,c)$

The functions are not metrics because it cannot be proven that if $d_p^F(a,b) = 0$ then $a = b$ (whereas the opposite implication easily holds). This is the case of *indiscernible* individuals with respect to the given set of features *F*. If the property were strictly required, a distance could be derived either by considering equivalence classes (Zezula, Amato, Dohnal, & Batko, 2007) or, if the *unique names assumption* were made, by introducing equality as a new meta-feature F_0.

Note that the projection functions for the individuals in the knowledge base can be computed in advance, thus determining a speed-up in the actual computation of the measure. This is very important for the measure integration in algorithms which massively use this distance, such as all instance-based methods.

As such, these projections elicit information for the (partially complete) knowledge base. This

is similar to the epistemic operator **K** proposed in (Donini, Lenzerini, Nardi, and Nutt, 1998). In our case, we use this information in order to induce a pseudo-metric.

It may be objected that, in our notion of similarity, we focus on membership involving concepts only, disregarding membership assertions involving roles which account for the configurations of the links between individuals, giving the actual structure of the domain of interest. Actually, role assertions are not disregarded since projections are computed through membership queries on defined features that may require links to other features. Even with very simple ontologies, one may express distinguishing features through the existence of chains of such links and we argue that such features can be learned.

The validity of the measure has been experimentally proven in (d'Amato et al., 2008), where it has been embedded in a K-Nearest Neighbor algorithm in order to classify individuals of an ontology with respect to several concepts.

OPTIMIZING THE FEATURE SET

The underlying idea in the measure definition is that similar individuals should exhibit the same behavior with respect to the concepts in *F*. Here, we make the assumption that the feature-set *F* represents a sufficient number of (possibly redundant) features that are able to discriminate really different individuals.

Preliminary experiments, where the measure has been exploited for instance-based classification (*Nearest Neighbor* algorithm) and similarity search (Zezula et al., 2007), demonstrated the effectiveness of the measure using even the very set of both primitive and defined concepts found in the knowledge bases. However, the choice of the concepts to be included in the committee *F* is crucial and may be the object of a preliminary learning problem to be solved (*feature selection for metric learning*).

Various optimizations of the feature set can be foreseen as concerns its definition. Among the possible sets of features we will prefer those that are able to discriminate the individuals in the ABox:

Definition 2.2 (good feature set): *Let F be a set of concept descriptions in the adopted DL language* $F = \{F_1, F_2, ..., F_m\}$. *F is a good feature set for the knowledge base* $\mathcal{K} = \langle \mathcal{T}, \mathcal{A} \rangle$ *iff*

$$\forall a, b \in Ind(\mathcal{A}), a \neq b, \exists i \in \{1,...,m\}:$$
$$\pi_i(a) \neq \pi_i(b)$$

Then, when the previously defined function is parameterized on a good feature set, it has the properties of a metric function.

Namely, since the function is strictly dependent on the committee of features F, two immediate heuristics arise:

- the *number* of concepts of the committee, and
- their discriminating power in terms of a *discernibility factor*.

Finding optimal sets of discriminating features should profit also by their composition employing the specific constructors made available by the representation language of choice.

These objectives can be accomplished by means of randomized optimization techniques, especially when knowledge bases with large sets of individuals are available. Namely, part of the entire data can be drawn in order to learn optimal F sets, in advance with respect to the successive usage for all other purposes. The space of the feature sets (with a definite maximal cardinality) may be explored by means of *refinement operators* (Iannone et al., 2007; Lehmann & Hitzler, 2008). The optimization of a fitness function based on the (finite) available dataset ensures that this process does not follow infinite refinement chains, as a candidate refinement step is only made when a better solution is reached in terms of the fitness function.

Optimization Through Genetic Programming

Rather than resorting to standard heuristic techniques (e.g., branch-and-bound search), initially we have cast the problem solution as an optimization algorithm founded in *genetic programming* (Mitchell, 1997). Essentially, these algorithms encode the traversal of the search space as a result of simple operations carried out on a representation of the problem solutions (*genomes*). Such operations mimic modifications of the solutions which may lead to better ones in terms of a fitness function, that in our case is based on the discernibility of the individuals.

The resulting algorithm is depicted in Figure 1. Essentially, it searches the space of all possible feature committees starting from an initial guess (determined by the call to the makeInitialFS() procedure) based on the concepts (both primitive and defined) currently referenced in the knowledge base K, starting with a committee of a given cardinality (INIT_CARD). This initial cardinality may be determined as a function of $\lceil \log_3(N) \rceil$, where $N = | Ind(\mathcal{A}) |$, as each feature projection can categorize the individuals in three sets.

The outer loop gradually augments the cardinality of the candidate committees. It is repeated until the threshold fitness is reached or the algorithm detects some fixpoint: employing larger feature committees would not yield a better feature set with respect to the best fitness recorded in the previous iteration (with fewer features). Otherwise, the extendFS() procedure extends the current for the next generations by including a newly generated random concept.

The inner while-loop is repeated for a number of generations until a stop criterion is met, based on the maximal number of generations maxGenerations or, alternatively, when a minimal fitness

Figure 1. Feature set optimization algorithm based on genetic programming

FeatureSet GP_Optimization(K, maxGenerations, fitnessThr)

input: K: current knowledge base
     maxGenerations: maximal number of generations
     fitnessThr: minimal required fitness threshold

output: FeatureSet: set of concept descriptions

static: currentFSs, formerFSs; arrays of current/previous feature sets
     currentBestFitness, formerBestFitness = 0;
     current/previous best fitness values offsprings;
     array of generated feature sets fitnessImproved;
     improvement flag generationNo = 0:
     number of current generation

Begin
currentFSs = makeInitialFS(K,INIT_CARD)
formerFSs = currentFSs
Repeat
currentBestFitness = bestFitness(currentFSs)
while(currentBestFitness<fitnessThr)**and**(generationNo<maxGenerations)
begin
offsprings = generateOffsprings(currentFSs)
currentFSs = selectFromPopulation(offsprings)
currentBestFitness = bestFitness(currentFSs)
++generationNo
end
if (currentBestFitness > formerBestFitness) **and** (currentBestFitness < fitnessThr) **then**
Begin
formerFSs = currentFSs
formerBestFitness = currentBestFitness
currentFSs = extendFS(currentFSs)
fitnessImproved = true
End
Else
fitnessImproved = false
End
until not fitnessImproved
return selectBest(formerFSs)
end

threshold *fitnessThr* is crossed by some feature set in the population, which can be returned.

As regards the *bestFitness*() routine, it computes the best fitness of the feature sets in the input vector. Fitness can be determined as the *discernibility factor* yielded by the feature set, as computed on the whole set of individuals or on a smaller sample. For instance, given the fixed set of individuals *IS* $\subseteq$ *Ind* ($\mathcal{A}$), the fitness function may be:

$$discernibility(F) :=$$

$$\nu \sum_{(a,b)\in IS^2} \sum_{i=1}^{|F|} |\pi_i(a) - \pi_i(b)|$$

where n is a normalizing factor that can depend on the overall number of couples involved.

As concerns finding candidate sets of concepts to replace the current committee (the generateOff-springs() routine), the function was implemented by recurring to some transformations of the current best feature sets:

- choose $F \in currentFSs$;
- randomly select $F_i \in F$;
- replace F_i with $F_i' \in randomMutation(F_i)$ randomly generated, or
- replace F_i with one of its refinements $F_i' \in ref(F_i)$vv

The possible refinements of concept description are language-specific. For example, for the case of $\mathcal{ALC}$ logic, refinement operators have been proposed in (Lehmann and Hitzler, 2008) and (Iannone et al., 2007).

This is iterated until a suitable number of offspring is generated. Then, these offspring feature sets are evaluated and the best ones are included in the new version of the currentFSs array; the best fitness value for these feature sets is also computed.

When the while-loop is over, the current best fitness is compared with the best one computed for the former feature set length; if an improvement is detected, then the outer repeat-loop is continued; otherwise (one of) the former best feature set(s) is selected and returned as the result of the algorithm.

Optimization Through Simulated Annealing

The randomized optimization algorithm based on genetic programming just described may suffer from being possibly caught in plateaux or local minima if a limited number of generations are explored before checking for an improvement. This is likely due to the extent of the search space, which, in turn, depends on the language of choice. Moreover, maintaining a single best genome for the next generation may slow down the search process.

To prevent such cases, different randomized search procedures which aim at global optimization should be adopted. Hence, a method based on *simulated annealing* (Aarts et al., 2007) has also been proposed (Fanizzi et al., 2007), whose algorithm is reported in Figure 2.

The algorithm searches the space of feature sets starting from an initial guess (determined by makeInitialFS(K)) based on the concepts (both primitive and defined) currently referenced in the knowledge base, which can be freely combined to form new descriptions.

The loop controlling the search is repeated for a number of times that depends on the temperature temp controlled by the cooing function $\Delta T()$ which gradually decays to 0, when the current feature committee can be returned. In this cycle, the current feature set is iteratively refined calling procedure randomSuccessor() which makes a step in the space by refining the current set. Then, the fitness of the new feature set is compared to that of the current one determining the increment of energy ΔE. If this is positive, then the candidate committee replaces the current one. Otherwise, it will (less likely) be replaced with a probability that depends on ΔE and on the current temperature.

The energy increase ΔE is determined by the *fitness*() function applied to the new and current feature sets, which can be computed as the average *discernibility* factor, defined as above.

As concerns finding candidates to replace the current committee, randomSuccessor() can be implemented by recurring to simple transformations of the feature set:

- add (resp. removing) a concept C: $nextFS \leftarrow currentFS \cup \{C\}$ (resp. $nextFS \leftarrow currentFS \setminus \{C\}$)

Figure 2. Feature set optimization procedure based on simulated annealing

FeatureSet SA_Optimization(K, ΔT)
input: K: knowledge base ΔT(): cooling function
output: FeatureSet: set of concept descriptions

static: currentFS: current Feature Set
     nextFS: new Feature Set
     time: time controlling variable
     ΔE: energy increment
     temp: temperature (probability of replacement)

Begin
currentFS = makeInitialFS(K)
for time = 1 **to** ∞ **do**
temp = temp $- \Delta T$(*time*)
if (temp == 0)
return currentFS
nextFS = randomSuccessor(currentFS, K)
$\Delta E = fitness(nextFS) - fitness(currentFS)$
if ($\Delta E > 0$)
// replacement
currentFS = nextFS
Else
// conditional replacement with given probability
currentFS = replace(nextFS, $e^{\Delta E/temp}$)
end

- randomly choose one of the current concepts from currentFS, say C; replace it with one of its refinements $C' \in ref(C)$

Note that these transformations may change the cardinality of the current feature set. As mentioned before, refining concept descriptions is language-dependent. Complete operators are to be preferred to ensure exploring the whole search space.

Given a suitable cooling schedule, the algorithm is known to find an optimal solution. More practically, to control the complexity of the process, alternate schedules may be preferred that guarantee the construction of suboptimal solutions in polynomial time (Aarts et al., 2007).

EVOLUTIONARY CLUSTERING PROCEDURE

Many similarity-based clustering algorithms (Jain et al., 1999) can be applied to semantically annotated resources stored in a knowledge base, exploiting the measures discussed in the previous section.

We focused on the techniques based on evolutionary methods which are able to determine also an optimal number of clusters, instead of requiring it as a parameter (although the algorithm can be easily modified to exploit this information that greatly reduces the search-space).

Conceptual clustering requires also to provide a definition for the detected groups, which may

Figure 3. ECM: The evolutionary clustering around medoids algorithm

medoidVector ECM(maxGenerations)
input: maxGenerations: max number of iterations;
output: medoidVector: list of medoids
static: currentPopulation: ordered vector of current best genomes offsprings: vector of generated offsprings fitnessVector: ordered vector of fitness values generationNo: generation number
begin
initialize(currentPopulation,popLength)
generationNo = 0
while (generationNo < maxGenerations)
Begin
offsprings = generateOffsprings(currentPopulation)
fitnessVector = computeFitness(offsprings)
currentPopulation = select(offsprings,fitnessVector)
++generationNo
end
return currentPopulation[0] // *fittest genome*
end

be the basis for the formation of new concepts inductively elicited from the knowledge base. Hence, the conceptual clustering procedure consists of two phases: one that detects the clusters in the data and the other that finds an intensional definition for the groups of individuals detected in the former phase (covered in section "Conceptual Clustering for Concept Formation").

The Evolutionary Clustering Algorithm

The first clustering phase implements a genetic programming learning scheme, where the designed representation for the competing genomes is made up of strings (lists) of individuals of different lengths, with each gene standing as prototypical for a cluster.

Specifically, each cluster will be represented by its prototype recurring to the notion of *medoid* (Kaufman & Rousseeuw, 1990; Jain et al., 1999) on a categorical feature-space with respect to the

distance measure previously defined. Namely, the medoid of a group of individuals is the individual that has the minimal distance with respect to the others. Formally, in this setting:

Definition 3.1 (medoid): *Given a cluster of individuals* $C = \{a_1, a_2, ..., a_n\} \subseteq Ind(\mathcal{A})$, *the medoid of the cluster is defined:*

$$medoid(C) := \underset{a \in C}{argmin} \sum_{j=1}^{n} d(a, a_j)$$

where $a \neq a_j$

In the proposed evolutionary algorithm, the population will be made up of genomes represented by a list of medoids $G = \{m_1, ..., m_k\}$ of variable lengths. The algorithm performs a search in the space of possible clusterings of the individuals, optimizing a fitness measure that maximizes the discernibility of the individuals of the different clusters (intercluster separation) and the intracluster similarity measured in terms of the d_p^F pseudo-metric.

On each generation those strings that are considered as best with respect to a fitness function are selected for passing to the next generation. Note that the algorithm does not prescribe a fixed length of the genomes (as, for instance in k-means and its extensions (Jain et al., 1999); hence it searches a larger space aiming at determining an optimal number of clusters for the data at hand.

Figure 3 reports a sketch of the algorithm, named ECM, *Evolutionary Clustering around Medoids*. After the call to the initialize() function returning (to currentPopulation) a randomly generated initial population of popLength medoid strings, it essentially consists of the typical generation loop of genetic programming where a new population is computed and then evaluated for deciding on the best genomes to be selected for survival to the next generation.

On each iteration new offsprings of current best clusterings in currentPopulation are computed. This is performed by suitable genetic operators explained in the following. The fitnessVector recording the quality of the various offsprings (i.e., clusterings) is then updated, and then the best offsprings are selected for the next generation.

The fitness of a single genome $G = \{m_1, \ldots, m_k\}$ is computed by distributing all individuals among the clusters ideally formed around the medoids in that genome. For each medoid m_i ($i = 1, \ldots, k$), let C_i be such a cluster. Then, the fitness is computed by the function:

$$fitness(G) = \left(\lambda(k) \sum_{i=1}^{k} \sum_{x \in C_i} d_p(x, m_i) \right)^{-1}$$

The function reflects the fact that the individuals within the same cluster should exhibit the least possible distances among themselves (this is similar to the least squares principle adopted in many optimization techniques). The factor $\lambda(k)$ is introduced in order to penalize those clusterings made up of too many clusters that could enforce the minimization in this way (e.g., by proliferating

singletons). A suggested value may be $\lambda(k) = \sqrt{k+1}$ which was used in the experiments (see section "Evaluation"). Better functions can be derived from the validity measures. We considered the simple function above also as a tradeoff between effectiveness and efficiency of the fitness computation, as this is the central operation of the genetic algorithm.

The loop condition is controlled by the maximal number of generation (the maxGenerations parameter) ensuring that eventually it may end even with a suboptimal solution to the problem. Besides other parameters can be introduced for controlling the loop based on the best fitness value obtained so far or on the gap between the fitness of best and of the worst selected genomes in currentPopulation. Eventually, the best genome of the vector (supposed to be sorted by fitness in descending order) is returned.

It remains to specify the nature of the generateOffsprings procedure and the number of such offsprings, which may as well be another parameter of the ECM algorithm. Three mutation and one crossover operators are implemented:

drop a randomly selected medoid:

$$G := G \setminus \{m\}, m \in G$$

select $m \in Ind(\mathcal{A}) \setminus G$ that is added to G:
$$G := G \cup \{m\}$$

randomly select $m \in G$ and replace it with $m' \in Ind(A) \setminus G$ such that

$$\forall m'' \in Ind(A) \setminus G \ d(m, m') \leq d(m, m''):$$
$$G' := (G \setminus \{m\}) \cup \{m'\}$$

select subsets $S_A \subset G_A$ and $S_B \subset G_B$ and exchange them between the genomes:

$$G_A := (G_A \setminus S_A) \cup S_B$$
$$\text{and } G_B := (G_B \setminus S_B) \cup S_A$$

DISCUSSION

The representation of centers by means of medoids has two advantages. First, it presents no limitations on attributes types, and second, the choice of medoids is dictated by the location of a predominant fraction of points inside a cluster and, therefore, it is less sensitive to the presence of outliers. In k-means case, a cluster is represented by its centroid, which is a mean (usually weighted average) of points within a cluster. This works conveniently only with numerical attributes and can be negatively affected even by a single outlier.

An algorithm based on medoids has several favorable properties. Since it performs clustering with respect to any specified metric, it allows a flexible definition of similarity. Many clustering algorithms do not allow for a flexible definition of similarity, but allow only Euclidean distance in current implementations. In addition, medoids are robust representations of the cluster centers that are less sensitive to outliers than other cluster profiles, such as the cluster means of k-means. This robustness is particularly important in the common context that many elements do not belong exactly to any cluster, which may be the case of the membership in DL knowledge bases, which may not be ascertained given the OWA.

A (10+60) selection strategy has been implemented, with the numbers indicating, respectively, the number of parents selected for survival and the number of their offspring generated employing the mutation operators presented above.

EVALUATION

The feasibility of the clustering algorithm has been evaluated with an experimentation on knowledge bases selected from standard repositories. Note that for testing our algorithm, we preferred using populated ontologies (which may be more difficult to find) rather than randomly generating asser-

tions for artificial individuals, which might have biased the procedure.

Assessing the semantic validity of the clustering results goes beyond the scope of this work and it is likely questionable. Indeed, it would require the assistance of the authors of the ontologies to judge whether the induced clusters (and derived concepts also) are significant with respect to the intended meaning that was encoded through the ontology.

More practically, we exploit modified versions of classic internal validity indices for clustering, that judge the induced clustering structure in terms of compactness (within the same cluster) and separation (among different clusters). This structure may be very handy for further applications related to abstracting (parts of) ontologies and providing alternate means for searching, matchmaking, and so forth.

Experimental Setup

A number of different populated knowledge bases represented in OWL were selected from various sources[5], namely: FSM, SurfaceWaterModel, Transportation, NewTestamentNames, and Financial. Table 1 summarizes important details concerning the ontologies employed in the experimentation. Of course, the number of individuals gives only a partial indication of the number of assertions (RDF triples) concerning them which affects both the complexity of reasoning and distance assessment.

For each populated knowledge base, the experiments have been repeated 10 times. In the computation of the distances between individuals (the most time-consuming operation) all concepts in the knowledge base have been used for the committee of features, thus guaranteeing meaningful measures with high redundancy. The Pellet reasoner[6] (ver. 1.5) was employed to perform the inferences (instance-checking) that were necessary to compute the projections.

Table 1. Ontologies employed in the experiments

Ontology	DL lang.	#concepts	#obj.prop.	#data prop.	#individuals
FSM	$\mathcal{SOF}(D)$	20	10	7	37
SurfaceWaterModel	$\mathcal{ALCOF}(D)$	19	9	1	115
Transportation	$\mathcal{ALC}$	44	7	0	331
NewTestamentNames	$\mathcal{SHIF}(D)$	47	27	8	676
Financial	$\mathcal{ALCIF}$	60	16	0	1000

The experimentation consisted of 10 runs of the algorithm per knowledge base. The indexes which were chosen for the experimental evaluation were the following: the *generalized* R-Squared (modRS), the *generalized* Dunn's index, the average Silhouette index, and the number of clusters obtained. In the following explanation of these quality measures, we will consider a generic partition $P = \{C_1,...,C_k\}$ of n individuals in k clusters.

The R-Squared index (Halkidi, Batistakis, & Vazirgiannis, 2001) is a measure of cluster separation, ranging in [0,1]. Instead of the cluster means, we generalize the measure by computing it with respect to their medoids, namely:

$$RS(P) := \frac{SS_b(P)}{SS_b(P) + SS_w(P)}$$

where SS_b is the *between clusters Sum of Squares* defined as follows:

$$SS_b(P) := \sum_{i=1}^{k} d(\overline{m}, m_i)^2$$

where $\overline{m}$ is the medoid of the whole dataset and SS_w is the *within cluster Sum of Squares* that is defined:

$$SS_w(P) := \sum_{i=1}^{k} \sum_{a \in C_i} d(a, m_i)^2$$

The generalized Dunn's index is a measure of both compactness (within clusters) and separa-

tion (between clusters). The original measure is defined for numerical feature vectors in terms of centroids and it is known to suffer from the presence of outliers. To overcome these limitations, we adopt a generalization of Dunn's index [6] that is modified to deal with medoids. The new index can be defined:

$$V_{GD}(P) := \min_{1 \le i \le k} \left\{ \min_{\substack{1 \le j \le k \\ i \ne j}} \left\{ \frac{\delta_p(C_i, C_j)}{\max_{1 \le h \le k} \{\Delta_p(C_h)\}} \right\} \right\}$$

where δ_p is the Hausdorff distance for **clusters derived[7] from** d_p, **while the cluster** diameter measure Δ_p is defined:

$$\Delta_p(C_h) := \frac{2}{|C_h|} \sum_{c \in C_h} d_p(c, m_h)$$

which is more noise-tolerant with respect to the original measure. Of course, this measure, ranging in $[0,+\infty[$, has to be maximized.

Conversely, the average Silhouette index (Kaufman & Rousseeuw, 1990) is a measure ranging in the interval [-1,1], thus suggesting an absolute best value for the validity of a clustering. For each individual x_i, $i \in \{1,...,n\}$, the average distance to other individuals within the same cluster C_j, $j \in \{1,...,k\}$, is computed:

$$a_i := \frac{1}{|C_j|} \sum_{x \in C_j} d_p(a_i, x)$$

Table 2. Results of the experiments: For each index, average value (±standard deviation) and [min,max] interval of values are reported

Ontology	R-Squared	Dunn's	Silhouette	#clusters
FSM	.39 (±.07) [.33,.52]	.72 (±.10) [.69,1.0]	.77 (±.01) [.74,.78]	4 (±.00) [4,4]
SurfaceWater-Model	.45 (±.15) [.28,.66]	.99 (±.03) [.9,1.0]	.999 (±.000) [.999,.999]	12.9 (±.32) [12,13]
Transportation	.33 (±.04) [.26,.40]	.67 (±.00) [.67,.67]	.975 (±.004) [.963,.976]	3 (±.00) [3,3]
NewTestament-Names	.46 (±.08) [.35,.59]	.79 (±.17) [.5,1.0]	.985 (±.008) [.968,.996]	29.2 (±2.9) [25,32]
Financial	.37 (±.06) [.29,.45]	.88 (±1.16) [.57,1.0]	.91 (±.03) [.87,.94]	8.7 (±.95) [8,10]

Then, the average distance to the individuals in other clusters is also computed:

$$b_i := \frac{1}{|C_j|} \sum_{x \in C_h}^{h \neq j} d_p(a_i, x)$$

Hence, the Silhouette value for the considered individual is obtained as follows:

$$s_i := \frac{(b_i - a_i)}{\max(a_i, b_i)}$$

Finally, the average Silhouette value *s* for the whole clustering is computed:

$$s := \frac{1}{k} \sum_{l=1}^{k} s_i$$

We also considered the average number of clusters resulting from the repetitions of the experiments on each knowledge base. A stable algorithm should return almost the same number of clusters on each repetition. It is also interesting to compare this number to the one of the primitive and defined concepts in each ontology (see Table 1), although this is not a hierarchical clustering method.

RESULTS

As mentioned, the experiment consisted in 10 runs of the evolutionary clustering procedure with an optimized feature set (computed in advance). Each run took from a few minutes to 41 minutes on a 2.5GhZ (512Mb RAM) Linux Machine. Note that these timings include the preprocessing phase, that was needed to compute the distance values between all couples of individuals. Indeed, the elapsed time for the core clustering algorithm is actually very short (max 3 minutes).

The outcomes of the experiments are reported in Table 2. For each knowledge base and index, the average values observed along the various repetitions is considered. Moreover, the standard deviation and the range of minimum and maximum values are also reported.

The R-Squared index values denote an acceptable degree of separation between the various clusters. We may interpret the outcomes observing that clusters present a higher degree of compactness (measured by the SS_w component). It should also be pointed out that flat clustering penalizes separation as the concepts in the knowledge base are not necessarily disjoint. Rather, they naturally tend to form subsumption hierarchies. Observe also that the variation among the various runs is very limited.

Dunn's index measures both compactness and separation; the rule in this case is *the larger the better*. Results are good for the various bases. These outcomes may serve for further comparisons to the performance of other clustering algorithms. Again, note that the variation among the various runs is very limited, so the algorithm was quite stable, despite its inherent randomized nature.

It can be observed that for the average Silhouette measure, that has a precise range of values, the performance of our algorithm is generally very good with a degradation with the increase of individuals taken into account. Besides, note that the largest knowledge base (in terms of its population) is also the one with the maximal number of concepts which provided the features for the metric. Thus, in the resulting search space there is more freedom in the choice of the ways to make one individual discernible from the others. Surprisingly, the number of clusters is limited with respect to the number of concepts in the KB, suggesting that many individuals gather around a restricted subset of the concepts, while the others are only complementary (they can be used to discern the various individuals). Such subgroups may be detected, extending our method to perform hierarchical clustering.

As regards the overall stability of the clustering procedure, we may observe that the main indices (and the number of clusters) show very little variations along the repetitions (see the standard deviation values), which suggests that the algorithm tends to converge towards clusterings of comparable quality with generally the same number of clusters. As such, the optimization procedure does not seem to suffer from being caught in local minima. However, the case needs a further investigation. Indeed, the optimization performed by the clustering procedure is two-fold: it does not only optimize the choice of the clustering medoids, but also their number, which

is normally considered as a fixed parameter for other algorithms (see section "Related Work").

Other experiments (whose outcomes are not reported here) showed that sometimes the initial genome length may have an impact to the resulting clustering, thus suggesting the employment of different randomized search procedures (e.g., again simulated annealing or tabu search) which may guarantee a better exploration of the search space.

CONCEPT EVOLUTION IN DYNAMIC ONTOLOGIES

In this section, we illustrate the utility of clustering in the process of the automated evolution of dynamic ontologies. Namely, clustering may be employed to detect the possible evolution of some concepts in the ontology as reflected by new incoming resources, as well as the emergence of novel concepts. These groups of individuals may be successively employed by supervised learning algorithms to induce the intensional description of revised or newly invented concepts.

Incremental and Automated Drift and Novelty Detection

As mentioned in the introduction, conceptual clustering enables a series of further activities related to dynamic settings: 1) concept drift (Widmer & Kubat, 1996): that is, the change of known concepts with respect to the evidence provided by new annotated individuals that may be made available over time; and 2) novelty detection (Spinosa et al., 2007): isolated clusters in the search space that require definition through new emerging concepts to be added to the knowledge base.

The algorithms presented above are suitable for an online unsupervised learning implementation. Indeed, as soon as new annotated individuals are made available these may be assigned to the *closest* clusters (where closeness is measured as the

Figure 4. Concept drift and novelty detection algorithm

(decision,NewClustering) Drift_Novelty_Detection(Model, CCluster)
input: Model: current clustering;   CandCluster: candidate cluster;
output: (decision, NewClustering);
Begin
$m_{CC} := medoid(CandCluster);$

for each $C_j \in Model \mid$ **do**
  $m_j := medoid(C_j);$
  $d_{overall} := \dfrac{1}{\mid Model \mid} \Sigma_{C_j \in Model} \left(\dfrac{1}{\mid C_j \mid} \Sigma_{a \in C_j} d(a, m_j) \right);$
  $d_{candidate} := \dfrac{1}{\mid CandCluster \mid} \Sigma_{a \in CCluster} d(a, m_{CC});$

if $d_{overall} \geq d_{candidate}$ **then** // *valid candidate cluster*
Begin
$\overline{m} := medoid(\{m_j \mid C_j \in Model\});$ // *global medoid*
$d_{max} := \max_{m_j \in Model} d(\overline{m}, m_j);$
If $d(\overline{m}, m_{CC}) \leq d_{max}$ **then**
return (drift, replace(Model, CandCluster))
else return (novelty, $Model \cup CandCluster$)
End
else return (normal, integrate(Model, CandCluster))
end

distance to the cluster medoids or to the minimal distance to its instances). Then, new runs of the evolutionary algorithm may yield a modification of the original model (clustering) both in the clusters composition and in their number.

Following (Spinosa et al., 2007, the model representing the starting concepts is built based on the clustering algorithm. For each cluster, the maximum distance between its instances and the medoid is computed. This establishes a decision boundary for each cluster. The union of the boundaries of all clusters is the global decision boundary which defines the current model.

A new unseen example that falls inside this global boundary is consistent with the model and

therefore considered *normal*; otherwise, a further analysis is needed. A single such individual should not be considered as novel, since it could simply represent noise. Due to lack of evidence, these individuals are stored in a short-term memory, which is monitored for the formation of new clusters that might indicate two conditions: novelty and concept drift.

Using the clustering algorithm on individuals in the short-term memory generates candidate clusters. For a candidate cluster to be considered valid, that is, likely a concept, the algorithm in Figure 4 can be applied.

The candidate cluster CandCluster is considered valid[8] for drift or novelty detection when the average mean distance between medoids and the respective instances for all clusters of the current model is greater than the average distance of the new instances to the medoid of the candidate cluster. Then, a threshold for distinguishing between concept drift and novelty is computed: the maximum distance between the medoids of the model and the global one[9].

When the distance between overall medoid and the medoid of the candidate cluster exceeds the maximum distance, then the case is of concept drift and the candidate cluster is merged with the current model. Otherwise (novelty case), the clustering is simply extended. Finally, when the candidate cluster is made up of normal instances, these can be integrated by assigning them to the closest clusters.

The main differences from the original method (Spinosa et al., 2007), lie in the different representational setting (simple numeric tuples were considered) which allows for the use of off-the-shelf clustering methods such as k-means (Jain et al., 1999) based on a notion of centroid which depends on the number of clusters required as a parameter. In our categorical setting, medoids substitute the role of centroids and, more importantly, our method is able to detect an optimal number of clusters autonomously; hence, the influence of this parameter is reduced.

Conceptual Clustering for Concept Formation

The next step may regard the refinement of existing concepts as a consequence of concept drift or the invention of new ones to account for emerging clusters of resources. The various cluster can be considered as training examples for a supervised algorithm aimed at finding an intensional DL definition for one cluster against the counterexamples, represented by individuals in different clusters (Fanizzi et al., 2004; Kietz & Morik, 1994).

Each cluster may be labeled with an intensional concept definition which characterizes the individuals in the given cluster while discriminating those in other clusters (Fanizzi et al., 2004; Kietz & Morik, 2004). Labeling clusters with concepts can be regarded as a number of supervised learning problems in the specific multirelational representation targeted in our setting (Iannone et al., 2007; Lehmann & Hitzler, 2008). As such, it deserves specific solutions that are suitable for the DL languages employed.

A straightforward solution may be found, for DLs that allow for the computation of (an approximation of) the *most specific concept* (*msc*) and *least common subsumer* (*lcs*) (2003) (such as $\mathcal{ALC}$). The first operator, given the current knowledge base and an individual, provides (an approximation of) the most specific concept that has the individual as one of its instances. This would allow for lifting individuals to the concept level. The second operator computes minimal generalizations of the input concept descriptions.

Indeed, concept formation can be cast as a supervised learning problem, once the two clusters at a certain level have been found, where the members of a cluster are considered as positive examples and the members of the dual cluster as negative ones. Then, any concept learning method which can deal with this representation (and semantics) may be utilized for this new task.

Given these premises, the learning process can be described through the following steps:

let C_j be a cluster of individuals

1. **for each** individual $a_i \in C_j$ **do** compute $M_i := msc(a_i)$ with respect to $\mathcal{A}$;
2. **let** $mscs_j := \{M_i \mid a_i \in C_j\}$;
3. **return** $lcs(mscs_j)$

As an alternative, more complex algorithms for learning concept descriptions expressed in DLs may be employed such as YinYang (2007) or other systems based on refinement operators (Lehmann & Hitzler, 2008). Their drawback is that they cannot deal with the most complex DL languages. However, a new language-independent method based on a notion of entropy, similarly to Foil (1997), has lately being developed (Fanizzi et al., 2008).

The concepts resulting from conceptual clustering can be used for performing weak forms of abduction that may be used to update the ABox; namely, the membership of an individual to a cluster assessed by means of the metric, may yield new assertions that do not occur in the ABox that can be added (or presented to the knowledge engineer as candidates to addition). Induced assertions coming for newly available individuals may trigger further supervised learning sessions where concepts are refined by means of the aforementioned operators.

RELATED WORK

The unsupervised learning procedure presented in this article is mainly based on two factors: the semantic dissimilarity measure and the clustering method. To the best of our knowledge, in the literature there are very few examples of similar clustering algorithms working on complex representations that are suitable for knowledge bases of semantically annotated resources. Thus, in this section, we briefly discuss sources of inspiration for our procedure and some related approaches.

Relational Similarity Measures

As previously mentioned, various attempts to define semantic similarity (or dissimilarity) measures for concept languages have been made, yet they have still a limited applicability to simple languages (Borgida et al., 2005), or they are not completely semantic, depending also on the structure of the descriptions (d'Amato et al., 2006). Very few works deal with the comparison of individuals rather than concepts.

In the context of clausal logics, a metric was defined (Nienhuys-Cheng, 1998) for the Herbrand interpretations of logic clauses as induced from a distance defined on the space of ground atoms. This kind of measures may be employed to assess similarity in *deductive databases*. Although it represents a form of fully semantic measure, different assumptions are made with respect to those which are standard for knowledgeable bases in the SW perspective. Therefore, the transposition to the context of interest is not straightforward.

Our measure is mainly based on Minkowski's measures (Zezula et al., 2008) and on a method for distance induction developed by (Sebag, 1997) in the context of *machine learning*, where *metric learning* is developing as an important subfield. In this work, it is shown that the induced measure could be accurate when employed for classification tasks even though set of features to be used were not the optimal ones (or they were redundant). Indeed, differently from our unsupervised learning approach, the original method learns different versions of the same target concept, which are then employed in a voting procedure similar to the Nearest Neighbor approach for determining the classification of instances.

A source of inspiration was also *rough sets* theory (Pawlak, 1991), which aims at the formal definition of vague sets by means of their approximations determined by an indiscernibility relationship. Hopefully, these methods developed in this context will help in solving the open points of our framework (see section "Conclusions and Possible Extentions") and suggest new ways to treat uncertainty.

Clustering Procedures

Our algorithm adapts to the specific representations devised for the SW context a combination of evolutionary clustering and the distance-based approaches (Jain et al., 1999). Specifically, in the methods derived from k-means and k-medoids, each cluster is represented by one of its points.

Early versions of this approach are represented by the systems PAM, CLARA (Kaufman & Rousseeuw, 1990), and CLARANS (Ng & Han, 1994). They implement iterative optimization methods that essentially cyclically relocate points between perspective clusters and recompute potential medoids. The leading principle for the process is the effect on an objective function. The whole dataset is assigned to resulting medoids, the objective function is computed, and the best system of medoids is retained. In CLARANS, a graph is considered whose nodes are sets of k medoids and an edge connects two nodes if they differ by one medoid. While CLARA compares very few neighbors (a fixed small sample), CLARANS uses random search to generate neighbors by starting with an arbitrary node and randomly checking maxneighbor neighbors. If a neighbor represents a better partition, the process continues with this new node. Otherwise, a local minimum is found, and the algorithm restarts until a certain number of local minima is found. The best node (i.e., a set of medoids) is returned for the formation of a resulting partition. (Ester et al., 1996) extended CLARANS to deal with very large spatial databases.

Our algorithm may be considered an extension of evolutionary clustering methods (Hall, Özyurt, & Bezdek, 1999), which are also capable of determining a good estimate of the number of clusters (Ghozeil & Fogel, 1996). Besides, we adopted the idea of representing clusterings (genomes) as strings of cluster centers (Lee & Antonsson, 2000) transposed to the case of medoids for the categorical search spaces of interest.

Other related recent approaches are represented by the UNC algorithm and its extension to the hierarchical clustering case H-UNC (Nasraoui & Krishnapuram, 2002). Essentially, UNC solves a multimodal function optimization problem seeking dense areas in the feature space. It is also able to determine their number. The algorithm is also demonstrated to be noise-tolerant and robust with respect to the presence of outliers. However, the applicability is limited to simpler representations with respect to those considered in this article.

Further comparable clustering methods are those based on an *indiscernibility relationship* (Hirano & Tsumoto, 2005). While in our method this idea is embedded in the semidistance measure (and the choice of the committee of concepts), these algorithms are based on an iterative refinement of an equivalence relationship which eventually induces clusters as equivalence classes.

As mentioned in the introduction, the classic approaches to conceptual clustering (Stepp & Michalski, 1986) in complex (multirelational) spaces are based on structure and logics. (Kietz and Morik, 1994) proposed a method for efficient construction of knowledge bases for the BACK representation language. This method exploits the assertions concerning the roles available in the knowledge base, in order to assess, in the corresponding relationship, those subgroups of the domain and ranges which may be inductively deemed as disjoint. In the successive phase, supervised learning methods are used on the discovered disjoint subgroups to construct new concepts that account for them. A similar approach is followed in (Fanizzi et al., 2004), where the supervised phase is performed as an iterative refinement step, exploiting suitable refinement operators for a different DL, namely $\mathcal{ALC}$. Alternative approaches based on the same metrics, yet applying partitional methods similar to bisecting k-medoids, have been investigated in other papers (Fanizzi et al., 2008). The limitation of this method is represented by the fact that parameter k must be known beforehand or it must be empirically determined by using validity measures (such as those introduced in the experimental section) in the clustering algorithm, so that no further bisection is performed when the quality of the resulting clustering would be compromised.

As mentioned, system OLINDDA (Spinosa et al., 2007) is, to the best of our knowledge, the first method exploiting clustering for detecting concept drift and novelty. Our method improves on it both in the representation of the instances and in being based on an original clustering method which is not parameterized on the number of clusters. This method has been coupled also with the other clustering method referred to above.

CONCLUSION AND POSSIBLE EXTENSIONS

This work has presented a framework for evolutionary conceptual clustering that can be applied to standard relational representations for knowledge bases in the SW context. Its intended usage is for discovering interesting groupings of semantically annotated resources and can be applied to a wide range of concept languages. Besides, the induction of new concepts may follow from such clusters, which allows for accounting for them from an intensional viewpoint.

The method exploits a dissimilarity measure, that is based on the underlying resource semantics with respect to a number of dimensions corresponding to a committee of features represented by a group of concept descriptions in the language of choice. A preliminary learning phase, based on randomized search, can be exploited to optimize the choice of the most discriminating features.

The evolutionary clustering algorithm is an extension of distance-based clustering procedures employing medoids as cluster prototypes so as to deal with complex representations of the target context. Variable-length strings of medoids yielding different partitions are searched guided by a fitness function based on cluster separation. As such, the algorithm can also determine the length of the list, that is, an optimal number of clusters.

As for the metric induction part, a promising research line, for extensions to matchmaking, retrieval and classification, is *retrieval by analogy* (d'Amato et al., 2006). A search query may be issued by means of prototypical resources; answers may be retrieved based on local models

(intensional concept descriptions) for the prototype constructed (on the fly) based on the most similar resources (with respect to some similarity measure). The presented algorithm may be the basis for the model construction activity. The distance measure may also serve as a ranking criterion.

The natural extensions of the clustering algorithm that may be foreseen are towards incremental and hierarchical clustering. The former may be easily achieved by assigning new resources to their most similar clusters, and restarting the whole algorithm when some validity measure crosses a given threshold. The latter may be performed by wrapping the algorithm within a level-wise procedure starting with the whole dataset and recursively applying the partitive method until a criterion based on quality indices determines the stop. This may produce more meaningful concepts during the next supervised phase.

Better fitness functions may be also investigated for both distance optimization and clustering. For instance, some clustering validity indices can be exploited in the algorithm as measures of compactness and separation.

REFERENCES

Aarts, E., Korst, J., & Michiels, W. (2005). Search methodologies. *Simulated annealing* (pp. 187-210). Springer-Verlag.

Bezdek, J. C., & Pal, N. R. (1998). Some new indexes of cluster validity. *IEEE Transactions on Systems, Man, and Cybernetics, 28*(3), 301-315.

Borgida, A., Walsh, T. J., & Hirsh, H. (2005). Towards measuring similarity in description logics. In I. Horrocks, H. Sattler, & F. Wolter (Eds.), *Working Notes of the International Description Logics Workshop: CEUR Workshop Proceedings*, Edinburgh, UK.

d'Amato, C., Fanizzi, N., & Esposito, F. (2006). Reasoning by analogy in description logics through instance-based learning. In G. Tummarello, P. Bouquet, & O. Signore(Eds.), *Proceedings of Semantic Web Applications and Perspectives: 3rd Italian Semantic Web Workshop, SWAP 2006, CEUR Workshop Proceedings*, Pisa, Italy.

d'Amato, C., Fanizzi, N., & Esposito, F. (2008). Query answering and ontology population: An inductive approach. In S. Bechhofer et al., (Eds.), *Proceedings of the 5th European Semantic Web Conference, ESWC 2008* (LNCS, pp. 288-302). Springer.

d'Amato, C., Staab, S., Fanizzi, N., & Esposito, F. (2007). Efficient discovery of services specified in description logics languages. In T. Di Noia et al., (Eds.), *Proceedings of the Workshop on Service Matchmaking and Resource Retrieval in the Semantic Web (SMRR 2007) at ISWC 2007, CEUR Workshop Proceedings*. Retrieved September 24, 2008, from www.CEUR-WS.org

d'Aquin, M., Lieber, J., & Napoli, A. (2005). Decentralized case-based reasoning for the Semantic Web. In Y. Gil, E. Motta, V. Benjamins, & M. A. Musen (Eds.), *Proceedings of the 4th International Semantic Web Conference, ISWC 2005* (LNCS 3279, pp. 142-155). Springer.

Donini, F. M., Lenzerini, M., Nardi, D., & Nutt, W. (1998). An epistemic operator for description logics. *Artificial Intelligence, 100*(1-2), 225-274.

Esposito, F., Fanizzi, N., Iannone, L., Palmisano, I., & Semeraro, G. (2004). Knowledge-intensive induction of terminologies from metadata. In F. van Harmelen, S. McIlraith, & D. Plexousakis (Eds.), *ISWC 2004: Proceedings of the 3rd International Semantic Web Conference* (LNCS, pp. 441-455). Springer.

Ester, M., Kriegel, H.-P., Sander, J., & Xu, X. (1996). A density-based algorithm for discovering clusters in large spatial databases. In *Proceedings of the 2nd Conference of ACM SIGKDD* (pp. 226-231).

Fanizzi, N., d'Amato, C., & Esposito, F. (2007a). *Approximate measures of semantic dissimilarity under uncertainty.* Working Notes of the ISWC Workshop on Uncertainty Reasoning in the Semantic Web: URSW 2007 in CEUR Workshop Proceedings, Busan, South Korea.

Fanizzi, N., d'Amato, C., & Esposito, F. (2007b). Evolutionary conceptual clustering of semantically annotated resources. In *Proceedings of the IEEE International Conference on Semantic Computing, ICSC 2007*, Irvine, CA (pp. 783-790). IEEE.

Fanizzi, N., d'Amato, C., & Esposito, F. (2007c). *Induction of optimal semi-distances for individuals based on feature sets.* In D. Calvanese, E. Franconi, V. Haarslev, D. Lembo, B. Motik, A.-Y. Turhan, & S. Tessaris (Eds.), Working Notes of the 20th International Description Logics Workshop, DL 2007: CEUR Workshop Proceedings, Bressanone, Italy.

Fanizzi, N., d'Amato, C., & Esposito, F. (2008a). DL-Foil: Concept learning in description logics. In *Proceedings of the 18th International Conference on Inductive Logic Programming, ILP 2008* (LNAI). Prague, Czech Republic: Springer. (in press).

Fanizzi, N., d'Amato, C., & Esposito, F. (2008b). Conceptual clustering for concept drift and novelty detection. In S. Bechhofer, M. Hauswirth, J. Hoffmann, & M. Koubarakis (Eds.), *Proceedings of the 5th European Semantic Web Conference, ESWC 2008* (LNCS, pp. 318-332). Springer.

Fanizzi, N., Iannone, L., Palmisano, I., & Semeraro, G. (2004). Concept formation in expressive description logics. In J.-F. Boulicaut, F. Esposito, F. Giannotti, & D. Pedreschi (Eds.), *Proceedings of the 15th European Conference on Machine Learning, ECML 2004* (LNAI, pp. 99-113). Springer.

Ghozeil, A., & Fogel, D. B. (1996). Discovering patterns in spatial data using evolutionary programming. In J. R. Koza, D. E. Goldberg, D. B. Fogel, & R. L. Riolo (Eds.), *Genetic Programming 1996: Proceedings of the First Annual Conference* (pp. 521-527). Stanford University, CA, USA: MIT Press.

Goldstone, R., Medin, D., & Halberstadt, J. (1997). Similarity in context. *Memory and Cognition, 25*(2), 237-255.

Halkidi, M., Batistakis, Y., & Vazirgiannis, M. (2001). On clustering validation techniques. *Journal of Intelligent Information Systems, 17*(2-3), 107-145.

Hall, L. O., Özyurt, I. B., & Bezdek, J. C. (1999). Clustering with a genetically optimized approach. *IEEE Transactions on Evolutionary Computation, 3*(2), 103-112.

Hirano, S., & Tsumoto, S. (2005). An indiscernibility-based clustering method. In X. Hu, Q. Liu, A. Skowron, T. Y. Lin, R. Yager, & B. Zhang (Eds.), *2005 IEEE International Conference on Granular Computing* (pp. 468-473). IEEE.

Iannone, L., Palmisano, I., & Fanizzi, N. (2007). An algorithm based on counterfactuals for concept learning in the Semantic Web. *Applied Intelligence, 26*(2), 139-159.

Jain, A. K., Murty, M. N., & Flynn, P. J. (1999). Data clustering: A review. *ACM Computing Surveys, 31*(3), 264-323.

Kaufman, L., & Rousseeuw, P. J. (1990). *Finding groups in data: An introduction to cluster analysis.* John Wiley & Sons.

Kietz, J.-U., & Morik, K. (1994). A polynomial approach to the constructive induction of structural knowledge. *Machine Learning, 14*(2), 193-218.

Kirsten, M., & Wrobel, S. (1998). Relational distance-based clustering. In D. Page (Ed.), *Proceedings of the 8th International Workshop, ILP98* (LNCS, pp. 261-270). Springer.

Lee, C.-Y., & Antonsson, E. K. (2000). Variable length genomes for evolutionary algorithms. In L. Whitley, D. Goldberg, E. Cantú-Paz, L. Spector, I. Parmee, & H.-G. Beyer (Eds.), *Proceedings of the Genetic and Evolutionary Computation Conference, GECCO00* (p. 806). Morgan Kaufmann.

Lehmann, J., & Hitzler, P. (2008a). A refinement operator based learning algorithm for the ALC description logic. In H. Blockeel, J. Ramon, J. Shavlik, & P. Tadepalli (Eds.), *Proceedings of the 17th International Conference on Inductive Logic Programming, ILP2007* (LNCS, pp. 147-160). Springer.

Lehmann, J., & Hitzler, P. (2008b). Foundations of refinement operators for description logics. In H. Blockeel, J. Ramon, J. Shavlik, & P. Tadepalli (Eds.), *Proceedings of the 17th International Conference on Inductive Logic Programming, ILP2007* (LNCS, pp. 161-174). Springer.

Mitchell, T.M. (1997). *Machine learning.* McGraw-Hill.

Nasraoui, O., & Krishnapuram, R. (2002). One step evolutionary mining of context sensitive associations and Web navigation patterns. In *Proceedings of the SIAM Conference on Data Mining,* Arlington, VA (pp. 531-547).

Ng, R., & Han, J. (1994). Efficient and effective clustering method for spatial data mining. In *Proceedings of the 20th Conference on Very Large Databases, VLDB94* (pp. 144-155).

Nienhuys-Cheng, S.-H. (1998). Distances and limits on herbrand interpretations. In D. Page (Ed.), *Proceedings of the 8th International Workshop on Inductive Logic Programming, ILP98* (LNAI, pp. 250-260). Springer.

Pawlak, Z. (1991). *Rough sets: Theoretical aspects of reasoning about data.* Kluwer Academic Publishers.

Sebag, M. (1997). Distance induction in first order logic. In S. Džeroski & N. Lavra (Eds.), *Proceedings of the 7th International Workshop on Inductive Logic Programming, ILP97* (LNAI, pp. 264-272). Springer.

Spinosa, E., Ponce de Leon Ferreira de Carvalho, A., & Gama, J. (2007). OLINDDA: A clusterbased approach for detecting novelty and concept drift in data streams. In *Proceedings of the 22nd Annual ACM Symposium of Applied Computing, SAC2007* (pp. 448-452). Seoul, South Korea: ACM.

Stepp, R. E., & Michalski, R. S. (1986). Conceptual clustering of structured objects: A goal-oriented approach. *Artificial Intelligence, 28*(1), 43-69.

The description logic handbook. (2003). Cambridge University Press.

Widmer, G., & Kubat, M. (1996). Learning in the presence of concept drift and hidden contexts. *Machine Learning, 23*(1), 69-101.

Zezula, P., Amato, G., Dohnal, V., & Batko, M. (2007). *Similarity search--the metric space approach of advances in database systems.* Springer.

ENDNOTES

[1] In relational databases the CWA yields that the absence of some assertion implies that its negation holds.

[2] Each individual can be assumed to be identified by its own URI; however, this is not bound to be a one-to-one mapping.

[3] This aspect has been investigated in cognitive science, for example, see [18]. Sometimes (part of) the context is known and can be supplied as background knowledge. We will not discuss this further, assuming that no such specific knowledge is available.

[4] See [8], § 2.2.4.4, Ex. 2.15

[5] See the Protégé library: http://protege.stanford.edu/plugins/owl/owl-library and the Web site: http://www.cs.put.poznan.pl/alawrynowicz/financial.owl

[6] http://pellet.owldl.com

[7] δ_p is defined $\delta_p(C_i,C_j) := \max\{d_p(C_i,C_j), d_p(C_j,C_i)\}$ where $d_p(C_i,C_j) := \max_{a\in C_i}\{\min_{b\in C_j}\{d_p(a,b)\}\}$

[8] This aims at choosing clusters whose density is not lower than that of the model.

[9] Clusters which are closer to the boundaries of the model are more likely to appear due to a drift occurred in the normal concept. On the other hand, a validated cluster appearing far from the normal concept may represent a novel concept.

This work was previously published in International Journal on Semantic Web & Information Systems, Vol. 4, Issue 3, edited by A. Sheth, pp. 44-67, copyright 2008 by IGI Publishing (an imprint of IGI Global).

Chapter 13
Nested Optional Join for Efficient Evaluation of SPARQL Nested Optional Graph Patterns

Artem Chebotko
University of Texas - Pan American, USA

Shiyong Lu
Wayne State University, USA

ABSTRACT

Relational technology has shown to be very useful for scalable Semantic Web data management. Numerous researchers have proposed to use RDBMSs to store and query voluminous RDF data using SQL and RDF query languages. This chapter studies how RDF queries with the so called well-designed graph patterns and nested optional patterns can be efficiently evaluated in an RDBMS. The authors propose to extend relational algebra with a novel relational operator, nested optional join (NOJ), that is more efficient than left outer join in processing nested optional patterns of well-designed graph patterns. They design three efficient algorithms to implement the new operator in relational databases: (1) nested-loops NOJ algorithm, NL-NOJ, (2) sort-merge NOJ algorithm, SM-NOJ, and (3) simple hash NOJ algorithm, SH-NOJ. Using a real life RDF dataset, the authors demonstrate the efficiency of their algorithms by comparing them with the corresponding left outer join implementations and explore the effect of join selectivity on the performance of these algorithms.

INTRODUCTION

The Semantic Web (Berners-Lee, Hendler, & Lassila, 2001; Shadbolt, Berners-Lee, & Hall, 2006) has recently gained tremendous momentum due to its great potential for providing a common framework that allows data to be shared and reused across application, enterprise, and community boundaries.

Semantic data is represented in Resource Description Framework (RDF) (W3C, 2004a, 2004b), the standard language for annotating resources on the Web, and queried using the SPARQL (W3C, 2008) query language for RDF that has been recently proposed by the World Wide Web Consortium. RDF data is a collection of statements, called *triples*, of the form $<s,p,o>$, where s is a subject, p is a predicate and o is an object, and each triple states the relation between the subject and the object. Such collection

DOI: 10.4018/978-1-60566-992-2.ch013

Copyright © 2010, IGI Global. Copying or distributing in print or electronic forms without written permission of IGI Global is prohibited.

of triples can be represented as a directed graph, in which nodes represent subjects and objects, and edges represent predicates connecting from subject nodes to object nodes. SPARQL allows the specification of triple and graph patterns to be matched over RDF graphs.

Increasing amount of RDF data on the Web drives the need for its efficient and effective management. In this light, numerous researchers (Abadi, Marcus, Madden, & Hollenbach, 2007; Agrawal, Somani, & Xu, 2001; Alexaki, Christophides, Karvounarakis, & Plexousakis, 2001; Beckett & Grant, 2003; Broekstra, Kampman, & Harmelen, 2002; Erling, 2001; Harris & Gibbins, 2003; Ma, Su, Pan, Zhang, & Liu, 2004; Narayanan, Kurc, & Saltz, 2006; Pan & Heflin, 2003; Sintek & Kiesel, 2006; Stoffel, Taylor, & Hendler, 1997; Theoharis, Christophides, & Karvounarakis, 2005; Volz, Oberle, Motik, & Staab, 2003; Wilkinson, 2006; Wilkinson, Sayers, Kuno, & Reynolds, 2003) have proposed to use RDBMSs to store and query RDF data using the SQL and SPARQL query languages. One of the most challenging problems in such an approach is the translation of SPARQL queries into queries formulated in relational algebra and SQL.

An important class of graph patterns that are mostly common in RDF queries in practice is the so called *well-designed* graph patterns (Perez, Arenas, & Gutierrez, 2006a). A well-designed graph pattern gp can contain arbitrary many optional graph patterns that can be nested in each other as in the following equation:

$$gp_1 OPT(gp_2 OPT(gp_3 OPT(...(gp_{n-1} OPT(gp_n))...)))$$
(1)

where each gp_1, gp_2, gp_3, ..., gp_{n-1}, gp_n can be a basic graph pattern (set of triple patterns) or another graph pattern with optional sub-patterns such as (1), OPT indicates an optional graph pattern that follows it, and parenthesis define the order of evaluation. In (1), gp_2, gp_3, ..., gp_1, gp_n

are optional graph patterns, and each gp_i, $i \geq 3$, is a nested optional graph pattern with respect to gp_{i-1}. By the definition of a well-designed graph pattern, the following property for gp holds: for any sub-pattern $(gp_x OPT(gp_y))$ in gp, if a variable $?v$ occurs both outside this sub-pattern and inside gp_y, then $?v$ also occurs in gp_x. The formal semantics of the well-designed graph patterns with nested optional patterns is defined by Perez et al. (2006a) and W3C (2008). Informally, it can be summarized as follows:

- *Basic semantics of optional graph patterns.* The evaluation of an optional graph pattern is not obligated to succeed, and in the case of failure, its variables are unbound. For example, in (1), gp_n does not have to succeed for gp_{n-1} to succeed.
- *Semantics of shared variables in optional graph patterns.* In general, shared variables must be bound to the same values. Variables can be shared among subjects, predicates, objects, and across each other. For example, in (1), if a variable $?v$ occurs both inside gp_1 and gp_2, it must be bound to the same value in both graph patterns.
- *Semantics of nested optional graph patterns.* Before a nested optional graph pattern can succeed, all containing optional graph patterns must have succeeded. For example, in (1), gp_3 corresponds to an optional graph pattern nested inside another optional graph pattern gp_2, and gp_3 can only succeed if gp_2 succeeds.

Therefore, a well-designed graph pattern gp as in (1) can have n-2 nested optional graph sub-patterns gp_3, ..., gp_{n-1}, gp_n, and an efficient evaluation of these nested patterns is very important. While the literature on the SPARQL-to-SQL translation is abundant (see the related work section), a few researches (Chebotko, Lu, Jamil, & Fotouhi, 2006; Cyganiak, 2005) study the translation of RDF queries with nested optional

Figure 1. Sample RDF graph and relational query over the graph

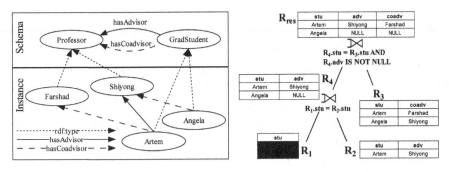

(a) Sample RDF graph   (b) Relational query with LOJs

patterns. In their work, the handling of these three semantics in a relational database relies on the use of the left outer join (LOJ) defined in the relational algebra and SQL: (1) basic semantics of optional graph patterns is captured by a LOJ; (2) semantics of shared variables is treated with the conjunction of equalities of corresponding relational attributes in the LOJ condition; (3) semantics of nested optional graph patterns is preserved by the *NOT NULL* check in the LOJ condition for one of the attributes/variables that correspond to the parent (containing pattern) of a nested pattern. In the following, we present our running example to illustrate the translation of a SPARQL query with a nested optional graph pattern into a relational algebra expression, in which a LOJ is used for implementing nested optional graph patterns; the example motivates the introduction of a new relational operator for a more efficient implementation.

Example 1 (*Sample SPARQL query and its relational equivalent*) Consider the RDF graph presented in Figure 1(a). The graph describes academic relations among professors and graduate students in a university. The RDF schema defines two concepts/classes (*Professor* and *GradStudent*) and two relations/properties (*hasAdvisor* and *hasCoadvisor*). Each relation has the *GradStudent* class as a domain and the *Professor* class as a range. Additionally, two instances of *Professor*, two instances of *GradStudent* and

relations among these instances are defined as shown in the figure.

We design an RDF query that returns (1) every graduate student in the RDF graph; (2) the student's advisor if this information is available; and (3) the student's coadvisor if this information is available and if the student's advisor has been successfully retrieved in the previous step. In other words, the query returns students and as many advisors as possible; there is no point to return a coadvisor if there is even no advisor for a student. The SPARQL representation of the query is as follows:

```
01 SELECT ?stu ?adv ?coadv
02 WHERE {
03 ?stu rdf:type:GradStudent .
/* R1(stu) */
04 OPTIONAL {
05 ?stu:hasAdvisor ?adv . /*
R2(stu,adv) */
06 OPTIONAL {
07 ?stu:hasCoadvisor ?coadv ./*
R3(stu,coadv) */
08 } } }
```

The query has three variables: *?stu* for the student, *?adv* for the advisor, and *?coadv* for the coadvisor. There are two *OPTIONAL* clauses, where the innermost one is the nested *OPTIONAL* clause. The graph pattern in the *WHERE* clause is well-designed and corresponds to the pattern $(gp_1 OPT(gp_2 OPT gp_3))$, where $gp_1 = \{?stu\ rdf{:}type{:}GradStudent\}$, $gp_2 = \{?stu{:}hasAdvisor\ ?adv\}$, and $gp_3 = \{?stu{:}hasCoadvisor\ ?coadv\}$. Variable *?stu* is a shared variable that occurs in gp_1, gp_2, and gp_3.

To translate this SPARQL query into an equivalent relational query, we use our translation strategy (Chebotko et al., 2006) as follows. Matching triples for the triple patterns gp_1, gp_2, and gp_3 are retrieved into relations R_1, R_2, and R_3, respectively. Note that the triple patterns are annotated with the corresponding relations and relational schemas in the SPARQL query above. Then the equivalent relational algebra representation is

$$R_4 = \pi_{R_1.stu,R_2.adv}\left(R_1 =\bowtie_{R_1.stu=R_2.stu} R_2\right),$$

$$R_{res} = \pi_{R_4.stu,R_4.adv,R_3.coadv}\left(R_4 =\bowtie_{R_4.stu=R_3.stu \wedge R_4.adv\ IS\ NOT\ NULL} R_3\right).$$

Each *OPTIONAL* clause corresponds to the left outer join ($=\bowtie$), shared variable *?stu* participates in the join conditions, and the nested *OPTIONAL* implements the *NOT NULL* check on the *adv* attribute to ensure that its parent clause has indeed succeeded. The graphical representation of the relational query is shown in Figure 1(b); the projection operators are not shown for ease of presentation. ◦

The running example motivates our research. The following is our insight to how the LOJ-based query in Figure 1(b) wastes some computations: (1) Based on the result of the first LOJ and the semantics of the nested optional graph pattern, we know that the *NULL* padded tuple (*Angela, NULL*) will also be *NULL* padded in the second LOJ. After all, there is no need for this tuple to participate in the second LOJ condition. (2) On the other hand, we know that the successful match in the tuple (*Artem, Shiyong*) contains no *NULLs*.

There is no need to apply the *NOT NULL* check to this tuple.

In this chapter, we propose to extend relational technology with an innovative relational operator that naturally supports the nested optional pattern semantics of well-designed graph patterns to enable their efficient processing in relational databases. The main contributions of our work include:

- We propose to extend relational databases with a novel relational operator, *nested optional join (NOJ)*, that is more efficient than left outer join in processing nested optional graph patterns of well-designed graph patterns. The computational advantage of NOJ over the currently used LOJ-based implementations comes from the two superior characteristics of NOJ: (1) NOJ allows the processing of the tuples that are guaranteed to be *NULL* padded very efficiently (in linear time) and (2) NOJ does not require the *NOT NULL* check to return correct results. In addition, (3) NOJ can significantly simplify the translation of RDF queries with well-designed graph patterns into relational algebra.

- We design three efficient algorithms to implement the new operator in relational databases: (1) nested-loops NOJ algorithm, *NL-NOJ*, (2) sort-merge NOJ algorithm, *SM-NOJ*, and (3) simple hash NOJ algorithm, *SH-NOJ*.

- Based on a real life RDF dataset, we demonstrate the efficiency of our algorithms by comparing them with the corresponding left outer join implementations. The experimental results are very promising; for RDF query processing with RDBMSs, NOJ is a favorable alternative to the LOJ-based evaluation of nested optional patterns in well-designed graph patterns.

- Based on both our theoretical analysis and empirical study, we give our recommendations for the use of the presented NOJ algorithms depending on the selectivity factor of the join.

This work extends our conference paper (Chebotko, Atay, Lu, & Fotouhi, 2007) in several directions. First, we address the changes in the SPARQL semantics, positioning our work for the evaluation of well-designed graph patterns which are most commonly used in real life RDF queries. Second, we present two new algorithms for nested optional join implementation; namely, a sort-merge NOJ algorithm, *SM-NOJ*, and a simple hash NOJ algorithm, *SH-NOJ*. These algorithms have better time complexity and show better performance on our test queries than our first proposed algorithm *NL-NOJ* (nested-loops NOJ algorithm). Third, we provide extensive details for our conducted experiments, including explanation of datasets, test queries, implementations, and observed results. Fourth, we conduct an additional performance study of the NOJ algorithm behavior with respect to varying join selectivity factor, giving our recommendations on the applicability of the three NOJ algorithms. This study is of high importance, because it suggests which specific algorithm (*NL-NOJ*, *SM-NOJ*, or *SH-NOJ*) should be used for the most efficient evaluation of a nested optional join with a known selectivity factor. Fifth, we implement our algorithm *NL-NOJ* in an existing RDBMS, MySQL, and compare the performance of our test queries evaluated with *NL-NOJ* and with MySQL's nested-loops join algorithm. Finally, we compare the performance of our in-RDBMS NOJ implementation with RDF stores Sesame and Jena.

NESTED OPTIONAL JOIN OPERATOR

In this section, we present our nested optional join operator that is used to evaluate nested optional patterns of well-designed graph patterns in relational databases and highlight its advantages over the left outer join.

The operands of NOJ are *twin relations* instead of conventional relations. The notion of twin relation is introduced as follows.

Definition 2 (*Twin Relation*) A twin relation, denoted as (R_b, R_o), is a pair of conventional relations with identical relational schemas and disjoint sets of tuples. The schema of a twin relation is denoted as $\xi(R_b, R_o)$. R_b with the schema $\xi(R_b, R_o)$ is called a *base relation* and R_o with the schema $\xi(R_b, R_o)$ is called an *optional relation*. A distinguished tuple $n_{\xi(R_b, R_o)}$ is defined as a tuple of $\xi(R_b, R_o)$ in which each attribute takes a *NULL* value. ⬦

Intuitively, a base relation is used to store tuples that have a potential to satisfy a join condition of a nested optional join. An optional relation is used to store tuples that are guaranteed to fail a join condition of a nested optional join. We incorporate the twin relation into the relational algebra by introducing the following additional operators, ⊎ and ‡, such that

- ⊎$(R_b, R_o) = R_b \cup R_o$, and
- ‡$(R) = (R, \varphi)$, where ϕ is an instance of empty relation with the same relational schema of R.

Note that ‡ is not a reversed operator of ⊎, because ‡$(⊎(R_b, R_o)) \neq (R_b, R_o)$ in general.

We also extend the *projection* and *selection* operators to a twin relation as $\pi[(R_b, R_o)] = (\pi[R_b], \pi[R_o])$ and $\sigma[(R_b, R_o)] = (\sigma[R_b], \sigma[R_o])$, respectively. The definition of a complete algebra for a twin relation is not our focus in this work; π and σ are sufficient for our running example and experimental study and, as we believe, for most SPARQL-to-SQL translations.

In the following, we define a novel relational operator, *nested optional join*, using the tuple calculus.

Figure 2. Nested optional join

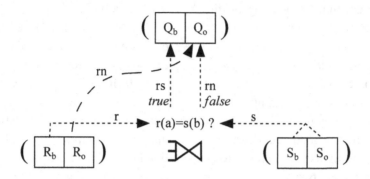

Definition 3 (*Nested Optional Join*) A nested optional join of two twin relations, denoted as $\equiv\bowtie$, yields a twin relation, such that $(R_b,R_o)\equiv\bowtie_{r(a)=s(b)}(S_b,S_o)=(Q_b,Q_o)$, where $Q_b=\{t|t=rs\wedge r\in R_b\wedge(s\in S_b\vee s\in S_o)\wedge r(a)=s(b)\}$ and $Q_o=\{t|t=rn\wedge(r\in R_o\vee(r\in R_b\wedge\neg\exists s[(s\in S_b\vee s\in S_o)\wedge r(a)=s(b)]))\}$, where $r(a)=s(b)$ is a join predicate, $r(a)\subseteq\xi(R_b,R_o)$ and $s(b)\subseteq\xi(S_b,S_o)$ are join attributes, $n=n_{\xi(S_b,S_o)}$. ⋄

In other words, the result base relation Q_b contains tuples t made up of two parts, r and s, where r must be a tuple in relation R_b and s must be a tuple in S_b or S_o. In each tuple t, the values of the join attributes $t(a)$, belonging to r, are identical in all respects to the values of join attributes $t(b)$, belonging to s. The result optional relation Q_o contains tuples t made up of two parts, r and n, where r must be a tuple in R_o with no other conditions enforced, or r must be a tuple in R_b and there must not exist a tuple s in S_b or S_o that can be combined with r based on the predicate $r(a)=s(b)$.

The graphical illustration of the NOJ operator is shown in Figure 2. Note how well it emphasizes one of the advantages of NOJ: the flow of tuples from R_o to Q_o bypasses the join condition and does not interact with tuples from any other relation. Obviously, the behavior of this flow can be implemented to have linear time performance in the worst case – the property that is, in general, not available in the LOJ implementations. The

second important advantage of NOJ – no need for the *NOT NULL* check – is discussed in the following example that describes the translation of our sample SPARQL query into a relational algebra expression with our extensions.

Example 4 (*Evaluation of the sample SPARQL query using NOJs*) We use the same RDF graph presented in Figure 1(a) and the SPARQL query described in Example 1. The translation strategy is similar to the one illustrated in Example 1 except that we use NOJ instead of LOJ. Matching triples for the triple patterns *?stu rdf:type:GradStudent*, *?stu:hasAdvisor ?adv*, and *?stu:hasCoadvisor ?coadv* are retrieved into relations R_1, R_2, and R_3, respectively. Then the equivalent relational algebra representation using NOJ is

$$(R_b^1,R_o^1)=\ddagger(R_1),(R_b^2,R_o^2)=\ddagger(R_2),(R_b^3,R_o^3)=\ddagger(R_3)$$

$$(R_b^4,R_o^4)=\pi_{(R_b^1,R_o^1).stu,(R_b^2,R_o^2).adv}((R_b^1,R_o^1)\equiv\bowtie_{(R_b^1,R_o^1).stu=(R_b^2,R_o^2).stu}(R_b^2,R_o^2))$$

$$(R_b^{res},R_o^{res})=\pi_{(R_b^4,R_o^4).stu,(R_b^4,R_o^4).adv,(R_b^3,R_o^3).coadv}((R_b^4,R_o^4)\equiv\bowtie_{(R_b^4,R_o^4).stu=(R_b^3,R_o^3).stu}(R_b^3,R_o^3)),$$

$$R_{res}=\uplus(R_b^{res},R_o^{res}).$$

The graphical representation of the relational query is shown in Figure 3; the conversion and

Figure 3. Nested optional join based evaluation of the SPARQL query in Example 1

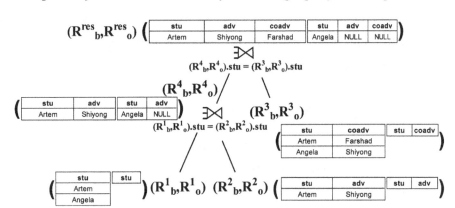

projection operators are not shown for ease of presentation. Note that this query does not contain the *NOT NULL* check, because all the tuples that have not succeeded in the first join are padded with *NULL* values and stored into the optional relation R_o^4; the tuples of R_o^4 bypass the second join condition and are copied directly to R_o^{res} with additional *NULL*-padding. ◇

Therefore, NOJ is superior to LOJ when we apply them to translate SPARQL nested optional patterns of well-designed graph patterns to relational queries. The main advantages of NOJ are (1) NOJ allows the processing of the tuples that are guaranteed to be *NULL* padded very efficiently (in linear time), (2) NOJ does not require the *NOT NULL* check to return correct results, and (3) NOJ can significantly simplify the translation of RDF queries with well-designed graph patterns into relational algebra, eliminating the need to choose a relational attribute for the *NOT NULL* check and, in some cases (Chebotko et al., 2006) when such an attribute cannot be chosen from available ones, the need to introduce a new variable or even a new triple pattern into a SPARQL query. Our performance study showed that these advantages bring substantial speedup to the query evaluation.

NESTED OPTIONAL JOIN ALGORITHMS

Previously, we defined NOJ through the tuple calculus, but it is also possible to express the NOJ result relations using standard operators of the relational algebra: $Q_b = R_b \bowtie_{r(a)=s(b)} (S_b \cup s_o)$ and $Q_o = R_o \cup [(R_b \bowtie_{r(a)=s(b)} (S_b \cup s_o)) - (R_b \bowtie_{r(a)=s(b)} (S_b \cup s_o))]$. However, it should be evident that this direct translation will be inefficient if implemented. Therefore, in this section, we design our own algorithms to implement NOJ in a relational database. Our algorithms, *NL-NOJ*, *SM-NOJ*, and *SH-NOJ*, employ the classic methods used to implement relational joins: nested-loops, sort-merge, and hash-based join methods, respectively.

Nested-Loops Nested Optional Join Algorithm

The simplest algorithm to perform the NOJ operation is the nested-loops NOJ algorithm, denoted as *NL-NOJ* (see Figure 4). The algorithm is self-descriptive. For each tuple r in relation R_b, twin relation (S_b, S_o) is scanned (lines 05-07) and tuples satisfying the join condition are merged into Q_b (lines 08-11). Tuples in R_b that have no matching tuples in (S_b, S_o) are *NULL* padded and placed in

Figure 4. Algorithm NL-NOJ

```
01   Algorithm: NL-NOJ
02   Input: twin relations (R_b, R_o) and (S_b, S_o)
03   Output: twin relation (Q_b, Q_o) = (R_b, R_o) ⋈_{r(a)=s(b)} (S_b, S_o)
04   Begin
05     For each tuple r ∈ R_b do
06       pad = true
07       For each tuple s ∈ (S_b, S_o) do
08         If r(a) = s(b) then
09           place tuple rs in relation Q_b
10           pad = false
11         End If
12       End For
13       If pad then
14         place tuple rn_{ξ(S_b,S_o)} in relation Q_o
15       End If
16     End For
17     For each tuple r ∈ R_o do
18       place tuple rn_{ξ(S_b,S_o)} in relation Q_o
19     End For
20     Return (Q_b, Q_o)
21   End Algorithm
```

Q_o (lines 13-15). Finally (lines 17-19), tuples in R_o are *NULL* padded and placed in Q_o.

The results of our complexity and applicability analysis are

- *NL-NOJ*   *complexity*: $\Theta(|R_b| \times (|S_b| + |S_o|) + |R_o|)$.
- *NL-NOJ applicability*: NOJs with high selectivity factors (see our performance study for more details).

The comprehensive analysis of the performance and applicability of the nested-loops join method is presented by Mishra and Eich (1992). In the join processing literature, there is a number of optimizations on the nested-loops join method that are also applicable to *NL-NOJ*: e.g., the block nested-loops join method (Elmasri & Navathe,

2004; Kifer, Bernstein, & Lewis, 2006) and "rocking" the inner relation optimization (Kim, 1980) that reduce the number of I/O operations.

Sort-Merge Nested Optional Join Algorithm

The sort-merge NOJ algorithm, *SM-NOJ*, is shown in Figure 5. *SM-NOJ* is executed in three stages. First (lines 05-07), relations R_b and S are sorted on the join attributes, where S contains all tuples of (S_b, S_o). Second (lines 08-36), R_b and S are scanned in the order of the join attributes and tuples satisfying the join condition are merged into Q_b; tuples in R_b that have no matching tuples in S are *NULL* padded and placed in Q_b. The scanning employs backtracking (lines 22-34), such that if r in R_b matches consecutive tuples in

Figure 5. Algorithm SM-NOJ

```
01   Algorithm: SM-NOJ
02   Input: twin relations (Rb, Ro) and (Sb, So)
03   Output: twin relation (Qb, Qo) = (Rb, Ro) ⋈r(a)=s(b) (Sb, So)
04   Begin
05     Sort Rb on r(a)
06     Let S = Sb ∪ So
07     Sort S on s(b)
08     r = first tuple of Rb
09     s = first tuple of S
10     While r ≠ EOF do
11       If s = EOF then
12         place tuple rnξ(Sb,So) in relation Qo
13         r = next tuple after r of Rb
14       Else
15         While r ≠ EOF and r(a) < s(b) do
16           place tuple rnξ(Sb,So) in relation Qo
17           r = next tuple after r of Rb
18         End While
19         While s ≠ EOF and s(b) < r(a) do
20           s = next tuple after s of S
21         End While
22         back = false
23         If r ≠ EOF and r(a) = s(b) then
24           backtrack = s
25           While s ≠ EOF and r(a) = s(b) do
26             place tuple rs in relation Qb
27             s = next tuple after s of S
28           End While
29           If r and next tuple after r of Rb have the same values of r(a) then
30             back = true
31           End If
32           r = next tuple after r of Rb
33         End If
34         If back then s = backtrack End If
35       End If
36     End While
37     For each tuple r ∈ Ro do
38       place tuple rnξ(Sb,So) in relation Qo
39     End For
40     Return (Qb, Qo)
41   End Algorithm
```

S, then *backtrack* remembers the first matching tuple (line 24), and if *r* and the next tuple after *r* have the same values of the join attributes (lines 29-31), then the scanning of *S* resumes from the tuple restored from *backtrack* (line 34). At the final, third stage (lines 37-39), the tuples in R_o are *NULL* padded and placed in Q_o.

The results of our complexity and applicability analysis are

- *SM-NOJ complexity*: $\Omega(|R_b|\times log|R_b|+(|S_b|+|S_o|)\times log(|S_b|+|S_o|)+|R_o|)$, $O(|R_b|\times(|S_b|+|S_o|)+|R_o|)$. The best case performance is achieved when there is no backtracking or, in other words, either R_b or *S* has no multiple tuples, such that these tuples have the same values of the join attributes and have at least one matching tuple in *S* or R_b, respectively. The more backtracking is involved, the worse the performance of *SM-NOJ*. The worst case performance occurs when all tuples in both R_b and *S* have the same values of the join attributes, such that for any $r\in R_b$ and $s\in S$, $r(a)=s(b)$ is always satisfied. In the cases close to the worst case, SM-NOJ does comparable number of computations to those of *NL-NOJ* and, additionally, sorts the relations and requires some extra operations that implement the backtracking mechanism; in the worst case, the relations are already sorted.
- *SM-NOJ applicability*: *SM-NOJ* is the best choice when *NL-NOJ* or *SH-NOJ* is not selected as the best performer; NOJs with median selectivity factors (see our performance study for more details).

The comprehensive analysis of the performance and applicability of the sort-merge join method is presented by Mishra and Eich (1992).

Simple Hash Nested Optional Join Algorithm

The simple hash NOJ algorithm, *SH-NOJ*, is presented in Figure 6. The algorithm uses a hash function *h* to hash the tuples of the twin relation (S_b, S_o) to a hash table *H* based on the values of the join attributes (lines 05-09). A perfect hash function hashes tuples with different values of the join attributes to different buckets, however in practice, such tuples may end up in the same bucket. Then for each tuple *r* in R_b, the hash value of the join attributes is computed using the same hash function *h* (line 12). If *r* hashes to a non-empty bucket of *H*, then all the tuples in the bucket are compared with *r* and merged to Q_b if the join condition is satisfied (lines 12-15) or *NULL* padded and copied to Q_o (lines 16-18) otherwise. Finally, the tuples in R_o are *NULL* padded and placed in Q_o (lines 20-22).

Note that the hash table should ideally be created for the (twin) relation with the fewest distinct values of the join attributes. When this information is not available, the hash table is usually created for the smallest of the (twin) relations R_b and (S_b, S_o) (Mishra & Eich, 1992).

The results of our complexity and applicability analysis are

- *SH-NOJ complexity*: $\Omega(|R_b|+|R_o|+|S_b|+|S_o|)$, $O(|R_b|\times(|S_b|+|S_o|)+|R_o|)$, depends on the efficiency of a hash function *h*. The linear performance is achieved for joins with empty results or joins with low selectivity factors. The higher the selectivity is, the slower *SH-NOJ* performs. In the worse case, when all tuples of R_b and (S_b, S_o) hash to the same bucket of the hash table, the algorithm has the quadratic performance.
- *SH-NOJ applicability*: NOJs with low selectivity factors (see our performance study for more details).

Figure 6. Algorithm SH-NOJ

```
01  Algorithm: SH-NOJ
02  Input: twin relations (R_b, R_o) and (S_b, S_o)
03  Output: twin relation (Q_b, Q_o) = (R_b, R_o) ⋈_{r(a)=s(b)} (S_b, S_o)
04  Begin
05    Let h be a hash function and H be an empty hash table
06    For each tuple s ∈ (S_b, S_o) do
07      hash on join attributes s(b) : h(s(b))
08      place s in the corresponding bucket of hash table H : H{h(s(b))} += s
09    End For
10    For each tuple r ∈ R_b do
11      pad = true
12      For each tuple s ∈ H{h(r(a))} and r(a) = s(b) do
13        place tuple rs in relation Q_b
14        pad = false
15      End For
16      If pad then
17        place tuple rn_{ξ(S_b,S_o)} in relation Q_o
18      End If
19    End For
20    For each tuple r ∈ R_o do
21      place tuple rn_{ξ(S_b,S_o)} in relation Q_o
22    End For
23    Return (Q_b, Q_o)
24  End Algorithm
```

The comprehensive analysis of the performance and applicability of the simple hash join method is presented by Mishra and Eich (1992). The simple hash join method (DeWitt et al., 1984) that is used to implement *SH-NOJ* is not the only hash-based join method that is found in the join processing literature. Other methods, such as simple hash-partitioned join, GRACE hash join, hybrid hash join, and hashed loops join (DeWitt & Gerber, 1985; Gerber, 1986; Lu, Tan, & Shan, 1990), can be also adapted to perform a hash-based NOJ.

PERFORMANCE STUDY

This section reports the performance experiments conducted using the NOJ algorithms coupled with an in-memory relational database and off-the-shelf RDBMS MySQL. The performance of the NOJ algorithms is compared with the performance of the corresponding LOJ-based implementations, as well as with existing RDF stores, and the behavior of the NOJ algorithms with respect to the NOJ selectivity factor is explored.

Figure 7. Simplified WordNet ontology

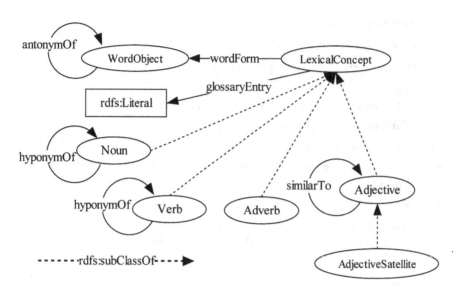

Experimental Setup

For the first five experiments, we used our in-memory relational database. We implemented in-memory representations of a relation and a twin relation, such that each relation was represented by a doubly-linked list of tuples, where each tuple corresponded to an array of pointers to attribute data values, and each twin relation was represented by pointers to two conventional relations. The memory to store relations and their tuples was allocated dynamically in the heap.

Our algorithms *NL-NOJ*, *SM-NOJ*, and *SH-NOJ* were implemented in C++. To compare the performance of queries evaluated with our algorithms and corresponding left outer join algorithms, we implemented nested-loops LOJ (*NL-LOJ*), sort-merge LOJ (*SM-LOJ*), and simple hash LOJ (*SH-LOJ*) algorithms (see, e.g., (Mishra & Eich, 1992)).

For the last two experiments, that required implementing NOJ in an RDBMS, we used MySQL 5.0. MySQL was selected because it is currently the most popular open source database system. For the evaluation of left outer joins, MySQL employed an optimized variation of a

nested-loops join algorithm, which we denoted as *NL-LOJ-MySQL*. In particular, nested joins of multiple relations were conducted concurrently, such that if *k* relations were joined, the join algorithm used *k* nested loops to compute one resulting tuple at a time (MySQL, 2008). Given a query with nested LOJs, MySQL did not perform any join reordering, but used B^+ tree indexes whenever applicable.

Our algorithm *NL-NOJ* was implemented within the MySQL relational engine. We denoted this implementation as *NL-NOJ-MySQL* and compared its performance to *NL-LOJ-MySQL* using our test queries. To keep with the spirit of conventional relational join algorithms, *NL-NOJ-MySQL* was only passed two names of relations, *R* and *S*, which served as a prefix to the names of the to-be-joined twin relations (R_b, R_o) and (S_b, S_o). For the very first (not nested) join in a query, when only conventional relations were available, $R_b = R$ and $S_b = S$, while R_o and S_o were considered to be empty. Even though each join result was a twin relation, this relation was represented by a single name prefix. Finally, the result of the last join in a query was combined into a single output relation.

Table 1. Property and resource statistics of WordNet

Property	Count		Resource	Count
type	251,726		WordObject	140,470
wordForm	195,802		Noun	75,804
glossaryEntry	111,223		Verb	13,214
hyponymOf	90,267		AdjectiveSatellite	11,231
similarTo	22,494		Adjective	7,345
antonymOf	7,115		Adverb	3,629
Others	36,225		*Others*	33
Total	714,852		**Total**	251,726

This way, we were able to completely hide twin relations outside of a query.

The experiments were conducted on the PC with one 2.4 GHz Pentium IV CPU and 1024 MB of main memory operated by MS Windows XP Professional.

The timings reported below are the mean result from five or more trials with warm caches.

Dataset

We conducted the experiments using the OWL representation of WordNet (Ciorascu, 2003), a lexical database for the English language, which organizes English words into synonym sets according to part of speech (e.g., noun, verb, etc.) and enumerates linguistic relations between these sets. In the *WordNet.OWL*, each part of speech is modeled as an *owl:Class*, and each linguistic relation is modeled as an *owl:ObjectProperty*, *owl:DatatypeProperty*, *owl:TransitiveProperty*, *owl:ObjectProperty*, or *owl:SymmetricProperty*. The simplified WordNet ontology is illustrated in Figure 7. The figure does not include some classes (e.g., *wn:Nouns_and_Verbs*) and properties (e.g., *wn:mMeronym*) that are not essential for the understanding of the dataset and the experiments.

The relevant statistics for the WordNet dataset is shown in Table 1. For example, *WordNet. OWL* contains 251,726 triples involving *rdf:type*

as the predicate, and 140,470 of them have *wn:WordObject* as the object.

Relational Storage of RDF Data

We stored the WordNet dataset into our in-memory relational database using *property relations*, where a property relation, e.g., *p(s,o)*, was created for each property *p* in the ontology and stored subjects *s* and objects *o* related by this property in the RDF dataset.

To store the WordNet dataset into MySQL, we employed our relational RDF store *RDF-Prov* (Chebotko, Fei, Lin, Lu, & Fotouhi, 2007; Chebotko, Fei, Lu, & Fotouhi, 2007). Based on the WordNet ontology, *RDFProv* generated a database schema, shredded RDF triples into tuples, and populated the relations. While *RDFProv* generated several kinds of relations, all the joins in our experiments were performed on property relations. In addition, *RDFProv* created B$^+$ tree indexes on every relational attribute of each property relation.

Test Queries

We chose 14 SPARQL queries to evaluate in our experiments based on the following criterion: (1) queries should contain well-designed graph patterns; (2) most queries should have nested optional graph patterns; (3) the input, intermediate,

Table 2. WordNet test queries

#	Query
Q1	W{?a rdf:type:Adjective O{?a:similarTo ?b}}
Q2	W{?a rdf:type ?b O{?c:wordForm ?a}}
Q3	W{?a rdf:type ?b O{?c:wordForm ?a O{?c:glossaryEntry ?d}}}
Q4	W{?a rdf:type ?b O{?c:wordForm ?a O{?c:glossaryEntry ?d O{?c:hyponymOf ?e}}}}
Q5	W{?n1:hyponymOf ?n2 O{?n2:hyponymOf ?n3 O{?n3:hyponymOf ?n4}}}
Q6	W{?n1:hyponymOf ?n2 O{?n2:hyponymOf ?n3 O{?n3:hyponymOf ?n4 O{?n4:hyponymOf ?n5 O{?n5:hyponymOf ?n6 O{?n6:hyponymOf ?n7}}}}}}
Q7	W{?n1 rdf:type ?t O{?n1:hyponymOf ?n2 O{?n2:hyponymOf ?n3 O{?n3:hyponymOf ?n4 O{?n4:hyponymOf ?n5 O{?n5:hyponymOf ?n6 O{?n6:hyponymOf ?n7}}}}}}}
Q8	Same as Q1, except ?b is substituted with:301947487
Q9	Same as Q2, except ?c is substituted with:100283103
Q10	Same as Q3, except all the occurrences of ?c are substituted with:100283103
Q11	Same as Q4, except all the occurrences of ?c are substituted with:100283103
Q12	Same as Q5, except all the occurrences of ?n3 are substituted with:100283103
Q13	Same as Q6, except all the occurrences of ?n3 are substituted with:100283103
Q14	Same as Q7, except all the occurrences of ?n2 are substituted with:100283226

and output (twin) relations involved in the query evaluation should fit into the main memory; and (4) some queries should have common patterns to reveal performance changes with increasing complexity of the queries.

The test queries are listed in Table 2, where W stands for *WHERE* and O stands for *OPTIONAL*. The SPARQL *SELECT* clause is omitted for brevity, and the projection includes all distinct variables of the query. The relevant characteristics of the test queries, such as the number of required joins (either nested optional or left outer joins) and the cardinality of participating twin relations (input, intermediate, output), are shown in Table 3. The cardinalities are presented for twin relations as ($Cardinality_b$; $Cardinality_o$); the corresponding cardinalities of conventional relations that participate in the left outer joins can be easily derived as $Cardinality_b + Cardinality_o$.

Q1 is interesting because the cardinalities of participating (twin) relations are relatively small. Both Q1 and Q2 have only one optional graph pattern and therefore require single join. This implies that the nested optional join has no advantages over the left outer join in Q1 and Q2, since there are no nested optional patterns in the queries. Queries Q2-Q4 and similarly Q5-Q7 are related and can be derived from each other. Q7 stands out from Q6 and Q5 in considerably larger values of $Cardinality_o$ in the intermediate twin relations. Queries Q8-Q14 resemble corresponding queries Q1-Q7, but substitute all the occurrences of one of the variables with a Uniform Resource Locator (URL). While Q1-Q7 involve quite expensive joins, Q8-Q14 are more specific and, in our setting, can take an advantage of database indexes. In addition, Q8-Q14 achieve the effect that all intermediate and output twin relations contain only a few tuples in their base relations, while optional relations are large.

An important characteristic of the test queries is that they only involve joins, whose selectivity factors are less than 0.0002 and, for most joins, are less than 0.00002. Join selectivity factor (JSF) is a

Table 3. Characteristics of the test queries

Query	#	Twin relation cardinality: (Cardinality$_b$; Cardinality$_o$)		
#	Joins	Input	Intermediate	Output
Q1	1	(7,345; 0) (22,494; 0)	N/A	(11,249; 4,653)
Q2	1	(251,726; 0) (195,802; 0)	N/A	(195,803; 111,255)
Q3	2	(251,726; 0) (195,802; 0) (111,223; 0)	(195,803; 111,255)	(195,803; 111,255)
Q4	3	(251,726; 0) (195,802; 0) (111,223; 0) (90,267; 0)	(195,803; 111,255) (195,803; 111,255)	(161,247; 149,656)
Q5	2	(90,267; 0) (90,267; 0) (90,267; 0)	(89,220; 3,416)	(88,213; 8,591)
Q6	5	(90,267; 0) (90,267; 0) (90,267; 0) (90,267; 0) (90,267; 0) (90,267; 0)	(89,220; 3,416) (88,213; 8,591) (86,323; 15,872) (81,263; 27,274)	(67,788; 45,800)
Q7	6	(251,726; 0) (90,267; 0) (90,267; 0) (90,267; 0) (90,267; 0) (90,267; 0) (90,267; 0)	(90,267; 163,343) (89,220; 166,759) (88,213; 171,934) (86,323; 179,215) (81,263; 190,617)	(67,788; 209,143)
Q8	1	Same as for Q1	N/A	(1; 7,344)
Q9	1	Same as for Q2	N/A	(2; 251,724)
Q10	2	Same as for Q3	(2; 251,724)	(2; 251,724)
Q11	3	Same as for Q4	(2; 251,724) (2; 251,724)	(2; 251,724)
Q12	2	Same as for Q5	(1; 90,266)	(1; 90,266)
Q13	5	Same as for Q6	(1; 90,266) (1; 90,266) (1; 90,266) (1; 90,266)	(1; 90,266)
Q14	6	Same as for Q7	(1; 253,609) (1; 253,609) (1; 253,609) (1; 253,609) (1; 253,609)	(1; 253,609)

factor to represent the ratio of the cardinality of a join result to the cross product of the cardinalities of the two join (twin) relations. The reason why we chose queries with only joins with low selectivity factors is that the result of a join should fit into the main memory. We use a different dataset to explore the effect of join selectivity on the performance of our algorithms.

To better understand how our test SPARQL queries are translated into relational algebra and SQL, and evaluated by the relational engine in our experiments, we provide the detailed description of the Q3 evaluation in the following example.

Example 5 (*Q3 translation and evaluation in our experiments*) Given the SPARQL query (see also Table 2)

```
01 SELECT ?a ?b ?c ?d
02 WHERE {
03 ?a rdf:type ?b . /*
R1(a1,a2,a3) */
04 OPTIONAL {
05 ?c:wordForm ?a . /*
R2(a1,a2,a3) */
06 OPTIONAL {
07 ?c:glossaryEntry ?d ./*
R3(a1,a2,a3) */
08 } } }
```

we perform the following operations to evaluate this query in our in-memory database:

Figure 8. Evaluation of query Q3. (a) NOJ-based evaluation (b) LOJ-based evaluation

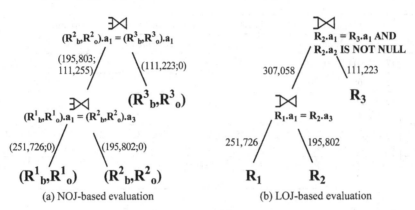

(a) NOJ-based evaluation   (b) LOJ-based evaluation

- *Query preparation.* All triple patterns in the query, *?a rdf:type ?b*, *?c:wordForm ?a* and *?c:glossaryEntry ?d*, are evaluated and the results are stored into the input (initial) relations, R_1, R_2, and R_3, respectively. The schema of each input relation has three attributes, denoted as a_1, a_2, and a_3, that correspond to a subject, a predicate and an object of a matching triple. For instance, $R_1.a_2$ always stores the value *rdf:type*, since all matching triples have this value as a predicate. The cardinalities of the input relations (see Table 3) are $|R_1|=251,726$, $|R_2|=195,802$, and $|R_3|=111,223$. The corresponding twin relations are computed as $(R_b^1,R_o^1) = \ddagger(R_1)$, $(R_b^2,R_o^2) = \ddagger(R_2)$, and $(R_b^3,R_o^3) = \ddagger(R_3)$, where $R_b^1 = R_1$, $R_b^2 = R_2$, $R_b^3 = R_3$, and R_o^1, R_o^2, R_o^3 are empty relations.

- *Query evaluation.* Each *OPTIONAL* clause of the query is translated into the NOJ or LOJ, such that the translation consistently uses one of the joins. The NOJ-based evaluation of Q3 is illustrated in Figure 8(a), and the LOJ-based evaluation – in Figure 8(b). In the figures, the edges are annotated with the cardinalities of the corresponding (twin) relations. Note that a LOJ that corresponds to a non-nested *OPTIONAL* has no *NOT NULL* check, while any LOJ that

corresponds to a nested *OPTIONAL* has such a check; a NOJ never requires this check.

For the in-RDBMS evaluation of Q3, the SPARQL query is translated into SQL. An equivalent SQL query that uses left outer joins is as follows:

```
01 Select * From
02 (Select t1.a as a, t1.b as b,
t2.c as c From
03 (Select s as a, o as b From
rdf_type) t1
04 Left Outer Join
05 (Select s as c, o as a From
rdf_wordForm) t2
06 On (t1.a=t2.a)
07) t3
08 Left Outer Join
09 (Select s as c, o as d From
rdf_glossaryEntry) t4
10 On (t3.c=t4.c And t3.a Is Not
Null)
```
◊

Further details on the translation of SPARQL queries into relational algebra and SQL can be found in the reports of Chebotko et al. (2006) and Cyganiak (2005). The description of the da-

Figure 9. In-memory evaluation of the NOJ and LOJ algorithms using the WordNet test queries. (a) Comparison of NL-NOJ and NL-LOJ (b) Comparison of SM-NOJ and SM-LOJ (c) Comparison of SH-NOJ and SH-LOJ (d) Comparison of SH-NOJ, SM-NOJ, and NL-NOJ

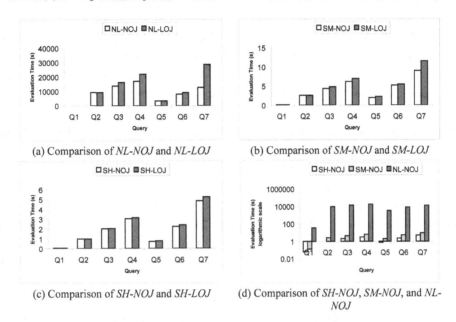

(a) Comparison of *NL-NOJ* and *NL-LOJ*

(b) Comparison of *SM-NOJ* and *SM-LOJ*

(c) Comparison of *SH-NOJ* and *SH-LOJ*

(d) Comparison of *SH-NOJ*, *SM-NOJ*, and *NL-NOJ*

Experiment I: Comparison of NL-NOJ and NL-LOJ

tabase schema generated by *RDFProv* in RDBMS MySQL can be found in reports of Chebotko, Fei, Lin, et al. (2007) and Chebotko, Fei, Lu, and Fotouhi (2007).

Figure 9(a) shows the in-memory evaluation time of queries Q1-Q7 using algorithms *NL-NOJ* and *NL-LOJ*. *NL-NOJ* significantly outperformed *NL-LOJ* for all queries, except for Q1 and Q2; however, the overall performance of these algorithms on the test queries was not satisfactory. For example, for the quite simple Q3, the *NL-NOJ* based evaluation took 13,755s and the *NL-LOJ* based evaluation took 16,262s. These algorithms are to be used for joins with high selectivity factors as we show later in this section.

The *NL-NOJ* and *NL-LOJ* performance for individual test queries is elaborated in the following. Query Q1 was evaluated in 34s by both

algorithms. The algorithms showed similar performance for Q1 and Q2, since these queries had no nested *OPTIONAL*s, and therefore *NL-NOJ* had no advantage over *NL-LOJ*. Queries Q3-Q7 (except perhaps Q5) showed substantial advantage of *NL-NOJ* over *NL-LOJ*. *NL-NOJ* was slightly faster (54s difference) than *NL-LOJ* for Q5, since the $Cardinality_o$ of the intermediate twin relation (see Table 3) was not significant. The *NL-NOJ* based evaluation of Q7 was roughly two times faster than the corresponding *NL-LOJ* based evaluation; the reason was in the large $Cardinality_o$ of the intermediate twin relations and relatively large number of performed joins that additionally required the *NOT NULL* check for the LOJ-based evaluation.

Experiment II: Comparison of SM-NOJ and SM-LOJ

Figure 9(b) shows the in-memory evaluation time of queries Q1-Q7 using algorithms *SM-NOJ* and

SM-LOJ. *SM-NOJ* outperformed *SM-LOJ* for all queries, except for Q1 and Q2. The performance difference between *SM-NOJ* and *SM-LOJ* was relatively smaller than the corresponding difference between *NL-NOJ* and *NL-LOJ* (e.g., see Q7), because the sort-merge implementations have better lower bound than the corresponding nested-loops implementations, and the *SM-NOJ* and *SM-LOJ* performance is closer to the best case performance for joins with low selectivity factors.

The discussion of the algorithm performance for individual test queries is similar to the one provided in Experiment I, except that query Q1 was evaluated in 0.12s by both algorithms.

Experiment III: Comparison of SH-NOJ and SH-LOJ

Figure 9(c) shows the in-memory evaluation time of queries Q1-Q7 using algorithms *SH-NOJ* and *SH-LOJ*. Although the time difference between *SH-NOJ* and *SH-LOJ* for most test queries may seem insignificant (3-8%), since the algorithms behave close to the linear lower bound for joins with low selectivity factors, the join processing that involves I/O operations can make this difference substantial.

The discussion of the algorithm performance for individual test queries is similar to the one provided in Experiment I, except that query Q1 was evaluated in 0.06s by both algorithms.

Experiment IV: Comparison of SH-NOJ, SM-NOJ, and NL-NOJ

Figure 9(d) shows the in-memory evaluation time of queries Q1-Q7 using algorithms *SH-NOJ*, *SM-NOJ*, and *NL-NOJ*. In the figure, the time axis has a logarithmic scale. For the WordNet test queries that involved only joins with low selectivity factors, *SH-NOJ* and *SM-NOJ* outperformed *NL-NOJ* in roughly three orders of magnitude. The *SH-NOJ*

based evaluation showed to be roughly twice as fast as the *SM-NOJ* evaluation. The observed trends are implied by the theoretical analysis of the algorithms for joins with low selectivity factors: *SH-NOJ* behaves close to the linear lower bound $\Omega(n)$; *SM-NOJ* behaves close to the lower bound $\Omega(n \log n)$; and *NL-NOJ* has the quadratic lower bound $\Omega(n^2)$.

Experiment V: Effect of Join Selectivity on the NOJ Algorithm Performance

To explore the effect of join selectivity on the NOJ algorithm performance, we evaluated a number of joins on artificially generated twin relations. In this experiment, we fixed the cardinalities of participating twin relations to (10,000; 0) and varied the join selectivity factor. Join selectivity factor (JSF) is a factor to represent the ratio of the cardinality of a join result to the cross product of the cardinalities of the two join (twin) relations. For the nested optional join of twin relations, we define JSF as

$$JSF = |(R_b, R_o) \equiv \bowtie (S_b, S_o)| / [|(R_b, R_o)| \times |(S_b, S_o)|]$$

where $|(X_b, X_o)|$ means the cardinality of twin relation (X_b, X_o) and $|(X_b, X_o)| = |X_b| + |X_o|$.

Note that, in this experiment, we did not materialize the output twin relations, because they did not fit into the main memory in case of joins with high selectivity factors. Our algorithm implementations allocated required memory for each output tuple, assigned attribute values of the tuple and deallocated the tuple memory without inserting it into the output relation.

Figure 10 shows the effect of join selectivity on the performance of *SH-NOJ*, *SM-NOJ*, and *NL-NOJ*. Figures 10(a) and 10(b) zoom in to the performance curves on the JSF intervals of 0.0001 $\leq$ JSF $\leq$ 0.005 and 0.005 $\leq$ JSF $\leq$ 0.01, respectively; Figure 10(c) is for the larger interval of 0.0001

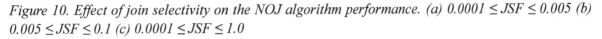

Figure 10. Effect of join selectivity on the NOJ algorithm performance. (a) 0.0001 ≤ JSF ≤ 0.005 (b) 0.005 ≤ JSF ≤ 0.1 (c) 0.0001 ≤ JSF ≤ 1.0

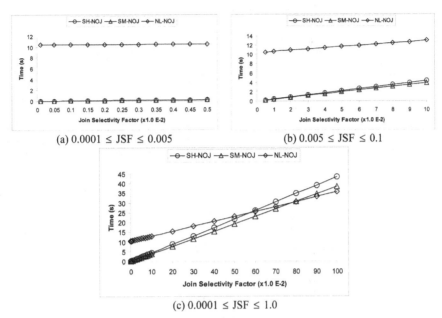

(a) 0.0001 ≤ JSF ≤ 0.005

(b) 0.005 ≤ JSF ≤ 0.1

(c) 0.0001 ≤ JSF ≤ 1.0

≤ JSF ≤ 1.0. The algorithm performance curves are monotonically increasing, because the number of processed output tuples increases with larger values of JSF. *SH-NOJ* showed the best performance for 0.0001 ≤ JSF < 0.005: e.g., *SH-NOJ* took 0.015s, *SM-NOJ* took 0.031s, and *NL-NOJ* took 10.48s for JSF = 0.0001. Both *SH-NOJ* and *SM-NOJ* took 0.219s for JSF = 0.005. *SM-NOJ* was the fastest for 0.01 ≤ JSF < 0.8, and *NL-NOJ* was the fastest for 0.8 ≤ JSF ≤ 1.0. The observed phenomenon can be explained by the following facts: when the processing of output tuples is neglected, (1) *SH-NOJ* has the constant hashing cost, however degrades from linear performance to quadratic performance with the growth of JSF, (2) *SM-NOJ* degrades from non-linear *nlogn* performance to quadratic performance with the growth of JSF, however, at the same time, the sorting cost decreases (e.g., for JSF = 1.0, input twin relations are already sorted on the join attributes), and (3) *NL-NOJ* has stable quadratic performance, but does not require neither hashing nor sorting.

Experiment VI: Comparison of NL-NOJ-MySQL and NL-LOJ-MySQL

The in-RDBMS evaluation of queries Q1-Q7 using implementations *NL-NOJ-MySQL* and *NL-LOJ-MySQL* revealed similar pattern as for the corresponding in-memory evaluations (see Figure 9(a)). Figures 11(a) and 11(b) show the evaluation time for queries Q8-Q12 and Q13-Q14, respectively, over the WordNet dataset stored into MySQL. Similarly to our previous experiments, queries with one join (Q8 and Q9) showed identical performance, since no nested *OPTIONAL*s were present. *NL-NOJ-MySQL* was considerably faster than *NL-LOJ-MySQL* for Q10-Q12 and several orders of magnitude faster for Q13 and Q14. Such a huge performance difference for queries Q13 and Q14 can be naturally explained by estimating the number of operations that each implementation did to compute the result. For example, to evaluate query Q13, *NL-NOJ-MySQL* roughly (neglecting indexes) required 90,267×90,267 operations for

Figure 11. Evaluation of the NL-NOJ-MySQL and NL-LOJ-MySQL implementations in RDBMS MySQL 5.0 using the WordNet test queries. (a) Queries Q8-Q12, WordNet dataset (b) Queries Q13 and Q14, WordNet dataset (c) Queries Q8-Q14, 10×WordNet dataset (over 7.1 mln triples)

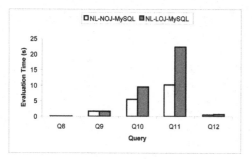
(a) Queries Q8-Q12, WordNet dataset

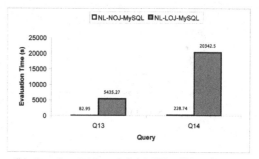
(b) Queries Q13 and Q14, WordNet dataset

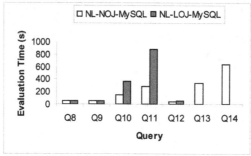
(c) Queries Q8-Q14, 10 × WordNet dataset (over 7.1 mln triples)

the first join (see Table 3), 1×90,267+90,266 for the second one, 1×90,267+90,266 for the third one, 1×90,267+90,266 for the fourth one, and 1×90,267+90,266 for the last one, resulting in ≈90,267^2+8×90,267 operations. On the other hand, *NL-LOJ-MySQL* roughly required 90,267×90,267×90,267×90,267×90,267=90,267^6 operations.

Additionally, Figure 11(c) reports the performance of *NL-NOJ-MySQL* and *NL-LOJ-MySQL* over 10 WordNet datasets stored into MySQL. Note that we did not evaluate Q13 and Q14 with *NL-LOJ-MySQL*, since these queries were extremely slow. As before, even though the dataset became 10 times larger and joins required to use more I/O operations, the NOJ performance showed to be much better than MySQL's LOJ performance.

Experiment VII: Comparison of NL-NOJ-MySQL with Sesame 1.2.6 and Jena 2.5.2

Figure 12 shows the comparison of *NL-NOJ-MySQL* and existing RDF store Sesame 1.2.6 (Aduna, 2008). This experiment used both systems to evaluate queries Q8-Q14 over one and 10 WordNet datasets stored into MySQL as reported in Figures 12(a) and 12(b), respectively. For all the queries, *NL-NOJ-MySQL* showed to be significantly faster than Sesame. Note that, for the larger dataset, Sesame could not evaluate Q14 reporting an insufficient memory problem. Nevertheless, Sesame's optimizations showed to be quite efficient in avoiding the complexity of left outer joins that we observed in the *NL-LOJ-MySQL* implementation (see Experiment VI). These optimizations might be also applicable to

Figure 12. Evaluation of the NL-NOJ-MySQL and Sesame 1.2.6 using the WordNet test queries. (a) Queries Q8-Q14, WordNet dataset (b) Queries Q8-Q14, 10×WordNet dataset (over 7.1 mln triples)

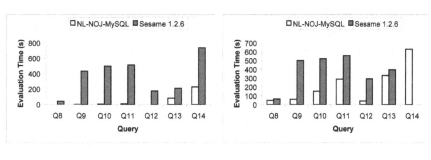

(a) Queries Q8-Q14, WordNet dataset

(b) Queries Q8-Q14, 10 × WordNet dataset (over 7.1 mln triples)

NOJ, which we will explore in future. An additional and very significant improvement of query response time may be achieved if sort-merge or hash NOJ algorithms are used to evaluate the above queries with low NOJ selectivity factors.

The comparison (not in the figures) of *NL-NOJ-MySQL* and RDF store Jena 2.5.2 (Wilkinson et al., 2003) showed that the former was several orders of magnitude faster for all the queries. For example, while *NL-NOJ-MySQL* took less than 1s on Q12 over a single WordNet dataset, Jena required over 19,000s to evaluate the same query.

Summary

In the following, we summarize the results of our performance study and present our recommendations for the usage of the presented NOJ algorithms:

- The nested optional join, $(R_b, R_o) \equiv \bowtie (S_b, D_o)$, showed the performance gain over the left outer join counterpart when used for the evaluation of nested optional graph patterns in both our in-memory relational database and existing RDBMS MySQL. The NOJ superior performance is due to the following computational improvements: (1) optional relation R_o is always processed in linear time by a NOJ algorithm and

(2) NOJ does not require the *NOT NULL* check. These improvements showed to significantly reduce the query response time in our experiments.

- For NOJs with JSF ≤ 0.005, algorithm *SH-NOJ* should be used for in-memory evaluation.

- For NOJs with JSF ≥ 0.8, algorithm *NL-NOJ* should be used for in-memory evaluation.

- For NOJs with $0.005 <$ JSF < 0.8, algorithm *SM-NOJ* should be used for in-memory evaluation.

RELATED WORK

The join operation defined in the relational data model (Codd, 1970, 1972) is used to combine tuples from two or more relations based on a specified join condition. Several types of joins, such as theta-join, equi-join, natural join, semi-join, self-join, full outer join, left outer join, and right outer join, are studied in database courses (Elmasri & Navathe, 2004; Kifer et al., 2006) and implemented in RDBMSs. We introduce a new type of join, nested optional join, whose semantics naturally supports the semantics of optional patterns in well-designed graph patterns (e.g., in SPARQL (W3C, 2008)). NOJ is defined on two twin relations, where each twin relation contains a base relation and an optional relation; therefore, NOJ can be viewed as a join of four conventional relations. The result of NOJ is also a twin relation, whose base relation stores tuples that have been concatenated and whose optional relation stores tuples that have been *NULL* padded. The above semantic and structural characteristics differentiate NOJ from any other join defined in the literature. We propose NOJ as a favorable alternative to the LOJ-based implementations for the nested optional graph pattern processing with relational databases. Note that NOJ is not a replacement of LOJ: their semantics are different, such as LOJ needs a special *NOT NULL* check to return similar results to the NOJ results and this check is not part of NOJ.

The join processing in relational databases has been an important research for over 30 years and the related literature is abundant (Mishra & Eich, 1992). To design algorithms for NOJ, we use three classical methods for implementing joins in RDBMSs: nested-loops, sort-merge, and hash-based join methods (Elmasri & Navathe, 2004; Kifer et al., 2006). These methods have numerous optimizations which are out of the scope of this work. Various techniques for estimating a join selectivity factor in database systems are surveyed by Mannino, Chu, and Sager (1988).

In this work, for the SPARQL-to-SQL translation, we use the translation strategy presented in our technical report (Chebotko et al., 2006). It is worthwhile to mention that SPARQL is not the only RDF query language that supports optional graph patterns. Other examples include SeRQL (Aduna, 2006) and RDFQL (Intellidimension, 2008). These languages can also benefit from the nested optional join.

Related literature on the SPARQL-to-SQL query translation, SPARQL query processing and optimization includes (Anyanwu, Maduko, & Sheth, 2007; Bernstein, Kiefer, & Stocker, 2007; Chebotko, Fei, Lu, & Fotouhi, 2007; Chebotko et al., 2006; Chong, Das, Eadon, & Srinivasan, 2005; Cyganiak, 2005; Harris & Shadbolt, 2005; Harth &

Decker, 2005; Hartig & Heese, 2007; Hung, Deng, & Subrahmanian, 2005; Polleres, 2007; Serfiotis, Koffina, Christophides, & Tannen, 2005; Udrea, Pugliese, & Subrahmanian, 2007; Zemke, 2006). Harris and Shadbolt (2005) show how basic graph pattern expressions, as well as simple optional graph patterns, can be translated into relational algebra expressions. Cyganiak (2005) presents a relational algebra for SPARQL and outlines rules establishing equivalence between this algebra and SQL. Chebotko et al. (2006) present algorithms for basic and optional graph pattern translation into SQL. The W3C semantics of SPARQL (W3C, 2008) has changed since then, which was triggered by the compositional semantics presented by Perez et al. (2006a); Perez, Arenas, and Gutierrez (2006b). The new semantics defines the same evaluation results for the most common in practice SPARQL queries with the so called well-designed patterns (Perez et al., 2006a), but it is different from the previously used semantics for other queries. Therefore, research results on the SPARQL-to-SQL translation described above need to be revisited to accommodate graph patterns which are not well-designed.

One of the first SPARQL-to-SQL translations that is based on the new semantics is outlined by Zemke (2006). More recently, Chebotko, Fei, Lin, et al. (2007); Chebotko, Fei, Lu, and Fotouhi (2007) define a SPARQL-to-SQL translation algorithm for basic graph pattern queries, which is optimized to select smallest relations to query based on the type information of an instance and the statistics of the size of the relations in the database, as well as to eliminate redundancies in basic graph patterns. Furthermore, Chebotko, Lu, and Fotouhi (2009) formalize a relational algebra based semantics of SPARQL and prove its equivalence to the mapping-based semantics of SPARQL (Perez et al., 2006a); based on this semantics, they propose the first provably semantics preserving SPARQL-to-SQL translation. Polleres (2007) and Schenk (2007) contribute with the translation of SPARQL queries into Datalog, along with other contributions on the extensions of SPARQL and its semantics. Anyanwu et al. (2007) propose an extended SPARQL query language called SPAR-Q2L which supports subgraph extraction queries. Serfiotis et al. (2005) study the containment and minimization problems of RDF query fragments using a logic framework that allows to reduce these problems into their relational equivalents. Hartig and Heese (2007) propose a SPARQL query graph model and pursue query rewriting based on this model. Harth and Decker (2005) propose optimized index structures for RDF that can support efficient evaluation of select-project-join queries and can be implemented in a relational database. Udrea et al. (2007) propose an in-memory index structure to store RDF graph regions defined by center nodes and their associated radii; the index helps to reduce the number of joins during SPARQL query evaluation. Weiss, Karras, and Bernstein (2008) introduce a sextuple-indexing scheme that can support efficient querying of RDF data based on six types of indexes, one for each possible ordering of a subject, predicate, and object. Bernstein et al. (2007) propose SPARQL query optimization techniques based on triple pattern selectivity estimation and evaluate them using an in-memory SPARQL query engine. Chong et al. (2005) introduce an SQL table function into the Oracle database to query RDF data, such that the function can be combined with SQL statements for further processing. Hung et al. (2005) study the problem of RDF aggregate queries by extending an RDF query language with the GROUP BY clause and several aggregate functions. Schenk and Staab (2008), Volz, Oberle, and Studer (2003), and Magkanaraki, Tannen, Christophides, and Plexousakis (2004) define RDF and SPARQL views for RDF data personalization and integration. Several research works (Bizer & Seaborne, 2004; Laborda & Conrad, 2006; Prud'hommeaux, 2004, 2005) focus on accessing conventional relational databases using SPARQL, which requires the SPARQL-to-SQL query translation. Finally, Guo, Qasem, Pan, and

Heflin (2007); Guo, Pan, and Heflin (2005) define requirements for Semantic Web knowledge base systems benchmarks and propose a framework for developing such benchmarks.

Our work is complementary to above research, as well as numerous projects on relational RDF stores, including Jena (Wilkinson et al., 2003), Sesame (Broekstra et al., 2002), 3store (Harris & Gibbins, 2003), KAON (Volz et al., 2003), RStar (Ma et al., 2004), OpenLink Virtuoso (Erling, 2001), DLDB (Pan & Heflin, 2003), RDFSuite (Alexaki et al., 2001), DBOWL (Narayanan et al., 2006), PARKA (Stoffel et al., 1997), RDFProv (Chebotko, Fei, Lin, et al., 2007), and RDFBroker (Sintek & Kiesel, 2006). While relational joins can be speeded up or even eliminated by various indexing techniques, query rewriting procedures, and database schema optimizations, they cannot be avoided completely in general case. When a join has to be computed for a nested optional graph pattern, a choice between NOJ or LOJ can make a difference. Additionally, supplemental index structures that reduce the size of to-be-joined relations can be applied in conjunction with NOJ. Therefore, NOJ can be beneficial to many existing relational RDF stores.

CONCLUSIONS AND FUTURE WORK

To support efficient processing of RDF queries with well-designed graph patterns and nested optional patterns in RDBMSs, we proposed a novel relational operator – nested optional join. We illustrated that such RDF queries can be translated into relational algebra using either left outer join (LOJ) or nested optional join (NOJ). The computational advantage of NOJ over the currently used LOJ-based implementations comes from the two superior characteristics of NOJ: (1) NOJ allows the processing of the tuples that are guaranteed to be *NULL* padded very efficiently (in linear time) and (2) NOJ does not require the *NOT NULL* check to return correct results. In addition, (3) NOJ can significantly simplify the translation of RDF queries with well-designed graph patterns into relational algebra. To facilitate the implementation of NOJ in relational databases, we designed three efficient algorithms: (1) nested-loops NOJ algorithm, *NL-NOJ*, (2) sort-merge NOJ algorithm, *SM-NOJ*, and (3) simple hash NOJ algorithm, *SH-NOJ*. Based on a real life RDF dataset, we demonstrated the efficiency of our algorithms by comparing them with the corresponding left outer join implementations using our in-memory database and popular open-source RDBMS MySQL. The experiments showed that NOJ is a favorable alternative to the LOJ-based evaluation of nested optional patterns in well-designed graph patterns. Moreover, we conducted a preliminary performance study of the NOJ algorithm behavior with respect to varying join selectivity factor (JSF). This study showed that: for NOJs with JSF ≤ 0.005, *SH-NOJ* should be used for in-memory evaluation; for NOJs with JSF ≥ 0.8, *NL-NOJ* should be used for in-memory evaluation; and for NOJs with $0.005 < \text{JSF} < 0.8$, *SM-NOJ* should be used for in-memory evaluation. Finally, our last experiment showed that our NOJ-based implementation outperformed existing RDF stores Sesame and Jena.

In the future, we would like to explore NOJ performance in an RDBMS using sort-merge and hash join algorithms, conduct a performance study on larger and diverse datasets, seek for additional optimization opportunities for NOJ and its implementations, and experiment with NOJ implementations in a column-oriented database (Abadi et al., 2007; Sidirourgos, Goncalves, Kersten, Nes, & Manegold, 2008). We would also like to compare *top-down* (Chebotko et al., 2006; Cyganiak, 2005) (also known as *bottom-up* (Chebotko et al., 2009; Perez et al., 2006a)) and *bottom-up* (Chebotko, Lu, & Fotouhi, 2007; Perez et al., 2006a) approaches to evaluation of nested optional patterns in well-designed graph patterns.

ACKNOWLEDGMENT

This book chapter is based on the original article on nested optional join, which was published in the International Journal on Semantic Web and Information Systems (IJSWIS) in 2008. We would like to thank our co-authors, Mustafa Atay and Farshad Fotouhi, for their contributions to that original article.

REFERENCES

W3C. (2004a). RDF Primer. W3C Recommendation, 10 February 2004. F. Manola and E. Miller (Eds.). Retrieved from http://www.w3.org/TR/rdf-primer/

W3C. (2004b). Resource Description Framework (RDF): Concepts and Abstract Syntax. W3C Recommendation, 10 February 2004. G. Klyne, J. J. Carroll, and B. McBride (Eds.). Retrieved from http://www.w3.org/TR/2004/REC-rdf-concepts-20040210/

W3C. (2008). SPARQL Query Language for RDF. W3C Candidate Recommendation, 15 January 2008. E. Prud'hommeaux and A. Seaborne (Eds.). Retrieved from http://www.w3.org/TR/2008/REC-rdf-sparql-query-20080115/

Abadi, D. J., Marcus, A., Madden, S., & Hollenbach, K. J. (2007). Scalable Semantic Web data management using vertical partitioning. In *Proceedings of the International Conference on Very Large Data Bases (VLDB)* (pp. 411-422).

Aduna. (2006). User guide for Sesame. Updated for Sesame release 1.2.6. Retrieved from http://www.openrdf.org/doc/sesame/users/index.html

Aduna. (2008). Sesame: RDF Schema querying and storage. Retrieved from http://www.openrdf.org

Agrawal, R., Somani, A., & Xu, Y. (2001). Storage and querying of e-commerce data. In *Proceedings of the International Conference on Very Large Data Bases (VLDB)* (pp. 149-158).

Alexaki, S., Christophides, V., Karvounarakis, G., & Plexousakis, D. (2001). On storing voluminous RDF descriptions: The case of Web portal catalogs. In *Proceedings of the International Workshop on the Web and Databases (WebDB)*.

Anyanwu, K., Maduko, A., & Sheth, A. (2007). SPARQ2L: Towards support for subgraph extraction queries in RDF databases. In *Proceedings of the International World Wide Web Conference (WWW)* (pp. 797-806).

Beckett, D., & Grant, J. (2003). SWAD-Europe Deliverable 10.2: Mapping Semantic Web Data with RDBMSes. Retrieved from http://www.w3.org/2001/sw/Europe/reports/scalable_rdbms_mapping_report

Berners-Lee, T., Hendler, J., & Lassila, O. (2001, May). The Semantic Web. *Scientific American*.

Bernstein, A., Kiefer, C., & Stocker, M. (2007, March). *OptARQ: A SPARQL optimization approach based on triple pattern selectivity estimation* (Tech. Rep. No. ifi-2007.03). Retrieved from http://www.ifi.uzh.ch/ddis/staff/goehring/btw/files/ifi-2007.03.pdf

Bizer, C., & Seaborne, A. (2004). D2RQ – treating non-RDF databases as virtual RDF graphs. In *Proceedings of the International Semantic Web Conference (ISWC)*. (Poster presentation)

Broekstra, J., Kampman, A., & van Harmelen, F. (2002). Sesame: A generic architecture for storing and querying RDF and RDF Schema. In *Proceedings of the International Semantic Web Conference (ISWC)* (pp. 54-68).

Chebotko, A., Atay, M., Lu, S., & Fotouhi, F. (2007). Relational nested optional join for efficient Semantic Web query processing. In *Proceedings of the joint conference of the Asia-Pacific Web Conference and the International Conference on Web-Age Information Management (APWeb/WAIM)* (pp. 428-439).

Chebotko, A., Fei, X., Lin, C., Lu, S., & Fotouhi, F. (2007). Storing and querying scientific workflow provenance metadata using an RDBMS. In *Proceedings of the IEEE International Workshop on Scientific Workflows and Business Workflow Standards in e-Science* (pp. 611-618).

Chebotko, A., Fei, X., Lu, S., & Fotouhi, F. (2007, September). *Scientific workflow provenance metadata management using an RDBMS-based RDF store* (Tech. Rep. No. TR-DB-092007-CFLF). Wayne State University. Retrieved from http://www.cs.wayne.edu/~artem/main/research/TR-DB-092007-CFLF.pdf

Chebotko, A., Lu, S., & Fotouhi, F. (2009). (in press). Semantics preserving SPARQL-to-SQL translation. [DKE]. *Data & Knowledge Engineering*. doi:10.1016/j.datak.2009.04.001

Chebotko, A., Lu, S., Jamil, H. M., & Fotouhi, F. (2006, May). *Semantics preserving SPARQL-to-SQL query translation for optional graph patterns* (Tech. Rep. No. TR-DB-052006-CLJF). Wayne State University. Retrieved from http://www.cs.wayne.edu/~artem/main/research/TR-DB-052006-CLJF.pdf

Chong, E. I., Das, S., Eadon, G., & Srinivasan, J. (2005). An efficient SQL-based RDF querying scheme. In *Proceedings of the International Conference on Very Large Data Bases (VLDB)* (pp. 1216-1227).

Ciorascu, C. (2003). WordNet, a lexical database for the English language. Retrieved from http://wordnet.princeton.edu/ (Version: 1.2)

Codd, E. F. (1970). A relational model of data for large shared data banks. *Communications of the ACM, 13*(6), 377–387. doi:10.1145/362384.362685

Codd, E. F. (1972). Relational completeness of data base sublanguages. In R. Rustin (Ed.), Database Systems (pp. 65-98). Prentice Hall and IBM Research Report RJ 987, San Jose, California.

Cyganiak, R. (2005). *A relational algebra for SPARQL* (Tech. Rep. No. HPL-2005-170). Hewlett-Packard Laboratories. Retrieved from http://www.hpl.hp.com/techreports/2005/HPL-2005-170.html

de Laborda, C. P., & Conrad, S. (2006). Bringing relational data into the Semantic Web using SPARQL and Relational.OWL. In *Proceedings of the ICDE Workshops* (pp. 55).

DeWitt, D. J., & Gerber, R. H. (1985). Multiprocessor hash-based join algorithms. In *Proceedings of the International Conference on Very Large Data Bases (VLDB)* (pp. 151-164).

DeWitt, D. J., Katz, R. H., Olken, F., Shapiro, L. D., Stonebraker, M., & Wood, D. A. (1984). Implementation techniques for main memory database systems. In *Proceedings of the SIGMOD International Conference on Management of Data* (pp. 1-8).

Elmasri, R., & Navathe, S. B. (2004). *Fundamentals of database systems*. Addison-Wesley.

Erling, O. (2001). Implementing a SPARQL compliant RDF triple store using a SQL-ORDBMS. OpenLink Software Virtuoso. Retrieved from http://virtuoso.openlinksw.com/wiki/main/Main/VOSRDFWP

Gerber, R. H. (1986). *Dataflow query processing using multiprocessor hash-partitioned algorithms* (Tech. Rep. No. 672). Dissertation, University of Wisconsin-Madison, Computer Sciences.

Guo, Y., Pan, Z., & Heflin, J. (2005). LUBM: A benchmark for OWL knowledge base systems. *Journal of Web Semantics, 3*(2-3), 158–182. doi:10.1016/j.websem.2005.06.005

Guo, Y., Qasem, A., Pan, Z., & Heflin, J. (2007). A requirements driven framework for benchmarking Semantic Web knowledge base systems. *IEEE Transactions on Knowledge and Data Engineering, 19*(2), 297–309. doi:10.1109/TKDE.2007.19

Harris, S., & Gibbins, N. (2003). 3store: Efficient bulk RDF storage. In *Proceedings of the International Workshop on Practical and Scalable Semantic Systems (PSSS)* (pp. 1-15).

Harris, S., & Shadbolt, N. (2005). SPARQL query processing with conventional relational database systems. In *Proceedings of the International Workshop on Scalable Semantic Web Knowledge Base Systems (SSWS)*.

Harth, A., & Decker, S. (2005). Optimized index structures for querying RDF from the Web. In *Proceedings of the Latin American Web Congress (LA-WEB)* (pp. 71-80).

Hartig, O., & Heese, R. (2007). The SPARQL query graph model for query optimization. In *Proceedings of the European Semantic Web Conference (ESWC)* (pp. 564-578).

Hung, E., Deng, Y., & Subrahmanian, V. S. (2005). RDF aggregate queries and views. In *Proceedings of the International Conference on Data Engineering (ICDE)* (p. 717-728).

Intellidimension. (2008). RDFQL database command reference. Retrieved from http://www.intellidimension.com/pages/rdfgateway/reference/db/default.rsp

Kifer, M., Bernstein, A., & Lewis, P. M. (2006). *Database systems: An application oriented approach*. Addison-Wesley.

Kim, W. (1980). A new way to compute the product and join of relations. In *Proceedings of the SIGMOD International Conference on Management of Data* (pp. 179-187).

Lu, H., Tan, K.-L., & Shan, M.-C. (1990). Hash-based join algorithms for multiprocessor computers with shared memory. In *Proceedings of the International Conference on Very Large Data Bases (VLDB)* (pp. 198-209).

Ma, L., Su, Z., Pan, Y., Zhang, L., & Liu, T. (2004). RStar: an RDF storage and query system for enterprise resource management. In *Proceedings of the International Conference on Information and Knowledge Management (CIKM)* (pp. 484-491).

Magkanaraki, A., Tannen, V., Christophides, V., & Plexousakis, D. (2004). Viewing the Semantic Web through RVL lenses. *Journal of Web Semantics*, *1*(4), 359–375. doi:10.1016/j.websem.2004.06.004

Mannino, M. V., Chu, P., & Sager, T. (1988). Statistical profile estimation in database systems. *ACM Computing Surveys*, *20*(3), 191–221. doi:10.1145/62061.62063

Mishra, P., & Eich, M. H. (1992). Join processing in relational databases. *ACM Computing Surveys*, *24*(1), 63–113. doi:10.1145/128762.128764

MySQL. (2008). MySQL 5.0 Reference Manual: 7.2.10 Nested Join Optimization [Computer software manual]. Retrieved from http://dev.mysql.com/doc/refman/5.0/en/nested-joins.html

Narayanan, S., Kurc, T. M., & Saltz, J. H. (2006). *DBOWL: Towards extensional queries on a billion statements using relational databases* (Tech. Rep. No. OSUBMI_TR_2006_n03). Ohio State University. Retrieved from http://bmi.osu.edu/resources/techreports/osubmi.tr.2006.n3.pdf

Pan, Z., & Heflin, J. (2003). DLDB: Extending relational databases to support Semantic Web queries. In *Proceedings of the International Workshop on Practical and Scalable Semantic Web Systems (PSSS)* (pp. 109-113).

Perez, J., Arenas, M., & Gutierrez, C. (2006a). Semantics and complexity of SPARQL. In *Proceedings of the International Semantic Web Conference (ISWC)* (p. 30-43).

Perez, J., Arenas, M., & Gutierrez, C. (2006b). Semantics of SPARQL. Retrieved from http://ing.utalca.cl/~jperez/papers/sparql_semantics.pdf

Polleres, A. (2007). From SPARQL to rules (and back). In *Proceedings of the International World Wide Web Conference (WWW)* (pp. 787-796).

Prud'hommeaux, E. (2004). Optimal RDF access to relational databases. Retrieved from http://www.w3.org/2004/04/30-RDF-RDB-access/

Prud'hommeaux, E. (2005). Notes on adding SPARQL to MySQL. Retrieved from http://www.w3.org/2005/05/22-SPARQL-MySQL/

Schenk, S. (2007). A SPARQL semantics based on Datalog. In *Proceedings of the KI 2007, Annual German Conference on AI* (p. 160-174).

Schenk, S., & Staab, S. (2008). Networked graphs: A declarative mechanism for SPARQL rules, SPARQL views and RDF data integration on the Web. In *Proceedings of the International World Wide Web Conference (WWW)* (pp. 585-594).

Serfiotis, G., Koffina, I., Christophides, V., & Tannen, V. (2005). Containment and minimization of RDF/S query patterns. In *Proceedings of the International Semantic Web Conference (ISWC)* (pp. 607-623).

Shadbolt, N., Berners-Lee, T., & Hall, W. (2006). The Semantic Web revisited. *IEEE Intelligent Systems*, *21*(3), 96–101. doi:10.1109/MIS.2006.62

Sidirourgos, L., Goncalves, R., Kersten, M., Nes, N., & Manegold, S. (2008). Column-store support for RDF data management: not all swans are white. In *Proceedings of the International Conference on Very Large Data Bases (VLDB)*.

Sintek, M., & Kiesel, M. (2006). RDFBroker: A signature-based high-performance RDF store. In *Proceedings of the European Semantic Web Conference (ESWC)* (pp. 363-377).

Stoffel, K., Taylor, M. G., & Hendler, J. A. (1997). Efficient management for very large ontologies. In *Proceedings of the American Association for Artificial Intelligence Conference (AAAI)*.

Theoharis, Y., Christophides, V., & Karvounarakis, G. (2005). Benchmarking database representations of RDF/S stores. In *Proceedings of the International Semantic Web Conference (ISWC)*.

Udrea, O., Pugliese, A., & Subrahmanian, V. S. (2007). GRIN: A graph based RDF index. In *Proceedings of the American Association for Artificial Intelligence Conference (AAAI)* (pp. 1465-1470).

Volz, R., Oberle, D., Motik, B., & Staab, S. (2003). KAON SERVER - a Semantic Web management system. In *Proceedings of the International World Wide Web Conference (WWW), Alternate Tracks - Practice and Experience*.

Volz, R., Oberle, D., & Studer, S. (2003). Implementing views for light-weight Web ontologies. In *Proceedings of the International Database Engineering and Applications Symposium (IDEAS)* (pp. 160-169).

Weiss, C., Karras, P., & Bernstein, A. (2008). Hexastore: Sextuple indexing for Semantic Web data management. In *Proceedings of the International Conference on Very Large Data Bases (VLDB)*.

Wilkinson, K. (2006). Jena property table implementation. In *Proceedings of the International Workshop on Scalable Semantic Web Knowledge Base Systems (SSWS)*.

Wilkinson, K., Sayers, C., Kuno, H., & Reynolds, D. (2003). Efficient RDF storage and retrieval in Jena2. In *Proceedings of the International Workshop on Semantic Web and Databases (SWDB)*.

Zemke, F. (2006, October). *Converting SPARQL to SQL* (Tech. Rep.). Retrieved from http://lists.w3.org/Archives/Public/public-rdf-dawg/2006OctDec/att-0058/sparql-to-sql.pdf

Chapter 14

An Associative and Adaptive Network Model for Information Retrieval in the Semantic Web

Peter Scheir
Styria Media Group AG, Austria

Peter Prettenhofer
Bauhaus University Weimar, Germany

Stefanie N. Lindstaedt
Know-Center Graz and Graz University of Technology, Austria

Chiara Ghidini
Fondazione Bruno Kessler, Italy

ABSTRACT

While it is agreed that semantic enrichment of resources would lead to better search results, at present the low coverage of resources on the web with semantic information presents a major hurdle in realizing the vision of search on the Semantic Web. To address this problem, this chapter investigates how to improve retrieval performance in settings where resources are sparsely annotated with semantic information. Techniques from soft computing are employed to find relevant material that was not originally annotated with the concepts used in a query. The authors present an associative retrieval model for the Semantic Web and evaluate if and to which extent the use of associative retrieval techniques increases retrieval performance. In addition, the authors present recent work on adapting the network structure based on relevance feedback by the user to further improve retrieval effectiveness. The evaluation of new retrieval paradigms - such as retrieval based on technology for the Semantic Web - presents an additional challenge since no off-the-shelf test corpora exist. Hence, this chapter gives a detailed description of the approach taken to evaluate the information retrieval service the authors have built.

DOI: 10.4018/978-1-60566-992-2.ch014

Copyright © 2010, IGI Global. Copying or distributing in print or electronic forms without written permission of IGI Global is prohibited.

INTRODUCTION

It is largely agreed that the semantic enrichment of resources provides for more information that can be used for search (see e.g. (Heflin & Hendler, 2000) or (Spärck Jones, 2004)). In turn, this can lead to greatly improved effectiveness of retrieval systems, not only for resources on the web but also for personal desktops. However, critics (McCool, 2005) as well as advocates (Sabou, d'Aquin, & Motta, 2006) of the Semantic Web agree that only a small fraction of resources on the current web are enriched with semantic information. The sparse annotation of resources with semantic information presents a major obstacle in realizing search applications for the Semantic Web that operate on semantically enriched resources. To overcome this problem, we propose the use of techniques from soft computing in order to find relevant resources, even if no semantic information is provided for those resources.

The main idea of our approach is to perform associative search using spreading activation in a two layer network structure (graphically illustrated in Figure 1) which consists of (1) a layer of concepts, used to semantically annotate a pool of resources, and (2) a layer of resources (documents). The combination of spreading activation in both layers, traditionally performed either to find similar concepts or to find similar text, allows a search to be extended to a wider network of concepts and resources, which can lead to the retrieval of relevant resources with no annotation.

In this chapter we describe our approach towards information retrieval in the Semantic Web and present a retrieval service. The rest of this chapter is organized as follows: in section *Terminology and Related Work* we introduce the main concepts of Associative Information Retrieval, Associative Networks and Spreading Activation that underlie our approach to retrieval and examine related work. In section *An Associative Information Retrieval Model for the Semantic Web*, we describe the retrieval model, which was

developed based on techniques from soft computing. In section *Application of the Retrieval Model within APOSDLE* we present the setting in which a retrieval service based on our retrieval model was realized. In section *Parametrization of the Retrieval Model* we describe which measures where used to parameterize the retrieval model. In section *Evaluation* we focus on the evaluation of the retrieval service. In section *Parameter Learning using Relevance Feedback* we present work on adapting the network structure based on relevance feedback by the user. We end the chapter with Conclusions and Future Work.

This invited book chapter contains work already published in (Scheir et al. 2008). In section *Parameter Learning using Relevance Feedback* we present recent – not yet published - research. Certainly this new aspects need to be better integrated in future versions of the retrieval model.

TERMINOLOGY AND RELATED WORK

The work presented in this chapter provides a retrieval model for the Semantic Web and an implementation of an associative retrieval service based on this model. In this section we briefly introduce the important terms underlying our work: Associative Information Retrieval, Associative Networks and Spreading Activation. Furthermore we briefly discuss other approaches to information retrieval in the Semantic Web and systems. In particular we review the efforts that have used the same or similar soft computing techniques.

Terminology

Associative (Information) Retrieval: Crestani (1997) understands associative retrieval as a form of information retrieval, which tries to find relevant information by retrieving information that is by some means associated with information that is already known to be relevant. Information items

Figure 1. The associative network model consisting of an interconnected term and document layer. Nodes are connected by directed, weighted edges. Edges between concept nodes represent semantic similarity, edges between document nodes represent content-based similarity, and an edge between a concept node and a document node represent the annotation of a document with a concept. Weights are calculated according equations 3, 4 and 5

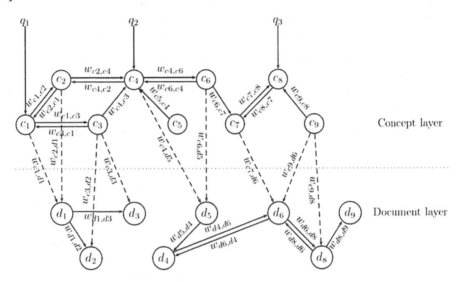

that are associated can be documents, parts of documents, extracted terms, concepts, and so on. The idea of associative retrieval dates back to the 1960s, when researches (Salton, 1963, 1968) in the field of information retrieval tried to increase retrieval performance using associations between documents or index terms, which were determined in advance.

Associative Networks: Association of information is frequently modeled as a graph, which is referred to as an associative network (Crestani, 1997). In the context of information retrieval these network structures are also referred to as neural networks (Wilkinson & Hingston, 1991) or connectionist approaches (Belew, 1989). Nodes in the network represent information items such as documents, terms or concepts. Edges represent associations between information items and can be weighted and/or labeled, expressing the degree and type of association between two information items, respectively.

Spreading Activation: A natural processing paradigm for network structures such as

Associative Networks is Spreading Activation. The spreading activation model originates from cognitive psychology (cf. (Anderson, 1983)) where it serves as a mechanism for explaining how knowledge is represented and processed in the human brain. The human mind is modeled as a network of nodes, which represent concepts and are connected by edges. Starting from a set of initially activated nodes, the activation spreads over the network.

Semantic Annotations: Semantic annotation is information about entities (or, more generally, semantic features), which appear in a text. Formally, semantic annotations represent a specific sort of metadata, which provides references to entities in the form of URIs or other types of unique identifiers. As Handschuh (2007) notes, different approaches to semantic annotation exist in literature. The authors refer to Bechhofer and Goble (2001) who differentiate between the following ways of semantic annotation:

- *Decoration:* Annotation of resources with a comment of the user.
- *Linking:* Annotation of resources with addition links.
- *Instance identification:* Annotation of resources with a concept. The annotated resource is an instance of the concept.
- *Instance reference:* Annotation of resources with a concept. The annotated resource references an individual in the world, which is an instance of the concept.
- *Aboutness:* Annotation of resources with a concept. The annotated resource is about the concept.
- *Pertinence:* Annotation of resources with a concept. The annotated resource provides further information about the concept.

Related Work

A growing amount of proposed models and implemented systems for information retrieval in the Semantic Web make use of semantic annotations. The work of Heflin and Hendler (2000), Shah, Finin, and Joshi (2002) or Guha, McCool, and Miller (2003) can be viewed as pioneering work in this domain. Kiryakov, Popov, Terziev, Manov, and Ognyano_ (2004) and Castells, Fernndez, and Vallet (2007) present logical consequences of this early work with fine tuned, evolved systems. Applications of semantic annotations in information retrieval in the Semantic Web lead from indexing them together with textual data (Shah et al., 2002; Chirita, Costache, Nejdl, & Paiu, 2006) over extensions of the vector space model (Kiryakov et al., 2004; Castells et al., 2007) to modeling documents as parts of probabilistic knowledge bases (Zhang, Yu, Zhou, Lin, & Yang, 2005) and ranking search results in semantic portals (Stojanovic, Maedche, Staab, Studer, & Sure, 2001; Stojanovic, Studer, & Stojanovic, 2003). Despite the quite extensive and sophisticated usage of semantic annotations, none of these aforementioned approaches employ measures of semantic association. The reader inter-

ested in a detailed overview can refer to (Esmaili & Abolhassani, 2006) and (Scheir, Pammer, & Lindstaedt, 2007).

Network models and spreading activation have found their way over applications in both neural and semantic networks to information retrieval as described in a detailed survey contained in (Crestani, 1997). The recent work of Mandl (2001) starts from the good results of spreading activation based text retrieval systems PIRCS (Kwok & Grunfeld, 1996) and Mercure (Boughanem, Dkaki, Mothe, & Soule-Dupuy, 1999) at the TREC[1] to conclude that Spreading Activation based retrieval models are comparable to other information retrieval approaches in their performance for the retrieval of text documents. Besides systems that use spreading activation for finding similarities between text documents or search terms and text documents (c.f. (Belew, 1989; Wilkinson & Hingston, 1991) or (Mothe, 1994; Crestani & Lee, 2000)), approaches exist, which employ spreading activation for finding similar concepts in knowledge representations (c.f. (Cohen & Kjeldsen, 1987; Alani, Dasmahapatra, O'Hara, & Shadbolt, 2003; Rocha, Schwabe, & Aragão, 2004)). Finally, Huang, Chen, and Zeng (2004) address the scarcity problem in recommender systems using a network-based associative retrieval approach. The novelty of our approach lies in combining spreading activation search in both layers using one and the same model (see Figure 1): the document layer, containing a document collection, and the concept layer, containing a knowledge representation of a domain. In addition, spreading activation is used for all three types of search: search for documents based on a set of concepts, associative search for concepts, and associative search for documents.

A recent stream of work makes use of ontology-based measures of association and evaluate them using spreading activation. Among them Ontocopi (Alani et al., 2003) identifies communities of practice in an ontology using spreading activation based clustering. Rocha et al. (2004) present a hybrid approach for searching the (semantic) web that combines keyword-based search and spreading activation search in an ontology for search on websites. Finally Berger, Dittenbach, and Merkl (2004) present a tourist information system whose underlying knowledge base is searched using spreading activation. The main difference between these approaches and our work is that they do not integrate text-based measures of association into their systems but only refer to measures of association within a structured representation of knowledge.

AN ASSOCIATIVE INFORMATION RETRIEVAL MODEL FOR THE SEMANTIC WEB

The model presented here relies upon the existence of two information sources and their interconnection: Firstly, a domain ontology which defines the vocabulary (concepts) used to annotate resources. Secondly, the resources themselves in the form of textual documents. On top of these two information sources we build an associative network consisting of two interconnected layers (see Figure 1). One layer C of nodes that represent concepts (c.f. equation 1)) and one layer D of nodes that represent documents (c.f. equation 2).

$$C=\{c_1,\dots,c_N\} \tag{1}$$

$$D=\{d_1,\dots,d_M\} \tag{2}$$

With:

- C ... layer of nodes representing concepts
- D ... layer of nodes representing documents
- $c_1,\dots,c_N$ ... concept node 1 to N
- $d_1,\dots,d_M$ ... document node 1 to M
- N equals the number of concepts in the system

- M equals the number of documents in the system
- $\forall c_i \in C : C(c_i) \in K$
- $\forall d_j \in D : D(d_j) \in S$
- $C(c_i)$ ... concept that is represented by concept node c_i
- $D(d_j)$ ... document that is represented by document node d_j
- K ... set of concepts in the ontology
- S ... set of documents in the system

Nodes in the concept layer correspond to concepts in the domain ontology. Nodes in the document layer correspond to documents. Concept nodes are associated by means of semantic similarity (cf. subsection *Modeling Semantic Similarity of Concepts*), while document nodes are associated by means of textual similarity (cf. subsection *Modeling Textbased Similarity of Documents*). The link between the two layers of the network is provided by annotations: a concept node is associated with a document node if the concept is used to annotate that document (cf. subsection *Modeling Semantic Annotation of Documents*).

Finally, the network is searched using a spreading activation algorithm which combines spreading of activation within the concept layer, spreading of activation from the concept to the document layer, and spreading of activation within the document layer (cf. subsection *Searching the Network*). Together this set of soft computing techniques constitutes a model for information retrieval on the Semantic Web.

Modeling Semantic Annotation of Documents

The link between the two layers of the network is provided by annotations of resources with ontological concepts (semantic annotation).

Semantic annotations in the present model and implementation are based on a specific way of annotations among the ones described in Bechhofer and Goble (2001) and presented in section *Terminology and Related Work: Aboutness*. This is, we annotate whole documents with a set of concepts the content of the document is about. This is partly due to the usage of annotations in the system that we use for experimentation. There, annotations are used to express exactly the *aboutness* of resources. The annotations are formally described with the property *deals with* and stored inside the knowledge base of the system.

In approaches based on *Instance identification or Instance reference* as (Castells et al., 2007) or (Kiryakov et al., 2004) annotation is treated on a more fine-grained level: Single words in documents are annotated with concepts stemming from the ontology.

We follow our approach for three reasons: (1) Although the complete semantics of words contained in a document are not recognized using this approach, the additional information added to the document still supports the retrieval of material (Spärck Jones, 2004), and requires only a limited amount of human involvement. (2) To make the Semantic Web a reality we need to focus on bringing *little semantics* (Hendler, 2007) into the current web and taking small steps. We follow this pragmatic approach and apply it in the context of our work. (3) The aboutness-based approach allows treating resources of different types equally. Documents containing text as well as video or audio can *deal with* a certain topic. The instance-based approaches used for textual documents cannot be applied easily to other types of material.

In our (and other) approach(es) to semantic annotation a document is either annotated with certain concepts or it is not. From a retrieval point of view this means that a document is either retrieved, if it is annotated with a concept present in the query, or it is not retrieved, if none of the concepts in the query are assigned to the document. Ranking the retrieved document set is impossible.

To allow for ranking the result set and increasing the performance of our service we weight the annotations between documents and concepts. The weight of the annotation between a concept node and a document node is represented by an edge weight (cf. equation 3). The greater the importance of a document for a concept is the higher the weight of the annotation. The model presented here is not restricted to a particular measure for weighting annotations. The only requirement for a similarity measure is that the weight values returned are in the range [0..1]. In the following section *Parametrization of the Retrieval Model* we present the measure used for the evaluation of our service.

$$w_{c_i,d_j} = weight(c_i, d_j) \qquad (3)$$

With:

- w_{c_i,d_j} ... weight of edge between node representing concept c_i and node representing document d_j
- $weight(c_i, d_j)$ ... weight of annotation of document d_j with concept x_i. (cf. section *Parametrization of the Retrieval Model* for actually used measure)
- $0 \leq weight(c_i, d_j) \leq 1$

Edges that represent semantic annotations are directed from concept nodes to document nodes. The reason for this is that in the presented model search for a set of documents is initiated from a set of concepts: activation spreads from concept nodes to document nodes. The direction of activation spread is indicated by the direction of the edge.

Modeling Semantic Similarity of Concepts

Concept nodes are associated in the concept layer by means of semantic similarity. The strength of the association between two concept nodes is represented by an edge weight (cf. equation 4). The more similar two concepts are, the higher the edge weight. For calculating the similarity of two ontological concepts a semantic similarity measure is used. The model presented here is not restricted to a particular measure for semantic similarity. The only requirement for a similarity measure is that the similarity values returned are in the range [0..1]. In the following section *Parametrization of the Retrieval Model* we present the three measures used for the evaluation of our service.

$$w_{c_i, c_j} = semsim(c_i, c_j) \qquad (4)$$

With:

- w_{c_i, c_j} ... weight of edge between node representing concept c_i and node representing concept c_j
- $semsim(c_i, c_j)$ ... semantic similarly between concept c_i and concept c_j (cf. section *Parametrization of the Retrieval Model* for actually used measures)
- $0 \leq semsim(c_i, c_j) \leq 1$

In the case that an asymmetric similarity measure is used the semantic similarity between concept c_1 and concept c_2 can be different from the semantic similarity between concept c_2 and concept c_1. To support this situation in the model presented the similarity between two concepts is modeled by two directed edges.

Modeling Text-Based Similarity of Documents

Document nodes are associated in the document layer by means of textual similarity. The strength of the association between two document nodes is represented by an edge weight (cf. equation 5). The more similar two documents are, the higher the edge weight. For calculating the similarity of

two documents a text-based similarity measure is used. The model presented here is not restricted to a particular measure for content-based similarity. The only requirement for a similarity measure is that the similarity values returned are in the range [0..1]. In the following section *Parametrization of the Retrieval Model* we present the measure used for the evaluation of our service.

$$w_{d_i, d_j} = contsim(d_i, d_j) \qquad (5)$$

With:

- n_j ... weight of edge between node representing document d_i and node representing document d_j
- $contsim(d_i, d_j)$ ... textual similarly between document d_i and document d_j (cf. section *Parametrization of the Retrieval Model* for actually used measure)
- $0 \leq contsim(d_i, d_j) \leq 1$

As with semantic similarity, textual similarity between two documents is modeled using two directed edges. Again two directed edges are used to provide support for asymmetric similarity measures.

Searching the Network

The network structure underlying the service is searched by spreading activation. Starting from a set of initially activated nodes in the network, activation spreads over the network and activates nodes associated with the initial set of nodes. The initial activation happens by an external stimulus (represented by q1, q2, q3 in Figure 1). The stimulus activates the nodes in the network that correspond to the concepts in the query. These nodes are assigned a fixed amount of activation. This initial amount of activation of the concept nodes is 1.0 divided by the number of concepts in the query. The amount of activation of further concept nodes is then calculated by the equation 6. Nodes representing concepts that are not part of the query are assigned an activation value of 0. Therefore for an empty query all nodes in the concept layer are assigned an activation value of 0.

$$\forall c_i \in C : \mathbf{A}(c_i) = \begin{cases} \dfrac{1.0}{|A|} & if\ \mathbf{C}(c_i) \in A \\ 0 & if\ \mathbf{C}(c_i) \notin A \end{cases} \quad (6)$$

With:

- c_i ... concept node c_i
- C ... layer of nodes representing concepts
- $\mathrm{A}(c_i)$ ... activation of concept node c_i
- A ... set of concepts in the query
- $|A|$ ... number of concepts in the query
- $\mathbf{C}(c_i)$ ... concept represented by concept node c_i

Equation 7 is used to calculate the spread of activation in our network. The activation of a node n_j is the sum of the activation of the nodes n_i that it is connected to. If a node does not receive activation from any other node its activation is = 0. The present approach to spreading activation is based on activation conservation, i.e. every node can only emit as much activation as it receives. To realize activation conservation the sum of the edge weights of all edges over which a node emits activation has to be = 1. In our case this is realized by dividing the weight of an edge through which a node n_i emits activation by the sum of all edge weights through which the node n_i emits activation. Thus, in total the outgoing activation of every node is multiplied by 1 and the node emits exactly as much activation as it holds. The use of activation conservation is an important factor in our approach. We have realized our algorithm in this way to avoid an increase of activation in the network after several cycles of activation spreading.

$$A(n_j) = \begin{cases} \displaystyle\sum_{i=1}^{t} \dfrac{A(n_i) \cdot w_{i,j}}{\displaystyle\sum_{k=1}^{s} w_{i,k}} & if\ t > 0 \\ 0 & if\ t = 0 \end{cases} \quad (7)$$

With:

- $\mathrm{A}(n_j)$ ... activation of node n_j
- $\mathrm{A}(n_i)$ ... activation of node n_i
- t ... number of nodes adjacent to node n_j
- $w_{i,j}$ ... weight of edge between node n_i and node n_j
- s ... number of nodes adjacent to node n_j
- $w_{i,k}$ ... weight of edge between node n_i and node

A central characteristic of the presented network model is its facility for associative search. In addition to search for documents based on semantic annotations, optionally associations between concepts and associations between documents can be taken into account. Thus four alternative ways of search in the network are possible:

1. Search based on semantic annotations of documents.
2. Search based on semantic annotations of documents and associations between concepts.
3. Search based on semantic annotations of documents and associations between documents.
4. Search based on semantic annotations of documents, associations between concepts and associations between documents.

Search in our network is performed as follows:

1. Search starts with a set of concepts, representing the information need of the user. The concept nodes representing these concepts are activated.

2. [Optionally, activation spreads from the set of initially activated concepts over the edges created by semantic similarity to other concept nodes in the network (c.f. equation 9).]
3. Activation spreads from the currently activated set of concept nodes to the document nodes over the edges created by semantic annotation to find documents that deal with the concepts representing the information need (c.f. equation 8).
4. [Optionally, activation spreads from the documents nodes currently activated to document nodes that are related by means of textual similarity and are therefore associated with the document nodes (c.f. equation 10).]
5. Those documents corresponding to the finally activated set of document nodes are returned as search result to the user.

Figure 2 shows the process of a search in the network as described above as an UML 2.0 activity diagram.

Equation 7 describes the spread of activation for a given moment in time only. It defines how the activation of a node is calculated without taking into account the temporal dimension. In the following equation 8 the temporal aspects of spreading activation are described.

The activation $A(d_j,\tau+1)$ of a document node in step $\tau+1$ is calculated based on the activation $A(c_i,\tau)$ of those nodes the document node receives activation from in step τ and the weight of the edges w_{c_i,d_j} to these nodes. Equation 8 expresses this relationship.

$$\forall d_j \in D : \mathbf{A}(d_j,\tau+1) = \begin{cases} \sum_{i=1}^{t} \dfrac{\mathbf{A}(c_i,\tau) \cdot w_{c_i,d_j}}{\sum_{k=1}^{s} w_{c_i,d_k}} & if\ t>0 \\ 0 & if\ t=0 \end{cases}$$

(8)

With:

- $A(d_j,\tau)$ ... activation of the document node to document j in step τ
- $A(c_i,\tau)$ ... activation of the concept node to concept i in step τ
- τ ... step of activation spreading
- t ... number of concept nodes from which node d_j receives activation
- w_{c_i,d_j} ... weight of edge between concept node c_i and a document node d_j
- $w_{c_i,d_j} = weight(c_i,d_j)$ (c.f. equation 3)
- s ... number of document nodes to which node c_i gives activation[2]
- w_{c_i,d_k} ... weight of edge between a concept node c_i and a document node d_k
- $w_{c_i,d_k} = weight(c_i,d_k)$ (c.f. equation 3)
- D ... layer of nodes representing documents

As expressed in equation 8 the activation of a document node d_j is calculated based on the sum of activations of those nodes from which the node receives activation. If a document node does not receive activation from any other node the activation of this document node equals zero.

The equations for calculating the spread of activation from concept nodes to concept nodes (equation 9) and from document nodes to document nodes (equation 10) are similar to equation 8. As with the spread of activation from concept nodes to document nodes in the spread of activation from concept nodes to concepts nodes the activation $A(c_i,\tau+1)$ of a node in step $\tau+1$ is based on the activation $A(c_i,\tau)$ of those nodes the node receives activation from in step τ and the edge weights w_{c_i,d_j} (c.f. equation 9). The same holds for the spread of activation from document nodes to documents nodes with the parameters $A(d_j,\tau+1)$, $\tau+1$, $A(d_j,\tau)$, τ and w_{d_i,d_j} respectively (c.f. equation 10).

Figure 2. Process of search in the network model. Depending on the configuration of the network model search is performed with or without semantic and/or textual similarity

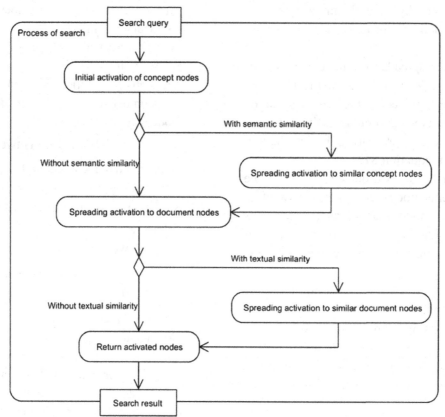

$$\forall c_j \in C : \mathbf{A}(c_j, \tau+1) = \begin{cases} \sum_{i=1}^{t} \dfrac{\mathbf{A}(c_i,\tau) \cdot w_{c_i c_j}}{\sum_{k=1}^{s} w_{c_i c_k}} + \mathbf{A}(c_j,\tau) & \text{if } t > 0 \\ \mathbf{A}(c_j,\tau) & \text{if } t = 0 \end{cases}$$

(9)

With:

- $A(c_j,\tau)$ ... activation of the concept node to concept j in step τ
- $A(c_i,\tau)$ ... activation of the concept node to concept i in step τ
- τ ... step of activation spreading
- t ... number of concept nodes from which node c_j receives activation
- $w_{c_i d_j}$ ... weight of edge between concept node c_i and a concept node c_j

- $w_{c_i c_j} = semsim(c_i, c_j)$ (c.f. equation 4)
- s ... number of concept nodes to which node c_i gives activation[3]
- $w_{c_i c_k}$ ... weight of edge between a concept node c_i and a concept node c_k
- $w_{c_i c_k} = semsim(c_i, c_k)$ (c.f. equation 4)
- C ... layer of nodes representing concepts

$$\forall d_j \in D : \mathbf{A}(d_j, \tau+1) = \begin{cases} \sum_{i=1}^{t} \dfrac{\mathbf{A}(d_i,\tau) \cdot w_{d_i d_j}}{\sum_{k=1}^{s} w_{d_i d_k}} + \mathbf{A}(d_j,\tau) & \text{if } t > 0 \\ \mathbf{A}(d_j,\tau) & \text{if } t = 0 \end{cases}$$

(10)

With:

- $A(d_j,\tau)$ ... activation of the document node to document j in step τ
- $A(d_i,\tau)$ ... activation of the document node to document i in step τ
- τ ... step of activation spreading
- t ... number of document nodes from which node d_j receives activation
- w_{d_i,d_j} ... weight of edge between document node d_i and a document node d_j
- $w_{d_i,d_j} = contsim(d_i,d_j)$ (c.f. equation 5)
- s ... number of document nodes to which node c_i gives activation[4]
- w_{d_i,d_k} ... weight of edge between a document node d_i and a document node d_k
- $w_{d_i,d_k} = contsim(d_i,d_k)$ (c.f. equation 5)
- D^i ... layer of nodes representing documents

As a central difference to equation 8, in equation 9 and equation 10 the activation $A(c_j,\tau)$ and $A(d_j,\tau)$ resp. of the current node in step τ is taken into account. Using this way of activation spreading the activation already present in a node is not replaced by the sum of activation of the node's neighbors, but these two values are added. This results in the situation that additional nodes in the concept layer and in the document layer are activated, while nodes already activated remain their activation or obtain additional activation from their neighbors.

APPLICATION OF THE RETRIEVAL MODEL WITHIN APOSDLE

We have applied the associative network model as presented above within the APOSDLE (Advanced Process-Oriented Self-Directed Learning Environment) project[5]. APOSDLE is a EU-funded integrated project (IST FP6) within the Technology Enhanced Learning Unit. The goal of the APOS-DLE project is to enhance knowledge worker productivity by supporting informal learning and collaborative learning activities in the context of knowledge workers' everyday work processes and within their computer based work environments. Support should be provided by means of a generic application that is not domain specific.

The foundation of the APOSDLE approach is to not rely on specifically created (e)Learning content, but to reuse existing (organizational) content which was not necessarily created with teaching in mind. We tap into all the resources of an organizational memory which might encompass project reports, studies, notes, intermediate results, plans, graphics, etc. as well as dedicated learning resources (if available) such as course descriptions, handouts and (e)Learning modules. The challenge we are addressing is: How can we make this confusing mix of information accessible to the knowledge worker in a way that she can advance her competencies with it?

In order to address this challenge APOSDLE needs a powerful retrieval mechanism. A frequently travelled path (specifically within eLearning systems) is the creation of fine-grained semantic models that allow for the categorization and retrieval of learning resources. But the creation of such models, their maintenance, and the annotation of resources with their concepts prove prohibitive within highly dynamic environments. Thus, the APOSDLE approach is a hybrid one: complementing coarse grained semantic models (maintained as much as possible automatically) with the power of diverse soft computing methodologies, improved over time through usage data and user feedback (collective intelligence) (Lindstaedt, Ley, Scheir, & Ulbrich, 2008).

Within APOSDLE the semantic models play two roles: on the one hand they serve as initial retrieval triggers and on the other hand they provide the basis for simple inferences and heuristics to interpret user interactions. A disadvantage of this approach is that 'statements' made by the system such as 'this resource helps you to understand the concept of use case modeling' or 'this person has expertise in use case writing' rely on

Figure 3. Instantiation of the network model for the domain of requirements engineering

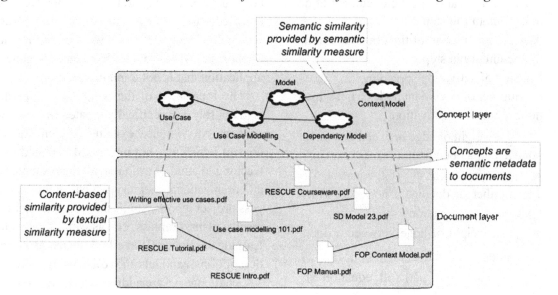

empirical observations with no claim to accuracy. We argue however, that users have become increasingly accustomed to handling uncertainty through their usage of (internet) search engines. Even more importantly, obsolete models do not provide any added value to the user and might provide a false sense of security. The APOSDLE approach is to apply a battery of soft computing technologies to bridge the gap between coarse-grained models and fine-grained learning needs. We employ this hybrid approach not only for the retrieval of resources but also for the identification of the user's current work context based on user interactions (Granitzer et al., 2008), for the determination of her competences based on task executions (Ley et al., 2008), and for the recommendation of people based on their competences and collaboration habits (Ähnelt, Ebert, Beham, Linstaedt, & Paschen, 2008).

Here we report on the application of the associative information retrieval model within the first APOSDLE prototype. The goal of this prototype is to support software engineers in advancing their requirements engineering skills. We employ the RESCUE (Jones & Maiden, 2005) requirements engineering process developed by the City University London (a partner within the APOSDLE project). Within the first prototype APOSDLE uses a knowledge base in the form of the RESCUE domain ontology and a document base that contains textual resources about requirements engineering that are partly annotated with concepts from the domain ontology. Figure 3 shows the instantiation of the network model for RESCUE.

The retrieval service implemented in the first APOSDLE prototype relies on knowledge contained in an ontology and the statistical information in a collection of documents. The service is queried with a set of concepts from the ontology and returns a set of documents. Documents in the system are (partly) annotated with ontological concepts if a document deals with a concept. For example, if the document is an introduction to use case models it is annotated with the corresponding concept in the ontology. In APOSDLE, the notation process is performed manually but is supported by statistical techniques (e.g. identification of frequent words in the document collection) (Pammer, Scheir, & Lindstaedt, 2007).

Concepts from the ontology are used as metadata for documents in the system. Opposed to classical metadata, the ontology specifies relations between the concepts. For example, class-subclass relationships are defined as well as arbitrary semantic relations between concepts are modeled (e. g. UseCase isComposedOfAction). The structure of the ontology is used for calculating the similarity between two concepts in the ontology according to the measure presented in the subsection (Semantic Similarity Measures Used) below. This similarity is then used to expand a query with similar concepts before retrieving documents dealing with this set of concepts. After thus retrieving documents based on metadata, the result set is expanded by means of textual similarity as introduced in the subsection (Text-based Similarity Measure Used) below. The implementation of the associative network inside the APOSDLE system allowed us to develop and test different combinations of query and result expansions that are based on the spreading activation algorithm presented in the previous section.

PARAMETRIZATION OF THE RETRIEVAL MODEL

In the following subsections we present the actual measures used for weighting the edges in the associative network structure that represent annotations and semantic and text-based similarity.

Measures Used for Weighting the Annotations

We weight the annotations between documents and concepts using a tf-idf-based weighting scheme. This is a standard instrument in information retrieval to improve retrieval results (Robertson & Spärck Jones, 1994). The higher the importance of a concept is for a document the higher the weight of the annotation. Our weighting approach is related to the one presented by Castells et al. (2007), who are also weighting semantic annotations using a tf-idf-based measure. The calculation

of the annotation weight is performed according to equation 11

$$weight(c,d) = \begin{cases} tf(c,d) \cdot idf(c) = tf(c,d) \cdot \log \dfrac{D}{a(c)} & if \ a(c) > 0 \\ 0 & if \ a(c) = 0 \end{cases}$$

$$(11)$$

With:

- c ... a concept
- d ... a document
- $tf(c,d)$ ... 1 if d is annotated with c, 0 otherwise
- $idf(c)$ ... inverse document frequency of concept c
- D ... total number of documents in system
- $a(c)$ ... number of documents annotated in system[6]

Semantic Similarity Measures Used

Within the work presented here, three different similarity measures where used for calculating the semantic similarity between concepts from an ontology. The determined similarity was used for weighting the edges in the concept layer of the Associative Network. All three measures where used for evaluation of the service that is presented in the next section.

The three similarity measures used are: a measure based on the shortest path between two concepts in the same class hierarchy, the measure of Resnik (1999) and a vector measure based on the properties which relate concepts in an ontology. All three measures share the fact, that for calculating the semantic similarity between two concepts these two concepts have to originate from the same ontology. In the case of our service all concepts are modeled in an ontology about Requirements Engineering.

If the similarity between two concepts from different ontologies should be calculated based on one of the three measures the approach described in (Ziegler, Kiefer, Sturm, Dittrich, & Bernstein, 2006) can be followed. There, an additional class called Super Thing is introduced as a direct superclass of all owl:Thing classed. owl:Thing stands for the superclass of all classes in every ontology formalized using OWL. Thus the class hierarchies of separated ontologies are connected. Alternatively, measures designed for determining the similarity between concepts from different ontologies can be applied. In this case measures for the alignment and mapping of ontologies (Euzenat & Shvaiko, 2007), which have been designed for this task can be applied.

The Shortest Path Measure

One of the measures used for determining the similarity between two concepts from one ontology is based on the number of edges in the shortest path between two concepts in the class hierarchy they share. This measure is a symmetric similarity measure. For calculating the measure the SimPack-Framework (Bernstein, Kaufmann, Kiefer, & Brki, 2005; Ziegler et al., 2006) was used.

The similarity between two concepts is calculated as shown in equation 12. The similarity measure is based on the shortest path (sp) between two concepts, being the number of edges in the hierarchy the two concepts are part of. The determined path length is increased by 1 and inverted afterward. The shortest path between a concept and itself is of length 0. In this case the calculated semantic similarity = 1.

$$sim(c_1, c_2) = \frac{1}{sp(c_1, c_2) + 1} \qquad (12)$$

With:

- c_1 ... first concept
- c_2 ... second concept
- sp ... number of edges in the shortest path between concept c_1 and concept c_2

Based on the characteristics of an ontology, different measures for calculating the semantic similarity between two concepts can be used. We applied the shortest path measure, as one feature of our ontology that is exploitable for the calculation of semantic similarity is the hierarchy of concepts.

Resnik's Measure (Resnik, 1999)

An additional measure that was used for calculating the similarity between two concepts from one ontology was the variant proposed by Resnik (1999) of the measure originally presented by Wu and Palmer (1994). Like the shortest path measure it builds on the position of two concepts in the same hierarchy. The measure is a symmetric similarity measure. The implementation was conducted during the APOSDLE project.

The method calculates the semantic similarity between two concepts according to equation 13. This similarity measure builds on the number of nodes in the path from the root node to the least common subsumer (lcs) of the two concepts, which is the most specific concept they share as an ancestor.

This value is scaled by the sum of the path lengths from the individual concepts to the root. When determining the number of nodes in a path the start and the end node are counted as well. If a path contains only one node its length is = 1, resulting in *depth*(root node) = 1.

$$sim(c_1, c_2) = \frac{2 \cdot depth(lcs(c_1, c_2))}{depth(c_1) + depth(c_2)} \qquad (13)$$

With:

- c_1 ... first concept
- c_2 ... second concept
- lcs ... least common subsumer of two concepts

- *depth* ... depth of concept in the class hierarchy (nodes in path from root node to concept node, including start and end node)

Depending on the features present in an ontology different similarity measures qualify to be applied. We chose the measure presented in (Resnik, 1999), as a prominent feature of our ontology are taxonomic relations between concepts. An advantage of the used measure (opposed to the shortest path measure) is that it tries to address one of the typical problems of taxonomy-based approaches to similarity: Relations in the taxonomy do not always represent a uniform (semantic) distance. The more specific the hierarchy becomes the more similar a child node is to its father node in the taxonomy. This situation is addressed in Resnik's measure by the introduction of the least common subsumer.

The Trento Similarity Measure

The Trento[7] similarity measure determines the similarity between two concepts in an ontology based on the properties (relations) in the ontology that are connecting the concepts. Two concepts that are related by a property are considered as similar. The more properties connect two concepts the more similar the two concepts are considered. For calculating the similarity between concepts based on the properties connecting them a vector based similarity measure is used. Concepts are represented as vectors and properties are used as features of the concept vectors. Every relation in the ontology is represented as a dimension in the vector space spanned by the concept vectors. Every relation in the ontology is represented as a dimension in the vector space spanned by the concept vectors. The similarity between two vectors is calculated based on the cosine measure (see equation 15). The cosine measure is a classic measure in text retrieval. It calculates the similarity between two vectors based on the angle between them. The more features two vectors share the smaller the angle between them and the more similar they are considered. By applying the cosine to the angle the similarity is represented by a value in the interval of [0..1]. This measure is a symmetric similarity measure.

The implementation of the measure presented here is again based on the SimPack-Toolkit (Bernstein et al., 2005), which provides means for representing classes as vectors and the computation of the cosine measure between two vectors. A procedure for filling the vectors was implemented building upon the existing functionality.

Equation 14 shows the representation of a concept as vector that is used by the Trento measure. Equation 15 shows the calculation of the semantic similarity based on the cosine measure.

$$\vec{c} = (d_1, d_2, \ldots, d_n) \tag{14}$$

With:

- $\vec{c}$ ... vector representing concept c
- d_n ... n-th dimension of vector representing concept c
- n ... number of properties in the ontology[8]
- $d_n=0$ if concept c is neither domain nor range of property n
- $d_n=1$ if concept c is domain or range (or both) of property n

$$sim(c_1, c_2) = sim_{cos}(\vec{c}_1, \vec{c}_2) = \frac{\vec{c}_1 \cdot \vec{c}_2}{|\vec{c}_1| \cdot |\vec{c}_2|} \tag{15}$$

With:

- c_1 ... first concept
- c_2 ... second concept
- $\vec{c}_1$ ... vector representing the first concept
- $\vec{c}_2$ ... vector representing the second concept
- $sim_{cos}(\vec{c}_1, \vec{c}_2)$ ... similarity between the two vectors $\vec{c}_1$ and $\vec{c}_2$ based on the cosine measure

This measure was chooses as an alternative to the measures based on the class hierarchy of the ontology (shortest path, Resnik). Based on the properties of an ontology it exploits a different feature of the knowledge representation.

Text-Based Similarity Measure Used

As similarity measure for textual documents we use an asymmetric measure based on the vector space model implemented in the open source search engine Lucene[9]. The similarity between two documents is calculated as shown in equation 16.

$$Sim(d1,d2)=score(d1_{25},d2) \qquad (16)$$

With:

- $d1$ ... document vector of the first document
- $d2$ ... document vector of the second document
- $d1_{25}$ ... document vector of the first document with all term weights removed except the 25 highest terms weights

$_{d125}$ is used as query vector for the score-measure of Lucene. For extracting the 25 terms with the highest weights, both the document content and the document title are taken into account. The calculation of Lucene's score is depicted in equation 17.

$$score(q,d)=coord(q,d)\cdot queryNorm(q)$$

$$\cdot \sum_{t\_in\_q} (tf(t\_in\_d) \cdot idf(t)^2 \cdot t.getBoost() \cdot norm(t,d))$$

$$(17)$$

With:

- q ... query vector
- d ... document vector

- $coord(q,d) = \dfrac{numberOfMatchingTerms}{numberOfQueryTerms}$
- *numberOfMatchingTerms* ... number of terms in document matching query
- *numberOfQueryTerms* ... number of terms in the query
- $queryNorm(q)$ ... normalization of the query vector, Lucene default used
- $tf(t\_in\_d)$ ... term frequency of current term in document, Lucene default used
- $idf(t)$ ... inverse document frequency of current term in the document collection, Lucene default used
- $t.getBoost()=tf(t\_in\_q)\cdot idf(t)$
- $tf(t\_in\_q)$ ... term frequency of current term in query
- $norm(t,d) = \dfrac{1}{\sqrt{(numberOfDocumentTerms)}}$
- *numberOfDocumentTerms* ... number of terms in the current document

Out of the various components that control the final score of a document matching a query, $coord(q,d)$ deserves special attention because it has shown in practice to contribute much to the final result. Thus, a document that matches the set of query terms will be ranked higher than a document that only contains a smaller subset of all input query terms. Another important aspect of the scoring function is the document normalization factor, $norm(t,d)$. Documents that contain fewer terms will yield a higher score than long documents. This applies not only to the document content but also to the document titles. Therefore, the similarity of the title terms contributes more to the final score than the terms from the document body. On the other hand, the $t.getBoost()$ factor can be ignored in our case because all query terms are weighted equally.

A detailed and in-depth explanation of the various parameters that can be used to adapt the behavior of Lucene can be found in the Javadoc of the org.apache.lucene.search.Similarity class.

EVALUATION

In this section we describe the evaluation that we performed. We introduce the evaluation measures, the queries used for evaluation; we discuss how we collected relevance judgments, and how the service configuration rankings are obtained.

Semantic Web Information Retrieval and Evaluation

At present information retrieval in the Semantic Web is an inhomogeneous research field (c.f. (Scheir, Pammer, & Lindstaedt, 2007). Although a good amount of approaches does exist, different information is used for the retrieval process, different input is accepted and different output is produced. This makes it difficult to define generally applicable rules for the evaluation of an information retrieval system for the Semantic Web and to create a test collection for this application area of information retrieval.

The present approach to retrieval on the Semantic Web is different from current attempts to retrieval: (1) the semantic information present in an ontology is taken into account for retrieval purpose; (2) the query to the retrieval service is formulated by a set of concepts stemming from an ontology as opposed to a set of terms (words) as typically used in the context of search engines. As we are not aware of any standard test corpora for the evaluation of an information retrieval service for the Semantic Web we have created our own evaluation environment.

The Test Corpus

A major obstacle for readily evaluating Semantic Web technology based information retrieval systems is the absence of standardized test corpora, as they exist for text-based information retrieval. We are unaware of any standard text retrieval corpora for evaluating a service with characteristics similar to ours. In our attempt to use a standard corpus we considered treating the ontological concepts used for querying our retrieval service equivalent to query terms of a text retrieval system. In order to do so, we would have needed some semantic structure relating the terms contained in the documents equivalent to our ontology that defines relations between concepts. For this task we could have used a standard thesaurus. But, since thesauri are structured differently to our original RESCUE ontology (and therefore different similarity measures had to be applied to it), this would have led us to evaluating a service with different properties than our original one.

We also considered the INEX[10] test collection for evaluating our service. INEX provides a document collection of XML documents that would have provided us with textual data associated with XML structure information. Unfortunately, again an ontology relating the metadata used as XML markup is unavailable. This would have prevented us from employing (and evaluating) the functionality provided by the query expansion technique, which is based on the ontology.

Due to these considerations we have built our own test corpus based on the data available in the first release of the APOSDLE system (Lindstaedt & Mayer, 2006). As discussed above, the first version of APOSDLE was built for the domain of Requirements Engineering (specifically RESCUE). The RESCUE domain ontology and the RECSUE document base together provide the knowledge base. The domain ontology consists of 70 concepts, 21 of which are used to annotate documents. The document base consists of 1016 documents, 496 documents of which are annotated with one or more concepts from the knowledge base. As these numbers show, the APOSDLE project provides a typical example of scarce annotation: only parts of the ontology are used for annotation and only parts of the documents are annotated. This setting illustrates the coverage problematic as discussed in the introduction. It prompts us to employ techniques from soft computing appropriate to finding relevant resources, which were not originally annotated with concepts from the domain ontology. In its size our test collection is comparable to test collections from early information retrieval experiments as the Cranfield or the CACM collections[11].

Measures Used For Evaluation

The central problem in using classic IR measures as recall or mean average precision is that they require complete relevance judgments, which means that every document is judged against every query (Buckley & Voorhees, 2004). Fuhr (2006) notices that recall cannot be determined precisely with reasonable effort. Finally Carterette, Allan, and Sitaraman (2006) states that: Building sets large enough for evaluation of realworld implementations is at best inefficient, at worst infeasible.

Therefore we opted for using evaluation measures that do not require that every document is judged against every query. We decided for using precision (P) at rank 10, 20 and 30. In addition we made use of infAP (Yilmaz & Aslam, 2006), which approximates the value of average precision (AP) using random sampling.

For calculating the evaluation scores we have used the trec_eval[12] package, which origins from the Text REtrieval Conference (TREC) and allows for calculating a large number of standard measures for information retrieval system evaluation.

Queries Used For Evaluation

The queries that were used for the evaluation of the service are formed by sets of concepts.

The first version of the APOSDLE system presents resources to knowledge workers to allow them to acquire a certain competency. To realize search for resources that are appropriate to build up a certain competency, competencies are represented by sets of concepts from the domain ontology. These sets are used as queries for the search for resources. For the evaluation of the

APOSDLE system all distinct sets of concepts representing competencies[13] were used as queries. In addition all concepts from the domain model not already present in the set of queries were used for evaluation purposes.

Collecting Relevance Judgments

Twelve different service configurations were tested and compared against each other based on the chosen evaluation measures. 79 distinct queries were used to query every service configuration. Queries were formed by sets of concepts stemming from the domain ontology.

For every query and service configuration the first 30 results were stored in a database table, with one row for every query-document pair. Query-document pairs returned by more than one service configuration were stored only once. The query-document pairs stored in the database-table were then judged manually by a human assessor. All query-document pairs were judged by the same person. The assessor was not involved in defining the competency to concept mappings uses as queries.

After relevance judgment, both, the results obtained by the different service configurations and the global relevance judgments have been stored into text files in a format appropriate for the trec_eval program. We then calculated the P(10), P(20), (P30) and infAP scores for the different service configurations.

The Obtained Service Configuration Ranking

Table 1 shows the calculated P(10), P(20), (P30) and infAP scores for the 12 different service configurations. The columns SemSim, TxtSim indicate whether semantic similarity or text-based similarity was used for the search. In addition, in column SemSim the name of the used semantic similarity measure is given. This can be the Shortest Path measure, the measure of Resnik, and the

Table 1. Evaluation scores of service configurations calculated using P(10), P(20), P(30) and infAP

Conf.	SemSim	TxtSim	P(10)	P(20)	P(30)	infAP
conf_1	No	No	0.2481	0.2089	0.1726	0.1523
conf_2	No	Yes	0.3127	0.2823	0.2540	0.2706
conf_3	Shortest Path (>0.4)	No	0.3177	0.2620	0.2122	0.2029
conf_4	Resnik (>0.5)	No	0.3228	0.2646	0.2156	0.2134
conf_5	Resnik (.0.7)	No	0.3177	0.2620	0.2122	0.2029
conf_6	Trento Vector (>0.1)	No	0.2772	0.2259	0.1907	0.1809
conf_7	Trento Vector (>0.4)	No	0.2608	0.2228	0.1865	0.1687
conf_8	Shortest Path (>0.4)	Yes	0.3962	0.3544	0.3135	0.3552
conf_9	Resnik (>0.5)	Yes	0.3886	0.3456	0.3089	0.3502
conf_10	Resnik (>0.7)	Yes	0.3962	0.3544	0.3135	0.3551
conf_11	Trento Vector (>0.1)	Yes	0.3785	0.3278	0.2928	0.3432
conf_12	Trento Vector (>0.4)	Yes	0.3367	0.2962	0.2679	0.3017

Trento Vector measure. All three measures are presented in section Semantic Similarity Measures Used. The value in brackets in column SemSim represent the threshold that is used for associative search. Shortest Path (> 0.4) stands for the Shortest Path measure from section Semantic Similarity Measures Used with a threshold of 0.4. This means that for associative search only concepts with a semantic similarity higher than 0.4 to the current concept from the query are taken into account. The thresholds used have been determined empirically.

Configuration 1 (conf_1) is the baseline configuration of our service, i.e. all other configurations are compared against it. The results delivered by this configuration are comparable to the use of a query language as SPARQL combined with an idf-based ranking (based on documents annotated with concepts) and no associative retrieval techniques used. Exactly those documents are retrieved that are annotated with the concepts present in the query.

All other configurations take semantic and/or textual similarity into account. While semantic similarity is used to extend the query set and thus indirectly extends the result set, textual similarity directly focuses on an extension of the result set.

Configurations 3 to 12 perform query expansion based on semantic similarity calculated with one of measure presented in previous section *Parametrization of the Retrieval Model*. Configurations 2 and 8 to 12 perform result expansion based on textual similarity calculated with the measure presented in previous section *Parametrization of the Retrieval Model*.

All associative search approaches employing semantic similarity (configurations 3 to 7), text-based similarity (configuration 2) or both (configurations 8 to 12) increase retrieval performance compared to the baseline (configuration 1). Additional relevant documents are found which are not annotated with the concepts used to query the service. With each of these configurations additional relevant documents are found, which would not have been found using the basic search functionality, as they are not annotated with the concepts that were used to query the service.

Table 2 shows the service configuration ranking based on the obtained evaluation scores of the measures P(10), P(20), P(30) and infAP. Those configurations returned by the majority of measures are marked bold.

Figure 2 shows the retrieval effectiveness of the evaluated service configuration based on the

Table 2. Ranking of service configurations based on P(10), P(20), P(30) and infAP. Configuration returned by the majority of measures marked bold

Rank	P(10)	P(20)	P(30)	infAP
1 (best)	**conf_8, conf_10**	**conf_8, conf_10**	**conf_8, conf_10**	conf_8
2				conf_10
3	**conf_9**	**conf_9**	**conf_9**	conf_9
4	**conf_11**	**conf_11**	**conf_11**	conf_11
5	**conf_12**	**conf_12**	**conf_12**	conf_12
6	conf_4	**conf_2**	**conf_2**	conf_2
7	conf_5, conf_3	**conf_4**	**conf_4**	conf_4
8		**conf_5, conf_3**	**conf_5, conf_3**	conf_5, conf_3
9	conf_2			
10	**conf_6**	**conf_6**	**conf_6**	conf_6
11	**conf_7**	**conf_7**	**conf_7**	conf_7
12 (worst)	**conf_1**	**conf_1**	**conf_1**	conf_1

measures infAP, P(10), P(20) and P(30) side to side. A higher bar corresponds to higher retrieval effectiveness. The configuration with the highest retrieval effectiveness is placed on the left hand side of the chart. The ranking (left to right) of the service configurations in Figure 4 was performed according the infAP measure.

Discussion of Service Configuration Ranking

All configurations using textual similarity lead to higher retrieval effectiveness than the respective configurations not using textual similarity (but employing the same semantic similarity measure). We believe that one reason for this is that textual similarity is a well-explored tool that can be used efficiently and rather independent of the application domain. Another even more important reason for the success of the textual similarity measure is the way it is currently employed in our service: The documents are retrieved using quality assured semantic annotations. This means, that for a given query either no resources will be retrieved (if no annotations are present) or documents will be retrieved that are of high relevance to the concepts

in the query. This is an ideal setting for result set expansion as highly relevant documents will be used to identify additional relevant documents based on term co-occurrences (this is the way the vector space based similarity measure described in section Text-based Similarity Measure Used works). The presented approach to result set expansion would fail if lots of noise (i.e. irrelevant results) is in the result set. This situation could occur in our setting if: (1) faulty semantic annotations are present, (2) an incorrect measure for semantic similarity is used, or (3) the threshold for semantic similarity is too low, which results in semantically broadening the query too much.

Conf_2 does not employ a measure for semantic similarity but only one for textual similarity. This configuration performs better than any of the configurations that only make use of semantic similarity. Again we see the way textual similarity is applied in our service as a reason for this situation: By exclusively using textual similarity the result set can be extended from a pool of 1016 documents (all documents in the document base are retrievable via textual similarity), while by exclusively using semantic similarity a smaller pool of 496 documents exists (the documents

Figure 4. Retrieval effectiveness of the evaluated configurations

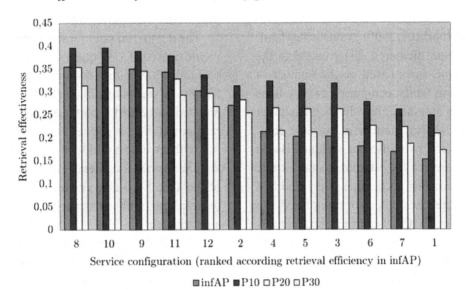

semantically annotated and thus retrievable giving a concept).

Of all tested configuration that make use of semantic similarity, those configurations employing the Trento Vector measure perform worst[1415]. We see the reason for this in the combination of the ontology we have used for testing with the algorithms used for determining semantic similarity. We assume that the Trento Vector measure least fits the way the ontology was modeled. Investigating this issue we thought of two potential problems occurring by the combination of the ontology currently used and the Trento Vector algorithm: (1) The ontology contains fewer properties than hierarchical relations, which entails that with the Trento Vector measure for fewer concepts associated concepts can be found than with the path-based measures. (2) Ontological properties in general have a lower semantic similarity than hierarchical relations. For the ontology given we expect (2) to be the reason for the lower performance of the measure. We have analyzed the structure of the concept layer of the associative network and found that for the Trento Vector measure 63 edges with a weight higher than 0.1

are available (these are the edges used for query expansion). For the measure of Resnik 173 edges with a weight higher than 0.5 are available. For the Shortest Path measure 67 edges with a weight higher than 0.4 are available. Although for the configurations using the Trento Vector measure almost the same number of edges are available for query expansion as for the configurations using the Shortest Path measure the Shortest Path measure did perform better in our evaluation. Therefore we do not think of (1) to be the reason for the lower performance of the Trento Vector measure.

Finally it has to be noted that those configuration that employ both, semantic similarity and textual similarity (i.e. configurations 8 to 12) perform best.

Discussion of the Performed Evaluation

We now discuss the evaluation measures used and why we think that the amount of relevance judgments collected is sufficient for a proper evaluation of our service.

P(10), P(20) and P(30)

Buckley and Voorhees (2000) evaluate the stability of evaluation measures. They calculate the error rate of measures based on the number of errors occurring whilst comparing two systems using a certain measure. They divide the number of errors by the total number of possible comparisons between two different systems. Based on previous research they state that an error rate of 2.9% is minimally acceptable. They find that P(30) exactly reaches this error rate of 2.9% in their experiment with 50 queries used. Finally they suggest that the amount of queries should be increased for P(n) measures, where n < 30. And suggest that 100 queries would be safe if the measure P(20) is used.

We performed our experiment with 79 distinct queries and used the measures P(10), P(20) and P(30). Following the results of Buckley and Voorhees (2000) the size of our query set should be appropriate for P(30). We are fortified in this assumption as the ranking of the 12 service configurations is identical for P(20), P(30) and infAP.

infAP

The Trec 8 Ad-Hoc collection consists of 528,155 documents and 50 queries which make a total amount of 26,407,750 possible relevance judgments. 86830 query-document relevance pairs are actually judged. This set of pairs is created by depth-100 pooling of 129 runs. Therefore 0.33% of the possible relevance judgments are performed.

Our collection consists of 1026 documents and 79 queries, which results in a total of 81,054 possible relevance judgments. This set of pairs is created by depth-30 pooling of 12 runs and 855 additional relevance judgments that were performed for runs that were not part of the experiment. 2787 query document pairs were actually judged. Therefore 3.44% of all possible relevance judgments were performed.

The depth-100 pool for the 12 evaluated runs would consist of 5393 query-document pairs[16]. As we judged 2787 query-document pairs, we judged 51.68% of our potential depth-100 pool. Yilmaz and Aslam (2006) report a Kendall's tau based rank correlation of above 0.9 between infAP and AP with as little as 25% of the maximum possible relevance judgments of the depth-100 pool of the Trec 8 Ad-Hoc collection. They consider two rankings with a rank correlation of above 0.9 as equivalent.

With 51.68% of our potential depth-100 pool judged, we are confident that the infAP measure produces a sufficiently accurate estimation. Again our confidence in the results of infAP is assured by the equivalence of the ranking of the 12 service configurations for P(20), P(30) and infAP.

PARAMETER LEARNING USING RELEVANCE FEEDBACK

In section *Parameterization of the Retrieval Model* we introduced various heuristics to parameterize the associative network structure. One current stream of our research is to investigate if feedback provided by the user on the retrieved documents can be facilitated to (re-)estimate the network parameters, so that it better reflects the user's intuition of relevance. In the following section we propose an extension of the associative retrieval model introduced in section *An Associative Information Retrieval Model for the Semantic Web* in which relevance feedback data is used to adjust the network parameters in order to improve retrieval effectiveness.

Extension of the Network Model by Relevance Feedback Based Learning

Traditional relevance feedback approaches in IR aim at a better understanding of the user's information need by using the evidence provided by the user to change the representation of the query (Rocchio, 1971; Robertson, Spärck Jones, 1976). These approaches can be considered as a form of transient learning which is limited to a single query session. In contrast, our approach changes the representation of the documents in a persistent manner and bears similarities to probabilistic indexing models (Fuhr, 1989) and connectionist approaches to IR (Belew, 1989; Kwok, 1995).

The proposed extension builds upon the theory of probabilistic indexing (Maron, Kuhns, 1960), which aims at estimating the probability that document is judged relevant given the query by regarding a single document to a number of queries. The theory is implemented by turning the associative network into a feed-forward neural network, a special case of an artificial neural network which underlying graph is directed and acyclic. Given a training set of explicit relevance judgments, we derive the model parameters (i.e. the network weights) by maximum likelihood. We use a gradient-based method known as stochastic gradient descent, to maximize the likelihood function. As an on-line method, stochastic gradient descent enables the network to be trained one training example at a time, rather than with a batch of examples. This allows the instant adaption of the model to user feedback rather than having to wait until a sufficient number of training examples have been aggregated. We use the efficient backpropagation algorithm to evaluate the gradient of the likelihood function w.r.t. the model parameters.

Fuhr (1992) points out, that traditional probabilistic indexing approaches fail due to insufficient training data since too many model parameters need to be estimated. However, because of the initialization of the associative network based on the heuristics described in section *Parameterization of the Retrieval Model*, the "untrained" model has already desirable retrieval capabilities. This initialization can be regarded as a reasonable initial estimate of the model parameters which we

would like to further improve based on relevance feedback. The Probabilistic Indexing and Retrieval Component System (PIRCS) by Kwok (1995) uses a similar strategy by utilizing (established) IR heuristics to *bootstrap* the feed-forward network underlying PIRCS in order to overcome the problem of insufficient training data. Schütze, Hull, and Pedersen (1995) point out that this approach has potential for enhancing the effectiveness of IR models based on neural networks. However, in contrast to our work, Kwok (1995) does not use the backpropagation algorithm for network training.

As introduced in subsection *Searching the Network* the spreading activation procedure can be expressed by a network which implements a feed-forward topology comprising four[17] node layers $C, \widehat{C}, D,$ and $\widehat{D}$, referring to the concept, expanded concept, resultset and expanded resultset layer, respectively. A depiction of the network is shown in Figure 5. Query processing proceeds from left to right: the activation $\mathrm{A}(n_j, \hat{o}+1)$ of node n_j in node layer $\hat{o}+1$ is given by a weighted sum of the activation values of all nodes in the preceding node layer $\hat{o}$,

$$\mathrm{A}(n_j, \tau + 1) = \sum_i w_{ji}^{(\tau)} \mathrm{A}(n_i, \tau) \qquad (19)$$

With:

- $\mathrm{A}(n_j, \tau+1)$... activation of node n_j in node layer τ.
- $\mathrm{A}(n_i, \tau)$... activation of node n_i in node layer τ
- $w_{ji}^{(\tau)}$... weight of the edge from node n_i to node n_j. The superscript refers to the τ-th weight layer.

Finally, the ranking is given by the activation level of the document nodes in node layer $\widehat{D}$.

In order to implement the theory of probabilistic indexing we propose the following modifications to the associative retrieval model:

Figure 5. The extended associative retrieval model. The network is modified by introducing logistic sigmoid activation functions in the output layer. The arrows on the top and bottom of the figure indicate the direction of information processing at retrieval and training time, respectively

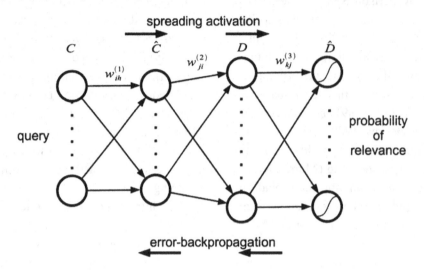

1. We constrain the activation level of the document nodes in the node layer $\hat{D}$ to the interval $[0,1]$ and interpret the activation of a document node d_k in layer $\hat{D}$ as an estimate of the probability of relevance of that document w.r.t. the query. The transformation is indicated by the logistic sigmoid units in the rightmost layer of Figure 5.

2. We map the relevance feedback data onto an estimate of the probability of relevance of that document w.r.t. the query. In the following, we restrict ourselves to the case of binary relevance, $R \in \{0,1\}$. Thus, the fact that a document is judged relevant is mapped onto a probability estimate of 1, and non-relevant is mapped onto an estimate of 0.

The modified network can be regarded as implementing multiple independent binary classification tasks, one for each document in the collection. Given a query q, we compute the estimate of the probability of relevance $P(R=1|d_k,q)$ of each document d_k by the network function $y_k(q,\vec{w})$ given by,

$$y_k(q,\vec{w}) = \sigma\left(\sum_{j=1}^{|D|} w_{kj}^{(3)} \sum_{i=1}^{|\hat{C}|} w_{ji}^{(2)} \sum_{h=1}^{|C|} w_{ih}^{(1)} \mathrm{A}(c_h)\right)$$

(19)

With:

- $\vec{w}$, ... weight vector comprising the network parameters $w_{ji}^{(\tau)}$
- $w_{ji}^{(\tau)}$ ... weight of the edge connecting node n_i to node n_j. Located in weight layer τ
- q ... query comprising a number of concepts c_h and their corresponding activation levels $\mathrm{A}(c_h)$
- σ... logistic sigmoid function given by,

$$\sigma(a) = \frac{1}{1+e^{-a}}$$

(20)

In the following subsection we describe how to derive the network parameters $\vec{w}$ from a training sample of explicit relevance judgments.

Network Training using Error-Backpropagation

Similar to other probabilistic indexing models such as the binary independence indexing model (Fuhr, 1992), we use the method of maximum likelihood to fit our model to the observed data. Given a training sample of queries Q, documents D and corresponding relevance judgments[18] $J = \{(q,d_k,r_k)|q \in Q, d_k \in D, r_k \in \{0,1\}\}$, maximizing the likelihood of the parameters given the data is equivalent to minimizing the negative log-likelihood given by,

$$E(\vec{w}) = -\sum_{q,d_k,r_k \in J} r_k \ln y_k + (1 - r_k)\ln(1 - y_k)$$

(21)

With:

- $\vec{w}$ ... weight vector comprising the network parameters
- $r_k \in \{0,1\}$ ... relevance judgment of document d_k w.r.t. query q
- y_k ... network function $y_k(q,\vec{w})$.

We minimize the above error function using *stochastic gradient descent*. This gradient-based technique updates the network parameters to comprise a small step in the direction of the negative gradient of the error function w.r.t. the current parameters by examining a single training example at a time. The weight update is given by,

$$\vec{w}^{t+1} = \vec{w}^t - \eta \nabla E_n(\vec{w}^t)$$

(22)

With:

- $\vec{w}^t$ ... weight vector at time t
- $\eta > 0$ ... hyperparameter known as the *learning rate* that controls the step size in the parameter space
- $\nabla E_n(\vec{w}^t)$ ... gradient of the error function w.r.t. the weight vector evaluated at

the *n*-th relevance judgement (i.e. the n-th term in the summation in Equation 21).

We use the backpropagation algorithm (c.f. (Bishop 2006; MacKay 2002)) to evaluate the gradient of the error function w.r.t. the network parameters. In the following, we give a brief summarization of the main steps of the algorithm.

For a given training example comprising a query q a document d_k and a relevance judgment r_k, network training proceeds as follows:

1. The error of the *k*-th output unit δ_k is computed according to,

$$\delta_k = y_k - r_k$$

(23)

With:

- δ_k ... error of the *k*-th output unit
- y_k ... network function $y_k(q,\vec{w})$.
- r_k ... relevance judgment of document d_k w.r.t. query q.

2. The error δ_k is propagated back through the network to set the values δ_j of the preceding node layers,

$$\delta_j = \sum_k w_{kj}\delta_k$$

(24)

With:

- δ_j ... error of the node n_j in the node layer τ
- δ_k ... error of the node n_k in the node layer $\tau+1$.
- w_{kj} ... weight of the edge between node n_j and n_k.

Thus, the value δ_j of a node n_j in the current layer is computed based on the (weighted) error of each node n_k in the proceeding node layer.

3. The partial derivative of the error function w.r.t. each connection weight is evaluated,

$$\frac{\partial E_n}{\partial w_{ji}} = \delta_j \mathrm{A}(n_i, \tau) \tag{25}$$

With:

- δ_j ... error of the node n_j in the node layer τ
- δ_k ... error of the node n_k in the node layer $\tau+1$.
- w_{kj} ... weight of the edge between node n_j and n_k.

Thus, the gradient w.r.t. the connection weight w_{ji} is simply the product of the error of the target node n_j and the activation level of the source node n_i.

4. Finally, each connection weight w_{ji} where $\frac{\partial E_n}{\partial w_{ji}} \neq 0$ is updated according to,

$$w_{ji}^{t+1} = w_{ji}^{t} - \eta \frac{\partial E_n}{\partial w_{ji}} \tag{26}$$

With:

- w_{ji}^{t} ... weight of the edge between node n_i and n_j at time t
- η ... learning rate, controls step size in parameter space
- $\frac{\partial E_n}{\partial w_{ji}}$ ... partial derivative of the error function w.r.t. the weight w_{ji} evaluated at the nth training example

The above procedure is applied to each training example in the training set and the process is repeated until a predefined stopping criterion is met (e.g. convergence, a fixed number of iterations, error on held-out data increases). The learning procedure outlined above is generic, meaning that it can be used for different feed-forward topologies with any number of weight layers.

The value of η is crucial to the success of the training procedure. If η is too small, the algorithm progresses slowly and a large number of iterations is needed for convergence. On the other hand, if η is too large, the algorithm might "jump over" minima in the error function or might even start oscillating around a minimum hence making no progress at all. A good value for η is usually obtained by means of cross-validation[19] or held-out data.

Variants of the Learning Algorithm

Considering the associative network depicted in Figure 5, we observe that different weight layers exhibit different levels of sparsity. This sparsity results from poor initialization of connection weights in certain weight layers. In particular, the concept to document layer is relatively sparse compared to the other two layers. This sparsity is due to the fact that the semantic annotations are created manually in a process where a person selects concepts the documents deal with. On the other hand associations between concepts and concepts and documents and documents are created automatically using similarity algorithms. Retrieval effectiveness might be improved by using as much training data as possible to derive better estimates for poorly initialized weights. In the following, two variants of the generic learning algorithm are proposed: a) Backprop $C - \hat{C} - D$ and b) Backprop $\hat{C} - D$. Both variants use the associative network as outlined above for forward propagation, however they restrict learning to certain weight layers.

Variant 1: Backprop $C - \hat{C} - D$

The use of cosine similarity in the vector-space model is an established means to estimate the similarity of documents and its effectiveness has been proven in many experiments and real life applications (c.f. (Baeza-Yates, Ribeiro-Neto,

1999)). Therefore, we might conclude that the third weight layer is properly initialized and we restrict network training to the first two weight layers.

Another fact why we would like to disregard the third weight layer during learning is that in general many more nodes in layer D are "active" compared to the preceding node layers C and $\hat{C}$ Thus, the gradients w.r.t. the weights in third weight layer $\vec{w}^{(3)}$ are much more likely to be non-zero than the gradients w.r.t. $\vec{w}^{(2)}$ and $\vec{w}^{(1)}$. Again, because of the density of the third weight layer this causes a fine grained distribution of the errors among the connection weights in $\vec{w}^{(3)}$. The runtime performance of the learning procedure is proportional to the number of non-zero gradients. Thus, a fine grained distribution of the errors considerably degrades the runtime efficiency of the system.

To restrict the learning procedure to the first two weight layers we make use of the simplifying fact that the node layers D and $\hat{D}$ consist of the same document nodes. We compute the probabilities of relevance and errors δ_k as described above. However, we alter the backpropagation procedure by skipping the error backpropagation from node layer $\hat{D}$ to node layer D and simply carry the error over to the corresponding document nodes in D.

Variant 2: Backprop $\hat{C} - D$

By restricting the adaption of the network solely to the second weight layer we focus on the worst initialized weight layer only. Note that this variant employs a notion of *adaptive indexing*. Again, the errors δ_k are carried over to the corresponding nodes in D and the gradients w.r.t. the weights in the second weight layer are simply the product of the activation level of the source node in $\hat{C}$ and the error of the target node in D. Note that this is essentially the application of the delta-rule,

$$w_{ki}^{t+1} = w_{ki}^t - \eta(y_k - r_k)A(n_i) \quad (27)$$

With:

- w_{ki}^t ... weight of the edge between node n_i and n_k at time t
- η ... learning rate
- y_k ... network function $y_k(q, \vec{w})$
- r_k ... binary relevance judgment of document d_k w.r.t. query q
- $A(n_i)$ ... activation of node n_i

Evaluation

In the following we evaluate the effectiveness of our parameter learning approach relative to the baseline model presented in section *An Associative Information Retrieval Model for the Semantic Web*. For this propose, we conduct an experiment based on a subset of the test collection presented in section *Evaluation*. To evaluate the effectiveness of the learning procedure we considered two approaches to system evaluation of interactive IR systems: a) residual ranking and b) train-test set (c.f. (Chang, Cirillo and Razon, 1971)). Both approaches evaluate different aspects of an interactive IR system. The residual ranking method evaluates the effectiveness of the system on a per query basis. For each query some evidence is given and the method evaluates how the system uses this evidence to increase retrieval effectiveness on the residual collection[20] of this query. On the other hand the train-test set method evaluates how well the system "generalizes" from a given set of queries (i.e. the training set) to new unseen queries (i.e. the test set). We choose the latter approach due to the fact that most of the queries in our test collection exhibit a small number of relevant documents. Reducing the number of relevance judgments – in particular positive judgments – for each query would compromise the reliability of the evaluation results.

The train-test set method is usually performed using a technique known as cross-validation. That is, the whole data set is partitioned into k partitions and each partition i is used once as the test set, while all other partitions but partition i comprise the training set. The size of k is a tradeoff between computational costs and the amount of data that is used for training. In general, one wants to use as much data as possible for training since the process of labeling (judging) the data is costly. To maximize the amount of training data we choose k to be the number of examples in the data set. This special case of cross-validation is referred to as *leave-one-out cross-validation*.

Test Corpus

The effectiveness of the system was evaluated using a subset of the test collection presented in section *Evaluation*. In particular, we choose our subset to be all queries comprising a single concept for which Configuration 10[21] of the associative retrieval model returned a non-empty result set. The resulting subset contains 26 queries.

Evaluation Setup

The associative network is initialized according to the second best performing run in section *Evaluation* (i.e. Configuration 10). One run is performed using solely the initialized system without any learning at all. The effectiveness of this run is considered as the baseline. The retrieval effectiveness of the proposed extensions will be evaluated relative to this baseline. As stated above, the system effectiveness of the learning runs is measured based on leave-one-out cross-validation. That is, for each of the 26 queries, the network is trained on all but the query in question. Then the effectiveness of the system is measured on the single query that was not considered during training. After each measurement, the network parameters are reset.

In order to determine the number of iterations of the training procedure, we randomly selected four queries as our validation set and trained the network on the remaining 22 queries. After each iteration of the training procedure we measured the error on the validation set and stopped the training as soon as the error on the validation set started to increase. This provided evidence that 30 iterations is a reasonable number to balance under- and overfitting.

We determine the learning rate η (c.f. subsection *Network Training using Error-Backpropagation*) using the same subsample of queries. The value of $\eta=0.01$ turned out to work best – lower values caused only minor changes in the ranking, whereas a larger value caused very unstable results and in general resulted in a weaker effectiveness on the subsample.

In line with the experiment described in section *Evaluation*, we use infAP and precision at various cut-off levels (10, 20, 30) as the target measures for determining retrieval effectiveness.

Evaluation Results

In the following section we report the results of the evaluation of the extended system. Three different runs of the extended system are considered. The first, Backprop, refers to the generic learning algorithm described in subsection *Network training using Error Backpropagation*. The second, Backprop $C - \hat{C} - D$, refers to variant 1 (described in subsection *Variants of the learning algorithm*) that restricts parameter adaption to the first and second weight layers. The third run, Backprop $\hat{C} - D$, refers to variant 2 (described in subsection *Variants of the learning algorithm*) that restricts learning solely to the second weight layer. Table 3 shows the evaluation results of the three runs compared to the baseline run. The empty and filled points refer to statistically significant improvement or degradation over the baseline, respectively. Following Sanderson and Zobel (2005) we use the

Table 3. Evaluation scores of the three runs and the baseline system. Statistically significant improvement or degradation over the baseline is based on a 95% confidence interval

Run.	P(10)	P(20)	P(30)	infAP
Baseline	0.7885	0.6846	0.5808	0.7609
Backprop	0.6154 (-21.95%) ●	0.5308 (-22.46%) ●	0.4679 (-19.43%) ●	0.6933(-8.88%)
Backprop $C - \hat{C} - D$	**0.8385** (+6.34%) ○	0.7038 (+2.80%)	0.5782 (-0.45%)	**0.7974** (+4.80%) ○
Backprop $\hat{C} - D$	0.8308 (+5.36%) ○	**0.7058** (+3.10%)	**0.5846** (+0.65%)	0.7810 (+2.64%) ○
○, ● statistically significant improvement or degradation				

Figure 6. The relative difference in terms of infAP of the Backprop and the baseline runs. A positive ΔinfAP indicates superior performance of Backprop

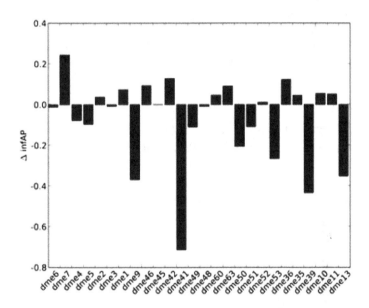

dependent t-test with a confidence interval of 95% to test statistical significance.

The results show that the generic approach performs worse than the baseline and the two variants w.r.t. all effectiveness measures. Considering Figure 6 which shows the per query difference in terms of infAP between the generic approach and the baseline, we observe that the differences are very instable. On the one hand, the effectiveness on queries 1, 2, 10, 11, 35 and 36 is superior to the baseline (and even to both variants). On the other hand, the effectiveness deteriorates on other queries. We assume that the weaker performance is due to the fact that there is not sufficient training data to train the document to document layer properly, following that the network completely overfits the training data and gives poor performance on the test data.

On the other hand, the two variants significantly outperform the baseline in terms of infAP

Figure 7. The relative difference in terms of infAP of the Backprop $C - \hat{C} - D$ *and the baseline runs. A positive ΔinfAP indicates superior performance of Backprop* $C - \hat{C} - D$

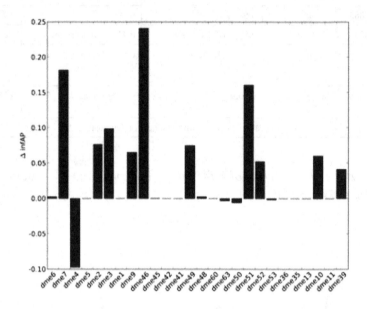

Figure 8. The relative difference in terms of infAP of the Backprop $\hat{C} - D$ *and the baseline runs. A positive ΔinfAP indicates superior performance of Backprop* $\hat{C} - D$

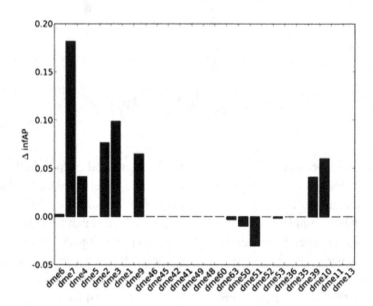

and P(10). The relative performance increase in terms of infAP of Backprop $C - \hat{C} - D$ over the baseline is 4.8%. A statistically significant increase in effectiveness of about 5% is very promising and can be considered as a positive result. Figure 7 shows the relative difference in terms of infAP between Backprop $C - \hat{C} - D$ and the baseline on a per query basis. One can see that the variant consistently outperforms the baseline on all but one query.

The effectiveness of Backprop $\hat{C} - D$ is slightly worse than Backprop $C - \hat{C} - D$, the relative increase in effectiveness with respect to the baseline is 2.64% compared to 4.8% for Backprop $C - \hat{C} - D$. However, Backprop $\hat{C} - D$ turns out to be more robust than the latter. Considering Figure 8, Backprop $\hat{C} - D$ does not fail miserably on any query compared to the baseline. The inferior effectiveness on query 51 is hardly recognizable (below 0.03).

CONCLUSIONS AND FUTURE WORK

We have presented an information retrieval model for the Semantic Web and an implementation of the model as service within the APOSDLE system. Both the model and its implementation rely on techniques from soft computing. We have evaluated the presented service using standard measures for information retrieval system evaluation. As classic measures for evaluation, as recall and average precision require that every document is judged for every query we have chosen precision at ranks 10, 20 and 30 as evaluation measures. In addition we made use of the random sampling approach performed by the infAP measure. Following recent works (Buckley & Voorhees, 2004; Yilmaz & Aslam, 2006) in information retrieval system evaluation we are confident that our chosen approach reflects the actual relation between the service configurations as the ranking of the

service configurations remains identical for the measures P(20), P(30) and infAP.

Our experiments encourage us, that the application of associative retrieval techniques to information retrieval on the Semantic Web is an adequate strategy. We tend to conclude that text-based methods for associative retrieval result in a higher increase in retrieval performance; therefore we want to explore the approach of attaching a set of terms to every concept in our domain ontology during modeling time to provide search results even for concepts that are not used for annotation. In addition we want to extend our research towards the application of different semantic similarity measures within our service. A key research question for the future is the appropriate selection of similarity measures for given ontologies. Therefore further experiments with different ontologies than the one used have to be conducted.

In this invited chapter we also gave insight to recent work on adapting the network structure to increase retrieval effectiveness. We proposed an extension to the associative network model which uses relevance feedback by the user to re-estimate the model parameters. We evaluated this approach relative to the original model. The results of the experiment show a significant increase in retrieval effectiveness, providing preliminary evidence of the benefit of incorporating relevance feedback into the associative retrieval model. To strengthen evidence on the usefulness of adapting the network structure further experiments with larger corpora have to be conducted.

ACKNOWLEDGMENT

We thank the anonymous reviewers of the International Journal of Semantic Web and Information Systems for their valuable comments.

While an earlier version of this chapter focusing on the description of the retrieval approach was presented at ISEMANTICS 2007 (Scheir, Ghidini,

& Lindstaedt, 2007) an in depth description of the approach to the evaluation of the developed service was presented at FGIR 2007 / LWA 2007 (Scheir, Granitzer, & Lindstaedt, 2007). We thank the anonymous reviewers of our submissions at I-SEMANTICS 2007 and LWA 2007 for their constructive feedback.

This work has been partially funded under grant 027023 in the IST work programme of the European Community. The Know-Center is funded within the Austrian COMET Program - Competence Centers for Excellent Technologies - under the auspices of the Austrian Ministry of Transport, Innovation and Technology, the Austrian Ministry of Economics and Labor and by the State of Styria. COMET is managed by the Austrian Research Promotion Agency FFG.

REFERENCES

Ähnelt, M., Ebert, M., Beham, G., Lindstaedt, S., & Paschen, A. (2008). A socio-technical approach towards supporting intra-organizational collaboration. In *Proceedings of ECTEL 2008, Maastricht, the Netherlands.*

Alani, H., Dasmahapatra, S., O'Hara, K., & Shadbolt, N. (2003). Identifying communities of practice through ontology network analysis. *IEEE Intelligent Systems, 18*(2), 18–25. doi:10.1109/MIS.2003.1193653

Anderson, J. R. (1983). A spreading activation theory of memory. *Journal of Verbal Learning and Verbal Behavior, 22,* 261–295. doi:10.1016/S0022-5371(83)90201-3

Baeza-Yates, R., & Ribeiro-Neto, B. (1999). *Modern Information Retrieval.* New York: Addison-Wesley & ACM Press.

Bechhofer, S., & Goble, C. (2001). Towards annotation using DAML+OIL. In K-cap 2001 workshop on knowledge markup and semantic annotation.

Belew, R. K. (1989). Adaptive information retrieval: using a connectionist representation to retrieve and learn about documents. In *Sigir '89: Proceedings of the 12th annual international acm sigir conference on research and development in information retrieval* (pp. 11–20). New York: ACM Press.

Berger, H., Dittenbach, M., & Merkl, D. (2004, January 18–22). An adaptive information retrieval system based on associative networks. In S. Hartmann & J. Roddick (Eds.), *Proceedings of the 1st asia-pacific conference on conceptual modelling (apccm 2004)* (Vol. 31, pp. 27–36). Dunedin, New Zealand: Australian Computer Society Inc.

Bernstein, A., Kaufmann, E., Kiefer, C., & Bürki, C. (2005, August). *Simpack: A generic java library for similarity measures in ontologies* (Tech. Rep.). [Zurich, Switzerland: University of Zurich, Department of Informatics.]. *Winterthurerstrasse, 190,* 8057.

Bishop, C. M. (2006). *Pattern Recognition and Machine Learning.* Springer.

Boughanem, M., Dkaki, T., Mothe, J., & Soule-Dupuy, C. (1999). Mercure at trec7. In The sevent text retrieval conference (trec- 7).

Buckley, C., & Voorhees, E. M. (2000). Evaluating evaluation measure stability. In *Sigir '00: Proceedings of the 23rd annual international acm sigir conference on research and development in information retrieval* (pp. 33–40). New York: ACM Press.

Buckley, C., & Voorhees, E. M. (2004). Retrieval evaluation with incomplete information. In *Sigir '04: Proceedings of the 27ᵗʰ annual international acm sigir conference on research and development in information retrieval* (pp. 25–32). New York: ACM Press.

Carterette, B., Allan, J., & Sitaraman, R. (2006). Minimal test collections for retrieval evaluation. In *Sigir '06: Proceedings of the 29th annual international acm sigir conference on research and development in information retrieval* (pp. 268–275). New York: ACM Press.

Castells, P., Fernandez, M., & Vallet, D. (2007). An adaptation of the vector-space model for ontology-based information retrieval. *IEEE Transactions on Knowledge and Data Engineering, 19*, 261–272. doi:10.1109/TKDE.2007.22

Chang, Y. K., Cirillo, C., & Razon, J. (1971). Evaluation of feedback retrieval using modified freezing, residual collection & test and control groups. In Salton, G. (Ed.), *The SMART retrieval system - experiments in automatic document processing* (pp. 355–370).

Chirita, P.-A., Costache, S., Nejdl, W., & Paiu, R. (2006). Beagle ++: Semantically enhanced searching and ranking on the desktop. In *The semantic web: Research and applications* (*Vol. 4011*, pp. 348–362). Berlin, Heidelberg: Springer. doi:10.1007/11762256_27

Cohen, P. R., & Kjeldsen, R. (1987). Information retrieval by constrained spreading activation in semantic networks. *Information Processing & Management, 23*(4), 255–268. doi:10.1016/0306-4573(87)90017-3

Crestani, F. (1997). Application of spreading activation techniques in information retrieval. *Artificial Intelligence Review, 11*, 453–482. doi:10.1023/A:1006569829653

Crestani, F., & Lee, P. L. (2000). Searching the web by constrained spreading activation. *Information Processing & Management, 36*(4), 585–605. doi:10.1016/S0306-4573(99)00073-4

Esmaili, K. S., & Abolhassani, H. (2006). *A categorization scheme for semantic web search engines. In 4th acs/ieee int. conf. on computer systems and applications (aiccsa-06).*

Euzenat, J., & Shvaiko, P. (2007). *Ontology matching.* Heidelberg: Springer-Verlag.

Fuhr, N. (1989). Models for retrieval with probabilistic indexing. *Information Processing & Management, 25*(1), 55–72. doi:10.1016/0306-4573(89)90091-5

Fuhr, N. (1992). Probabilistic Models in Information Retrieval. *The Computer Journal, 35*(3). doi:10.1093/comjnl/35.3.243

Fuhr, N. (2006). *Information Retrieval: Skriptum zur Vorlesung im SS 06, 19.* Dezember 2006.

Granitzer, M., Kröll, M., Seifert, C., Rath, A. S., Weber, N., Dietzel, O., et al. (2008). Analysis of machine learning techniques for context extraction. In *IEEE Proceedings of ICDIM 08, Third International Conference on Digital Information Management.*

Guha, R., McCool, R., & Miller, E. (2003). Semantic search. In *WWW '03: Proceedings of the 12th international conference on world wide web* (pp. 700–709). New York: ACM Press.

Handschuh, S. (2007). Semantic annotation of resources in the semantic web. In Studer, R., Grimm, S., & Abecker, A. (Eds.), *Semantic web services: Concepts, technologies, and applications* (pp. 135–155). Secaucus, NJ, USA: Springer-Verlag New York, Inc.

Heflin, J., & Hendler, J. (2000). Searching the web with SHOE. In Artificial Intelligence for Web Search. Papers from the AAAI Workshop. WS-00-01. (p. 35-40). Menlo Park, CA: AAAI Press.

Hendler, J. (2007). The dark side of the semantic web. *IEEE Intelligent Systems, 22*, 2–4. doi:10.1109/MIS.2007.17

Huang, Z., Chen, H., & Zeng, D. (2004). Applying associative retrieval techniques to alleviate the sparsity problem in collaborative filtering. *ACM Transactions on Information Systems, 22*(1), 116–142. doi:10.1145/963770.963775

Jones, S., & Maiden, N. (2005). Rescue: An integrated method for specifying requirements for complex socio-technical systems . In Mate, J. L., & Silva, A. (Eds.), *Requirements Engineering for Sociotechnical Systems*. Hershey, PA: Idea Group Inc.

Kiryakov, A., Popov, B., Terziev, I., & Manov, D., & Ognyano_, D. (2004). Semantic annotation, indexing, and retrieval. *Journal of Web Semantics*, *2*, 49–79. doi:10.1016/j.websem.2004.07.005

Kwok, K., & Grunfeld, L. (1996). Trec-4 ad-hoc, routing retrieval and filtering experiments using pircs . In Harman, D. K. (Ed.), *The fourth text retrieval conference (trec-4)*.

Kwok, K. L. (1995). A network approach to probabilistic information retrieval. *ACM Transactions on Information Systems*, *13*(3), 324–353. doi:10.1145/203052.203067

Ley, T., Ulbrich, A., Scheir, P., Lindstaedt, S. N., Kump, B., & Albert, D. (2008). Modelling competencies for supporting workintegrated learning in knowledge work. *Journal of Knowledge Management*, *12*(6). doi:10.1108/13673270810913603

Lindstaedt, S. N., Ley, T., Scheir, P., & Ulbrich, A. (2008). *Applying scruffy methods to enable work-integrated learning. To appear in*. The European Journal for the Informatics Professional.

Lindstaedt, S. N., & Mayer, H. (2006). A storyboard of the aposdle vision. In *Innovative Approaches for Learning and Knowledge Sharing, First European Conference on Technology Enhanced Learning*, ec-tel 2006, crete, greece, october 1-4, 2006 (p. 628- 633).

Mackay, D. J. C. (2002). *Information Theory, Inference & Learning Algorithms*. Cambridge University Press.

Mandl, T. (2001). *Tolerantes information retrieval. neuronale netze zur erhöhung der adaptivität und flexibilität bei der informationssuche*. Unpublished doctoral dissertation, University Of Hildesheim.

Maron, M.E. and Kuhns, J.L. (1960). On relevance, probabilistic indexing, and information retrieval. *Journal of the Association for Computing Machinery*, 7.

McCool, R. (2005). Rethinking the semantic web, part 1. *IEEE Internet Computing*, *9*(6), 88–87. doi:10.1109/MIC.2005.133

Mothe, J. (1994). Search mechanisms using a neural network model. In Proc. of the riao 94 (recherche dinformation assiste par ordinateur).

Pammer, V., Scheir, P., & Lindstaedt, S. N. (2007). Two protégé plug-ins for supporting document-based ontology engineering and ontological annotation at document level. In *10th International Prot'eg'e Conference - July 15-18, 2007 - Budapest, Hungary*.

Resnik, P. (1999). Semantic similarity in a taxonomy: An information-based measure and its application to problems of ambiguity in natural language. [JAIR]. *Journal of Artificial Intelligence Research*, *11*, 95–130.

Robertson, S., & Spärck Jones, K. (1976). Relevance weighting of search terms. *Journal of the American Society for Information Science American Society for Information Science*, *27*(3). doi:10.1002/asi.4630270302

Robertson, S., & Spärck Jones, K. (1994). *Simple, proven approaches to text retrieval* (Tech. Rep.). University of Cambridge, Computer Laboratory. Available from http://www.cl.cam .ac.uk/techreports/UCAM-CL-TR-356.pdf

Rocchio, J. J. (1971). *Relevance Feedback in Information Retrieval. Englewood*. Cliffs, New Jersey: Prentice Hall.

Rocha, C., Schwabe, D., & de Aragão, M. P. (2004). A hybrid approach for searching in the semantic web. In *Proceedings of the 13th international conference on world wide web, www 2004.*

Sabou, M., d'Aquin, M., & Motta, E. (2006). Using the semantic web as background knowledge for ontology mapping. In *International Workshop on Ontology Matching* (om-2006).

Salton, G. (1963). Associative document retrieval techniques using bibliographic information. *Journal of the ACM, 10,* 440–457. doi:10.1145/321186.321188

Salton, G. (1968). *Automatic information organization and retrieval.* McGraw Hill.

Sanderson, M., & Zobel, J. (2005). Information retrieval system evaluation: effort, sensitivity, and reliability. In *Sigir '05: Proceedings of the 28th annual international ACM SIGIR conference on Research and development in information retrieval* (pp. 162–169). New York: ACM Press.

Scheir, P., Ghidini, C., & Lindstaedt, S. N. (2007). Improving search on the semantic desktop using associative retrieval techniques. In Proceedings of i-semantics 2007 (p. 221-228).

Scheir, P., Granitzer, M., & Lindstaedt, S. N. (2007). Evaluation of an information retrieval system for the semantic desktop using standard measures from information retrieval. In Lwa 2007, lernen - wissensentdeckung - adaptivität, 24.-26.9. 2007 in halle/saale (p. 269-272).

Scheir, P., Lindstaedt, S. N., & Ghidini, C. (2008). A network model approach to retrieval in the Semantic Web. *International Journal on Semantic Web and Information Systems, 4*(4), 56–84.

Scheir, P., Pammer, V., & Lindstaedt, S. N. (2007). Information retrieval on the semantic web - does it exist? In Lwa 2007, Lernen - Wissensentdeckung - Adaptivität, 24.-26.9. 2007 in Halle/Sale (pp. 252-257).

Schütze, H., Hull, D. A., & Pedersen, J. O. (1995). A Comparison of Classifiers and Document Representations for the Routing Problem. In Research and Development in Information Retrieval, pages 229–237.

Shah, U., Finin, T., & Joshi, A. (2002). Information retrieval on the semantic web. *In Cikm '02: Proceedings of the Eleventh International Conference on Information and Knowledge Management* (pp. 461–468). New York: ACM Press.

Spärck Jones, K. (2004). What's new about the semantic web? Some questions. *SIGIR Forum, 38,* 18–23.

Stojanovic, N., Maedche, A., Staab, S., Studer, R., & Sure, Y. (2001). Seal: A framework for developing semantic portals. In *Proceedings of the first international conference on knowledge capture (k-cap 2001), October 21-23, 2001, Victoria, BC, Canada* (p. 155-162).

Stojanovic, N., Studer, R., & Stojanovic, L. (2003). An approach for the ranking of query results in the semantic web. In International semantic web conference (p. 500-516).

Wilkinson, R., & Hingston, P. (1991). Using the cosine measure in a neural network for document retrieval. In *Sigir '91: Proceedings of the 14th annual international acm sigir conference on research and development in information retrieval* (pp. 202– 210). New York: ACM Press.

Wu, Z., & Palmer, M. S. (1994). Verb semantics and lexical selection. In *Meeting of the association for computational linguistics (ACL)* (pp. 133-138).

Yilmaz, E., & Aslam, J. A. (2006). Estimating average precision with incomplete and imperfect judgments. In *Cikm '06: Proceedings of the 15th ACM international conference on information and knowledge management* (pp. 102–111). New York: ACM Press.

Zhang, L., Yu, Y., Zhou, J., Lin, C., & Yang, Y. (2005). An enhanced model for searching in semantic portals. In *Www '05: Proceedings of the 14th international conference on world wide web* (pp. 453–462). New York: ACM Press.

Ziegler, P., Kiefer, C., Sturm, C., Dittrich, K. R., & Bernstein, A. (2006). Detecting similarities in ontologies with the soqasimpack toolkit. In Y. Ioannidis et al. (Eds.), *10th international conference on extending database technology (EDBT 2006)* (Vol. 3896, pp. 59-76). Springer.

ENDNOTES

[1] Text REtrieval Conference

[2] $s > 0$ if $t > 0$ as c_i and d_j are connected. Therefore c_i gives activation to at least one node if d_j receives activation from one node

[3] $s > 0$ if $t > 0$ as c_i and c_j are connected. Therefore c_i gives activation to at least one node if c_j receives activation from one node

[4] $s > 0$ if $t > 0$ as d_i and d_j are connected. Therefore d_i gives activation to at least one node if d_j receives activation from one node.

[5] http://www.aposdle.org/(29.04.2008)

[6] if no document in the system is annotated with concept c, also document d is not annotated with concept c, this leads to the case $a(c)=0$

[7] This measure was created during a research visit of the first author at FBK-irst in Trento

[8] in the used formalism for ontologies - OWL - properties are not, as in object-oriented programming, parts of classes, but classes are defined as domain and range of a property

[9] http://lucene.apache.org/ (29.04.2008)

[10] http://inex.is.informatik.uni-duisburg.de/ (29.04.2008)

[11] http://www.dcs.gla.ac.uk/idom/ir resources/ test collections/ (29.04.2008)

[12] http://trec.nist.gov/trec eval/ (29.04.2008)

[13] Different competencies can be represented by the same concepts.

[14] Note that the Trento Vector measure is fundamentally different from the two path based measures Shortest Path and Resnik, c.f. section *Semantic Similarity Measures Used*.

[15] Interestingly for the second prototype of the APOSDLE system, which makes use of different ontologies than the first prototype, the Trento Vector measure seems to provide the most benefit in combination with one of the new ontologies.

[16] this value was determined experimentally

[17] In the following we assume that both concept and document similarity are used.

[18] We use the term relevance judgment to refer to both, a binary variable indicating the relevance of a document w.r.t. a query and a training example (q, d_k, r_k) comprising a query, a document and a relevance judgment.

[19] See subsection *Evaluation*.

[20] The residual collection refers to the set of documents which have not been used for feedback.

[21] See section *Evaluation*.

Compilation of References

Aarts, E., Korst, J., & Michiels, W. (2005). Search methodologies. *Simulated annealing* (pp. 187-210). Springer-Verlag.

Abadi, D. J., Marcus, A., Madden, S., & Hollenbach, K. J. (2007). Scalable Semantic Web data management using vertical partitioning. In *Proceedings of the International Conference on Very Large Data Bases (VLDB)* (pp. 411-422).

Abulaish, M., & Dey, L. (2007). A fuzzy ontology generation framework for handling uncertainties and non-uniformity in domain knowledge description. In *Proceedings of the International Conference on Computing: Theory and Applications*, Kolkata, India (pp. 287-293).

ActivePrint. (2007). *Active Print Web Site*. Retrieved Sept 13, 2007, from http://www.activeprint.org/

Adams, R. (2007, April 04) *2-D Bar Code Page*. Retrieved September 11, 2007, from http://www.adams1.com/pub/russadam/stack.html

Adida, B., & Birbeck, M. (2006). *RDFa Primer 1.0 Embedding RDF in XHTML*. Technical report, World Wide Web Consortium. Retrieved from http://www.w3.org/TR/xhtml/rdfa/primer/

Aduna. (2006). User guide for Sesame. Updated for Sesame release 1.2.6. Retrieved from http://www.openrdf.org/doc/sesame/users/index.html

Aduna. (2008). Sesame: RDF Schema querying and storage. Retrieved from http://www.openrdf.org

Agrawal, R., Somani, A., & Xu, Y. (2001). Storage and querying of e-commerce data. In *Proceedings of the International Conference on Very Large Data Bases (VLDB)* (pp. 149-158).

Ähnelt, M., Ebert, M., Beham, G., Lindstaedt, S., & Paschen, A. (2008). A socio-technical approach towards supporting intra-organizational collaboration. In *Proceedings of ECTEL 2008, Maastricht, the Netherlands*.

Alani, H., Dasmahapatra, S., O'Hara, K., & Shadbolt, N. (2003). Identifying communities of practice through ontology network analysis. *IEEE Intelligent Systems*, *18*(2), 18–25. doi:10.1109/MIS.2003.1193653

Alexaki, S., Christophides, V., Karvounarakis, G., & Plexousakis, D. (2001). On storing voluminous RDF descriptions: The case of Web portal catalogs. In *Proceedings of the International Workshop on the Web and Databases (WebDB)*.

Alien Technology. (2005). *EPCglobal Class 1 Gen 2 RFID Specification*. Whitepaper. Morgan Hill, CA: Alien Technology Corporation.

Anagnostopoulos, A., Broder, A., & Punera, K. (2008). Effective and efficient classification on a search-engine modeling. *Knowledge and Information Systems*, *16*(2), 129–154. doi:10.1007/s10115-007-0102-6

Anderson, J. R. (1983). A spreading activation theory of memory. *Journal of Verbal Learning and Verbal Behavior*, *22*, 261–295. doi:10.1016/S0022-5371(83)90201-3

Copyright © 2010, IGI Global, distributing in print or electronic forms without written permission of IGI Global is prohibited.

Andersson, M. (1994). Extracting an entity relationship schema from a relational database through reverse engineering. In *Proceedings of the 13rd International Conference of the Entity-Relationship Approach*, Manchester, UK (LNCS 881, pp. 403-419).

Anick, P. (1994). Adapting a full-text information retrieval system to the computer troubleshooting domain. *17th Annual International ACM SIGIR Conference on Research and Development in Information Retrieval* (pp. 349-358).

Antoniou, G., & van Harmelen, F. (2004). *A Semantic Web Primer.* Cambridge, MA: The MIT Press.

Anyanwu, K., Maduko, A., & Sheth, A. (2007). SPARQ2L: Towards support for subgraph extraction queries in RDF databases. In *Proceedings of the International World Wide Web Conference (WWW)* (pp. 797-806).

Aphinyanaphongs, Y., Tsamardinos, I., Statnikov, A., Hardin, D., & Aliferis, C. F. (2005). Text categorization models for high-quality article retrieval in internal medicine. *Journal of the American Medical Informatics Association, 12*(2), 207–216. doi:10.1197/jamia.M1641

Apte, C., Damerau, F., & Weiss, S. (1994). Automated Learning of Decision Rules for Text Categorization. *ACM Transactions on Information Systems, 12*, 233–251. doi:10.1145/183422.183423

Auer, S., Bizer, C., Lehmann, J., Kobilarov, G., Cyganiak, R., & Ives, Z. (2007). DBpedia: A nucleus for a web of open data. In *Proceedings of the International and Asian Semantic Web Conference (ISWC/ASWC2007)* (pp. 718–728). Busan, Korea.

Baader, F., Horrocks, I., & Sattler, U. (2003). Description logics as ontology languages for the semantic Web. *Lecture Notes in Artificial Intelligence.* Springer.

Baader, F., McGuinness, D. L., Nardi, D., & Patel-Schneider, P. F. (2003). *The description logic handbook: Theory, implementation, and applications.* Cambridge University Press.

Baeza-Yates, R., & Ribeiro-Neto, B. (1999). *Modern Information Retrieval.* New York: Addison-Wesley & ACM Press.

Balzer, S., Liebig, T., & Wagner, M. (2004). Pitfalls of OWL-S: a practical semantic web use case. In *Proceedings of the Second International Conference on Service-Oriented Computing* (ICSOC2004), New York, NY, USA.

Bansal, A., Blake, M. B., Kona, S., Bleul, S., Weise, T., & Jaeger, M. C. (2008). WSC-08: Continuing the web services challenge. In *Proceedings of the 10th IEEE International Conference on E-Commerce Technology (CEC2008) / 5th IEEE International Conference on Enterprise Computing, E-Commerce and E-Services (EEE2008)* (pp. 351–354). Washington, DC, USA.

Barranco, C. D., Campana, J. R., Medina, J. M., & Pons, O. (2007). On storing ontologies including fuzzy datatypes in relational databases. In *Proceedings of the 16th IEEE International Conference on Fuzzy Systems*, London, UK (pp. 1-6).

Basili V. R. (1992). *Software modeling and measurement: the goal/question/metric paradigm.* Technical report. College Park, MD, USA: University of Maryland at College Park.

Baziz, M., Boughanem, M., Aussenac-Gilles, N., & Chrisment, C. (2005). Semantic cores for representing documents in IR. *ACM Symposium on Applied Computing, Santa Fe, New Mexico* (pp. 1011-1017).

Bechhofer, S., & Goble, C. (2001). Towards annotation using DAML+OIL. In *K-cap 2001 workshop on knowledge markup and semantic annotation.*

Bechhofer, S., Möller, R., & Crowther, P. (2003). The DIG description logic interface. *Proceedings of the 16th International Workshop on Description Logics (DL'03).*

Beckett, D. (2004). *RDF/XML syntax specification* (revised). Retrieved September 24, 2008, from http://www.w3.org/TR/2004/REC-rdf-syntax-grammar-20040210/

Beckett, D., & Grant, J. (2003). SWAD-Europe Deliverable 10.2: Mapping Semantic Web Data with RDBMSes. Retrieved from http://www.w3.org/2001/sw/Europe/reports/scalable_rdbms_mapping_report

Behrendt, W., Gangemi, A., Maass, W., & Westenthaler, R. (2005). Towards an ontology based distributed architecture for paid content. *Proceedings of the European Semantic Web Conference (ESWC 2005)* (pp. 257-271). Herakion, Greece. May 29 - June 1, 2005. London: Springer-Verlag.

Belew, R. K. (1989). Adaptive information retrieval: using a connectionist representation to retrieve and learn about documents. In *Sigir '89: Proceedings of the 12th annual international acm sigir conference on research and development in information retrieval* (pp. 11–20). New York: ACM Press.

Ben Mokhtar, S., Kaul, A., Georgantas, N., & Issarny, V. (2006). Efficient semantic service discovery in pervasive computing environments. *Proceedings of the ACM/IFIP/USENIX 7th International Middleware Conference, Middleware '06.*

Berger, H., Dittenbach, M., & Merkl, D. (2004, January 18–22). An adaptive information retrieval system based on associative networks. In S. Hartmann & J. Roddick (Eds.), *Proceedings of the 1st asia-pacific conference on conceptual modelling (apccm 2004)* (Vol. 31, pp. 27–36). Dunedin, New Zealand: Australian Computer Society Inc.

Berners-Lee, T. (1994). *IETF RFC (Informational) 1630 Universal Resource Identifier (URI).* http://www.ietf.org/rfc/rfc1630.txt.

Berners-Lee, T. (1999). *Weaving the Web.* San Francisco: Harper.

Berners-Lee, T. (2002). *What do HTTP URIs Identify?* http://www.w3.org/DesignIssues/HTTP-URI.html.

Berners-Lee, T., et al. (1998). *RFC 2396: Uniform Resource Identifiers (URI): Generic Syntax.* http://www.ietf.org/rfc/rfc2396.txt.

Berners-Lee, T., Fielding, R., & Masinter, L. (1998). *IETF RFC (Obsolete) 2396 Uniform Resource Identifier (URI): Generic Syntax.* http://www.ietf.org/rfc/rfc2396.txt.

Berners-Lee, T., Fielding, R., & Masinter, L. (2005). *IETF RFC 3986 Uniform Resource Identifier (URI): Generic Syntax.* http://www.ietf.org/rfc/rfc3986.txt.

Berners-Lee, T., Hall, W., Hendler, J., O'Hara, K., Shadbolt, N., & Weitzner, D. (2006). A framework for Web science. *Foundations and Trends in Web Science, 1*(1).

Berners-Lee, T., Hall, W., Hendler, J., Shadbolt, N., & Weitzner, D. J. (2006). Creating a science of the Web. *Science, 313*(11), 769-771.

Berners-Lee, T., Hendler, J., & Lassila, O. (2001). The semantic Web. *Scientific American, 248*(4), 34-43. doi:10.1038/scientificamerican0501-34

Berners-Lee. Fielding, R., & McCahill, M. (1994). *IETF RFC (Obsolete) 1738 Uniform Resource Locators (URL).* http://www.ietf.org/rfc/rfc1738.txt.

Bernstein, A., Kaufmann, E., Kiefer, C., & Bürki, C. (2005, August). *Simpack: A generic java library for similarity measures in ontologies* (Tech. Rep.). [Zurich, Switzerland: University of Zurich, Department of Informatics.]. *Winterthurerstrasse, 190,* 8057.

Bernstein, A., Kiefer, C., & Stocker, M. (2007, March). *OptARQ: A SPARQL optimization approach based on triple pattern selectivity estimation* (Tech. Rep. No. ifi-2007.03). Retrieved from http://www.ifi.uzh.ch/ddis/staff/goehring/btw/files/ifi-2007.03.pdf

Bezdek, J. C., & Pal, N. R. (1998). Some new indexes of cluster validity. *IEEE Transactions on Systems, Man, and Cybernetics, 28*(3), 301-315.

Bishop, C. M. (2006). *Pattern Recognition and Machine Learning.* Springer.

Bizer, C., & Seaborne, A. (2004). D2RQ – treating non-RDF databases as virtual RDF graphs. In *Proceedings of the International Semantic Web Conference (ISWC).* (Poster presentation)

Bizer, C., Cygniak, R., & Heath, T. (2007). *How to Publish Linked Data on the Web.* http://www4.wiwiss.fu-berlin. de/bizer/pub/LinkedDataTutorial/

Black, J. (2006). Creating a common ground for URI meaning using socially constructed Web sites. *Proceedings of Identity, Reference, and the Web (IRW2006), WWW2006 Workshop.* Edinburgh, United Kingdom. May, 22nd 2006. http://www.ibiblio.org/hhalpin/irw2006/jblack.pdf.

Blake, M. B., Cheung, W. K.-W., Jaeger, M. C., & Wombacher, A. (2007). WSC-07: evolving the web services challenge. In *Proceedings of the 9th IEEE International Conference on E-Commerce Technology (CEC 2007),* Tokyo, Japan.

Blake, M. B., Cheung, W., Jaeger, M. C., & Wombacher, A. (2006). WSC-06: the web service challenge. In *Proceedings of the Eighth IEEE International Conference on E-Commerce Technology (CEC 2006) and Third IEEE International Conference on Enterprise Computing, E-Commerce and E-Services (EEE 2006),* Palo Alto, California, USA.

Bleul, S., Weise, T., & Geihs, K. (2009). The web service challenge - a review on semantic web service composition. In *Proceedings of the Workshop on Service-Oriented Computing at KIVS 2009,* Kassel, Germany.

Bobillo, F., & Straccia, U. (2008). fuzzyDL: An expressive fuzzy description logic reasoner. In *Proc. FUZZ-IEEE-2008,* pp. 923-930. IEEE Computer Society.

Bobillo, F., & Straccia, U. (2008). Towards a crisp representation of fuzzy description logics under Łukasiewicz semantics. In *Proc. ISMIS-2008,* (LNCS 4994, pp. 309-318).

Bobillo, F., Delgado, M., & Gómez-Romero, J. (2006). A crisp representation for fuzzy SHOIN with fuzzy nominals and general concept inclusions. In *Proc. URSW-2006, CEUR Workshop Proceedings* 218. CEUR-WS.org.

Bobillo, F., Delgado, M., & Gómez-Romero, J. (2008). Optimizing the crisp representation of the fuzzy description logic SROIQ. In *Proc. URSW-2007, CEUR Workshop Proceedings* 327. CEUR-WS.org.

Booth, D. (2003). *Four uses of a URL: Name, concept, web location, and document instance.* Retrieved from http://www.w3.org/2002/11/dbooth-names/dbooth-names_clean.htm

Booth, D. (2009). *Denotation as a Two-Step Mapping in Semantic Web Architecture.* Paper presented at IJ-CAI-2009, Pasadena, California. Retrieved from http://dbooth.org/2009/denotation/

Borgida, A. (1995). Description logics in data management. *IEEE Transactions on Knowledge and Data Engineering, 7*(5), 671-682.

Borgida, A., Walsh, T. J., & Hirsh, H. (2005). Towards measuring similarity in description logics. In I. Horrocks, H. Sattler, & F. Wolter (Eds.), *Working Notes of the International Description Logics Workshop: CEUR Workshop Proceedings,* Edinburgh, UK.

Borsje, J., Levering, L., & Frasincar, F. (2008). Hermes: a Semantic Web-Based News Decision Support System. *23rd Annual ACM Symposium on Applied Computing (SAC 2008)* (pp. 2415-2420).

Boughanem, M., Dkaki, T., Mothe, J., & Soule-Dupuy, C. (1999). Mercure at trec7. In The seventh text retrieval conference (trec- 7).

Bouquet, P., Stoermer, H., Mancioppi, M., & Giacomuzzi, D. (2006). OkkaM: Towards a solution to the "identity crisis" on the semantic Web. *Proceedings of the Italian Semantic Web Workshop (SWAP 2006).* Pisa, Italy, December 18-20, 2006.

Bouquet, P., Stoermer, H., & Giacomuzzi, D. (2007). OKKAM: Enabling a Web of Entities. In *Proceedings of I3: Identity, Identifiers, Identification. Proceedings of the WWW2007 Workshop on Entity-Centric Approaches to Information and Knowledge Management on the Web,* Banff, Canada, May 8, 2007., CEUR Workshop Proceedings.

Bouquet, P., Stoermer, H., Niederee, C., & Mana, A. (2008). Entity Name System: The Backbone of an Open and Scalable Web of Data. In *Proceedings of the IEEE International Conference on Semantic Computing*. Retrieved from http://www.okkam.org/publications/stoermer-EntityNameSystem.pdf

Brachman, R., & Levesque, H. (1984). The tractability of subsumption in Frame-based description languages. *4th National Conference on Artificial Intelligence – AAAI-84* (pp. 34-37).

Brambilla, M., Ceri, S., Passamani, M., & Riccio, A. (2004). Managing asynchronous Web services interactions. *Proceedings of the IEEE International Conference on Web Services (ICWS)*.

Brewster, C., & O'Hara, K. (2007). Knowledge representation with ontologies: Present challenges—Future possibilities. *International Journal of Human-Computer Studies 65*, 563-568.

Brickley, D., & Guha, R. (2004). *RDF Vocabulary Description Language 1.0: RDF Schema*. W3C Recommendation. Retrieved from http://www.w3.org/TR/2004/REC-rdf-schema-20040210/

Broekstra, J., Kampman, A., & van Harmelen, F. (2002). Sesame: A generic architecture for storing and querying RDF and RDF Schema. In *Proceedings of the International Semantic Web Conference (ISWC)* (pp. 54-68).

Broll, G., Keck, S., Holleis, P., & Butz, A. (2009). Improving the Accessibility of NFC/RFID-based Mobile Interaction through Learnability and Guidance. In Proc. of MobileHCI'09. Bonn, Germany, September 15 - 18, 2009.

Broll, G., Siorpaes, S., Rukzio, E., Paolucci, M., Hamard, J., Wagner, M., & Schmidt, A. (2006) Supporting Service Interaction in the Real World. Permid Workshop in conjunction with Pervasive 2006, Dublin, Ireland, May 7 2006.

Broll, G., Siorpaes, S., Rukzio, E., Paolucci, M., Hamard, J., Wagner, M., & Schmidt, A. (2007). *Supporting Mobile Service Usage through Physical Mobile Interaction*. In Proc. of PERCOM'07 (pp. 262-271). IEEE Computer Society, Washington, DC.

Buckles, B. P., & Petry, F. E. (1982). A fuzzy representation of data for relational database. *Fuzzy Sets and Systems, 7*(3), 213-226.

Buckley, C., & Voorhees, E. M. (2000). Evaluating evaluation measure stability. In *Sigir '00: Proceedings of the 23rd annual international acm sigir conference on research and development in information retrieval* (pp. 33–40). New York: ACM Press.

Buckley, C., & Voorhees, E. M. (2004). Retrieval evaluation with incomplete information. In *Sigir '04: Proceedings of the 27th annual international acm sigir conference on research and development in information retrieval* (pp. 25–32). New York: ACM Press.

Buhler, P., & Vidal, J. (2004). Enacting BPEL4WS specified workflows with multi-agent systems. *Proceedings of the Workshop on Web Services and Agent-Based Engineering (WSABE04)*. New York, NY.

Buhler, P., et al. (2003). Adaptive workflow = Web services + agents. *Proceedings of the International Conference on Web Services (ICWS03)*. Las Vegas, NV.

Calegari, S., & Ciucci, D. (2007). Fuzzy ontology, fuzzy description logics and fuzzy-OWL. In *Proceedings of the 7th International Workshop on Fuzzy Logic and Applications*, Camogli, Italy (LNAI 4578, pp. 118-126).

Calì, A., & Lukasiewicz, T. (2007). Tightly integrated probabilistic description logic programs for the Semantic Web. In *Proc. ICLP-2007* (LNCS 4670, pp. 428-429).

Calì, A., Lukasiewicz, T., Predoiu, L., & Stuckenschmidt, H. (2008). Tightly integrated probabilistic description logic programs for representing ontology mappings. In Proc. FoIKS-2008 (LNCS 4932, pp. 178-198).

Calvanese, D., De Giacomo, G., Lembo, D., Lenzerini, M., & Rosati, R. (2007). Tractable reasoning and efficient query answering in description logics: The *DL-Lite* family. *Journal of Automated Reasoning, 39*(3), 385–429. doi:10.1007/s10817-007-9078-x

Carterette, B., Allan, J., & Sitaraman, R. (2006). Minimal test collections for retrieval evaluation. In *Sigir '06: Proceedings of the 29th annual international acm sigir conference on research and development in information retrieval* (pp. 268–275). New York: ACM Press.

Castells, P., Fernandez, M., & Vallet, D. (2007). An adaptation of the vector-space model for ontology-based information retrieval. *IEEE Transactions on Knowledge and Data Engineering, 19*, 261–272. doi:10.1109/TKDE.2007.22

Chamberlain, J., Blanchard, C., Burlingame, S., Chandramohan, S., Forestier, E., Griffith, G, et al. (2006). *IBM WebSphere RFID handbook: A solution guide,* 1st ed. IBM International Technical Support Organization.

Chandrasekaran, B., Josephson, J., & Benjamins,V. (1999). What are ontologies, and why do we need them?. *IEEE Intelligent Systems, 14,*(Jan.-Feb.), 20-26,

Chang, Y. K., Cirillo, C., & Razon, J. (1971). Evaluation of feedback retrieval using modified freezing, residual collection & test and control groups . In Salton, G. (Ed.), *The SMART retrieval system - experiments in automatic document processing* (pp. 355–370).

Chang, Y.-C., & Chen, S.-M. (2006). A new query reweighting method for document retrieval based on genetic algorithms. *IEEE Transactions on Evolutionary Computation, 10*(5), 617–622. doi:10.1109/TEVC.2005.863130

Chebotko, A., Atay, M., Lu, S., & Fotouhi, F. (2007). Relational nested optional join for efficient Semantic Web query processing. In *Proceedings of the joint conference of the Asia-Pacific Web Conference and the International Conference on Web-Age Information Management (AP-Web/WAIM)* (pp. 428-439).

Chebotko, A., Fei, X., Lin, C., Lu, S., & Fotouhi, F. (2007). Storing and querying scientific workflow provenance metadata using an RDBMS. In *Proceedings of the IEEE International Workshop on Scientific Workflows and Business Workflow Standards in e-Science* (pp. 611-618).

Chebotko, A., Fei, X., Lu, S., & Fotouhi, F. (2007, September). *Scientific workflow provenance metadata management using an RDBMS-based RDF store* (Tech. Rep. No. TR-DB-092007-CFLF). Wayne State University. Retrieved from http://www.cs.wayne.edu/~artem/main/research/TR-DB-092007-CFLF.pdf

Chebotko, A., Lu, S., & Fotouhi, F. (2009). (in press). Semantics preserving SPARQL-to-SQL translation. [DKE]. *Data & Knowledge Engineering.* doi:10.1016/j.datak.2009.04.001

Chebotko, A., Lu, S., Jamil, H. M., & Fotouhi, F. (2006, May). *Semantics preserving SPARQL-to-SQL query translation for optional graph patterns* (Tech. Rep. No. TR-DB-052006-CLJF). Wayne State University. Retrieved from http://www.cs.wayne.edu/~artem/main/research/TR-DB-052006-CLJF.pdf

Cheng, S., et al. (2002). A new framework for mobile Web services. *Proceedings of the Symposium on Applications and the Internet (SAINT '02w).* Nara City, Japan.

Chiang, R. H. L., Barron, T. M., & Storey, V. C. (1994). Reverse engineering of relational databases: Extraction of an EER model from a relational database. *Journal of Data and Knowledge Engineering, 12*(2), 107-142.

Chinnici, R., Moreau, J., & Ryman, A. *Web Services Description Language (WSDL) Version 2.0 Part 1: Core Language.* W3C Candidate Recommendation 27 March 2006; http://www.w3.org/TR/2006/CR-wsdl20-20060327

Chirita, P.-A., Costache, S., Nejdl, W., & Paiu, R. (2006). Beagle ++: Semantically enhanced searching and ranking on the desktop . In *The semantic web: Research and applications* (Vol. 4011, pp. 348–362). Berlin, Heidelberg: Springer. doi:10.1007/11762256_27

Choi, B., & Peng, X. (2004). Dynamic and hierarchical classification of web pages. *Online Information Review*, *28*(2), 139–147. doi:10.1108/14684520410531673

Chong, E. I., Das, S., Eadon, G., & Srinivasan, J. (2005). An efficient SQL-based RDF querying scheme. In *Proceedings of the International Conference on Very Large Data Bases (VLDB)* (pp. 1216-1227).

Ciorascu, C. (2003). WordNet, a lexical database for the English language. Retrieved from http://wordnet.princeton.edu/ (Version: 1.2)

Clack, C., Farringdon, J., Lidwell, P., & Yu, T. (1997). Autonomous document classification for business. *1st International Conference on Autonomous Agents, Marinadel Rey, CA* (pp. 201-208).

Clark, K. G. (2002). *Identity Crisis*. http://www.xml.com/pub/a/2002/09/11/deviant.html.

Clark, K. G. (2003). *The Social Meaning of RDF*. http://www.xml.com/pub/a/2003/03/05/social.html

Cobo, J. M. L., Losada, S., Corcho, Ó., Benjamins, V. R., Niño, M., & Contreras, J. (2004). SWS for financial overdrawn alerting. In *Proceedings of the Third International Semantic Web Conference (ISWC2004)*, Hiroshima, Japan.

Codd, E. F. (1970). A relational model of data for large shared data banks. *Communications of the ACM*, *13*(6), 377–387. doi:10.1145/362384.362685

Codd, E. F. (1972). Relational completeness of data base sublanguages. In R. Rustin (Ed.), Database Systems (pp. 65-98). Prentice Hall and IBM Research Report RJ 987, San Jose, California.

Cohen, P. R., & Kjeldsen, R. (1987). Information retrieval by constrained spreading activation in semantic networks. *Information Processing & Management*, *23*(4), 255–268. doi:10.1016/0306-4573(87)90017-3

Cohen, W. W., & Singer, Y. (1999). Context-sensitive learning methods for text categorization. *ACM Transactions on Information Systems*, *17*(2), 141–173. doi:10.1145/306686.306688

Colucci, S., Di Noia, T., Di Sciascio, E., Donini, F., Ragone, A., & Rizzi, R. (2006). A semantic-based fully visual application for matchmaking and query refinement in b2c e-marketplaces. *8th International conference on Electronic Commerce, ICEC 06* (pp. 174-184).

Colucci, S., Noia, T. D., Sciascio, E. D., Donini, F. M., & Mongiello, M. (2005). Concept abduction and contraction for semantic-based discovery of matches and negotiation spaces in an e-marketplace. *Electronic Commerce Research and Applications*, *4*(4), 345–361. doi:10.1016/j.elerap.2005.06.004

Connolly, D. (2000). *IETF RFC (Informational) 2854 The 'text/html' Media Type*. http://www.ietf.org/rfc/rfc2854.txt.

Connolly, D. (2006). A Pragmatic Theory of Reference for the Web. Proceedings of the Identity, Reference, and the Web (IRW2006) Workshop at the World Wide Web Conference (WWW2006). Edinburgh, United Kingdom. May 22nd 2006.

Cover, T., & Thomas, J. (1991). *Elements of information theory*. John Wiley and Sons Inc.

Crestani, F. (1997). Application of spreading activation techniques in information retrieval. *Artificial Intelligence Review*, *11*, 453–482. doi:10.1023/A:1006569829653

Crestani, F., & Lee, P. L. (2000). Searching the web by constrained spreading activation. *Information Processing & Management*, *36*(4), 585–605. doi:10.1016/S0306-4573(99)00073-4

Cunningham, H., Maynard, D., Bontcheva, K., Tablan, V., Ursu, C., Dimitrov, M., et al. (2009). *Developing language processing components with GATE*. Retrieved from http://gate.ac.uk/sale/tao

Cyganiak, R. (2005). *A relational algebra for SPARQL* (Tech. Rep. No. HPL-2005-170). Hewlett-Packard Laboratories. Retrieved from http://www.hpl.hp.com/techreports/2005/HPL-2005-170.html

d'Amato, C., Fanizzi, N., & Esposito, F. (2006). Reasoning by analogy in description logics through instance-based learning. In G. Tummarello, P. Bouquet, & O. Signore (Eds.), *Proceedings of Semantic Web Applications and Perspectives: 3rd Italian Semantic Web Workshop, SWAP2006, CEUR Workshop Proceedings*, Pisa, Italy.

d'Amato, C., Fanizzi, N., & Esposito, F. (2008). Query answering and ontology population: An inductive approach. In S. Bechhofer et al., (Eds.), *Proceedings of the 5th European Semantic Web Conference, ESWC 2008* (LNCS, pp. 288-302). Springer.

d'Amato, C., Staab, S., Fanizzi, N., & Esposito, F. (2007). Efficient discovery of services specified in description logics languages. In T. Di Noia et al., (Eds.), *Proceedings of the Workshop on Service Matchmaking and Resource Retrieval in the Semantic Web (SMRR 2007) at ISWC 2007, CEUR Workshop Proceedings*. Retrieved September 24, 2008, from www.CEUR-WS.org

d'Aquin, M., Lieber, J., & Napoli, A. (2005). Decentralized case-based reasoning for the Semantic Web. In Y. Gil, E. Motta, V. Benjamins, & M. A. Musen (Eds.), *Proceedings of the 4th International Semantic Web Conference, ISWC 2005* (LNCS 3279, pp. 142-155). Springer.

Davidson, D. (1973). Radical Interpretation. *Dialectica, 27*, 314–328. doi:10.1111/j.1746-8361.1973.tb00623.x

de Laborda, C. P., & Conrad, S. (2006). Bringing relational data into the Semantic Web using SPARQL and Relational.OWL. In *Proceedings of the ICDE Workshops* (pp. 55).

De, P., Basu, K., & Das, S. (2004). An ubiquitous architectural framework and protocol for object tracking using RFID tags. *The First Annual International Conference on Mobile and Ubiquitous Systems, Networking and Services, MOBIQUITOUS 2004* (pp. 174-182).

Delugach, H. (2007). *Common Logic (CL): a framework for a family of logic-based languages. ISO/IEC 24707.* http://www.iso.org/iso/iso_catalogue/catalogue_tc/catalogue_detail.htm?csnumber=39175

Deutsche Bahn, A. G. (2007). *Handy-Ticket.* Retrieved Sept 11, 2007; www.bahn.de/p/view/planen/reiseplanung/mobileservices/handy_ticket.shtml.

DeWitt, D. J., & Gerber, R. H. (1985). Multiprocessor hash-based join algorithms. In *Proceedings of the International Conference on Very Large Data Bases (VLDB)* (pp. 151-164).

DeWitt, D. J., Katz, R. H., Olken, F., Shapiro, L. D., Stonebraker, M., & Wood, D. A. (1984). Implementation techniques for main memory database systems. In *Proceedings of the SIGMOD International Conference on Management of Data* (pp. 1-8).

Di Noia, T., Di Sciascio, E., Donini, F., & Mongiello, M. (2004). A system for principled matchmaking in an electronic marketplace. *International Journal of Electronic Commerce, 8*(4), 9-37.

DLMedia. (2008). Retrieved from http://gaia.isti.cnr.it/straccia/software/DLMedia/DLMedia.html.

Dolin, R. (2006). Deploying the Internet of things. *Proceedings of the International Symposium on Applications on Internet (SAINT 2006)* (pp. 216-219). Phoenix, USA. Los Alamitos, CA: IEEE Computer Society.

Donini, F. M., Lenzerini, M., Nardi, D., & Nutt, W. (1998). An epistemic operator for description logics. *Artificial Intelligence, 100*(1-2), 225-274.

Donini, F., Lenzerini, M., Nardi, D., & Schaerf, A. (1996). Reasoning in description logics. In: G. Brewka (Ed.), *Principles of knowledge representation: Studies in logic, language and information* (pp. 191-236). CSLI Publications.

Dridi, O., & Ahmed, M. B. (2008). Building an ontology-based framework for semantic information retrieval: application to breast cancer. *3rd International Conference on Information and Communication Technologies: From Theory to Applications, ICTTA 2008, v2* (pp. 1-6).

Du, L., Jin, H., de Vel, O., & Liu, N. (2008). A latent semantic indexing and WordNet based information retrieval model for digital forensics. *IEEE International Conference on Intelligence and Security Informatics, ISI 2008* (pp. 70-75).

Duerst, M., & Signard, M. (2005). *Internationalized resource identifiers (IRIs). RFC 3987*, Internet Society, January 2005. Retrieved from http://www.ietf.org/rfc/rfc3987.txt

Dumais, S. T., Platt, J., Heckerman, D., & Sahami, M. (1998). Inductive learning algorithms and representations for text categorization. 7th ACM International Conference on Information and Knowledge Management CIKM-98, Bethesda, MD (pp. 148-155).

ebXML. (2007). Retrieved June 1, 2007 from http://www.ebxml.org

ECMA International. (Sept. 2006). *Near Field Communication White paper*; Ecma/TC32-TG19/2004/1 EPCGlobal *RFID Implementation Cookbook, 2nd Release*. Retrieved September 11, 2007, from http://www.epcglobalinc.org/what/cookbook/

Eiter, T., Ianni, G., Lukasiewicz, T., Schindlauer, R., & Tompits, H. (2008). Combining answer set programming with description logics for the Semantic Web. *Artificial Intelligence, 172*(12/13), 1495–1539. doi:10.1016/j.artint.2008.04.002

Eiter, T., Ianni, G., Schindlauer, R., & Tompits, H. (2006). Effective integration of declarative rules with external evaluations for Semantic Web reasoning. In *Proc. ESWC-2006* (LNCS 4011, pp. 273-287).

Eiter, T., Lukasiewicz, T., Schindlauer, R., & Tompits, H. (2004). Well-founded semantics for description logic programs in the Semantic Web. In Proc. RuleML-2004 (LNCS 3323, pp. 81-97).

Elmasri, R., & Navathe, S. B. (2004). *Fundamentals of database systems*. Addison-Wesley.

EPCglobal Inc. (2005). *EPC Radio-Frequency Identity Protocols Class-1 Generation-2 UHF RFID Protocol for Communications at 860 MHz-960 MHz*. January 2005.

EPCglobal Inc. (2005). *Object Naming Service (ONS - ver. 1.0)*. October 2005.

Erling, O. (2001). Implementing a SPARQL compliant RDF triple store using a SQL-ORDBMS. OpenLink Software Virtuoso. Retrieved from http://virtuoso.openlinksw.com/wiki/main/Main/VOSRDFWP

Esmaili, K. S., & Abolhassani, H. (2006). *A categorization scheme for semantic web search engines. In 4th acs/ieee int. conf. on computer systems and applications (aiccsa-06)*.

Esposito, F., Fanizzi, N., Iannone, L., Palmisano, I., & Semeraro, G. (2004). Knowledge-intensive induction of terminologies from metadata. In F. van Harmelen, S. McIlraith, & D. Plexousakis (Eds.), *ISWC2004: Proceedings of the 3rd International Semantic Web Conference* (LNCS, pp. 441-455). Springer.

Ester, M., Kriegel, H.-P., Sander, J., & Xu, X. (1996). A density-based algorithm for discovering clusters in large spatial databases. In *Proceedings of the 2nd Conference of ACM SIGKDD* (pp. 226-231).

Euzenat, J., & Shvaiko, P. (2007). *Ontology matching*. Heidelberg: Springer-Verlag.

Fanizzi, N., d'Amato, C., & Esposito, F. (2007). *Approximate measures of semantic dissimilarity under uncertainty.* Working Notes of the ISWC Workshop on Uncertainty Reasoning in the Semantic Web: URSW2007 in CEUR Workshop Proceedings, Busan, South Korea.

Fanizzi, N., d'Amato, C., & Esposito, F. (2007). Evolutionary conceptual clustering of semantically annotated resources. In *Proceedings of the IEEE International Conference on Semantic Computing, ICSC2007,* Irvine, CA (pp. 783-790). IEEE.

Fanizzi, N., d'Amato, C., & Esposito, F. (2007). *Induction of optimal semi-distances for individuals based on feature sets.* In D. Calvanese, E. Franconi, V. Haarslev, D. Lembo, B. Motik, A.-Y. Turhan, & S. Tessaris (Eds.), Working Notes of the 20th International Description Logics Workshop, DL2007: CEUR Workshop Proceedings, Bressanone, Italy.

Fanizzi, N., d'Amato, C., & Esposito, F. (2008). Conceptual clustering for concept drift and novelty detection. In S. Bechhofer, M. Hauswirth, J. Hoffmann, & M. Koubarakis (Eds.), *Proceedings of the 5th European Semantic Web Conference, ESWC2008* (LNCS, pp. 318-332). Springer.

Fanizzi, N., d'Amato, C., & Esposito, F. (2008). DL-Foil: Concept learning in description logics. In *Proceedings of the 18th International Conference on Inductive Logic Programming, ILP2008* (LNAI). Prague, Czech Republic: Springer. (in press).

Fanizzi, N., Iannone, L., Palmisano, I., & Semeraro, G. (2004). Concept formation in expressive description logics. In J.-F. Boulicaut, F. Esposito, F. Giannotti, & D. Pedreschi (Eds.), *Proceedings of the 15th European Conference on Machine Learning, ECML2004* (LNAI, pp. 99-113). Springer.

Fensel, D. (2004). *Ontologies, a silver-bullet for knowledge management and electronic commerce*, 2nd ed. Berlin: Springer Verlag.

Fensel, D., Hendler, J., Lieberman, H., & Wahlster, W. (2003). *Spinning the Semantic Web*. Cambridge, MA: MIT Press.

Fensel, D., Wahlster, W., Lieberman, H., & Hendler, J. (Eds.). (2002). *Spinning the Semantic Web: Bringing the World Wide Web to Its Full Potential*. MIT Press. fuzzyDL (2008). Retrieved from http://gaia.isti.cnr.it/straccia/software/fuzzyDL/fuzzyDL.html.

Fielding, R., Gettys, J., Mogul, J., Frystyk, H., & Berners-Lee, T. (1997). *IETF RFC 2068 - Hypertext Transfer Protocol – HTTP/1.1*. http://www.ietf.org/rfc/rfc2068.txt.

Fielding, R., Gettys, J., Mogul, J., Frystyk, H., Masinter, L., Leach, P., & Berners-Lee, T. (1999). *IETF RFC 2616 - Hypertext Transfer Protocol – HTTP/1.1*. http://www.ietf.org/rfc/rfc2616.txt.

FIPA. (2007). *Foundation for the intelligent physical agents*. Retrieved June 1, 2007 from http://www.fipa.org.

Fischer, T. (2005). *Entwicklung einer Evaluationsmethodik für Semantic Web Services und Anwendung auf die DIANE Service Descriptions* (in German). Master's thesis, IPD, University Karlsruhe.

Flickr Virtual Community. (2007). www.flickr.com.

Folksonomies. (2007). www.wikipedia.org/folksonomy

Frege, G. (1892). Uber sinn und bedeutung. Zeitshrift fur Philosophie and philosophie. *Kritic, 100*, 25–50.

Friend-of-Friend Virtual Community. (2007). www.foaf-project.org

Friesen, Λ. & Grimm, S. (2005). *DIP deliverable D4.8: Discovery specification*. Technical report.

Friesen, A., & Namiri, K. (2006). Towards semantic service selection for B2B integration. In *Proceedings of the Joint Workshop on Web Services Modeling and Implementation using Sound Web Engineering Practices and Methods, Architectures and Technologies for e-service Engineering (SMIWEP-MATeS'06) at the Sixth International Conference on Web Engineering (ICWE06)*, Palo Alto, CA, USA.

Fuhr, N. (1989). Models for retrieval with probabilistic indexing. *Information Processing & Management, 25*(1), 55–72. doi:10.1016/0306-4573(89)90091-5

Fuhr, N. (1992). Probabilistic Models in Information Retrieval. *The Computer Journal, 35*(3). doi:10.1093/comjnl/35.3.243

Fuhr, N. (2006). *Information Retrieval: Skriptum zur Vorlesung im SS 06, 19*. Dezember 2006.

Fuhr, N., Hartmann, S., Knorz, G., Lustig, G., Schwantner, M., & Tzeras, K. (1991). AIR/X—a rule-based multistage indexing system for large subject fields. *3rd International Conference "Recherche d'Information Assistee par Ordinateur" RIAO-91, Barcelona, Spain* (pp. 606-623).

Gangemi, A. (2008). Norms and plans as unification criteria for social collectives. *Journal of Autonomous Agents and Multi-Agent Systems, 16*(3).

Gangemi, A., & Mika, P. (2003). Understanding the semantic Web through descriptions and situations. *Proceedings of International Conference of Ontologies, Databases, and Applications of Semantics (ODBASE2003)* (pp. 689-706). Catalina, Italy. November 3-7th 2003. London: Springer-Verlag.

Gangemi, A., & Presutti, V. (2006). The bourne identity of a Web resource. *Proceedings of the Identity, Reference, and the Web (IRW2006) Workshop at the World Wide Web Conference (WWW2006)*. Edinburgh, United Kingdom. May, 23rd 2006. http://www.ibiblio.org/hhalpin/irw2006/presentations/-vpresutti.pdf.

Gangemi, A., Borgo, S., Catenacci, C., & Lehmann, J. (2005) *Task taxonomies for knowledge content*. Deliverable D07 of the Metokis Project. Retrieved from http://www.loa-cnr.it/Papers/D07_v21a.pdf

Gangemi, A., Guarino, N., Masolo, C., Oltramari, A., & Schneider, L. (2002). Sweetening Ontologies with DOLCE. In *Proceedings of International Conference on Knowledge Engineering and Knowledge Management. Ontologies and the Semantic Web.* Siguenza, Spain. 1-4 October 2002 (pp. 166-181). London: Springer-Verlag.

Gelfond, M., & Lifschitz, V. (1991). Classical negation in logic programs and disjunctive databases. *New Generation Comput.*, 9(3/4), 365–386. doi:10.1007/BF03037169

General Formal Ontology. (2007). Retrieved May 30, 2007 from http://www.onto-med.de/ontologies/gfo.owl

Gerber, R. H. (1986). *Dataflow query processing using multiprocessor hash-partitioned algorithms* (Tech. Rep. No. 672). Dissertation, University of Wisconsin-Madison, Computer Sciences.

Geven, A., Strassl, P., Ferro, B., Tscheligi, M., & Schwab, H. (2007) Experiencing real-world interaction: results from a NFC user experience field trial. In Proc. of MobileHCI '07, vol. 309 (pp. 234-237). ACM, New York, NY.

Ghozeil, A., & Fogel, D. B. (1996). Discovering patterns in spatial data using evolutionary programming. In J. R. Koza, D. E. Goldberg, D. B. Fogel, & R. L. Riolo (Eds.), *Genetic Programming 1996: Proceedings of the First Annual Conference* (pp. 521-527). Stanford University, CA, USA: MIT Press.

Gibbins, N., Harris, S., & Shadbolt, N. (2004). Agent-based Semantic Web services. *Journal of Web Semantics, 1.*

Ginsberg, A. (1983). *Quantum Statistics, Quantum Field Theory, and The Interpretation Problem*. Ph.D. dissertation.

Ginsberg, A. (2006). *The Big Schema of Things: Two Philosophical Visions of the Relationship Between Language and Reality and Their Implications for the Semantic Web*. Paper presented at WWW 2006, Edinburgh, Scotland. Retrieved from http://www.ibiblio.org/hhalpin/irw2006/aginsberg.pdf.

Ginsberg, A. (2008). Ontological Indeterminacy and The Semantic Web. *International Journal on Semantic Web and Information Systems*, 4(2), 19–48.

Glaser, H., Millard, I., & Jaffri, A. (2008). RKBExplorer.com: A knowledge driven infrastructure for Linked Data providers. In *Proceedings of European Semantic Web Conference (ESWC)*, Tenerife, Spain. (pp. 797–801).

Goldstone, R., Medin, D., & Halberstadt, J. (1997). Similarity in context. *Memory and Cognition*, 25(2), 237-255.

Gomez-Perez, A., Fernadez-Lopez, M., & Corcho, O. (2003). *Ontological engineering*. London: Springer Verlag.

Gong, Z., Cheang, C., & L. H. U., (2005). Web query expansion by WordNet (LNCS 3588, pp. 166-17).

Granitzer, M., Kröll, M., Seifert, C., Rath, A. S., Weber, N., Dietzel, O., et al. (2008). Analysis of machine learning techniques for context extraction. In *IEEE Proceedings of ICDIM 08, Third International Conference on Digital Information Management.*

Grosof, B. N., Horrocks, I., Volz, R., & Decker, S. (2003). Description logic programs: Combining logic programs with description logics. In *Proc. WWW-2003* (pp. 48-57). ACM Press.

Gruber, T. (1993). A translation approach to portable ontology specification. *Knowledge Acquisition, 5*(2), 199-220. Retrieved October 14, 2007 from http://tomgruber.org/writing/ontolingua-kaj-1993.pdf

Gruber, T. (2007). Ontology of folksonomy: A mash-up of apples and oranges. *Journal on Semantic Web & Information Systems, 3*(2).

Guarino, N. (1998). Formal ontology and information systems. In: N. Guarino (Ed.), *Formal ontology in information systems. Proceedings of FOIS'98* (pp. 3-15). Trento, Italy, Amsterdam: IOS Press. http://www.loa-cnr.it/Papers/FOIS98.pdf

Guarino, N., Masolo, C., & Vetere, G., Ontoseek. (1999). Content-based access to the web. *IEEE Intelligent Systems, 14*(3), 70–80. doi:10.1109/5254.769887

Gugliotta, A., Tanasescu, V., Domingue, J., Davies, R., Gutiérrez-Villarías, L., Rowlatt, M., Richardson, M., & Stinčić, S. (2006). *Benefits and challenges of applying semantic web services in the e-government domain.* Semantics 2006.

Guha, R., McCool, R., & Miller, E. (2003). Semantic search. In *WWW '03: Proceedings of the 12th international conference on world wide web* (pp. 700–709). New York: ACM Press.

Guo, Y., Pan, Z., & Heflin, J. (2005). LUBM: A benchmark for OWL knowledge base systems. *Journal of Web Semantics, 3*(2-3), 158–182. doi:10.1016/j.websem.2005.06.005

Guo, Y., Qasem, A., Pan, Z., & Heflin, J. (2007). A requirements driven framework for benchmarking Semantic Web knowledge base systems. *IEEE Transactions on Knowledge and Data Engineering, 19*(2), 297–309. doi:10.1109/TKDE.2007.19

Haartsen, J., & Zürbes, S. (1999). *Bluetooth voice and data performance in 802.11 DS WLAN environment.* Ericsson Sig Publication.

Hájek, P. (1998). *Metamathematics of Fuzzy Logic.* Kluwer.

Halkidi, M., Batistakis, Y., & Vazirgiannis, M. (2001). On clustering validation techniques. *Journal of Intelligent Information Systems, 17*(2-3), 107-145.

Hall, L. O., Özyurt, I. B., & Bezdek, J. C. (1999). Clustering with a genetically optimized approach. *IEEE Transactions on Evolutionary Computation, 3*(2), 103-112.

Halpin, H., & Presutti, V. (2009). An Ontology of Resources: Solving the Identity Crisis. In *Proceedings of European Semantic Web Conference (ESWC)*, Heraklion, Greece (pp. 521-534).

Halpin, H., & Thompson, H. (2005). *Web Proper Names: Naming Referents on the Web.* Chiba, Japan: The Semantic Computing Initiative Workshop.

Halpin, H., Hayes, P., & Thompson, H. S. (Eds.). (2006). *Proceedings of the WWW2006 Workshop on Identity, Reference, and the Web,* Edinburgh, United Kingdom, May 23, 2008, CEUR Workshop Proceedings. http://www.ibiblio.org/hhalpin/irw2006.

Hamming, R. (1986). *Coding and information theory.* Prentice Hall.

Handschuh, S. (2007). Semantic annotation of resources in the semantic web. In Studer, R., Grimm, S., & Abecker, A. (Eds.), *Semantic web services: Concepts, technologies, and applications* (pp. 135–155). Secaucus, NJ, USA: Springer-Verlag New York, Inc.

Harman, D. (1992). Overview of the first Text REtrieval Conference (TREC-1). In *Proceedings of the first Text REtrieval Conference (TREC-1)*, Gaithersbury, MD, USA.

Harris, S., & Gibbins, N. (2003). 3store: Efficient bulk RDF storage. In *Proceedings of the International Workshop on Practical and Scalable Semantic Systems (PSSS)* (pp. 1-15).

Harris, S., & Shadbolt, N. (2005). SPARQL query processing with conventional relational database systems. In *Proceedings of the International Workshop on Scalable Semantic Web Knowledge Base Systems (SSWS)*.

Harth, A., & Decker, S. (2005). Optimized index structures for querying RDF from the Web. In *Proceedings of the Latin American Web Congress (LA-WEB)* (pp. 71-80).

Hartig, O., & Heese, R. (2007). The SPARQL query graph model for query optimization. In *Proceedings of the European Semantic Web Conference (ESWC)* (pp. 564-578).

Hayes, P. (2006). In defense of ambiguity. *Proceedings of the Identity, Reference, and the Web (IRW2006), WWW2006 Workshop.* Edinburgh, United Kingdom. May, 23rd 2006. http://www.ibiblio.org/hhalpin/irw2006/presentations/-HayesSlides.pdf.

Hayes, P. J., Andersen, P. M., Nirengurg, I. B., & Schmandt, L. M. (1990). Tcs: a shell for content-based text categorization. *6th IEEE Conference on Artificial Intelligence Applications CAIA-90, Santa Barbara, CA* (pp. 320-326).

Hayes, P., & Halpin, H. (2008). In defense of ambiguity. *International Journal on Semantic Web and Information Systems, 4*(3), 1–18.

Hazas, M., Scott, J., & Krumm, J. (2004). Location-aware computing comes of age. *Computer, 37*(2), 95–97. doi:10.1109/MC.2004.1266301

Heflin, J., & Hendler, J. (2000). Searching the web with SHOE. In Artificial Intelligence for Web Search. Papers from the AAAI Workshop. WS-00-01. (p. 35-40). Menlo Park, CA: AAAI Press.

Hendler, J. (2007). The dark side of the semantic web. *IEEE Intelligent Systems, 22*, 2–4. doi:10.1109/MIS.2007.17

Herre, H., Heller, B., Burek, P., Hoehndorf, R., Loebe, F., & Michalek, H. (2007). *General formal ontology (GFO); A foundational ontology integrating objects and processes. Part I, v.1.0.1.* Retrieved May 30, 2007 from http://www.onto-med.de/en/theories/gfo/part1-drafts/gfo-part1-v1-0-1.pdf

Hirano, S., & Tsumoto, S. (2005). An indiscernibility-based clustering method. In X. Hu, Q. Liu, A. Skowron, T. Y. Lin, R. Yager, & B. Zhang (Eds.), *2005 IEEE International Conference on Granular Computing* (pp. 468-473). IEEE.

Hölldobler, S., Störr, H.-P., & Khang, T. D. (2004). The subsumption problem of the fuzzy description logic ALC_{FH}. In *Proc. IPMU-2004* (pp. 243-250).

Horrocks, I., & Patel-Schneider, P. F. (2004). Reducing OWL entailment to description logic satisfiability. *Journal of Web Semantics, 1*(4), 345–357. doi:10.1016/j.websem.2004.06.003

Horrocks, I., & Patel-Schneider, P. F. (2006). Position paper: A comparison of two modelling paradigms in the Semantic Web. In *Proc. WWW-2006* (pp. 3-12). ACM Press.

Horrocks, I., Patel-Schneider, P. F., & van Harmelen, F. (2003). From SHIQ and RDF to OWL: The making of a Web ontology language. *Journal of Web Semantics, 1*(1), 7–26. doi:10.1016/j.websem.2003.07.001

Horrocks, I., Sattler, U., & Tobies, S. (1999). Practical reasoning for expressive description logics. In *Proc. LPAR-1999*, LNCS (LNCS 1705, pp. 161-180). Springer.

Horrocks, I., van Harmelen, F., Patel-Schneider, P., Berners-Lee, T., Brickley, D. (2001). *DAML+OIL specifications.* Retrieved May 01, 2007 from http://www.daml.org/2001/03/daml+oil-index.html.

Huang, Y., & Chung, J. (2003). A Web services-based framework for business integration solutions. *Electronic Commerce Research and Applications, 2*(1), 15-26.

Huang, Z., Chen, H., & Zeng, D. (2004). Applying associative retrieval techniques to alleviate the sparsity problem in collaborative filtering. *ACM Transactions on Information Systems, 22*(1), 116–142. doi:10.1145/963770.963775

Huffman, D. (1952). A method for the construction of Minimum Redundancy Codes. *IRE*, 1098-1101.

Hung, E., Deng, Y., & Subrahmanian, V. S. (2005). RDF aggregate queries and views. In *Proceedings of the International Conference on Data Engineering (ICDE)* (p. 717-728).

Iannone, L., Palmisano, I., & Fanizzi, N. (2007). An algorithm based on counterfactuals for concept learning in the Semantic Web. *Applied Intelligence, 26*(2), 139-159.

IDTechEx. (2007); *RFID Logistics Case Studies: Thirty detailed RFID logistics case studies.* From. http://www.idtechex.com/products/en/view. asp?productcategoryid=49. Retrieved September 22, 2007, Kerer, C., Dustdar, S., Jazayeri, M, Gomes, D., Szego, A., & Burgos Caja, J.A. (2004). *Presence-Aware Infrastructure using Web services and RFID technologies.* 2nd European Workshop on Object Orientation and Web Services, ECOOP Workshop, 14 June 2004, Oslo, Norway, Springer LNCS

Intellidimension. (2008). RDFQL database command reference. Retrieved from http://www.intellidimension. com/pages/rdfgateway/reference/db/default.rsp

Ishikawa, F., Tahara, Y., Yoshioka, N., & Honiden, S. (2004b). Behavior descriptions of mobile agents for Web services integration. *Proceedings of the IEEE International Conference on Web Services* (ICWS) (pp. 342-349). San-Diego, CA.

Ishikawa, F., Yoshioka, N., Tahara, Y., & Honiden, S. (2004). Mobile agent system for Web services integration in pervasive networks. *Proceedings of the International Workshop on Ubiquitous Computing* (IWUC) (pp. 38-47). Porto, Portugal.

ISO. (2003). *Industrial automation systems and integration — Integration of life-cycle data for process plants including oil and gas production facilities — Part 2: Data Model.* International standard, 1ST ed. www.iso.org

Ittner, D. J., Lewis, D. D., & Ahn, D. D. (1995). Text categorization of low quality images. In *Proceedings of SDAIR-95, 4th Annual Symposium on Document Analysis and Information Retrieval, Las Vegas, NV* (pp. 301-315).

Jacobs, I., & Walsh, N. (2004). *Architecture of the World Wide Web.* W3C Recommendation. Retrieved from http:// www.w3.org/TR/Webarch

JADE. (2007). *Java agent development environment.* Retrieved June 1, 2007 from http://jade.tilab.com

Jain, A. K., Murty, M. N., & Flynn, P. J. (1999). Data clustering: A review. *ACM Computing Surveys, 31*(3), 264-323.

Joachims, T. (1988). Text Categorization with Support Vector Machines: Learning with Many Relevant Features. *Machine Learning, ECML-98*, 137–142.

Jones, S., & Maiden, N. (2005). Rescue: An integrated method for specifying requirements for complex socio-technical systems . In Mate, J. L., & Silva, A. (Eds.), *Requirements Engineering for Sociotechnical Systems.* Hershey, PA: Idea Group Inc.

jUDDI. (2007). *Open source Java implementation of the universal description, discovery, and integration (UDDI) specification for Web services.* Retrieved June 1, 2007 from http://ws.apache.org/juddi/

Kagal, L., et al. (2002). Agents making sense of the semantic Web. *Proceedings of the First International Workshop on Radical Agent Concepts, (WRAC).* McLean, VA.

Kalfoglou, Y., Domingue, J., Motta, E., Vargas-Vera, M., & Shum, S. B. (2001). myPlanet: An Ontology-Driven Web-Based Personalized News Service. *Workshop on Ontologies and Information Sharing - IJCAI 2001* (pp. 44-52).

Kaufman, L., & Rousseeuw, P. J. (1990). *Finding groups in data: An introduction to cluster analysis.* John Wiley & Sons.

Kawakita, Y., & Mistugi, J. (2006). Anti-collision performance of Gen2 Air Protocol in Random Error Communication Link. *International Symposium on Applications and the Internet Workshops, SAINTW'06* (pp. 68-71).

Kawakita, Y., Wakayama, S., Hada, H., Nakamura, O., & Murai, J. (2004). Rendezvous enhancement for conference support system based on RFID. *International Symposium on Applications and the Internet Workshops, SAINT2004* (pp. 280-286).

Kawamura, T., Ueno, K., Nagano, S., Hasegawa, T., & Ohsuga, A. (2004). Ubiquitous service finder discovery of services semantically derived from metadata in ubiquitous computing. *Proceedings of International Semantic Web Conference (ISWC 2005)* (pp 909-915). Galway, Ireland. November 6-10th 2004. London: Springer-Verlag.

Kent, W., Ahmed, R., Albert, J., Ketabchi, M., & Shan, M. (1992). Object identification in multi-database systems. *Proceedings of Conference on Semantics of Interoperable Databases* (pp. 313-330). Lorne, Australia. November 16-20th 1992. Amsterdam: Elsevier.

Khusraj, D., & Lassila, O. (2005). Ontological approach to generating personalized user interfaces for Web services. In: Y. Gil, et al. (Eds.), *ISWC 2005, LNCS 3729* (pp. 916-927). Berlin/Heidelberg: Springer.

Kietz, J.-U., & Morik, K. (1994). A polynomial approach to the constructive induction of structural knowledge. *Machine Learning, 14*(2), 193-218.

Kifer, M., Bernstein, A., & Lewis, P. M. (2006). *Database systems: An application oriented approach*. Addison-Wesley.

Kim, W. (1980). A new way to compute the product and join of relations. In *Proceedings of the SIGMOD International Conference on Management of Data* (pp. 179-187).

Kim, Y.-B., & Kim, Y.-S. (2008). Latent semantic kernels for WordNet: Transforming a tree-like structure into a matrix. *IEEE International Conference on Advanced Language Processing and Web Information Technology, ALPIT '08, Dalian Liaoning* (pp. 76-80).

Kindberg, T., & Barton, J. (2001). A Web-based nomadic computing system. *Computer Networks, 35*(4), 443–456. doi:10.1016/S1389-1286(00)00181-X

Kindberg, T., Barton, J.J., Morgan, J., Becker, G., Caswell, D., Debaty, P., Gopal, G., Frid, M., Krishnan, V., Morris, H., Schettino, J., Serra, B., & Spasojevic, M. (2002). People, Places, Things: Web Presence for the Real World. *MONET, 7*(5).

Kirsten, M., & Wrobel, S. (1998). Relational distance-based clustering. In D. Page (Ed.), *Proceedings of the 8th International Workshop, ILP98* (LNCS, pp. 261-270). Springer.

Kiryakov, A., Popov, B., Terziev, I., & Manov, D., & Ognyano_, D. (2004). Semantic annotation, indexing, and retrieval. *Journal of Web Semantics, 2*, 49–79. doi:10.1016/j.websem.2004.07.005

Klein, M., König-Ries, B., & Müssig, M. (2005). What is needed for semantic service descriptions - a proposal for suitable language constructs. [IJWGS]. *International Journal on Web and Grid Services, 1*(3/4), 328–364. doi:10.1504/IJWGS.2005.008393

Klusch, M. (2008). Semantic web service coordination. In SchumacherH. H. M. (Ed.), CASCOM - Intelligent Service Coordination in the Semantic Web. Springer.

Klusch, M. (2008). Semantic web service description. In M. Schumacher, H. H., editor, CASCOM - Intelligent Service Coordination in the Semantic Web, chapter 3. Springer.

Klusch, M., & Zhing, X. (2008). Deployed semantic services for the common user of the web: A reality check. In *Proceedings of the 2nd IEEE International Conference on Semantic Computing (ICSC2008)*, Santa Clara, CA, USA.

Kobayashi, M., & Takeda, K. (2000). Information retrieval on the web. *ACM Computing Surveys, 32,* 144–173. doi:10.1145/358923.358934

Koivunen, M-R. (2006). Annotea and semantic-Web-supported collaboration. Retrieved October 31, 2007 from http://kmi.open.ac.uk/events/usersweb/papers/01_koivunen_final.pdf

Koller, D., & Sahami, M. (1997). Hierarchically classifying documents using very few words. *14th International Conference on Machine Learning ICML-97, Nashville, TN* (pp. 70-178).

Kolte, S., & Bhirud, S. (2008). Word sense disambiguation using WordNet domains. *1st IEEE International Conference on Emerging Trends in Engineering and Technology, ICETET '08, Nagpur, Maharashtra* (pp. 1187-1191).

Korzybski, A. (1931). A Non-Aristotelian System and Its Necessity for Rigour in Mathematics. In *Proceedings of the American Mathematical Society.* New Orleans, Louisiana. December 28 1931 (pp. 747-761). Providence, RI: American Mathematical Society.

Kripke, S. (1980). *Naming and Necessity.* Cambridge, MA: Harvard University Press.

Küster, U., & König-Ries, B. (2007). Supporting dynamics in service descriptions - the key to automatic service usage. In *Proceedings of the Fifth International Conference on Service Oriented Computing (ICSOC07),* Vienna, Austria.

Küster, U., & König-Ries, B. (2008). Evaluating semantic web service matchmaking effectiveness based on graded relevance. In *Proceedings of the 2nd International Workshop SMR² on Service Matchmaking and Resource Retrieval in the Semantic Web at the 7th International Semantic Web Conference (ISWC08),* Karlsruhe, Germany.

Küster, U., & König-Ries, B. (2008). On the empirical evaluation of semantic web service approaches: Towards common SWS test collections. In *Proceedings of the 2nd IEEE International Conference on Semantic Computing (ICSC2008),* Santa Clara, CA, USA.

Küster, U., & König-Ries, B. (2008). Towards standard test collections for the empirical evaluation of semantic web service approaches. *International Journal of Semantic Computing, 2*(3), 381–402. doi:10.1142/S1793351X0800052X

Küster, U., & König-Ries, B. (2009). Relevance judgments for web services retrieval - a methodology and test collection for sws discovery evaluation. In *Proceedings of the 7th IEEE European Conference on Web Services (ECOWS09),* Einhoven, The Netherlands.

Küster, U., König-Ries, B., Klein, M., & Stern, M. (2007). DIANE - a matchmaking-centered framework for automated service discovery, composition, binding, and invocation on the web. *International Journal of Electronic Commerce (IJEC) - . Special Issue: Semantic Matchmaking and Resource Retrieval on the Web, 12*(2), 41–68.

Küster, U., Lausen, H., & König-Ries, B. (2007). Evaluation of semantic service discovery - a survey and directions for future research. In *Proceedings of the 2nd Workshop on Emerging Web Services Technology (WEWST07) at the 5th IEEE European Conference on Web Services (ECOWS07),* Halle (Saale), Germany.

Kwok, K. L. (1995). A network approach to probabilistic information retrieval. *ACM Transactions on Information Systems, 13*(3), 324–353. doi:10.1145/203052.203067

Kwok, K., & Grunfeld, L. (1996). Trec-4 ad-hoc, routing retrieval and filtering experiments using pircs . In Harman, D. K. (Ed.), *The fourth text retrieval conference (trec-4).*

Laboratory for Applied Ontologies. (2007). *LOA site.* Retrieved October 31, 2007 from http://wiki.loa-cnr.it/index.php/Main_Page; http://www.loa-cnr.it/ontologies/EVAL/oQual.owl

Lam, T. H. W. (2006). Fuzzy ontology map—a fuzzy extension of the hard-constraint ontology. In *Proceedings of the 5th IEEE/WIC/ACM International Conference on Web Intelligence,* Hong Kong, China (pp. 506-509).

Lange, D., & Oshima, M. (1998). *Programming and deploying Java mobile agents with aglets*. Addison-Wesley.

Larkey, L. S., & Croft, W. B. (1996). Combining classifiers in text categorization. *19th ACM International Conference on Research and Development in Information Retrieval SIGIR-96, Zurich, Switzerland* (pp. 289-297).

Lausen, H., Petrie, C., & Zaremba, M. (2007). W3C SWS testbed incubator group charter. Available online at http://www.w3.org/2005/Incubator/swsc/charter.

Lee, C.-Y., & Antonsson, E. K. (2000). Variable length genomes for evolutionary algorithms. In L. Whitley, D. Goldberg, E. Cantú-Paz, L. Spector, I. Parmee, & H.-G. Beyer (Eds.), *Proceedings of the Genetic and Evolutionary Computation Conference, GECCO00* (p. 806). Morgan Kaufmann.

Lehmann, J., & Hitzler, P. (2008). A refinement operator based learning algorithm for the ALC description logic. In H. Blockeel, J. Ramon, J. Shavlik, & P. Tadepalli (Eds.), *Proceedings of the 17th International Conference on Inductive Logic Programming, ILP2007* (LNCS, pp. 147-160). Springer.

Lehmann, J., & Hitzler, P. (2008). Foundations of refinement operators for description logics. In H. Blockeel, J. Ramon, J. Shavlik, & P. Tadepalli (Eds.), *Proceedings of the 17th International Conference on Inductive Logic Programming, ILP2007* (LNCS, pp. 161-174). Springer.

Lewis, D. D. (1992). *Feature selection and feature extraction for text categorization* (pp. 212–217). San Francisco, USA: Speech and Natural Language Workshop.

Lewis, D. D. (1998). Naïve (Bayes) at forty: The independence assumption in information retrieval. *10th European Conference on Machine Learning ECML-98, Chemnitz, Germany* (pp. 4-15).

Lewis, D. D., & Ringuette, M. (1994). A comparison of two learning algorithms for text categorization. *3rd Annual Symposium on Document Analysis and Information Retrieval SDAIR-94, Las Vegas, NV* (pp. 81-93).

Lewis, R. (Ed.). (2007). *Dereferencing HTTP URIs, Draft Tag Finding*. Retrieved from http://www.w3.org/2001/tag/doc/httpRange-14/2007-08-31/HttpRange-14.html.

Ley, T., Ulbrich, A., Scheir, P., Lindstaedt, S. N., Kump, B., & Albert, D. (2008). Modelling competencies for supporting work integrated learning in knowledge work. *Journal of Knowledge Management, 12*(6). doi:10.1108/13673270810913603

Li, K., Verma, K., Mulye, R., Rabbani, R., Miller, J., & Sheth, A. (2006). Designing semantic Web processes: The WSDL-S approach. In: J. Cardoso & A. Sheth (Eds.), *Semantic Web services, processes and applications*. Springer-Verlag.

Li, L., & Horrocks, I. (2003). A software framework for matchmaking based on semantic web technology. In *Proceedings of the 12th World Wide Web Conference (WWW2003)*, Budapest, Hungary.

Li, Y. H., & Jain, A. K. (1998). Classification of text documents. *The Computer Journal, 41*(8), 537–546. doi:10.1093/comjnl/41.8.537

Liefke, H., & Suciu D. (2000). XMill: An efficient compressor for XML data. *SIGMOD Rec., 29*(2), 153-164.

Lindstaedt, S. N., & Mayer, H. (2006). A storyboard of the aposdle vision. In *Innovative Approaches for Learning and Knowledge Sharing, First European Conference on Technology Enhanced Learning*, ec-tel 2006, crete, greece, october 1-4, 2006 (p. 628- 633).

Lindstaedt, S. N., Ley, T., Scheir, P., & Ulbrich, A. (2008). *Applying scruffy methods to enable work-integrated learning. To appear in.* The European Journal for the Informatics Professional.

Lu, H., Tan, K.-L., & Shan, M.-C. (1990). Hash-based join algorithms for multiprocessor computers with shared memory. In *Proceedings of the International Conference on Very Large Data Bases (VLDB)* (pp. 198-209).

Lukasiewicz, T. (2005). Probabilistic description logic programs. In *Proc. ECSQARU-2005* (LNCS 3571, pp. 737-749). Extended version: *Int. J. Approx. Reason., 45*(2), 288-307, 2007.

Lukasiewicz, T. (2006). Fuzzy description logic programs under the answer set semantics for the Semantic Web. In Proc. RuleML-2006 (pp. 89-96). IEEE Computer Society. Extended version: Fundam. Inform., 82(3), 289-310, 2008.

Lukasiewicz, T. (2006). Stratified probabilistic description logic programs. In *Proc. URSW-2005, CEUR Workshop Proceedings* 173. CEUR-WS.org.

Lukasiewicz, T. (2007). A novel combination of answer set programming with description logics for the Semantic Web. In *Proc. ESWC-2007* (LNCS 4519, pp. 384-398).

Lukasiewicz, T. (2007). Tractable probabilistic description logic programs. In *Proc. SUM-2007* (LNCS 4772, pp. 143-156).

Lukasiewicz, T., & Straccia, U. (2007). Description logic programs under probabilistic uncertainty and fuzzy vagueness. In *Proc. ECSQARU-2007* (LNCS 4724, pp. 187-198). Springer.

Lukasiewicz, T., & Straccia, U. (2007). Top-k retrieval in description logic programs under vagueness for the Semantic Web. In *Proc. SUM-2007* (LNCS 4772, pp. 16-30). Springer.

Lukasiewicz, T., & Straccia, U. (2008). Managing uncertainty and vagueness in description logics for the Semantic Web. *Journal of Web Semantics, 6*(4), 291-308. doi:10.1016/j.wcbsem.2008.04.001

Luntley, M. (1999). *Contemporary Philosophy of Thought*. Oxford, UK: Blackwell.

Lv, Y., Ma, Z. M., & Yan, L. (2008). Fuzzy RDF: A data model to represent fuzzy metadata. In *Proceedings of the 17th IEEE International Conference on Fuzzy Systems*, Hong Kong, China (pp. 1439-1445).

Ma, L., Su, Z., Pan, Y., Zhang, L., & Liu, T. (2004). RStar: an RDF storage and query system for enterprise resource management. In *Proceedings of the International Conference on Information and Knowledge Management (CIKM)* (pp. 484-491).

Ma, Z. M., & Mili, F. (2002). Handling fuzzy information in extended possibility-based fuzzy relational databases. *International Journal of Intelligent Systems, 17*(10), 925-942.

Ma, Z. M., & Yan, L. (2007). Fuzzy XML data modeling with the UML and relational data models. *Data & Knowledge Engineering, 63*(3), 970-994.

Ma, Z. M., & Yan, Li (2008). A literature overview of fuzzy database models. *Journal of Information Science and Engineering, 24*(1), 189-202.

Mackay, D. J. C. (2002). *Information Theory, Inference & Learning Algorithms*. Cambridge University Press.

Maedche, A., Naumann, G., & Staab, S. (2002). *Bootstrapping an Ontology-based Information Extraction System for the Web. Intelligent Exploration of the Web, Series - Studies in Fuzziness and Soft Computing*. Springer/Physica-Verlag.

Magkanaraki, A., Tannen, V., Christophides, V., & Plexousakis, D. (2004). Viewing the Semantic Web through RVL lenses. *Journal of Web Semantics, 1*(4), 359–375. doi:10.1016/j.websem.2004.06.004

Mahoney, M. (2005). *Adaptive weighing of context models for lossless data compression*. Florida Tech. Technical Report, CS-2005-16.

Mäkelä, K., Belt, S., Greenblatt, D., & Häkkilä, J. (2007). *Mobile interaction with visual and RFID tags: a field study on user perceptions*. In *Proc. of CHI '07*(pp. 991-994). New York: ACM.

Mandl, T. (2001). *Tolerantes information retrieval. neuronale netze zur erhöhung der adaptivität und flexibilität bei der informationssuche*. Unpublished doctoral dissertation, University Of Hildesheim.

Manning, C. D., & Schutze, H. (1999). *Foundations of Statistical Natural Language Processing*. Cambridge, MA: MIT Press.

Manning, C. D., Raghavan, P., & Schutze, H. (2008). *Introduction to information retrieval*. New York: Cambridge University Press.

Mannino, M. V., Chu, P., & Sager, T. (1988). Statistical profile estimation in database systems. *ACM Computing Surveys, 20*(3), 191–221. doi:10.1145/62061.62063

Maron, M.E. and Kuhns, J.L. (1960). On relevance, probabilistic indexing, and information retrieval. *Journal of the Association for Computing Machinery, 7*.

Martin, D., Burstein, M., Hobbs, J., Lassila, O., Mc-Dermott, D. (n.d.). *OWL-S: Semantic markup for Web services*. Retrieved May 01, 2007 from http://www.daml.org/services/owl-s/1.1/overview/.

Martin, D., Burstein, M., McDermott, D., McIlraith, S., Paolucci, M., & Sycara, K. (2007). Bringing Semantics to Web Services with OWL-S. *World Wide Web (Bussum), 10*(3). doi:10.1007/s11280-007-0033-x

Martin, T. (2004). Searching and smushing on the semantic web-challenges for soft computing. In Nikravesh, M., Azvine, B., Yager, R. R., & Zadeh, L. A. (Eds.), *Enhancing the Power of the Web* (pp. 167–188). Heidelberg: Springer.

Masolo, C., Gangemi, A., Guarino, N., Oltramari, A., & Schneider, L. (2004). *WonderWeb EU project deliverable D18: The WonderWeb Library of Foundational Ontologies*. Retrieved from http://wonderWeb.semanticWeb.org/deliverables/documents/D18.pdf

Mazzieri, M., & Dragoni, A. F. (2005). A fuzzy semantics for Semantic Web languages. In *Proceedings of the 4th ISWC2005 Workshop on Uncertainty Reasoning for the Semantic Web*, Galway, Ireland (pp. 12-22).

McCool, R. (2005). Rethinking the semantic web, part 1. *IEEE Internet Computing, 9*(6), 88–87. doi:10.1109/MIC.2005.133

McGuinness, D., Fikes, R., Hendler, J., & Stein, L. (2002). DAML+OIL: An ontology language for the semantic Web. *IEEE Intelligent Systems, 17*(5), 72-80.

McIlraith, S. A., Son, T. C., & Zeng, H. (2001). Semantic web services. *IEEE Intelligent Systems, 16*(2), 46–53. doi:10.1109/5254.920599

McIlraith, S., & Martin, D. (2003). Bringing semantics to Web services. *IEEE Intelligent Systems, 18*(1), 90-93.

Mealling, M., & Daniel, R. (1999). *IETF RFC (Experimental) 2483 URI Resolution Services Necessary for URN Resolution*. http://www.ietf.org/rfc/rfc2483.txt.

Meloan, S. (2003). *Toward a Global "Internet of Things"*. Sun Developers Network. November 11, 2003. Retrieved on September 22, 2007 from http://java.sun.com/developer/technicalArticles/Ecommerce/rfid/

Mika, P. (2005). Ontologies are us: A unified model of social networks and semantics. *Proceedings of International Semantic Web Conference (ISWC 2005)* (pp. 522-536). Galway, Ireland. November 6-10th 2004. London: Springer-Verlag.

Miles, A. (2005). *Working around the identity crisis*. Retrieved from http://esw.w3.org/topic/SkosDev/IdentityCrisis

Miller, G. A. (1995). WordNet: a lexical database for English. *Communications of the ACM, 38*(11), 39–41. doi:10.1145/219717.219748

Mishra, P., & Eich, M. H. (1992). Join processing in relational databases. *ACM Computing Surveys, 24*(1), 63–113. doi:10.1145/128762.128764

Mitchell, T. M. (1996). *Machine Learning*. New York: McGraw Hill.

Moats, R. (1997). *IETF RFC (Proposed) 2141 Uniform Resource Names*. http://www.ietf.org/rfc/rfc2141.txt.

Montanari, R., Tonti, G., & Stefanelli, C. (2003). A policy-based mobile agent infrastructure. *Proceedings of the 3rd IEEE International Symposium on Applications and the Internet Workshops (SAINT03) IEEE Computer Society Press*. Orlando, FL.

Montanari, R., Tonti, G., & Stefanelli. C. (2003). Policy-based separation of concerns for dynamic code mobility management. Proceedings of the 27th International Computer Software and Applications Conference, (COMPSAC'03). Dallas, TX: IEEE Computer Society Press.

Mothe, J. (1994). Search mechanisms using a neural network model. In Proc. of the riao 94 (recherche d information assiste par ordinateur).

Motik, B., Horrocks, I., Rosati, R., & Sattler, U. (2006). Can OWL and logic programming live together happily ever after? In *Proc. ISWC-2006* (LNCS 4273, pp. 501-514).

Mukhopadhyay, D., Banik, A., & Mukherjee, S. (2007). A technique for automatic construction of ontology from existing database to facilitate Semantic Web. In *Proceedings of the 10th International Conference on Information Technology*, Rourkela, India (pp. 246-251).

MySQL. (2008). MySQL 5.0 Reference Manual: 7.2.10 Nested Join Optimization [Computer software manual]. Retrieved from http://dev.mysql.com/doc/refman/5.0/en/nested-joins.html

Narayanan, S., Kurc, T. M., & Saltz, J. H. (2006). *DBOWL: Towards extensional queries on a billion statements using relational databases* (Tech. Rep. No. OSUBMI_TR_2006_n03). Ohio State University. Retrieved from http://bmi.osu.edu/resources/techreports/osubmi.tr.2006.n3.pdf

Nasraoui, O., & Krishnapuram, R. (2002). One step evolutionary mining of context sensitive associations and Web navigation patterns. In *Proceedings of the SIAM Conference on Data Mining,* Arlington, VA (pp. 531-547).

Nethercote, N., & Seward J. (2007). Valgrind: A framework for heavyweight dynamic binary instrumentation. *Conference on Programming Language Design and Implementation - PLDI 07.* ACM SIGPLAN.

Ng, R., & Han, J. (1994). Efficient and effective clustering method for spatial data mining. In *Proceedings of the 20th Conference on Very Large Databases, VLDB94* (pp. 144-155).

Nielsen, J. (2003). *Paper Prototyping: Getting User Data Before You Code.* Retrieved on September 22, 2007 from http://www.useit.com/alertbox/20030414.html

Nienhuys-Cheng, S.-H. (1998). Distances and limits on herbrand interpretations. In D. Page (Ed.), *Proceedings of the 8th International Workshop on Inductive Logic Programming, ILP98* (LNAI, pp. 250-260). Springer.

O'Neill, E., Thompson, P., Garzonis, S., & Warr, A. (2007). Reach out and touch: Using nfc and 2d barcodes for service discovery and interaction with mobile devices. In Proc. of Pervasive'07 (LNCS 4480, pp. 19-36).

Ontomed. (2006). *Ontomed ontology.* Retrieved October 31, 2007 from http://www.onto-med.de/ontologies/gfo.owl

Open Mobile Alliance. (2006). *User Agent profile ,Version 2.* Retrieved February 28, 2007 from http://www.openmobilealliance.org/release_program/docs/UAProf/V2_0-20060206-A/OMA-TS-UAProf-V2_0-20060206-A.pdf

OSGi Alliance. (2005). *About the OSGi service platform* (rev. 4.1). San Ramon, CA: OSGi Alliance.

OWL-S. (2007). *OWL Web ontology language for services (OWL-S).* Retrieved June 1, 2007 from http://www.w3.org/Submission/2004/07/

OWL-S/UDDI Matchmaker Web Interface. (2007). Retrieved June 1, 2007 http://www.daml.ri.cmu.edu/matchmaker/

OWLSM. (2007). *The TUB OWL-S Matcher.* Retrieved June 1, 2007 from http://kbs.cs.tu-berlin.de/ivs/Projekte/owlsmatcher/index.html

OWLS-MX. (2007). *Hybrid OWL-S Web Service Matchmaker.* Retrieved June 1, 2007 from http://www.dfki.de/~klusch/owls-mx/

Pammer, V., Scheir, P., & Lindstaedt, S. N. (2007). Two protégé plug-ins for supporting document-based ontology engineering and ontological annotation at document level. In *10th International Prot'eg'e Conference - July 15-18, 2007 - Budapest, Hungary.*

Pan, Z., & Heflin, J. (2003). DLDB: Extending relational databases to support Semantic Web queries. In *Proceedings of the International Workshop on Practical and Scalable Semantic Web Systems (PSSS)* (pp. 109-113).

Paolucci, M., Broll, G., Hamard, J., Rukzio, E., Wagner, M., & Schmidt, A. (2008). *Bringing semantic services to real-world objects.* In this issue.

Paolucci, M., Kawamura, T., Payne, T., & Sycara, K. (2002). Semantic matching of Web services capabilities. *Proceedings of the International Semantic Web Conference (ISWC)*. Sardinia, Italy.

Papazoglou, M., & Heuvel, W. (2007). Service oriented architectures: approaches, technologies and research issues. *The VLDB Journal, 16*(3). doi:10.1007/s00778-007-0044-3

Parsia, B., & Patel-Schneider, P. F. (2006). *Meaning and the semantic Web. Proceedings of Identity, Reference, and the Web (IRW2006), WWW2006 Workshop*. Edinburgh, United Kingdom. May, 23rd 2006. http://www.ibiblio.org/hhalpin/irw2006/bparsia.pdf.

Pawlak, Z. (1991). *Rough sets: Theoretical aspects of reasoning about data*. Kluwer Academic Publishers.

Pepper, S. (2006). The case for published subjects. *Proceedings of Identity, Reference, and the Web (IRW2006), WWW2006 Workshop*. Edinburgh, United Kingdom. May, 23rd 2006. http://www.ibiblio.org/hhalpin/irw2006/spepper2.pdf.

Pepper, S., & Schwab, S. (2003). *Curing the Web's identity crisis: Subject indicators for RDF*. Technical report, Ontopia, 2003. Retrieved from http://www.ontopia.net/topicmaps/materials/identitycrisis.html

PERCI. (PERvasive ServiCe Interaction) website (2005). Retrieved on July 15, 2009 from http://www.hcilab.org/projects/perci

Perez, J., Arenas, M., & Gutierrez, C. (2006). Semantics and complexity of SPARQL. In *Proceedings of the International Semantic Web Conference (ISWC)* (p. 30-43).

Perez, J., Arenas, M., & Gutierrez, C. (2006). Semantics of SPARQL. Retrieved from http://ing.utalca.cl/~jperez/papers/sparql_semantics.pdf

Peterson, E. (2006). Beneath the metadata; Some philosophical problems with folksonomy. *D-Lib Magazine 12*(11). Retrieved May 31, 2007 from http://www.dlib.org/dlib/november06/peterson/11peterson.html

Petrie, C., Küster, U., & Margaria-Steffen, T. (2008). W3C SWS challenge testbed incubator methodology report. *W3C incubator report, W3C*. Retrieved from http://www.w3.org/2005/Incubator/swsc/XGR-SWSC/

Petrie, C. Lausen, H. Zaremba, M. Margaria, T. (Eds.). (2008). Semantic Web Service Challenge - Results from the First Year. *Semantic Web and Beyond* (Vol. 8). Springer.

Pohjola, P. (2007). *Technical artefacts, an ontological investgation of arfacts*. Jyväskylä Studies in Education, Psychology and Social Research, Report No. 300. Retrieved October 14, 2007 from http://dissertations.jyu.fi/studeduc/9789513927561.pdf

Polleres, A. (2007). From SPARQL to rules (and back). In *Proceedings of the International World Wide Web Conference (WWW)* (pp. 787-796).

Pour, G., & Laad, N. (2006). Enhancing the horizons of mobile computing with mobile agent components. *Proceedings of the 5th IEEE/ACIS International Conference on Computer and Information Science and 1st IEEE/ACIS International Workshop on Component-Based Software Engineering, Software Architecture and Reuse (ICIS-COMSAR'06)* (pp. 225-230).

Prade, H., & Testemale, C. (1984). Generalizing database relational algebra for the treatment of incomplete or uncertain information and vague queries. *Information Sciences, 34*, 115-143.

Predoiu, L., & Stuckenschmidt, H. (2007). A probabilistic framework for information integration and retrieval on the Semantic Web. In *Proc. InterDB-2007 Workshop on Database Interoperability*.

Preist, C. (2004). *A conceptual architecture for semantic web services (extended version)*. Technical Report HPL-2004-215, HP Laboratories Bristol.

Preist, C. (2007). Goals and vision: Combining web services with semantic web technology. In *Semantic Web Services: Concepts, Technologies, and Applications* (pp. 159–178). Springer-Verlag New York, Inc.

Preist, C., Cuadrado, J. E., Battle, S. A., Grimm, S., & Williams, S. K. (2005). Automated business-to-business integration of a logistics supply chain using semantic web services technology. In *Proceedings of the Fourth International Semantic Web Conference, Galway, Ireland.*

Prud'hommeaux, E. (2004). Optimal RDF access to relational databases. Retrieved from http://www. w3.org/2004/04/30-RDF-RDB-access/

Prud'hommeaux, E. (2005). Notes on adding SPARQL to MySQL. Retrieved from http://www.w3.org/2005/05/22-SPARQL-MySQL/

Puttonen, J. (2006). *Mobility management in wireless networks.* Doctoral Thesis. Jyväskylä Studies in Computing # 69, University of Jyvaskylä, Jyväskylä, Finland.

Quack, T., Bay, H., & Van Gool, L. J. (2008). Object Recognition for the Internet of Things. *IOT, 2008,* 230–246.

Quan, T. T., Hui, S. C., Fong, A. C. M., & Cao, T. H. (2006). Automatic fuzzy ontology generation for Semantic Web. *IEEE Transaction on Knowledge and Data Engineering, 18*(6), 842-856.

Quine, W. (1960). *Word and Object.* Cambridge, MA: MIT Press.

Quine, W. V. O. (1951). Two Dogmas Of Empiricism. *The Philosophical Review, 60,* 20–43. doi:10.2307/2181906

Quine, W. V. O. (1969). Ontological Relativity . In *Ontological Relativity and Other Essays.* Columbia University Press.

RACER. (2007). *DL reasoner.* Retrieved June 1, 2007 from http://www.racer-systems.com

Raggett, D., Le Hors, A., & Jacobs, I. (1999). *HTML 4.01 Specification.* W3C Recommendation 24 December 1999. Retrieved from http://www.w3.org/TR/html401/

Raghavan, V., & Wong, S. (1986). A critical analysis of vector space model for information retrieval. *JASIS, 37*(5), 279-287.

Ragone, A., Straccia, U., Noia, T. D., Sciascio, E. D., & Donini, F. M. (2007). Vague knowledge bases for matchmaking in P2P e-marketplaces. *In Proceedings of the 4th European Semantic Web Conference (ESWC2007),* Innsbruck, Austria.

Raju, K. V. S. V. N., & Majumdar, A. K. (1988). Fuzzy functional dependencies and lossless join decomposition of fuzzy relational database systems. *ACM Transactions on Database Systems, 13*(2), 129-166.

Ramakrishnan, K., & Deavours, D. (2006). Performance benchmarks for passive UHF RFID tags. *Proceedings of the 13th GI/ITG Conference on Measurement, Modeling, and Evaluation of Computer and Communication Systems.* Nurenberg, Germany.

Ramanathan, S., & Hodges, J. (1997). Extraction of object-oriented structures from existing relational databases. *ACM SIGMOD Record, 26*(1), 59-64.

Reilly, D., Dearman, D., Welsman-Dinelle, M., & Inkpen, K. M. (2005, October-December). Evaluating Early Prototypes in Context: Trade-offs, Challenges, and Successes. *IEEE Pervasive Computing / IEEE Computer Society [and] IEEE Communications Society, 4*(4), 10–18. doi:10.1109/MPRV.2005.76

Resnik, P. (1999). Semantic similarity in a taxonomy: An information-based measure and its application to problems of ambiguity in natural language. [JAIR]. *Journal of Artificial Intelligence Research, 11,* 95–130.

Riekki, J., Salminen, T., & Alakärppä, I. (2006). Requesting Pervasive Services by Touching RFID Tags. *IEEE Pervasive computing.*

Robertson, S., & Spärck Jones, K. (1976). Relevance weighting of search terms. *Journal of the American Society for Information Science American Society for Information Science, 27*(3). doi:10.1002/asi.4630270302

Robertson, S., & Spärck Jones, K. (1994). *Simple, proven approaches to text retrieval* (Tech. Rep.). University of Cambridge, Computer Laboratory. Available from http://www.cl.cam .ac.uk/techreports/UCAM-CL-TR-356.pdf

Rocchio, J. J. (1971). *Relevance Feedback in Information Retrieval. Englewood.* Cliffs, New Jersey: Prentice Hall.

Rocha, C., Schwabe, D., & de Aragão, M. P. (2004). A hybrid approach for searching in the semantic web. In *Proceedings of the 13th international conference on world wide web, www 2004.*

Rohs, M., & Gfeller, B. (2004). Using Camera-Equipped Mobile Phones for Interacting with Real-World Objects. In Advances in Pervasive Computing, Austrian Computer Society (OCG) (pp. 265-271).

Roman, D., Keller, U., Lausen, H., deBruijn, J., Lara, R., Stollberg, M., et al. (2005). Web service modeling ontology. Applied Ontology, *1*(1), 77-106.

Römer, K., Schoch, T., Mattern, F., & Dübendorfer, T. (2004). Smart identification frameworks for ubiquitous computing applications. *Wireless Networks, 10*(6), 689-700.

Rosati, R. (2006). DL+*log*: Tight integration of description logics and disjunctive Datalog. In *Proc. KR-2006* (pp. 68-78). AAAI Press.

Rukzio, E., Leichtenstern, K., Callaghan, V., Holleis, P., Schmidt, A., & Shiaw-Yuan Chin, J. (2006). *An Experimental Comparison of Physical Mobile Interaction Techniques: Touching, Pointing and Scanning* (pp. 87–104). Proc. of Ubicomp.

Rukzio, E., Wetzstein, S., & Schmidt, A. (2005). *A Framework for Mobile Interactions with the Physical World.* Wireless Personal Multimedia Communication (WPMC'05). Aalborg, Denmark, 2005.

Russell, B. (1911). Knowledge by acquaintance, knowledge by description. In . *Proceedings of the Aristotelian Society, 11*, 197–218.

Ruta, M., Di Noia, T., Di Sciascio, E., & Donini, F. (2006a). Semantic-enhanced Bluetooth discovery protocol for M-Commerce applications. *International Journal of Web and Grid Services, 2*(4), 424-452.

Ruta, M., Di Noia, T., Di Sciascio, E., Donini, F., & Piscitelli, G. (2006b). Advanced resource discovery protocol for semantic-enabled M-commerce. *Encyclopaedia of Mobile Computing and Commerce (EMCC).* Hershey, PA: Idea Group.

Sabou, M. (2004). Extracting ontologies from software documentation: A semi-automatic method and its evaluation. In *Proceedings of the 16th European Conference on Artificial Intelligence Workshop on Ontology Learning and Population*, Valencia, Spain.

Sabou, M., d'Aquin, M., & Motta, E. (2006). Using the semantic web as background knowledge for ontology mapping. In *International Workshop on Ontology Matching* (om-2006).

Salminen, I., Lehikoinen, J., Huuskonen, P. (2005). Developing and extensible metadata ontology. In: W. Tsai & M. Hamza (Eds.), *Procedings of the 9th IASTED Intl. Conference on Software Engineering and Applications (SEA)* (pp. 266-272). .Phoenix, AZ: ACTA Press.

Salton, G. (1963). Associative document retrieval techniques using bibliographic information. *Journal of the ACM, 10*, 440–457. doi:10.1145/321186.321188

Salton, G. (1968). *Automatic information organization and retrieval.* McGraw Hill.

Sanchez, E. (2006). *Fuzzy Logic and the Semantic Web.* Amsterdam: Elsevier.

Sanchez, E., & Yamanoi, T. (2006). Fuzzy ontologies for the Semantic Web. In *Proceedings of the 7th International Conference on Flexible Query Answering Systems*, Milan, Italy (pp. 691-699).

Sanderson, M., & Zobel, J. (2005). Information retrieval system evaluation: effort, sensitivity, and reliability. In *Sigir '05: Proceedings of the 28th annual international ACM SIGIR conference on Research and development in information retrieval* (pp. 162–169). New York: ACM Press.

Sarvas, R. (2006). *Designing user-centric metadata for digital snapshot photography*. Doctoral Dissertation, Helsinki University of Technology, Department of Computer Science and Engineering/Soberit, and Helsinki Institute for Information Technology (HIIT)/HUT. http://lib.tkk.fi/Diss/2006/isbn9512284448/isbn9512284448.pdf

Scheir, P., Ghidini, C., & Lindstaedt, S. N. (2007). Improving search on the semantic desktop using associative retrieval techniques. In Proceedings of i-semantics 2007 (p. 221-228).

Scheir, P., Granitzer, M., & Lindstaedt, S. N. (2007). Evaluation of an information retrieval system for the semantic desktop using standard measures from information retrieval. In Lwa 2007, lernen - wissensentdeckung - adaptivität, 24.-26.9. 2007 in halle/saale (p. 269-272).

Scheir, P., Lindstaedt, S. N., & Ghidini, C. (2008). A network model approach to retrieval in the Semantic Web. *International Journal on Semantic Web and Information Systems*, *4*(4), 56–84.

Scheir, P., Pammer, V., & Lindstaedt, S. N. (2007). Information retrieval on the semantic web - does it exist? In Lwa 2007, Lernen - Wissensentdeckung - Adaptivität, 24.-26.9. 2007 in Halle/Sale (pp. 252-257).

Schenk, S. (2007). A SPARQL semantics based on Datalog. In *Proceedings of the KI 2007, Annual German Conference on AI* (p. 160-174).

Schenk, S., & Staab, S. (2008). Networked graphs: A declarative mechanism for SPARQL rules, SPARQL views and RDF data integration on the Web. In *Proceedings of the International World Wide Web Conference (WWW)* (pp. 585-594).

Schmidt, A., Gellersen, H., & Merz, C. (2000). Enabling implicit human computer interaction: A wearable RFID tag reader. *The 4th International Symposium on Wearable Computers* (pp. 193-194).

Schütze, H., Hull, D. A., & Pedersen, J. O. (1995). A Comparison of Classifiers and Document Representations for the Routing Problem. In Research and Development in Information Retrieval, pages 229–237.

Schwatrz, A. (2004). IETF RFC 3870 application/rdf+xml Media Type Registration. http://www.ietf.org/rfc/rfc3870.txt

Scott, F., Lewis, W. D., & Langendoen, D. T. (2002). An ontology for Linguistic Annotaion 1-2. *14th Innovative Applications of AI Conference, Edmonton, Canada* (pp. 11-19).

Sebag, M. (1997). Distance induction in first order logic. In S. Džeroski & N. Lavra (Eds.), *Proceedings of the 7th International Workshop on Inductive Logic Programming, ILP97* (LNAI, pp. 264-272). Springer.

Sebastiani, F. (2002). Machine Learning in Automated Text Categorization. *ACM Computing Surveys*, *34*(1), 1–47. doi:10.1145/505282.505283

Semacode.org. (2007). *Semacode SDK technical paper*. Retrieved September 21, 2007, from http://semacode.org/about/technical/

Serfiotis, G., Koffina, I., Christophides, V., & Tannen, V. (2005). Containment and minimization of RDF/S query patterns. In *Proceedings of the International Semantic Web Conference (ISWC)* (pp. 607-623).

Shadbolt, N., Berners-Lee, T., & Hall, W. (2006). The Semantic Web revisited. *IEEE Intelligent Systems*, *21*(3), 96–101. doi:10.1109/MIS.2006.62

Shah, U., Finin, T., & Joshi, A. (2002). Information retrieval on the semantic web. *In Cikm '02: Proceedings of the Eleventh International Conference on Information and Knowledge Management* (pp. 461–468). New York: ACM Press.

Shen, D., Chen, Z., Zeng, H.-J., Zhang, B., Yang, W.-Y., Ma, Q., & Lu, Y. (2004). Web-page classification through summarization. *27th Annual International ACM SIGIR Conference on Research and development in information retrieval, Sheffield, United Kingdom* (pp. 242–249).

Sheth, A., Arpinar, I. B., & Kashyap, V. (2004). Relationships at the heart of Semantic Web: modeling, discovering and exploiting complex semantic relationships . In Nikravesh, M., Azvine, B., Yager, R. R., & Zadeh, L. A. (Eds.), *Enhancing the Power of the Web* (pp. 63–94). Heidelberg: Springer.

Sidirourgos, L., Goncalves, R., Kersten, M., Nes, N., & Manegold, S. (2008). Column-store support for RDF data management: not all swans are white. In *Proceedings of the International Conference on Very Large Data Bases (VLDB)*.

Siegemund, F., & Florkemeier, C. (2003). Interaction in pervasive computing settings using Bluetooth-enabled active tags and passive RFID technology together with mobile phones. *Proceedings of the 1st IEEE International Conference on Pervasive Computing and Communications, PerCom 2003* (pp. 378-387).

Sim, S. E., Easterbrook, S. M., & Holt, R. C. (2003). Using benchmarking to advance research: A challenge to software engineering. In *Proceedings of the 25th International Conference on Software Engineering (ICSE2003)*, Portland, Oregon, USA.

Sintek, M., & Kiesel, M. (2006). RDFBroker: A signature-based high-performance RDF store. In *Proceedings of the European Semantic Web Conference (ESWC)* (pp. 363-377).

Siorpaes, S. (2006). *A Physical Mobile Interactions Framework based on Semantic Descriptions*. Diploma Thesis, Institut für Informatik, Ludwig-Maximilans-Universität München; July 2006.

Sîrbu, A. (2006). *DIP deliverable D4.14: Discovery module prototype*. Technical report.

Sîrbu, A., Toma, I., & Roman, D. (2006). A logic based approach for service discovery with composition support. In *Proceedings of the ECOWS06 Workshop on Emerging Web Services Technology, Zürich, Switzerland*.

Sirin E. (2004). OWL-S API. Retrieved on Sept 22, 2007, from hwww.mindswap.org/2004/owl-s/api/

Smith, B. (2003). Ontology. An Introduction . In Floridi, L. (Ed.), *Blackwell Guide to the Philosophy of Computing and Information* (pp. 155–166). Oxford: Blackwell.

Smith, B. (2004). Beyond concepts, or: Ontology as reality representation systems. In: A. Varzi & L.Vieu (Eds.), *Proceedings of the 3rd International Conference on Formal Ontology in Information, Systems , Turin 4-6 (FOIS 2004)* (pp. 73-84). Amsterdam: IOS Press. Retrieved May 29, 2007 from http://ontology.buffalo.edu/bfo/BeyondConcepts.pdf

Smith, B. (2006). Against fantology. In: M. Reicher & J. Marek (Eds.), *Experience and analysis (pp. 153-170)*.

Smith, B. (2006). Against idiosyncrasy in ontology development. In: B. Bennett & C. Fellbaum (Eds.), *Formal ontology in information systems: Proceedings of the 4th International Conference (FOIS 2006). Frontiers in Artificial Intelligence and Application, 150*. New York, NY: IOS Press. Retrieved October 14, 2007 from http://ontology.buffalo.edu/bfo/west.pdf

Smith, B., & Ceusters, W. (2007). Ontology as the Core Discipline of Biomedical Informatics . In Crnkovic, G. D., & Stuart, S. (Eds.), *Computing, Information, Cognition* (pp. 104–122). Newcastle: Cambridge Scholars Press.

Snyder, C. (2003). *Paper Prototyping: The Fast and Easy Way to Design and Refine User Interfaces*. The Morgan Kaufmann Series in Interactive Technologies.

Spärck Jones, K. (2004). What's new about the semantic web? Some questions. *SIGIR Forum, 38*, 18–23.

Spinosa, E., Ponce de Leon Ferreira de Carvalho, A., & Gama, J. (2007). OLINDDA: A clusterbased approach for detecting novelty and concept drift in data streams. In *Proceedings of the 22nd Annual ACM Symposium of Applied Computing, SAC2007* (pp. 448-452). Seoul, South Korea: ACM.

Srinivasan, N., Paolucci, M., & Sycara, K. (2004). Adding OWL-S to UDDI, implementation and throughput. *Proceedings of the First International Workshop on Semantic Web Services and Web Process Composition (SWSWPC)*. San Diego, CA.

Staab, S., & Studer, R. (Eds.). (2004). *Handbook on ontologies*. Berlin-Heidelberg, Germany, New York, NY: Springer Verlag.

Stepp, R. E., & Michalski, R. S. (1986). Conceptual clustering of structured objects: A goal-oriented approach. *Artificial Intelligence, 28*(1), 43-69.

Stoffel, K., Taylor, M. G., & Hendler, J. A. (1997). Efficient management for very large ontologies. In *Proceedings of the American Association for Artificial Intelligence Conference (AAAI)*.

Stoilos, G., Stamou, G., Tzouvaras, V., Pan, J., & Horrocks, I. (2005). Fuzzy OWL: Uncertainty and the Semantic Web. In *Proc. OWLED-2005, CEUR Workshop Proceedings* 188. CEUR-WS.org.

Stojanovic, N., Maedche, A., Staab, S., Studer, R., & Sure, Y. (2001). Seal: A framework for developing semantic portals. In *Proceedings of the first international conference on knowledge capture (k-cap 2001), October 21-23, 2001, Victoria, BC, Canada* (p. 155-162).

Stojanovic, N., Studer, R., & Stojanovic, L. (2003). An approach for the ranking of query results in the semantic web. In International semantic web conference (p. 500-516).

Stollberg, M. (2004). SWF use case. *WSMO working draft D3.5*. Retrieved from http://swf.deri.at/usecase/20041019/SWFUseCase-20041019.pdf.

Straccia, U. (2004). Transforming fuzzy description logics into classical description logics. In *Proc. JELIA-2004*, (LNCS 3229, pp. 385-399). Springer.

Straccia, U. (2005). Towards a fuzzy description logic for the Semantic Web (preliminary report). In *Proc. ESWC-2005* (LNCS 3532, pp. 167-181).

Straccia, U. (2006). A fuzzy description logic for the Semantic Web . In Sanchez, E. (Ed.), *Fuzzy Logic and the Semantic Web, Capturing Intelligence* (pp. 73–90). Elsevier.

Straccia, U. (2006). Fuzzy description logic programs. In *Proc. IPMU-2006* (pp. 1818-1825).

Straccia, U. (2006). Uncertainty and description logic programs over lattices . In Sanchez, E. (Ed.), *Fuzzy Logic and the Semantic Web, Capturing Intelligence* (pp. 115–133). Elsevier.

Straccia, U., & Visco, G. (2007). DLMedia: An ontology mediated multimedia information retrieval system. In *Proc. DL-2007, CEUR Workshop Proceedings* 250. CEUR-WS.org.

Stuckenschmidt, H., Hartmann, J., & van Harmelen, F. (2002). Learning Structural Classification Rules for Web-Page Categorization. *FLAIRS Conference* (pp. 440-444).

SWSL Committee. (2007). *Semantic Web services framework (SWSF)*. Retrieved June 1, 2007 from http://www.daml.org/services/swsf

Sycara, K., Paolucci, M., Ankolekar, A., & Srinivasan, N. (2004). Automated discovery, interaction and composition of semantic Web services. *Journal of Web Semantics, 1*.

The OBO foundry. (2007). Retrieved October 31, 2007 from http://obofoundry.org/

Theoharis, Y., Christophides, V., & Karvounarakis, G. (2005). Benchmarking database representations of RDF/S stores. In *Proceedings of the International Semantic Web Conference (ISWC)*.

Tho, Q. T., Hui, S. C., Fong, A. C. M., & Tru Hoang, C. (2006). Automatic Fuzzy Ontology Generation for Semantic Web. *IEEE Transactions on Knowledge and Data Engineering, 18*, 842–856. doi:10.1109/TKDE.2006.87

Tohamy, N. (2005). *The Present and Future of RFID in Logistics*. Forrester Research. Retrieved November 16, 2005 from http://www.rfidupdate.com/articles/?id=998

Toma, I., Iqbal, K., Roman, D., Strang, T., Fensel, D., & Sapkota, B. (2007). Discovery in grid and web services environments: A survey and evaluation. *International Journal on Multiagent and Grid Systems, 3*(3).

Toye, E. (2007, January). Interacting with mobile services: an evaluation of camera-phones and visual tags. *Personal and Ubiquitous Computing, 11*(2), 97–106. doi:10.1007/s00779-006-0064-9

Traub, K., Allgair, G., Barthel, H., Bustein, L., Garrett, J., et al. (2005). *EPCglobal architecture framework.* Technical report, EPCglobal Inc., July 2005.

Tresp, C., & Molitor, R. (1998). A description logic for vague knowledge. In *Proc. ECAI-1998* (pp. 361-365). J. Wiley & Sons.

Trinh, Q., Barker, K., & Alhajj, R. (2006). RDB2ONT: A tool for generating OWL ontologies from relational database systems. In *Proceedings of the 2nd Advanced International Conference on Telecommunications and International Conference on Internet and Web Applications and Services*, Guadeloupe, French Caribbean (pp. 170-178).

Tsetsos, V., Anagnostopoulos, C., & Hadjiefthymiades, S. (2006). On the evaluation of semantic web service matchmaking systems. In *Proceedings of the 4th IEEE European Conference on Web Services (ECOWS2006)*, Zürich, Switzerland.

Tsetsos, V., Anagnostopoulos, C., & Hadjiefthymiades, S. (2007). Semantic Web service discovery: Methods, algorithms and tools. In: J. Cardoso (Ed.), *Semantic Web services: Theory, tools and applications.* Hershey, PA: IGI Publishing.

Udrea, O., Pugliese, A., & Subrahmanian, V. S. (2007). GRIN: A graph based RDF index. In *Proceedings of the American Association for Artificial Intelligence Conference (AAAI)* (pp. 1465-1470).

Umano, M., & Fukami, S. (1994). Fuzzy relational algebra for possibility-distribution-fuzzy-relational model of fuzzy data. *Journal of Intelligent Information Systems, 3*, 7-27.

Umsoy, M. (2007). *3GSM Congress 2007 Notes.* Retrieved February 27, 2007 from http://cartagena-capital.com/pdfs/3gsm_congress_2007_notes.pdf

Vallet, D., Fernandez, M., & Castells, P. (2005). An ontology-based information retrieval model. *2nd European Semantic Web Conference, ESWC 2005, Springer, Grete, Greece* (pp. 455-470).

van Fraassen, B. (1969). Presuppositions, Supervaluations, and Free Logic . In Lambert, K. (Ed.), *The Logical Way of Doing Things* (pp. 67–91). New Haven: Yale University Press.

van Heijst, G., Schreiber, A., & Wielinga, B. (1997). Using explicit ontologies in KBS development. *International Journal of Human-Computer Studies, 46*(2-3), 183-292.

Van Rijsbergen, C. J. (1986). A new theoretical framework for information retrieval. In *Proceedings of the 9th Annual International ACM SIGIR Conference on Research and Development in Information Retrieval*, Pisa, Italy (pp. 194-200).

Vaneková, V., Bella, J., Gurský, P., & Horváth, T. (2005). Fuzzy RDF in the Semantic Web: Deduction and induction. In *Proceedings of the 6th Workshop on Data Analysis*, Abaujszanto, Hungary (pp. 16-29).

Veijalainen, J. (2007). Developing mobile ontologies; who, why, where, and how?. *Mobile Services-oriented Architectures and Ontologies Workshop (MoSO 2007).* Mannheim, Germany.

Veijalainen, J., Nikitin, S., & Törmälä, V. (2006). Ontology-based semantic Web service platform in mobile environments. *Proceedings of Mobile Ontologies Workshop.* Nara, Japan. http://csdl2.computer.org/persagen/DLPublication.jsp?pubtype=p&acronym=MDM

Venetis, T., Stoilos, G., Stamou, G. B., & Kollias, S. D. (2007). f-DLPs: Extending description logic programs with fuzzy sets and fuzzy logic. In *Proc. FUZZ-IEEE-2007* (pp. 1-6). IEEE Computer Society.

Vidulin, V., Lustrek, M., & Gams, M. (2007). Training a genre classifier for automatic classification of web pages. *Journal of Computing and Information Technology, 15*(4), 305–311.

Volz, R., Oberle, D., & Studer, S. (2003). Implementing views for light-weight Web ontologies. In *Proceedings of the International Database Engineering and Applications Symposium (IDEAS)* (pp. 160-169).

Volz, R., Oberle, D., Motik, B., & Staab, S. (2003). KAON SERVER - a Semantic Web management system. In *Proceedings of the International World Wide Web Conference (WWW), Alternate Tracks - Practice and Experience.*

Voorhees, E. M. (1994). *Query expansion using lexical-semantic relations. 17th Annual ACM SIGIR conference on research and development in information retrieval* (pp. 61–69). Springer-Verlag.

W3C (2004). OWL Web Ontology Language Overview. W3C Recommendation (10 February 2004). Retrieved from www.w3.org/TR/2004/REC-owl-features-20040210/.

W3C. (2004). RDF Primer. W3C Recommendation, 10 February 2004. F. Manola and E. Miller (Eds.). Retrieved from http://www.w3.org/TR/rdf-primer/

W3C. (2004). Resource Description Framework (RDF): Concepts and Abstract Syntax. W3C Recommendation, 10 February 2004. G. Klyne, J. J. Carroll, and B. McBride (Eds.). Retrieved from http://www.w3.org/TR/2004/REC-rdf-concepts-20040210/

W3C. (2008). SPARQL Query Language for RDF. W3C Candidate Recommendation, 15 January 2008. E. Prud'hommeaux and A. Seaborne (Eds.). Retrieved from http://www.w3.org/TR/2008/REC-rdf-sparql-query-20080115/

Want, R. (2006). An Introduction to RFID Technology. *IEEE Pervasive Computing / IEEE Computer Society [and] IEEE Communications Society, 5*, 25–33. doi:10.1109/MPRV.2006.2

Want, R., Fishkin, K. P., Gujar, A., & Harrison, B. L. (1999). Bridging physical and virtual worlds with electronic tags. In *Proc. of CHI 1999* (pp. 370-377). New York: ACM.

Web Services Modeling Ontology. (2007). http://www.wsmo.org/

Weiss, C., Karras, P., & Bernstein, A. (2008). Hexastore: Sextuple indexing for Semantic Web data management. In *Proceedings of the International Conference on Very Large Data Bases (VLDB).*

Widmer, G., & Kubat, M. (1996). Learning in the presence of concept drift and hidden contexts. *Machine Learning, 23*(1), 69-101.

Wilkinson, K. (2006). Jena property table implementation. In *Proceedings of the International Workshop on Scalable Semantic Web Knowledge Base Systems (SSWS).*

Wilkinson, K., Sayers, C., Kuno, H., & Reynolds, D. (2003). Efficient RDF storage and retrieval in Jena2. In *Proceedings of the International Workshop on Semantic Web and Databases (SWDB).*

Wilkinson, R., & Hingston, P. (1991). Using the cosine measure in a neural network for document retrieval. In *Sigir '91: Proceedings of the 14th annual international acm sigir conference on research and development in information retrieval* (pp. 202– 210). New York: ACM Press.

Wittgenstein, L. (1921) *Tractatus Logico-Philosophicus.* Retrieved from http://www.gutenberg.org/etext/5740.

Wittgenstein, L. (1963). *Philosophical Investigations.* New York: The Macmillan Company.

Woods, W. A. (1997). *Conceptual indexing: a better way to organize knowledge.* Retrieved from http://research.sun.com/techrep/1997/abstract- 61.html.

Wooldridge, M. (2002). *An introduction to multi-agent systems.* John Wiley & Sons.

World Intellectual Property Organisation. (2007). *Berne convention.* Retrieved April 3, 2007 from http://www.wipo.int/treaties/en/ip/berne/

Wu, Z., & Palmer, M. S. (1994). Verb semantics and lexical selection. In *Meeting of the association for computational linguistics (ACL)* (pp. 133-138).

Yager, R. R. (1988). On ordered weighted averaging aggregation operators in multi-criteria decision making. *IEEE Transactions on Systems, Man, and Cybernetics, 18*, 183–190. doi:10.1109/21.87068

Yager, R. R. (1993). Families of OWA operators. *Fuzzy Sets and Systems, 59*, 125–148. doi:10.1016/0165-0114(93)90194-M

Yager, R. R. (2000). A Hierarchical Document Retrieval Language. *Information Retrieval, 3*, 357–377. doi:10.1023/A:1009911900286

Yang, Y. (1994). Expert Network: Effective and Efficient Learning from Human Decisions in Text Categorization and Retrieval. *17th Annual International ACM-SIGIR Conference on Research and Development in Information Retrieval, Dublin, Ireland* (pp. 3-6). ACM/Springer.

Yilmaz, E., & Aslam, J. A. (2006). Estimating average precision with incomplete and imperfect judgments. In *Cikm '06: Proceedings of the 15th ACM international conference on information and knowledge management* (pp. 102–111). New York: ACM Press.

Yoshinaga, H., Hattari, Y., Sato, T., Yoschida, M., & Washio, S. (2003). i-Mode FeliCa. *NTT DoCoMo Technical Journal, 6*(3).

Youtube Virtual Community. (2007). www.youtube.com

Zadeh, L. A. (1965). Fuzzy sets. *Information and Control, 8*(3), 338-353.

Zadeh, L. A. (1978). Fuzzy sets as a basis for a theory of possibility. *Fuzzy Sets and Systems, 1*(1), 3-28.

Zahreddine, W., & Mahmoud, Q. (2005). An agent-based approach to composite mobile Web services. *Proceedings of the 19th IEEE International Conference on Advanced Information Networking and Applications (AINA05)*. Taipei, Taiwan.

Zanella, A., Tonello, A., & Pupolin S. (2002). On the impact of fading and inter-piconet interference on Bluetooth performance. *The 5th International Symposium on Wireless Personal Multimedia Communications, 1*, 218-222.

Zemke, F. (2006, October). *Converting SPARQL to SQL* (Tech. Rep.). Retrieved from http://lists.w3.org/Archives/Public/public-rdf-dawg/2006OctDec/att-0058/sparql-to-sql.pdf

Zezula, P., Amato, G., Dohnal, V., & Batko, M. (2007). *Similarity search--the metric space approach of advances in database systems.* Springer.

Zhang, L., Yu, Y., Zhou, J., Lin, C., & Yang, Y. (2005). An enhanced model for searching in semantic portals. In *Www '05: Proceedings of the 14th international conference on world wide web* (pp. 453–462). New York: ACM Press.

Zhanova, A. (Ed.). (2006). *Deliverable 3.1, Ontology definition for the DCS and DCS resource description, User rules. EU-IST SPICE project.* Retrieved February 28, 2007 from http://www.ist-spice.org/documents/D3.1_061017_v1_final_bis.pdf

Ziegler, P., Kiefer, C., Sturm, C., Dittrich, K. R., & Bernstein, A. (2006). Detecting similarities in ontologies with the soqasimpack toolkit. In Y. Ioannidis et al. (Eds.), *10th international conference on extending database technology (EDBT 2006)* (Vol. 3896, pp. 59-76). Springer.

Ziv, J., & Lempel, A. (1977). A universal algorithm for sequential data compression. *IEEE Transactions on Information Theory, 23*(3), 337-343.

About the Contributors

Amit Sheth is an educator, researcher, and entrepreneur. He is a LexisNexis Eminent Scholar (an endowed faculty position, funded by LexisNexis and the Ohio Board of Regents) at Wright State University. He directs the Kno.e.sis center for Knowledge enabled Information & Services Science; which conducts research in Semantic Web, services computing, and scientific worklfows. He was a professor at the University of Georgia where he founded and directed the LSDIS Lab. Prior to that, he served in R&D groups at Bellcore, Unisys, and Honeywell. His research has led to several commercial products and two companies which he founded and managed in various executive roles: Infocosm, which had products in enterprise workflow management and Taalee/Voquette/Semagix, which was one of the earliest companies with Semantic Web applications and application development platforms. Professor Sheth is an IEEE Fellow and has received recognitions such as the IBM Faculty award. He has published over 250 papers and articles many of which are highly cited (h-index > 54 based on Google scholar citations), given over 200 invited talks and colloquia including over thirty keynotes, (co)-organized/chaired forty-five conferences/workshops, and served on over 125 program committees. He is on several journal editorial boards, is the Editor-in-Chief of the *International Journal on Semantic Web and Information Systems (IJSWIS)*, and the joint-EIC of *Distributed & Parallel Databases Journal*.

Miltiadis D. Lytras is an assistant professor in the Computer Engineering and Informatics Department-CEID (University of Patras). His research focuses on Semantic Web, knowledge management, and e-learning with more than 100 publications in these areas. He has co-edited/co-edits, 25 special issues in International Journals (e.g. *IEEE Transaction on Knowledge and Data Engineering, IEEE Internet Computing, IEEE Transactions on Education, Computers in Human Behaviour*, etc.) and has authored/[co-]edited 12 books (e.g. *Open Source for Knowledge and Learning Management, Ubiquitous and Pervasive Knowledge Management, Intelligent Learning Infrastructures for Knowledge Intensive Organizations*, and *Semantic Based Information Systems*). He is the founder and officer of the Semantic Web and Information Systems Special Interest Group in the association for information systems (http://www.sigsemis.org). He serves as the (Co) Editor-in-Chief of 12 international journals (e.g. *International Journal of Knowledge and Learning, International Journal of Technology Enhanced Learning, International Journal on Social and Humanistic Computing, International Journal on Semantic Web and Information Systems, International Journal on Digital Culture and Electronic Tourism, International Journal of Electronic Democracy, International Journal of Electronic Banking*, and *International Journal of Electronic Trade)* while he is an associate editor or editorial board member of seven more.

* * *

Copyright © 2010, IGI Global, distributing in print or electronic forms without written permission of IGI Global is prohibited.

Birgitta König-Ries holds the Heinz-Nixdorf Endowed Chair for Practical Computer Science at the University of Jena, Germany. Prior to this she has worked with the Technical University of Munich, Florida International University, the University of Louisiana at Lafayette, and the University of Karlsruhe. Birgitta holds both a diploma and a PhD from the latter. Her research is focused on the transparent integration of both information and functionality. In particular, her group is working on semantic web services and on portal technology.

Ulrich Küster holds a diploma in computer science from Friedrich-Schiller-University Jena, Germany. Since 2005, he is working as a researcher in the group of Prof. König-Ries at that university. His main research interests are on semantic web services, service discovery and matchmaking languages and frameworks and evaluation of semantic service technology.

Matthias Klusch is Senior Researcher and Research Fellow of the German Research Center for Artificial Intelligence (DFKI) where he is co-head of the Multiagent Systems (MAS) group and its research team on Intelligent Information Systems and Agents (I2S). He is also Adjunct Professor of Computer Science at Swinburne University of Technology in the Center for Complex Software Systems and Services. He received both his MSc (1992) and PhD (1997) in computer science from the Christian-Albrecht University of Kiel, and his Habilitation (2009) in computer science from the University of the Saarland, Germany. He published widely and serves as editorial member of several major journals on the Semantic Web, service-oriented computing, multi-agent systems, and distributed rational decision-making. He is member of the GI, IEEE, and ACM. Full biography available at: http://www.dfki.de/~klusch/CV-Klusch.pdf

Vasileios Baousis received his B.Sc from the Hellenic Air Force Academy and his M.Sc. Degree in Networking and Telecommunications Engineering in 2001 from the University of Athens, Dept. of Informatics and Telecommunications, Greece. In 2003, he received a M.Sc. titled 'Mobile and Satellite Communications' from the University of Surrey, Dept. of Electronics and Physical Sciences, UK. Currently, he is a PhD student at the University of Athens, Dept. of Informatics and Telecommunications and a staff member of the Communication Networks Laboratory and Pervasive Research Laboratory. His research interests include semantic web and Mobile Agent Technology (MAT) integration, UMTS/ Virtual Home Environment (VHE) architectures in conjunction with MAT, artificial intelligence, distributed programming and game theory.

Vassilis Spiliopoulos received his B.Sc in 2005 from National and Kapodistrian University of Athens, Greece, Department of Informatics & Telecommunications. Currently he is pursuing a PhD degree at the Department of Information and Communication Systems Engineering (Artificial Intelligence Laboratory) of the University of the Aegean, Greece, in collaboration with the National Center of Scientific Research "Demokritos", Institute of Informatics & Telecommunications (Software & Knowledge Engineering Laboratory). His research interests include Multi-Agent Systems, Machine Learning, Semantic Web and Ontology-based Information Extraction.

Elias Zavitsanos received his B.Sc from the National and Kapodistrian University of Athens, Greece, Department of Informatics and Telecommunications. Since December 2005, is a PhD student at the Department of Information and Communication Systems Engineering (Artificial Intelligence Lab) of the University of the Aegean, Greece, in collaboration with the National Center of Scientific Research

''Demokritos'', Institute of Informatics and Telecommunications (Software and Knowledge Engineering Lab). His research interests are Multi-Agent Systems, Machine Learning, Artificial Intelligence and Probabilistic Models.

Stathes Hadjiefthymiades received his B.Sc., M.Sc. and Ph.D. in Informatics from the Department of Informatics and Telecommunications at the University of Athens, Greece. He has also received a joint engineering-economics M.Sc. from the National Technical University of Athens. In 1992 he joined the Greek consulting firm Advanced Services Group, Ltd., where he was extensively involved in the analysis and specification of information systems and the design-implementation of telematic applications. In 1995 he became a member of the Communication Networks Laboratory of the University of Athens. During the period 2001-2002, he served as a visiting assistant professor at the University of Aegean, Department of Information and Communication Systems Engineering. In July 2002 he joined the faculty of the Hellenic Open University (Department of Informatics), Patras, Greece, as an assistant professor. Since December 2003, he belongs to the faculty of the University of Athens, Dept. of Informatics and Telecommunications. He has participated in numerous projects realized in the context of EU programs (ACTS, ORA, TAP, and IST), EURESCOM projects, as well as national initiatives. His research interests are in the areas of wireless/mobile computing, web engineering, and networked multimedia applications. He is the author of over 100 publications in these areas.

Lazaros Merakos received a Diploma in electrical and mechanical engineering from the National Technical University of Athens, Greece, in 1978, and M.S. and Ph.D. degrees in electrical engineering from the State University of New York, Buffalo, in 1981 and 1984, respectively. From 1983 to 1986 he was in the faculty of Electrical Engineering and Computer Science at the University of Connecticut, Storrs. From 1986 to 1994 he was in the faculty of the Electrical and Computer Engineering Department at Northeastern University, Boston, Massachusetts. During the period 1993-1994 he served as director of the Communications and Digital Processing Research Center at Northeastern University. During the summers of 1990 and 1991, he was a visiting scientist at the IBM T. J.Watson Research Center, Yorktown Heights, New York. In 1994 he joined the faculty of the University of Athens, Greece, where he is presently a professor in the Department of Informatics and Telecommunications, and director of the Communication Networks Laboratory (UoA-CNL) and Networks Operations and Management Center. His research interests are in the design and performance analysis of broadband networks, and wireless/mobile communication systems and services. He has authored more than 150 papers in the above areas. Since 1995 he has led the research activities of UoA-CNL in the area of mobile communications, in the framework of the Advanced Communication Technologies and Services (ACTS) and Information Society Technologies (IST) programs funded by the European Union (projects RAINBOW, MagicWAND, WINE, MOBIVAS, POLOS, ANWIRE). He is Chairman of the Board of the Greek Universities Network, the Greek Schools Network, and member of the board of the Greek Research Network. In 1994 he received the Guanella Award for the best paper presented at the International Zurich Seminar on Mobile Communications.

Jari Veijalainen is a full professor at the Department of Computer Science and Information Systems of University of Jyväskylä, Finland, since August 1996. He is also a Docent in Computer Science at the University of Helsinki, Finland since May 1996. He holds a M.Sc. degree from Univ. of Helsinki, Finland (1983), and Dr-Ing. degree from TU Berlin, Germany (1989), both in computer science. He has published tens of scientific papers in conference proceedings, monographs, and journals and is a member of editorial board of IJWET and WINE. He has just retired from the editorial board of the VLDB Journal.He has been participating in Adaptive Services Grid project (EU-IST2002-004617, 2004-2007) as a partner and was also a member of its scientific board, contributing to the project as a visiting professor at Hasso-Plattner-Institut, University of Potsdam, Germany. During 2003 he has spent six months at Waseda University, Tokyo, working as a visiting professor and studying the Mobile Internet in Japan. He is currently leading an international Master's program "Mobile Technology and Business" at the University of Jyväskylä. Dr. Veijalainen was one of the initiators of MoSo workshop series at MDM conference and has been a co-chair in them and a co-editor of this special issue. He was a key note speaker at MDM 2005. He is a member of ACM, IEEE Computer Society, and the Finnish Computer Science Association

Massimo Paolucci is a Senior Scientist at DoCoMo European Laboratories. His research interests include discovery and composition of Semantic Web services with a specific focus on mobile computing. Mr Paolucci received an MS in Computatioal Linguistics from Carnegie Mellon University and an MS in Intelligent Systems from the University of Pittsburgh and a Laurea from Universita' di Milano. He is a member of the OWL-S coalition and a former member of the UDDI Technical Committee and of the Architecture committee of the SWSI initiative. He served in the Program Committees of numerous conferences including WWW, ISWC, ICWS, AAAI and AAMAS

Gregor Broll is a PhD candidate from the Media Informatics Group at Ludwig-Maximilians-Universität München, where he also received his Ms in Media Informatics from. He was also a visiting researcher at the Mixed Reality Laboratory at the University of Nottingham. His research interests include Mobile Computing, mobile interaction with the real world, pervasive gaming and persuasive technology.

John Hamard has participated as Senior Interaction Designer, Usability Expert, Information Architect, and HCI Researcher in a wide variety of international projects and applications. High interest is in contributing to successful projects in industries such as Advertising/Marketing/Communication, Media/Entertainment, Publishing and Industrial Design. He received a Master in Ergonomics from Université René Descartes (Paris V) and a Bachelor degree from Université de Provence (Aix-Marseille I)

Enrico Rukzio is an Academic Fellow and Lecturer at the Computing Department at Lancaster University. Dr Rukzio received his doctorate at the University of Munich, Germany, his MSc in Computer Science at the Technical University of Dresden. Dr Rukzio's research interests include mobile and pervasive computing, human-computer interaction and software engineering.

Matthias Wagner is a Senior Manager of the Evolutionary Applications and Services Research at DoCoMo Euro-Labs. In his research he mainly focuses on proactive services, context awareness, personalization and on leveraging the Semantic Web in mobile applications. Dr Wagner has numerous scientific publications in international journals, conferences and workshops. He holds a Master degree and a Ph.D. degree in Computer Science, and on behalf of DoCoMo he acted in different coordinating roles within the IST research programs of the European commission.

Albrecht Schmidt is a professor for Pervasive Computing and User Interface Engineering at the University of Duisburg-Essen in Germany. Previously he was head of department at the Fraunhofer institute for intelligent information and analysis systems. From 2003 to 2006 he headed the embedded interaction research group at the University of Munich. Albrecht studied in Ulm, Karlsruhe and Lancaster, where he completed his PhD on the topic "ubiquitous computing – computing in context". His teaching and research interests are in media informatics and ubiquitous computing, and in particular in the area of user interface engineering.

Tommaso Di Noia (t.dinoia@poliba.it) is an assistant professor in Information Technology Engineering at Technical University of Bari (Politecnico di Bari). He got his Ph.D. from Technical University of Bari. His main scientific interests include: Description Logics - Theoretical and Practical Aspects; Resource Matchmaking; Knowledge Representation Systems for Electronic Commerce; Automatic (Web) Services Discovery and Composition; Knowledge Representation Systems and Applications for the Semantic Web. He co-authored papers which received the best paper award at conferences ICEC-2004, IEEE CEC-EEE-2006 and ICEC-2007.

Eugenio Di Sciascio (disciascio@poliba.it) received the master's degree with honours from University of Bari, and the Ph.D. from Politecnico di Bari (Technical University of Bari). He is currently full professor of Information Technology Engineering at Technical University of Bari, and leads the research group of SisInfLab, the Information Systems Laboratory of Technical University of Bari. Formerly, he has been an assistant professor at University of Lecce and associate professor at Technical University of Bari. His research interests include multimedia information retrieval, knowledge representation and e-commerce. He is involved in several national and European research projects related to his research interests. He co-authored papers that received best paper awards at conferences ICEC-2004, IEEE CEC-EEE-2006 and ICEC-2007.

Francesco Maria Donini (donini@unitus.it) is a full professor at the Università della Tuscia Viterbo, Italy. Formerly, he was an assistant professor at the Università La Sapienza, Rome, and associate professor at Politecnico di Bari. His Ph.D. thesis was on description logics; he has subsequently worked on many aspects of knowledge representation in artifi cial intelligence, both on theoretical issues and practical applications. His research interests range from description logics to non-monotonic reasoning, abduction, algorithms, and complexity of reasoning in KR formalisms to their application in a variety of practical contexts. He co-authored papers that won awards at the IJCAI-1991, ICEC-2004, and IEEE CEC EEE -2006 conferences.

Michele Ruta (m.ruta@poliba.it) received the master's degree in Electronic Engineering from Politecnico di Bari (Technical University of Bari) in 2002 and his Ph.D. in Information Engineering from the same University in 2007. His research interests include pervasive computing and ubiquitous Web, mobile service discovery and composition, Knowledge Representation systems and applications for wireless ad-hoc contexts. On these topics he has co-authored various papers in international journals and conferences. He is involved in various research projects related to his research interests. He co-authored a paper which received the best paper award at the conference ICEC-2007.

Floriano Scioscia (f.scioscia@poliba.it) received the master's degree in Information Technology Engineering from Politecnico di Bari (Technical University of Bari) in 2006. He is currently pursuing his Ph.D. in Information Engineering at the same University. His research interests include pervasive computing, mobile service discovery and composition, knowledge representation systems and applications for wireless ad-hoc contexts. He co-authored a paper which received the best paper award at the conference ICEC-2007.

Eufemia Tinelli (e.tinelli@poliba.it) has a master's degree in information technology engineering from the Technical University of Bari (Politecnico di Bari), Italy, and is currently pursuing her Ph.D. in computer science at the University of Bari. Her research interests are in the areas of efficient storage and retrieval techniques for very large knowledge bases and applications of Semantic Web technologies to e-commerce.

Harry Halpin is a W3C Fellow at MIT in the Technology and Society Domain. He received his B.A. in Mathematics from University of North Carolina at Chapel Hill and his Ph.D. in Informatics from the University of Edinburgh. He was the Chair of the GRDDL (Gleaning Resource Descriptions from Dialects of Language) Working Group that has produced standards on how to extract RDF semantics from XML documents and microformats, serves of the W3C Semantic Web Co-ordination Group, co-chairs the W3C Social Web Incubator Group, and is staff contact for the RDB2RDF Working Group charged with mapping relational data into RDF. Guiding all of his work is a long-standing interest in the philosophical background of Web architecture, he has published some of the first work in this area, including being the primary organizer of the IRW (Identity, Reference, and the Web) workshop, and a series of workshops at conferences as diverse as IJCAI and WWW on this topic.

Pat Hayes is a Senior Research Scientist at the Institute for Human and Machine Cognition. He re ceived a BA in mathematics from Cambridge University and a PhD in Artificial Intelligence from Edinburgh. He has held academic positions in computer science at the University of Essex, in philosophy at the University of Illinois and as the Luce Professor of cognitive science at the University of Rochester and has directed applied AI research at Xerox-PARC, SRI and Schlumberger, Inc. At various times, Pat has been secretary of AISB, chairman and trustee of IJCAI, associate editor of Artificial Intelligence, a governor of the Cognitive Science Society and president of AAAI. He is the editor of the W3C Recommendation for RDF Semantics and co-editor of the OWL Web Ontology Language Semantics and Abstract Syntax.

Valentina Presutti is a research fellow at the Laboratory for Applied Ontology of the Institute for Cognitive Sciences and Technology at the Italian National Research Council. She received her PhD in computer science at the University of Bologna. Her research interests include ontology design, semantic web, and semantic Web-oriented software engineering. She is currently working under the EU funded ontology engineering project NeOn.

Aldo Gangemi (born Rome, 1962) is senior researcher at the Institute for Cognitive Sciences and Technology at the Italian National Research Council. He is co-founder of the Laboratory for Applied Ontology, a leading research unit in the areas of conceptual modeling, formal ontology, and ontology engineering. His research topics include knowledge engineering, the semantic Web, NLP, and business modeling, with about 100 publications on international refereed journals, books and conferences. He has been working in many national and EU projects, spanning from the pioneering biomedical ontology project GALEN to the current largest ontology engineering project NeOn. He is currently coordinating the work package on collaborative aspects of ontology design in NeOn, and an Italian project on the use of semantic technologies in organizational intranets. He is reviewer for the EU and Italian governmental agencies, and consultant for Italian and international organizations.

Allen Ginsberg holds doctorates in Computer Science (1986) and Philosophy (1983) from Rutgers, The State University of New Jersey. In Philosophy he specialized in the Philosophy of Physics with emphasis on the interpretation problem of Quantum Mechanics. In Computer Science he specialized in Artificial Intelligence, writing his thesis on the problem of automatic refinement of expert system knowledge bases (rules) using known cases in order to improve performance. He was a Member of Technical Staff at Bell Labs for over 15 years, during which time he worked, and published papers, on a wide variety of research problems. He joined MITRE as a Lead Artificial Intelligence Engineer in 2005. At MITRE he worked on the development of ontologies and associated research involving semantic technologies. He is now a consultant in the Washington D.C. area.

Marek Reformat received his M.Sc. (with honors) from Technical University of Poznan, Poland, and his Ph.D. from University of Manitoba, Canada. Currently, he is with the Department of Electrical and Computer Engineering at the University of Alberta. His research interests are in the areas of application of Computational Intelligence techniques, as well as probabilistic and evidence theories to intelligent data analysis and modeling leading to translating data into knowledge.

Ronald R. Yager has worked in the area of fuzzy sets and related disciplines of Computational Intelligence for over twenty-five years. He has published over 500 papers and fifteen books. He received IEEE Pioneer award in Fuzzy Systems and is a fellow of the IEEE and the International Fuzzy Systems Association (IFSA).

Zhan Li is a PhD student in the Electrical and Computer Engineering Department at the University of Alberta. His research interests include the Semantic Web, Computational Intelligence, and Information Retrieval of web documents. He received his B.Sc. and M.Sc. degrees from the Department of Electronic Information at Wuhan University, Wuhan, China.

Z. M. Ma received his PhD degree from City University of Hong Kong. He is currently a full professor of the College of Information Science and Engineering at Northeastern University, China. His research interests include database modeling, XML data management, as well as knowledge representation and reasoning with a special focus on information imprecision and uncertainty. He has published many papers in high quality international conferences (e.g., ER, DEXA and WI) and in highly cited international journals (e.g., Information Systems and Data & Knowledge Engineering). He has also published two monographs with Springer.

Yanhui Lv received the MS degree in computer application and technology from Shenyang Ligong University in 2005 and she is an associate professor of computer science at Shenyang Ligong University, China. She is studying for a doctor degree in computer application and technology from Northeastern

University, China. Her current research interests include ontology modeling, learning and alignment related to representing uncertain information.

Li Yan received her PhD degree from Northeastern University, China. She is currently an associate professor at Northeastern University, China. Her research interests include database modeling, XML data management, as well as imprecise and uncertain data processing. She has published papers in several journals such as Data & Knowledge Engineering, Information and Software Technology and International Journal of Intelligent Systems.

Thomas Lukasiewicz is currently holding a Heisenberg Fellowship by the German Research Foundation (DFG), affiliated both at the Computing Laboratory of the University of Oxford and at the Institute of Information Systems of the Vienna University of Technology. He holds the Dipl.-Inf. degree (M.Sc.) in Computer Science from the Clausthal University of Technology, Germany, the Doctorate (Ph.D.) in Computer Science from the University of Augsburg, Germany, and the Universitätsdozent degree (venia docendi) in Practical and Theoretical Computer Science from the Vienna University of Technology, Austria. Thomas Lukasiewicz's main research interests are in databases, the Web, and Artificial Intelligence.

Umberto Straccia is currently researcher at the "Istituto di Scienze e di Tecnologie dell'Informazione" (ISTI) of the Italian National Council of Research (CNR). His main research interests include in the broad sense Knowledge Representation and Reasoning (KRR), Information Retrieval (IR), and their combination. In particular, he has interests in logics for KRR and the Semantic Web (in particular, logic programming and description logics), the management of uncertainty and vagueness, top-k retrieval and logic-based approaches to multimedia information retrieval.

Nicola Fanizzi, PhD, is assistant professor at the computer science department of the University of Bari. His research focuses on Machine Learning and Knowledge Discovery, and particularly on methodologies that can be applied complex (multi-relational) representations. Currently he is interested in uncertainty reasoning with the standard Semantic Web representations (and Description Logics) and in its related problems: classification, clustering, retrieval, matching, ranking, etc. He was an invited expert of the W3C Uncertainty Reasoning for the World Wide Web Incubator Group. He is serving as an organizer and program committee member in international conferences and workshops on the topics of interest.

Floriana Esposito has been an associate professor of computer science at University of Bari since 1984 and Full Professor of Computer Science and Chair of Knowledge Engineering since 1994. Her scientific interests are in the area of Artificial Intelligence and concern the logical and algebraic foundations of Machine Learning: more in particular, the integration of numerical and symbolic methods in learning and classification, the logical foundations of conceptual learning techniques, the automated revision of logical theories, multistrategy learning for discovery in data bases, inductive logic programming. The major application fields are Document processing and Digital Libraries and, recently, Bioinformatics. Floriana Esposito is author of more than 250 papers which have been published in international journals and Proceedings. On August 2006 she received the ECCAI Fellowship in recognition for Pioneering Work in the field of artificial intelligence.

Claudia d'Amato received her PhD in 2007 at the University of Bari, defending a thesis focused on the definition and implementation of Machine Learning methods, and specifically instance based learning methods, for the Semantic Web. She received the nomination from the Italian Artificial Intelligence community, as one of the best Italian PhD contribution in the area. Currently, she is research fellow at the University of Bari - Department of Computer Science and visiting researcher at University of Koblenz-Landau - ISWeb Lab. She is investigating on supervised and unsupervised methods for ontology management and approximate and uncertain reasoning for the Semantic Web.

Artem Chebotko is an assistant professor in the Department of Computer Science at the University of Texas - Pan American. He received his PhD and MS in computer science from Wayne State University in 2008 and 2005, respectively, MS in management information systems from Ukraine State Maritime Technical University in 2003, and BS in computer science from Ukraine State Maritime Technical University in 2001. His research interests include semantic web data management, scientific workflow provenance metadata management, and database systems. Dr. Chebotko has published a number of papers in refereed journals and conference proceedings and currently serves as a program committee member of several international conferences and workshops on scientific workflows and semantic web. He is a member of IEEE.

Shiyong Lu is currently an associate professor in the Department of Computer Science at Wayne State University and the director of the Scientific Workflow Research Laboratory. Dr. Lu received his PhD from the State University of New York at Stony Brook in 2002, ME from the Institute of Computing Technology of Chinese Academy of Sciences at Beijing in 1996, and BE from the University of Science and Technology of China at Hefei in 1993. His research interests include scientific workflows and semantic web. He has published over seventy refereed international journal and conference papers in the above areas. Dr. Lu is the founder and currently a program co-chair of the IEEE International Workshop on Scientific Workflows (2007~2009), an editorial board member for International Journal of Semantic Web and Information Systems and International Journal of Healthcare Information Systems and Informatics. He also serves as a program committee member for several top-tier IEEE conferences, including ICWS, SCC, and CLOUD. He is a member of IEEE.

Peter Scheir is project manager at the staff unit Business Development at Styria Media Group AG, Austria's largest privately held media company. There he signs responsible for coordinating and consulting various projects on new media. Until 2008 he was a scientific assistant at the Knowledge Management Institute of Graz University of Technology and a member of the Knowledge Services division at the Know-Center in Graz. He received a master's degree in 2003 and a doctoral degree in 2008, both in Telematics from Graz University of Technology. In 2001 Peter joined the Know-Center, Austria's Competence Center for Knowledge Management, where he began to work in the area of information and knowledge management systems. Since 2006 he has been working in the field of web science at the Knowledge Management Institute of Graz University of Technology. In his doctoral studies he focused on the intersection of information retrieval and the Semantic Web. Peter's current research interests include Semantic Web, information retrieval based on knowledge organization systems, ontology enabled information systems and web analytics.

Peter Prettenhofer received the master's degree in software development and business management from Graz University of Technology. He is currently a research assistant at the web technology and information systems group, Bauhaus University Weimar. His research focuses on information retrieval and machine learning.

Stefanie Lindstaedt is head of the research division Knowledge Services at Know-Center in Graz and Assistant Professor at Graz University of Technology. She acts as scientific coordinator of the EU-funded project APOSDLE (www.aposdle.org), is engaged in the MATURE integrated project (www.mature-ip.eu) and the STELLAR network of excellence (www.stellar.eu). Her research interests are in knowledge technologies, technology enhanced learning, and requirements engineering. Specifically, her research focuses on hybrid knowledge services. Knowledge (web) services aim at discovering relationships between people (usage), content, and semantic structures. Hybrid knowledge services combine semantic approaches with methods from soft computing in order to handle uncertainty.

Stefanie holds a PhD and a M.S. both in Computer Science from the University of Colorado (CU) at Boulder (USA). She is member of the Center for Lifelong Learning and Design and the Institute of Cognitive Science at CU. She has co-organized eight I-Know conferences (www.i-know.at), acted as PC member of over 50 international conferences on knowledge management and technology enhanced learning, and chaired more than 20 workshops on process-oriented knowledge management, work-integrated learning, and Science 2.0. Stefanie has published more than 100 scientific publications.

Chiara Ghidini is a Senior Research Scientist at FBK-irst where she works in the Data & Knowledge Management unit. Dr. Ghidini completed her PhD in Computer Science Engineering in 1998 at the University of Rome "La Sapienz". Between September 1998 and May 2003 she worked first at the Centre for Agent Research and Development (CARD), Manchester Metropolitan University, and then at the Department of Computer Science, University of Liverpool. Her work in the area of context-based reasoning and in the area of logics for agent-based systems is well known and internationally recognized and she has published over 40 conference and journal papers on the topics. She has served as programme committee and reviewer in many journals, international conferences and workshops and she was directly involved in the organization of several scientific events. Among them she served as general co-chair of the 2nd European workshop on multi-agent systems (EUMAS 2004), as programme co-chair of the 1st Annual International Conference on Mobile and Ubiquitous Systems: Networking and Services (MobiQuitous 2004) and of the 4th International and Interdisciplinary Conference on Modeling and Using Context (CONTEXT 2003), and as tutorial co-chair of the 6th Annual European Semantic Web Conference (ESWC 2009).

Index

A

access relation 102, 103, 104, 106, 107, 112, 113, 114, 115, 116, 117, 118, 119

adopted language 257

advanced process-oriented self-directed learning environment (APOSDLE) 310, 319, 320, 321, 322, 325, 326, 339, 344

agents 148, 150, 151, 152, 153, 158, 162, 163, 165, 168

ambiguity 102, 106, 108, 110, 111, 112, 118, 119, 120, 121, 122

analogical reasoning 258

annotations 222

answer set semantics 237, 238, 244, 246, 247, 248, 249, 251, 252, 253

Architecture of the World Wide Web (W3C) 125, 141

Aristotle 46

associations 186, 211

associative information retrieval 310, 330, 335

associative networks 310, 311, 313, 319, 321, 329, 330, 331, 334, 336, 339

associative retrieval 309, 310, 311, 312, 327, 330, 331, 332, 336, 339, 341, 343

associative retrieval model 309, 330, 331, 332, 336, 339

associative retrieval techniques 309, 327, 339, 341, 343

attributes 222, 224, 225, 227, 230, 231, 258, 269

B

background knowledge 258, 280

backward compatability 76

being, study of 46

benchmarks 1, 3, 10, 11

Berners-Lee, Tim 103, 110, 111, 114, 115, 120, 121, 122

bit pipes 45

Bluetooth 62, 64, 76, 77, 78, 79, 80, 81, 82, 83, 86, 87, 88, 89, 90, 91, 94, 95, 96, 97, 98, 99, 100

Bluetooth service discovery 76, 77, 78

Bluetooth service discovery protocol 76, 78

C

card, passive 62

case-based reasoning 258, 278

categories 187, 188, 189, 191, 197, 198, 200, 205, 206, 207, 209, 211, 212, 214, 220

centroid 259, 269, 274

classes 187, 191, 196, 197, 200, 203, 205, 209, 210, 219, 220, 222, 227, 228

closed world assumption (CWA) 259, 280

clustering 257, 258, 259, 260, 261, 266, 267, 269, 270, 271, 272, 273, 274, 275, 276, 277, 278, 279, 280

clustering methods, similarity-based 258

clustering techniques 257

clustering validity indices 257, 277

clusters 257, 258, 259, 266, 267, 268, 269, 270, 271, 272, 273, 274, 275, 276, 277, 278, 279, 280

cognitive psychology 311

communication delays 77

comparative evaluations 1, 2, 3, 10, 11, 16

compression 76, 77, 84, 85, 86, 88, 91, 92, 94, 95, 98, 100, 101

compression tool, dedicated 76

Copyright © 2010, IGI Global, distributing in print or electronic forms without written permission of IGI Global is prohibited.